CHATEAUGAY BLOCKHOUSE

THE HISTORY OF THE
COUNTY OF
HUNTINGDON

❧ CANADA ❧

AND OF THE SEIGNIORIES OF
CHATEAUGAY AND
BEAUHARNOIS

FROM
THEIR FIRST SETTLEMENT
TO THE YEAR
1838

Robert Sellar

HERITAGE BOOKS
2007

HERITAGE BOOKS

AN IMPRINT OF HERITAGE BOOKS, INC.

Books, CDs, and more—Worldwide

For our listing of thousands of titles see our website
at
www.HeritageBooks.com

A Facsimile Reprint
Published 2007 by
HERITAGE BOOKS, INC.
Publishing Division
65 East Main Street
Westminster, Maryland 21157-5026

International Standard Book Number: 978-0-7884-1929-4

PREFACE.

THE following work was undertaken with reluctance and solely from a sense of duty. Soon after coming to Huntingdon I perceived that the first-settlers were fast passing away and I considered it would be deeply deplored by future generations that no narrative of when and how they redeemed the wilderness, no sketch of the kind of men and women they were, should have been preserved. Feeling thus I repeatedly suggested to different friends, qualified by education and long-residence in the district, that they ought to prepare a local history. Not one would listen to my representations. As time passed on I perceived that soon the preparation of such a work would be impossible, and if it was to be done at all I must needs do it myself. My occupation was a serious hindrance to its prosecution. The publisher of a country newspaper so indifferently supported that its punctual appearance weekly depended as much on my labor as a printer as its editor, I could not leave my office to gather information except at rare intervals and for short periods, and this circumstance has materially affected the completeness of the work.

As the value of a history, however humble, depends upon its authenticity, the reader has a right to know the sources from which I drew my information. When I began to prepare for the work, I counted on finding much documentary material. My hopes were quenched in a very short time. Not a letter, diary, or memorandum could I obtain. Repeatedly have I gone with confidence to the families of clergymen and other educated men to ask to be permitted to examine the papers they had left, only to be disappointed. Documents which, to me, would have been of the last consequence I could not obtain. Speaking from my experience, I would say the idea entertained by Mr Brymner, the keeper of the archives at Ottawa, and others, that there is much documentary material lying hid in families similar to that of the muniment-chests of Great Britain, is a delusion. The destruction of the papers of the seigniory-office was an irreparable loss to me, which would have been avoided had I assumed the task ten years sooner. Mr Browning did his best to assist me, and his kindness I here acknowledge.

Failing to secure documentary sources of information, I had
to depend almost entirely upon what I could glean in conversations with early settlers, and if there ever was a history
written as taken from the lips of actors in or eye-witnesses
of the scenes depicted, it is that now submitted. I visited
every old settler I could learn of, and thus listened to what
over 300 had to say. There is such a difference among men
and women in accuracy of observation and power of memory,
that information of this nature has to be carefully dealt with,
and the narratives I obtained I compared and sifted, and
when I found serious discrepancies or had doubts as to the
correctness of what had been told me, I paid more than one
visit to the same person; in a few instances, as many as
four or five. The work of interviewing was not only laborious, but too often disagreeable, for my reception was not
always gracious. That a sane man should neglect his business and spend his substance on horse-hire to collect old-world
stories, and, above all, do so from disinterested motives, was
beyond the comprehension of many, and curt answers, suspicious questions, and downright refusals were sometimes my
reward for a cold and fatiguing drive over bad roads. In the
majority of instances, however, I was kindly received and all
the information desired readily conveyed to me. The defects
of the book, (and despite all my efforts, I know they are
numerous) arise largely from those unavoidable in verbal
sources of information, such as inaccuracy in details and in
the sequence of events, and the omission of important particulars. Those who note errors or the absence of facts which
ought to find a place in its pages, will oblige me by communi-
cating them, so that, should a second edition be called for, the
necessary changes may be made. I have scrupulously avoided
genealogical details or anything approaching to family histories, seeking to supply a narrative of the settlement of the
district and nothing else. To the general reader it will be
too minute; to the inhabitants of the several concessions it
will not be minute enough. To hit a medium that would
satisfy both was impossible, and I have sought rather to meet
the expectations of the residents, without including so many
details as to make it tiresome to those who know of Huntingdon and her sister-counties only by name. On the lists of old
settlers much labor has been spent, and yet I know they are de-
fective. The man who cleared a lot seldom had the patent
issued in his name, so that in the books of the crown lands
department I found little information as to Huntingdon, and
the destruction of the seigniory books left no other recourse

as to the other two counties than the memories of old residents. The lists for Franklin and Havelock that I compiled were so incomplete that I could not print them. Of Hemingford I could obtain none. In speaking of that township, I would express my obligations to Mr Scriver, M. P., for the great trouble he took in obtaining for me all the information that lay in his power regarding it. No one, with the exception of my friend Mr Younie, did as much to assist me.

Touching the sources from which I have drawn my material for the chapters relating to the war of 1812 and the rebellion, I would state that I supplemented what oral information I obtained, by a conscientious examination of all the histories and documents I could obtain access to in Ottawa, Montreal, and Quebec. Because my narrative of the campaign of Hampton and of the encounters at Odelltown differ widely from those previously printed, the reader is not to conclude I am in error. My investigations into the campaign on the Chateaugay gave as great a shock to my own preconceptions of it as the account in these pages can to any of its readers. My duty was to follow the best authorities I could find, and I could not reject the despatches and statements of those engaged on both sides in the campaign and accept the figments that have passed current in Canadian histories. In this, as in other parts of the work, I have reproduced to the best of my ability a true picture of what actually occurred, without considering who would be pleased or offended thereby. In the chapter on the rebellion I have drawn largely from the evidence given in the State Trials.

The book is a realization of only part of my design, for I had in view a history of the district to the close of the second Fenian raid. That would have brought in the transition-period in its history, the stage between that of bush-farming and modern culture, the volunteer movement of 1838 and the establishment of the Huntingdon Troop; the introduction of the principle of self-government into scholastic and municipal affairs, a most important yet unwritten chapter in Canadian history; the forming of congregations, and over half came into being after 1838; the building of the Beauharnois canal, with its riots and the creation of Valleyfield; the drift in political events, from Dunscomb's stormy return to the first election under Confederation; the rebellion losses; the social changes wrought in those years; in short, have completed my picture of what I consider to be the formative-period in the life of Canada. I was unable to do so, however, not from want of will or material, but of means, for in publishing the book as it stands, I had trenched so far upon my resources that I dared not go farther. Although disappointed in being prevented from carrying out my design, I have the satisfaction of knowing that the narrative is complete as an account of the settlement of the three counties.

I believe that the book will be of more than local value, and found my belief on these reasons :

1. That it is the first to give a full account, prepared from original sources, of the events of the war of 1812 in this province, for the operations in the first county of Huntingdon comprise all that happened in Quebec during these three eventful years, excepting Wilkinson's repulse at Lacolle mill.

2. That it is original in giving a minute yet comprehensive picture of how Canada was made : of how its pioneers subdued the wilderness and left the country what we find it. There are numberless narratives of life in the bush, there are many county histories ; but this is the first attempt to give the experience not of one or two settlers, but of scores, not colored to make a fascinating book, or told by persons of a romantic disposition, but the unvarnished narratives of men and women whose hands were stiffened and backs bent by the toils and sufferings they relate, and not one of whom would have reduced their stories to writing. How Huntingdon and its sister counties were made is a sample of how Ontario and Canada were made, and the making of Canada must form at the base of all true histories of our country.

3. It gives an almost complete history of the rebellion of 1838, for the head and front of the rising of that year was in the district that falls within its scope, while it takes up a subject which other histories have ignored, the relations of the two races.

That the book will be of permanent value I am somewhat doubtful, and while engaged in its preparation I often asked myself, Is the play worth the candle? and considered whether I should not abandon it. After debating the matter the conclusion I always reached was, that though the present generation might possibly regard a record of the settlement of the district of Beauharnois as trite and commonplace and dismiss it with disdain, a time would come when some future Buckle or Macaulay would turn to its pages for information on subjects preserved nowhere else, and the thought (possibly a foolish one) that I was working for future generations, encouraged me to persevere and complete my task, when I had naught else to cheer me.

To the Youth of the District of Beauharnois
I Dedicate This Book, in the Hope that the
Record it Preserves of the Sacrifices its First
Settlers Made, of the Privations they Endured
in Redeeming It from the Wilderness, and in
Defending It against Invasion and Rebellion,
may Incite them to Emulate their Self-denying
Thrift and Persevering Industry, and Deepen
in their Hearts the Sentiment of Loyalty to
The Mother Land and of Devotion to The
Land of their Birth.

Robt. Sellar.

THE DISTRICT OF BEAUHARNOIS.

CHAPTER I.

THE CREATION OF THE SEIGNIORIES.

AT the beginning of the present century the hardy emigrant, as he toiled upon his weary way from lake Champlain to the west, on looking down from one of those spurs of the Adirondacks which nearest approach Canada, could see a great plain, stretching northward until ended by a range of hills similar to that on which he stood, whose isolated peaks alone indicate their presence. In the centre of this vast plain, the gleam of the St Lawrence would catch his eye, and the thought could hardly fail to occur to him, that, at some distant period in the past, the forest-covered flat which stretched beneath him, must have been the bed of a great inland sea, with the Adirondacks on the south and the Laurentian range on the north as its shores, and that the mighty river before him is merely its residuum. With that portion of the plain that lies south of the St Lawrence, and is formed into a triangle by the international boundary-line, the base starting at Chateaugay Basin and the apex at St Regis, I have to deal, and my purpose is to tell how this section which, at the opening of the century, was a howling-wilderness, impenetrable save to the Indian as he sought the wild-beast in his lair, has become transformed into one of the most highly cultivated districts in the Dominion. And not alone the interest that must ever attach to narratives of early settlement belongs to the story I have to tell, for it will comprise the history of a community distinct from every other in the province of Quebec. With the Eastern Townships, with which they are often erroneously classed, the English-speaking settlements of the district of Beauharnois have no affinity. The first settlers of the Eastern Townships were Americans, and between the customs and habits of their descendants and those of the people who live to the south of them there is no material difference, but they who dwell by the Chateaugay and its tributaries are of Old Country stock, and in character, ways of life, and speech present nearly as striking a contrast to the Americans, who are divided from them by an imaginary boundary-line, as they do to the French Canadians who are found among them and who hem them in to the north and east. Thus it comes that my narrative deals not only with an isolated and peculiarly situated portion of the Dominion, but with a community distinct from the neighboring populations and possessing a marked individuality. My story is that of the chief settlement in Quebec of Old Country immigrants, of their struggles, their trials, and their triumphs in subduing an inhospitable tract of country, and of their relations with the French-Canadian people, amidst whom they exist like a sand bank in the sea, always threatened with overflow and extinction, yet unchanged and unmoved by the surrounding waters.

Of the history previous to the year 1800 of that portion of Canada which lies between the mouths of the Chateaugay and of the St Regis little can be said, and it is a satisfaction to the enquiring mind to know, that this is not only because little has been preserved but that there was little to tell. The country was in a state of nature, and its chief inhabitants were wandering bands of Indians. There had, indeed, been a time when a race superior to Huron or Iroquois possessed the land, for the striking eminence on Nuns' island, and the smaller one on the mainland to the south of it, tell of the presence of that singular people, the Mound Builders. The mound on the island is in admirable preservation and the largest in the Dominion. No attempt at excavation has yet been made. Considering that the district was a favorite hunting-ground, the fewness of the Indian relics preserved is singular, and attributable, probably, to the heedlessness of the settlers, who cast aside the fragments the plow turned up. Along the river-banks, stone arrow-heads, tomahawks, and pottery have been frequently found. On the point on the north bank of the Chateaugay, where the English river unites with it, was a considerable clearing, which the first settlers believed had been made by the Indians and which they named Indian point. From the quantity of stone weapons and implements which were unearthed, their surmise that the clearance had been the site of an Indian village was a reasonable one. They discovered no iron relic of these times with the exception of a pronged spear, which must have required a handle two inches thick.

The traces of the presence of the French during what may be termed the romantic period—the age of exploration and missionary journeyings—are equally dim. While passing over lake St Francis, nightfall overtook Champlain off the mouth of the Laguerre, and drawing up his canoes on the shingly beach he kindled his camp fire. From a very early date there must have been a portage-trail along the bank from Hungry bay to Melocheville, for the south channel was used by the voyageurs.

Although the great river that bounded it was thus a highway, the French obtained no foothold in the district until long after their taking possession of the country. This arose from the insecurity caused by hostile Indians, and it was not until the subjugation of the tribes by Frontenac, after the massacre at Lachine, that it became safe to attempt a foothold on the south bank. Isle Perrot and the north shore, as far west as the Cascades, had been dotted with houses, before a single clearance had been made on the other bank. During Frontenac's time a seigniory 6 miles broad and 9 deep, was carved out of the bush, and given to Charles L. Lemoine, seignior of Longueuil. The deed bears date Sept. 29th, 1673, and the title given to the seigniory was Chateaugay, a name probably derived from some place in

France.* Thirteen years afterwards the seigniory was still a wilderness, but in 1687 it is believed that, in order to hold it, Mr Lemoine caused to be built on the western point of l'isle St Berñard (Nuns' island) the windmill which still stands there, but now converted into an oratory, and the land bounded by the lake and river was surveyed. The lots were laid out long and narrow, so that the settlers could build their houses close together for mutual defence. When the first, clearance was made is unascertainable, but from the fact that the Jesuits, who held the neighboring seigniory of Sault St Louis, and had opened a church at Caughnawaga half a century before, deemed it advisable to establish a mission at Chateaugay Basin in 1736, it may be concluded that there existed by that time a respectable settlement.† The log church they erected was used until the end of the century. It stood about a quarter of a mile below the bridge, on the west bank, where its site is indicated by a row of elms. In 1759 one hundred lots had been conceded, the habitants paying an easy rental of 1 sol (2 cents) for each of the ordinary arpents and a fat fowl for each front arpent. The following year, a band of Indians, belonging to General Amherst's army, traversed the infant settlement. The only

*Among the pioneers of Louisiana was a Chateaugay, who afterwards became governor of the French colony of Cayenne. I have been somewhat perplexed as to the spelling of the word. Up to within half a century it was more commonly written without the final u than with it. DeSalaberry, who helped to make the name famous and who was an admirable French scholar, wrote the word Chateaugay, at once preserving the correct pronunciation and keeping in unison with the rules that govern the spelling of modern French, for the "guay" is antique if not barbarous. In the consolidated statutes for U. & L. C. the name is given as Chateaugai.

† The Jesuits visited the settlement before 1736, however, which is the date when they built a church. The edicts and ordinances of 1722, by which so many parishes were established, says : "This fief having no parish adjoining it, and not being sufficiently settled for one to be erected therein, shall continue to be served as a mission by the missionary to the Iroquois Indians of Sault St Louis."

incident of their incursion preserved, is that they scalped a man and woman while working in a corn-field, and that one of the two recovered. As it was part of Amherst's policy to conciliate the habitants, the probability is that the settlement was left unharmed, and that the outrage mentioned was exceptional.

On the 25th August, 1764, Miss Marie Anne Robutel de Lanoue sold the seigniory to Madame Youville, foundress of the convent of Grey Nuns at Montreal, for $1322 and a pension of $900 a year. When the transfer took place, 1542 arpents had been conceded on the north side of the river and 2875 on the south, the settlement extending from the St. Lawrence to the bridge. Except a small fringe of clearance on either bank of the river, no impression had been made on the forest, and the probability is that the settlers depended more upon hunting and fishing than on cultivating the soil. When the nuns took possession, they adopted Isle St. Bernard for a country residence, there being then an old log-house upon it, 20 x 50 feet, and about 100 arpents under cultivation, but they never lived there in any numbers, and, save in summer, seldom more than three or four were to be found. Five years after becoming owners of the seigniory, the nuns built the first dam, a short distance above the bridge, and a grist-mill, which shows that the settlement had so increased that the old windmill was no longer sufficient. In 1774 they built the present manor-house, and the old Jesuit church was replaced by a spacious stone edifice, dedicated to St John.

While a sleepy little settlement was thus vegetating at the mouth of the Chateaugay, no movement was to be marked either south or west of it. Over fifty years after the creation of the seigniory of Chateaugay, that of Beauharnois, or Villechauve, took place. It was made an exact square, 18 miles each way, and was ceded by the French king to Charles, Marquis de Beauharnois, who was then governor, so that the gift was like one to himself. His brother Claude, a former intendant, was made a partner in the gift. Neither of the brothers availed themselves of the estate, magnificent in extent at least, though the deed states that it was conveyed to them because they had formed a design of bringing out a colony from France, and because they had given assurance that the land was to be "cleared immediately." The grant to the Beauharnois brothers bears date April 12, 1729. On June 14, 1750, the French king signed a new deed, ceding the seigniory to Lieutenant de Vaisseau, Marquis de Beauharnois, for the reason that he (the king) wished to favor the design, which the marquis had formed, of planting a large settlement upon it.* Nothing was done, and, in 1763, his representative transferred his rights to the Marquis deLotbiniere for $8000. He, also, did nothing towards improving the property, leaving it in a state of nature, for, beyond a few habitants who had crossed over from Isle Perrot and squatted along the lake shore between the foot of the rapids and where Beauharnois now stands, there was not a sign of clearance in its 324 square miles. One of these was Joseph Hainault, grandfather of the late sheriff, who left Isle Perrot for the mainland about 1782. The number did not increase until towards the close of the century, when a steady influx from Isle Perrot and the north shore began. DeLotbiniere retained his unproductive purchase until the 30th July, 1795, when he sold it to Alexander Ellice, a member of a great commercial house in London, for 36,000 Spanish dollars. The deed states that Mr Ellice was present at its execution, and that, as he could not speak French nor the notary English, Mr Richardson acted as interpreter. One clause bound Mr Ellice to grant deeds to those who had squatted on the seigniory, and whose number is given as about 60. The price seems excessive, and may be accounted for by supposing that the seigniory was either taken in payment of a bad debt, or that there was at the time a speculative demand for wild lands. In support of the latter supposition, it may be stated that Mr Ellice seems to have had a craze

*What the cause was for the second deed, which is simply a regrant, I have been unable to ascertain. There may have been some dispute between the heirs of the original grantees.

for land, and through his agent in Montreal, Mr Richardson of the firm of Richardson, Forsythe & Co., hardware merchants, was a large buyer of the land scrip offered by militiamen and others. Francis Winter, an American, was engaged to act as local agent, and William Waller to make a general survey of the seigniory and lay out in lots a portion of the lands bordering the St Lawrence and the Chateaugay, and this task he seems to have fulfilled in the summer of 1800. In laying out the seigniory he divided it into sections, giving them the names they still bear—Catherinestown, Helenstown, Marystown, Annstown, North and South Georgetown, Ormstown, Jamestown, Williamstown, Edwardstown, and Russeltown, being the Christian names of Mr Ellice's children. The seigniory itself was named Annfield, after Mrs Ellice, and the chef lieu Annstown (now the town of Beauharnois), which had been selected on account of its being the only bay between Chateaugay Basin and the foot of the rapids, and the only place having water-power, which, even at that date, was utilized, for there was a small sawmill at the mouth of the St Louis, which apparently as early as 1780 began changing the noble pine-trees that overhung its waters into boards, which were sold to the habitants on the north shore and rafted to the city. Beyond surveying it, Mr Ellice did nothing towards settling his great estate. He died in 1804. From several old deeds I have examined, I am disposed to believe that he intended each of his children should inherit the portions to which he gave their names.

CHAPTER II.

WITH the overthrow of French rule ceased, of course, the creating of seigniories, so that, after the American revolution, when the southern boundary of Canada was established, there lay a vast tract of territory between the seigniories and the frontier, which was called "waste lands." As the seigniories of Chateaugay and Beauharnois occupied the greater part of the wedge-shaped piece of land west of Caughnawaga, there was only a ragged fringe of waste land between them and the United States. The necessity of providing for the soldiers who had served in the American war apparently first suggested the propriety of surveying this tract and dividing it into townships. This was done by Mr Chewett, deputy-surveyor-general, in 1788-9, when he defined the boundaries of the non-fief land west of the Richelieu, and which constitutes the present county of Huntingdon, its singular shape arising from its being formed of the gores left after forming the seigniories. Before Mr Chewett sent in his report, the political status of the province underwent a change. Up to 1791 it had been under military rule, which suited the requirements of the country very well. The Canada act ended this, and substituted a modified constitutional system. The sole territorial division heretofore had been that of the seigniories, but now the English plan of counties, and, where they did not interfere with the seigniories, of townships, was introduced. In May 1792 a proclamation was issued dividing the province into 21 counties, all of them, with six exceptions, bearing such English names as Devon, Hertford, Kent, and York. Out of the district lying west of the Richelieu a large county was formed and named Huntingdon. The choice of name governed the subdivisions, and Mr Chewett, who did not file his report until

1795, took from old Huntingdon the names Hemingford,* Godmanchester, Hinchingbrook for three of his townships. Each county was allotted the right to send two members to the legislative assembly then constituted. The election was held in June, the month following the issue of the proclamation, when Hypolite St George Dupre and C. C. Larimier were returned for Huntingdon. The poll was opened at St Phillipe and probably the two members were from that neighborhood. The thus forcing constitutional government upon the habitants was a great absurdity, for they had no conception of it and were unfitted for self-government. They took what was meant by the Imperial authorities to be a privilege as a deep-laid plot to tax them, and regarded the poll as a place to be tabooed, and whoever voted as an enemy of the country. So strong was this ignorant delusion, that twenty years after the electoral system was introduced, there were large parishes whose inhabitants boasted that a vote had never been given by them. The consequence was, that, outside the towns, for many years, the holding of elections was nominal, and the members returned went in by acclamation. These members were, with few exceptions, so ignorant that they could not read or write.

The intention of dividing the land surveyed by Mr Chewett among the veterans of the American war was carried out to a limited extent only. A large portion of Godmanchester (which then included St Anicet) was so ceded and a small part of Hinchinbrook. The recipients sold their claims, which were bought up mainly for Mr Ellice at trifling cost, with the exception of a party of them who formed a settlement on the 2nd range of St Anicet, and which dotted the ridge from Ogilvie's hill to the Laguerre. When that settlement was formed, who belonged to it, and what its experience was, I have been unable to ascertain. This alone is known,

---

* The additional m seems to have crept in from an idea that the township was named after a person by the name of Hemming. The dropping of the g in Hinchinbrook followed its ordinary pronunciation.

that, at the outbreak of the war in 1812, it was abandoned, and when the first immigrants came, they found a row of some ten roofless shanties and of clearings covered with saplings.

What was to be done with ·the wild lands outside the seigniories perplexed the executive very much. The simple plan of throwing them open to actual˙settlers does not seem to have occurred to those who then governed the province. Being deeply imbued with aristocratic ideas, they sought after the creation of a territorial gentry, and proposed to grant the townships to cadets of English houses, who, they expected, would get the land settled by a class of farmers who would pay them rent. Nay more, one-seventh of the land was to be reserved for the support of a clergyman of the Church of England, so that each township would have its rector as well as its magnate.

Had the plan worked, we would have had in the townships the Old Country system of tenants and landlords—of a hundred farmers paying rent to a little autocrat. They might as well have proposed to establish the ·Highland clan system. It was impracticable, and the only result of the attempt was that a number of favorites got large grants of wild lands which they did nothing whatever to improve. The plan was subsequently modified by granting each township to a leader and associates, the former paying the survey and patent-fees and selling the lots at what he could to 'his ·associates and others. It is pitiful to see how, in these critical years, the rulers of the province were trammelled by antiquated and impracticable ideas, when, under a common-sense policy of selling to whoever would clear the land, the townships might have been thickly settled by Old Country-men.

In 1792 Walter Dibblee of St Johns was instructed to survey Hemingford, and was followed the next year by Joseph Kilburn, who was directed to lay it out into farms, excepting the portions reserved for the·clergy and for the crown. He completed his field-work that fall, and drew his plans at his home at Longueuil, transmitting them to Quebec in March, 1794. In his report, he stated that he had made the lots as uniformly 200 acres in extent as possible, with an allowance of 5 per cent. for roads, and that he had left two blocks undivided, one of 8,075 acres for the clergy and one of 7,220 for the crown. The total acreage he had divided into lots was 58,600, and of it he wrote: "The land is very good, and fit for the cultivation of any kind of grain peculiar to this country. Timbered chiefly with birch, basswood, maple, hemlock, some pine, butternut and elm, except the swamps, which are cedar and spruce. The land is well-watered, and there are some falls in the different rivers which will admit of good mill seats." In 1793 W. Walker was sent to begin the survey of Hinchinbrook and was followed by Henry Holland the same season. They did not complete their task, however, for in 1801 J. Rankin finished what they had left undone. Hemingford and Hinchinbrook were erected into townships by proclamation of Governor Sir A. Clarke.

The first large grant in the Huntingdon townships is dated January 3, 1779, when General Prescott deeded over 7000 acres in Hinchinbrook to Gilbert Miller, and in March following nearly 40,000 acres to Robert Miller. Of these persons, I can learn nothing, and they were probably given these grants as being favorites of the government. They and others, to whom like grants were subsequently made, never visited their domains nor did anything towards settling them. Of all to whom grants were made, probably Robert Ellice and the other heirs of Alexander Ellice, alone realized anything. In 1811 they got a grant of 25,592 acres in Godmanchester and of 3719 in Hinchinbrook, in settlement of the land claims their father had bought from old soldiers. These lands were held, some as long as 70 years, by the Ellice family until sold to actual settlers at high prices.

While the government was moving thus bunglingly in the matter of settling the townships, a movement set in which resulted in a portion of them being taken up. The agitation of the American colonists to throw off their allegiance to Great Britain was not the unanimous one that is generally

supposed. There was no inconsiderable number who held
that so extreme a step was unjustifiable and who exerted
themselves in opposition to it. When hostilities began, many
who thought thus left their homes and joined the king's
troops. Those who remained on their farms, where the insurgents had control, were subjected to cruel persecutions by
their neighbors. The legislatures of several states passed
acts confiscating the property of-all who refused to swear
fealty to the new republic; that of Massachusetts went
further, it ordered them into banishment. Wherever deprived of the protection of the British army, those who
remained true to the king, had neither liberty of speech nor
pen. It became the fashion to organize mobs to visit the
houses of people whose only crime was devotion to the government of their fathers, and outrages, often too disgraceful
to detail, were perpetrated upon them and their families.
When a man like John Adams recommended "to fine, im-
prison, and hang all inimical to the cause" of separation
from Great Britain, it may be imagined to what excesses
the lower classes would proceed. Many loyalists from terror,
for the sake of their children, or to save their property, took
the oath of allegiance to the republic, but there was a noble
remnant, who would not do violence to their principles, and,
abandoning all their hard earnings, fled to some place where
they could enjoy peace and liberty under the British flag.
Of the tens of thousands who, at the end of the war, thus
left the United States for conscience' sake, a number sailed
to Great Britain, many to the West Indian islands, but the
greater part emigrated to Nova Scotia, New Brunswick, and
Canada. Many of the latter number came by way of lake
Champlain, and of those who did, not a few took up land
on the banks of the Richelieu. As the families of these
loyalists grew up, the sons had to find homes for themselves,
and naturally did so by moving back into the bush, and so
became the first settlers of Hemingford.

Another, and much more powerful agency in settling the
townships came into being about the same time. The sterile
New England States had become overpopulated, and as the

manufacturing interest was then in its infancy, the rising generation was forced to look for other lands to till. In reading the chronicles of these times, it is curious to note how the country west of lake Champlain was regarded in the same light as the people of our day look upon the North-west—as a field for immigration. The talk of the groups who gathered in Vermont stores or Massachusetts taverns of an evening was of the level plains that lay between the Richelieu and lake Ontario, and every summer prospecting parties set out whose reports were awaited with feverish anxiety. Every excellence under the sun was attributed to the western country, and it is not wonderful that, even to its climate, it should have deeply impressed those who, until then, had known nothing better than the stony ridges and narrow intervales of New England. Shrewd men were not slow in turning the emigration-movement to their own profit. Speculators bought up great tracts of land as far west as the Genessee valley and then sent agents to go from one New England school district to another, lecturing on the Arcadias of Clinton or St Lawrence counties and selling lots at from $2 an acre upwards. From this great column of emigrants, who kept streaming towards the Black river and the St Lawrence, and settling the intervening places on the way to them, there were not a few stragglers who left the beaten path, and of those a large number of families turned northward and sought homes in what is now the district of Beauharnois.

CHAPTER III.

WHO was the first to enter the townships with the intention of making them his home, it is impossible to ascertain. That they had settlers at a much earlier date than is commonly supposed is certain. Henry Holland, while surveying Hinchinbrook, casually jots down in his field notes that he had to suspend work on the first concession from want of provisions, that he made a raft to go down the Chateaugay to get those he had left on lot 7, and that about four miles down he met the first settlement, which must have been near Huntingdon village. Who that settler was is unknown; it may have been Baxter, or some other American, on lot 24 or 25. That was in 1793. In a legal document, Squire Manning affirmed that Asa Smith, from whom he bought 48, second range of Hinchinbrook, had taken possession in 1788. That the French Canadians at the Basin must have become familiar, while lumbering or hunting, with the upper reaches of the Chateaugay is obvious, and that some straggler from the column of emigrants who were passing from lake Champlain to lake Ontario may have raised his caboose in the woods to the north of the frontier-line, is probable. Of these adventurers, whether Leatherstockings tempted by the game that abounded, plunderers of the magnificent groves of oak that bordered the rivers, or humble potash-makers, no record is now to be recovered. All that can be said with certainty is, that up to 1800 such settlers must have been few and far between. The earliest settler of whom I have been able to ascertain any particulars is Eustache Dupuis, and his story has a touch of the romantic. When Nova Scotia passed under the British sway, there dwelt in the Western settlement of Acadia an old French couple, named

Dupuis, who had four sons, all of whom had served in defence of the colony. Resolute in their determination not to take the oath of allegiance, the four brothers decided on fleeing to Canada, where the French flag still waved. The waters of the Gulf being blockaded by British cruisers, their only hope of reaching their compatriots on the St Lawrence was by going through New England. Shouldering their muskets and carrying a small iron pot and some peas, they traversed the shores of the Bay of Fundy, and after a journey of many privations and which lasted 9 weeks, they walked into Boston, where, owing to word coming of Wolfe's victory on the plains of Abraham, they stayed. Events moved fast. The downfall of French rule on this continent removed the great obstacle to the American colonies leaving the protection of the Mother Country, and the revolution began. As was generally the case, our four Acadians sided with Britain, and, after a stay of some 8 or 9 years in Boston, made for Canada. One brother found a home at L'Acadie in Laprairie, where his descendants, a numerous host, still are, another settled at Jacques Cartier, and a third went to the Northwest. The fourth, Eustache, found a wife at LaPierre river, opposite the Sault, and stayed there some time, leaving it for Chateaugay Basin, where two of his sons, Benjamin and Norbert, were baptized. A proclamation being issued, declaring Godmanchester open for American refugees, and offering all who would go 3 years' provisions, Eustache, who had no land of his own, accepted the offer. In 1795 he moved his young family, the oldest being six, to lots 48 and 49, 1st range. When he came, there was no settler west of where Valleyfield now stands, though then, or soon after, Knight, of Dutch origin, built a shanty on what is now known as Knight's point. East of Knight, opposite Grande isle, lived Dunn, of like descent. Hungry bay and all west of it was a desolation, the only frequenters being the Indians, whose occasional wigwams were seen, where they pitched them for fishing or hunting, and, in winter the shanties of lumbermen, as they plundered the woods. Dupuis, himself a lumberman, attacked the giant pines, that grew

thick behind his humble shanty on the lakeshore, and by the
sale of masts maintained his family.   His third son, Norbert
Benjamin, was an infant when he came, and he was baptized
at the church at the Cedars.   The nearest mill was at Cornwall, and to it he went until that of Fort Covington was
built, and that at St Timothy.   To reach the latter was
dangerous, and skill was needed to save the flour from being
wetted by the foaming waters of the rapids.   Dupuis had no
neighbor for a year or so, when Genier, a retired officer, who
had been granted lot 26 for his services, came, and was
followed by Chretien, on lot 28, and by Delorme dit LeMay
on No. 32.   The Cazas came next, and being a large family
of stout young men, they made their mark, all taking up lots,
except Baptiste, who lumbered along the Laguerre.   L'Ecuyer
took up lot 27.   All these men were Acadians.   Cascagnette
squatted on lot 50, and so became neighbor to Dupuis.   On
the point of Cascagnette's lot were buried those who died in
the infant settlement, but so great was Dupuis' repugnance to
using unconsecrated ground, that, when his wife died in 1828,
he placed the coffin in a canoe and paddled it to the church-
yard of St Regis.   He was a famous builder of large canoes,
which were called in those days peeros, a corruption of pi-
rogue.   These canoes were hollowed out of the largest pines
obtainable and were blunt at both ends.   For common use
the smaller and speedier canoes of Indian model superseded
them.   In 1835 the old pioneer sank to his rest at the good
old age of 84, and was placed beside his wife.   Up to the last,
though most anxious to hear of their fate, he never learned
aught of the parents he left so sadly in Acadia.   In addition
to those enumerated, J. B. Cartier took up his abode at a
very early date on the site of St Anicet village, a little west
of Masson's store.   He lived to see his 101st year.   Bercier,
Quenneville, Saucier, and Desvoyans were on the shore west
of him.   Dupuis and the other settlers named were, in the
eyes of the law, squatters, for, whether entitled or not to
their lots, they neglected to draw patents for them, and held
them, when their titles were questioned, by prescription.
Dupuis' claim to the lots he lumbered on was disputed by

Ellice, but unsuccessfully. His son Antoine, for services during the war of 1812, in carrying despatches from Chateaugay Basin to Coteau and Cornwall, was rewarded by a grant of 200 acres and the title of major. He died at St Anicet village when 94 years old. He was wont to relate the dangers he ran of being captured and shot when the American flotilla under Wilkinson blocked the river below Cornwall.

Meanwhile a settlement was growing up at the other extremity of the county. At an early period, possibly 1795, a Dutch American, Jonathan Wettson, took up land on the front range of Hemingford and others squatted near him. None of them remained long. The first influx of permanent settlers was in 1800, when several families of U, E. Loyalists moved from Lacolle and neighborhood into Hemingford. The first to go was a Scotchman, James Fisher. He was a native of Killin, Perthshire, could speak Gaelic, and his parents emigrated to the United States when he was 12 years of age. Following the fortunes of the British arms, he left all and sought a new home at the head of lake Champlain, near Alburgh. On the townships being surveyed it was found that the boundary-line, established in 1771-2, was wrongly located in places, and that Fisher was actually in the United States and not in Canada as he supposed. Determined to make sure this time, he sought and obtained a lot in Hemingford, receiving the patent for No. 4, 1st range, in March, 1799. While at Alburgh he had married. Before sleighing went, in the spring of 1800, he moved his family, all young, on to his new possession. He had for his neighbor, Squire Wettson, who, by this time, had a large clearing. The road was a mere ox-track, and on the north side of it, Fisher built his house, the site of which is still marked by the apple-trees he planted and the family-graveyard, in which the hardy pioneer rests. He was followed by Frederick Scriver, who left his home in Duchess county, N.Y., in 1790, the year when it became apparent to the most sanguine loyalists that they could not remain and hold their property without taking the oath of allegiance to the republic. He followed the stream of those, like-minded with himself, who were going up lake Champlain,

and took up land near Lacolle. After remaining there ten
years he considered he could improve his circumstances by
joining in the westward movement, and accordingly took up
lots 61 and 62 in Hemingford. He, also, built on the north
side of the road, and a ruined foundation and the remains of
an orchard mark the site. As the stream of immigrants
increased, he accommodated them by opening a house of
entertainment, which proved to be of great convenience. A
rude road was made north of his house, winding along the
low ridges to avoid the marshy land, and on the west side
of it Hypolite Senecal squatted, and a little north of him,
on the east side, another French Canadian, named Durivage.
This crooked road was joined by a path which led between
the 3rd and 4th ranges. On the east end of it, along the
Little Montreal river, a number of Americans squatted, and
made such extensive clearances that, when they abandoned
them in 1812, they came to be known as "the commons,"
and cattle were sent from a distance to graze upon them.
At the west end of the road, on 48, was Messenger, on 154
Daniel Norton, who lived on the west branch of the creek
to which his family gave the name, and north of him, on
the main branch of it, on 189, Ebenezer Norton, all Americans. Northeast of the Nortons, an important settlement
was begun in 1802 by the moving in from Duanesburgh, N.Y.,
of John Manning, who took up 183 and 184 on the 4th
range. Whether Isaac Wilsea, familiarly styled Colonel
Wilsea, preceded him on 182, it has been impossible to ascertain, but the probability is that he did by a year or two.
Of Mr Manning, who proved a leading spirit in the eastern
end of the county, I will have a good deal to say. The inducement to select his lot was the abundance of ash and
elm that covered an old beaver-meadow. The place is now
desolate, a few poplar-trees and the remains of an old wall
alone indicating where once a bustling homestead stood.
One of Mr Manning's children dying, he fenced in a portion
of his clearance, and it, by his consent, became the common
burying-place for the northern part of Hemingford. In the
spring of 1809 he was appointed a justice of the peace, and

took the qualifying oath in August, before David Ross of Montreal. In 1810 he and S. Z. Watson (presumably a son of Jonathan Wettson), were appointed commissioners to take oaths per dedimus potestatem, to facilitate crown lands' transactions.

All the settlers named found much difficulty in getting into their new homes, for the country between the Richelieu and Hemingford was not merely a wilderness, but one broken by wide swamps. Those unable to move during winter, had to drag their goods on oxsleds over bush-tracks frequently covered by a foot of water. The late Colonel Scriver was wont to relate how he, although only a boy of ten years of age, was entrusted, when his family journeyed to their new home, with an oxsled. Falling behind, he lost his way in the long hollow a mile east of Clelland's Corners. To add to his perplexity, while making his slow way through a long stretch of water, something broke about the sled, and while engaged in vain efforts to repair the injury, darkness overtook him. Realizing the danger of his situation, he abandoned the oxen, and groping his way through the thick forest, his bare feet sore and bleeding, he finally found the little opening in the leafy wilderness where his father had raised a new home. Among the sorest trials of this particular family, was the loss of their only cow, during the second winter, by the awkwardness of a chopper in felling a tree.

Of these early days of Hemingford little can be said. Apparently less progress was made than in Franklin or on the Chateaugay. The mainstay of the settlers was potash, and, as it rose as high as $60 a barrel, and two men could fill a barrel in a month, the making of it yielded good wages. It was hauled on ox-sleds to Montreal by way of St Remi, which, it is right to observe here, was then an American settlement, and there were no French to be met for 4 miles north of it. Both Roxham and Odelltown were also purely American settlements, and more populous and thriving than they are to-day. On getting seed into the land it yielded heavy crops of wheat, corn, and potatoes; the wheat sometimes gave 30 bushels to the acre. The nearest mill was

Judge Moore's, at Champlain, N.Y., and it was not until 1810 that the road to it became fit for wheeled vehicles. Boards had to be drawn from there, so that it was long before sawn lumber was used largely in building. Without having much variety of food, the settlers were never pinched. At first, Indian meal had to be mixed with the flour to make it go further, and there was no pork save what was bought in Montreal or Champlain, but that did not last long. Game, which was abundant in all the other settlements, was particularly so in Hemingford, and venison and bear's-meat, "bush-pork" the settlers called it, were frequently on the table. The country at that time was visited by immense flocks of pigeons, and John Manning, who had a net for snaring them, was in the custom of salting hundreds of them for winter.

While the south-eastern part of Hemingford was thus slowly filling up, another settlement was in progress on the eastern slope of Covey Hill. It was apparently begun by James O'Neill in the spring of 1797. He was a native of Limerick, and had been educated for the Church of England. Instead of taking orders, he emigrated to Pennsylvania, where he married. On the war of the revolution breaking out, he enlisted, and served in the Royal Regiment of Highland Emigrants, seeing some active service. On the war ending he was discharged, and proceeded to Canada. After some delay, a grant of 200 acres, lot 32, was allotted to him, and he proceeded to occupy it, arriving on the 18th April, 1797. The country was in its primitive state, wild beasts abounding. O'Neill used to relate that they never caused in him a feeling of dread save once when, while returning from Champlain with a bag of flour on his shoulders, a pack of wolves suddenly rushed past, a little in front of him; happily for him, too much engaged in the object of their pursuit to see him. The year following, he got neighbors, though not near ones, in the persons of Nicholas Sweet and his two brothers-in-law. Sweet was a native of Vermont. During the war he served as a soldier on the revolutionary side, was made a prisoner at the battle of Bennington, and was sent to Montreal, where he took the oath of allegiance to King George and enlisted in the British service as a drummer. At the peace he got his discharge, returned home, and married. Having a hankering for Canada, he determined to make it his home, and with two brothers-in-law, Grouse and Oliver, started northward about 1798, and squatted on the three first lots of Havelock, their inducement in choosing them being the bonus of $200 offered by Woolrich to those who would clear 30 acres on any of his lots. At the same time as Sweet and his relatives came, a family, probably Scotch and loyalist refugees from the States, moved in from Sorél, the father, Rach Gordon, taking up lot 17 and the son 16. The very day they arrived, the old man lifted his gun and a small keg of liquor they had brought, saying he would look around and see if there was anything to shoot, his purpose being to hide the keg for his own use. He did not return and all search proved futile. Half a century after, when the family had gone, a rusty musket barrel, with the rings that bound it to the stock, and a few scraps of hoop-iron, were found in the woods towards the Flats, and those who had heard their parents talk of the disappearance of old Gordon, believed the relics were of him; that he had got drunk and, wandering in the woods, lost his way, and perished. Thus the liquor-habit began its history of woe in Huntingdon.

In 1801 the settlement received a large accession, the most prominent of the new-comers being Andrew Gentle, of whom, as a leading settler, a few details are required. He was a native of Stirlingshire, Scotland, and was born the year when the hopes of the Stewart dynasty were blasted on Culloden Moor. He was brought up to the business of maltman and brewer, which, in those days, when milk was scarce and tea almost unknown, was a good one, every town and village in Scotland having its brewer of table-beer, which was the only beverage used at meals by the middle classes. A certificate, as to his good character and standing, from the parish minister of Dunblane, shows he had been a resident of that place for 12 years in 1784, the year when he emigrated to America. On reaching the United States he got employment at his calling in New Jersey, where he lived several years and where he married again (for he was a widower when he left the Old Country), his choice being Anne Yale of Connecticut, a member of the well-known New Haven family. They moved to Vermont, where in Charlotte, a small village on Lake Champlain, he found employment at his business, which he afterwards left upon purchasing a farm of 50 acres some distance from it. Cherishing a deep love for the mother land, the abuse of Great Britain and her institutions, epidemic among our neighbors during the French Revolution, and which they carried to a great length, was distasteful to him and he wanted to get back under the old flag, to which he was the more urged by the heavy taxes that then pressed upon the republic. Packing up his effects, he moved, as stated, into Hemingford, and occupied lot 19. Opposite to him, on 70, was Dady, on 69 was James Gilfillan, a Highlander, and adjoining were Oliver Hubbell, William Brisbin, and Samuel Covey, all Americans. The little community lived in great harmony and in a state of mutual helpfulness. When Sweet had earned the bonus, he bought lot 20 from Captain Ephraim Sanford, who was on half-pay, for $150, and which he designed as a homestead. He moved on to it in 1805, which was a memorable year from a cyclone visiting the settlement. It was in June, while he was logging on his new lot, assisted by neighbors, that Sweet observed a fearful looking cloud suddenly loom up in the north-west, and move in their direction with incredible speed. The men fled for shelter, and in the rush the oxen got abeam of a big rock (still to be seen on the south side of the road), when the yoke snapped and they ran different ways. The men got into Gentle's shanty, but the first blast lifted off the roof, when they rushed out and flung themselves on the ground, amid the roar of the storm and the crashing of falling trees. The blast soon passed to the southeast, and the men looked with awe on the destruction it had wrought. For about 1½ miles in width it had mown a clear track through the forest, the trees being levelled. One of the oxen was found killed, the other could not be seen, and it was only after searching

a day or two that it was found pinned in a hollow by a
fallen tree, and with its back worn bare in the effort to
escape. The poor beast was released and did good service
after that. Several cows were killed, and a man, who happened to be passing over the hill at the time, had a narrow
escape. Sweet had sown two acres with wheat, and it was
so covered with debris that it was lost. The calamity was
so discouraging, that the settlers were for abandoning their
homes, believing that to clear up the land, encumbered with
the fallen trees, was impossible for them. The year after,
Covey moved to 33, beside O'Neill, and although he was not
the first settler upon it, for O'Neill was 9 years before him,
the hill came to be known by his name. With his life
on Covey hill I will deal presently. Up to 1812 a number
of Americans came in and there was quite a settlement from
Covey's down to Sweet's. A school was opened in the barn
of one of Sweet's brothers-in-law, who lived on the Havelock
line, and there was preaching occasionally by itinerant ministers from across the frontier. Sweet had brought with him
from Vermont a mare, and, by-and-by, had a team, which, as
the only horses in the settlement, were in request when a
couple had decided to face life together, and wanted to go
to Mooers, N.Y., to find a justice to make them one.

After a prosperous career of eight years or so, the settlement began to decay, the cause being the inability of the
settlers to buy their lots out and out. A wealthy Montreal
merchant, James Woolrich, believing that wild lands would
prove a good investment, began, as Mr Ellice was doing in
the western end of the county, to buy up the claims and
patents of those to whom land had been granted in Hemingford, and few of whom had gone to see them. In this way,
for a nominal sum, he acquired, between the years 1798 and
1816, about 12,000 acres. He purposed to hold the land in
his own name, renting to tenants on terms somewhat similar
to those of the seigniories. To actual settlers he would sell
for a nominal price, subject to a perpetual low yearly rental,
payable to him and his successors. His design was to create,
as near as might be, a seigniory out of township land. He

did little to facilitate the settlement of the blocks of land he acquired beyond building a small grist and sawmill on the English river, on lot 117, about 1808. It had a run of stones for wheat and another for corn, and the miller was a Scotchman, Archibald Muir, who subsequently settled in Franklin. When the settlers (several of whom had taken up lots under the belief that they belonged to the crown) came to understand that Mr Woolrich would not give them absolute possession of the land, but that, on getting over their first difficulties, they would have to begin and pay him rent, they were much annoyed and contemplated abandoning their improvements and taking up land of which they would be unconditional owners. They were the more disposed to do so, from their knowledge that, west of them, lay a country superior to that in which they were. Every season families went past their doors to settle in what was then called Russeltown, now Franklin, and several of them, among them Mr Gentle, resolved to do likewise. The finishing-blow to the settlement came in the summer of 1812, when a proclamation was issued requiring all foreign-born residents to take the oath of allegiance or leave the country. With a few exceptions, the Americans declined to become British subjects, and left.

Covey was among those who left at the outbreaking of the war, and his life during his stay on Covey hill was so peculiar that it deserves describing. His father, Samuel Covey, was reputed to be of Irish descent, and moved from New York state at the close of the revolution and settled at Alburgh with the other loyalists. In recognition of his sacrifices for the British cause, he received a grant of lot 33, on the 1st range of Hemingford, and not caring to live upon it himself, he gave it to his oldest son, Samuel, on his marriage with the daughter of a neighbor-loyalist, and they went through the wilderness to take possession. They stayed (as has been related) for some time in the Sweet settlement, and then moved upwards to their lot. While building a shanty, they lodged in Gilfillan's, which had for a door a large piece of elm-bark. Gilfillan was among those who had moved off

Woolrich's land and had squatted on 134. Covey was a cooper and he raised beside his shanty a log-shop, where he made the wooden-dishes, called keelers, used in the dairy before tin-pans were known, and tubs and pails and potash barrels. Small as was his custom he did not attend to it, for he was a born-hunter, and gloried in the wilderness in which he was placed. He shot moose and trapped beaver, being, probably, the last to do so in Huntingdon, together with innumerable deer and smaller game. The spoil he thus obtained mainly furnished his table, and Mrs Covey found the flesh of the moose to more nearly resemble beef than anything he brought, and the bones to be full of marrow. During his frequent absences, she passed the nights in terror of wild beasts, but her fear of Indians was still greater. These denizens of the forest roamed the slopes of Covey hill and the wilderness to the south of it in search of game, and keenly resented the intrusion of white men in their pursuits, holding that all wild animals pertained to them and carrying out their doctrine by confiscating any skins they found in their possession. Knowing this, when she saw Indians approach, Mrs Covey hid any furs there might be in the house. Her greatest fright was caused by the sudden appearance of two Indians and four squaws, who coolly appropriated the cooper-shop as their place of abode. The untutored savages had no more conception of the rights of property than of the proprieties, and with stolid unconsciousness that they were doing anything wrong, plucked the ears of the corn on the scanty patch and searched over the little shanty as if it were their own. Only one place they failed to explore, the bed, and under it Mrs Covey had concealed the furs then on hand. She had raised some flax the summer before, had spun it, and got it woven at some distant settlement, and was now cutting the cloth so obtained into garments. She missed a sleeve and other portions, and managed to make known her loss to an Indian, who could speak a few words of English. He said nothing, but, when leaving, a young squaw, who had purloined the cloth, at his instance, restored it, with a pair of moccasins and some toys for the infant,

showing that the sense of right survives in the human breast
even when the conscience is unenlightened. To Mrs Covey's
great relief, her unwelcome visitors then left. Mention has
been made of an infant. When it was about to be born, she
had gone on a visit to her father's, where she was delivered,
and returned again to her lonely home on the hill-top, clasping the little Rachel to her bosom. Necessarily a close
intimacy grew between her and her nearest neighbor, the
O'Neills, so much so that when either she or Mrs O'Neill
had occasion to leave home, they entrusted to one another
the care of their children. Before she left the hill, four
children were born to Mrs Covey. To fill their little mouths,
Covey still, with the carelessness of a hunter, relied more
on his gun than on enlarging and cultivating his clearance,
and moose meat was more common than bread. When he
had a grist, or had money, obtained by selling furs, to purchase flour, he went to Chateaugay. At first he made the
journey on foot, carrying the bag, but latterly he got a pony
to bear it, and he would start out with a hatchet in his belt
to blaze the trees and his gun over his shoulder. When the
pony had to be fed, he fastened a rope to its neck and
wrapping the other end round his wrist he slept while it
grazed. For this rude life Covey was adapted by nature, for
though under the average stature, he was thickset and of
great strength. He was wont to relate that he was only
once in peril of his life. He fired at a large bull moose and
wounded it, when the infuriated animal dashed at him before
he could reload. His presence of mind did not desert him,
and as the brute neared him he stepped behind a small tree.
With lowered head the animal did not see him move, and
ran against the tree, its horns branching on either side.
Before it could recover from the stun, Covey had killed it.
The lake and gulf were part of his trapping-ground, and
he stated, when he first saw the latter, its sides were so
thickly covered with large trees, that their tops almost met.
Several years afterwards, in 1825, when the Huckleberry
rock was swept bare by fire, these trees were destroyed. The
food of the little household consisted of the fruits of the

chase, boiled corn, and occasionally wheat-bread. The wheat he raised was so affected by smut, that it had to be washed before taking to mill. The cause of his not going to Woolrich's mill, was that the intervening country was so wet that he could seldom reach it with a horse. When war broke out in 1812, he listened at last to the entreaties of his wife, who had long desired to leave the hill, and, selling his lot to Woolrich, he retired to La Tortue, so far inland as to be out of reach of the coming storm, having lived on the hill 7 years. At La Tortue he stayed a year and moved to Clarenceville, when he entered the army, and was one of the guides in Prevost's expedition to Plattsburgh, during which he was threatened with death on suspicion of misleading a column of the army. About 1830 he moved into Franklin and settled down with his brothers, James, Enos, and Archibald, on 51 of the 1st range. His love of the chase clung to him and, like all hunters, he was poor. While on a visit to his son John at Gananoque, Ont., he died, at the age of 86, and the following year his faithful partner, who had accompanied him to their son's, was laid beside him. I have been minute in describing the fortunes of Samuel Covey, because no ordinary interest attaches to him, from his name being associated for all time with the only hill in the district.

North of Covey hill, on Russeltown Flats, a settlement sprung up at the beginning of the century. I do not here speak of it, reserving what little I have been able to recover of its early days for the chapter on Havelock, and pass on to note the successive steps by which the settlers pushed westward from Covey's shanty on the brow of the hill, where the road, or, more properly speaking, track, bent northwards and passed over the shoulder of the hill and came out at the line between 134 and 136, where lived Levi Stockwell and his son David, whose name has been perpetuated in that of the postoffice. Stockwell had served on the American side in the war of the revolution and to qualify him to draw his pension lived part of the year on the American side of the line. He was much addicted to drink, and the surprise was common that one so dissipated should live so long.

The road from Stockwell's west followed, with slight varia-
tions, its present course, and grew out of the track made by
those journeying into Franklin to take up land. The first
shanties encountered were those of Jacob Manning, lots 15
and 16, and his brother-in-law, Gilbert Mayne, lots 13 and
14. Manning's father, though a loyalist, was several times
drafted, and escaped serving in the American army by supplying substitutes. When the Royalist cause became hopeless
he left Poughkeepsie and settled at the head of lake Champlain. His son Jacob, when old enough to be doing for
himself, went to Montreal and worked with Mayne on several
contracts, one of which was macadamizing St Paul-street,
about the first, if not the first, attempt of the kind in
Canada. Resolving to have homesteads of their own, they
visited Huntingdon, and decided on Franklin. They moved
in the spring of 1804, going by way of läke Champlain.
At that time there was no road, merely a rude track through
the woods. Having some money, they both brought considerable stock and made a good start. Their choice of lots
was guided by the splendid timber for ashes that covered
them, and they did not see that the land was as stony as
it proved. The potash they made, they hauled on sleds by
a bush-track to a point on the Chateaugay a little below
the blockhouse, whence it went by canoe to the Basin.

At the same time, or the year before, a German, Jacob
Mitchel, who had long been resident in the United States
and where he had got an Irish wife, penetrated deeper into
Franklin and squatted on 48 of the second range. His name
has been preserved by being associated with the brook whose
crystal waters danced swiftly by his lonesome hut. He was
followed by a large number of Americans, who came in both
by Chateaugay, N.Y., and the Covey hill road. Strange to
say, Franklin was of high repute among the land-hunters
of these days. The grass was greener and more abundant
than in Hemingford, abounding with springs and brooks
there were no swamps, and the seasons were deemed earlier
and milder. The magnificent growth of hardwood that clad
the pleasant slopes was looked upon not merely as valuable

for potash but as an indication of the richness of the soil, the stones in which were not discerned, being buried deep in the forest-litter of ages. Settlers kept streaming in, so that when the war broke out in 1812, Franklin was more thickly populated than Havelock or Hemingford. Of those who came in during this period, few proved permanent settlers. The chief of them was Andrew Gentle, who, moved by the reports of the superiority of Franklin, visited it 'in 1808 with the view to pick out a lot, when he selected No 3 on the 2nd range. His choice was decided by a spring which poured forth an abundant stream of the purest water, and beside which he built a shanty, which stood where the road now runs. It was somewhat better than common, for it had 3 windows of 5 panes each, the flooring was basswood slabs, and for the loft there were sawn boards, drawn laboriously from Woolrich's mill and which were the only ones in the settlement. These boards had a singular destiny, for they were taken one by one to make coffins as deaths occurred. Having got a place ready, he moved his family in the following March, the household goods being packed in two sleds, each drawn by an ox, the sleighs being made narrow to pass between the trees on the rude track that led to his new home. He also brought four cows with him. That spring he got a good piece of ground cleared and planted with corn. He was not a handy man for a bush farm and never became expert with the axe, so that he had to manage to get along by exchanging day's work, he going with his oxen to log or drag for some neighbor who would chop or do other service for him. Though sometimes short he was never bare of food in those early years, which was more than some of his less provident neighbors could say, for there were instances of their having to go to Rouses Point, returning with a bag of cornmeal, which cost $3, borne by horse or ox, but by not a few of them on their own backs.

The seignior, who claimed the surrounding territory though he did not attempt to collect rent, had built a small gristmill on the Outarde, and which stood on the north side of the bridge. It was a most primitive affair, having a wheel like a tub, the water striking an arm, and one run of stones, which ground coarsely. There was a sort of a bolt on an upper story, which was turned by hand. The first miller was an American, Sherman, and his death, in 1809, was the first in the settlement; he was buried in the graveyard to the west of Mr Gentle's, being its first occupant. The mill in summer was often stopped from want of water, when an old malt-mill, which Mr Gentle had brought with him, was of service, for it could grind corn roughly.

In 1809 the immigration into Franklin was large, and what had been an untrodden forest was fast becoming a lively community. The inclination was to settle along the track which in time came to be the main road, and very few were out of sight of it. Among the few was Soper, who lived where the village of St Antoine now is. The magnificent growth of hardwood the settlers coined into cash, by making potash, which was in eager demand then at high prices. The labor in getting it to market was very great however, for in summer the only means of doing so was to drag it on oxsleds by way of St Remi to Laprairie and thence by batteaux to Montreal. Each settler generally made two trips in the year, and brought back flour aud groceries. The land, as cleared in the making of ashes, was planted with corn and potatoes and some fall wheat was sown, all of which yielded abundantly. The conveniences of the settlement increased. A physician came to it in person of an American, Dr Buck, who, his practice being limited, filled up his spare time by keeping school, and in 1811 another American, Ketchum, opened a small store alongside the gristmill. There were tradesmen of different kinds, among them being a Scotchman, Dewar, a blacksmith, who had his shop on lot 4, 1st range of Russeltown. The want of lumber was so severely felt by the settlers that they clubbed together to secure a sawmill. The machinery was brought from the States, and the mill set agoing on lot 6 of the ninth range. It was run by Joseph Towns, an American.

CHAPTER IV.

THE FIRST SETTLERS ON THE CHATEAUGAY AND TROUT RIVER.

At the time its eastern frontier was being fringed with the petty clearings of first settlers, the district was penetrated by the Chateaugay by a considerable body of men in search of land. Those who first traversed its waters with the view of establishing homes upon its banks were Americans, and, unlike those who moved in by Hemingford, without admixture of United Empire Loyalists. In 1790 the New York legislature had voted a sum to make a road westward from lake Champlain to the St Lawrence, and in 1796 a trail was cut out from Plattsburgh to what ultimately became the village of Four Corners, now known as Chateaugay, N.Y. In the early spring of that year Benjamin Roberts moved from Vermont with his family and established himself on a lot about a mile north of the present village. To get there, during the latter part of his journey, he had to drag his household goods on handsleds over the snow, the brush being too thick for ox or horse, his wife walking with an infant in her arms and he himself carrying his youngest boy. He was the first settler in Franklin county, and when Nathan Beman followed in the summer, his wife was the first woman Mrs Roberts had seen for three months. These two families were the advance-guard of the great body of immigrants which, from that year, began to pour into Franklin and St Lawrence counties. As they settled down, they naturally turned to exploring the country in their vicinity, and those in the neighborhood of Chateaugay very speedily followed the course of the river that bounded northward in a succession of impetuous rapids, and found, after descending the hills, that its turbulent waters expanded into a noble and placid river, which, with many a curve, wound through a wide-

4

spreading plain of fertile soil. The advantages presented by the country they thus explored over the sandhills on which they had built their shanties, they were quick to perceive: the land was better and the river afforded an easy mode of access to Montreal, which then was the only possible market for the entire country south of the St Lawrence as far west as Ogdensburg. The great objection to their moving on to this new land was the fact that it was in Canada and that the more desirable portions were within the seigniories, where, in time, they would have to pay rent. Despite those hindrances, (of the latter the first-comers were ignorant, for no attempt was made to collect rent until after 1806), many ventured, and soon the smoke from the shanties of American settlers curled over the waters of the Chateaugay. When the first ventured in is not known, but there were few, if any, before 1800, in which year a number began to make clearances on the north bank from where the village of Ormstown now is to Logan's Point. They made a sort of road from Chateaugay, N.Y., to what they called "The Cove," being the pool on lot 16, 3rd range of Hinchinbrook, where the shallow rapids end. From there, they drove on the ice in winter or proceeded by canoe in summer. At a very early date, probably in 1802, a road was brushed across the country from the settlement to Chateaugay N.Y., which could be used in sleighing-time. These settlers were, without exception, from the New England states, very many of them from Massachusetts, and, as became their ancestry, were industrious and handy. During winter they lumbered or made cordwood, so that every settler, when the ice broke up, had a raft of either square timber or cordwood to take to Montreal, and the rest of the year they spent in clearing and cultivating the land and making potash. They were thrifty and became comfortable much sooner than had they remained on the sandy knolls of Franklin county. Though they labored under the disadvantages always attendant upon living in a wilderness, yet, as they expressed it in a song that was popular among them, they were independent, having no taxes to pay and being free from judge and bailiff. The same immunity

from social restraint which has such a fascination for the
pioneers of the territories, charmed those early dwellers by
the Chateaugay, and, also like the population of the territories, they had among them not a few who were refugees
from justice.

It is either a peculiar or a very small community which has
not a Scotchman. As has been seen, there was one in Hemingford, and this infant settlement on the Chateaugay had
also a representative of the omnipresent race. In 1800 one
Goudy took up the lot west of Georgetown church. He did
not stay long, and seeing he could do better in Montreal, he
gave his place to his relative, William Ogilvie, who came from
Scotland in 1802. Goudy was the forerunner of that body of
Scotch emigrants who, before other 30 years, were to possess
the land between the St Louis river and the Beech Ridge.

The unlooked for influx of settlers from the United States,
compelled the agents for Mr Ellice to make arrangements for
granting them lots. They would sooner the Americans had not
come, but as they were taking possession of the banks of the
Chateaugay in spite of them, the best that could be done was
to induce them to accept deeds, which were based on double
the rental that the other seigniories were exacting. Otherwise the terms were considerate. The settlers were to be
allowed to sit free of rent for the first two years, and at the
expiration of the third were charged $1, and for each of the 4
succeeding years $1.50. In the eighth year the rent rose to
$2.20, and increased one shilling (20 cents) per year until the
12th year, when $3 was exacted for it and the 13th. After
the 13th year, the rent was $5, and at the end of the 15th,
year, 5 bushels of merchantable wheat was exacted in addition. The principle upon which the rent was based, was to
give the settler time to make his clearance and to exact rent
in proportion as his holding increased in productiveness.
Each deed was coupled with such galling reserves as that the
settler had no right to the minerals or the stone on his lot,.
that he could utilize no water-power that might be upon it,.
build no mill, not even one driven by wind, while the seignior
could take off whatever timber he might see fit. The seignior

also exacted that the settler should build a house within a
year and have, within five years, 4 arpents under grain or
pasture, while, under a penalty of double toll, he bound himself to carry all his grain to be ground at the seigniory mills,
for which a toll of one-tenth would be exacted. If the lot
was left without a tenant for a year and a day, the seignior
could resume possession, or if the settler sold his lot, he had
to pay a fine to the seignior of one-twelfth of the purchase-
price, who, if he saw fit, could take possession of the lot on
paying the sum the intending purchaser had offered. Such
were the restrictions of the seigniory system, differing only
from the feudalism of France in that personal service in the
field was not required. As stated, the rent exacted was in
excess of what had been customary for the few to whom
lots were ceded, during deLotbiniere's tenure, paid 5 cents
per arpent only and that is all their lots are still liable for.
As will be seen subsequently, Ellice's exaction of 10 cents
per arpent was disputed as unauthorized by the French law,
which governed seigniories. On the terms named, a number
of lots between Dewittville and the forks of the English river
were taken up by settlers between 1800 and 1812. The agent
who negotiated the majority of these deeds, Francis Winter,
died about the year 1808, and was buried by the roadside,
where some poplars still grow, on the farm he had occupied,
west of Baker's (lot 1). That was the first burying-ground,
and for many years was surrounded by a railing. Thomas
McCord (father of the late Judge) succeeded as agent and
he lived at Beauharnois, until the first seigniory-house was
accidentally destroyed by fire. He did not hold the office
long, only for a year or two, and was followed by John Milne,
who, apparently, had been sent out by Mr Ellice in Winter's
time. He was an Aberdonian, and, though a man of education, of coarse, despotic disposition, greedy, and given to drink.
He also took up his abode at Beauharnois, and when he came
there were only a few habitants, whose huts were scattered
along the shore, for they depended for a living as much upon
hook and line as spade and hoe. Of one of these habitants,
the late sheriff Hainault has preserved a few particulars.

His grandfather, Joseph Hainault, born on Isle Perrot in 1752, took up his abode where Melocheville now stands in 1782, and the following year his father was born. "On his marriage in 1802 the old man gave him a lot near his own, which was almost entirely covered with bush, but had a small house and barn upon it. Here he labored until 1808, when he exchanged for a lot farther east and off the river, so that he was deprived of fishing, which then formed part of his living; on the other hand, game was very abundant, being in the midst of a boundless forest. One fine evening in summer, returning from the field with his loaded gun on his shoulder, he saw before him, through the trees, a deer running. He fired, and though it was 3 acres and 3 rods distant from him, he succeeded in bringing it down with the one shot. One evening towards the end of winter, returning from the forest, with no other weapon than his axe, he heard his dog barking at a little distance, and saw it scratching around a hole in the trunk of a tree. He cut into the hole, and in so doing cut the nose off a young bear cub, which at once set up a howl. Then he saw the trunk of the tree shaking, and an enormous she-bear descending upon him. He waited till she was just going to seize him, and then struck her a blow on the head with his axe that caused her to fall. Another well-aimed blow finished her. My father was a great bear-hunter; he killed no fewer than nine in one fall."

The increase in the number of settlers made the erection by the seignior of a gristmill a necessity, and Mr Ellice sent out (probably in 1800, if not the year before) John Simpson, a Scotch millwright, who built a small mill at Beauharnois, well out in the channel of the St Louis, containing two run of stones. It had not been many months in operation, until it was found to be of little use from the insufficiency of the power. In summer the St Louis dwindled to a brook; in winter the current was choked by ice. If the mill, which had cost a considerable sum, was to be of any value, a better supply of water had to be got. This the agent, Francis Winter, proposed to do by cutting a feeder from the St

Lawrence to the head-waters of the St Louis, and in 1806 a contract was made with Thomas Fingland, a lumberer who lived at Lachine, to do the work. He dug the feeder sufficiently deep where the ground was soft, but owing to his merely making a shallow channel across the ridge that lies north of the St. Louis, the water did not run over except when the St Lawrence happened to be high. The seignior was reluctant to bear the cost of making a sufficient cut across this stony ridge, with the result that the mill was so little to be depended upon, that the settlers continued to go to the mills at the Basin and La Tortue. After finishing the Beauharnois gristmill, Simpson, by order of the seigniory, built a smaller one at Howick, a sawmill at Dewittville, for Daigneault & Moreau, and a sawmill for himself at the mouth of the Outarde.

The seigniory-house at Beauharnois, burned in McCord's time, was replaced by a commodious one, which still stands, and beside it, in 1810, Milne opened a small store, which was of great convenience not only to those in its neighborhood but also to the settlers on the Chateaugay, for by this time the Beauce road had been cut out. Besides keeping some drugs, Milne made pretensions to a knowledge of medicine, so that he was often consulted and sent for, which became risky latterly, when he was seldom free from the influence of drink. On one settler asking for medicine for a sick boy, Milne declared he knew his complaint, and lifted a bottle to fill a small vial. ` In doing so his shaky hands let a few drops fall on the brass buttons of his vest. The settler had not been gone long, when Milne ran shouting after him. He said he had noticed the liquid had turned his buttons green, and concluded he had filled the vial out of the wrong bottle! His sense of humor was of a mischievous cast, as when he got a bundle of old almanacs and, neatly changing the date with the pen, sold them to the settlers at a yorker (an English sixpence, 12½c) apiece, and his encouraging them to clear up a bit of land for turnips with the promise of free seed, and giving them what turned out to be poppy-seed.

The settlement on the Chateaugay extended rapidly, and soon there was a succession of clearings that reached from Ste Martine to Dewittville. Opposite the first named village was William Reed, whose name was given to the rapids, by which they are known to this day. On the rapids above (called by the habitants "la rouge") an American, John Perry, had a small sawmill on the south bank. The shanties were thickest between Logan's point and Ormstown, and, with the exceptions I am about to note, were on the north bank and inhabited by Americans. The causes for keeping to the north bank were palpable, for apart from the circumstance that the land was better on that bank, as evidenced by its being covered with hardwood, while the trees on the south side were mainly tamarac and soft wood, it was only natural that the settlers should seek to be close to the only road, and that they should shun the difficulty of crossing the river, which they had no means of bridging. While each year saw an increase in the number of settlers from the United States, not one passed without a Scotch family also finding its way in. Alexander Hassack arrived from Cromarty in 1801 and settled on lot 17, North Georgetown. Being pleased with the country, he sent for his niece and her husband, James Williamson, who arrived at Montreal in August, 1803, the journey having taken them over four months, half of which time, however, was lost in sailing round from Cromarty to Tobermory, from whence the good ship finally sailed. The same year that Hassack came, there settled to the west of him, on lot 21, John Ralston, also a bachelor, who had been a hind in Ayrshire and boasted of his acquaintance with Burns, with whom, he said, he had worked at making roads. He had a strange peculiarity of eating earth, and while engaged in conversation would nibble at the mortar of the wall adjoining or the clay at his feet.

In 1802 the English river received its first settler, James Wright, a Cupar shoemaker, who left Scotland in 1801, and worked at his trade in Montreal for a year. Wages being very low, he considered he could do better by taking up land, and so moved with his wife and two infant sons to a lot on

the south bank of the English river, about half way between
its mouth and Howick. Mr Wright lived there for several
years, but from the isolated situation he had chosen, no neighbor came. Up to (apparently) 1808 settlers, both on the
Chateaugay and at Beauharnois, had to go to the Basin with
their grist, which they did in canoes, involving an absence
from home of, at least, two days and much hard work, for in
addition to paddling, the recurring rapids made it necessary
to get out and carry both canoe and grist around them.
About that time, the seignior erected a small gristmill very
nearly on the same spot where the Howick mills now stand.
Like the nuns' mill, it only ground the wheat, and the bran
had to be sifted out by hand on reaching home. A sad accident attended the opening of the mill. The dam having
sprung a leak, a Frenchman and his boy were engaged to
draw gravel to repair it, and, in doing so, the canoe upset and
both were drowned, for those who saw the accident could not
swim and there was no other canoe. The miller was a
Scotchman by the name of Somerville, a bachelor, an in-
veterate snuffer, much given to drink, and rather useless
generally, much to the annoyance of the settlers, for, on the
erection of the new mill, according to seigniorial law, they
could no longer go to the Basin. The lot opposite the mill
was held by Somerville, who managed to make a considerable
clearance along the river. A track was bushed from the mill
to the Chateaugay, and was difficult to struggle through, for
the intervening country was then a swamp. West of the
mill, and north of Ogilvie's creek, another Scotchman, Andrews, settled in course of time, and proved great society to
the Wrights, for, though some distance apart, they almost
daily saw each other. One night, when Wright was on his
way to see them, he heard what sounded like a human cry,
and was going towards whence it proceeded, when a second
shriek convinced him it was a wolf. He fled back to his
home, and being swift of foot outstripped the pack. Some
time afterwards, Mr Wright had another narrow escape.
While chopping, his axe glanced and cut a terrible gash in
his leg above the foot. He struggled to the house and Som-

erville, as the nearest neighbor, was sent for. He came, but did nothing but stand and glower at the spouting blood, with his mull in hand, from which he, ever and anon, mechanically took a pinch. Knowing he would soon bleed to death, the sufferer exerted himself, and asked to have his shoemaker's bench drawn near him. With great composure he made a very strong and long wax-end, which he wound around his leg above the wound and, then using his pawl, twisted the thread until the blood was stopped. There was a doctor by this time in the settlement at Russeltown, and being sent for, he dressed the wound, which soon healed. This accident, in connection with another, which happened a little while afterwards, decided him on moving to the Chateaugay. He wanted a cow but could not find a neighbor who had one to sell. One day, Mr Ogilvie told them he was going to Montreal, and if Mrs Wright would go with him he would help her to buy one and drive it back. This was done, and a weary journey the faithful wife had. To feed this cow during the winter, there being neither hay nor straw, Wright cut saplings on the north side of the river for her to browse upon. As spring drew on, the ice grew rotten, and to keep poor bossie from following him, for she ran after him like a dog whenever she saw him go out with his axe, he put up a rough enclosure. One day she managed to break through this and went on to the ice to reach the spot where the browse was generally got for her. When half way over the river, the ice broke under her. Mr Wright fortunately happened to be near, and, with the help of his wife, he took the loose boards that formed the ceiling of the shanty and laid them on the crumbling ice. Standing on these they, with great difficulty, dragged crummie out, but, no sooner was she on her feet than she broke through again, and a second effort had to be made to get her to land. While working to save the cow, Wright saw his three infant children standing on the bank watching the rescue, when the thought struck him, if he and his wife were drowned in their exertions, what would become of them. This consideration determined him to leave the English river and go where he would have neighbors. He accordingly bought a lot east of Williamson's, No 15, which was occupied by an American named Finch, to whom he paid $100 for his betterments. The Andrews also left, going to the States, where the sons became clockmakers, and, long after, one of them revisited the district peddling wooden clocks of their own manufacture. With their departure and that of Wright, all attempt at settlement on the lower portion of the English river ceased. The mill fell into disuse from want of custom and was shut up by Milne, and the miller, Somerville, sold his lot to Reeves, who did not occupy it. The contents of the mill were appropriated piecemeal by those who needed them, until nothing movable remained, and the building became a resting-place for the parties of young folk who went berrying on the rocks east of the English river. A fire lit by those pleasure-makers, one raw morning, set fire to the mill, which was consumed, and the dam fell into ruins. The presence of the few settlers named, together with those on its upper waters, had given the river its name, for the French Canadians had come to know it as the rivière Anglaise. Twelve years and more elapsed before another attempt was made to settle by its pond-like waters.

The settlement on the Chateaugay, which Mr Wright joined, continued to prosper, as, indeed, it could hardly fail to do, for its inhabitants had not the great drawback of new countries to contend with—namely, want of the means of communication with the outside world. The river that flowed by them afforded an easy and cheap outlet to Montreal, and a good deal of money was made by the sale of square timber, masts, cordwood, and potash, the settlers bringing back in their canoes groceries, clothing, and other necessaries. The roads, moreover, were yearly growing better. The grand voyer visited the settlement, and ordered the seignior to construct bridges across the creeks as far up as Dewittville. Long timber being plenty, high ones, on trestles, were erected, flush with the banks—better bridges, indeed, than any that have replaced them. From Dewittville a rude track, with the worst places corduroyed, led by way of Athelstan to Chateaugay, N.Y. There was no bridge either at Athelstan or Huntingdon. The ford at the latter place was at the head of the rapids. Then, from near where the blockhouse stood, a blazed track, fit for ox-sleds in summer and sleighs in winter, ran to Franklin, coming out near Ames's, and thence there was a practicable road across the lines and on to Chateaugay. To the north, as already stated, the settlers had a road (a very bad one, to be sure) by the Beauce to Beauharnois, and another along the west bank to the Basin. Carts and horses came into use and other facilities enjoyed rarely known to settlers at so early a date.

The rapid progress thus made was largely to be attributed to the Americans, and their presence was of vital consequence to the Scotch, for they showed them how to handle the axe, how to fell trees, to build log-houses, to make potash, to plant corn, and a thousand other arts peculiar to the American backwoods. If handy and full of resources, the Americans, in the long run, began to fall behind the Old Countrymen. The former did not like prolonged hard work and were ever ready to do a little trading or speculating among themselves or by going to Montreal, while the latter plodded on, day after day, laboriously clearing the land of its covering of trees and bringing it into cultivation. The Americans teased the Scotch about their broad speech, their clumsiness, their want of sharpness, and the Scotch retorted as to the shallow character and the questionable morality of the "cuteness" on which their critics prided themselves. They were very friendly, however, and so freely intermixed that marriages took place. The American wives were of equal benefit to the Scotch women. They taught them those household economies unknown save in the backwoods; to make maple sugar, to bake, to cure meat, to make cloth. One new-come out Scotch woman, on paying a visit to her American neighbor, was struck with amazement to see how she took a quantity of Indian corn, ground it, sifted the meal, made it into a savory cake, and then served it up steaming hot at the supper-table with honey. The presence of the Americans was as that of schoolmasters to teach the Old Country folk how to farm in the backwoods, their lessons smoothed the way and hastened their progress, and what they taught became a common inheritance for all who came thereafter to settle, for what the first new-comers learned they taught to those who afterwards joined them.

Of the Old Countrymen who lived on the Chateaugay before the war it is impossible now to obtain the names, for there were a number who came, and, after a brief trial, went away. Of those who remained over the war the following is a complete list: On the point, at the junction of the English river, was Alex. Logan, a Rossshire Highlander, who had lived some time in the States. On coming to the Chateaugay he first settled on No 34, South Georgetown, afterwards moving to the point. He was a hardy, energetic man, retaining to the last many of the characteristics of his native hills. In person, he was short and muscular, and in winter wore a buckskin coat, which had a fringe similar to that of the Indians. His farming was rough and careless, yet he generally managed to keep a quantity of wheat for the spring, when he would give it to any newly-come settler on the condition that it be repaid in the fall at the rate of two bushels for one. He kept a large flock of sheep, for which the point was favorable in requiring little fencing, and wool, which was very scarce, he sold at 50 cents a pound. He lumbered a good deal and had the faculty of getting a great deal of work out of his men. The money he made he entrusted to no bank. Changing it into Mexican dollars or gold he buried it in the earth on his farm. He lived to a good age and was drowned in 1853 while crossing one night from Reeves' tavern to his own house.

Alexander Reeves was a London tailor who came out in 1811, in a ship that had 4 guns in apprehension of the impending war. Among her passengers was Thomas Dawes, and a strong intimacy sprang up between the two. After remaining at Montreal for 9 months, they resolved to take up land and try farming, and, in the spring of 1812, moved to the Chateaugay and raised a joint shanty on lot 10, S. Geo. Reeves followed his trade and farming, for, though lame, he was active, and his wife was of singular energy and strength.

After a brief partnership and not agreeing very well, Dawes sold his share to Reeves, and going to Montreal got work in Chapman's brewery. Marrying a widow with some money, he started for himself in 1826 at Lachine, and largely supplied the district with the beer it consumed. In his tours of collecting and taking orders, Dawes, who was a rugged and energetic man, scorned both horse and vehicle, and made his rounds on foot. Finding living on the south side of the river inconvenient, Reeves bought lot 6, N.Geo., from a Canadian and moved across in 1816, when he began storekeeping in a small way and gradually fell into the habit of entertaining travellers. Of him frequent mention will be made in subsequent chapters. To Ogilvie, Williamson, Hassack, and Ralston allusion has already been made. On 22 settled John Harvie, and on 26 Captain Morrison, and on the lot on the opposite side of the river his brother Neil, both natives of Lochgilphead, Scotland. Neil was by trade a mason, but had taken to the sea, shipping under his brother. In 1801 their ship, of which the one was mate and the other captain, visited Montreal when they determined, before leaving, to find homesteads, for they had become tired of the sea and Neil wished a home so far inland that his boys would not know of it. Hearing of land being open for settlement on the Chateaugay, they walked up, when the captain selected the lot mentioned and Neil the one opposite, 30, South Georgetown, whereon he built a shanty large enough to serve also as a store, which he opened with a small stock of groceries. On the death of the captain, in Scotland, who never lived on his lot, Neil bought it and moved over on to it, as more convenient. Near Morrison lived John Stewart, who removed to the States. The only other Scotch settler on the south side of the river besides Neil Morrison, was one named Thomson, who built his shanty on 23, which became the scene of a tragical event. On one of his visits to Montreal, Goudy had engaged a young carpenter, fresh from Ayrshire, named James McClatchie, to work for him. He developed a taste for hunting, and one day, when out scouring the woods, entered Thomson's house, and, before doing so, left his gun at

the door. While conversing with Mrs Thomson, the children
spied the gun, and the oldest boy, Archie, 8 years of age, took
it and said he would shoot the rooster. He inadvertently
pulled the trigger in handling it, when the bullet pierced his
mother. She died that night, her last entreaty being to spare
her boy. The event cast a gloom over the settlement, and its
inhabitants attended her funeral in a body. She was buried
in the Georgetown graveyard, and was the first committed to
its dust. This was probably in 1806. Thomson left some
time afterwards. The foundation of his shanty can still be
traced. A long way up the river, on 14, Ormstown, settled
Thomas Marratt, an Englishman.

Of Old Countrymen who did not stay long, may be mentioned an enterprising man named Rankin, who built a two-
story house on the line between Annstown and N. Geo., intending to keep tavern. It was built of sawed lumber, with board
partitions, and well-finished for the times, being accounted
a remarkable structure by the settlers. Rankin built beyond
his means, and in 1804 was glad to sell house and lot for
$600 to Nahum Baker, a New Englander, and who, as his
son after him, became the most noted of the Americans on
the Chateaugay. He had served in the war of the Revolution,
fighting on the insurgent side at Lexington and Bunker's hill.
What is of more interest, is the circumstance that he was
one of the guard over Major André, the night before his
execution. Baker was wont to tell, that when the guard was
detailed, a quiet hint was given them that if they allowed
their prisoner to escape no fault would be found with them.
They accordingly gave him every chance, pretending to fall
asleep, while the door was left unwatched. Baker perceived
the gallant soldier get up more than once as if to leave, but
each time honor conquered the desire for life, and he heard
him mutter "No, I shall not!" and resume his hard bed.
When he saw him led out next morning to the gallows,
Baker wept. Baker removed to Burlington, Vt., where he
suffered heavy losses from the rascality of a partner, which
caused him to leave. Reaching Franklin county he penetrated
into Canada by following the banks of the Chateaugay.

The settlement progressed slowly, owing to the land being hard to bring in. The stumps being hardwood rotted slowly, which was a great hindrance. No fall wheat was sown, and the main crops were spring wheat, oats, and potatoes, which grew remarkably, for the land was strong. For many years after it was cleared, from three to four hundred bushels of potatoes per acre was common. The Americans raised much corn. Below Round Point little potash was made, the bush not suiting, but above there was much fine elm, which induced many to settle. From the same motive, several Americans went into the bush on the 2nd concession of, North Georgetown and to the ridges on the south lots on the lower concession of Ormstown.

The Americans were careless alike of religion and education, and Sunday was poorly observed. An itinerant preacher visited the settlement, Dr Rogers, who made pretensions to be a physician. He stayed with Root, who lived on 25, preaching in what was at once his kitchen and sitting-room. On Rogers removing to the States, he wrote Root, telling him he had found a home at last, and as he observed people were more ready to pay to save their bodies than their souls, he had given up preaching and devoted himself entirely to medicine. The first attempt at education was made in the shanty of another American, Beech, near the mouth of English river, where a man named Haldane acted as schoolmaster, and was apt enough with the strap at least. After that school was kept in a settler's house farther up the river, by a Scotchman named Renshaw, who was well-liked. Beech, above-mentioned, moved to the Basin, where there were two or three American families at the outbreak of the war, but no Scotch.

All the Americans were hunters, but a few of them made the shooting and trapping of wild animals a regular business, taking the skins and furs to Montreal to sell. The Scotch lads acquired a taste for the chase, and made it their recreation. One of them, Sandy Williamson, had an exciting adventure with a bear. While chopping, he struck a hollow tree, and the crash of the axe speedily aroused a huge bear

within it, which rushed out, felling the dog that was with
Williamson with a blow from a forepaw and eluding the
stroke of the axe. Going for Henry Wright to assist, they
tracked the animal until they lost the trail. On returning
they told their story, and the following day a French-Canadian hunter started. He traced the brute to a new lair it
had formed under a tree in an inaccessible position. Sending
in his dog to start it out, he stood ready and on the bear's
appearing fired. Unhappily the dog got between at that
moment and received the charge, falling dead while the bear
scampered off. After skinning his faithful friend, the hunter
followed the bear's tracks, came up with it, shot it, and
brought back both skins. There were not many bears, but
deer were exceedingly plentiful.

Leaving for a while the settlement I have been endeavoring to depict, I would lead the reader up the stagnant waters
of the Bean river, from where it sluggishly unites with the
Chateaugay, through the dense forest that enveloped it,
across the ridges in whose recesses lie the springs that form
its source, to a settlement of Highlanders who, by a series of
singular events, had been led to plant themselves in the midst
of an untracked wilderness.

Among the grants of land with which the Imperial government rewarded Sir John Johnson for his sacrifices and
services during the American war, was a property in Chambly, which he endeavored to settle with emigrants from the
Mother-country. In the summer of 1802 the Nephton arrived at Quebec with 700 Highlanders, mostly from Glenelg,
Rossshire. Of these a considerable portion were induced to
proceed to Sir John's property. Those who got lots on the
slopes of Mount Johnson (now called Chambly mountain) did
tolerably well, but the surrounding land was so wet that
the Highlanders could make nothing of it, and, after enduring
much privation, determined on looking out another place for
their abode. Three of the shrewdest of their number, John
Roy McLennan, John Finlayson, and Finlay McCuaig, were
selected in the spring of 1812 to go out and spy the land to
'the west. On reaching St Remi, which was occupied by

quite a little colony of Americans, one of them, Abram Welch, hearing of their errand, came to them, and told them there was a fine tract of land near by of which they could take possession. They went with him and were satisfied, for they saw that though the flat land was wet there were many creeks by which it could be drained and that the ridges were extensive. On consulting with the notary at St Remi, they were told that they would be quite safe in settling on the land, that it was part of the seigniory of Beauharnois, and' that once located upon it the seignior would have to recog-nize them as tenants. They engaged Welch (who though a farmer knew something of surveying) to run a base-line, which he did, and which after-surveys showed to be correct. The messengers, wearied with their journey, for they had walked the whole distance, gladly turned their faces home-ward and reported to their brethren their success. That fall, led by the three explorers named, several moved over and founded what came to be known as the Scotch settle-ment. Others followed, until, by 1816, the 1st, 2nd, and 3rd concessions of Williamstown were fairly occupied. The Am-erican squatters at St Remi and along the Norton creek, were very kind, helped them to put up shanties and showed them how to make potash. Those who did not come to Williams-town, went to Glengarry, so that not a single Highlander was left on Mount Johnson. Altogether 60 families took up their abode in Williamstown. They prospered exceedingly. In the forest they had an apparently inexhaustible bank, and, besides making potash, which sold high, they made en-ormous quantities of oak staves for shipment to the West Indies. The flats were covered with magnificent oaks, many trees yielding 18 $3\frac{1}{2}$ foot staves before a knot was reached. Both potash and staves were hauled to Laprairie on ox-sleds, and thence ferried to Montreal; the return-load being pro-visions. They had no facilities as to mills, and when they had wheat to grind they had to haul it all the way to the King's mills on the La Tortue. To the Basin there was only a blazed track, and to Ste Martine not even that much. Boards for their houses they obtained by making saw-pits.

and cutting them with whip-saws, for among their number were several who had been sawyers in Scotland. At Mount Johnson they had been joined by Norman McLeod, a schoolmaster, sent out by the Royal Institution, which allowed him £60 a-year, and whose services Sir John had obtained for them. On the breaking up of the settlement at the Mount, he elected to go with the division that had selected Williamstown, and choosing a lot in the Scotch settlement, he continued to hold school in his own house, so that the rising generation was more favored in this than in any other of the early settlements. On Sundays he gathered the people together and held divine service in Gaelic, which was the language of the settlement. So remote was the settlement that the seignior left them undisturbed for 8 years, after which rents were exacted, but no deeds were given until Manuel surveyed the settlement in 1821.

Along both sides of the Norton creek there were a considerable number of Americans, who had come from Connecticut, the only exception being William Struthers, who was Scotch by his father's side and German by his mother's, and who had moved over from Caldwell's manor. The most friendly relations existed between the Americans and the Highlanders.

Returning to the Chateaugay, I resume the description of the settlements along its banks, ascending its waters from the point I heretofore treated of. There were at least 20 American families from the mouth of the English river to Morrison's rapids,* above which the bush solidly presented

*As possibly a matter of interest to a few I give the names of the American families so far as I have been able to recover them and the number of their lots : Hall, probably 93, Annstown; Nahum Baker, 94; George Perry, who from being weatherwise was known best as Old Almanac, on No 1 North Georgetown, where he was buried; opposite him Beech seems to have lived. Nathan Baxter, No 10; Baxter, jnr, 17; Bill and Ike Davis on 19 and 20; Auldjo probably on 25; Root on 26; Goodwin, a turner by trade, who made furniture and moved to Montreal, on 26; William Dunsmuir, commonly styled Doctor, on 29, who came very early. In 1807 he sold

itself with few breaks until Round Point was reached. From there the country was uncleared save the flats along the river, which had been brushed and raised large crops of natural hay, which was cut and stacked and drawn away on the ice by the settlers who lived farther down. Where the village of Ormstown now stands, lived Jones, whose house was a little to the east of the grist-mill, and next to him, was one Spears, who was a leading man among the settlers, and who gave a piece of land for a burial-place, which long afterwards was adopted by the Presbyterians and adjoins their church. Above Spears was another family of Shurtleffs, and at the mouth of the Outarde lived the Scotchman, John Simpson, already referred to as having been engaged by the seignior to build mills. Here he had thrown a dam across the Outarde and raised a sawmill, which he managed himself, and which was of great value to the settlers both above and below it. The dam led to the river changing its outlet, it breaking out a new channel a little farther west, so that where the mill stood is now dry land.*

At McClintock's creek was a path that led back to a settlement that had been formed on the upper Ormstown concession. Attracted by the fine cut of timber for potash-making, they had gone in until no fewer than 9 families were gathered together. They cleared a road, fit for ox-sleds, along the banks of the creek to the Chateaugay, and the

to his friend and neighbor Ebenezer Rodgers, who turned it over to the care of Isaac Davis. Where Allan's Corners now stands lived an American family named Bullen, and two children of it are buried in the island that is near. On lot 42 was Cummings, a blacksmith, and on No 1, Ormstown, Johnson. Two families of the same name, Philips, were on No 5, on 19 one Sylvester, and on the point of No 12 lived Shurtleff, who gave his name to the point. At the mouth of Stony creek lived Poulin.

* In the great freshet in April, 1886, the ice choked the mouth of the Outarde, when its heaped up waters sought escape by the channel it had deserted some 60 years before. In rushing through it, trees of ample girth, the growth of the intervening period, were snapped like pipestalks.

bridges they built over the runlets were serviceable when the
first Scotch settlers moved in a quarter of a century afterwards. Of these 9 families, who left on the breaking out
of the war, all record has perished. When the Scotch came
they found great heaps of ashes on the lower end of 29,
where they had been leached, a succession of small patches
of clearances, bearing traces of potato-hills and corn-drills,
and on 27 a well: these were all that remained to tell of their
years of toil, that there men and women once lived and loved
and children romped and grew. From McClintock's creek
to Dewittville shanties peeped out from the bush at irregular
intervals. Their inmates were all Americans, and had come
in much later than those east of Ormstown, so that when
they left, on the breaking out of the war, their clearances were
small and soon lapsed into the forest again. At Dewittville
there were several families, and it may be here noted that
there is a tendency among pioneers to prefer settling beside
rapids, the advantage of a ford being an inducement, while
there is the prospect of the power being applied to run mills,
and the unacknowledged liking even the roughest have for
the motion and foaming sparkle of broken water. On the
north side lived two Scotchmen, McCallum, from Odelltown,
and James McClatchie (page 45) who lived first at the mouth
of the creek on lot 3, but finding it wet, moved to a few
rods east of where the church now stands. McClatchie was
a carpenter by trade and a native of Ayr, where he was born
in 1780. In 1801 he emigrated and had for fellow-passenger
John Ralston (page 39) and was brought, as already narrated,
by Goudy to the Chateaugay settlement, and in one of the
humble homes of which he found a wife, in the person of
Lucinda, daughter of William Reed (page 39). The difficulty
they had in getting the marriage ceremony performed, will
show how isolated the settlement was. They had their
choice of going to Montreal, where there was a solitary
Protestant minister, the Rev Mr Esson, or to Chateaugay,
N.Y. They chose the latter, because there would be no
delay from banns, and drove all the way from Georgetown
to that village in a traineau, where they were married, on the

6th January, 1803, by Judge (in reality only a justice of the peace) Baillie, there being no minister. The young couple began life as stated at Dewittville, and remained for 7 or 8 years, making potash, lumbering, hunting and fishing. Here their first child was born, Charles, probably the first of Saxon parentage in Godmanchester, and his earliest recollection was seeing his father kill an otter in the Chateaugay. On the Hinchinbrook side was Monica, part German and part French, and who had something to do with a small sawmill, probably put up by the seignior about 1810, and there were one or two French-Canadians besides.

Between Dewittville and Huntingdon there was only one clearance, on the river bank of No 9 Hinchinbrook, made by two Englishmen named Hall, who after putting up a good shanty with a cedar-lined cellar, and making a small clearance, at the outbreak of the war left for Montreal, where they entered into business and became well-known merchants. Where Huntingdon now stands the primeval forest still waved undisturbed, but at the head of the rapids, on Somerville's point, there stood a half finished shanty, put up by an American of the name of Sutherland, who, for some reason, gave up his intention of settling there.

Of the settlement on the Trout River, made by the Americans, no satisfactory account can be given, because, unlike that on the Chateaugay, there were no Old Countrymen among them, and, therefore, no recollections of the settlement previous to 1818 are to be got. It is possible there may have been a few American squatters on its banks as early as the beginning of the century, but of that there is no certainty, and the likelihood is that, until the war broke out, no settlement worth speaking of was to be found. While the war was in progress a number found refuge on the banks of Trout River from the draft, and eked out a living by lumbering and making potash. Reed squatted on lot 38 in 1810 or 1811, and it is highly probable that, about the same time, a small sawmill was put up at the mouth of Beaver creek. In St Anicet there were no settlers beyond those mentioned in chapter 3. Dundee (then known as "Indian Lands"), was in the possession of the Indians, apart from an occasional American squatter along the Salmon river and Brunson on the lake. But to return to the Chateaugay. Its solitude continued unbroken until a little above the forks, where on the bank of lot 24, Hinchinbrook, was the shanty of an American, Zebulon Baxter, the forest closing in again until 28, where, in about 1809, a drunken, thriftless American, Jonathan Elliot, drifted in with the tide from across the lines, and raised a shanty below Seely's bridge. He had two sons and a number of daughters, one of whom married a Dutch shoemaker, Daniel Vosburgh, who had come from the States and built a shanty on the Chateaugay at the Cove above Athelstan. A short time before he did so, an American, Truesdell, built a small sawmill on the Hinchinbrook, and was thus the founder of Athelstan. From that place the road followed pretty nearly its present course to nigh the frontier, where a blazed track branched off, leading eastward, and which led, by many crooks and turns, to Russeltown and Hemingford. On this road there were several settlers. The first was William Reed, already mentioned as living near Ste Martine, and who afterwards moved up to lot 32, N. Geo., but when he came to understand the nature of the seigniorial tenure and that he would have to pay rent, determined to have land of his own, and in 1807 he moved up to the first concession of Hinchinbrook and settled on the Burnbrae farm (lot 25). His departure was regretted by the settlers of the Chateaugay settlement on account of losing the society of his wife, who was a clever and very eccentric woman, and who spent a good deal of her time in visiting, being welcome at every house, for she supplied the place of a newspaper and had an inexhaustible flow of caustic and humorous small talk, which she varied by songs. Her visits she generally made on the back of a bull, whose horns were ornamented with ribbons, and with which she even made trips to Montreal. She was, despite her birth, a loyal British subject. It is related of her that she fearlessly visited relatives in Vermont during the war, and on returning found no canoe wherewith to cross the Richelieu to the

Canadian side. Presently the British sentry saw something white waving on the opposite shore, and taking it to be a flag of truce reported, when the guard turned out, and a canoe was sent off, to find Mother Reed standing alone, and chuckling at the success of her ruse. James Wright said: When I was a boy, she came in late one evening, when we were all in bed, and told my father she had made a song on the war. He asked to hear it, when she replied he would have to get up. He retorted he could listen as well in bed. We boys, who had risen on hearing her, sat beside her at the glowing chimney-nook, and she began, snapping her toothless jaws, to bawl out her ballad, of which I do not remember a word, but it amused us highly. On a subsequent visit, my father hailed her as Mother Reed, when she sharply responded that was no longer her name; she was Mrs Turner. Turner was a shiftless, drunken Englishman and she was, when she married him, of the mature age of 72!

Three years after Reed had made a home for himself in Hinchinbrook, two Old Countrymen took up their abode some distance to the east of him. One of them was Captain Barron the other John Nichols. Garret Barron was an Irish Protestant, from the county Wexford, and had served in the army. During the American war he rose to be quartermaster's sergeant of his regiment, and, at the close of the struggle, got his discharge and a grant of land in Caldwell's manor, where he became very comfortable. One of his neighbors was John Nichols, from the English side of the Borders, and his daughter he married as his second wife. When father and son-in-law sold their places on the Champlain and moved into Hinchinbrook Barron (called captain from his rank in militia) when asked why he moved, gave as his reason that he wanted to be again in the woods. Barren squatted on 33 and Nichols on 34. Mrs Barron felt very lonesome in her new home, when her husband remarked that with 5 gallons of rum she had all the company needed. Like all old soldiers of that time, he was fond of his dram, but never got intoxicated. He was tall, over 6 feet, and in his prime must have been a powerful man. He was rough-spoken, and fond

of contradiction, and especially prone to controversy with
Presbyterians (he was an Episcopalian) and Catholics. There
were two large stones, one on each side of his door, on one
or other of which he was generally to be found in fine
weather, ready for a talk with the first passer-by. He left
work to his sons, and they lived poorly, as was indicated by
his remark to a stranger whom he had invited to share their
dinner, "Eat away; it will be long before you get as good
a meal again," the bill of fare beginning and ending with
potatoes and milk. Despite his provoking mode of speech,
he was at heart a kindly man, and ready to share his last
loaf with a neighbor. He was a Freemason and regularly
attended the lodge at Chateaugay, N.Y., which he continued
to call by its old name of Seventhtown. Dying at a great
age, he was buried on his own lot. At his funeral, old Mr
Gentle got annoyed at the long continued hammering, for
there were no screws then, in putting on the coffin-lid, and
exclaimed, "That will do." "Abundance of law is no breaking of it," retorted the carpenter, a bachelor named Fisher,
as he drove in another nail. None of Barron's descendants
remain in the county.

In the fall of 1810 another settler came, in the person of
James McClatchie, who had resolved to follow his father-in-
law, Wm. Reed. It was in September that he was ready to
move from where he was living at the time in North Georgetown. He borrowed the largest canoe in the settlement,
which had been formed by hollowing out the trunk of a
gigantic pine, and in it he put his wife, their four children,
and all his household effects, placing it in charge of his wife's
uncle, John Cantello, while he himself kept to the road and
drove his live stock,—a yoke of oxen and 4 cows. That year
lumbering had been unusually active, there being a great
demand for oak and masts for the royal navy. Of the magnificent character of the trees that then covered the district
some idea may be formed from the fact that when the little
party got near Ormstown they found a mast, which had got
adrift from a raft, lying across the river, at least 100 feet
wide, from bank to bank. The only way to make a passage

for the canoe was to chop it in two, which Cantello did. He was a big man, and propelled the heavy-laden canoe by oars in deep water and by a pole in shallow, the oxen being brought into service to tow it up the rapids. .On reaching the Cove, the canoe had to be left, and the rest of the journey made on foot. McClatchie lost no time in putting up a shanty on lot 29, where a small clearance had been made by an American, Peter Comstock, who had moved next to Reed, and cut and stacked some marsh hay along the Walker brook for his cattle. It ran short, however, for the snow of that winter was of unprecedented depth and continuance, being 4 feet on the level, and with a crust on it. The year following, the snowfall was equally great. To keep his beasts alive, he had every day to fell trees for them to browse upon, which he did very unwillingly on Sundays, for he was a strict Presbyterian, as was also his wife. The crops the following season were abundant, and after that they knew no scarcity.

East of this small settlement of five families, the bush was unbroken for 4 miles, there being no clearance between that of Nichols and Jacob Mitchel (page 30) so that my description of the settlements previous to the outbreak of the war is complete, having led the reader back to the point where the preceding chapter closed.

CHAPTER V.

THE WAR—THE FIRST YEAR.

THE War of the Revolution left, as a bad legacy, to the Americans a most intense hatred of Great Britain. This hatred, in time, came to be regarded as an essential element of American patriotism, and the rising-generation, from their childhood, by schoolbooks and otherwise, had their minds inflamed against the Mother Country. When misfortune befell her, the tidings were hailed with delight at Boston and New York, and whoever assailed her was welcomed as a friend. This senseless and wicked feeling received an impetus from the French revolution, for the Americans sympathized warmly with the effort to establish a republic in France, and as warmly resented Great Britain's opposition. When the republic failed and Napoleon rose from its ruins as dictator, public sentiment changed but little, for the dictator, though the most absolute of military tyrants, was seeking the destruction of Great Britain, and that purpose covered a multitude of sins in the eyes of the Americans. Among the most ardent of his admirers was President Madison, who persistently endeavored to get the United States to assist him by declaring war against Great Britain. Justification for doing so was found in two causes. One of Napoleon's devices to ruin Great Britain was the issuing of decrees forbidding all countries occupied by his armies, which was the whole Continent, from having any commercial dealings with Great Britain and her colonies, and ordering the confiscation of all goods, ships, and other property owned by British subjects. The effect of these decrees was to ruin British trade, for it closed her best markets, and, in self-defence, her government issued a retaliatory decree, declaring every country occupied by the armies of Napoleon to be in a state of blockade, and, consequently, that any ships caught endeavoring to enter or leave their ports would be seized and confiscated by her cruisers. The Americans exulted over the promulgation of Napoleon's decrees, but when Great Britain imitated them as a measure of self-defence, there was a great outcry that the rights of neutrals were violated, which was true, but the complaint came ill from a nation that had approved of and loudly applauded the principle when used by Napoleon against Britain, and who only realized its enormity when it was going to affect themselves. This was the first reason given by President Madison for asking the United States to declare war against Great Britain—that, by her orders-in-council, she was infringing on the rights of free trade. His second reason was, that Great Britain, when any sailors deserted from her men-of-war in foreign ports, claimed the right to follow them on board United States' ships and take them back. The captains of too many American ships had habitually made it a practice, when they anchored near a British man-of-war, to entice her sailors to desert, offering them higher wages and better berths, and so recruiting their crews at the expense of Great Britain. To put an end to such a course, the outraged captains took the only effectual means, namely, to follow the deserters and bring them back. This right of search was no new proceeding, it was universal among the navies of Europe; captains giving every facility to one another to put down the great evil of the service, desertion. It was not until the American navy came into existence, that a body of officers was known who encouraged desertion and took deserters under their protection.

On these two grounds, the British orders-in-council and the exercise of the right-of-search, the United States declared war against Great Britain. These, however, were only pretended reasons, the real ones being a desire to assist Napoleon to crush Great Britain and to take possession of Canada. The declaration of war was not endorsed by the great body of respectable people in the United States, and even in congress there was a large minority who opposed it. The minority in the house of representatives, which formed one-third, issued a protest, in which they solemnly disavowed the iniquity of siding with Napoleon and characterized the contemplated seizure of Canada as unjust.

The declaration of war was signed by President Madison on the 19th June, 1812, and it shows how imperfect were the means of communication in those days, that news so important did not reach Quebec until 6 days afterwards. The province was literally defenceless. The sore straits to which the Motherland had been reduced in her gigantic struggle against the all-conquering Napoleon, had compelled her to withdraw regiment after regiment from Canada, so that beyond a few thousand militia there were no troops. Sir George Prevost, who was then governor, called the legislature together, which voted $248,000 to enable him to raise an army and take steps to defend the province. While preparations were going on, the English mail came in with tidings that the Imperial government had repealed the orders-in-council several weeks before the United States' declaration of war had reached London. Thinking that the Americans would abandon their purpose of making war, on learning that what they professed to be the chief cause of it had ceased to exist, Sir George Prevost, a shallow, flighty man, ordered a pause, to hear from Washington of their determination: it was, that the war would go on, thus confirming what everybody knew, that the alleged reasons for it were hypocritical.

The levying of the militia was not effected without trouble. The habitants felt no interest in the impending struggle, were quite indifferent whether the British or American flag fluttered over the bastions on Cape Diamond, and disliked military service, so that the draft was carried out under difficulties. At Pointe Claire the habitants rose en masse, drove away the officers sent to enroll them, and moved in a body towards Montreal to coerce the government. Their numbers were swelled as they marched along, and what might have proved a disastrous movement to British supremacy was happily nipped in the bud by Major Penderleath, who, with a single company of regulars, suddenly attacked them before they had left Lachine, and dispersed them, killing one habitant and fatally wounding another.

Thus forced, the habitants submitted to the inevitable, and were formed into regiments, each of which was supplied with officers from the regular army.

On the first whisper of war, the chiefs of the Indian tribes hastened to Quebec to offer their services, one of them declaring with much pathos, "The Americans are taking our lands from us every day; they have no hearts; they have no pity for us; they want to drive us beyond the setting sun." These Indians were given muskets, organized into bands to act as scouts, and, so far as possible, a white was sent with each band to take control.

On the 12th July the first invasion of Canada took place. Gen. Hull crossed the Detroit river and issued a proclamation in which he declared his confidence as to his success and said he had come to emancipate the people of Canada from the tyranny and oppression of Great Britain and restore them "to the dignified status of freemen." The United Empire Loyalists, who then composed almost the entire population west of Kingston, had a lively remembrance of the wrongs they had suffered at the hands of the United States and flew to arms. Led by Gen. Brock, and supported by a small body of regulars, they attacked Gen. Hull, when the braggart and his whole army surrendered. This discomfiture, followed afterwards by the victory of Queenstown Heights, had the effect of delaying the invasion of Quebec, which was of essential consequence, as it enabled Governor Prevost to complete his arrangements for its defence.

On receiving word of the declaration of war, he issued a proclamation notifying all American citizens, who declined to take the oath of allegiance, to leave the Province by the 14th of July. This proclamation was carried into the settlements of the county of Huntingdon by special messengers, and the news fell like a thunderbolt. Of the Americans, few had any desire to leave. Their mingling with Old Countrymen had rubbed off their absurd prejudices, and it was their intention to become subjects of the Crown. They were assured that they would not be meddled with nor required to bear arms, but a vague panic seized them. They perceived that this part of the frontier must necessarily be the scene of conflict, while they were filled with terror of the Indians, with whose acts in the Revolutionary War they were acquainted, and the rumor was that a strong body of them were on their way from Caughnawaga to rob and destroy. Their fields gave promise of an unusually abundant harvest, but the Americans would not wait to reap them. Packing what they could of their movables, they fled across the lines. So precipitate was their flight that there were instances where they left bread in the oven. A few on leaving said they would soon be back, that the American armies would speedily conquer Canada, but the majority at once made for Western New York, a great many taking up land in the Genessee valley, which was then being opened. From Georgetown all left save three families—the two Baxters and Baker. The latter stayed because the father was too old and the son too young to move. At Ormstown a few remained, among them Horace Hibbard, who entered the British service and was made a captain in the 1st battalion of militia, which was quickly organized. In Franklin the exodus was equally complete, one or two Old Countrymen, alarmed at the prospect of the Indians coming, joining in it. Two days after the proclamation was received all had left except the two Mannings, Mayne, Calkins, Gentle, Pettis, and Adams. In Hemingford fully half of the families left, among those who remained being Scriver, Delong, Fisher, Norton and Brayton. None of those who remained were in the slightest degree molested, and the statements in American histories, that those who left were driven away and despoiled of their property, have no foundation.* Urged by

* Subjoined are the "regulations respecting American subjects now residing in the province of Lower Canada":

First—That all American subjects who shall refuse to take the oath of allegiance, and also refuse to take up arms, must leave the country, unless they shall obtain the permission of His Excellency the Governor, to remain for a limited time, for the purpose of settling their affairs.

Secondly—That all American subjects, having visible property and of good character, and who will take the oath of allegiance, with the exception of not being obliged to bear baseless fears they fled of their own freewill, and against the advice of their Old Country neighbors. The best proof of the truth of this lies in the fact that many who fled thus precipitately, on afterwards seeing that they had nothing to fear, returned to their farms in Franklin and on the Chateaugay, and in the former place still live many of their descendants. John Manning of Hemingford was appointed commissioner to administer the oath of allegiance.*

A proclamation advised settlers on the frontier to go to Montreal or to the "blockade" formed east of where the village of St Chrysostome now stands, on the Norton Creek, for protection. That blockade consisted of a slash of timber, about half a mile long and 50 rods wide. The idea was, that

arms against the United States of America, be allowed to remain without being compellable to bear arms against the United States; but subject to leave the province whenever government shall deem it necessary.

Thirdly—That all Americans, being immediate grantees of the Crown, be allowed to remain, but to take the general oath of allegiance to His Majesty, and consequently must bear arms.

Fourthly—That all Americans, subjects of good character, holding lands from grantees of the crown, or from seigneurs, if approved of by a committee, consisting of not less than 3 members of His Majesty's executive council, may remain on taking the general oath of allegiance to His Majesty, and consenting to bear arms; but this oath must be taken in Quebec, Montreal, or Three Rivers, before the police magistrates.

Fifthly—Any American subjects of good character may, if approved by a committee of the executive council as aforesaid, be allowed to remain on taking the oath of allegiance and consenting to bear arms; the oath to be taken before the police magistrate as aforesaid.

Sixthly—That the foregoing regulations shall take effect, notwithstanding the proclamation of the 30th June last.

Government House, July 10, 1812.   GEORGE PREVOST.

*A copy of the private instructions sent to him are before me. They, in effect, tell him not to insist upon American settlers taking the oath of allegiance unless he has reason to suspect them of being spies.

the felled trees would be an insuperable obstacle to the advance of the American army and that the settlers would be safe behind it. A very few of the families in Russeltown did go, but on Jacob Manning's anxiety about his crops leading him to steal back to his farm, and finding everything as he left it, he felt convinced that nothing was to be feared, while everybody, except the English officers, perceived how sorry a defence the blockade would be against born-axemen like the Americans. After a stay of a fortnight the blockade was abandoned, though it long remained a monument of the troublous times and proved for years afterwards a great obstacle to travellers on the road to St Remi.

The Indians, of whom such apprehensions were entertained, soon appeared, the first band being one of about a hundred braves, commanded by a French-Canadian, Capt. Versailles. Their appearance was terrifying enough, for beyond a girdle they were naked, their bodies and faces streaked with the war paint, and feathers stuck in their hair. Among them was a Flathead Indian, who had strayed from the Pacific coast, and whose English consisted of "Good George," "Much war." They were very civil to the settlers, much more courteous, indeed, than the regular soldiers proved to be, and would touch not even an apple tree without permission. One good woman who regarded a band of them, who came to her house one evening, with terror, had all her apprehensions set at rest when, on looking into the shed where they were to pass the night, she witnessed several on their knees in prayer. They were divided into bands of 40, and were constantly on the move along the frontier from Lake Champlain to St Regis, doing service as scouts and patrols which was simply invaluable, for while they watched the enemy like the hawk, they were as stealthy in their movements and as difficult to catch as the snake. Though the Americans repeatedly endeavored to surprise these Indians bands, and though they were constantly hovering around their lines, it is a curious fact, illustrative of their consummate craft, that not a single Indian was captured during the war. Of the captains in command of them, besides Versailles, there were Lamothe and

Perrigo; the latter afterwards married a squaw. When they became acquainted with them, the settlers rather liked to have a visit from an Indian patrol, as it gave them a sense of security. These children of the forest carried their food in small haversacks, and, except when the weather was cold or wet, rarely went near a house save to buy provisions.

On the American side the alarm, on receipt of the news of war being declared, was hardly less than on the Canadian side. The settlers believed that the Indians would be let loose by the British government and, expecting that they would appear at any moment, they became panic-stricken and most of them fled West or into the interior of the country. In some cases so great was their trepidation, that they took none of their effects and even left the tables spread for the meal of which they were about to partake. The settlers who remained in the town of Chateaugay clubbed together and built a blockhouse by voluntary labor on the hill above the river, opposite the graveyard, about 3 miles northwest of the village. The State afterwards allowed them $100 towards its cost. The intention was that it would prove a defence against any invading party, as it commanded the only road that then led from Canada. Cols. Wool and Snelling soon appeared with a body of troops. They were heartily welcomed by the settlers, and a detachment of them was placed in the blockhouse. In October 100 of them were sent to make an incursion into Canada. Mr Gentle and his son Hiram were at the Centre when they were surprised to meet them. The commanding officer told Mr Gentle he had been sent, at the instance of the settlers who had fled, for the property they had left behind them, but could only find old barrels and like lumber about their deserted shanties. Placing father and son under arrest, they marched to their house, where they halted all night. The rank-and-file camped out-of-doors. Seizing all Mrs Gentle's poultry they wrung their necks, and making a roaring fire they swung a cooler over it, and cooked the poultry and potatoes together. In the morning, they left the family without doing any further molestation than devouring their little store of food, and for

6

which they did not pay. They wore a light blue uniform. In addition to the Indians sent to patrol the Huntingdon frontier, Governor Prevost, on the arrival of a few regulars from England in the fall, sent a company of the 8th regiment, under the charge of Captain Mundy, to form a depot of provisions at the junction of the English river with the Chateaugay. The headquarters were on the south bank, opposite Dumochelle's rapids, and the men were quartered upon the habitants. Capt. Mundy, a Scotchman of excellent character and who was much liked by the settlers, showed great energy in the task entrusted to him. He built a small blockhouse, which he filled with all the wheat and oats he could buy, and made arrangements for the supply of pork, beef, and fodder, if needed. The following letter from him shows how he carried on his operations :

6th November, 1812.

Sir,—I am directed by his excellency the governor-in-chief, to order you to use every method possible for immediately sending down the grain, potash, cattle, &c., the property of any settler who may have quitted his land. You will also cause, with all exertion in your power, grain of every description, as well as cattle, to be brought below the mouth of the English river, the property of the present settlers, to prevent its falling into the hands of the Americans, who are about to invade this country. I will endeavor to cause a lodgement for it, and, if necessary, a guard to be stationed for its protection. The consequence of non-compliance with this order, will my being obliged to resort to a very painful measure, to wit, that of destroying it on your farms, to prevent the enemy reaping the benefit thereof. You will make this known to any settlers in your neighborhood.

I remain, your most obedient servant,

J. Mundy,

Capt. commanding

To Andrew Gentle, Russeltown.   Posts of Chateaugay.

The plan devised by Prevost for the defence of the province, was that as large an army as possible should be assembled at Montreal, and that depots of provisions should be established at intervals along the frontier. When word should be received from the scouting parties of the likelihood of an invasion, this army would march to the point threatened, when the depots of provisions would be of service. Gen. Dearborn in October took up his quarters in Plattsburgh, where he assembled a large army, with which he designed invading Canada. It was the knowledge of this fact that caused Capt. Mundy to order the destruction of all supplies that could not be moved to his post, and the falling-back of the settlers, for it was possible that General Dearborn might cross at the Huntingdon frontier, when it would be of consequence that he should encounter a wasted country and that the British troops, who would come to meet him, should find plenty of provisions at the English river forks. After long hesitation, Gen. Dearborn approached the frontier, and on the night of the 29th November, his advance left Champlain and began crossing the Lacolle river before daylight. Captain McKay, who was in charge of the post, gave the alarm, when a desultory musketry fire was opened, and in the darkness two columns of the enemy fired into each other by mistake. Disheartened by this misadventure and finding the roads very bad, the Americans retreated to Champlain, and all intention of invading that season was given up.

Mr Gentle (who had received a commission as lieutenant in the militia) knew that there was no reason for obeying the order in the latter part of Captain Mundy's letter, for there was no prospect of an invasion by way of Franklin. He, however, did what he could to send provisions to his post, and took the grain that had been cut on the deserted farms and threshed it, and Captain Mundy sent up ox-sleds and drew it away. That winter Mr Gentle had a serious illness, which ended in a large gathering on his right arm. On application, Capt. Mundy sent a pass, and Drs. Moss and Powell of Malone attended him until he was convalescent. He never recovered his former strength, and the whole burden of the household fell on his only son, Hiram.

With the advent of cold weather, all fears of an invasion for that season passed away, and during the winter Captain Mundy and Lieutenant Boyd were frequent visitors to the houses of the Old Countrymen on the Chateaugay. One of the subalterns, Sergeant Henderson, was a pious man who tried to do all the good in his power. Seeing that the children of the settlers were growing up in ignorance, he organized a class, which he taught in the intervals of his military duties, and from the lips of that honest soldier not a few of the second generation of settlers received about all the schooling they ever got. In the spring Capt. Mundy and his company got orders to return to Montreal, from whence they were sent to Upper Canada. In the carnage of Little York they suffered so fearfully that the only one who escaped unwounded was Sergt. Henderson. When, at the close of the war, the survivors were on their way to England, a few of the settlers made a journey to Montreal with the express purpose of seeing them once more and bidding them farewell.

The defence of the frontier, however, was not left to depend upon the regulars alone. Every settler, capable of bearing arms, was enrolled by a draft. Those of the district of Beauharnois were formed into battalions, of which the captains of the first were Isaac Wilsie for Hemingford; Archibald Ogilvie for Georgetown and lower end of Ormstown; Horace Hibbard for upper Ormstown; Garret Barron for Hinchinbrook, and Louis Demers and A. Dumochelle for the Basin. The 2nd battalion was an exclusively French one, and included all the inhabitants between the Chateaugay and the St Lawrence. It was commanded by Charles Grant, lieut.-col., E. Henry, major; M. O. Sullivan, adjutant. The names of two of the captains were Ed. Hainault and A. Vallé. An incident of the formation of the 1st battalion is worth recalling. When Ezra Baxter of N. Georgetown was drafted, his father, Nathan, an old veteran of Washington's army, presented himself in his stead, telling the officer he knew a great deal more about soldiering than his son and could be much better spared on the farm.

While the first year of the war passed without an encounter on the Hinchinbrook and Hemingford frontier, a gallant affair took place at French Mills, as Fort Covington was then called. Its settlement dates back to 1793, in which year the Indians, at a nominal rent, leased to William Gray a tract of land on the Salmon river, on condition that he would build a sawmill. In 1798 the property passed into the hands of James Robertson of Montreal, who added a gristmill, and both mills were in operation until 1804 when a great freshet swept them away. Mr Robertson at once began to rebuild but died before the mills were finished, when his heirs leased them to the millwright, Robert Buchanan, who had built them. There were three of the Buchanans, Walter and Duncan being the names of the other brothers, and they came from Stirlingshire, Scotland. They were, in many respects, worthy men, and were the founders of the settlement on the Salmon river. No Americans came in until after the beginning of the century, and for a long time the main part of the inhabitants were the half dozen French Canadian families who got work about the sawmill, and from whose presence the name French Mills arose. When war was declared, however, the Americans were largely in the majority and the place had begun to assume the aspect of a village, there being a store or two and at least two taverns. On the Canadian side there were a few settlers, French or American, along the lake-shore and on the Salmon river; with these trifling exceptions Dundee was still a wilderness, and the silence of its woods disturbed alone by the hunter and lumberer. The magnificent timber that fringed the Salmon river was the great attraction, for oaks 5 feet across, and pines unequalled in quality elsewhere, grew upon the knolls that bordered it.

Dundee was then known as the Indian Lands, and constituted part of the St Regis reservation. The story of the origin of St Regis is romantic. During the interminable wars between the French Canadians and the New Englanders, a raiding party set out in 1676 which penetrated as far as Gorton, Massachusetts. Among the prisoners taken by the Indians were two boys, whom they brought back to Caughnawaga and adopted into their tribe. When they became men the difference in intellect and taste showed itself, and the superiority they affected was resented by the chiefs. The disagreements rose to such a height that they determined on leaving, and, with their wives and children and a few followers, ascended the St Lawrence and raised their wigwams at the mouth of the St Regis river. Half a century later, a Jesuit, Father Gordon, joined them with a body of Mohawks, and he named the village St Regis, after the great French Jesuit, who had not long before been canonized by the Pope. In 1812 the place differed little from what it is to-day, being a collection of mean, dirty shanties with a squalid population. On the breaking out of the war, a division took place, part of the Indians siding with Britain, part with the Americans, and a still larger number remaining neutral. They quarrelled and even fought among themselves as to the respective flags they should follow. Those who cast in their lot for King George, at once enlisted into the bands that were formed for the patrolling of the frontier, so that the village was left entirely at the mercy of the neutrals and of the American partizans. In order to prevent its being occupied, Colonel McGillivray of Glengarry got together and sent over 48 voyageurs—French Canadian canoemen and lumbermen —commanded by captain McDowell. This was on the 16th of October. On the 18th lieutenant Hall learned that the Americans contemplated an assault upon the picket, and advised his captain to withdraw to the small island that lies opposite the village, where they would be safe from surprise. Both he and De Montigny, the interpreter, treated the information and advice with disdain. On the 22nd a loyal Indian came with like information, declaring he had seen the preparations for the attack. His advice to retire to the island was also disregarded. The night that followed was intensely dark and favorable for a surprise, so that the sentinels were on the alert. No cause for alarm occurred and as it drew towards the hour of dawn, their apprehensions grew less. About 5 o'clock the two officers of the guard, lieutenant Hall and ensign Rottot, were seated with sergeant McGillivray around the camp-fire, that blazed in front of the house where the captain and the men not on duty were fast asleep. The subject of conversation of the trio was the danger of their situation, and the ensign had just said: "Is it possible that the obstinacy of our captain exposes us thus to death without profit or glory!" when a volley was suddenly

fired from the bush, and he fell dead and the sergeant
mortally wounded. Lieutenant Hall sprang into the house
when a second volley was poured forth, which killed a French
Canadian private and wounded several others, who had hardly
been fairly aroused from their night's sleep. Not a shot was
fired by the Canadians, who at once surrendered. One of
the missionaries was caught and told to shrive the wounded
and bury the dead ; the other escaped by hiding in the cellar.
The Americans ransacked the houses, among other spoil,.
plundering a girl of 13 years of age of the box that held her
Sunday-clothes and playthings and her savings in pennies,
amounting to $3. Worse than that, they stripped the body
of ensign Rottot. Satisfied they had left nothing they could
carry, the force, which numbered 200 men under command of
major Young, marched to French Mills, carrying the paltry
spoil they had found and 25 prisoners. From French Mills the
party proceeded to Plattsburgh. Among the plunder was a
small Union Jack, which they found in a cupboard in the
house of the interpreter, and which he was in the custom of
hoisting on saints' days and other notable occasions. This
flag Major Young declared to be the stand of colors that
belonged to the detachment, and he was sent to Albany with
the trophy. His arrival in the capital of the state was made
the occasion of a solemn ceremony. Escorted by all the troops
in the city, and with a band before him playing "Yankee
Doodle," he solemnly stalked along the streets of Albany,
crowded by cheering multitudes, holding aloft the flag of the
Indian interpreter, until the capitol was reached, when, with
spread-eagle speeches, it was received from his hands and
hung upon its walls as "the first colors captured from the
enemy." The major was rewarded with a colonelcy.

On receipt of the news of the declaration of war a blockhouse was ordered by the American authorities to be built at
French Mills. The site chosen was less than a mile from the
boundary, being the first knoll met with in ascending the
Salmon river on its west bank, and commanding an unob-
structed view northward and westward and across to the
rising ground on the east bank, and close to the road that

then connected Malone with St Regis. It was made of elm logs, with loop-holes 10 inches long and 18 inches apart. It was occupied by a volunteer company from Moira, and, owing to many of them having served in the Revolutionary War, modestly assumed the name of "Silver Greys." They were destined to bear the brunt of the act of retribution the British had in store for the devastation of St Regis. Col. McMillan was entrusted with the expedition. He assembled at Cornwall a small but motley force of 250 men. It included a detachment of Royal Artillery and of the 49th regt., companies of the Cornwall and Glengarry militia and 30 Indians from Oka. At 11 o'clock at night of the 22nd November they silently embarked at Glengarry House, rowed across the St Lawrence, and landed at a point where the road from St Regis comes out on the southern bank of the St Lawrence. Here 100 men under Colonel McLean were left to protect the line of communication, and the remainder of the force advanced on French Mills. Though the distance was not great the road was execrable and it was 5 o'clock before the bridge across the Little Salmon was reached, which was crossed without discovery, there being no sentry. About half way to the bridge across the Big Salmon, however, a sentry was met, who fired his musket, to give the alarm. The advance discharged their guns, and the faithful sentinel fell, pierced with 3 balls. A rush was made for the village, and at the end of the bridge another sentry was found posted, who fired at the advancing force and turned to flee, when he also was killed. A few shots from the dwelling-houses, evoked the order to fire a volley, when one man, who stood at the door, fell dead, and resistance ceased. It was now learned that the surprise had not been so complete as anticipated; that scouts had brought in word of their approach 3 hours before, and that the garrison had all withdrawn into the blockhouse, to which the British now marched. Drawing up in front, prepared to storm it, a messenger was sent demanding their surrender, coupled with a threat to destroy the village. The Revolutionary veterans at once marched out and gave up their arms. They comprised 1 captain, 2 subalterns, and 41 men. Besides, 4 batteaux and 57 stand of arms were taken. Col. McMillan returned with deliberation, bearing his spoil and prisoners, to Cornwall, from whence the latter were sent to' Montreal, where they were, in the following month, exchanged for the Canadians captured at St Regis. Col. McMillan did not destroy the blockhouse, probably because too green to burn, and to hold it 2 companies were at once detached by the American general from the force at Chateaugay, who stayed there until March, when a Constable company, under Capt. Erwin, took their place.

CHAPTER VI.

THE SECOND YEAR OF THE WAR.

THE winter passed quietly, the only alarm being caused by a sensational report in February that the enemy had gathered 2000 men at French Mills with the intention of crossing on the ice to Cornwall and so cutting communication between the provinces. The fact is, neither side cared for a winter campaign, and both were engrossed in getting ready for the summer. The Americans had great difficulty in getting men, and after trying volunteering had to resort to drafting. Among their contrivances to fill their ranks was that of bestowing commissions on sheriff's deputies and constables, who raised companies by imprisoning debtors who would not enlist. A bounty of $40 was offered, and the pay of a private in the regulars was $8 a month. In June Cuvillier, a resident of the Cedars, was sent disguised as a French merchant, to reconnoitre French Mills, and he reported that the soldiers consisted of waiters, servants, journeyman shoemakers and a tanner.* He found the garrison so inefficient that he recommended an attack upon it, to which Col. Lethbridge, who commanded the fort at Coteau, would not consent, as the

---

* Cuvillier's report goes on to say that of this noble host "not more than 10 or 12 sleep in the blockhouse, the others staying in the village. The captain lodges at Stutson's tavern, the ensign at another, and the lieutenant in the blockhouse. There are 5 or 6 French families in the village, the men of which serve in the militia, receiving $10 and $11 a month with rations. These families were there before the war, with the exception of that of Lorraine, who was a leader in the Pointe Claire party. (See page 60). The sentries had no ammunition in their pouches." Cuvillier was politely treated and being a French Canadian and known as a travelling merchant no suspicion of his being a spy was entertained. His report, apparently written by himself, is couched in excellent English.

Captain had found no British deserters at the Mills. Up to this time, desertion had caused much annoyance to the British officers, and they had resorted to extreme measures to stop it. In illustration of this, one incident will be sufficient. An American settler lived on what was called Marsh island, Dundee, and one day two deserters entered his house and asked if they were yet in the States. A deceptive answer was given, when, feeling safe, they ate what was set before them and then lay down to rest their exhausted bodies. Brunson went out and, getting the assistance of a neighbor, seized and bound the two poor men, and took them in his canoe to the fort at Coteau, where they were at once shot. The reward, $20 for each, was placed on their coffins, from which their captor had to pick it up. This shooting of captured deserters was invariable, and knowing the danger to which they were exposed, the Americans generally sent them on to Albany. The captors were not always so successful as in the case mentioned. In the east end of the county, a settler named Moore, greedy of the reward, seized a deserter, placed him on horseback behind him, and started for Lacolle. On the way, the deserter managed to get his hands free, and pulling out a knife, suddenly plunged it into the bowels of his captor, and escaped across the lines. As the war progressed there was less desertion, for the hard usage to which the American soldiers were subjected became widely known.

Beyond the continual excitement and apprehension inseparable from a state of war, the settlers along the Huntingdon frontier had little to complain of. Those living east of Hemingford, near the lake, were plundered of provisions without conscience by the American soldiers and once had their horses taken away, on the pretence that they had been used for drawing supplies to the British garrisons, but the settlers in the west had no such wrongs and indignities to undergo. The only instance of plundering by soldiers was experienced in Franklin. One day three American soldiers suddenly emerged from the woods and entering the open door of Andw. Gentle's shanty one of them discharged his musket into the log wall, apparently to frighten the inmates. Placing one of their number to stand as sentinel at the door, the others ransacked the house for plunder. From a pedlar, who happened to be in the house, they took his pack of dry goods and $50. On opening a trunk, one was for appropriating its contents, when the other protested against taking "the old man's clothes." Making up what they had stolen from the pedlar, into three bundles, each lifted one on his back, and departed. A more serious attempt at plundering was made by three French Canadians who had been employed in making ashes on the St Antoine Abbé road, and who, on the outbreak of the war, had fled to Plattsburgh. One night they returned and stole Jacob Manning and Andrew Gentle's oxen and cows, leaving not a trace behind. During the day a messenger came from Chateaugay, N.Y., stating that early that morning, Mr Douglas, the miller, had seen three French-men pass with a drove of cattle, among them a yoke of oxen which he recognized as having often been at the mill with Mr Gentle. Believing the men were thieves, he and his neighbors seized the cattle, the Frenchmen flying on per-ceiving that they were suspected. The cattle were restored to their owners, with the exception of one of Mr Manning's cows, which had died from being over-driven. The most friendly relations subsisted between the people on both sides, and despite the patrols from Chateaugay, N.Y., there was an interchange of neighborly favors. The war had deprived the American settlers of a market for their potash, and they now, at night-time, drew the barrels over to their British neighbors, who sold them on their behalf in Montreal. Then there was considerable smuggling done in the way of spirits, which the war had made scarce and very dear in the United States. In this infamous trade Milne, the seigniory agent, engaged largely and made much money. He brought the liquor, in 10-gallon kegs, from Montreal to Franklin, by the way of the Chateaugay and the track that led southwards from the Georgetown settlement, and it was drawn across the lines in handsleds by a number of men he employed.

A more peculiar contraband traffic was that in cattle. The country on the Canadian side of the lines was almost a wilderness and, necessarily, could supply few cattle, while the habitants of the old parishes had none to spare. The consequence was, that the government found the greatest difficulty in providing beef for the troops. Their perplexity was relieved to a large extent by a set of daring men who, knowing that there was no lack of cattle on the American side, and that their owners were eager to exchange them for the Spanish dollars which the British commissariat so lavishly spent, engaged in making the transfer. At a pre-arranged time and place, invariably in some lonely part of the woods, the American farmers were in waiting with their beasts, when the Canadian drovers appeared, paid their price, and drove them into Canada. The American military authorities were perfectly cognizant of the traffic, and did their best to end it, and so anxious were they to cut off all supplies from their opponents, that they announced whoever was caught engaged in it would be hanged on the spot. This proved no deterrent and it is additional proof of the good understanding that subsisted between the settlers along the Huntingdon frontier, that no instance occurred of either betraying the other to the respective governments in the dealings they had. A track was made through the woods by the cattle smugglers from the Hinchinbrook frontier to the St Lawrence, going by Cazaville, across the Scotch ridge, fording the Laguerre at what came to be known as la traverse aux vaches, a little north of the fourche à brûler, and thence to Chretien's point, where they were ferried across to supply the troops at Coteau and Cornwall. Those engaged in the traffic made enormous profits.*

The omnipresence and unceasing watchfulness of the Indian bands, which prevented the American officers from guarding the frontier sufficiently to stop the illicit intercourse that was going on under their noses, exasperated

---

*A leading spirit in the traffic was an American who lived on the lake shore, Josiah H. Classon. On tar running short for the gunboats then being built at Coteau for cruising on the lake, he contrived to distill a sufficient quantity from pine knots, secured on the pine plains of St Anicet.

them greatly, and they made repeated attempts to break them up. Their efforts to catch them resembled those of a turtle in pursuing a lizard. When a detachment of a hundred men or so had laboriously marched to the point where the Indians had been seen, they had vanished to assail the enemy at some other point. Time and again when the American commanders thought they had cornered a portion of their detested foe beyond all possibility of escape, they found they had slipped away. In one instance they were nearly successful. Sam Hatch, an American, who had lived until the war broke out on lot 39 of the 1st range of Hinchinbrook, became a spy for the American camp and haunted the woods in the vicinity of his old home. One day he took word to Four Corners that a patrol was staying at James McClatchie's. 300 men were detailed, and sent in haste, guided by Hatch, through the bush. They silently surrounded the house, when, hearing a slight rustle, Mrs McClatchie looked out of the window, when an American officer made a cut at her with his sword, which she narrowly escaped. He afterwards apologized for his cowardly act by declaring he had mistaken her head of black hair for that of an Indian. They were much provoked to find the patrol had left and that they had lost their journey. The evening had turned out cold and wet, and, not daring to risk a night march through the bush back to their barracks, they encamped until daylight should return. They were clad in blue swallow-tailed coats, and had neither blankets nor overcoats, so that they spent an uncomfortable night, the only shelter for the rank-and-file being what they could secure by breaking down the corn. The officers were very civil and, on departing in the morning, offered to pay Mr McClatchie for the provisions they had taken, which he refused.

The summer passed in constant apprehension of invasion by the enemy, who had gathered a considerable force on the New York frontier, styled The Army of the North. It did not at any time exceed 18,000, but in those days that was a great number to concentrate on so remote and wild a frontier. It is to be remembered that in 1813 there were no rail-

ways and that steamboats were only beginning to be introduced. The consequence was, that the regiments had,
generally, to march every mile of the distance from where
they were recruited to the field of action. A large proportion
of the regiments composing The Army of the North had been
raised in the Southern States, so that to reach lake Champlain or the foot of lake Ontario (both headquarters of the
army) they had to undergo fatiguing and prolonged marches.
The intention was to have invaded Canada early in June,
but it was well on in August before a sufficient force was
concentrated. The chief command was given to Wilkinson,
who had been bred a physician, but having entered the army
and served through the Revolutionary war was looked upon
as an invincible soldier. Hampton, who was a Southern
planter, had also served in the Revolutionary war, and was
likewise held in popular esteem as a veteran hero. The most
extravagant estimates were indulged in by the American
papers as to what they would effect, and it was regarded as
certain that they would gain possession of Montreal by the
4th of July. A false report having reached New York that
the army had crossed the frontier, one leading journal announced the news thus, "Our armies have entered Canada
and it is ours." The conquest of Canada was spoken of as
an accomplished fact.

To repulse the threatened invasion Governor Prevost had
very inadequate means at his command. Engaged as she
was in a death-struggle with Napoleon, her utmost resources
needed to enable her to hold her ground on the Continent,
the Motherland was utterly unable to spare troops to carry
on the contest in America which the United States had
forced upon her, and it was late in the summer before the
few she ventured to withdraw from facing the French
arrived at Quebec, and these were mostly sent on to Upper
Canada, where there was more need. The defence of this
province would have to rest largely upon the militia raised
between Prescott and New Brunswick. The tactics of the
preceding fall were persisted in—that of keeping a strong
patrol along the frontier threatened, with depots and garri-

sons at central points. Ile aux Noix was headquarters for lake Champlain, then there was a body of troops kept at Lacolle, another at St Phillipe, and a fourth was formed on the Chateaugay. On the withdrawal of Capt. Mundy and his company, Major-General Stovin was sent to form a camp, which he did on Nahum Baker's farm. In addition to doing so, he looked more closely after the drafting and drilling of the habitants. There were no uniforms for them, but they were fairly armed and had for their chief officers men of experience. The service was intensely disliked by the habitants, and when there was word of their being likely to march or of having a brush with the enemy, they deserted by the score. The Old Country settlers were also formed into a company, of which James Wright was made captain and Neil Morrison lieutenant. Those of them who lived along the river road and had oxen or horses were excused from drill, as their services were needed for teaming. The reason for keeping the camp near the forks, was that it was uncertain which way the Americans would come in, and from Baker's the men could follow either the English river or the Chateaugay, strike north towards Coteau or fall back to cover Montreal. A detachment of troops under Col. Williams was placed to cover the ferry at Caughnawaga and Col. d'Archambault was posted at Melocheville, as it was expected a part of the American army might descend in boats.

Of the social life of the officers while waiting at Baker's for the approach of the enemy, a glimpse is given by an unfriendly observer. Mrs Baker said their house was made headquarters without asking leave or offer of payment. Her husband being an American they seemed to think he had no rights they were bound to observe. They killed his cattle to supply their table, used his grain and fodder for their horses, and occupied every room in the house except a small one, which they left for Mrs Baker. The officers were full of life, boisterous, and given to pranks. One evening, when the fun ran fast and furious, an officer caught up a little dog and exclaiming, "Here is a Yankee!" flung it into the big box stove, which was almost red hot at the time. Another, catching up the cat, shouted "Here is another," and sent it after the dog. Baker dared not complain, but he took a strange revenge. For want of room a number had to sleep on the floor, which they did with their feet to the stove. When all were sound asleep, he crept into the room, laid a train of powder along the stockinged feet, and going out, reached to the end of the train from the open door with a stake. There was a flash, a cry of pain, and the sound of confusion. Deep and loud the officers swore, but the trick had been so neatly done that they could not conjecture how their feet came to be scorched, and one of them declared the cat must have come alive again. On returning from delivering a despatch, Baker led out an officer's horse to make room for his own overheated animal. He was observed, and ordered to be confined in the guard-house, which was one of his own outbuildings. Subsequently, on being taunted about his countrymen and his declining to take the oath of allegiance, Baker retorted so warmly, that he was ordered again into confinement, this time for a day and a night, and the weather being cold and damp, he became affected with inflammatory rheumatism, which made him useless for work ever after. Mrs Baker said deSalaberry was courteous to her though rough-spoken with his men. When he came first he was very hungry and enquired what she could give him. She answered either fowl or ham. He replied he would have no ham, and to cook a fowl, with which, when served, he was much pleased, saying he did not expect so good a meal in the bush. With Sir George Prevost she was highly pleased, declaring him to be a perfect gentleman. DeWatteville she did not like. The house was empty during the day, the officers riding to the front after breakfast and not returning until towards dark. Her trouble did not last long, for immediately after the fight they left as abruptly as they had come. The rank-and-file were miserably lodged in sheds hurriedly nailed together near Baker's and Morrison's, and in barns and stables, and the over-crowded shanties of the settlers.

While preparations were going on along the Chateaugay, and men waited impatiently for the onset, the army of the enemy on the northeast frontier was growing stronger and its plans of operation were maturing. The secretary of war, Gen. Armstrong, meant to take chief command himself, but did not do so, when it devolved upon Wilkinson. On the 15th August he wrote from Albany to Gen. Hampton, who received the letter at Burlington, informing him of the fact and asking details as to his force. Hampton, who resented Wilkinson's being placed above him, replied not to him but to Armstrong, stating that if he was placed under Wilkinson he would resign, and urged that his command was a distinct one, and therefore independent. Armstrong, who was .friendly towards Hampton, persuaded him to continue, but weakly left the point undecided whether or not he was subject to Wilkinson. The result was, that Wilkinson continued to regard Hampton as his subordinate, and issued orders to him. which the haughty Southerner treated with contempt. The defeat which awaited both generals did not arise from this jealousy, but undoubtedly made more complete by it.

The intention from the first was, that The Army of the North should not enter Canada in a body, but that it should be divided and, striking at two different and distant points, distract the attention of the small force at Governor Prevost's command. By this simple stratagem, an easy victory was confidently counted upon. In accordance with this plan, Gen. Wilkinson moved his headquarters to Sackett's Harbor, where he had 9000 men, while Hampton embarked his army on boats and crossed the lake from Burlington to Cumberland Head. These movements perplexed Prevost, who believed the intention was to unite both armies and attack Kingston, and to that place he proceeded with all speed. It did, indeed, look as if Hampton's army was to go west, for large reinforcements arrived at Chateaugay Four Corners and French Mills, and another camp was formed a little east of the former place, at Colonel Smith's, named Fort Hickory, where preparations were made as if a permanent garrison was designed. These were merely feints, however, for Hampton's instructions were to invade Canada near Hemingford, and penetrate to the shore of the St Lawrence above Caughnawaga, where he would find Wilkinson's army encamped on Ile Perrot, conveyed thither by boats from the head of the St Lawrence, and, uniting with him, they were to cross to the Island of Montreal and capture the city. In compliance with this plan, General Hampton broke up camp at Cumberland Head on the morning of the 20th September, and, embarking again in boats, landed at the foot of the rapids on the Big Chazy river, close to the village of Champlain, and at once began the march to Odelltown.

On hearing of the landing at Cumberland Head the probability of an invasion by way of Odelltown and L'Acadie was palpable, and Major deSalaberry, who was in command at that part of the frontier, ordered a great slash to be made in the bush on either side of the road, which was barricaded also by felled trees, forming abattis at convenient intervals, and to guard which a number of Indians were left under Captain Mailloux. In the afternoon the reconnoitring-party thrown out by Hampton came up to these obstructions, when a skirmishing-fire was opened by the Indians, who fell back as they were pressed, for they were only a handful. The alarm was now given, however, and reinforcements were hurrying up. Major Perrault first came with a couple of militia companies, and was followed by Major deSalaberry himself with his Voltigeurs. Instead of spreading out their men into the bush and advancing in skirmishing order, the Americans persisted in keeping the road, which subjected them to losses from the desultory fire kept up by the Indians and French Canadians under cover of the woods that lined it.* The road, which led through a black-ash swamp, seemed to the Americans to be interminable. They were now nearing that part of it where a gang of men was busy getting out logs for the fortifications at Ile aux Noix. At the first intimation of the approach of the Americans, these logs were piled into a rude breastwork, and on coming in sight of it, the officer com-

---

* Among the Huntingdon settlers in the fight was Platt Stafford of Covey Hill. His brother Joseph served in the 100th regt. in Ontario.

manding the invaders cried halt and then began to fall back.
Had they persevered, after suffering some loss, they would,
unquestionably, have penetrated the woods, when they would
have emerged on the cleared country which then extended,
as now, from Lacolle to the St Lawrence. Fortunately for
Canada, they knew neither of this nor of the insignificance of
the force in their front. On hearing the report of the officers
in command of the advance, Hampton fell back next day to
Champlain, and sent a despatch to Washington, stating that
he found the route to Montreal by Odelltown impracticable,
owing to the great dryness of the season and the absence of
rivers along it !* On the 22nd the army took the road for
Chateaugay Four Corners, where it encamped on the 24th.
The tents were pitched in the field south and west of the
present railway station ; log houses being put up for the
officers. Gen. Hampton and his staff boarded at Smith's
tavern, which stood on the ground now covered by Beman's
brick-block. His haughty manners repulsed and disgusted
the settlers around, who, for the first time, saw a Southern
planter and the commander of no mean army. Of the many
thousands of slaves he was reputed to have in the Carolinas,
he had a number waiting upon him as servants. One incident of his residence at Chateaugay, N.Y., is still remembered.
The proud old man had a magnificent black charger, which a
reckless fellow, named Hamilton, determined to steal. He
coolly entered the stable while the hostlers were in the tavern,
led out the horse, mounted, dashed past the sentinel, took the
road for Athelstan, and was soon beyond pursuit. As fate
would have it, when some distance off, he saw a patrol returning to Four Corners, when, the road being narrow and the
bush impenetrable for a horse, he sprung from its back and
escaped into the woods, and the charger was recovered.

* The drouth of the summer of 1813 was unparalleled. As
an instance of its effects, the English river ceased to flow and
the pools became too shallow for big fish. On going to fetch
a pail of water on the morning of the 26th September, Benj.
Roberts found one floundering about. He jumped into the
water, caught the fish in his arms, and flung it upon the bank.

Day after day slipped by in inaction, apparently because Hampton was afraid to venture into Canada with the force at his command. The regulars were mainly Southerners, and on their march northwards had suffered much from sickness, which rather increased while in camp, owing to the coldness of the nights and the insufficiency of their clothing.. One regiment which had left Virginia with 1000 men could not muster 500 fit for a march, and there were others nearly as bad. To make up for his disabled men, Hampton sent to Plattsburgh and other points for militia, but as they had been enlisted for defence only, they refused to join an expedition intended to invade Canada. While wasting time at Chateaugay, Hampton kept a number of men improving the road to Plattsburgh, the turnpiking of which was completed on the 4th October. On the afternoon of the same day a scouting party of Indians and French Canadians crept up to the outskirts of the American camp, killing Lieut. Nash and a private of the 33rd regt. and taking 2 prisoners, and then retreated. in safety. One of the prisoners escaped and the other was allowed to follow him. This incident greatly annoyed the Americans and caused them to use increased vigilance, and intensified the dread of the average soldier of the Indians,. who he knew were continually lurking in the woods to the north of the camp.

On word reaching Montreal that Hampton was at Chateaugay, N.Y., his design of penetrating into Canada by following the windings of the river of that name was apparent, and preparations made to defeat it. Every available man was hurried to Baker's, and the additions to the barracks on the river-point were so numerous, that the place looked like a town. General DeWatteville, one of the numerous foreign officers then in the British service, was sent to take command of all the forces west of the Richelieu. He was a soldier of experience, having seen much service on the Continent, been taken prisoner by Napoleon and exchanged on condition of not serving against the French. He was accompanied by several staff-officers who, like himself, had belonged to the foreign legion, and, after examining the country, he selected

the house of James Wright, North Georgetown, as his headquarters. He was a plain, unostentatious man, exceedingly
attentive to his duties, and liked by the settlers. The force
he found at his disposal was small and inefficient, and can be
described in a few sentences.

The main-camp was at Baker's, or LaFourche as it had
been named, and was occupied chiefly by sedentary militia,
composed of material in whom the regulars despaired of
arousing anything like military spirit. In the ravine on lot
14, North Georgetown, formed by the creek, were encamped
several hundred embodied militia, and at Morrison's was a
smaller detachment. From there to the mouth of the Outarde
were posted, at intervals, pickets, varying in strength from a
score to a company, and beyond them were the Indian patrols,
reinforced by whites who volunteered as scouts. Among the
corps of embodied militia was the regiment of Voltigeurs,
which had for its colonel Chas. M. deSalaberry, the son of a
Frenchman who had been an officer in the British army, and
to which he became so attached that he destined his four sons
to the same noble service. On retiring on half-pay, he had
taken up his residence at Beauport, a suburb of Quebec, and
while living quietly there the Duke of Kent (father of Queen
Victoria) arrived as commander of the forces, and a warm
friendship sprung up between him and the retired officer,
whose necessities he delicately relieved by procuring commissions for his sons as they came of age. Two of them
died in India, and another was killed at the storming of
Badajoz. The fourth, Charles Michel, entered the Duke's
own regiment, and was stationed in the West Indies for 11
years, and where he saw some active service against both the
Spanish and the French. While there an event happened
which caused him much remorse. One morning, sitting at
breakfast, a German officer swaggered in and, with an insulting air, said to him, "I have just come from sending a
French-Canadian to the other world." DeSalaberry at once
understood that he had killed in a duel his comrade Des
Rivieres, the only other French Canadian in the garrison,
and indignantly sprang from his seat, but recovering himself

replied, "I will finish breakfast and then you shall have the pleasure of finishing another French Canadian." They fought with swords, and, despite a severe cut on the forehead he received at the outset, he killed the insolent German. A score of years afterwards, his boy asked, "Were you ever wounded in battle, father?" "No, my son." "How then did you get that scar on your forehead?" The father staggered as if shot as he recalled that fatal morning, and turning left the room without uttering a word. The Duke of Kent took a fatherly interest in the young officer, and on the regiment proceeding to England befriended him in many ways. In one curious instance his counsel changed the tenor of his protege's life. While on a visit to Ireland, where he had relations, he fell in love with a cousin and wanted to marry her. On hearing of this, the Duke wrote him a long letter, in which he pointed out how' he would blast his own prospects and bring misery upon the lady by marrying on his limited pay. DeSalaberry had the good sense to take the advice, and as an aide on General deRottenburgh's staff, he accompanied the Walachren expedition, after which disastrous affair, on his general's being ordered to Canada to take chief command of the forces, he followed him to his native country. His long absence, nearly 18 years, had made an Englishman of him in speech and tastes, and he probably wrote English with greater facility than French. At the outbreak of the war he married a daughter of the seignior of Chambly, and when militia regiments came to be raised, he was appointed commander of one, the Voltigeurs, which he brought into so high a state of discipline that it was the best in the service. Composed not of habitants, but of lumbermen, voyageurs, and young men from the cities and towns, irrespective of nationality, he had material into which it was possible to impart a martial spirit. When ordered to the Chateaugay he was 35 years of age and is described by those who remember him on that occasion as short in stature, and stout and strong in make; energetic and decisive in character and, probably the result of camp and barrack-life, coarse and peremptory in speech with his men. He left the impression of being a man of ability in his profession, and if he did not achieve anything like what is attributed to him, it was owing to want of opportunity and not of capacity. His regiment consisted of about 600 men; their uniform was a grey blouse. Another noted regiment of embodied militia was the 5th battalion, whose members had green coats with red facings, and who were commonly called "the Devil's Own," owing to their thieving and disorderly propensities. They had been enlisted in Montreal and Quebec, and were largely composed of the offscourings of those cities. They were encamped in the ravine on lot 14, already referred to, and the second son of James Wright, then a boy of 13, was sent daily to sell potatoes to them, when he was cautioned to stand on the bridge and, on a yorker being handed up, to give back the measure of potatoes, but on no account to give the potatoes without first receiving the coin. There were no regulars except a battery of field artillery, under charge of Captain McKay.

Such was the force gathered on the north bank of the Chateaugay to repulse the threatened invasion—small in number and crude in material. Whatever its commander's perplexity may have been as to its inadequacy, it was excelled by the uncertainty as to the direction from which the assault would come. The common conjecture was that Hampton would go to St Regis, and there unite with Wilkinson, sailing down the St Lawrence in company to Montreal. Then there were those who held that it was Hampton's intention to strike across the country and meet Wilkinson where Valleyfield now stands, while others, who knew the country better, held it to be plain he would have to keep along the Chateaugay to its mouth, or striking off at Ste Martine, go by St Phillip to Laprairie. These doubts caused the small British force to be divided, in order to cover the exposed points, and DeWatteville ordered Major Stovin, who continued to hold the command at Baker's, to be in readiness to march to any one of them. The vigilant watch that had been maintained along the frontier was redoubled, and, in addition to the Indian guard, a body of spies was formed from among the settlers in Hemingford and Hinchinbrook, who, from their situation and the intimate relations they kept up with the neighboring settlers on the south side of the line, had great facilities in finding out what was going on in the camp at Chateaugay, N. Y., and without exciting the slightest suspicion on the part of the enemy. Among the most active of these secret-service agents was David Manning, and from the few of his reports still preserved it can be seen that he was a man of education and great shrewdness. Another of the agents, Morris Simpson, from Lacolle, was detected by the enemy, who made arrangements to capture him. Receiving word from a spy that he was staying at Gentle's in Franklin, a detachment was sent from Smith's, and surrounding the house at night found him asleep in bed and took him prisoner without resistance. On their return march, they halted on the flat rock south of Rockburn for breakfast, when Simpson seized his opportunity and made a rush for the bush, escaping unscathed amid a volley of bullets, and made his way back to Gentle's. This was followed by an equally daring descent in the night-time on the house of Jacob Manning, when they arrested him and David Manning and Sam. Place, who were together in bed. They were ordered to dress and then hurried away, amid the entreaties of a distracted household. Neither of the Mannings had any apprehension of danger, but they knew that Place would be recognized at Chateaugay as a spy, and would be punished as such, so they whispered to him to try and escape, and they would assist him. The detachment halted on lot 48, of the 2nd range of Hinchinbrook, when Place affected to be taken suddenly ill and going apart to where a large log lay, suddenly rolled over it and fled. The Americans started in pursuit when the Mannings shouted if they did not come back they would run too, a consideration which, added to their fear of the Indians, caused them to return and hurry forward with their prisoners to Chateaugay, when they were consigned for safe keeping to a log-stable, where they were kept for 18 days. At the end of that time they were unexpectedly led out and conducted to Smith's hotel and brought into the general's room. Addressing Jacob, Hampton asked if he would not take his best horse and go to Montreal and bring back word of the strength of the army he would have to meet. There was no danger, he would not be suspected, and if he did his errand faithfully he would be richly rewarded. Manning refused. "Are you not an American?" demanded Hampton. "Yes," said the sturdy settler, "I was born on the American side, and have many relations still there, but I am true to the British flag." Annoyed at the bold bearing of the U.E. Loyalist, Hampton got angry and spoke roughly. He told Manning he was in his power. and he would send them to Green Bush, which was the name of the military prison near Albany. The undaunted backwoodsman said they would be glad to go, that they were sick of being confined in a filthy stable, and would, at least, be treated like human beings at Green Bush. Seeing he was not to be frightened, Hampton took another tack, and asked if there was a fort at Montreal and when Manning told him there was not, he would not believe him. Taking him to the window, Hampton showed him his army encamped on Roberts' farm, a scene full of life, for its thousands were striking tent and getting under arms, Manning particularly admiring the cavalry and the fine physique of the infantry. Waiting until he thought the magnificent spectacle had made a due impression, Hampton asked proudly, "How far an army like that would go?" "If it has good luck, it may get to Halifax," Manning at once replied, meaning that they would be taken captive and sent to Halifax, which was the place where all prisoners-of-war were sent. Seeing he could make nothing of the loyal men, Hampton ended the interview, by ordering Hollenback, who was officer of the guard, to take them back to their wretched quarters and keep them there for 3 days, so as to prevent them carrying information of the army's moving to the British camp. Hollenback who, as a resident of Chateaugay, was acquainted with them, was either more merciful or desired to get rid of the charge of them. "Do you want anything to eat?" he asked. "No," Jacob answered. "Well, then, put for home." Advice of which they gladly availed themselves.* That afternoon, the 21st October, the American army marched into Canada.

The decisive step was taken after long hesitation, and after more than one abortive start. One Sunday, the 10th October, Hampton went so far as to send out detachments to press into service all the farmers' teams for miles around, and when gathered, changed his mind. The fact is, he hesitated between contending passions—that of fear, which caused him to shrink from the dangers he would encounter in Canada, and that of jealousy of Wilkinson, which urged him to risk all and snatch the laurels that might fall to his rival. It was under the stimulus of the latter motive that he moved at last. Word reached him that Wilkinson was about to take to his boats and sail down the St Lawrence, when he resolved to march at once upon Montreal and achieve its capture before his competitor could reach it. So far as regards provisions and transport, Hampton had nothing to complain of, for both were ample. The great lack was that of winter clothing. After a hot, dry summer, the fall had set in early, and so cold and wet that late corn did not ripen. The soldiers, particularly those from the South, suffered extremely, and were more anxious to get into winter-quarters than to undertake a campaign. The few winter garments that had been received had been divided by lot, and the overcoats were reserved for those who stood guard. The army which crossed the line numbered about 5000, of whom 400 were cavalry, and 100 artillery-men with 8 six-pounders, 1 twelve-pounder, and a howitzer. Before leaving Chateaugay, where he had dallied 26 days, Hampton sent a despatch to Washington, in which he pompously declared: "The Rubicon is now passed, and all that remains is to push forward to the capital"—Montreal.†

* Jacob Manning lost no time on his return in becoming a Free Mason, for he said, while held a prisoner, he saw a number brought in like himself, discharged at once, because of their connection with the mystic tie.

† The American people had formed extravagant expectations of what The Army of the North would accomplish. A

The first column to move was that commanded by Brig.-Gen. Izard, who was ordered by Hampton to move easterly from camp Douglas, familiarly known as Fort Hickory, and possess the country at the junction of the Outarde with the Chateaugay, and so protect the main army on its march on the east flank, the only one that, from the nature of the country, would be exposed, and to clear' the way for its advance. On the morning of the 21st October, Izard, who was an active and skilful soldier, guided by Judge Smith, who knew the country, struck boldly into the woods, near to or on lot 36 of the 1st concession of Hinchinbrook, and made straight for the mouth of the Outarde, by way of Black's church and the Gore.* Preceded by a band of axemen, a tolerable path was easily made for the passage of his corps and the few waggons he had with him, for he went in light marching order, and carried only 5 days' rations. Without misadventure they struck the Outarde on the west side of lot 40, which they crossed by the ford that exists there, and then, turning east, passed down the island of Jamestown. While the rank and file fell to, in order to form a camp, which extended from lot 3 to 1, an advance guard waded the Chateaugay, and, at 4 p.m., surprised the British outpost that

Congressman (Gardiner of N. Y.), although not in sympathy with the war-party, was so infected by the popular sentiment that he was constrained to write: "Wilkinson sounded his bugle: Hampton rose in his strength. From east to west was nothing heard but the dreadful note of preparation. From both armies came letters teeming with assurances of victory. Victory! was the cry of a thousand trumpets."

* The only remains of·this road are a few logs near Black's church—the survivors of those that formed a corduroy across the beaver meadow swamp that existed there. For many years the road was used as a means of communication between the 1st and 2nd concessions. The road from Rennie's to the Chateaugay was little used, owing to the British authorities, after the retreat of the Americans, closing it by frequent slashes. One of the Mathers (Mrs Lewis McKay) said about 1830 she travelled the road, her companions helping her to surmount the heaps of logs.

had been established a few days before at Ormstown, and who fled, astounded at the unexpected appearance of the enemy. They carried the tidings to the camp at Baker's, of which Major Henry happened to be in command. Gen. DeWatteville had just arrived on a tour of inspection of the posts under his charge, and he at once detached about 300 men as a corps of observation, who reached Allan's Corners that night, where they halted. He also sent word to the outlying detachments to fall in, among which was a small body of men at the Basin under deSalaberry. He was awakened from sleep to receive the despatch, when, with soldierly alertness, he aroused his men, and marched for Baker's at daylight. DeWatteville also sent a messenger to Montreal with a despatch for Governor Prevost, informing him of the startling fact that the long-anticipated American invasion had taken place.

Meanwhile General Izard was busy in preparing for the arrival of the main army, which he knew was on the way. Selecting the clearance on lot 33, Ormstown, which was occupied by an American named Spears, he began to form a camp. The infantry were the first to leave Chateaugay, and followed what is substantially the existing road to Athelstan. At that time it followed the crooks of the river and straggled over hills, and, rather than keep to it the engineer-corps, with a strong working party, who went in advance, where they saw fit cut out new bits of road. The advance-brigade reached Spears' (a distance of 22 miles) on the evening of the 22nd, where they found Izard's men in camp. In passing Athelstan they burned Truesdell's sawmill; Simpson's mill at the mouth of the Outarde had before met the same fate at the hands of Izard's corps. So slow was the progress of the main-body, that, on the evening of the 22nd, it had only reached near where Athelstan now is, where it halted for the night; while the baggage-train was far in the rear, so that the last detachment did not leave Chateaugay until the 23rd. Hampton himself left on the 22nd, and, with an escort of 20 cavalrymen, rode rapidly down the track cut out by Izard, and joined him in a few hours in the camp at Spears'. This movement on his part was so sudden and unexpected that the British scouts were unaware of it until he had passed, greatly to their chagrin, more especially that of the Indians. Much expedition was shown in getting the main-army forward, which, considering that new roads had to be made at frequent intervals and that the soil was so saturated by the continued rain that the waggons soon converted them into a quagmire, was creditable to the energy of the enemy. The road from Athelstan to Huntingdon was so bad that portions had to be corduroyed by felling trees, in order to get the waggons and cannon past. In passing Baxter's lot (page 54) the soldiers appropriated his entire crop of potatoes, for which they refused to pay, although he was an American. The river was forded at the head of the rapids above the village of Huntingdon, and from the Methodist church to the end of Hunter street there was so deep a swamp that it had to be corduroyed. On Sunday, the 24th, all difficulties were surmounted and the last detachment of the army reached the camp at Spears'.

It is necessary now to turn and see what preparations were being made to receive the enemy who had thus penetrated 16 miles into Canada without molestation. The morning after Izard's column had passed, a boy of 14 years of age rode along the track that led from Gentle's to the McClatchie settlement. He was a son of Frederick Scriver and was carrying a despatch from Hemingford to Chief Lamothe of the frontier guard, and had been chosen for the duty on account of his youth, it being supposed the enemy would not suspect one so young being entrusted with despatches. The road was a mere by-way, and as the fallen leaves covered the track he had to keep a sharp lookout for the blaze-marks on the trees, when all at once he emerged on a broad open road, freshly hewn out of the woods, and he at once knew that the enemy had crossed. With beating heart he quickened the pace of his pony and soon reached Reed's (Burnbrae), where he found the chief with 20 of his men, and to him he delivered the letter, and which he had carried in the sole of one of his boots. The chief was communicative, and told the boy (Joseph Scriver) that he knew of the Americans having crossed and supposed, from their being so very strong in numbers, that they would not be offered battle until near Montreal. Soon after the band took their way through the forest to unite with DeWatteville's force in the impending struggle. Following them went a strange volunteer. The loyal soul of old Barron (page 55) was stirred by the tidings that the Americans had at last crossed on to British soil, and stiffened as were his arms he thought he could deal one more blow for his king and country. Keeping quiet his purpose, he one night took possession of his father-in-law's horse, the only one in the settlement, and getting on its back, clad in his old regimentals and his sergeant's sword by his side, struck through the woods to gain the British camp by the Chateaugay. When Nichols went out in the morning to his barn, he discovered his loss and guessed the perpetrator of it. Running into the shanty he cried to his wife, "Barron's gone to the camp and taken the old mare, and won't bring back even a hair of her tail." In this he erred, for both Barron and the mare came back safe and sound, the former much disappointed that he failed to reach the British lines until after the fighting was over.

Governor Prevost remained at Kingston until it became apparent from Wilkinson's movements that he had no intention of attacking that place, and that Montreal was his objective point. Once satisfied of this, Prevost resolved on withdrawing a portion of the force there and sending it to the Chateaugay, and the battalion that could best be spared was one of the Canadian Fencibles, lately formed by Colonel Macdonell. It was, unlike the other battalion, which was French Canadian, a mixed one, the greater portion being from Glengarry, mixed with numerous U.E. Loyalists from New Brunswick and not a few Scotch and Irish from the newly-formed settlements in the country south of Quebec. Sending for the colonel, the governor asked him how soon he could be ready to move with his battalion. "As soon," said he, with Highland promptitude, "as my men have done dinner." That afternoon he embarked in boats with his men, descended the St Lawrence with its perilous rapids, and, on the evening of the second day, landed with them in the bay at Valleyfield, and at once marched them through the forest to the Chateaugay, apparently striking the Grande Marais road south of Beauharnois. Robert Morrison, who still survives among us, remembers seeing the long line of redcoats approach his father's house, where they were quartered. The journey from Kingston was made in 60 hours, and not a man fell out by the way. They arrived on the evening of the 24th October and had not come an hour too soon to prepare for the defence.

Gen. DeWatteville knew that the army of the enemy, now fast approaching him, numbered at least 5000, that they were all regulars, and had an efficient artillery-train and a squadron of cavalry. To meet this formidable force he had only 1600, who, with the exception of Captain McKay's artillery corps and the Indian bands, were all militia, and a large proportion sedentary-militia, upon whom no reliance could be placed. It does not appear, however, that even for a moment he contemplated allowing the enemy to advance without a struggle. On Sunday, the 24th October, he, accompanied by Adjutant-Gen. Baynes, Colonel deSalaberry, and Colonel Hughes of the Royal Engineers, reconnoitred their camp at Ormstown, and, observing that they would soon be ready to make another advance, saw the time had come to concert a plan of action, and this he did before returning to his quarters.

The present aspect of the country between Ormstown and Allan's Corners is very different from that presented to the eyes of the four officers on that memorable Sunday. It is now a great smooth plain, calculated to excite the admiration of every lover of good farming, level as a floor, edged on one side by the Chateaugay and on the other by a thin fringe of bush, the sole remnant of the primeval forest. In 1813 the square flat fields, which now present themselves in unvarying succession, were represented by a narrow strip of clearance, full of tree-stumps, which ran along the riverbank, with the forest, from which it had been carved, walling it in and occasionally, where the backwoodsman's axe had so far spared it, intervening. The thick foliage of the all-pervading bush sheltered the soil from the sun and wind, with the result that the rain accumulated on its level surface and formed a marsh, from which, at frequent intervals, there were small creeks flowing into the Chateaugay. This, too, has changed. With the clearing of the bush, the land has become dry, and it is hard to realize that those fields, covered with waving grain, were once so swampy that they could only be traversed when the winter's frost made them solid. With the drying of the land, the creeks have all but disappeared, and water only flows over their beds in the fall and spring. In 1813 the creeks were always full and their banks were densely covered with trees. In the course of the centuries, their currents washed away the deep clay soil until they had made beds for themselves at the bottom of ravines varying from 10 to 25 feet below the surrounding level and in breadth from 20 to 100 yards.

General DeWatteville's plan was to convert these ravines into rude lines of fortification. The road that ran parallel with the Chateaugay, the only possible avenue by which the Americans could advance, crossed, between Allan's Corners and Neil Morrison's, no fewer than six of these gullies. First tearing up the bridges, he ordered that the trees be felled on the east bank of each ravine, so as to form a barricade, behind which he would post his men. By such a plan it was plain the Americans would be at a great disadvantage, that as they came to each successive ravine, they would have to rush down and struggle through the waters of the creek, all the time exposed to the fire of a foe safely ensconced behind an impenetrable slash of felled trees, and which they could leave in time and fall back to the next ravine to repeat the same opposition with perfect safety to themselves. The entrenching of the three first ravines on lots 34, 29 and 28 he entrusted to Colonel deSalaberry, who, at once, set his men to work in felling trees, though they did not make much speed from scarcity of axes. The second line, which included the ford at Morrison's, the key of his defensive plan, he left in the hands of Colonel Macdonell. The main body he concentrated at Gardner's creek, where the artillery was posted. Of this he retained command, ready to make a final stand should his front lines be forced.

The weak point in the plan was the possibility of the enemy going round the entrenchments, and this General DeWatteville foresaw. On the north side there was no possibility of flanking, for the barricades were carried into the bush a short distance, and through the bush, so swampy was it, no troops could move. Where the danger lay, was in the Americans moving down the south side of the Chateaugay, and crossing it, at either of the two fords, taking the fortified ravines in the rear. The ford at Grant's rapids was, at that time, so obstructed by large stones, that it was rarely used and only at low water, but to make sure a body of militia was stationed behind a rude breastwork facing it, and 150 Indians placed in the ravine above it. The other ford (Morrison's) perfectly practicable and easy of passage, was entrusted to Col. Macdonell, who quickly threw up an entrenchment which fully commanded it. In all these works, Col. Hughes took little part, for, despite his position, he was far from being respected, and he and Col. deSalaberry had a quarrel on his interfering. On the afternoon of the 25th, DeWatteville inspected the works, and approved of all that had been done. Although he did not know it, at that very time the Americans were preparing for the attack, and the gloomy October day, now darkening in its close by the rain clouds that swept the sky, was the eve before the battle.

General Hampton was fully informed of the preparations made to resist his farther progress, and resolved that he would not force his way but endeavor to turn the British line of defence by a bold flank movement. The south side of the Chateaugay was an unbroken forest, and he conceived that it would be possible for a detachment of light troops to cross at Rapid Croche (Ormstown) and march downwards to the ford at Morrison's, where, regaining the north bank, they would take the 7 fortified ravines with their defenders in rear and easily capture them, when the main army would move down unopposed. Without enquiring into the feasibility of a brigade penetrating 6 miles of thick woods, interspersed with hemlock swamps, he at once set about carrying his plan into operation. The flower of his army, comprising the best conditioned of the infantry, to the number of 1500, were got in readiness and, at sunset, on the evening of the 25th Oct., they were marched to the river side and waded through the rapids to the southern bank. Before they had advanced many hundred yards, it became apparent that it was impossible to proceed. The guides, two in number, had assured Hampton before starting that they were not very well conversant with the country on the south bank, and soon proved to Purdy that they were incompetent. The night was dark and cold and rain began to fall, while the advance was thrown into confusion by unexpectedly finding themselves floundering in the waters of a creek, which, in the darkness, they had not perceived. Gen. Purdy was compelled to call a halt and wait for daylight. The long night wore wearily on for the Americans in their wretched condition, for they dared not light camp-fires to warm and dry themselves, and their only food the little in their haversacks. Clad in their summer uniforms, they felt the cold and wet very much. At the first streak of day the expedition silently resumed its march, but its progress was necessarily slow, for, apart from the guides not having a competent knowledge of the ground, their route was over what was little better than a hemlock swamp, through which they could only advance as a body of axemen in front of the column brushed a road. Had the guides kept closer to the river all might yet have gone well, but instead of seeking the comparatively dry ground that skirted the Chateaugay, they led the army into the intricacies of the creek that empties near Morrison's rapids.

Informed of the nature of the bush on the southern side of the Chateaugay, Colonel deSalaberry, who had been entrusted with the picket service, had sent no scouts across the river, so that the Americans continued their advance unobserved until several hours after daylight, when the guards at deSalaberry's position near Allan's Corners were astonished to see several American soldiers, who had straggled out towards the river, when the alarm was sent to Col. Macdonell, who, as already stated, had been assigned the guarding of the ford at Morrison's, which was evidently the point aimed at. He at once ordered Captains Daly and Bruyère to cross the ford with their companies and reconnoitre, while a body of the sedentary militia, composed of habitants from the adjoining parishes, followed in support. Capt. Daly, threading his way quickly through the woods, came upon a party of the enemy, consisting of about 100 men of the advance, who had made their way through the bush in single file, until they had nearly reached the river bank on lot No 36, when a brisk engagement ensued. At the sound of the first shot, the sedentary militia, reluctantly following behind, were seized with panic and fled wildly back to the ford, their blue tuques streaming behind. So provoked were the spectators on the north bank, who saw them plainly, that they were strongly inclined to open fire upon them. The Fencibles were of other stuff and aided by a few Indians, kept up a skirmishing fire, during which several on both sides were hit. The Americans behaved badly, for after feebly returning the fire of the Fencibles, and not seeing their supports, they broke and fled,[*] one portion rushing backwards over the route they had come and another taking the more solid footing that led out to the river. The first squad had not run far, when they came in sight of the companies behind, hurrying to reach the place from whence they heard the sound of musketry. Never dreaming that the men they saw running towards them were their countrymen, and supposing them to be British troops rushing to assault them, they began to fire, and several were killed before the mistake was discovered.[†] The second squad,

---

[*] Colonel King, who was with the detachment, said his "countrymen behaved in the most cowardly manner and disgraced themselves."

[†] Edward Wilkins, a U. S. private who was taken prisoner, said, "I saw one man dead, and there was 1 captain, 1 lieutenant, and several privates wounded; shot by ourselves in mistake."

on coming out on the river's edge on lot 43, found, the moment they exposed themselves, that they were under the fire of a corps on the opposite bank and surrendered, when 5 French Canadians* swam across, and making the Americans hold on to a pole, brought them over.

With the return of the men of his advance companies, who, as they came straggling in, brought exaggerated reports of the strength of the foe and the difficulties of the country to justify their ignominious rout, Colonel Purdy gave up all intention of further aggressive movement. It was true that his force was practically intact, but they were exhausted and dispirited and filled with nervous apprehensions of the Indians, whom they believed to be watching behind every tree. The design had been that he should surprise the guard and carry the ford with a rush at daybreak, and here it was wearing on to the afternoon, and he still two miles distant from the ford, and the British fully apprised of his presence and intent, and filling the woods in front of him. He resolved to await where he was until he received further orders, and proceeded to post his men on the angle of land that lies between Round Point and lot 46, he covering the two river-faces with lines of men, while his eastern and southern approaches were protected by impassable swamps.

Leaving him in this strong position, we turn to see what Gen. Hampton with the main army has been doing. Preparatory to his proposed advance, when Purdy left, he threw forward a strong scouting party to clear the route along which he would move. A body of Indians, who had hung round Hampton's camp all day, proceeded at nightfall to a hollow by the river on lot 19, and then, unconscious of the contemplated movement, lay down to sleep. As the Americans advanced, they came upon the hollow, and saw the redmen stretched in slumber around a small fire. They pounced upon them, killed two or three, and captured the others, which was fortunate for the enemy, as it prevented

---

*Their names have been preserved: Vincent, Pelletier, Vervais, and Caron—all privates in the Voltigeurs regt.

word being carried to deSalaberry of their approach, and
who, not hearing from the Indian scouts, supposed all was
well and was unaware of the Americans being near him until
late in the following forenoon.

Long before daybreak, the camp at Sear's was astir, and
after a hurried breakfast the army filed on to the road, and
began their march for Allan's Corners. Hampton's design,
as already stated, was to attack the British lines in front as
soon as the sound of musketry told that Purdy was assail-
ing the defenders of the ford at Morrison's. As he advanced,
and the sluggish dawn of that dull October morning broad-
ened into day, signs were noted that indicated that Purdy
was still far from the point of attack and though glimpses of
part of his force could be caught in the openings of the bush,
it was impossible, owing to the British scouts who lurked on
both banks, to hold communication.

This advance of the main army had been unanticipated by
the British. The day previous, deSalaberry had set his
working party, on completing the inside lines, to strengthen
the front one at Allan's Corners by thickening the abatis,
cutting down trees so that their tops fell outwards and inter-
laced. Pushing rapidly forward, Hampton's skirmishers came
suddenly upon a party of French Canadians engaged upon
this work and guarded by 20 men, whom deSalaberry speaks
contemptuously of as "habitant chasseurs." The guard, discharging their muskets at random, promptly ran with the
axemen, and did not draw breath until they passed the line
of defence on lot 37. At sight of the fleeing men, the Americans cheered, and pushed on faster, but were speedily brought
to a halt, for when they came up to the abatis at Allan's
Corners, which was flanked on the river's bank by a small
blockhouse, the guard, composed of Voltigeurs under command of Lieut. Johnson, turned out and opened fire, which
the Americans returned, and skirmishing was kept up for
over half an hour.

DeSalaberry, unconscious of the approach of the Americans
in front, had gone a short distance down the river, but, on

PLAN OF MOVEMENTS AT CHATEAUGAY.

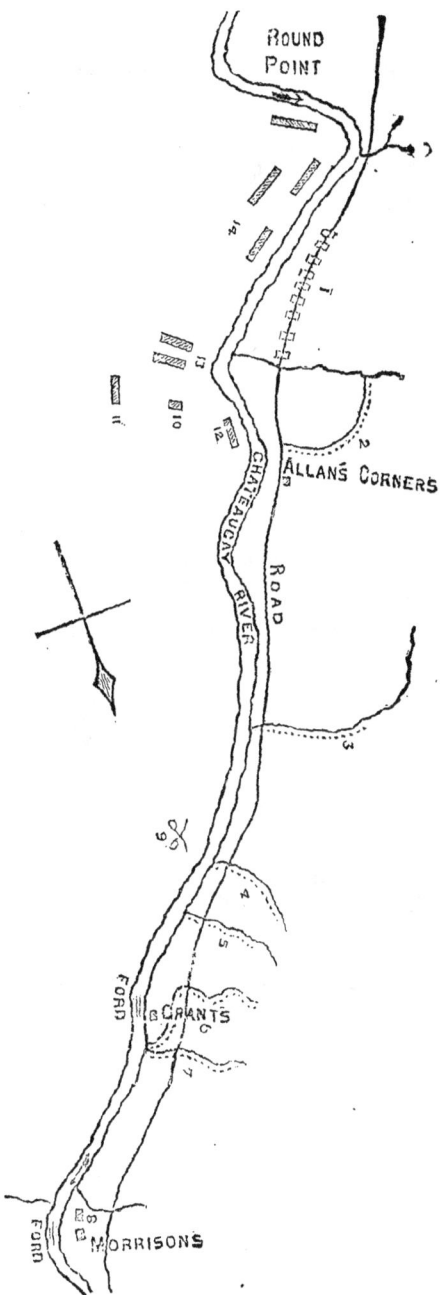

1 Column of Hampton's division that made the attack.   3 Second line, composed largely of Indians.
2 First British line of defence, in charge of Lt.-Col. deSalaberry.   8 Colonel Macdonell's position.
    4, 5, 6 and 7 lines of defence, of which 4, 5, and 7 were protected by abatis.
9 Where Capt. Daly encountered the Americans advancing on the ford and defeated them.
    10 Capt. Daly's position in the afternoon.
    11, 12, and 13. Americans trying to surround Daly's company.
14 Where Purdy encamped.   Scale 1000 yards to the inch.
    The engraver omitted the Blockhouse. It stood between the road and the river at the end of line 2.

hearing the shots hurried to his post,* accompanied by Capt. Ferguson with a company of the Glengarry Fencibles and 3 companies of the regiment Canadien, to reinforce the Voltigeurs and militia. When he arrived the American skirmishers had ceased firing and fallen back upon their supports.

Satisfied that an attack in force was to be made, deSalaberry prepared for it. The abatis, or timber-slash, began at the point on Bryson's creek where the clearance ended, and then bent westward and southward, following the windings of the creek, and describing a quarter circle, until the other end rested on the small blockhouse on the river-bank. At the upper end of the abatis deSalaberry posted 22 Indians, while the Voltigeurs and the companies of the regiment Canadien occupied the rest of the line, and waited in silence for the approach of the foe. In order to see him, deSalaberry went a short distance in front of the abatis, to where a large hemlock lay that had been overturned by the wind (about a rod west of the existing church), and mounting it, concealed by a couple of trees in front, he rapidly took in the situation. He could see the Americans slowly moving along the road until they came to a clearance on lot 42, where they halted, and where a temporary camp had been formed, and preparations made to give the men something to eat. After a short interval, the roll of drums was heard and a brigade fell in for the attack, the main-body awaiting the result. This brigade was commanded by Gen. Izard, and consisted of 1500 men, covered on the left flank by a troop of cavalry, who, however, from the soft nature of the ground, could not help him. The American column advanced along the road with the precision of well-drilled soldiers, and on coming within

* Had the Americans proved successful, deSalaberry would have had to justify his absence before a court-martial. An official report, dated May 13, 1814, states Lt.-Col. deSalaberry "was culpable in a high degree in neglecting to report to his commanding-officer (Maj.-Gen. DeWatteville) the approach of the enemy, which must have originated either in being surprised or from a wilful neglect, in either case highly censurable."

range of the abatis, the order to halt was given, when a tall officer rode forward a few yards and cried out in French, "Brave Canadians, surrender yourselves : we wish you no harm!" Before he could say more, deSalaberry fired point-blank, when he dropped from his horse. DeSalaberry shouted to the bugler, standing behind him, to sound the call to begin firing, and instantly puffs of smoke from discharged muskets issued from the circle of fallen trees, while the yells of the Indians, who filled the woods to the north, mingled with their reports. As if undecided which part of the line to assail, the Americans held their fire, and silently the column wheeled on to the clearance into line, and when the order to fire was given, and several volleys belched forth. At this the skir-mishers, thrown out by deSalaberry along the road, jumped up and ran for cover, causing the Americans to burst into cheering, under the idea that the British were giving way. Their shouts were returned with interest, and as the Ameri-cans pressed forward to improve their supposed advantage were checked by the increasingly rapid fire of a foe they could not see. Halting within musket-range, the Americans poured in volley after volley. The rattle of musketry was now incessant. The fire of the companies behind the fallen trees was that of half-disciplined men—sputtering and irregu-lar, while that of the Americans was delivered in the form of regular volleys, they firing by battalion. The parties kept blazing at one another for fully an hour, and with slight result. The British force were bad shots under the best of circumstances, and at long range, as now, were mere wasters of ammunition, for only 1 American fell under their fire and 4 were wounded. On the other hand the American volleys were almost as ineffective. At first they supposed their antagonists were posted in the woods to the north of them, and blazed in that direction until they discovered their error. Their bullets were harmless to those behind the abatis, the greater proportion lodging in the tree-tops that rose behind it.

With the sound of this noisy but harmless contest in his ears, Colonel Purdy resolved to co-operate with the column, whose movements he could partially trace from where he was entrenched. Encouraged by his success in the morning, Capt. Daly had proceeded to feel his way cautiously forward, until he ascertained where the American mainbody was posted, when he halted on lot 42 to watch its movements. Colonel Purdy was aware of Daly's proximity, and he resolved to capture him, and, after that, it might be, to advance even yet on the ford. Daly's south-flank being unapproachable from the swampy nature of the ground, Purdy detached a body of his troops to move down the river-bank and hem him in from the north. The Americans advanced so quickly that Daly had not time to extricate himself from his dangerous position, and ordered his men to defend it. The exchange of shots was lively for a minute or so, resulting in the wounding of both Daly and Bruyére. To find solid ground, in their effort to get round to where the beset British stood, the Americans, who were cheering lustily in anticipation of routing them, had to come out close to the edge of the river. The moment they left cover, the British on the opposite bank (lot 38), which is higher, opened fire, which so disconcerted the Americans that they gave up their project, at the very moment Daly's men were hurrying away, bearing him and his wounded brother-officer. This failure, coupled with the fact that the firing in front showed that Macdonell held the woods with a strong skirmish line on lot 39, caused Colonel Purdy to conclude that it would not be prudent to push farther, and he gave the order to retire, when the men whom he had detached moved back to the position they had left near the river on lot 47, and there he awaited instructions from General Hampton.

It was still in the power of that officer to redeem the fortunes of the day. Experience having convinced him that firing volleys into the abatis was as useless as shooting in the air, he had issued the order to cease firing when Purdy began to move, awaiting the result of his advance to decide what he should do next himself. For an hour, there was not a shot fired between the two armies facing each other on the north bank, save when two skirmishers happened to get into line. When it became apparent Purdy had failed, two courses were open to Hampton, first, to order an assault on the abatis, and he had men enough to have carried it at the point of the bayonet; or, second, to have his field-pieces brought up and clear a lane through it. He did neither. Apparently he desired nothing more than an excuse for retiring to the United States, and, finding that Purdy was unable to make any progress, and that Izard's volleys were futile, he sent word to the latter officer to fall back on the main-body, which he did slowly and in good order, deSalaberry not following him, and the only annoyance sustained being from the Indians who lay hid in the edge of the bush. By nightfall the army had reached lot 7, where the baggage-train had been ordered forward, and where they encamped for the night.

To Purdy no order was sent, and on that officer despatching a messenger to ask General Hampton for a regiment to cover the crossing of his men on rafts, he was astonished to learn that the main army had fallen back two miles, while Hampton's command to him was to march his men to rapid Croche and rejoin him.* As Purdy did not choose that his men should undergo the sufferings of another night march, and this time to be tracked by a victorious foe, he ventured to disobey his superior by deferring to move until daylight, and issued the order to his troops to encamp where they were until morning. His men were in a miserable plight, exhausted by fatigue and suffering from cold and hunger, to which was added anxiety as to their safety. They knew the enemy was watching them from every point in the surrounding bush and from the opposite bank, and that an attack was possible at any moment. Their sentries had instructions to be extra vigilant, which they scarcely needed, for the apprehension among the rank and file of the Indians was such that it amounted almost to a panic. Towards midnight, the sentries on watch on the river-bank fancied they saw a movement of troops on the opposite, or north, bank. At once

---

* In a letter Purdy indicates that Hampton consoled himself for the day's discomfitures with the bottle, and was in an unfit condition to take care of the army.

supposing a night-attack was about to be made, they discharged their muskets, and in a few minutes their comrades sprang from their comfortless places of repose, and slumbers made uneasy by dread of the Indian knife and tomahawk. A moment before all was silence, but now the air was filled with shouts and cries, and under the trees the men responded to the commands of the officers and got into some sort of order. The officers themselves were deceived by the movements they could dimly discern through the gloom, into the belief that the enemy was massing on the opposite bank preparatory to plunging into the river to attack them. The order came quick and sharp to fire, and the flash of volleys gleamed on the dark waters of the Chateaugay and their sound rolled far and near, carrying alarm alike to Hampton's camp and the shanties of the settlers, who believed the enemy to be again advancing. No response came from the north-bank, save a desultory shot or two, and before many seconds Colonel Purdy was startled on learning that the men he was firing upon was a detachment sent by Hampton to cover his flank—a night attack by the British across the river being deemed possible—and that he had been shooting his fellow-countrymen and not the British. There was no more sleep and at the first streak of day the men silently fell into Indian files, and, bearing their wounded, returned without molestation to the ford at Ormstown and joined the main camp, where the tidings of the unfortunate mistake of the preceding night deepened the despondency which prevailed and strengthened the feeling in favor of abandoning the expedition. In the afternoon Gen. Hampton held a council-of-war, at which he laid before them a despatch which had arrived by a courier the evening before, to the effect that Gen. Wilkinson had not yet moved, and submitted this question, "Is it advisable under existing circumstances to renew the attack on the enemy's position, and, if not, what position is it advisable for the army to take until it can receive advices of the advance of the grand army down the St Lawrence?" After long deliberation the council returned the answer, "It is our unanimous opinion, that it is necessary,

for the preservation of this army and the fulfilment of the
ostensible views of the government, that we immediately
return by orderly marches to such a position as Chateaugay
(Four Corners) which will preserve our communications with
the United States, either to retire into winter-quarters or to
be ready to strike below." This decision gave great satisfaction to the army, which began to prepare for its return to
Chateaugay by immediately marching to its old camp at
Spears', Ormstown. The Indians, under Lamothe, were watching their every move, and caused their sentries much uneasiness. On the 28th they surprised a picket, killing one or
more and wounding several.* On that day, after dinner, the
first division started for Chateaugay, for the army retired as
they advanced, in separate detachments, and moved so slowly,
owing to the state of the roads and the length of their
baggage-train, that their old camp at Four Corners was not
reached until the end of the week. From that place, on the
1st November, Hampton sent a letter to Washington, tendering his resignation, and another to Wilkinson, to inform him
that he could not, from want of supplies, form the junction
with him at St Regis which he now asked, and proposing,
instead, that they should combine their forces at the head of
Lake Champlain and attack Montreal from there. After a
brief rest, the wearied soldiers resumed their march for
Plattsburgh, where they went into winter-quarters, the
greater part being soon disbanded and Gen. Hampton relieved of his command.

* I have been unable to locate with certainty the scene of
this midnight surprise, but am disposed to assign it to the
river-bank on lot 11, where the skeletons of two men were
turned up by the plow many years afterwards. The tra-
ditional account is, that the Indians were lurking in the
vicinity afraid to advance farther from being unable to see.
While watching, an American, presumably to light his pipe,
struck a light, revealing his surroundings, when the Indians
fired and rushing to the spot would have killed all, had the
darkness not favored the escape of the Americans. On the
river-bank on lot 13 a skeleton was exhumed with buttons
bearing the stamp U. S. 11th regt.

Having now given a description of what is popularly
known as battle of the Chateaugay, but which, in reality,
was only a bungling attempt by the Americans to force the
British position, needlessly abandoned after some skirmishing,
I will give details of the encounter which would have ob-
scured the preceding narrative, necessarily somewhat confused, as it involved the description of the simultaneous
movements of two bodies of troops, one on either bank of the
Chateaugay. In brief, the fight consisted in Hampton's de-
taching, at the site of the present village of Ormstown, a
strong brigade across the river, to carry the ford at Morrison's
and take the British lines in the rear, and the plan miscarried
in the manner already described, whereupon, after a weak
effort of his own with the main-army to force the lines in
front, Hampton gave up his projected march on Montreal
and went back to whence he came. Considering that the
Americans had three men to one, and had the advantage in
discipline, equipment, and artillery, their conduct is indefen-
sible, and it is not surprising, that one of the officers engaged,
Major-General Wool, afterwards wrote : "No officer who had
any regard for his reputation, would voluntarily acknowledge
himself as having been engaged in" the Chateaugay encounter.

To turn now to the episodes and consequences of the collision between the two armies, I may remark that the settlers
along the Chateaugay looked forward to the invasion with
well-grounded apprehensions that it would end in their ruin:
instead, it resulted in improving their circumstances. The
presence of the troops at Baker's camp and all along the road
to Allan's Corners, caused a keen demand for whatever surplus provisions they had, and which they sold at what they
considered extravagant prices, while any service they rendered was well-paid. The English speaking settlers had been
formed, as stated in a former chapter, into a militia company,
with James Wright captain and Neil Morrison lieutenant, but
they were never called out, being of more service as teamsters,
and were kept engaged in conveying stores and supplies from
the Basin.

From the moment they heard of Hampton's arrival at

Chateaugay, the settlers lived in a state of constant apprehension, and were ready for flight at any moment. When the Americans did come, the news was unexpected, and the day of the contest saw each family prepared to fly should they force the first line. When the word came towards nightfall, that the Americans had been baffled on both sides of the river, and were falling back to their camp, they were far from feeling secure. Their belief, and it was shared in by the troops, was that the Americans would renew the attempt, and that they would ultimately succeed. The day had been an exciting one. First the roll of hostile musketry in the south woods and the hurrying forward of men and stores to the front, then the dreadful pause before Hampton made his attack, broken by the arrival of the wounded. The first of these poor sufferers, were several men of Purdy's command brought in by soldiers of Macdonell's regiment, who carried them out of the woods and across the ford to Neil Morrison's. Two doctors were in waiting, and a room was emptied and placed at their disposal. Of the wounded 2 died, and their bodies were buried by the river's edge, close to the ford. Others of the wounded, especially those from deSalaberry's position, were placed in canoes and taken down to the camp at Baker's, the groans of the poor men, as they floated past, sinking deep into the hearts of the compassionate dwellers by the tranquil river. Among those most active in thus conveying the wounded, was Sandy Williamson. The surgeon at Baker's was rough and harshly treated the poor fellows, which evoked the compassion of Mrs Baker, who slipped in, while he was absent, to ease their pain or to give them some dainty. The doctor suspected this, and once asked "If that woman had been giving them anything?" to which the orderly replied evasively. Their groans at first were terrible but they all eventually recovered.

Sixteen prisoners were taken in all, and of these the first three that were captured were brought to Gen. DeWatteville's headquarters at Wright's, where they were examined. One of them was so ravenously hungry that he paid more attention to the piece of bread that had been given him than to the general's questions, when an officer remarked, "Let him .eat first and then he will speak."

On word reaching him that the Americans had attacked·in force, General DeWatteville despatched every man that could be spared to reinforce deSalaberry and hurried forward supplies of ammunition, while he superintended the preparations for a final stand on Gardner's creek, should the advance-lines be abandoned. In the course of the afternoon, while all were busy, the governor, Sir George Prevost, arrived from Montreal accompanied by Colonel Baynes, adjutant-general. After a short conference with DeWatteville, that officer and Lieut.- Colonel Hughes rode with the governor to the front. When they reached Allan's Corners, the enemy had desisted from the attack, and deSalaberry made his report of the engagement in·person, on hearing which Prevost said, "The action which you have performed does you and your countrymen great honor, the whole of you being Canadians." DeSalaberry, who reports this speech of the governor, adds, "I hope he is satisfied, though he appeared cold." The vice-regal party remained until dark, when it became evident fighting was over for the day, when the governor rode back.

The story has been preserved that, on his way, he halted to speak to Macdonell, who had moved forward with his men to reinforce deSalaberry if required and lay in waiting at the second ravine. After some conversation, the governor, who recalled his parting with Macdonell at Kingston six days before, asked, "And where are your men?" "There, sir," replied the hardy Highlander, pointing to the sleeping forms that covered the sides of the ravine, and then he added significantly, "there is not one man absent."

The governor stayed at Baker's overnight and returned to Montreal next morning, where his presence was necessary owing to the uncertainty regarding Wilkinson's movements. His last command to DeWatteville was to stand on the defensive, which was, as we will see, too literally obeyed.

When the firing had ceased and it was known there would be no more fighting that day, the belief was that the Americans had merely suspended the struggle until next morning. General DeWatteville, whose instructions were to keep on the defensive, and whose plan was to fall back on Montreal as pressed by the enemy, stubbornly contesting every inch of the way and laying waste the country, sent his orderlies round to the shanties of the settlers, to tell them to pack up their movables and to be ready to leave with their families as the army fell back, setting fire to their buildings and all property they could not carry, so that the Americans would find nothing in the shape of subsistence. The order brought consternation into every household. Carts were hurriedly packed with what was deemed most valuable, and stood at the door, while the horses munched their hay in harness ready to be hitched. Children were dressed for the journey and on every hearth there was a fiercer blaze than usual, so that the supply of brands should not fail when the moment came to apply the torch to hay-stack and rooftree. If the invader came, the loyal settlers by the Chateaugay were determined he should find neither shelter for himself nor fodder for his horses, and resolute men sat by their glowing chimneys awaiting the command to sacrifice all they had accumulated by years of painful labor.

The anxiety at the front was scarcely less, for a night attack was looked for. The Indians were thrown out on both sides of the river as scouts, and the troops slept with their guns in hand around the camp-fires. At one of them, probably that which blazed in front of the small blockhouse on lot 38, deSalaberry wrote the following account of the part borne by his command during the day:

ON THE CHATEAUGAY RIVER,
26th October, 8 P.M.

SIR,—In the action of this day, which began by the enemy attacking our advanced pickets, in great strength, on both sides of the river, the enemy has been obliged to abandon his plan. Our pickets, supported in time by the Canadian Light company, 2 companies of Voltigeurs, and the light company of the 3rd Embodied Militia, behaved in the bravest manner. After the action, we remained in quiet possession of the abatis and posts we occupied previously.

The enemy's force appeared to me to have been at least

1500 men, with 250 dragoons and 1 piece of cannon. Three of our men, who saw the American army passing at best part (place) make it out amount to more. There were about 30 cannon with them.

I cannot conclude without expressing the obligations I owe to Capt. Ferguson, for his cool and determined conduct and his extreme readiness in executing of orders. Capt. Daily, of the 3rd Batt., in gallantry cannot be surpassed ; he contended with 50 men against a force ten times in number. Captain Daily is wounded in three places. Capt. Bruyére behaved with gallantry and was wounded. Capt. J. Robertson and Jochereau Duchesnay have evinced great gallantry, and so, indeed, have many officers employed, particularly aide Major Sullivan, whose bravery has been so conspicuous. Capt. Lamothe, with a few Indians, exposed himself very much, and so did Capt. Hebden of the Voltigeurs.

By correct information there appears no doubt the enemy have returned to the Outarde.

This report is made by woodfire light.

I have the honor to be, Sir,

Your most obedt. servt.,

DESALABERRY.

To Major-Genl. DEWATTEVILLE.

Two officers wounded.

Light company, Canadian regiment, 3 killed and 4 privates wounded.

Voltigeurs, 4 wounded.

3rd Batt., light company, 2 killed, 6 wounded, 4 missing.

DESALABERRY, Lt.-Col.

This letter, like all the others preserved, is in English, and written neatly and correctly; indeed, to judge from his letters, nobody would suspect the nationality of the gallant colonel. The seal is apparently a bit of moistened biscuit, wax not being available at his outpost.

The night wore away amid painful apprehensions, intensified for a time by an outburst of musketry, and much relief was felt among the settlers, when the news came in the morning that no Americans were visible from the British lines, and that the report of the scouts was that they were falling back to their old camp ground at Ormstown. With this welcome news, came fresh reinforcements from Montreal, chief among which was 250 men under Captain deRouville, a brother-in-law of deSalaberry's. At the same time Macdonell moved up with his command to Allan's Corners, where as strong a force was concentrated as possible, in anticipation of a second attack.

In compliance with the order of his general, deSalaberry detached Capt. Ducharme with 150 men to reconnoitre in front, which he proceeded to do with all caution. Feeling their way up the river bank, they came upon the scene of Purdy's night-mistake, the river-edge being strewn with dead. Continuing their stealthy course, they surprised several pickets, whom they made prisoners, and finally came in sight of Hampton's camp on lot 7, which they carefully prospected. Satisfied that the enemy had abandoned the country between their new camp and Allan's Corners, Ducharme returned, and as he did so ordered a party to dig two trenches on lot 41, in which were laid the dead of the night-mistake, and among whom were two officers. Two elms mark their last resting-place by the river-edge. Swimming the river to the other bank, Purdy's late camp was explored, and a large quantity of guns, haversacks, provisions, and the like, were picked up. The bodies of two dead horses were also found. Ducharme's report did not shake the belief of DeWatteville and his officers that the Americans intended to renew the attack ; that they would go back to their own country without making a second trial does not seem to have been conceivable by them. The day was spent in preparation, and the mystery as to the enemy's intentions was deepened when, towards night, word was brought in by the scouts that they were falling back to the camp at Spears'. Next morning, the 28th, Lamothe with his Indians was ordered forward to watch the enemy and during the day a party of militia went up the road for a couple of miles to destroy the bridges built by the Americans across the creeks and so hinder their anticipated return. On that day, when the first detachment took the route for Chateaugay, the astounding fact that the American army, substantially intact, had abandoned its purpose of marching to Montreal and was in full retreat to whence it came, flashed upon the minds of the handful of soldiers now concentrated at Allan's Corners, and their rejoicing was in proportion to their astonishment. The greatness of the result, revealed to them the importance of the encounters in which they had been engaged, and, thenceforth, for all time, what would otherwise have been passed over by the historian as skirmishes incident to every campaign and unworthy of narration, came to be regarded by him among those conflicts which decide the fate of peoples and nations. Had the American army been less cowardly, they could have captured Montreal, and the fall of Montreal would have resulted in the forcible annexation of Canada to the United States. Never did consequences of greater moment result from so insignificant operations. Those engaged in them were rewarded in proportion to their issues and not their severity, and it is unfortunate that those, like Macdonell and DeWatteville, when rewards were being bestowed by the provincial authorities, were beyond the Atlantic and had no representatives in Canada to urge their claims, although it is possible neither of these war-worn veterans attached any importance to the skirmishing in which they took part on the banks of the Chateaugay.

Owing to Prevost's injunction, on no account to assume the offensive, the Americans were not assailed in their retreat. On the 28th, Neil Morrison was given $16 to induce him to go as a spy on the enemy's movements. He penetrated as far as McClatchie's, on the 1st concession of Hinchinbrook, and ascertained beyond all doubt that Hampton was falling back to his old quarters at Chateaugay. Despite this positive information, not the slightest attempt was made to molest the retreating army, which moved safely back through 20 miles of bush, where 50 men could have seriously harassed them and a few hundred might have routed them. Much to their surprise, the Americans had not a single shot fired at them from the moment they broke up camp at Ormstown, and reached Chateaugay with the loss of a few waggons, that broke down or for which the horses died. In all the course of the war no better opportunity of inflicting a heavy blow on the enemy was allowed to slip. After they had gone, an officer indeed arrived capable of such exploit, the gallant Gordon Drummond, who must have chafed when he learned of the invader escaping with impunity.*

The curiosity felt by the settlers in the fighting, led them to visit the scenes of it the day after, and they examined everything minutely. The slight execution done by the American volleys was explained by the appearance of the trees under which the British had lurked, for their branches were lopped off and their trunks high up studded with bullets, so that, in after days, the youth of the settlement when in need of ball, would go to the scene of encounter and fell a .tree, in order to pick the lead out of it. The equal harmlessness of the fire of the British was explained by their lack of practice and the steadiness which drill can alone give. James Wright relates that, when deSalaberry and his regiment, returning to the camp at Baker's, halted at his father's house, "the men amused themselves during their rest by setting up a mark and discharging their guns of the loads they had put in on the day of the fight. DeSalaberry, who had a beautiful double-barrelled piece, joined in, but he and all his men made such very bad shooting, that I no longer wondered that so few Americans had been killed."

Of the enemy's loss nothing certain can be said. DeSalaberry, in a letter to his wife, puts it down at 100, but that is a gross overestimate. A contemporary American account puts it at 36, and Gen. Hampton himself at under 50. The British loss is given in the general-orders at 5 killed, 16 wounded, and 4 missing. It is a curious commentary on the popular impression which ascribes to the Voltigeurs the sole

* One officer, Major Perrault, who had charge of the post at Lacolle, realizing the opportunity that had been missed, was for pursuing the enemy across the frontier. Writing on the 9th November, he states that the scout, Simpson, had just come in and informed him that Hampton's force was retreating in divisions to Plattsburgh at the rate of 10 miles a day, and were in a wretched state. He proposed to his commander, Colonel Williams, that they should be cut off, but nothing was done. In a few days more they were beyond reach.

credit of the engagement that their only loss was 4 wounded.*

The settlers of those days believed that not all who died were so fortunate as to get graves. They had stories of stragglers who lost themselves in the woods and perished, and from the cries of the wolves, which were unwontedly loud, they suspected they nightly banquetted on their remains. A relief to these dismal surmises, is this authentic incident. After it was well assured that the Americans had gone, the soldiers in front were either withdrawn to the camp at Baker's, or despatched to meet Wilkinson. A sergeant with 12 of the Voltigeurs, however, were left as an outpost in the blockhouse at Allan's Corners. This blockhouse, which has been so frequently mentioned, was a small log building, intended for a guardhouse. For many years after the war it was used as a barn and stable. One night they came rushing tumultuously into James Wright's house, declaring ghosts were abroad. Mr Wright got up and went back to ascertain the cause of their fright. They had been scared by the unearthly cries of a catamount !

A counterpart to this, as showing a woman's courage, was an incident at Baker's. Some time after the fight, 3 Indians entered the kitchen, when all were out save Mrs Baker and her husband, who was lying near the fire unfit to move from rheumatism. They demanded rum, knowing it was from there that the daily ration was served to the troops. Mrs Baker answered it was locked up. Crazy for drink, an Indian seized an axe and swung it over her head, without changing her determination. He then advanced towards her husband and declared he would split open his head unless she showed them where the rum was. On the stove stood a

---

* The general-order is that of the 27th October, 1813, and gives the details of loss thus :

	Killed.	Wounded.	Missing.
Glengarry Light Infantry	3	4	
Voltigeurs		4	
3rd Batt., flank co'y (Capt. Daly's)	2	7	4
Chateaugay Chasseurs		1	
	5	16	4

cooler of boiling water. Stepping up to it, Mrs Baker quickly scooped up a dipperful, and told them quietly if they did not go out, she would scald them to death. They left and on the officers returning she told them of her adventure, when they caused search to be made for the Indians, who were punished by being confined for a while in the guardhouse.

The ration of rum here alluded to had a disastrous effect upon the morals of the whole country. The physicians of those days believed spirits were an essential to the maintenance of health, so that each soldier got his daily glass of Jamaica rum. The militia-men being treated in like manner, habitants, who had hardly known the taste of liquor before, became habituated to it, while intemperance among the Old Country settlers got a fatal stimulus.

It was apparently the second week in November before any reconnaissance of the frontier was made, when Lieut. Powell was sent by Gen. DeWatteville with a strong patrol. Lieutenant Powell found the country clear and penetrated into the United States as far as the blockhouse, 2 miles from Chateaugay, which he burned.* He reported that he would have gone farther, but had no guide.

When Powell returned to Wright's from his excursion, which was on the 13th November, he found that Gen. Gordon Drummond had arrived, who, being DeWatteville's superior, assumed command. He had come to complete preparations for disputing Wilkinson's passage down the St Lawrence and to prevent Hampton's co-operating with him. To effect the first purpose, he sent over the two 3-pounders which they had at Baker's to strengthen the batteries that had been erected along the river above Melocheville, and personally inspected the positions taken up there by Col. Deschambault, who was in command. To effect the second, the checkmating of Hampton, he ordered DeWatteville with his force to march

* In all U.S. local histories, the burning of the blockhouse is represented to have been done by the Americans themselves. The official correspondence preserved at Ottawa settles the point, it being perfectly explicit. It was burned in the afternoon.

to Lacolle, where, with other detachments posted there, he intended, aided by the fleet, to have attacked Hampton. This design was frustrated by that general falling back from Chazy to Plattsburgh, and was happily rendered superfluous by the tidings of Wilkinson's defeat at Crystler's Farm. Gen. Drummond appears to have stayed at Wright's until the end of November, when the troops went back to Montreal for winter-quarters. Their discomfort on the Chateaugay had been extreme—wretched accommodation, scant rations, cold wet weather, and marches over roads deep with mire. One French officer wrote that his experience at Baker's and Allan's Corners had led him to "believe that a man is capable of enduring, without breaking down, more misery than a good dog."

Before all left a reconnaisance was made of the frontier, apparently with a view to ascertaining whether it was possible to attack the enemy's position at Chateaugay Four Corners, and to obtain information of the situation there the seigniory-agent, Milne, was engaged. His connection with the illicit traffic that was going on (page 76) had made him familiar with the frontier and brought into his employ a number of reckless Americans who would not hesitate to act the spy on their countrymen. Accompanied by Milne, deSalaberry marched with his force from Allan's Corners after dinner on the 23rd November, having, in addition to the infantry, a detachment of the 19th Dragoons. Next morning, he sent forward Milne and Barron, who had been sent as a guide, to secure intelligence. Milne's letter is so interesting in its details, that it would not be well to relegate it to the appendix :

DAVIS HOUSE,
CHATEAUGAY, 26th November, 1813.

SIR,—In obedience to your orders, I proceeded, in advance of your party, at 8 o'clock on the morning of the 24th, with Capt. Barron, by the road followed by Gen. Hampton's army in their retreat, and, from near the Lines, went eastward to the first house, from whence I sent a man, under pretext of business, towards Four Corners, to ascertain, as far as possible, the strength of the enemy's force, the position of the

pickets, &c., and to return to me at Capt. Barron's. From
thence, I proceeded to Capt. Barron's, where we got at 4
o'clock p.m. He sent his wife across the Lines 5 miles, for
one Hollenback (from whom he has occasionally received
intelligence), in order that he might affirm before me on oath
his losses by the Indians, for which Colonel Boucherville
promised remuneration. Mrs Barron returned at 8 o'clock,
saying that Hollenback having killed a heifer, had baked it,
and was gone to the camp to sell it in pieces, and that on his
return, which was hourly expected, his father would send
him forward. The night becoming exceedingly dark and
rainy, so much so that he could not have found his way
(having only a footpath through the woods) I, for the same
reason, was obliged to remain till morning to wait him.

At 9 o'clock a.m. of the 25th his father came to Barron's.
He stated that the weather having been so bad, his son had
not returned, but that he had brought the account to which
he would swear. This I put off, by saying that the person
who had produced the account must qualify it, and desired
him to send down his son directly. The old man, who had
no knowledge of the force at Four Corners, said that 4 days
before there was no guard at Major Smith's, but there was
one between that and Four Corners. Leaving Capt. Barron
to collect intelligence from the son, I went to Reed's, where,
after waiting about an hour, he arrived. Reid had been at
several houses on the main road leading from Four Corners
to Salmon river, where he had an opportunity of seeing
several people who had been lately at Four Corners, some
of whom state the force there at 1000 men, others at 800,
and 600 men, with 2 pieces of heavy ordnance, at or near the
camp in the S. E. section of Four Corners. Small parties
were marching and countermarching from Four Corners to
Salmon river, numbers of waggons were passing towards
Salmon river with provisions, &c., for Gen. Wilkinson's army.
It is said the men at Four Corners compose one regiment and
a small party of Gen. Hampton's army left in charge of his
sick and wounded. A sergeant of the regiment informed
him that they were 1000 strong, and expected to winter
there. He was informed that they were lodged in huts and
branch tents on the edge of the woods, at the S. E. section of
Corners, on an eminence. He cannot state what number of
dragoons there are, but that they ride much in patrols during
the night, and he has seen their tracks. On his way up, he
saw, at about 100 rods from the blockhouse, towards the
Corners, a small patrol of men about twilight. * * *

Capt. Barron was to have followed me down as soon as Hollenback came to his house. I presume he will be here to-day, and I will report to you the information he has got from Hollenback.

Apprehensive that your men would be short of provisions, I caused Capt. Barron to send his son and another with 3 head of cattle. I suppose they have come as far as Trout river forks last night, where they have been benighted.

I arrived at (Neil) Morrison's last night, an hour after midnight, and from the horrible state in which you found the roads you will allow I have not lost time. The roads from the Forks to the Province Line are much worse (if possible) than those you passed, the thin mud among the logs and tree roots being near belly-deep.

I have the honor to be, &c.,

J. MILNE,
Lieut -Col. DESALABERRY,   Asst. Q. M.
   Command advance of Chateaugay.   Emb. Militia.

On the 27th, deSalaberry reported to Gen. DeWatteville that he had arrived at Vallee's (who probably lived at Dewittville), and enclosed Milne's letter. It is questionable if the expedition went any farther, for it appears to have returned to the camp at Baker's at once without having effected anything, and to find that Gen. Drummond had gone to Cornwall.

With the retreat of Hampton all anxiety as to his movements ceased on the Huntingdon frontier, and, instead, those of Wilkinson filled the minds of its settlers with apprehension. Every resource at the disposal of the military authorities had been exhausted to prevent the expedition passing down the St Lawrence, from lake St Francis to lake St Louis. At Coteau a really strong fort grew up under the direction of Colonel Scott, and the same energetic officer undertook even a greater task, that of so obstructing the south channel that boats could not pass it. This he effected by sinking rafts of huge logs. On the island below Port Lewis he threw up a battery* and from the guard there stationed it got the name it bears, Grenadier island. The gunboats on lake St Louis were

---

* On Caza's point, below St Anicet village, there is apparently the remains of an earthwork. That it was a battery, thrown up at this time, I have no proof.

too few and small to engage the approaching flotilla, for the dispersion and wreck of which the batteries and the violence of the rapids were relied upon. After spending two months at Sackett's Harbor preparing for the descent on Montreal, Wilkinson set sail, the first week in November, with 7000 men in over 300 boats. No opposition of consequence was encountered until Hamilton's Island was reached, when the Americans learned that the passage of the Long Sault rapids would be disputed by 800 men under Gen. Boyd. On this, Wilkinson landed a detachment of 2000 of his force, who, after a well-fought engagement, were beaten back, losing 102 killed and 339 wounded, the British loss being 22 killed and 147 wounded. Leaving 1 cannon and a number of their wounded behind, the Americans regained their boats, and ran the rapids, the British having no guns of sufficient weight to command the river. This battle, that of Crystler's farm, was fought on the 11th November; on the following day Wilkinson called a halt on Barnhart's Island, near Cornwall, and held a council-of-war, when a letter from Hampton was read, dated Chateaugay, Nov. 1st, stating that he had decided on going to Plattsburgh and would not meet Wilkinson either at Ile Perrot, or, as had been suggested, at the mouth of the Salmon river. This letter decided men whose only wish was to get out of the enemy's reach, and it was agreed to give up the idea of going to Montreal and to retire to French Mills. By this time the army was very disorganized and all discipline lost. Hundreds had rowed ashore and openly deserted and, what was morally worse, officers enriched themselves by selling the stores entrusted to them, and were not particular whether the purchaser was British or American. Word was sent to the small garrison at French Mills of the decision arrived at, and on the 13th the obstructions placed in the river were removed, the chief one being a boom, which was chopped away. It was late that night before the first boats rowed up the river, and they were laden with the wounded, who formed a ghastly and horrible spectacle. So far as its capacity permitted, the wounded were carried into the block-house. One boat bore a peculiarly mournful load. At Crystler's farm General Covington had been wounded in the bowels, and while being rowed as gently as might be, breathed his last on the midnight waters. His body was buried close to the blockhouse with military honors. Afterwards his remains, with those of two other officers, were sent to Sackett's Harbor for final interment, but Gen. Covington's name has been perpetuated by the citizens of French Mills, for when they formed a municipal organization in 1817, they named their town after him, prefixing the word "Fort" to distinguish it from Covington in Kentucky.

Landed opposite Barnhart's Island the cavalry marched at once, part going to Utica the other to Sackett's Harbor, leaving the infantry and artillery to go into camp at French Mills, and it shows to what an extent desertion had prevailed, that, on the roll being called, only 4482 answered their names. The wretchedness of their condition can hardly be exaggerated. The country was a wilderness, with no stores of provisions to draw upon within a week's journey, and no shelter save their tents. There had been sleet and snow before their arrival, but no sooner had they pitched their tents around the blockhouse (into which the artillery was moved and port holes cut for their guns) than steady frost set in, and the men, clad in their summer uniforms, and with few blankets, suffered untold agonies. Their rations were of the most meagre quantity, some regiments being actually without biscuits for 4 days, and, what made it worse, of such a quality that even starving men loathed them. The biscuits were mouldy and had been made from the flour of sprouted wheat. The meal designed as poultices for wounds, the doctors had to order to be made into bread for the sick, and they reported that, without proper food and medicines, it was impossible for those under their care to recover. Dysentery, inflammation of the lungs, and typhus-fever soon became prevalent, but, more frightful than these dread diseases, was a withering of the limbs—a dry rot of the extremities—attended by pain. The physicians ascribed its cause to the bread made from smutty flour, and were happy, in prescribing opium to relieve the pain of the sufferers, to find that the drug also counteracted the disease. Before Christmas one-third of the army was unfit for duty; how many died during those six dismal weeks is unknown. By that time, lumber had been obtained and huts were erected* and the sick and wounded had been conveyed to Malone, which village was converted into an hospital.

The officers of the small British force at Cornwall were aware of the state of matters at French Mills and were eager to attempt the capture of the camp, but were forbidden. The energetic commandant at Coteau, Col. Scott, wrote Sir George Prevost asking permission, which was refused. One dark November night a midshipman, whose name deserves to be preserved, Master Harvey, left Cornwall in a canoe with 3 carcas to set fire to the flotilla of boats that were moored in Salmon river. Having succeeded in getting on board one of the largest he was preparing to fire a carca when the crackling of the ice, as his canoe floated at her side, alarmed a sentry, who shouted to the guard-boat, which put-off and rowed twice past the canoe without discovering her. Finding it impossible to effect his purpose, he returned to Cornwall. By the 1st of December the frost was intense enough to close the river and with the ice a new avenue for escape was afforded the American soldiers. Handbills had been sent from Cornwall promising that deserters would receive any arrears of pay that might be due them, and pathways through the woods were blazed to guide them to

* The encampment was on both sides of the river, and wherever there was a cleared and sloping piece of ground. The chief cantonment was on the rising ground on the east side, less than half a mile from the frontier. On the knoll to the nor-east was the look-out post. When Wilkinson left for Malone the command devolved on Generals Lewis and Boyd, who lived in a long, one-storied, red-painted house, on the west bank of the Salmon river and a few yards north of the lower bridge. The house was standing and inhabited when I visited it in 1883. After they left on leave of absence, General Brown took command, and his headquarters were a house on the corner of Water and Chateaugay streets, where P. A. Mathews long kept a hardware store. It was Brown who ordered the men to build huts.

friendly houses on the banks of the St Lawrence, the chief
of which was Captain Moquin's, with whom rations were
left and batteaux to cross the deserters to Cornwall. Among
the many who accepted the offer, was an Englishman, who
offered to conduct a party to the log barn in which the ammunition was stored and blow it up, but Sir George Prevost's
orders were peremptory not to assume the offensive.

When General Wilkinson arrived at French Mills he hardly
stayed a day, and was carried in a litter, borne by 8 men, to
Malone, where he took up his abode in the house of a leading
citizen. Whether his illness was the result of unavoidable
causes or arose from drink, to which he was a slave, is uncertain, but it certainly had no effect in checking his boastful
inclinations. He who wrote on the 6th November, "I am
destined to and determined on the attack of Montreal, if not
prevented by some act of God," and then fled up the Salmon
river when almost within sight of Mount Royal, now threw
the cause of his failure on Hampton. "What a golden opportunity has been lost by the caprice of Major-General
Hampton," he exclaims in a despatch to the secretary of war,
and, ignoring the fact that his men were unfit for service,
haggard from cold and hunger, sick and dying within 15
miles of him, he, who had so wretchedly failed in carrying
any out, goes on to suggest new schemes. If Hampton would
advance from Plattsburgh, he would join him to capture St
Phillip, L'Acadie, St John, and Ile aux Noix, or if Secretary
Armstrong would only let him, he would capture Cornwall
and so cut the Provinces in two, and then take Prescott and
Kingston at his leisure. Anything was possible (on paper)
for this Bobadil, who, no doubt, secretly rejoiced when, the
last week in January, 1814, he received orders to send 2000
of his men to Sackett's Harbor and to take the rest himself
to Plattsburgh. The order came none too early, for the rank
and file at French Mills were almost in a state of mutiny,
one day a large portion of them having actually started to
march to Sackett's Harbor and being with difficulty persuaded by their officers to return. Their only excuse was,
that anything was better than their present situation, of

being starved to death by cold and want. When the pay-master arrived, they spent their few dollars in buying food from the settlers, who came in sleighs from a great distance to find a market for their produce in the stricken camp. What was peculiarly galling to the soldiers was, that many of their officers were making money out of their sufferings; that they did not revise the rolls, and were drawing pay and rations for men who had long before deserted or found graves on the banks of the Salmon river. The pay they pocketed and the rations they sold to the survivors. That there were honorable and patriotic men in the army is undeniable, but the majority of the officers were ignorant and unscrupulous; school-district and ward politicians, who owed their position to the influences of caucus and partyism, and who viewed the campaign as a means of enriching themselves. As depicted by those who served under them, a more despicable set of men never officered an army; blatant as to their patriotism and hatred of Great Britain, yet pilfering their own government and making secret offers to that they opposed of intelligence and of the provisions and war-material they had meanly pur-loined.

On the 3rd February preparations for abandoning camp were begun. The masts of part of the boats were cut and the hulls then sunk. The remainder were set fire to and burned to the water's edge. The barracks and what stores they could not move, were also burned, and as one great barn, on falling a prey to the flames, gave forth the odor of burning biscuit, the bitterness of the men against their officers was intensified, for they believed it had been saved, while they were hungering, in the expectation of selling it. The troops destined for Plattsburgh were the first to leave, and on Sunday, 6th February, the main body for Sackett's Harbor took their departure. To part of the provisions the commis-sariat-officers were unable to move, the settlers were allowed to help themselves.

Kept fully acquainted of all that was happening in the camp at French Mills, the British officers at Cornwall and Coteau were most anxious to attempt an expedition to capture it, but the cautiousness of Sir George Prevost was not to be overcome, and to every request, he returned a peremptory refusal. It was not until the middle of February, when it was notorious the camp was deserted, that he sent permission from Montreal, where he was staying. On the 18th, Lieut.-Colonel Pearson sent 500 regulars to join the force of Indians and militia collected by Col. Scott, who had also got together about 100 sleighs, furnished by the farmers of Dundas and Glengarry, in which the solders sat. At 9 o'clock on the morning of the 19th, the expedition left Edwardstown, both weather and roads being favorable, and all in high spirits at the prospect of a raid. The ice being in splendid condition, such good time was made, that in the evening the cavalcade swept into French Mills and took possession of what remained of the American camp without opposition. Requisitioning all the horses he could find, after a brief halt, and leaving a strong guard behind, Col. Scott pushed on with fresh teams for Malone, which he entered in a few hours, and found its inhabitants cowed with fear. A small detachment got orders to go on to Chateaugay, and reached that place, then a hamlet, at 4 o'clock in the morning. There was a light in the barroom of Smith's tavern, which was crowded with teamsters having loads of stores for the army at Plattsburgh, and who were wiling away the time until their horses had finished their oats. Suddenly the door was flung open and a tall soldier-like man entered, who, in a tone of command, said he made them his prisoners in the name of King George. The sight of a company of soldiers, drawn up behind him, showed resistance was futile, and the astonished teamsters surrendered. Hearing that a messenger had been sent to Plattsburgh with news of the raid, a party was sent in pursuit and overtook him near the bridge across Marble river. At daylight, the captured teamsters had to harness up and turn back to Malone, with the addition of a great quantity of other stores that were found in Chateaugay. The farmers' houses* along the road were searched for government

---

*The late Wolcott Thayer of Burke, N.Y., told me he

great excitement, the citizens being terrified that their village would be given up to be sacked by the Indians. Colonel Scott assured them that if they would deliver the government stores concealed in their houses and barns, no violence would be done, and he was as good as his word. One Indian, mad from drink, and angry at not being permitted to plunder, aimed his musket at the colonel, who coolly knocked the fellow down. A large building used as an arsenal and the only one owned by the government, the colonel gave orders to burn, but, at the request of the inhabitants, he spared it and gave it to them for a schoolhouse. Gathering up their spoils, the British returned to Fort Covington in the afternoon, and halted. Colonel Scott receiving information that a quantity of stores were lying at Hopkintown, he secured fresh teams for a small detachment, who drove the distance, 27 miles, that night, and reached the village while its inhabitants were sleeping. Sentinels were posted at each door, while a searching party went from house to house. 300 barrels of flour was found in a barn and a number of cases of muskets scattered among the houses. All was taken that sleighs could be got for, and the provisions that had to be abandoned were distributed among the inhabitants, who were loud in their praises of the conduct of the redcoats, who scrupulously respected private property and paid for what they required. The expedition then returned to the Fort and the journey across the St Lawrence was set about and before nightfall Summerstown was safely reached, where they rested, and entered Cornwall in triumphal procession on

assisted his father, who was captain of a militia company, to hide a number of muskets he had been served with under the pig-pen. A government teamster had eased his load by leaving 500 ℔ of cheese in their house to take away again on a second trip. "It was put in the cellar and before the British searching-party came in, my mother placed her chair over the trap-door and sat down, and the soldiers did not ask her to stir. When private property was taken, it was restored on complaint to the officers, who said they did not wish to harm the people. When they passed our house, they had a long string of loaded waggons."

10

the 22nd, amid great rejoicings. Immense quantities of pork, beef, flour, and whisky were thus captured, with not a few muskets. The farmers were dismissed to their homes, after being paid $4 a day for their teams, and those Americans who had been pressed into service with their horses were now given permission to return. The only casualty that attended the raid was the loss of a team in the ice on the return journey. Considering that the enemy's country was penetrated for 25 miles and held for 2 days, a more gallant and better managed raid is not on record, and its success indicates what Colonel Scott would have done had he been permitted, as he asked, to attack French Mills two months sooner. The one provoking feature of the war of 1812, is that the cautious and vacillating policy of Sir George Prevost should have stifled the genius of such officers. When too late, the Americans from Plattsburgh detached a force to meet the raiders.

This was the last overt act of war on the Huntingdon frontier, for although peace was not proclaimed until a year afterwards, the tide of battle did not again touch our borders. Reviewing the circumstances that caused the discomfiture of the two large and well-appointed armies who invaded this district, and who ought to have, so weak was the opposition, conquered all before them, it is impossible to escape the conclusion that God was on the side of our forefathers, and co-operated with them in their efforts to preserve our country's independence. That the fate of Hampton and Wilkinson may overtake each invading army that may dare to put a foot on our soil, must be the prayer of every Canadian patriot.

NOTE.—On page 118 the name James Wright was inadvertently printed instead of Neil Morrison. It was Mr Morrison who went back with the scared guard. His oldest son, Robert, is the last survivor of those who took part in these critical days, and his kindness and patience in answering my questions, I gladly take this opportunity of acknowledging.

CHAPTER VII.

WHEN peace was declared, a number of Americans came back to resume possession of the lots they had left when the war broke out. Fresh from a struggle in which national emotions had been aroused, and foreseeing the danger of an American population along the frontier should that struggle be resumed, the feeling was against permitting them to re-possess the properties they had abandoned, and to which they had only the claim of squatters, for they had not received patents for their lots. In Hemingford a number were turned back, but west of that there was no impediment placed in their way until the Chateaugay was reached, and scores crowded into their old clearances in Russeltown Flats and Franklin. Milne, the seigniory agent, strenuously resisted the Americans getting back to their old homesteads on the Chateaugay. He burned their shanties, obstructed the road by tearing up the rude bridges that spanned the creeks, and threatened to set the Indians upon them. His motive was a purely selfish one, he designing to appropriate their lots for his own benefit. To Ellice's agents in Montreal, Forsythe, Richardson & Co., he represented that he had bought the claims of those people, none of whom had received concession of the lots they had lived upon, and got himself so registered in the seigniory books. When the actual facts came to the knowledge of the firm, it was too late to obtain either full proof against Milne or to afford redress to the claimants, who had disappeared. Unable to disprove Milne's title to all he claimed, a compromise was made with him, by which he got a block of 500 acres near Ormstown on sur-rendering all the rest. A few of the Americans did get their lots and lived upon them for several years, selling out to the Old Countrymen when they began to come.

The years 1815 and 1816 were peculiarly trying, owing to their extraordinary coldness. In 1815 snow fell on the 14th June and the settlers planted corn in tight-buttoned overcoats. Little more of the corn matured than served for seed. The next year was worse, there being a continuance of bleak, dry weather, with steady north winds, which blasted vegetation and prevailed all summer. On the 8th of June there was a fall of 6 inches of snow, followed by frost at night, and it snowed again on the 16th, while there was frost every month of the year. Corn was a complete failure and starvation stared not a few families in the face. Indeed, the settlements would have been depleted had it not been for ashes and lumber, the money so obtained enabling them to buy provisions, and, as it seemed to them, providentially the price of potash bounded up at the close of the war until, in the summer of 1816, it brought from $10 to $12 per hundred-weight, a price it never afterwards approached. The settlers east of Hinchinbrook had to tramp as far as Rouses Point for Indian meal, a bag of which they carried home on their shoulders and which cost them $3 a bushel. One household had eaten the last mouthful of food before the husband and father had returned. The children went hungry to bed and when, at daybreak, the honest man returned exhausted from his long tramp, they all eagerly rose and clustered impatiently round their mother as she mixed a jonny-cake, which she cut, on turning, into as many portions as there were mouths. With hungry eyes the little ones watched what seemed to them the slow-cooking of the cake, until one boy, unable to resist, snatched the hot, half-baked morsel that would have fallen to him and, rushing out of doors to escape punishment, devoured it. Fodder was as scarce as grain, and that winter Sandy Williamson went as far as the Richelieu for a load of hay, which cost him $40 a ton. Poorer neighbors kept their cattle alive by felling trees and feeding them browse. The greed of Milne intensified to the settlers on the Chateaugay the general distress. At that time half the rent was payable in cash, the other in wheat. This arrangement, devised by the old French law to press more lightly on the censitaires, was, in years of scarcity, made a means of extortion by unjust seigniors, and was taken advantage of by Milne, who demanded the wheat or $5 for each bushel. As hardly one of the settlers on the Chateaugay had a bushel to spare, they had to pay the money. That winter, flour sold in Montreal for $15 a barrel. There being a prospect of a continuance of the scarcity from want of seed, the legislature voted $80,000 for that purpose. None of the help was accepted by the English-speaking settlers of this district, many of whom, in the spring of 1817, paid a dollar a bushel for seed-potatoes.

It was in the year of scarcity that a few of the English settlers went for the first time to vote. The poll was held then at St Phillipe, and one of the candidates took the trouble to send a messenger to ask the settlers to come and vote for him. There being good sleighing at the time, many went. Owing to their distance from the polling-place little or no interest was then felt in politics.

The most important event on the Chateaugay was the construction of a fortification on its south bank by the Imperial government. Experience had made plain the value of rallying-points on the frontier, and the military-authorities decided on erecting a fortalice that would be at once a point of observation, a storehouse of supplies, and command the Chateaugay route to Montreal. The nature of the country, level and wooded, suggested a blockhouse, and, in the spring of 1815 the construction of what proved to be the finest specimen in Canada of that species of fortification, peculiar to North America, was begun. The spot chosen was a dry portion of the river bank a little east of Allan's Corners. Baxter was engaged to fell the trees for a space of several acres, so that no enemy would find shelter within musket-range. The blockhouse was placed near the edge of the south bank, and the drawing, given in the frontispiece, gives a good idea of its appearance. An excavation 4 feet deep was made, and a wall begun 5 feet 8 inches wide. This thickness was continued for 6 feet above the ground, or to the first floor, from thence it was 5 feet, the wall sloping in, until an additional height of 14½ feet was completed, when the second floor was reached. The building was an exact square, the masonry measuring at the level 40 feet and at the top 38. The wooden portion of the structure was wider and hung over the walls of masonry like a cap. The wood-work was 45½ feet square, 10 feet high, and 4 feet thick. It was framed of a double tier of 11-inch pine-logs, and the hollow of 2 feet between was packed with rubbish, to make it perfectly bullet-proof. There were no windows in the masonry, the only apertures being 6 slits on three faces and 8 on the side looking up the river, for muskets, with the addition of a door, high up, in the wall that looked down the river. The basement was divided into 4 rooms, intended for storing ammunition and provisions. The flat above the cellar formed a single apartment, with platforms below the portholes for the marksmen to stand on. The top-flat, which comprised the portion built of logs, was a roomy apartment, 10 feet high. On each side of it was a long slit, for the defenders to fire through, with two square holes, 22 × 22 inches, at the side of each corner for a small cannon, and which, in after years, were changed into windows. The roof was pavilion-shaped and covered with sheet-iron. A member of the Royal Engineer corps, Capt. Jebb, superintended the work, for which a mason of the name of Dupuis had the contract. There being no stone in the vicinity, it had to be floated down on rafts from the Outarde and the lime was brought from the Basin. It was mounted with two small cannon and was ready for occupation in the fall of 1815, when a company was detached to garrison it under command of Capt. Christie, the future historian. He did not stay with his men, preferring to board at Morrison's. On peace being assured, a sergeant's guard was considered sufficient, and, eventually, it also was dispensed with and the building locked up.

In 1822 Hendry Craige bought the lot upon which it is situated from the seignior, when he occupied it as a house. Strange to say, the Imperial government had never got a deed for the site, and, when danger had passed, had abandoned what must have cost them several thousand dollars. Craige continued to live in the stronghold until 1838, when, on the rebels gathering at Baker's, it was made the point of assembly for the loyalists, when Craige and his family moved out and lived in the bakehouse. On the suppression of the rebellion, the government deemed it prudent to retain the blockhouse, and bought it from Craige along with 4 acres of land for $800. During the winter of 1838 the company of Captain John Tate, which had been organized into a volunteer corps, kept guard, and on their being disbanded in the spring, the government gave the blockhouse a thorough overhauling, the floors being relaid, windows placed in the portholes, and the roof covered anew with iron. Thus made more habitable, Sergt. James Thomson of the Huntingdon volunteers was placed in charge, and he had a guard of 4 men, who were relieved monthly. In May, 1842, even this guard was dispensed with, and an old pensioner, Sergeant Dalton, sent as caretaker. He was relieved by another pensioner, Sergt. John Riddell, a Waterloo veteran, who, with his family, proved to be the last occupant of the blockhouse. Besides his pension, he had 50 cents a day as its governor, with fuel and light, and the use of its 4 acres. On his death in May, 1858, the imperial authorities sold the movables and locked up the now historic building.

As time wore on and the memories of past events on the Chateaugay grew dim, the old building became associated in the popular mind as the centre of deSalaberry's imagined exploit, until even those in authority fell into the same belief, and on the report of the officer of ordnance-lands, in 1859, Sir Geo. E. Cartier announced, amid great applause, to the legislature that an order-in-council had been passed, reserving the blockhouse and the lot on which it stood as "a monument commemorative of that distinguished feat of arms, the battle of Chateaugay." No precaution was taken to preserve the building, and neighboring farmers helped themselves to the flooring and partitions and even to stone where the masonwork crumbled. Despite all this, the outer-frame stood good, and the blockhouse remained the most picturesque object

from Dundee to Montreal, and bid good to withstand the
tooth of time for many generations. In 1881, John Hastie,
owner of the farm on which the blockhouse was situated,
applied to the Crown lands department to purchase it, and,
with no demur, it was sold to him, with the 4 acres of land,
for $70! No sooner did he receive the patent, than he pro-
ceeded to remove the roof and demolish the woodwork. His
cupidity was not rewarded, for little of the timber was of
value, being full of spikes and affected with rot. The walls
were afterwards levelled. The dismantling of this old landmark was much deplored, and there was general surprise
that Sir John Macdonald should have consented to such an
act of disloyal vandalism.

But I have got beyond the period to which this chapter is
devoted. To return to the settlement on the Chateaugay, we
find that the lands along the river, abandoned by the Americans, from below the village of Ormstown to Allan's Corners,
grew up in grass, and came to be known as "the meadows."
In 1817 Milne engaged David Bryson, who had shortly before
arrived from Perthshire. His duty was to cut the hay that
grew in great luxuriance on these meadows, stack it, and feed
to stock which Milne sent up. The cattle were kept out all
winter, and fed by pulling down the fence that surrounded a
new stack of hay as they finished one, they being allowed to
help themselves. They throve well and when fat were sold at
a profit. Besides the cattle were several horses, bought by
Milne from the government when the war ended. The hay,
as might be expected in a country covered by forest, was
coveted by the settlers and lumbermen, and they endeavored
to help themselves, stealing a stack at a time, and requiring
vigilant watch on the part of Bryson and his sons. What
meadows Milne did not require, he sold to Canadians, who
cut and stacked the hay on them, and removed in the winter.

During the interregnum that followed the disappearance of
George Ellice there was an entire cessation of lumbering in
the seigniory and Milne's duties were more those of a forest-
ranger than of anything else. On Robert being declared
heir, this inaction was ended, and the timber along the Cha-

teaugay and its tributaries was sold to Macaulay, a Glengarry lumberman, who was given ten years to remove it He sublet portions of his limits to Thomas Fingland, Moreau, and others, while keeping large gangs at work himself. Several winters he sent no fewer than 200 men into the woods, and when the ice broke up, covered the Chateaugay with rafts of the finest cut of oak and pine. This industry furnished welcome work to the settlers and their grown-up sons during the winter, but did not help their market for oats, of which they had then little to sell. Macaulay brought his supplies from Montreal, where oats were generally 20 cents a bushel and only in one or two years rose as high as 30. The wages paid axemen was $8 to $10 a month.

About the time lumbering revived it became obvious that the making of potash could be carried on more profitably to all concerned as a separate business than otherwise, and asheries were started. The first to establish one was Reeves, who carried on the manufacture of salts on the river-bank beside his house, buying the ashes at 10 cents a bushel from the settlers. The next step was the building of an oven and the manufacturing of pearl-ash. Reeves soon had opposition in the person of James Perrigo, who was destined to play a prominent part in the affairs of the locality he joined. He was born at Burlington, Vt. His father was an Italian, and on his death the mother removed to Montreal, where she remarried and young Perrigo was given to Dr Pomeroy to bring up. When old enough to do for himself, he set up a small store at Caughnawaga, which, before the Lachine canal was made, was a stirring-place, as the Durham boats touched there before running the rapids and had often to wait in scores when the wind was unfavorable. Perrigo kept 8 batteaux for taking part of the cargo of boats that drew too much water for running the rapids. Fond of hunting he, accompanied by an Indian, frequently visited the Chateaugay and, on the death of his wife, who was a French Canadian, and with the prospect of the destruction of his trade by the opening of the canal, he bought the river-point from Baker and opened a store and ashery. He did not do well, and, becoming insolvent, gave up business and assumed the role of physician, obtaining much repute among the habitants, and his tall figure, heightened by a hat and draped by a long cloak, was a conspicuous and frequent object on the road as he made his rounds. His lack of knowledge of the medical art being tempered by caution, he did little harm. Appointed a J.P. while at Caughnawaga, he was the first magistrate on the Chateaugay and continued to be such for a number of years. From his first appearing on the river, he was a keen politician, espousing extreme republican views.

Up to 1820 the population gained slowly. In 1817 William Brown, who had arrived from Neilston, Scotland, the year before, rented a farm at the eastern end of the Grand Marais, and afterwards moved to the western end of it, becoming its first and only Old Country inhabitant, for the seigniory-office designed this concession for the French. The stone-tavern at the corner of the Beauce road was the first tavern; it was erected by a French Canadian, and was a place of call for all who were journeying either by way of Beauharnois or the Basin.

In 1819 there was an addition made to the settlement in North Georgetown, of four families of Highlanders, who came out together in the brig Favorite, of which the father of Sir Hugh Allan was captain. They were Duncan Mc-Cormick, Peter McKellar, and two Archibald Campbells. They had been old neighbors of Neil Morrison in Argyle-shire, and were induced to leave Scotland by him. They took up lots near him.

Moving up the river, the country between Ormstown and Dewittville was a solitude, the old American clearances being unoccupied. At Dewittville there was some stir, caused by the sawmill, which did a good business. One of its owners, Moreau, happened, in the summer of 1817, to fall in with a newly-landed immigrant, John Todd, a native of Monaghan, Ireland, and being in want of a man to manage it, engaged him, and he proceeded with his family to his new home. Finding that Daigneault & Moreau wanted to sell, he per-suaded an old neighbor in Ireland, Lyttle, who had come out, to join him in buying it. After two years' possession Lyttle died while on a visit to Quebec, whereupon Todd assumed possession, paying the debts and undertaking the contracts of Lyttle. He did a large business. From Dewittville upwards the solitude was unbroken until Huntingdon was reached, where there was a solitary settler. Apparently in 1817 Benjamin Palmer, a native of Vermont, found it necessary to leave Franklin county for an infraction of the law, and determined on squatting on the north-bank at the head of the rapids. Using the logs of Sutherland's old shanty and the logs the Americans had laid down as a road for their waggons and artillery from the ford to the top of the bank, he erected a comfortable house, the cellar of which could be traced as late as 1870. Palmer proceeded to clear the point, but rested content when he had a patch large enough for corn and potatoes, for he was no farmer, and depended more on hunting and fishing. He trapped and shot a large number of wolves, whose heads were bought by Americans, who used them in obtaining the bounty paid by the towns, which gradually rose to $20 a head, when the frauds to obtain it grew to such a magnitude that the law was repealed in 1821. Palmer was of kindly disposition and was blessed with children who turned out well. Soon after he came, three brothers of the name of Percy erected a small sawmill on the south bank and about a hundred yards above the upper bridge, obtaining power by throwing a low dam across the river. They came from Chateaugay, N.Y., where, in Brighton Hollow, their father had a small grist and saw-mill, which David assisted to work, occasionally visiting the Huntingdon mill, which was managed by James and Robert, of neither of whom can much good be said. Their dwelling-house they built of planks on the river-bank at the east side of the bridge, and made a clearance which ran back across the concession road.

About 4 miles above the forks, the beginning of the settlement on Trout river was encountered, and which was almost exclusively composed of Americans, who were a poor lot, indolent and shiftless, and earning a precarious living by potash-making and lumbering. The first Old Countryman to take up his abode on Trout river was George Elder, a cooper by trade, who came from Glasgow in 1817, and stayed the winter of that year with David Bryson, getting out oak staves. When summer came, he went up the river, and arranged with one of the American squatters on Trout river, Abram Sutton, who lived on 48, to stay with him and make staves, which he did until 1819, when he bought the betterments of a squatter named Brewster on lot 50, Godmanchester, and his family arrived from Scotland. About the same time, James Terry, an Englishman, and who had served in the navy, came in and squatted on the Elgin side, building a shanty, 10 × 12, a little to the east of where the Holbrook bridge stands. He was undoubtedly the first Old Country settler in Elgin. As a stout Englishman, Terry kept up Christmas, inviting Elder to his feast, which was primitive enough, and when New Year's day came Elder reciprocated. Besides, these isolated representatives of the two nationalities celebrated the respective anniversaries of their country. In 1821 Brewster got into trouble. Going to Montreal and representing his circumstances as good, he had purchased largely on credit from Moreau & Daigneault, who, on discovering the truth, sent a bailiff to take him prisoner. Getting wind of this, he fled across the Lines, when the defrauded firm seized his betterments on lot 1, 3rd range of Elgin, consisting of a clearance along the river, and sold them to George Elder, who did not like the lot he was on, for $200. Moving across the river he put up a shanty and now began in earnest to make some clearance, which he had not attempted on his old lot, and which he sold to John Massam, an English Catholic and unmarried, who lived for several years alone, his sole companion being a dog. His son Robert, a cabinet-maker, he sent for from Quebec, but a short time's experience disgusted him with the privations of bush-life, and he fled by night to Quebec, where he stayed until he married, when he came to Trout river and lived with his father, who, until a very old man, was the only wheelwright from Huntingdon to Fort Covington, and made all the ox and horse carts needed.

Beyond a few additional American families, there was no change in the settlements in Hinchinbrook, and except the isolated clearances on the Chateaugay between Huntingdon and Athelstan and on the first concession, it remained in a state of nature. On the 1st concession, John Campbell settled on 600 acres which had been granted to his father, a U.E. Loyalist who lived at Caldwell's Manor, for having served in the militia during the war.

With the declaration of peace Franklin gained largely in population. Doubtful of the seignior's title to the lands, Milne dared not prevent their former occupiers returning to them, while the locality was too remote for any agent of the crown to know of what was being done, for the decision had been come to, that no person who declined taking the oath of allegiance should be eligible to own land in Canada. Among the new-comers was Jonathan Priest, a native of Massachusetts, who moved on to a part of Jacob Mitchel's lot in 1816, and who was the first to introduce a wheeled vehicle, for he brought a waggon and team. He was instrumental in making the road to Montreal somewhat more passable, for, at his solicitation, several settlers went with him in 1818 and helped to corduroy the worst of the sloughs near St Chrysostome. Up to that time, the settlers had dragged their barrels of potash on sleds to St Remi, where they hired carts. In 1817 Aram Moe left Caldwell's Manor and bought the lot opposite Mr Gentle's. His wife, who lived to over 90 years of age, in speaking of their moving into Franklin, said:

We bought from an American named Masting, paying him $200 for his improvements. Before the sleighing was over, we drove to it, following the bush-track that led over Covey Hill and down to Stockwell's. We carried an axe to remove any tree that might have fallen on the track. We stayed to rest in Gilfillan's and when I saw the hens roosting in one end of it, I thought they would get their eggs handy and without hunting for them. There was an apple-tree in front of our lot when we got it, which had been in bearing several years. We got in a good crop and it yielded well, for 1817, unlike the two years before, was one of plenty. The old seigniory-mill (page 31) was going at Ames's, and made such coarse flour that we had to sift it before using. I did not like the work, and said one day I hoped it would burn down so that we might get in its place a decent mill with bolts. Sure enough, the first word we got next morning was that the mill had been burned down. That would be about 1825. The seignior did not rebuild the mill, however, and we had to go to Chateaugay; N.Y. My husband drew the potash he made through a track in the woods that came out below the blockhouse. People were very friendly and shared everything they had. I have had a neighbor send 6 miles for a drawing of tea on hearing I had got some from Montreal.

With the year 1820 the decadence of the district as a hunting-field may be said to date, for then settlers began to flock in. Of the abundance of game that prevailed previous to that period, we can have little conception. In every direction the deer-runs could be met with in the woods, all leading to some creek or river. Deer were to be met not singly, but in herds, and as the early settlers, more manly than the pretended sportsmen of our own day, never shot them unless when needed for food, they multiplied long after the settlement of the district began. Old Mr McClatchie boasted that 365 deer had fallen to his rifle, and of these he had only killed one on the crust, and then from the necessity to get food. To his rifle fell probably the last moose seen in the district, and which he shot near where the bridge crosses the Hinchinbrook south of Herdman. Catamounts were rarely met with, but bears, especially near swamps, were plentiful, and occasional stragglers have been killed in Teafield as late as 1870. Of all wild beasts, wolves were the most annoying, and they (for the safety of sheep and young cattle) were hunted and shot without mercy. Beavers were trapped as late as 1820, and otters were also occasionally shot. It has often been denied that salmon frequented the Chateaugay, but on this I have had abundant evidence. Up to the time the sawmills got fairly going, they were plentiful during their season, and in the rapids opposite Huntingdon were speared as late as 1825. Of the flocks of pigeons, quails, ducks, and, more rarely, of geese, the statements of the early settlers would be incredible were they not so well substantiated. In the spring and fall they darkened the sky like clouds and where they lit vegetation was destroyed.

Few of the Americans who left at the breaking out of the war, returned to Hemingford, and up to the period when the tide of immigration set in from the Motherland it was sparsely settled, there being a thin fringe of clearances on the front range and, scattered here and there in the woods to the north, the shanties of migratory French Canadians and Americans, who earned an irregular livelihood by making potash and by hunting. Few as the permanent settlers were, they made an effort to establish a school, and securing the services of a daughter of Squire Manning, turned a log shanty, which stood on a knoll by the roadside on Senecal's lot (page 20), into a schoolhouse. This was during the second year of the war, when the teacher was a girl still in her teens, She had had no opportunities of learning beyond those afforded under her father's roof, where, in the long winter evenings, the younger members of the family received lessons from him and their oldest brother David (page 89) who, like his father, was an excellent English scholar and well-informed. From want of text-books, her teaching was mainly oral, but with the help of a copy of Hume's England, Webster's Speller and the Bible she succeeded in turning out creditable scholars. She taught until 1816, when she became the wife of John, oldest son of Frederick Scriver (page 19), and around whom, for the ensuing years, the history of Hemingford may be said to centre. His quiet though laborious life on the paternal bush-farm was interrupted by the war, when he was drafted with the other young men of the settlement into a battalion of the militia. Stationed at Isle aux Noix, his ability in managing men and his handiness in woodcraft did not remain long unobserved, and he was taken from the ranks to assist in raising of fortifications, the construction of barracks and on any outside service that required tact and knowledge of the country. When the U.S. men-of-war Julia and Growler attacked the island, he was assigned the responsible post of commanding a squad of volunteer sharpshooters, who poured in so galling a fire from the bushes that lined the shore, that it hastened the striking of the flag of the enemy and the surrender of the two ships. When peace was declared the gallant young backwoodsman returned to Hemingford with a considerable sum in silver—the pay he had received for his services and which he had, with characteristic thrift and self-denial, saved. The money thus obtained he devoted to securing a home of his own. In the fall of 1815 he bought lots 105 and 106 and the following spring made a considerable clearance, and on the east side of the road erected suitable barns and a stone-house, in which he installed Lucretia Manning as mistress, and to her assistance his after-success was, in no small measure, due, and, probably, to her influence in part, at least, may be attributed a meeting of the settlers held in her new home, on the 19th October, 1816, to endeavor to build a better schoolhouse and to secure a grant from the fund of the Royal Institution for the Advancement of Learning. The meeting decided upon building a schoolhouse on the south-west corner of the cross-roads on lot 105, and resolved "that it shall always, on the Sabbath-day, be devoted to the use of religious worship." John Manning, John Henigan, and Frederick Scriver were appointed to carry the project into effect, and a subscription-list was opened, which is so curious that I print it in full:

We, the subscribers, being desirous to promote literature in the township of Hemingford, promise to pay towards building a house for that purpose on lot No 105, in the said township, the several sums in cash, and quotas in labor, to our several names respectively annexed.

October 19, 1816.

	Cash Dollars.	Days Labor.	
John Manning	20	15	paid
John Schryver	10	10	
Frederick Schryver	15	20	paid
Wm. Schryver	5	6	paid
John Hennagin, jr.	2	6	
Nathan Peterson		3	paid
Joseph Hennagin	2	6	paid
Joseph Clevelin	2	6	Recd $3.90

		Days Work.	
Louis × Eshten Derwazh	$4	5	Judgment on the
James Cross	1	4	same by me, Joseph
Eward Simson	2	4	Churchill, J.P. for
Daniel Hennagin	2	6	the town of Mooers
Samuel B. Hudson	2	4	paid
John Lindsay	2	6	
David H. Hennigan	1	4	paid
Joseph Lindsay	1	3	
John Henegin		4	paid
S. Sewell	16		paid
John Wallis	5		paid
Aaron Smith	10		paid
Zekiel Dewey	10		paid
Freeman Sweet	5	2	
Rolleat Snickall		5	
Richard Lindsay	2	4	paid in wood
Joseph Brisben	2	4	
William Wallace	3		
Isaac Wilsey	5		paid in shingles
James Woolrich	6		paid.

The names being evidently all autographs, I print them as written.

The enterprise, thus spiritedly begun, dragged from want of means, and it was not until 1820 that the schoolhouse, which also served as church and town-hall for over a score of years, was finished. The effort to obtain a grant from the Royal Institution was not successful.*

The Nathan Peterson, mentioned in the foregoing list, had squatted on lot 100 and on that opposite to him afterwards came Truman Cleveland, both Dutch Americans. The side-road they opened came to be known as Cleveland-street. In 1821 Cleveland, on the north side of the concession road, built a sawmill on the Little Montreal river, which, despite its paltry appearance now, had in those days an abundance of water and the mill cut 100 M feet of lumber each season. Below the mill was the landing-place for the canoes in which

---

*When the old schoolhouse, which was a fairly-finished block-building, came to be superseded by a better, it was sold and moved to another site. It is now (1887) occupied by Mrs Thomas McClelland.

the settlers made the difficult and tedious passage to the Richelieu with their potash. In 1819 Isaac Proper, a Vermonter, moved in from Chazy, and settled on lot 9, having for neighbor, on 10, Daniel Scriver, a brother of Frederick. Mr Proper's oldest son, Nelson, said:

We moved into Canada in May, when there was only one road, that by Clelland's corners. There were very few settlers in the township and they were all Americans or of American descent, depending wholly on potash, and living poorly. There was no house between Clelland's corners and Sweet's, and I remember the swamp on 66 was crosswayed and floated. There was no house between that of Frederick Scriver and of his son John. The road that passed my lot (150) followed the ridge to Nesbit's mill, whence there was a bush-track to Russeltown, that was little used.

The roads thus referred to were mere sled-tracks, and Hemingford's lack of means of communication was the great obstacle to its progress. Its isolated situation can hardly be exaggerated. Cut off by great swamps to the north, bounded by the United States to the south, and without navigable rivers, the settlers underwent the most exhausting toil in getting their potash to market. When the water was high enough, they floated the barrels down the Little Montreal river, having frequently to plunge into the current to lift the canoes over shallows, or to drag them on ox-sleds to Champlain, and send them by the Chazy to Montreal. During the season of sleighing, they were driven to the city by Laprairie. It is 30 miles to Laprairie from Hemingford, and St Edward is half-way. As far as the latter place the country was in a state of nature, forest and swamp, the one so rugged and the other so deep, that to traverse the 15 miles with an ox-sled was a day's journey when everything was most favorable. Colonel Scriver perceived that if the township was to be peopled, an outlet must be secured, and his opportunity soon came. In 1817 the legislature passed an act to provide for better communications in the county of Huntingdon (that is, the old county, which stretched eastwards to the Richelieu) and Colonel Scriver urged, upon the commissioners appointed under it, the claims of Hemingford. They examined the ground, and decided on opening two roads, for which they gave out contracts. The first was from the farm of William Struthers, near St Remi, to the farm of James Allen, Russeltown Flats, which was taken by William Brisbin for $1600, but owing to the governor's declining to ratify it, the work was not done. The second contract was for cutting out a road from La Tortue to the Hemingford line, which was taken by Colonel Scriver for $2000. It was 9 miles long and crossed three swamps which had to be crosswayed. The work was of a most difficult nature but by October, 1819, the contract was fulfilled and the amount paid. The new road was exceedingly rough and one or two seasons passed before wheeled vehicles could go over it with ease. The swamps so difficult to span then, now comprise the finest land in the province. From the opening of this road, the prosperity of Hemingford dates.

It will now be perceived that during the interval between the close of the war and the setting-in of immigration, the English-speaking settlements made little progress, and, apart from that of Franklin, barely held their own. The lands thrown open in Western New York and in Ohio were more attractive to the New Englanders, and they no longer came to Canada in any numbers, while to the British immigrants, who were being landed by the shipload at Quebec, this district up to 1821 was barred, for the representatives of the seignior could not concede lots and the crown would not sell. There were divided opinions among military men as to what was best to be done with Huntingdon. Believing that a renewal of war with the United States was probable, a number contended that leaving the country along the frontier a wilderness was the best defence for the settlements behind, while others held that an invading-army would meet with more serious hindrances were it peopled with loyal settlers. That was General Drummond's view, and he advised the Imperial government to divide up the county of Huntingdon among such of the regulars as had served under Macdonell, Meuron, and DeWatteville as would consent to stay in Canada and become farmers. The government did nothing.

Some time after, the provincial legislature passed an act to reward all who had served in the militia with grants of wild land, and to which the Imperial consent was obtained. Under this act the larger portion of St Anicet was drawn by officers of the French battalions, and part of Godmanchester and Hinchinbrook. The grant to a lieutenant-colonel was 1200 acres and ranged downwards to 100 to a private. Owing to the number of formalities and the amount of fees exacted by each official, few of the rank-and-file proved their claims, and they sold their rights for mere trifles to the landsharks who haunted taverns and market-places, and Ellice and Woolrich obtained the larger share of the grants made in Huntingdon. The officers, however, drew their land and then did nothing with it, complying with none of the conditions upon which the grants were made, and waiting until they became valuable from the labors of settlers on adjoining lots. About 165,000 acres were thus granted of the township land in the province, and, in subsequent years, these militia grants caused no end of wrong and hardship to actual settlers, who unwittingly went on improving lots, believing them to be crown lands, which they discovered in course of time were claimed by French gentlemen or their heirs who lived in Quebec and more remote parts of the province.

The seignior's agent declining to concede lots did not deter the habitants of the north shore and of Longueuil from pressing into Beauharnois, and the settlements near Ste Martine and the town of Beauharnois increased rapidly after the peace. On the census being taken in 1820 it was found there were 2205 people living in the seigniory of Beauharnois, of whom fully half were French. Of the 433 families who lived by farming, none (whether French or English-speaking) had received titles from the seignior. The population of the seigniory of Chateaugay was more dense than it is to-day, for it numbered 3530, accounted for by the number who lived by lumbering and boating.

CHAPTER VIII.

ON the 21st April, 1820, there beat down the Firth of Clyde a small barque, named the Alexander. Her passengers were not numerous and came chiefly from Lanarkshire: weavers, shepherds, and farm-laborers who determined to improve their condition by emigrating to Canada. They proved to be so congenial in disposition that, before a week was over, they were as one family, and before anchor was dropped at Quebec, after a weary voyage of 45 days, they had become so attached to one another that those who intended taking up land resolved not to separate, but endeavor to settle together. Taking the steamer for Montreal, the Lady Sherbrooke, they landed there after a passage of 36 hours. Enquiring for lodgings, they found that a brother Scotchman, Shields, who had been out a year, had rented a house which was too large for him, and they bargained with him for several rooms, into which they crowded, and lived, of course, as befitted their means, very economically. Having thus provided for their wives and children, the heads went to search for land, which, strange to say, though the province, with the exception of narrow strips along the St Lawrence, was in a state of nature, was not easy to get. There was land, they were told, to be had in Terrebonne and to the south of Chambly, and on examination it was found to be of fair quality, but they were surprised to learn that they could not obtain an absolute title, and would have to pay a small perpetual rent. Still greater was the astonishment of the Scotchmen when informed that the priests levied tithes and the large churches they saw were built by taxes levied by law. Ardent Radicals one and all, and, as such, detesters

of all union between church and state, such a condition of
affairs on American soil and under British rule, shocked
them, and after debating the matter over they resolved that,
on no condition, would they settle upon parish-land, and they
turned their attention to the townships, where, they were
told, British and not French law prevailed. One of their
number, who had relatives in Vermont, went to see the land
there, and others visited the Eastern Townships. When they
came back and compared notes, they decided that no place
they had visited would do. Vermont was hilly and stony
and the desirable lands in the Eastern Townships were held
by companies who asked extortionate prices for them. When
despairing of finding homes in this province and about to set
out for Upper Canada, which in those days, when even the
Lachine canal was not built, was a terrible journey, they
learned that the government was giving out lots in Dundee.
A delegation of three was despatched to report, the others
agreeing to wait until they returned. They walked all the
way up to Cornwall. While resting in the inn at Beaudette
they met surveyor-general Bouchette, who, on learning their
errand, directed them how to proceed, and told them if they
were not satisfied with Dundee, they would be sure to get free
township land in Godmanchester, for his errand had been to
prepare for opening it and Hinchinbrook for settlement.
They asked when lots would be given out, and on his answering in a year, they said that would not do, they must get
homes for their families at once. Pointing across lake St
Francis, to where the wooded shores of the county of Huntingdon swam in the distance, Mr Bouchette told them they
could go and squat there, and he would see that the lots would
be secured to them when the surveys were made. They
parted; Mr Bouchette going to Quebec and the prospectors
holding on their way to Dundee. Crossing to St Regis they
saw the agent, and he had no sooner told them that the lands
he had to give out were subject to Indian-rent, than they gave
up all thought of them, and started to make their way back
to Montreal by the Basin. With two Indians as guides, they
had their first experience of travelling through the bush.

One of them, in relating what happened, said while they were struggling with the branches, which scratched their faces and tore their clothes, the Indians glided through the thickest bush like fish in water. On reaching what seemed to them civilization at Fort Covington, though the settlement was primitive enough, they were able to find their own way, and striking Trout river at the lines walked on to Huntingdon, resting at Palmer's, who, from his own door, shot a duck for their entertainment. Next day, as they trudged along the west bank of the Chateaugay and had passed the meadows, they were surprised and delighted to encounter a settlement of their own countrymen, who hailed them with rapturous welcome, and, learning their story, urged them to come and live with them. They would gladly have consented, had it not been that the words parish and seigniory terrified them. They would not become subject to French law and they would not pay rent. Ferried from the Basin to Lachine, they rejoined their companions in Montreal and related all they had seen and heard. The immigrants had been 3 weeks now in Montreal, and it was necessary they should come to a decision as to what they should do. After long consultation they resolved that they would trust Bouchette's word and go to Huntingdon. It was, they argued, township land, was free from rent and French law, and therefore equal in privilege to any they could get in Upper Canada. A bateau was hired, and a portion of the party, for a number of the women and children were to follow, sore wearied by delay and strangers in a strange land, walked out to Lachine and embarked upon it; in all, representatives of 17 families. On the 1st of August they were landed on a point on lot 17, close to the line of 16. The point, which would have been the Plymouth rock of Huntingdon, was afterwards washed away by the rising waters of the lake. Standing on the bank was a negro, Henry Bullard, who came running from his cabin, which stood on lot 20, now Port Lewis, on seeing the bateau steer for the shore. The day was rainy and comfortless, and a sort of shelter was made for the women and children by piling up chests and boxes and forming a roof with blankets and brush, laid on poles. They had barely finished it and crowded under its shelter to escape a thunder-shower, when the rain penetrated the frail covering and left them soaking wet. Despite their discomfort, the poor people were pleased with what they saw. The noble trees, that thickly covered the ground, were their admiration, and they did not know enough to be aware that the location was hardly one that an agriculturalist would have chosen, for while there was much good land it was broken by low ridges, and had great stretches of marsh both in front and rear. The latter feature, however, was not so prominent as it is now, for when they landed the lake was exceptionally low, and continued to be so for several years. Whether the soil was good or bad gave them no concern, for, singular to say, among the 17 there was not a single farmer. Two or three had done farm-work in their capacity as day-laborers, but the only one among them who had ever held a plow was David Anderson, and he was a shepherd.* Their notion was that whoever got to be proprietor of 100 acres became a laird, and passing rich. The first duty was to get up shanties, and here they were at a disadvantage, for, excepting the negro, they had no neighbors to direct them, and none of them knew how to raise a shanty in Canadian fashion. Several of them were tradesmen, however, and rigging up a whip-saw turned the trees into boards. So slow was their progress, that it was six weeks before enough houses were up and the tents abandoned, greatly to the joy of the women, who long remembered what they suffered until the shanties were ready. Bullard's wife was a French Canadian and she was forward in showing the Scotch gudewives how to cook bush-fashion, making rum an indispensable ingredient, even in baking. As they soon found where the liquor went, they dispensed with her tuition. She subsequently deserted Bullard, who disap-peared soon after. He had moved over from Glengarry that

---

* He left Scotland in 1819 for Miramichi, but not liking New Brunswick had moved west. In Montreal he fell in with the Alexander party and decided to go with them.

spring, and when the party arrived was eking out a miserable living by fishing and hunting.

After they had taken possession, one of their number, James Brown, was sent to Quebec to secure titles to the lots. He had an interview with the governor, Lord Dalhousie, who listened with deep interest to the narrative he had to tell and assured him of his aid. In the fall, Mr Bouchette visited them, and arranged for laying out the lots. He was exceedingly friendly and gave many hints as to bush-life and farming. He had much difficulty in understanding the broad Scotch of the settlers, and made himself popular with some of them by making a present of snuff. There was no order in the locating of 'the settlers, who, indeed, worked very much in common. The most western shanty was that of Thomas Marshall on 19, and they straggled along the lake shore eastward to 14, where James Paul 'and Robert Barrie lived together in a low caboose. As shelter was provided, word was sent to Montreal for their families, who came as opportunity presented itself. The captain of the bateau which brought the first party, took a kindly interest in the settlement, and stopped whenever he passed. On one occasion he sold them a quantity of flour at $3 a barrel, for it was cheap that fall. Of the experience of one family I can give a few details. Marshall, having got everything ready, went to the city to bring up his family. Early in November, they left in a Durham-boat, and in three days reached Coteau, where, frost having set in, she could not get into the lake for ice. A canoe being expected, the wayfarers made beds of their wraps and lay down by the water's edge to be in readiness, the mother having for her pillow the weaver's stone, for the loom formed part of their baggage. The canoe at last came, and was that of the negro, Bullard. When Mrs Marshall stepped into the humble shanty her husband had provided, she said she considered it a palace, so proud was she of the first house she could call their own property, though she complained of the floor being "shoogly," owing to the uneven sawing of the boards. The Durham-boat continuing fast, the canoe had to make several trips for their effects.

The fall was a remarkably fine one, and the leaves being perfectly dry, the children were set to gathering and packing them into bolster-slips for the beds. December, though colder, was equally fine, and no severe weather was experienced until near its close, after which there were heavy falls of snow. The settlers found the cold very trying, owing to their ignorance in choosing fire-wood. Not knowing the difference in trees, and naturally inclining to those easiest to chop, they cut all sorts, and it was hard to keep up a blaze with swamp-elm and green basswood. Their houses, too, except the few that had been built shanty-fashion, were very cold, and they huddled around the great open fire-places when the west wind came screeching across the lake. In the mornings, they noted often that the blankets were frozen stiff with their breath. None of the women had ever baked bread in Scotland, and Mrs Bullard's lessons were not first-class. They had no hops, and preserved leaven by covering it in a chaudron, for there was not a stove in the settlement, so the bread was sour and heavy.

With the advent of the ice, their communication was restored with Montreal, and they had many visitors to view the country and see about joining them. That winter, Peter McFarlane, a book-keeper fresh from a Glasgow counting-house, with his worldly goods stowed in a traineau, drove up the Chateaugay from the Basin to above Huntingdon, where there was a lumber-road to the Laguerre, and thence made his way to the settlement, of which he became an active member. Every one was welcomed and the settlement grew until the string of shanties reached from Port Lewis to Hungry bay, when it was considered worthy of a name, and was duly called "Dalhousie Settlement," in honor of the governor. On New Year's morning its inhabitants were aroused at daybreak by Black Bullard firing a shot before each door, when he was rewarded by a glass from the carefully hoarded bottle. The day so ushered in, their first New Year in Canada, the settlers observed with the hearty customs of their mother-land and that night, from the shanties where they held their merry-making, rose in the frosty air

the sound of Scotland's songs and many an old story was re-
told of the land their heartstrings were knit tó. I may note
that the settlers retained not only the social but the moral customs of their native land. Of their number, Hart and Dick
had been prepared as secession preachers, and they, on alternate Sundays, preached in the house of Thomas Brown, which
happened to be the largest. Neither was adapted for the
toils of the bush, and both left the following summer, but
after their departure, though no public services were held,
Sunday was rigidly observed, and there was none of the
hunting, fishing and card-playing that was too common in
other settlements. Of Hart's unfitness for the bush, it is
enough to relate that, on going out, he would wrap the edge
of his axe with rags, to prevent its cutting him should it fall.

The Scotch citizens of Montreal, then few in number and
bound together by closest bonds, took a deep interest in the
new settlement, the first of its kind in Lower Canada, and
did what they could to assist it. Two active promoters were
Alexander Shaw and John Hunter. Sandy Shaw kept a
tavern on the corner of Commissioners and Grey Nun streets,
which had been a place of resort for the immigrants while in
the city. He died of the cholera in 1834. Hunter had been
a ship-chandler in Leith, and emigrated in 1819, opening a
grocery-store on Bleury-street. During the early winter of
1820, he heard of a young Scotchman lying ill of the jaundice,
and went to see him. Finding he was poorly attended, he
induced his wife to take him into their house, and where he
speedily recovered. The young man was James Brown, on
his way back from seeing the governor at Quebec. The topic
uppermost in his mind, and of which he was never tired
talking, was the settlement on the shore of lake St Francis.
Hunter, who was of a singularly sanguine temperament,
caught his guest's enthusiasm, and recommended all whom
he could influence to throw in their lot with the party in
Huntingdon. While hopeful as to their future, the settlers
were uneasy as to the delay in securing deeds for their land,
and had sent James Brown to Quebec to see about them,
when he took ill on the journey as stated. He brought with

him no patents, but his report was favorable. He had seen Lord Dalhousie, who told the settlers not to be discouraged, and the head of the crown lands department led him to believe he (Brown) would be appointed agent. A stone-mason by trade, his father had given him an education to fit him to be an architect, and his knowledge of civil engineering he now turned to account. He defined the limits of the lots of the settlers, and, on the occasion of a visit from his friend Hunter, after the New Year, he explored with him the country to the south, and determined on opening a road to the Chateaugay. Accordingly in February all the settlers who could be spared from home followed him to brush the line as he defined it. His object was to open the road left between 16 and 17, and considering that his only instrument was a make-shift theodolite he had contrived out of a field-compass, he ran it with singular straightness, for he came out on the Chateaugay within an acre or two of the true line. One evening, after a hard day's work running the line, the party made preparations to camp. The snow was trodden down, a fire lit, and branches cut for sleeping upon. While the two chain-boys were felling a dry pine to replenish the fire, it, proving hollow, suddenly fell, and nearly killed Mr Brown, grazing one of his legs. While sitting round the camp-fire after supper, singing songs, and all grateful for the narrow escape, one of the party proposed that the swamp should be named in memory of the event, when it was agreed that it should be known as Teafield—from their having par-taken of their supper upon it. On the line thus run, a road was finally brushed out by 7 of the young sons of the settlers, so that it was possible to pass from the lake to the Chateau-gay. In the middle of March, Hunter made a second visit, examined the land, and accepted from Brown the lot at the outlet of the road, 17, range 5, on which he at once erected a shanty, and left his eldest son, John, and a Canadian in charge.

There were other visitors; among them several who had been passengers on the Alexander. As the lake-front was taken up, Brown proposed they should settle on the new line, which he designed as a concession, the farms to run east and west. Peter and Parlan McFarlane were given the first lot and the next lot fell to William Caldwell. To get to them, it was necessary to do some brushing and to blaze a track, which done, Caldwell moved in during April, taking the McFarlane brothers, who were unmarried, as boarders. John and William Hamilton had to go farther to get lots, for the Teafield spread its dreary waste to the south of Caldwell's, and they settled on 17, 4th range.

As spring approached, Thomas Brown crossed the lake to secure a cow. There were several old country families along the river front, and back of the stage-road. From one of these he bought a cow and calf. On reaching the lake, he found that the frost which had followed the thaw had covered it with glare-ice. Borrowing a horse and traineau, he tied the cow on the sled, and it being too small for the calf also, he swung her round his neck, and holding her legs drove safely across. When spring came, there was no grass for bossy nearer than the point on 20, which had been chopped some years before by lumbermen in getting out masts. The neighbors wondered what Mrs Brown would do with a cow, for she had been city-bred. She soon showed that where there is a will there is a way, for she not only found out how to milk but to make excellent butter, as much as 7 ℔ a week. The calf was a heifer. The cow's two subsequent calves were steers, and those came to be the first yoke of oxen in the settlement, for, like most Scotchmen, the first effort of the settlers was to get horses, though they soon found they were not adapted for the work they had for them to do. That spring, the trees were tapped, and the first maple-sugar made ; several families managed to secure enough sap to make 60 ℔. With the reappearance of bare ground, began preparations for getting in the crop on the small patches they had chopped around their shanties. Potatoes were planted and a little wheat sown. Ignorant of the use of the hoe, the settlers spaded the soil around the stumps. They had a long wait until harvest, and it needed all their courage to sustain them. Provisions could be only obtained by going to Coteau or Fort Covington, long distances to sail in the canoes they managed to buy or make, and often they were in sore need. One family lived on peas alone, and the diet of others, who had some money left, was not much more varied. Every day saw the bush driven farther back, for, despite heat and mosquitoes, the settlers did not relax their exertions in chopping. The trees that were suitable they burned, and converted into ashes, which they paddled in canoes up to the newly-opened store of Alex. Ogilvie on the Laguerre, and sold them for 12½c a bushel, which was a perfect godsend. An honest penny was also earned by making cordwood, which was sent on rafts to Montreal.

During the summer two of the settlers left, Barrie and Rorison, for Scotland, the former for his wife the latter to see to some business. They were wrecked on the coast of Ireland, and reached Glasgow in a destitute condition. Barrie safely returned, but Rorison, whose craze for bush-life had not been satisfied, started to resume it, was again wrecked, and this time was lost with the ship. A number of settlers came in during the summer and took up land beside the Caldwells in what is now known as Newfoundout.

The harvest proved a bountiful one, the yield of potatoes being marvellous in the eyes of those whose experience had been confined to Scotland, and of wheat one settler could boast of having 20 bushels from one he had sown. This ended all fears of scarcity, and the winter was faced with good spirits and much better preparations to resist the cold. Their great anxiety was the delay in issuing patents for their land. They had now ascertained that the lots they occupied had been granted many years before to militiamen and to officers who had taken part in the war of the American revolution, and of the purchasers of the claims of these men or their representatives, Edward Ellice was the most uncompromising. His agents in Montreal told the settlers they had either to buy or leave, and laughed on being asked if, choosing the latter alternative, they would pay for the betterments. Platt and McDonell, who held from 16 to 19, were equally firm, but asked more moderate prices. The settlers contended that as the conditions upon which the grants had been made had not been complied with, as no settlement duties had been done and no patents issued, the lands had reverted to the crown; that they had gone on them in good faith, at the recommendation of the surveyor-general and on assurances from the governor, and therefore they should be conceded to them. The settlers had both equity and law on their side ; Ellice and his co-proprietors had political influence, and the latter prevailed. Lord Dalhousie was much annoyed at the situation in which they were placed, and assured James Brown, who went to see him, that the best that could be done was to give them lots in other parts of the county. The settlers would gladly have paid for their land and remained where they were, but they had no money, so, perforce, had to accept the new lots, which were mainly in Elgin. Adam Patterson was the first to move, and the entire settlement turned out in the spring of 1822 to tramp the road to the Chateaugay to permit of his going to his new lot, which was on the 1st concession of Elgin.

While troubled with the prospect of being compelled to abandon the improvements they had made by so much painful self-denial, two incidents occurred to them of a trivial nature, but which are deserving of record as they served to distract the minds of the settlers from the seriousness of their situation. Thomas Marshall, despite his being a weaver by trade, was the most handy man in the settlement with tools, and was never at a loss to provide a makeshift on meeting difficulties. He had brought the works of a clock with him from Scotland, and made a case wherein to set them, which was of shape and material so strange that Barrie declared it might be worshipped without breaking the commandment, for it was like nothing on the earth and he was positive there could be nothing like it in heaven. Marshall grew most expert with the axe, and when a boasting Yankee lumberman chanced their way and declared he had never seen the man who would chop with him, he took him up. The American chopped 5 cords in two days, Marshall $5\frac{1}{2}$, and would have done more but for well-meant interruptions by his neighbors

who, at first, considered him foolish to have accepted the
wager. The other incident was less pleasant. A straggling
American named Cunningham had been given shelter for the
winter by Paul and Barrie in return for his work. One
Saturday night Wylie gave a merry-making, at which every
soul in the settlement was there. Cunningham and Paul were
the fiddlers. During the evening Cunningham left, saying he
needed a new string and shortly after returned. On Thomas
Brown and his wife returning to their shanty, they found
the dog, which had been left outside, inside, and knew it had
been entered. Flying to the chest where they kept their
money, they found the lid open and their own little stock of
cash safe, but a sum of money entrusted to their safe-keeping
by Barrie, stowed at the other end, had been taken away.
The deed caused the greatest excitement, and it was agreed
that every house and individual should be searched. Next
morning (Sunday) Paul who had his suspicions of him, saw
Cunningham go towards the bush and watched him. He cut
some cedar and in gathering it up, made a motion as if thrusting something into the snow. On coming in Paul reproached
him for cutting brush on such a day, the more so as their
broom was good enough, when he replied that the bush was
such a nice one he could not resist lopping its branches.
Watching his chance, Paul went to the spot, and underneath
the snow found Barrie's money. Afraid of the consequences
if he told Barrie, who was an exceedingly strong man and who
he knew would be very angry, he did not tell him, but reproached the thief privately, who confessed all, and accepting
a few coins to carry him back to the States, disappeared.

That winter the first death took place, an infant of 13
months, the daughter of Thomas Brown. She was buried in
an island that lay near his house, and, by common consent, it
was used for many years as the burial-ground of the settlement.

The settlers were in no way troubled by wild beasts. There
were bears in the Teafield, but they never strayed their way,
and wolves were equally unknown. Deer were abundant,
however, and venison in its season was a welcome variety to

their monotonous diet. Of fish they had a fair supply, the
lake at that period abounding in them. Black Bullard would
come in with his canoe filled, and let the settlers help themselves without price. There was no Indian camp near them,.
and the only redman seen by them, was when one would pass
on a hunting-expedition. A queer encounter with one was
that of two of the settlers, who, while far down towards
Valleyfield in search of a horse that a Canadian had stolen,.
came suddenly upon an Indian in full costume, with rifle and
tomahawk—"a perfect picture" as they described him. They
were abashed and somewhat terrified by the imposing appearance of the savage, and one of the canny Scots sought to
propitiate him by offering "the piece" he had brought with
him. The Indian graciously accepted the bread, and though
he could not speak English showed his good-will by signs.

The hopes of the settlers as to a favorable solution of their
land difficulties were revived in the summer by Bowron, who,.
by political influence, had got the appointment as land-agent
which had been promised to James Brown, and who now left
for Quebec, where he was engaged to build lighthouses on
the island of Anticosti, and spent the remainder of his life in
building and overseeing such structures on the St Lawrence,.
dying at Quebec about 1845. Bowron sent for the settlers
to meet him at Hunter's house, when he made a plausible
speech, promising to faithfully fulfil to them all the assurances
the governor had made to Brown. Soon after they discovered that their ostensible friend was in treaty to buy up
the claims of the gentlemen who held grants for their land.
This decided them to leave at once for the lots for which
they held location-tickets. To the idea of moving they had
become more reconciled on finding out many of the drawbacks of their present situation, the greatest of which was
distance from mill. They had to go to Fort Covington,
Williamstown, Coteau, or St Timothy, all of them involving
long and dangerous voyages in frail canoes, which they were
awkward in managing. Often were they overtaken by those
sudden squalls characteristic of lake St Francis, and not only
had their bags of flour soaked by water but had hairbreadth

escapes with their lives. Thomas Brown with a neighbor on one occasion went to St Timothy mill. In returning, a storm arose and they had to make for the shore of Hungry bay. There was no house near and the marsh on every side was full of water. By chance, a hunter passed the second day and gave them a light, so that they had a fire. For two days and nights they were compelled by the storm to remain, their only food a fish thrown up wounded by the gale. Another settler who had gone to Williamstown to buy a bag of flour, was detained 3 days by the wind. So great was the difficulty in conveying boards from Fort Covington, that they found it easier to saw them by hand. On a boat that went to the Fort for supplies, the settler who held the paddle gave much uneasiness to the others by steering boldly across from headland to headland, instead of coasting along shore, and one of them repeatedly called out to him "Keep close to Crete; keep close to Crete." They brought back in their boat a young pig or two and other supplies.

It was true the lake had also its advantages, as it gave them water communication in summer and formed the best of roads in winter, but, on the other hand, the Teafield behind isolated them, except during sleighing, from the interior of the country, and by this time they had learned the soil was better along the Chateaugay and Trout river. Ellice's agent threatening to eject them unless they would buy their lots, the settlers almost unanimously determined upon leaving. The only concession they could wring from him was leave to return and cut the hay that might grow on their clearings until such time as new owners went into possession. The privilege was of no value, as their new lots were at too great a distance to allow of hauling it. In the fall (1823) they set out to see the lots provided for them in Elgin, and found a guide to them in a negro, Black William, who was an escaped slave and deformed from a timber having fallen upon him at a raising. He was unmarried and lived alone on 3, 1st concession, maintaining himself by hunting.* Be-

* The poor man died in Malone poorhouse at an advanced age.

side him there was only one other resident in the interior of the township, an American of the name of Palmer, who had temporarily left his own place in Constable in order to make potash in the Canadian woods. He had a shanty and a small clearance where the Presbyterian church now stands. On ascertaining their lots, the settlers put up shanties, and returned to their homes by the lake. All that winter was spent in preparations for moving, and early in the spring, while the sleighing was still good, they abandoned forever the clearings and betterments they had made with such incredible self-sacrifice. All did not leave that spring, a few remaining in the hope that the threat to eject them would not be acted upon, but they also, before other two years, had to follow, and only three remained and paid the claimants of their lots, and they did so because by this time they had livestock for which they could not get hay in Elgin.

Thus ended in disaster Dalhousie settlement, whose early days were so promising, furnishing an early warning, often since repeated, but of little influence upon public men, for the same mistake has been made in the Northwest, of allowing crown lands to pass into the hands of other than actual settlers. While the dispersion of the Old Countrymen led to the more rapid settlement of Elgin and the southern side of Godmanchester, it had a decided effect upon the future prospects of St Anicet, for had they been allowed to remain, they would have spread over the municipality, which would have become, like the others in the county, the seat of an English, instead of a French-speaking population.

The subsequent history of the settlement is so strikingly illustrative of the political changes in the province, that I give it, although it extends beyond the period to which this narrative is designed to be confined. The lots wrested from their first settlers found, in course of time, purchasers, and again the land along the lake was occupied by about a dozen Irish and Scotch families, who plodded on quietly, redeeming the wilderness and converting it into desirable farms. They lived in peace for over half a century and might have gone on in the even tenor of their ways had not Mr Ellice, in 1867, sold the seigniory and with it the land he owned in the county of Huntingdon. The company that bought his rights was active in realizing every dollar possible, and the portion of Teafield they had acquired, they sold, for a trifling sum, to the late Mr Demers of Valleyfield. After taking off the scrub bush that covered it, sawing what was large enough and selling the remainder as cordwood, he conceived the idea of disposing of it for cultivation. The proposal seemed to be preposterous. The land is lower than the St Lawrence and subject to frequent overflow, and where it is not covered with peat has a thick layer of black muck over the clay. Asking only a trifle down and giving long credit for the balance, secured by mortgage, there was no lack of applicants from the parishes adjoining Valleyfield. They managed to raise crops by burning the surface of the muck and sowing in the ashes. If they got a good burn and the season was dry, they raised fair crops of oats and barley; if the weather was unfavorable, they left. The population on the swamp has been a changeable one and, even now, few have their lots, miserable as they are, free of mortgage. In less than 10 years there was a row of shanties with stovepipes sticking out of the roof from Ogilvie's hill to the seigniory-line across land which it had been believed nobody could have been tempted to live upon. The Old Countrymen on the lake-shore viewed the unexpected incursion in their rear with astonishment, and believed it was only a matter of a few years when the poor people would be starved out, and Teafield, excepting the patches of good land, which rise above its dreary expanse like islands, would relapse into desolation. As they increased in numbers, it was suggested to the new-comers that they should have a church of their own, and there was an opportunity of buying a discarded wooden one in an adjoining parish which had erected a large stone edifice. The habitants fell in with the proposal and petitioned bishop Fabre to form them into a parish. The church was got cheap, was removed in pieces and re-erected on a knoll at the eastern extremity of the swamp. On the 6th February, 1882, the bishop issued his decree constituting all that portion of the county of Hunt-

ingdon that lies east of the plank-road and north of Godmanchester, a parish under the name of Ste Barbe. He referred
his decree to the commissioners of his diocese, who made their
report, when the lieutenant-governor issued his proclamation,
dated 12 June, 1882, declaring Ste Barbe to be a parish with
civil powers. Of these movements the Old Countrymen
knew nothing whatever, and when they did hear of their
French neighbors in the Teafield getting a church of their
own, they did not perceive that it was going to affect them.
They were rudely awakened to the fact that it was otherwise.
In the seigniories, when a new parish is formed as the Catholic bishop of Montreal constituted Ste Barbe, it is not only a
parish for ecclesiastical purposes but for municipal also, and
the dwellers in Teafield, all natives of seigniories, considered
they could do in Huntingdon what they could in Beauharnois,
and not only elect a fabrique and church-wardens, collect
tithes and levy assessments to pay for their church, but
organize a municipal council. A council was formed and
imposed a rate. The Old Countrymen were thunderstruck.
They knew that in seigniorial territory the Catholic bishops
can initiate the proceedings that result in the formation of
municipalities, but their belief, which had been shared in by
the entire English-speaking population since the conquest,
was, that outside the seigniories they had no such power and
that in township or non-fief land the legislature and the
county councils alone had the right to erect municipalities.
They asked if French law was to prevail in the county of
Huntingdon, and the Catholic bishop cut it up into municipalities at his pleasure? They appealed to the courts and to
the legislature to protect what they believed to be their rights,
and met with the reception to be expected from men dominated
by clerical influence. While the case is not finally decided at
the time this is written, the prospect is that the descendants
and successors of the men who chose the lake-shore as a place
of residence, because they believed in Huntingdon they would
be clear of seigniorial and parish law, will be driven from
their homes by the operation of the very laws they sought to
escape.

NOTE: An absolutely correct list of the settlers at the lake-shore it was impossible to compile when I began to collect information. The annexed is substantially correct. An asterisk indicates those who were passengers by the Alexander. All were natives of Scotland. Knowing nothing of the procedure in settlement, they fancied they could live together and have their farms adjacent, so the front on the lake was laid out so as to give each family 5 acres and the shanties were put in a line, forming a little village. For this reason, any attempt to give their location would be misleading. I should have liked to have given the names of those who landed on the 1st August, but failed to recover them :

*Robert Allan, only stayed a few weeks, and afterwards settled on the Chateaugay ; David Anderson, shepherd, Dumfries-shire ; *Robert Barrie, mason, New Monklands ; David Brown, plasterer, Beith ; *James Brown, mason, Glasgow ; *Thomas Brown, weaver, Campsie ; *Thomas Brown, carpenter, who kept with his brother James a grocery on the Spoutmouth, Glasgow ; William Caldwell, weaver, Pollokshaws ; —— Dick, who had studied for the ministry, entered into business at Glasgow and failed ; *Archd. Fleming, carpenter, Paisley ; *John Gillies, laborer, Ayrshire ; *John Harper, Paisley ; *Dr Fortune, Paisley ; *Wm. Hamilton, baker, and *James Hamilton, helper on farm, brothers, from Motherwell ; Jacob Hart, divinity-student, Hamilton ; *Robert Higgins, carpenter, Paisley; *Peter Horn, weaver, Campsie ; *Thomas Marshall, weaver, Wishaw ; *James McArthur, weaver, and *William McArthur, weaver, brothers, from Paisley; Gilbert MacBeth, weaver, and James MacBeth, mason, brothers, from Beith ; Parlan McFarlane, carpenter, and Peter McFarlane, book-keeper, brothers, from Glasgow; James McNair, farm-helper, Inverary ; Robert Nelson ; *Adam Patterson, plasterer, Glasgow ; *James Paul, mason, New Monklands ; John Potty, sailor ; *—— Rorison, merchant, Glasgow ; *James Tannahill, mason, Tinnock ; *Hugh Wiley and *John Wiley, masons, brothers, from Paisley.

CHAPTER IX.

DUNDEE.

FROM 1760 the western extremity of the county of Huntingdon was regarded by the government as an Indian reserve. The Indians clustered at the point, named St Regis, and did not occupy the country east of Salmon river, but when the townships came to be laid out, it was deemed desirable that sufficient territory should be kept for them to supply their prospective needs, and Chewett, the surveyor, left a length of ten miles of territory before running the line for Godmanchester. Bouchette, who visited St Regis at the close of the war, says about 50 dirty hovels, with enclosures attached, wherein potatoes and corn were raised, composed the village, and that its inhabitants were indolent and shiftless. A large church, 100 × 40 feet, had been erected in 1795 and there was a resident priest, who, however, made no effort to improve the temporal condition of his flock, and in 1820 the government agent reported that not half of the inhabitants derived any part of their living from tillage, they depending upon hunting and fishing alone, eking out a livelihood with the pensions, or presents, allowed by government, which, for a number of years after the close of the war, were much larger than they are now. As the Indians were making no use of their land and there being no prospect of their doing so, it was deemed better that they should be permitted to lease it to settlers, as had been done 50 years before with the lands they had held in Glengarry and Stormont. Repeated efforts had been made by the government to elevate the Indians, with no success. The agent, Chesley, told a parliamentary committee in 1846 that during his connection of 32 years with the tribe "several attempts had been made to establish schools at St Regis but they have been invariably opposed and put down by the priests." A philanthropic soldier, Major Penderleith Christie, took 6 Indian boys and placed them in the school, erected at Chateaugay, in 1829 at his own expense. On hearing of it the governor, Lord Sydenham, doubled the number and paid the expense out of the public funds, but from the inefficiency of the teacher the experiment was not successful. Not discouraged, on Major Christie's finding the right man for such work in the Rev. E. Williams, a Caughnawaga Indian who had become a Protestant and been educated for the Episcopal ministry in Connecticut, he opened a school at St Regis, the attendance at which rose from 17 to 40 in two months, when the priest interfered, and commanded the parents to withdraw their children from the school under the pain of his displeasure and the anathema of the church. All save 7 left, and with these Mr Williams persevered until the arrival of Earl Gosford as governor, who, at the request of the Catholic bishop of Montreal, withdrew the salary of $96 which the government had allowed and, what was more fatal, the permission of the government to live on the Indian reserve. The school was closed but not without fruit, for there are a few Protestant families belonging to the tribe, now resident on Cornwall island, who are by far the most comfortable and intelligent, and whose origin is to be traced to the forgotten labors of Mr Williams. The trite remark, of the Indians being a decaying race, is not sustained by records of this reserve. In 1820 its inhabitants numbered 300, in 1827, 348, in 1837, despite their losses from smallpox in 1829 and cholera in 1832, 381, and in 1885, 1,136.

Before the war of 1812 a few American families had settled in Dundee. Of these Benjamin Phillips lived on 12, Orlando Brunson on a point, or marsh island, farther west, and Joseph Spencer on 23, 2nd concession. On the Salmon river were a few families, of whom all record is lost. All were probably squatters, for there is no certainty that the Indians granted leases before 1817, on the 3rd of August of which year a marsh island on Salmon river, Portage island, was leased to Hypolite Emlotte dit Perikier, who several years afterwards transferred it to Peter Cameron, who made the island notorious by distilling whisky upon it. In the spring of 1818, an American, Jonas Schryer, from Alburg, Vermont, moved across the line and leased the east half of No 30 and all of 29 in the Broken Front. To shelter his wife and three children he raised a shanty of logs, having one gable built up with mud and stones for the fireplace, and roofed with splinters of cedar. He was very poor and to obtain provisions, had to labor at potash-making day after day. When winter came he borrowed a yoke of oxen and drew a load of boards from Fort Covington, with which he made his house somewhat more comfortable, though to the last, the children could amuse themselves by sitting at the fire and looking up the wide chimney watch the tree-tops waving overhead.

The same spring that Schryer moved into the western portion of Dundee, an important settlement was formed on the eastern extremity. Late in the fall of 1816 a ship arrived in Quebec with a number of Highland immigrants. The prolonged voyage made it impossible for them to proceed to Ontario, which was their intended destination, and they waited over the winter at Lancaster, being given the use of the barracks that had been erected during the war of 1812. While the women rested in this rude home in the new world, the men worked at what they could get, many hiring themselves to farmers. The people of the vicinity took an interest in them, and the Ross's, who were then the leading business firm, told them they believed land could be had on the south side of the St Lawrence by lease from the Indians, and a bargain was eventually struck with the chiefs for a range of lots starting from the Godmanchester line. During the winter of 1817 small clearings were made and shanties erected; the Glengarry farmers making several bees to do the work, and being aided by Ross the lumberer, who had men getting out masts, and who indicated the lines of the lots. These Glengarry men worked with a will all day and at night gathered in one of the new shanties and sang and danced and drank until a late hour, yet rose to renew their good-hearted task next morning with unimpaired vigor. Seven shanties in all were completed and, while the crossing was still good, their future occupants moved over and took sion. Starting at the east the order was Wm. Campbell, Angus McGillis, John Tolmie, Ronald, Angus and Norman McDonald and William McPhee. Except Tolmie all were from the Isle of Skye, and had come in the same ship, and they named the settlement New Skye, but in course of time it came to be known as the Isle of Skye. They brought over sufficient seed with them and the season proved favorable, for after that harvest they never knew want. Their Glengarry neighbors continued to take an interest in them, and often came over to help by bees. On one occasion the evening jollification was so prolonged that the keg ran dry, when the hosts, zealous for Highland hospitality, while their guests were sleeping, sent two of their number across the lake to get it refilled, and they were back long before the morning dram was needed. The liquor used at that time was Jamaica rum. Once started, the settlement grew. William McPhee, who was the most comfortably situated of the band, having brought over with him two cows and a yearling, got for his neighbor a very decent Irish couple, John Seaton and his wife. They had no family and left early. West of them was Roderick Murchison. To the east, the settlement extended rapidly down the lake shore, Duncan Stewart, Duncan McNicol, and 3 McMillans settling in 1820. The lake at that time was much lower than it is now, so low that there was a fine sandy beach, on which the young lads raced up and down on their horses, for they never troubled with oxen. The St Lawrence was then well-stocked with fish, which so swarmed in the bays that the habitants came from far and near to fish in them during the season, so that at night 40 or 50 canoes could be counted. The mode of fishing then was wholly by the spear, which was practised during the day as well as by night. The Highlanders, almost all of whom had fished at home, entered into the sport with gusto. The marshes were also valuable for more than the hay which they afforded, for they were visited by such flocks of geese and ducks that, when they rose, they darkened the air like a cloud. When the flocks of pigeons were seen coming from the Glengarry side, the men and boys hastened to the water's edge, each armed with a long pole. A peculiarity of the pigeon is that, while crossing water, it skims its surface, and rises as it reaches land. Noticing this, the settlers struck them down with their poles just as they rose from the water's surface to wing a higher flight, and those who were dexterous sometimes killed 4 at one blow. Wild swan were occasionally met with, but the king of American edible birds, the wild turkey, never, so far as I have been able to learn, visited Huntingdon. Deer came trotting daily in the dry season to drink at the lake.

The great river furnished a road to the settlement which was all they could desire, for, with one or two exceptions, they had all come from the Highland coast and boating to them was second nature. If the weather was fine, they crossed on Sundays to attend the services conducted by the Rev. John McKenzie at Williamstown, and to them he was pastor for many years. On sacramental Sundays the whole settlement was deserted. If any were sick, Dr McLeod of Williamstown was sent for, and his services were gladly given. To build a big boat, that would do to go to mill or market, was a joint undertaking, and it was duly launched and moored in the creek, named in old maps Sherwood. When salts were made, the settlers carried them through the woods in bags upon their backs to the creek, and when the big canoe was loaded, started for Salmon river, generally taking at the same time a grist. The round trip took two days and one night. For 10 years there was no road, except the footpath that connected shanty with shanty. The first road was that to Laguerre. In winter the custom was for each settler to make at least one trip to Montreal in a traineau with his surplus butter and pork. The road taken was by Laguerre to Huntingdon, and thence to the Basin.

In nearly every family Gaelic was the common language, but a reasonable desire was shown by the older people that their children should learn English, and a teacher was secured in Patrick McGregor, who continued to follow his profession in the neighborhood for many years. He was so cruel as to disgust his scholars with learning, and all the more so that he had little to impart. He was a spare, gaunt man, and his favorite mode of punishment, striking with the back of his hands, was so severe that the blow often drew blood. As his scholars declared, they might as well get a slap from a skeleton. He taught at first from house to house. The second teacher was Alexander Crawford, sadly given to drink, who gave place to Duncan Campbell, a lame weaver, who taught in a shanty on McDonald's point. Afterwards a school was erected farther west, at the creek, where a burial-place by common consent had been chosen. In 1821 the settlement got a blacksmith in Jas. Fraser, on Gardiner's point. He conducted business in primitive style. If the job was a small one, he told his customer to take up whatever task he was engaged upon on the farm, while he went to his shop and lit his forge. Customers complained that he kept them longer in the field than he ought, and that the change of work was not altogether to his disadvantage.

The clearances were confined for many years to the knolls, but gradually the swamps, which were covered with a splendid growth of black ash, were cleared and drained and fine farms formed. The fires of 1825 left Dundee untouched, and, alone in the county, it has never suffered to any extent from burned soil.

From the year 1820 the settlement of the township proceeded actively, the Indians in that year granting about 40 leases. The terms were liberal, $5 a year for 100 acres, the leases being for 99 years, and then renewable until 999 years elapsed. A few leases were for 1000 years, or so long as grass grew or water ran. The leases issued after 1822 were all for 30 years, unless the occupants could show they had a promise for a longer period. A condition was inserted in a majority of the leases inflicting a fine of 8 per cent. on the sum received when the land changed hands (lods et ventes), but was never exacted. The leases were negotiated for the Indians by Isaac LaClair, their agent, and signed by a majority of the chiefs—who were all men of mark. In all of these old leases, the reserve is styled "the Indian reservation of Kintail." The rents were made payable on the 1st of February in each year. The scarcity of money and the necessities of the Indians caused the amount generally to be taken in kind, and the Indian had often unhealthy pork or an undesirable heifer palmed upon him. For three days at the beginning of February the Indian chiefs attended at Dundee lines with their agent, and squared accounts with the settlers. Even with the privilege of paying in provisions, many settlers were most negligent in settling the rent, and as the agents were supine, arrears were allowed to accumulate for 20 years and over. From the first, the Indians were good neighbors, keeping to their reservation, and rarely seen east of the Salmon river unless hunting or seeking timber for making baskets, which they traded with the farmers. No objection was made by any settler to their felling trees suitable for their petty manufactures.

The free issue of leases stimulated the influx of immigrants. On leaving shipboard, Highlanders naturally gravitated towards Glengarry, the great settlement of their kindred, and where nearly all had relatives, more or less remote. Even those destined for the West made Glengarry their halfway stopping-place, to renew those old friendships which are so precious to the sons of the heather. Thus it came, that in those days there was always during the summer a floating population of immigrants in search of homes, and on Dundee being thrown open they naturally moved into it, the dividing line being only the St Lawrence. The abandoned clearances on Salmon river became again the scene of life and activity, and for over 3 miles below the boundary-line there was a succession of good farm-houses with an excellent road on the river-bank. At Peter Cameron's, referred to already as a distiller, there was a large and finely kept garden and a race-course. The rising of the lake-level and the crumbling away of the river bank, have destroyed these scenes of prosperity.

On Salmon river John Davidson established himself, and proved to be the leading-man of the young township. He was a native of Perthshire, and had gone a poor boy to Dundee, where he was taken into the household of a Mr

Ogilvie, who owned a small factory, and who gave him work and whose daughter he subsequently married. He was unfortunate enough to be drafted into the army and served 7 years abroad, and on his discharge at the peace in 1817, emigrated to Canada, where he earned sufficient money as a travelling-merchant to enable him to start in 1819 a small store at Dundee lines, and his log shanty, consisting of one room, was the nucleus of that village, to which he gave the name of the fair town by the Tay in which he had spent the greater part of his life—Dundee. His family, accompanied by his brother-in-law, Alex. Ogilvie, arrived during the following summer. The same season saw also two other arrivals. Henry McDonald, a miller by trade, from Melrose, Scotland, on landing at Montreal, heard of an opening at Fort Covington, and on going there was engaged by Robert Buchanan, the owner of the grist-mill, who had been there for 16 years.* Patrick Buchanan, a youth of 17, and a cousin of the Fort Covington Buchanan, arrived from Scotland the same year, and has left many descendants. He at once engaged in boating, and for half a century no one was better known than Captain Buchanan. It was either in 1819 or 1820 that the first Irish families settled in Dundee, and of whom the more prominent were Patrick Bannon on 28, B. F. and John Ashburn on 27. They were few, however, and it was not for over 20 years afterwards that they began to come in, and, buying out the Highlanders, formed the settlement in the neighborhood of St Agnes. Among those who came in 1820 to see the country was Alexander Gardiner, who had emigrated from Renfrewshire, Scotland, that summer, and who was in search of a farm. He hesitated between Dundee and St Andrews, when his brother-in-law, Hugh Brodie, Petite Côte, proposed to leave it to the lot,—a not infrequent mode of deciding a difficulty among the devout Pres-

---

* Mr Buchanan caught enough of salmon at his dam not only for immediate use but to fill several barrels for winter consumption. Although not one has been caught in it for half a century, Salmon river well deserved its name in those days.

byterians of the last century. After earnest prayer, a halfpenny was tossed up, and thrfce the side that stood for Dundee came uppermost. In February, 1821, Mr Brodie's team brought him and his family from Montreal to lot 19, the betterments on which he had bought from an Irishman, James Curran, and whose shanty stood a few yards west of the residence of Peter Gardiner. Glad to gain its shelter, they enjoyed their first meal in the form of a bowl of oatmeal brose. Though the oak had disappeared, the ridges were still crowned by great pines, one of which, having grown on its site, furnished Curran with the 3 lower logs of his shanty. The level land between the knolls and ridges was swampy and unfit for cultivation. Mr Gardiner was totally unacquainted with the use of the axe, and was afraid to cut down a tree in case it should fall upon him, but in this and other duties his neighbor Edward Aubrey, an American, who had come in two years before, taught him. On the ridges very good crops were raised, the grain having to be carried on the shoulder to mill, for the flats were too wet to admit of a horse going on them. That summer he had one cow and the following had 3, when Mrs Gardiner, who was a notable dairy-woman, began making cheese, for which a market was found in Montreal. Mr Gardiner was an exemplary man in more respects than those of thrift and industry. In the season of 1821, Father Brunton, as he afterwards came to be affectionately called, arrived in Fort Covington from Scotland, and began preaching to the people there, being greatly encouraged by Robert Buchanan, who was looked up to as the leader of the settlement. When, in 1827, the church was formally organized, Mr Gardiner was chosen one of its elders. The same year that he took up his land, there settled a short distance west of him, on lots 30 and 31, Broken Front, James Farlinger, of U. E. descent, and who in 1823 became his son-in-law.

The settlers along the lake in St Anicet and Dundee, had difficulties peculiar to themselves to contend with. The numerous marshes prevented the construction of roads, and up to 1835 there was hardly one fit for wheels. The grist

had to be shouldered by the settler and to drag his barrel of
potash he had to resort to the ox-sled. Horses were few
because of little use, and the first settler to own one was
Jonas Schryer. Mr Davidson's store was situated on the east
bank of Salmon river and behind it stretched a deep swamp,
impossible to cross unless when frozen, so that the settlers
could only get to it by going round by Fort Covington. The
customs' officer was vigilant, and extorted duties on what
they were taking home, for, in a petition to the legislature,
dated 12th November, 1820, Mr Davidson alleges "that the
prosperity of the settlement formerly called Indian lands,
now designated by the name of Dundee, is much retarded
from the want of a public road. In their present situation,
many of the inhabitants are under the necessity of passing
through a section of the U. S., in going to and returning from
market (Dundee lines), and are consequently liable to pay
heavy duties at the American custom-house. Under these
circumstances we pray for aid to enable us to open a road on
the British side of the lines." No notice was taken of this
representation, and two months afterwards he sent in a
petition from the settlers praying for aid to make a road
across the swamp to Davidson's store and wharf, which was
their outlet during navigation. The French Canadians dominated in the assembly and viewed with undisguised illwill
the progress of the townships. On the 17th February, the
committee to whom Davidson's petition and similar ones had
been referred, reported that the petitioners ought to have
considered the inconveniences of the places in which they
had settled while selecting them and that the law of the province they had come to was that roads are a charge upon the
soil, therefore no aid from the public purse could be given.
Undismayed by this rebuff, in the winter of 1823 Mr Davidson renewed his request, telling the assembly that: "A serious
inconvenience experienced in our settlement is want of roads,
the village of Dundee being separated from the rest by a
swamp nearly one mile wide, through which the inhabitants
have been unable from poverty to make a road, so that the
only way that they can have communication is by crossing

the province-line, in doing which they are exposed to the rapacity of the U.S. custom-house officers, who never fail to exact a duty of 16½ per cent. on whatever passes to or from our market, or, what is worse, detain our property." To help the settlers to make a road Mr Davidson asked $400. The assembly took no notice of the petition. Mr Davidson's representation as to smuggling had another side to it. Until the railway was built to Ogdensburg, the entire tract of country between that place and lake Champlain depended for its supply of manufactured goods being brought by teams from Plattsburgh and Rouses Point. The expense of the long land journey so added to their cost, that they were much dearer than goods brought from Montreal, so that the Americans along the lines bought the greater part of their dry-goods and hardware in Canada,' and while the Dundee storekeepers sold smuggled tea, tobacco and whisky to Canadians, they found their best customers for what they brought from Montreal in Americans, who were rarely interfered with by their customs officers, who interpreted the law to mean, that what a farmer bought for his own use was not smuggling.

The clearances were confined to the ridges and the knolls that so abound in Dundee, and on these crops of potatoes and corn were raised, the main dependence being potash-making and lumbering. In winter the woods were dotted with lumbering shanties and an immense quantity of timber taken out. On the Pine Plains, especially, the timber was magnificent, and so abundant that it withstood the ravages of the axe for over 20 years, when it became the desert sandy plain of to-day. Men acquainted with the lumber districts of the Ottawa declare that they saw nowhere pines to compare with those west of Hungry Bay; pines so straight and tall that they were made into masts, and sticks ranging from 80 to 120 feet long were hauled out to the lake every winter. From Moquin's bay, St Anicet, back to the 2nd range was a mast-road, and there were others, all straight and smooth, as they had need to be to permit the passing of the great spars, which would take several yoke of oxen to haul them or, as was preferred, horses in tandem. To drive the animals needed no small skill, and there were those who could boast of handling successfully 20 horses hitched in tandem to a mighty mast. Of the great lumberers were Angus Roy McDonald of Cornwall, Bagg & Waite, Perrault, and Moquin. The last was a Quebec merchant.

The making of potash was too profitable a trade to allow the storekeepers of Fort Covington to monopolise it, so, shortly after his coming, Mr Davidson added an ashery with pearling-oven to his establishment, and Charles Marsh who ·had opened store beside him, did likewise. He was an American and had been a clerk in Frothingham's, Montreal, who had started him in business. He entered into partnership with Peter Cameron, who had made a racecourse on Portage island, and, after a fast and short career, failed. Frothingham started him anew, when he showed he was a changed man and did a large business so long as Dundee retained its trade, especially in the manufacture of potash and pearl-ash. Other early storekeepers were McCutcheon and Wells & Cleveland. The first-named committed suicide from despair over losses in lumbering, when his clerk, Norman McDonald,* continued the business, and some time afterwards Patrick Buchanan added another store to the number, taking, in 1840, his brother-in-law, David Baker, as partner. Up to 1848, all these stores did a large and profitable business, which was by no means confined to trading with the settlers of Dundee. In those days tea, tobacco, whisky, and a few lines of dry-goods were much cheaper in the United States than Canada, and these stores, all situated within a stone-throw of the lines and with buildings built half across, sold more to customers in Glengarry than Dundee. During the war when the importation of spirits from the West Indies was stopped, the American distilleries received a great im-

---

*He published a book in New York in 1827 entitled "Moral Maxims and Reflections," which I have not seen. He was a man of education and talent. He prospered so well in business that, at one time, he was the largest shareholder in the City bank.

petus and they discovered the art of making mash from potatoes. By 1817 the country was overspread with small distilleries making potato-whisky and the use of their product became general in Upper Canada. The people of the lower province continued to prefer Jamaica rum and did not begin to look at whisky until it became so very cheap that the more ardent and palatable spirit had no chance. From 1822 whisky gradually superseded rum, until it finally supplanted it. St Lawrence county early became famous for its whisky, and Franklin county, at one period, had no fewer than 17 distilleries. The chief distiller was one Parish, who had a village named after him, and Parishville whisky was known far and wide. The importation of spirits from the States, under any conditions, was then illegal, but there was no serious attempt made to enforce the law, and, on summer nights, barrels were rolled by the dozen from the Dundee storehouses into boats that conveyed them to dealers on the north side of the St Lawrence, and in winter long strings of teams came from Glengarry and Stormont to exchange grain and pork for whisky, tobacco, and tea. By the barrel, Parishville whisky was sold as low as 18 cents a gallon. It is a striking fact, that not one of the merchants engaged in the traffic retained any portion of the immense profits they made for a long succession of years.

The contraband traffic was only a part of the trade of Dundee lines, which included large exports of potash and lumber, the former being conveyed to Montreal in the kind of barge called Durham boats, so named from being modelled on the boats used on the canals in the county of Durham, England. I have found reference to them in U.S. despatches during the war, but they were rare on the St Lawrence until 1817, when they began to be numerous, and were so palpably superior for river navigation to the bateaux then in use, that they superseded them. In 1817 the collector of customs reported that 835 bateaux had passed Coteau and only 268 Durham boats; in 1820 the proportion was reversed, 561 Durham boats to 430 bateaux, and the former carried four times the freight of the latter. The bateau of those days was an open boat of about 20 feet in length, 6 wide, and 3 deep, sharp-pointed at both ends, propelled by 4 oarsmen and steered by the captain with a long oar. When the wind favored, a square sail was set. On the downward trip they could carry 15 tons; on the upward, less than 5. Being open the freight was exposed to damage by wet, and the crew tied up the boat and went ashore to cook, and frequently did so at night to sleep. The French Canadians who manned these boats endured great hardship and were often in peril in running the rapids. The Durham-boat was in every way superior to the bateau. It was from 60 to 80 feet long and 12 to 15 feet wide, and decked, giving a roomy and dry hold. Flat bottomed, its cargo capacity was great, from 50 to 70 tons. There ran along each side, a broad plank with cleats, on which the men stood to pole the boat along in shallow water. In deep, a centre-board was let down and sail set, a large spread being made; the boat being sloop-rigged. Oars were only used when required in the rapids. The crew consisted of 8 men and a captain. Such were the boats that, for over quarter a century, maintained communication between Montreal and the country west of it. Their navigation required skill, boldness, and superhuman exertion. On getting into swift-water, the crew ranged themselves at the bow of the boat. One stepped on to the plank that ran along the side, dropped his long ash-pole into the water until it struck bottom, then placing the head of the pole against his shoulder-blade, pushed with all his might, walking, as the boat slowly stemmed the current, to the stern, when he returned to the bow and so on. As he passed down, another boatman stepped out with his pole, until all 8 would be so engaged. The work was most exhausting, and caused the skin on the forebreast and shoulder to become callused. Where the rapid was too swift to be thus overcome, or when the boat was heavily laden, oxen or horses were hitched on, as many, if the boat was large and the water low, as 9 span, and painful accidents were of occasional occurrence, from their being unable to overcome the rush of water, and the boat being swept backwards and dragging them to a watery grave.

To prevent such a calamity, each of the crew hung a small hatchet at his waist when the rapids were reached, so as to be ready to cut the tow-rope. Rounding the points was the critical operation, and at Split Rock there was a windlass to supplement the strength of the crew and tow-horses. In this slow and painful manner not only goods but immigrants were conveyed from Montreal, and hundreds of settlers in this district so made the journey. What some of them suffered is now inconceivable. With favorable weather and plenty of water in the rapids, the passage was endurable; when wet, water low, and winds contrary, it was worse than the ocean-voyage and what women and children endured is not to be described. They were usually overcrowded, perhaps 200 crowded into one, and if the weather was cold or wet, or the passage of the rapids difficult, they were forced into the hold to give the crew full scope on deck, perhaps required to land and walk to the head of the rapid to lessen the draft of the boat. The holds were low-ceiled, dark and foul-smelling, and without a vestige of accommodation for passengers, who slept on the floor, and from the time they went on board until they left would not taste cooked food. With a favorable wind, the trip from Montreal to Coteau would occupy a couple of days; when wind and draft of water were unfavorable, it took from 6 to 14 days. On the down-trip the boats dared not enter the rapids with a head-wind, and there was often a fleet of them anchored at Coteau waiting for a change of wind. The Lachine canal was not available until 1825 and the Beauharnois not for 20 years more. From a very early date the rapids between lakes St Louis and St Francis were partially avoided by four short canals cut across the points on the north shore. They were so very small, the locks being only 6 feet wide with 2½ feet of water, that they were of little use until 1817, when the width of the locks was doubled and the water deepened a foot. No further enlargement was attempted, and until the Beauharnois canal was opened any boat that drew more water than they afforded, had to be dragged and pushed up the rapids in the manner described.

The first Durham-boat that hailed from Salmon river was the Dundee, owned by Thos. Farlinger and Robt. Buchanan.* She was succeeded by a much larger boat, the Glengarry. Others followed, until Durham-boats that claimed Dundee as their port became numerous, for Fort Covington and Dundee were the outlets for the vast expanse of country that the Salmon river and its tributaries watered, and Captains Buchanan, Farlinger, and Lucas made regular trips.

The first steamboat to ply the waters of the Salmon river was a very small vessel that had been built in the States, named the Jack Downing. She ran as ferry between Fort Covington and Cornwall in 1835 or 1836, when her engine was taken out to be placed in the Henry Burden, popularly known as the cigar-boat, from her hull being composed of two cylinders, on which the deck rested like a raft, with the one paddle-wheel in the centre. On the opening of the Beauharnois canal, Masson, Finchley & Farlinger bought the Rob Roy, and as business increased built the Lord Elgin, which proved to be too long for the crooks of the Salmon river. Competition came from Augustus Martin of Trout river, who built at Dundee the George Frederick, which made regular trips to Montreal under Capt. Sawyer of Fort Covington, who claimed to be the first to run the north channel of the Long Sault. Then the Fashion, commanded by Captain Charles Dewitt, extended her route to Dundee. The Star, the Blue Bonnet, and the Salaberry succeeded those boats, the latter being the last that made Dundee a regular place of call, for, owing to trade changing to other channels, the traffic that once made Dundee lines the busiest place west of the Basin, deserted it.

The progress of Dundee furnishes nothing of special interest. More than those of any other part of the district, its inhabitants engaged in lumbering and boating, which had a hurtful influence on their habits and made farming a second-

* His eldest son, Thomas, went to Liberia as a missionary and subsequently became governor. He died there of fever, leaving a considerable fortune to his relations on the Salmon river.

ary consideration, so that, despite its land being taken up so early, it was later in being brought into cultivation than that of the adjoining townships. The establishing of schools and churches received little attention until 1830, and for many years the only school in the township besides the one in the isle of Skye was that at Schryer's corners, which opened with Hector McRae as master, who was given to drink and cruel in his punishments. The lot adjoining the school came to be used as a place of burial, and Edward Schryer and many others of the first generation rest there. In the schoolhouse the Fort Covington ministers occasionally preached. The Baptist, Rev Nathaniel Culver, made it one of his stations as early as 1824, and, during his incumbency of the Presbyterian church, the Rev John Savage preached frequently and acceptably. One of the first teachers was Alexander Cameron, who belonged to Dundee, Scotland, and had been a divinity-student. He exerted himself in several ways to benefit those he had come among, giving religious instruction to the young on Saturday afternoons, distributing tracts, of which he had brought with him across the Atlantic two boxes, and preaching on Sunday. He was a good singer. After making a trial of farming, he left for London, Ontario. No effort was made to secure regular religious services and the years passed until 1832, when the settlers were surprised and pleased by the arrival among them of the Rev Duncan Moody. He was born at Kilmailie, on the banks of Locheil, in 1808, and was educated for the ministry at Glasgow, whither his people had removed. On the completion of his studies he was urged by his older brother, Charles, to go to the East Indies as a missionary, but, on his dying from cholera, he followed his own inclination of going to Canada. He arrived at Montreal in the summer of 1832 and at once waited on Dr Mathieson, who had been at college with his brother. The doctor told him there were several openings, but that Dundee had a special claim upon him, seeing he could preach in Gaelic. He journeyed to Salmon river and met with a hearty welcome, a call being signed by nearly every Protestant in the township. On the 31st October the

Quebec Presbytery ordered his ordination and induction, which took place on the 28th December. The people were too poor to build a church and even if they had been able, it would have been of little service, for the roads were such that they were rarely fit for travel. He arranged to preach regularly at 4 stations—the lines, in the Skye and Aubrey schoolhouses, and at Laguerre, with occasional services in private houses. A kirk-session was formed March 21, 1833, and its first regular meeting was held in the house of Malcolm Smith, 3rd concession, on July 16, with the minister as moderator and James Fraser and Donald McFarlane as elders. In many ways James Fraser was an example of what an elder ought to be, and his influence was felt in Dundee long after he was laid to rest. In all difficulties that arose his advice was sought, and he was the means of settling many a dispute and of maintaining that harmony which is so grateful in a community. He was the originator of a Sunday-school in his neighborhood, maintained a prayer-meeting, and did much otherwise towards promoting a living-faith among his fellowmen. Mr Moody boarded at Dundee village and continued to do so after his marriage with Miss Farlinger until 1837, when he bought lot 12, 4th range. Mrs Moody says:

The township was well settled in 1837 but the people were very poor, so much so that when any of them would offer money to my husband, he, knowing their circumstances, would say, "Keep it for your children." Our lot had hardly any clearance on it, and the people were very kind in giving their assistance. My husband had only to mention that there was work to be done, and in the morning, a number would be at the door. "We have come," they would say, "to do so-and-so to-day, Mrs Moody; but we have had no breakfast." My father gave me a horse and 3 cows. Mr Moody being city-bred knew nothing about farming, and when he wanted the horse I had to harness it. He could make little use of the animal in his rounds, for the roads, except in the driest times or in winter, were only passable on foot. It was a day's journey for my husband to go to the Fort and back. He made his pastoral journeys on foot, and often had to sit on a log, take off his boots, and pour the water out of them. The journey to Laguerre he found the most fatiguing and on coming in he would often remark that he had felt so exhausted that he would have been thankful had any of us gone to meet him with a crust. Although the settlers were poor, there was no actual privation among them. There were very few Irish in the neighborhood of St Agnes when we came to live here; they moved in gradually, buying out the Highlanders.

The building of a church was begun in 1839 on lot 8, 2nd concession. It was a plain, frame building, and all the congregation was able to do was to enclose it. The seats were slabs laid on four water-beech legs, and the only one that had a back was the pew for the minister's family. The pulpit, which was high, had a canopy after the old-fashion in Scotland, and the precentor's box was set in front. In the forenoon the service was in Gaelic, the English in the afternoon, and both extremely long, which was rather trying where the seats were so contrived that they neither supported the back nor rendered a few winks possible. Books being scarce, the precentor read the psalms two lines at a time, which he did in a droning tone, so as to retain the run of the tune. The sacrament was administered once a year and was a season of great importance and solemnity. The services, in which Mr Moody was assisted by neighboring ministers, began on Thursday and did not close until Tuesday. Family worship was common in the township and on the catechising of the children great stress was laid. Before Mr Moody's death a sufficient sum was raised to plaster the church and put in pews. To the last he was no burden to his people, who gave little beyond presents of produce and aiding in bees. His modest wants were met by his farm and the small allowance from the clergy reserves. He died in 1855, and it can be said of him, that he did more to recommend the gospel to his people by his daily life than by his preaching.

Long before it had a minister, Dundee had a physician, and a well-educated one, in Dr John McGibbon. He was a graduate of Glasgow college, had made several voyages in a whaler, came to Canada, resided some time at Cornwall, and in 1824 moved over to lot 16, B. F., adding afterward several adjoining lots. The land he selected was wet and hard to manage, and in redeeming it he underwent much hardship.

His practice yielded him next to nothing. He was early appointed a justice of peace and agent for the lands owned by Ellice, and, as will be recorded in its place, took a prominent part in suppressing the rebellion of 1837-8. As showing the value of land when he came, it may be stated he bought a lot from Dupuis for a cow.

NOTE.—The following is a list of leases granted up to 1838. The date of lease does not always correspond with that of settlement, many lessees having lived on their lots some time before getting deeds and others delaying going on them after receiving leases, while a few resold without doing settlement duties. Where lots are passed the record has been lost or the leases are recent. Remarkable to say the government has not a complete list of the leases granted :

Lot.   1st Concession.
3 Angus McGillis 1819
5 Ronald McDonald 1819
6 Angus McDonald 1819
7 Norman McDonald 1819
8 William McPhee 1819
9 John Seaton 1819
10 Louis & Norbert Dupuis 1819
11 Antoine & Joseph Dupuis 1819
12 Benjamin Phillips 1819
13, 14 & 15 Robert Colquhoun 1821
16 & 17 John McGibbon 1819
18 & 19 John Handley 1819
20 & 21 Horatio Brunson 1819
27 Richard Fitzpatrick 1819
28 Henry Jackson 1819
30 Jonas Schryer 1819
30 Nicholas Farlinger 1819
32 & 33 Henry C. Bagley 1821
34 John Moore 1818

2nd Concession.
3 Duncan McMillan 1821
4 Donald McKinnon 1819
5 Dougald McKinnon 1819
7 William Frazer 1820
8 Murdoch McAuley 1819

14 Farquhar McLennan 1819
15 Farquhar McRae 1819
16 Alexander McRae 1819
19 Alexander Gardiner 1821
20 Jacob Aubrey 1819
24 Aaron Foster 1821
25 Henry C. Bagley 1821

3rd Concession.
5 & 8 Donald & Dougald McKinnon 1819
9 Finley McRae 1819
14 Murdoch McRae 1819
15 { Patrick Timmons } 1819
   { Patrick Garrity }
16 Donald McFarlane 1819
17 John Seaton 1819
19 Hiram Stockweather 1823
20, 21 & 22 James Curran 1821

4th Concession.
3 John Cameron 1821
5 Thomas Cross 1821
6 & 7 Allan Cameron 1824
8 Daniel O'Hare 1819
9 John Derry 1819
10 Francis Logan 1819
11 John Miller 1821
12 Duncan Moody
13 William Miller 1819
14 Samuel Miller 1821

15 Samuel Miller 1837
16   do   do   1822
17 John McRae 1821
18 Rufus Campbell 1819
19 & 20 James O'Brien 1821
  5th Concession.
  6 Oliver Classon 1821
  7 William Aubrey 1819
11 Malcolm Smith 1821
12 Moses Miller 1821
  7th and 8th Concession.
5 & 6 David Thompson 1819
  Broken Front.
26 Patrick Benson 1819
27 John Ashburn 1819
29 Jonas Schryer 1819
B, C, D & N John Davidson
  1819
A John Silver 1823
2 marsh lots, Lucy Brunson
  1821
Gardiner's Island, Angus
  Campbell 1819
Marsh Island, Amable Casinet
  1819

Sucker Island, Jacob Hollen-
  beck 1821
L Angus Plamondon 1821
I William Ross 1825
  Bittern Island.
1 Hyp. E. dit Perikier
Utley farm, Henry Utley 1825
2 Duncan Gillis 1820
3 Alexander Campbell 1820
7 Robert Colquhoun 1819
8 George Truax 1819
  Petite Chenail.
4 John Lamasney 1819
5 George Truax 1819
6 Patrick Gallagher 1819
8 Isaac Leclair 1818
10 William Empey 1820
11 James Summers 1820
12 Donald Grant 1820
13 John Grant 1820
  Village of Dundee.
1 George B. R. Gove 1821
2 Patrick Buchanan 1828
3 James Peck 1821
5 & 6 John Silver 1821

CHAPTER X.

ST. ANICET.

UNTIL the hapless Dalhousie settlement came into existence, the only habitations in that portion of Godmanchester township now known as the parish of St Anicet, were those of some dozen French Canadians on the lakeshore. The most easterly was Genier, and from his shanty paltry clearances occurred at intervals until Moquin's bay was reached. None of them paid attention to farming, their dependence being placed upon lumbering, so that their clearances were simply patches for corn and potatoes.* St Amour, by trade a blacksmith, came alone and squatted where the Catholic church stands. He kept two large black dogs and was suspicious of strangers. It was understood that he had fled from his native place, near Quebec, on committing some crime, and lived in dread of those he had injured coming to take vengeance upon him. After leading the life of a hermit for a number of years he went back to his native-place on learning that it was safe for him to do so. Out of sight of the lake there was only one settler, Antoine Bouthillier, who had received a grant of the land west of the Laguerre, and who lived in a house on the high bank of that river a short distance above its mouth.

The record of the first English-speaking settlement has been given in chapter 8. The second was begun in the fall of 1820, when Duncan McNicol crossed from Glengarry, where he had landed the year before, and squatted on 56,

---

* Their order, as near as I can ascertain, was, Genier lot 26, L'Ecuyer 27, Chretien 28, Delorme 32, J. Bpte. Caza 35, St Amour and Cartier on point where St Anicet village is built, Bercier 39, Quenneville 41, Saucier 42, Desvoyans 47, Dupuis 48, Cascagnette 50, Moquin 51, and Joseph Caza 52.

supposing it to be crown land, but afterwards learned it was part of a thousand-acre grant to deSalaberry. He soon had for neighbor Duncan Stewart, and the following spring, while the ice was good, three brothers of the name of McMillan, who had emigrated from Lochaber in 1819. Duncan, the last survivor of those who came out, and who was known better as "Torramore," said :

My father was working as gardener for Sir John Johnston at St Andrews when we heard of government land being thrown open in Huntingdon, and we crossed on the ice, bringing 3 cows with us, for which we found plenty of feed in the marsh hay, which then grew high enough to hide an ox. We put up a shanty, roofed with split basswood slabs, and hoed in potatoes and corn among the ashes of the little clearance we made, which yielded wonderfully, so that after that fall we had to buy little provisions. There was a lumber-road to Trout river, but no settlers off the lake. Lumbering was in full blast and the finest cedars I ever saw were taken out of the Beaver, as we called the swamp east of Dupuis' corners, many being $2\frac{1}{2}$ feet thick at the butt and straight as an arrow. The oak was all gone, but the pine was no more than touched. We all went into lumbering, which was an injury to us, and we would have done better to have stuck to our land. We rafted a good deal of cord-wood to Montreal, and I have stayed there a fortnight with a raft before I got it all sold. The price ranged from $2.50 to $4 per cord for maple, according to the supply. It cost so much for help to run the rapids and took so much time, that it seldom paid us. The only produce that brought money was potash. For the best, we got half money and half trade. For inferior, the storekeeper would pay only in goods. Our grist we took by canoe to Williamstown, or by canoe or on our backs to Fort Covington. In going by water to the Fort, we were subject to be detained by storms, and often had, in the spring and fall, to put in to some island and wait for one or two days for the lake to go down. I have known settlers to be thus caught without food and sleeping in the wet grass. Very often the grist got injured by the waves. Mrs Alex. Grant (lot 11) was the first to be buried on lot 12 and Benjamin Phillips was the second. The bit of land belonged to the Broken Front and the Indians gave a deed of it for a burial-place. The great fires of 1825 did not do damage west of the plank-road. All the land we and our neighbors had squatted on, proved to have been granted, mostly to French

Canadians who had served as officers in 1812, and we had to pay them for it, which we found hard, although they gave us easy terms.

In 1822 this settlement got an important addition in Donald Rankin, who came from Argyleshire with a large family of sons, who have many descendants. One of the sons opened a store, but the situation was not favorable for business. Like Dundee, the nature of the country was such that to make roads was beyond the ability of the settlers and the government would give no assistance. The chief means of communication was the lake with its numerous creeks, up which canoes penetrated distances which their present dimensions make incredible. Of the early settlers of St Anicet and Dundee it may be truly said the canoe was their waggon. As the largest of its streams, and with branches which traversed the country east and west, the Laguerre naturally became the centre of trade. Near the mouth of it, on the east bank, a French Canadian, Fortier, set up a blacksmith shop, and to reach him from the other side customers had to swim their horses. Alexander McBain, whose people lived on the north side of the lake, visited the Laguerre in search of timber limits, and in 1820 took out several rafts, and continued to lumber each winter thereafter. The canal-like reaches of the river, which with its branches penetrated a tract of country that could not otherwise be reached save when winter hardened the swamps they drained, were so many roads provided by nature, and McBain perceived the advantages they offered not only for lumbering but for trading. The lands along Trout river were filling up fast, and the Laguerre was the natural outlet for the back country to the south of it. Colonel Davidson also perceived the encouragement there was to commence business on the Laguerre and assisted his brother-in-law, Alexander Ogilvie, to open a store on its banks. The land along the west bank was owned by Bouthillier, who had inherited it from his father, who had received it for military service. A lot was bought from him where the west branch flows into the parent stream, and here Ogilvie built his store. He was the son of a Dundee manufacturer, had left Scotland in 1820, and clerked with Colonel Davidson, so acquiring a knowledge of storekeeping. Shaw, an American, who had squatted on the Ridge-road, agreed to put up the necessary buildings, and raised a store, dwelling-house, and ashery, with a wharf, part of which can still be traced. He was a handy man and did the work without a single bee, his only help being his son and a yoke of oxen. When Ogilvie took possession, the place was solitary enough, there being only one neighbor, a French Canadian, who had squatted on the opposite bank, named Monroi. Bouthillier's shanty was near the mouth of the river, where the site of his garden is marked by aged apple-trees. There was a foot-track to Huntingdon and a sort of a road that angled along the ridges to Dundee, over which oxen could struggle in a dry season, but which was little used, communication by water being so much more easy. Recognizing that connection with Trout river was essential to his prosperity, he engaged Shaw to cut out an ox-track to the Ridge, where it connected with the one that led to Trout river. The first immigrants to settle near him were John Harvey and William Brodie, Lowland Scotchmen, who went on to 42 and 43, 2nd range, which they reached by blazed tracks from his store. Both were industrious men, and Brodie was the first in the township to have a field entirely clear of stumps.

In 1823 Lalanne laid out the south end of lot 35, facing the concession-line into a village, which he named Godmanchester. The lots were issued in 1824 to whoever would pay $2.70 per half acre lot. Part of these McBain had pre-empted, and in the fall of 1823 built a store. Immigrants were now arriving weekly, seeking by the Laguerre a way across to Trout river and Elgin, but, so far, none had sought homes near its banks. McBain was now the means of inducing several to come, and the best description I can give is in the words of John McPherson :

We belonged to Strathspey and with a number of neighbors left in the spring of 1823. We embarked on the Monarch at Fort William, which sailed round to Tobermory and lay there for a fortnight, for the remainder of those who had engaged passage. The price of tickets was $25, and the ship provided rations. In other 6 weeks we arrived at Quebec. Our intention was to settle in Glengarry, and we made our way to Lachine, where there was a great number of Durham boats, loading and unloading. Our baggage was carefully weighed, and the charge was 50 cents the hundred-weight. It took the boat 10 days to reach Lancaster. We were detained off Ile Perrot by a head wind, but the length of the passage was mainly due to the difficulty in poling and towing the boat up the rapids. There were 8 men and the captain, four to each side with poles, and as the boat was overcrowded, it was a wonder none of the children were knocked overboard. At the foot of the first rapid, a number of us got out, we being told we could get in at the village above, which, they said, was only two or three miles away. But we found it a weary journey, and when we got there, not a sign of the boat, and it was next day before she arrived, the rapids having been extra difficult to overcome. We bought bread from the habitants, and I recollect one of the passengers on coming out with a black loaf being asked what it was, answering, "They told me it was bread." Ill-looking as it was, we were glad of it. Well, we were landed at last at Lancaster and my father, whose first name was Donald, and others went out to look for land and were disappointed, for the lots that were not taken up were either very wet or stony. Hearing there was land at Beaudette,* he walked to that place but found that all the vacant lots were swimming in water. While there he met McBain, who suggested to him to cross the lake to Huntingdon, and, on his persuasion, got into his wherry, for he was about starting for Laguerre. He led him to the land west of where he was erecting his store, and advised him to squat on it, saying he believed it was still owned by the crown. He did so, and began to raise a shanty on 37, second range of 1st concession, and that fall, when the ice was forming, the family moved over, and we were not alone, for four others of our fellow-passengers came also and settled beside us, namely, William Campbell, who was a shoemaker and who was going to work for McBain, on lot 36, John Grant, also a blacksmith, on 38, and another blacksmith, Angus McIntosh, on the west half of

---

*In an old map, this is given as Baudet, the French word for monkey. It is curious if that is the original word and that it came to be corrupted into Beaudette, which signifies nothing, so far as I am aware.

38, and with Wm. Campbell stayed Alex. McDonald, a shoemaker, who took up the other half of lot 39. There were no
roads and the paths that led from the landing-place on the
river to our shanties we blazed with the axe; during the first
year, we often lost ourselves. It was a hard winter for all of
us, being new to the country and having to carry all our provisions from the Glengarry side. One day, towards spring,
my father with McDonald and McIntosh went over for
potatoes, and on returning found the crack had so widened
that they could not jump it with the bags on their back.
McIntosh pitched his own and father's to the other side and
offered to do the same with McDonald's, who, however,
thought he could fling it himself; he did so, and it landed
partly in the water. Well, they fished it out, and before they
got to their journey's end, that bagful was frozen. So little
did any of us know about chopping, that a tree my father
felled came crashing down on our shanty, and had the basswood scoops that formed the roof not been strong, it would
have done damage. Because it was so easy to chop and split,
we preferred basswood for firewood, leaving the beech and
maple, and had poor fires in consequence. By spring we had
a good clearance, and got in corn and potatoes with some
wheat. That summer we bought a cow from McBain. It
was curious how animals were brought across the lake in
canoes. Two canoes were lashed together, and the forelegs
were in one and the hindlegs in the other. If it came on to
blow, cattle would not balance themselves, but horses would.
I only know of one instance of a cow being brought over in
a single canoe. One of the Cazas did it, and charged a dollar.
Any of the habitants on the lakeshore would ferry a passenger over for 50 cents. We cut hay for the cow on the
Beaver, and carried it two miles in bundles on our backs. We
had a good crop that fall, and never wanted for food thereafter, and the only time of scarcity was in 1836, when early
frosts prevented the grain ripening, so that, the following
summer, oatmeal was not to be had, and I travelled to
Huntingdon and Dewittville and as far as several miles
below Ormstown before I could find anybody who had a
quintal to sell. We got William Breaky, who had settled
on part of lot 28, 2nd con., and the only one near us who had
a yoke of oxen, to come occasionally to help to log and break
up the ground, and I may tell you that oxen will not drag
more land in a day than a bushel will sow. The country was
so wet between our place and Breaky's that it was a day's
journey for him to reach us, and he had himself to carry

the yoke in crossing the swamp between the hill and the river. By-and-by we managed to get a pair of steers, and when they grew to be oxen we counted ourselves rich, for then we made great progress in clearing the land. We made a good deal of blacksalts, and that was our only way of getting money. We went to mill by canoe to Fort Covington, and if the weather was not favorable, it would be a week before we got back; sleeping on the islands and bringing back the bags wet on the outside from the spray of the waves. Old Kerr, the baker, used to say we left with flour and brought back dough. With our neighbors we had a share in a large canoe, which would carry ten hundredweight. The bush was so thick and high that we never knew when there was a storm except by the sound in the tree-tops, and often we have gone down the river anticipating no trouble, to find, when we left the mouth, that the waves were chasing each other on the lake. Our first school was in Grant's house, Mrs Grant being the teacher. After that we managed to get a schoolhouse built, when Robert E. King, who had been a clerk with McBain and was well qualified in every way except his habits, taught. The Rev John McKenzie of Glengarry visited our settlement, baptizing and marrying as was required. It turned out that the land we had settled upon had been conceded to the Hon Mr deBoucherville, and we had to pay him for it.

The nationality of the first settlers determined the character of the settlement, which became an almost exclusively Highland one. Angus McPherson adds many interesting details:

My father belonged to Invernessshire, and sailed for Canada in 1826. He took up lot 39, for which he paid $2.50 an acre to Colonel deRouville, who claimed a large tract. Like our neighbors we built our shanty on the front of the lot, but finding it wet and unpleasant my father raised another on the ridge, and, in course of time, his neighbors to the east of him did likewise, and it came to be known as the Scotch or Highland ridge. There was a good deal of fever and ague in those days and the storekeepers sold quite a quantity of quinine. There was much in Canada that struck the settlers with surprise, and they, coming from where game-laws were strictly enforced, wondered to see men freely fishing, and shooting deer and partridge at pleasure. My mother had never seen a snake until she came here and the first warm night, when the air was filled with sparks, she was greatly alarmed, thinking it was raining fire, and could not believe the spectacle was due to flies. Knowing no better, my father, on cutting up the trees, dragged the pieces with a rope to the house, and continued to do so until a neighbor showed him how to construct a handsled. It was a long while before my father got a yoke of oxen, and until he did, Breaky would come with his, receiving payment in day's work in return on his own farm. During the first winter, my father had occasion to be away one night and before leaving forgot to show my mother how to heap the ashes and keep a gathering-coal for the morning. She thought she left it as usual, but, on rising on the morning, found the fire had burned out. There were no matches in those days and there was no flint and steel in the house, and it was too far to go through the snow to the next house. So she went back to bed to keep warm and remained in it until father came. He took down the musket he had brought with him from Scotland, and pouring some powder on the pan and placing a bit of punk in it, drew the trigger, and secured the means of restoring the fire. To take our first grist to mill, my father gave a blanket to a Canadian, who hauled it in his traineau through the woods to Fort Covington and back again. Our shanty was so buried in the bush, that in chopping a tree in front of it, it fell differently from the direction my father expected, and crashed against the door, which it forced open and the tree-top lodged on the shanty-floor, giving my mother a fright. There were wild beasts around us, and we lost a 3-year old heifer, which was found dead, with the marks of a bear's claws in its torn back. There was a clearing on the top of a knoll on our lot, in which, on hoeing in corn and potatoes, we found bits of pottery, shells, and arrowheads, leading us to suppose that Indians had once had a camp there. As no bones were found, it could not have been a burial-place. Among the settlers we had a poet, Wm. McEdward, who lived a little west of us, and who came in 1830. He had been a shepherd in Scotland and his education was limited to the ability to read print, so he composed his verses mentally and then dictated them to someone who could write Gaelic. In 1836 he went to Montreal to have the poems of Peter Grant and Dougald Buchanan, copies of which he had brought with him, reprinted, and added 17 hymns of his own, one of which has Canada for its subject, and is devoted mainly to reproving the laxity with which its people keep the Sabbath and the like. When he came back with the book he was thin and pale, and his friends believed he had denied himself in the city to make ends meet. The book was printed by J. Starke & Co. in 1836, and the edition was disposed of by the poet's travelling far and near among his kindred Celts, he realizing sufficient to pay off the balance due on his farm. McEdward sang his own hymns, and as he had a soft, sweet voice, it was pleasant to hear him. He always wore, winter and summer, a Scotch bonnet, and a hoop was slipped into the crown to extend it to shade his eyes in summer. When the weather required it, he enveloped himself in a large Rob Roy plaid. He never worked much but went about among the neighbors a good deal, and was a capital story-teller, delighting to relate ghost and fairy tales. When, at the end of one, he would be asked "Is it true?" he would reply, "Weel, weel, I don't know; I just tell it you the way I heard it." His visits were other than social however. He was a Baptist and of a pious spirit, and never failed to visit those who suffered under sickness or other trial, and his prayers were devout and earnest. His ideas of Sabbath observance were very strict. Thus one day he saw a settler come into church with a fine new blue bonnet of genuine Scotch shape. To have asked him where he had bought his cap would have been to violate the Sabbath, so he refrained, and next day walked 5 miles to get the desired information, which resulted in his renewing his headgear. His daughter married John Campbell, who had been a fisherman in Scotland, and who lived on lot 60, 1st range, who was also a Baptist and travelled about a good deal, preaching when he found opportunity. He went as far in his trips as Hemingford. His sermons were very tiresome. McEdward one day was complaining of the laziness of his son-in-law, remarking that fishermen were always lazy. "Ay, and shepherds too," caustically rejoined his neighbor. The poet died in 1856 when 80 years of age and is buried in Laguerre churchyard. Campbell moved to Michigan three years afterwards.

The hamlet at Laguerre, which was the centre of this and the other settlements adjoining, promised during its early years to become a village. Ogilvie and McBain employed many men in their asheries and in lumbering, and blacksmiths, coopers, shoemakers and other tradesmen gathered around them. All winter the country presented a busy scene from the teams hauling timber and cordwood to the river-bank and the oxsleds of settlers, many of whom came from a considerable distance, with black salts and potash to exchange for store goods. When the ice left, the river was so full of rafts that canoes had difficulty in picking their way, and bateaux came in from Montreal with goods and later on in the season, with immigrants. The trade in ashes was large and remunerative, as may be judged when Ogilvie averaged 250 barrels each season, and pearled 50 barrels. McBain did as large a business in ashes, although he directed his attention mainly to lumbering. On the flats along the river he cut a great quantity of oak and pine, immense lots of masts, oars, and flatted timber of all sorts. The bateaux could not take full loads from the wharves owing to the sandbar at the mouth, so the balance of their lading was sent off to them in another boat. The freight to Montreal was $1 the barrel of potash.

An interesting subject connected with the early days of the district, is that of prices. Up to 1835, when the supply began to be exhausted, the great article of export was timber. What was most sought for was masts and oars, and as the woods were plundered of these, square timber grew in importance. The mast-trade was exceedingly profitable, and as the price was in proportion to the length, exertions were made to get them out of the woods without trimming. To this end, mast-roads were formed, and of these there were two of such length that they led from the lake to the 4th range. The oldest ran back by where Cazaville now is, and after it had ceased to be needed for lumbering, was used as an ordinary road, so that when the side-line between 48 and 49 was opened, Castagenet had difficulty in getting people, who preferred the old to the new road, to cease trespassing on his lot. A little to the east of this road, Bagg & Waite cut out another which angled across the country to the west-branch of the Laguerre. It passed over several hills, one so steep that a rope was attached to the mast and given a turn round a beech tree, and two men paid it off to let the mast go down gradually. One day the rope snapped, when the nigh team were rendered unfit for further service. After that a chain was used. The sled that bore up the head of these masts, was so massive that, by itself, it was as much as a yoke of oxen could draw. With 20 horses, or as many oxen, attached to a mast, and with many men, the noise made the woods ring, and they could be heard long before they hove in sight. Of one white-pine mast, got out for McBain, a memorandum has been preserved It was 84 feet long, 25 inches at the butt and 18 at the small end. The average price settlers received for delivering pine at the stump was $20, and rock elm $25, paid in goods. It was worth as much more if delivered on the rafting-ground. White-ash oars, from 15 to 19 feet long, $4\frac{1}{2}$ inches square at one end and 2 at the other, and 6 inches wide at the blade, averaged 80 cents a pair. Cordwood was almost given away. The most of the maple on the Scotch-ridge was sold standing at $12\frac{1}{2}$ cents a cord to French Canadians, who rafted it to the city, and as late as 1834 it was only worth 15c. Delivered at Laguerre it was worth $1 a cord. Ashes seldom went below $12\frac{1}{2}$c the bushel.

The growth of the place suggested the building of a church and a knoll on the east side of the river was selected. Ogilvie offered to give the lumber on condition that the others paid him in ashes and farm-produce for the labor. He put up the frame and piled beside it the boards he had brought from Dundee, but the settlers were inert and nothing more was done, the frame standing until blown down. The knoll, however, was utilized as a place of burial. A negro, known by the name of Cyrus, on returning in a canoe with John Bartly from Dundee, was drowned near the place of landing and was buried there. Soon after a Mrs McManus died, it was supposed of ship-fever, and the woman who had attended her, Mrs Duhême, had the body hurriedly committed to the same place. Some time after, Mrs Duhême alleged that on going to milk her cow in the pasture one evening, the ghost of Mrs McManus appeared and reproached her for placing her body in unconsecrated ground. Next day, Mrs Duhême got men to exhume the body and placing the coffin in her canoe took it to the burial-place at Caza's point. The third body to find a resting-place was that of William, father of Angus McPherson, who passed away, at a good age, in May, 1828. The change that came over the place ere long postponed the project of building a church, and it was not until 1847 that work was begun on the church that now stands, and which was completed about 1850.

The school alluded to by John McPherson as the first built, was erected in the village during the summer of 1829, and that winter, Robert King, who had been a clerk with McBain for a number of years, engaged as master, the rate of fees to be 25c per month for reading, 12½c extra each for writing and ciphering; "grammar and book-keeping to be paid for as may be agreed for with the schoolmaster." The trustees, the three leading men of the place, Ogilvie, McBain, and L. Duhême, undertook to see that the agreed number of scholars attended, that the fees were collected, and fuel provided. Doubtless they had to advance the fees and take them out in trade from the parents, for money was not in circulation. Thus in 1835 we find Ogilvie arranging with the farmers to pay at the rate of a bushel of corn per scholar for a winter's schooling of 155 days, the corn being valued at 70c a bushel. This reduction in fees is accounted for by the government's then contributing a grant of $80. The second signature to this list is that of John Kerr, a Greenock baker, who had to flee from his connection with the radicals, and was a passenger on the Alexander in her memorable voyage of 1820. After working a short time at St Johns, he took up lot 37, 2nd range.

An irreparable blow was dealt the place in July, 1830, by the death of McBain. He had gone to Quebec with timber, which he had sold well, and on his way back bought a boatload of goods for his store, which he accompanied. Leaving the boat at Coteau he was rowed home by his brothers, and joined his family in great spirits. It being Sunday, business was suspended, and after dinner, on his father and brothers preparing to go back, it was proposed that the family should accompany them as far as the lake. The day had been sultry and they had not gone far until it was seen a thunderstorm was approaching. They hauled up at Dr Fortune's, who was living in Bouthillier's old house, to wait until it passed over. While gathered in the sitting-room, McBain's father, who had been sitting at the window, rose, and asked his son to take his chair. He did so, and drew his eldest daughter on to his knee. A minute or so after, there was a vivid flash, followed by a stunning crash of thunder. When the occupants of the room recovered their sight after the dazzling light, they saw McBain and his daughter stretched on the floor. Their first impression was that he had fallen in a faint, but on loosening his clothes it was seen that the bolt had traversed his body, which quickly turned black. A steel watch-chain that he wore was conjectured to have conducted the fatal bolt. His daughter was prostrated for some time, but ultimately recovered. The sudden and entire suspension of his business and the removal of its leading-spirit, gave a blow to the embryo village from which it never rallied. After an interval of some two years, his widow married John MacDonald, who had come to Canada shortly before. He was a native of Alvie, Invernessshire, had seen much of the world, and was an excellent man of business. With indomitable energy and good management he did much to restore the prosperity of the place, and would have succeeded but for circumstances over which he had no control, and which will be noted presently. He lumbered and made both pot and pearl ashes on a large scale, shipping between four and five hundred barrels yearly on his own Durham boats. He had opposition in John Gibson, Baker & Buchanan, Alex. McDonald, J. B. Charlebois, and John Graham. Associated with his father-in-law, Colonel Davidson, he assisted in getting the road made from Huntingdon to Dundee, towards which a grant was made by government in 1831, on the report of grand-voyer deLery, who visited the county in October of that year. The contract for forming a crossway over the swamp on lot 32 was taken by David Hunter, and was long known as the Hunter road.

The constructing of this road was of great consequence to the settlement that had grown up to the east of it, and to which one of its first settlers, John Higgins, gave the appropriate name of Newfoundout, for it was, indeed, a new discovery in the labyrinth of swamps that surrounded it.

James Higgins was the first to move into it. He came from Limerick in 1826 and went to work on the Rideau canal, leaving his family in Glengarry. The second spring he took up part of lot 36 on the 3rd range of Godmanchester, which he soon left on finding it was claimed, and went on to 39, second range, where he was joined by several of his country-men, who, like himself, had a hard time of it. One spring there was great shortness of provisions, the boats being de-layed in making their first trip to the Laguerre from Mon-treal. One day, when there was not a mouthful of solid food in one of their houses, two Americans came who desired to cross the lake. Higgins conducted them to the lake-shore and ferried them over, and with the money they paid him he bought peas, which he shared on his return, and before they were done supplies had arrived. The record of the settlers in Newfoundout is simply a repetition of that of other portions of St Anicet—a contest with low-lying ground, hard to clear and worse to drain, with the added drawback of fever and ague. That affliction was almost unknown in other parts of the district, but in the Newfoundout settlement no family escaped. It was, however, of the mildest type, the tertiary, and yielded readily to treatment. As the land was brought into cultivation it disappeared. The shanties clustered closely on the ridge that runs across the lots, and the road naturally grew out of the track that was made from one door to the next, which accounts for its crookedness. On the ridge they grew corn and potatoes and depended on selling ashes and timber for money to buy other necessaries and pay for their lots, many of which were claimed by Ellice. The eastern end of the settlement was mainly occupied by Highlanders; the western by Irish Catholics; all living in a state of harmony and mutual helpfulness. The extreme eastern end of the concession was occupied in the days of Dalhousie settlement (page 158) and two brothers, John and Malcolm Currie from Cantyre, settled on lot 20 as early as 1824. They were followed by Archibald McMillan, Andrew McFarlane, John Sterling, Malcolm McLellan, Hugh McIntyre, Duncan Living-stone, and in 1830, by Peter McNaughton. In 1827 an event happened in the settlement which shocked the neighborhood. James Feeny, an Irish Catholic, well-known subsequently as a bailiff, had come in 1826. He had a bee, which was well attended, and towards the close of which, as the drink took effect, there was some quarreling. The day had been warm, and after all had left a thunderstorm, of unusual violence and continuance, burst. The night was so dark and wild, that few were able to reach their homes. James Macarthur (page 166) never reached his. Search was made in vain. Not a trace could be discovered and his disappearance was a mystery until, a number of years afterwards, a skeleton was found in the bush at the rear of the lake lots. From the brass buttons among the shreds of clothing there was no doubt about the remains being those of the missing man. Whether he had been murdered by a neighbor, whose violence was notorious and with whom he had words at the bee, or been killed by a tree falling upon him, was never ascertained.

The change which steam was working in the modes of transport, was quietly superseding the Laguerre as a port. Steamers began calling at St Anicet village and wharves near it, and trade was diverted to them, and Laguerre decayed with the Durham boat and the bateau, which alone could navigate its waters. The final blow to its prospects was dealt in 1849, when the dam at Valleyfield was completed. Low-lying at the best, the additional height of water overspread the flat on which the streets and square of Godmanchester had been laid out, and, one by one, the owners left, selling out to Mr MacDonald, until, from the road to the lake there was not a house left, and where once stood stores and dwellings, asheries and wharves, there now remains hardly a vestige, and what from 1822 to 1850 was a scene of activity and the chief business-centre of the county, is now pervaded by rural calmness and the river drifts sluggishly to the St Lawrence unfretted by the keels of the bateaux that once traversed it in quick succession and of the rafts that concealed it.

The village of St Anicet had no existence until the church was built and no trade until the Beauharnois canal was opened. Its site and the land in rear of it were held by deBoucherville. In 1823 he sold lot 37 to James Leslie, a mason, and his brothers and father joined him two years afterwards. They were from Badenoch, Scotland. The year after Leslie sat down by the lake, a hive of habitants was thrown off by the overcrowded seigniory of Berthier, who bought the land in Godmanchester owned by gentlemen in that vicinity. The newcomers sent back such good reports, that a furore arose, and French Canadians from Berthier and De l'Isle came crowding in, so that by 1826 all the unoccupied lots in the front ranges were taken up. With their advent, Father Lavallé, the missionary of St Regis, began to make regular visits, and held service in the houses of Dupuis, Caza, and others on the lakeshore, for in 1820 the bishop formed the western end of Huntingdon into the mission of St Anicet. Fathers Dufresne, Blyth, and Marceau kept these services up. On Caza's point were a few graves, where were buried those who died at a season when it was impossible to convey the bodies to a cemetery, for well on to 1830 it was the custom of both Irish and French Catholics to take their dead in canoes to Flanaghan's point, near Summerstown, or to St Regis. To remedy this, during a 40 hours' devotion, when several priests were in attendance, the burial-place at Caza's point, lot 35, was blessed and a large cross erected, and it was used until the church was built. In the spring of 1827 the bishop of Montreal issued a decree constituting Godmanchester a parish under the name of St Anicet, but no steps towards getting a church were taken until 1835, when subscription-lists were passed round and the contract given to John McIntosh and Baptiste Caza, who began to build it in 1837. The site chosen was the point on which the village now stands, although it had then only one resident, Bouthillier, who had removed from the Laguerre. In 1838 Edward Dupuis put up a house near him. The building of the church proceeded slowly and was not finished until 1840, when it stood a commodious and substantial stone-edifice of the ordinary design of those days. The priest appointed, and who came in 1835, Father Poirier, lived in the vestry until 1843, when a presbytere was provided. It deserves to be carefully noted, that no pretension was made at that time to the Church of Rome having power to levy either fabrique taxes or tithes in township lands. The parish constituted by the bishop in Godmanchester was merely a canonical parish, the church was built by voluntary contributions, and the salary of the priest was met in the same way, by subscription. When, in 1845, St Anicet was set off from Godmanchester, and constituted a distinct municipality, the proceedings were civil and wholly independent of ecclesiastical authority; indeed the limits of the municipality and of the parish were not the same. It was not until after 1850 that the hierarchy felt themselves in a position to extend French law to the free townships, and claim the power to tithe and tax in them and to initiate proceedings to cut them up and create parish-municipalities.—Once the St Anicet church was up, houses began to cluster round it. Dr Fortune built the third house and ended there his days. Joseph Parent opened the first store where the present church stands, and in 1841 Dr Masson came beside him. Parent built a wharf, and induced the Porcupine to call on her round trip, for she went from Montreal to Ottawa, thence by the Rideau canal to Kingston, and then back to Montreal by the St Lawrence. She was a small vessel with a high-pressure engine, and called regularly for two seasons. She was supplanted by the Rob Roy, which, plying between Montreal and Cornwall, made more frequent visits. Before Parent built his wharf, Delorme on lot 32 had erected one, at which the Highlander (brought to the lake in 1837 to convey troops) called a few times, without finding sufficient inducement to continue. The French had no school until 1834, when one was opened on 38 and a second was started on the Quesnel concession.

Having now given an outline of the manner in which the front rangés were settled, I turn to those in their rear, and as the opening up of the southern part of St Anicet and the northern of Godmanchester is due to Irish Catholics, I cannot do better than give the narrative of the oldest of them, Patrick Curran :

I was born in Kilkenny in 1798, and left Ireland in the spring of 1820 with a number of other emigrants for Newfoundland. When I reached St John I found that, owing to the large number who had come out that season, work was hard. to get. I got odd jobs on the wharves and remained until August, when I left in a trading schooner for Quebec, with the intention of going to my cousin James Curran, who lived then near the lines at Fort Covington, but shortly afterwards moved into Dundee. The journey from Quebec to Montreal I made in a small steamer, one of the two then running. From Montreal I started on foot. The Lachine canal had been begun and there had been trouble between the French and Irish laborers on it, ending in riots. I was told it would not be safe for me to go through the French country just then, when there was such a bitter feeling against the Irish, but I started, worked a while for a habitant near Coteau, shearing wheat, which I did not like as it was thistly, and reached McKie's point, when one of the famiiy agreed to cross me. There was a strong wind blowing down the lake, so that the canoe drifted as far as lot 7. I started at once to walk to Fort Covington, following the shore. For a long way there was not even a foot-track, but I came to one at last, and the first house I saw was Genier's. J. Bte. Caza ferried me over the Laguerre. The road, or track, followed the shore, going out to the points, so I passed St Amour's, saw his two big black dogs and his bit of clearance, which was planted with corn. I got to Joseph Caza's hut, which stood west of Moquin's, and stayed overnight. In the morning Mr Caza launched his canoe and conveyed me to the Fort and I joined my relative. I worked about the Fort for a year, when I resolved to take up land, and hearing that lots were going to be issued in Godmanchester I went with John Smyth, an Irish Catholic, who had been working at an ashery in the Fort, in December, 1821, and squatted on lot 44, 4th range, and spent the winter in making a clearance and some potash. There was not a road then in the township, only the tracks made by the lumbermen, who had just then begun to get out square timber. Up to then they had only taken masts, and the woods were not plundered. We worked hard, living by ourselves in a little shanty, with no neighbors, and before the snow left had two barrels of potash, which we drew to old Marsh at Fort Covington, and got $5 the cwt., or $40 the barrel. It paid good wages then to make potash. That summer (1822) Lalanne and his men stayed in our place while engaged in surveying the township into lots, and on Bowron's coming and being made agent I drew a location-ticket for 37 on the 5th range, but I did not go on to it. That summer Shaw and Force, both Americans, came to live on the Ridge and were followed by a number of their countrymen, until from Clyde's Corners to Lee's came to be known as the Yankee-ridge. They had no intention of staying, but just came to make potash and do something at lumbering. They went through the woods plundering the best of the timber. There might be about 30 families of Americans on the Ridge and near it. That winter I hired with Shaw who was getting out square timber, and in the spring of 1823 took up 38, 1st range, and went to live on it, afterwards moving to 33, 2nd range. The first time I passed where Laguerre village was laid out, there was just one hut, inhabited by a Canadian named Monroi. Alex. McBain had come in 1820 from Glengarry to begin lumbering, and two or three years afterwards he built a store where Monroi's house stood. I was married in June, 1823, and had to go to St Regis, where Father Lavallé performed the ceremony. The Irish came in strong every summer, especially between 1832 and 1836, filling up the back ranges, the French keeping near the lake. The first Irish settlers besides myself and Smyth, were Edward Walsh, Edward Smyth, William and Jas. Higgins, James and Michael Finnegan, Cornelius Daly, and the McGintys. They were from all parts of Ireland and most of them had worked on the Rideau canal. There was nothing else but Irish on what is known as the Irish ridge. They did not know then of the stones, but looked at the fine cut of timber for ashes and the dry soil. At the end of the 2nd range, several of the Irish who first came out lived for a while, the Higgins, John Murphy, William Sullivan, and Daniel Keefe, who had to move, from the land having been granted and those who held it asking more than they could pay. The great want of the country was roads, and for many years we had no other way of drawing anything than in woodshod sleds, or jumpers, dragged by oxen through the roads, to the Laguerre, where both McBain and Ogilvie had stores and asheries. I built a big canoe, that would hold 2 barrels of potash or take 50 bushels of grain to the mill at the Fort, and the custom of the settlers on the Ridge was to haul their ashes or grain as far as the creek (the east branch of the Laguerre) at my place, and take the one to the stores at Laguerre or the other to the mill. When a canoe could not be used, a bag of wheat was thrown across a horse's back and a way found through the woods by the blazes on the trees to the Fort. The first

road to be opened was one from Huntingdon to Laguerre, for
which the government gave a grant. That was in 1834.
Barlow had the contract for the portion between lots 32 and
33, and had to crossway the swampy portions. There were
two springs near O'Hare's corners that you could not pass
until that was done. The roads in Newfoundout and the
Irish ridge were not laid out, and grew from the tracks that
were naturally made between shanty and shanty, which
accounts for there being so crooked. There was splendid
pine all over, and I have seen masts 110 feet long and trees
that squared 32 inches. Our being near the St Lawrence
was an advantage to us, for it made the timber on our lots
be of value, and brought us in money we sorely needed. The
fire of 1825 did not do much damage to the growing timber.
It ran over about 30 acres on Castagenet's lot and burned deep
holes in the swamps, which are still to be seen, and the creek
went dry. Wild beasts were plentiful for over 20 years after
I came, and I shot from first to last a great many bears. The
largest one, I killed on lot 30, 3rd range. I heard one was in
the habit of jumping into an old log shanty in which a neighbor had stored his oats. I watched and when he came and
stood up scenting round before entering, I sent a ball clear
through him and carrying with it a streak of fat. He turned
on me quite fierce, and it took two more shots to kill him
He was rolling in fat. Deer were plentiful, and I ran down
with the dogs one winter 7. There were a few wolves.
James Higgins, I remember, shot one that had killed a
number of sheep. There was a good-sized beaver-meadow on
my lot, with the dams still remaining, but the beavers had
gone before I came. The meadow yielded hay, which was of
great service. I was the first settler to get a yoke of oxen,
which was in 1822, and their services being in great demand
I had to change work with my neighbors very often. It was
a long while before horses were of any use to us. The settlers
were often bare enough, but I never knew of anything like
want. They had always enough to eat. You may say the
land was at first cleared by whisky. It was bee after bee to
log and burn, and there was no bee without whisky, and after
the work was done, they would stay to talk and drink. The
bane of these times was whisky. It was about 1829 that the
first school was opened. The government gave a small grant,
with which an old log-house that stood on lot 31, 1st range,
was bought from James Higgins and another was put up on
lot 41, 3rd range, at the same time. The first teacher in
Higgins' school was a Scotchman named King, who was very

capable. He lived in the attic above the schoolroom, and there he died the first winter. He was succeeded by Finlay McPherson.

NOTE.—The following is a list of the first occupants of lots. Like the lists that will be appended to other chapters, it is only approximately correct, for it is compiled from the recollections of old settlers, there being no written data available. The omission of the names of French settlers is not through design. Repeated attempts in St Anicet and other parishes, demonstrated that, from the frequent changes and other causes, it was impossible to obtain of them the required information with anything like fulness or accuracy. I gratefully acknowledge the assistance given me by Mr John D. MacDonald of Laguerre in preparing this chapter. He is one of those who take a patriotic pride in the history of the country of their birth.

3RD RANGE.

20 Matthew Mathieson
Neil Mathieson
21 John Rankin
22 Thomas O'Leary
23 Terrence Quinn, jr.
24 Henry Thomson, a negro
25 Heny Jackson, a negro
26 Thomas R. Higgins
Peter Beauchêne, jr.
27 Michael Gaynor
28 Patrick Reardon
Timothy O'Ready
29 Dennis O'Connor
James O'Connor
30 James Higgins
John Mulverhill
31 James B. O'Connor
James Clyde
32 James O'Connor
Charles O'Connor
33 Murdoch McPherson
34 Thomas Glynn
34 Maurice O'Connor
35 Thomas O'Rielly
John Moriarty
36 Richard Savage
William Kelly

37 William O'Leary
Martin Curran
38 Patrick Finnigan
James Finnigan
39 Edward Walsh
Michael Griffin
40 Maurice Leehy
Thomas Leehy
41 Thomas Shane
Patrick Barrett
42 Thomas McGinnis
Bernard Cosgrove
43 W. & J. McGinnis
Thomas Gilassy
44 David McCarty
Allen Watson
45 William Watson
John Harvey
46 Jean B. Hart
Xavier Quenneville
47 Jere. Stowell, who sold to
Hugh Curran and
Samuel Clark
43 Samuel McNarland
William Hassan
49 John Doyle
Michael Moore
50 Moses Clark

2ND RANGE.

20 John Bartly
   Malcolm Currie
21 Bernard Bartly
   Richard Finn
22 Patrick Ferris
   Thomas Quinn
23 Archd McMillan
   Peter Qinn
24 Andrew McFarlane
   Dennis Sullivan
25 Peter McNaughton
   John Sterling
26 Malcolm McLellan
   John Currie
27 Peter Currie
   Hugh McIntyre
28 Duncan Livingstone
   John Breaky
29 Michael Quinn
   Terrence Quinn
30 Michael Kerby
   Lawrence Sullivan
31 John Higgins
   James Higgins
32 Richard Higgins
33 Leandre Duhême
   Patrick Curran
   Amable Charlebois
34 M. & P. Beauchêne
35 Theodore Caza
   Alexis Bray
36 John MacDonald
   Wm. and Thos. Gold
37 John Kerr
   Patrick Finnigan
40 Henry Thomas, a negro
   James McGauly
   William Smyth
41 John Sinclair
   William Sullivan
42 John Murphy
   Cornelius Daly
43 P. Shaughnessy
   Joseph Adams

44 William Brodie
   John Harvey
45 Edward Smyth
   William Alsopp
46 John Stewart
49 Duncan McIntosh
52 James Black
53 Andrew Thompson
   James Black
54 Alex. McLachlan
55 Angus McDonald
   Neil McGillis
56 Duncan McNicol
57 Donald McLean
58 John McLean
59 Dougald McLachlan
   John Loney
60 James D. Stewart
   Peter Stewart
61 Alex. Stewart

1ST RANGE.—DUNDEE ROAD.

36 Wm. Campbell James Leslie
37 John McPherson
38 John Grant
   Angus McIntosh
39 Alex. McDonald
   Angus McPherson
40 Alex. & Donald McGregor
41 William McEdward
   George Dupuis
42 Harvey Stowell
   Alex. Stewart
   "   & Colin McIntosh
44 Josiah Classon
   Ewen Cattanach
45 Amable & Francois Quesnel
56 Duncan McNicol
57 Donald McLean
58 Hugh McLean
   Alex. Cameron
59 Neil Ferguson
   Malcolm McLean
60 Hector McLean
   Neil Chisholm
61 Duncan Stewart

15

THE LAKE FRONT.

As regards the lots east of 20, the names given are those who succeeded the occupiers during the days of the Dalhousie settlement. (chap. 8). In a few instances, the lots west of 20 were held by squatters or tenants before those whose names are given, who were the first to make improvements as proprietors.

8 David Dourie
12 Wm. H. & Thomas Evatt*
13 James Feeny
14 William Macarthur†
   Thomas Brown
15 John Wiley
16 James Cluff
17 John McDonell
18 Malcolm Campbell
19 Finlay Campbell
   Donald Campbell
20 Thomas Kennedy
21 Donald McKillop
23 Archd. Cameron
24 Malcolm Stalker
   James McGowan
25 Duncan Rankin
   Dennis Martin
26 Honore Genier
27 David L'Ecuyer
28 John Ross
   Hugh Rankin
   Patrick Curran

29 The Chretien family
30 James Curran
   Donald McKenzie
31 Donald Livingstone
   Antoine Quesnel, who sold
     to Edward Chapman,
     who opened a tavern.
32 Amable Lemay, dit Delorme
   John Sinclair
33 John McIntosh
34 and 35 J. Bte. Caza
   Antoine Bouthillier and son
     Michael
36 John MacDonald
37 Peter Leslie
   John Leslie
38 Bouthilliers
39 Benj. Norbert Dupuis
40 Registe Belanger
   Benj. Bercier
41 Frs. Lajeunesse
   J. Bte. Paride dit Aubin
52 John Black
53 Donald Rankin
54 Alex. Roy Cameron
55 Peter McNicol
56 Donald McNicol
57 John, Peter, and Angus
     McMillan
58 Hugh McLean
   Alex. Cameron
59 John Ferguson
   John Campbell
60 Neil Chisholm
   Duncan Stewart

*They were the sons of an officer who sent them to Canada to make homes for themselves, and were intelligent and well-educated. They put up a sawmill driven by wind, and sold to James Tully, who came from Griffintown. He put an engine into the mill, which did not pay.

†By a slip of the pen, his name is given on page 202 as James, which was that of his brother, who succeeded him.

CHAPTER XI.

UNTIL the canal was opened, Beauharnois was the only village on the river-bank between Caughnawaga and St Regis. St Timothy consisted of a mill and a few houses ; Valleyfield had no existence. The traffic was all on the north bank, along which there was a continuous settlement, with several villages, larger and more prosperous then than they are now. The building of the canal and the growth of Valleyfield I will treat of further on. Beauharnois as a village may be said to date from 1820, when the bishop formed that portion of the seigniory that lies between the St Lawrence and the Chateaugay into a mission, named St Clement, and a church was begun. How meagrely populated the country was is evidenced by the register, for in the wide extent of it comprised in the mission there were only in

1820 - - 142 baptisms - - 26 marriages - - 63 deaths
1821 - 148   "   - 24   "   - 112   "
1822 - - 142   "   - - 16   "   - - 57   "

The cause of the large number of deaths in 1821 I have been unable to ascertain; probably it was due to smallpox, which periodically visited the parishes. The agent for the seigniory, Milne, made no effort to induce people to settle, and it does not appear that any lots were conceded in his time. Those who desired were allowed to take up lots and paid rent, but received no deeds. This was partly due to a legal doubt as to who had authority to act for the seigniory. One of the heirs, George, sailed in a ship for South America, which was never heard of, and a certain number of years had to pass before his estate could be administered. The other reason was the desire of the 3rd son, Edward, to have the tenure of the seigniory changed to free and common soccage, so that he could give purchasers absolute possession. The Imperial government in 1822 had passed an act giving power to seigniors to so commute the tenure, and Mr Ellice tried twice, in 1823 and 1826, to take advantage of the new law, but was baffled by the officials at Quebec, the whole sentiment in that city being against the destruction of the seigniorial system, and who raised all manner of technical objections. The grist-mill having fallen into a state of disrepair, Milne, in 1820, employed two immigrants, newly arrived from Scotland, to refit it, and those two men, Peter Macarthur and William Donaldson, became prominent in the district. They had intended going to Ontario and it illustrates the then travelling facilities, to state that Macarthur, as the quickest mode at the season when the roads were deep with mud, walked from Montreal to Kingston. While resting at Cornwall, he called to his companions to look out of the tavern window and see the mail, an ox-team yoked with beech-withe traces to a cart. Disappointed with the stony character of the country on the route, he returned to Montreal, where his two younger brothers, Daniel and Alexander, had hired out as shearers until he came back with his report. His employment by Milne decided their destination, they taking up farms on the Chateaugay. The fall (1820) was an exceedingly dry one, and on Macarthur's hurrying to Milne's house to inform him the mill was in danger of catching fire from the adjoining bush, he was told it would be no great loss, as it was about worn out and was insured. The machinery of the mill was very primitive, the power being derived from a wheel set in a chamber that had been hollowed out of the rock at the rapids and driven by the force of the current. After renewing the machinery, Macarthur built several mills for the seignior, putting up no fewer than four in the following eight years—Ste Martine, Howick, St Timothy, and Norton Creek. The renewal of the Beauharnois mill was Milne's last official act. He had been detected by Richardson, Forsythe & Co. in misappropriating funds, and retired to Ste Martine, where he led a disreputable and secluded life, losing the esteem even of his poorest neighbors, and on his death there was buried in

Georgetown churchyard, where he fills an unmarked grave. In June, 1821, the new agent, Lawrence George Brown, arrived. He was a member of a respectable Aberdeen-shire family and was of good education. When he visited Beauharnois, he found only two houses besides the manor-house and a church in course of construction, where the present stone-edifice rears its front. Arrangements were made* with Richardson, Forsythe & Co. to give up their agency, so that the entire management was vested in Brown. To assist him,† Robert H. Norval, who belonged to Fifeshire, arrived during the fall, and he was to keep the books, a set of which were opened with the year 1822. Brown's in-structions were to develop the resources of the seigniory and render it a source of profit. The first step in the new policy was to induce immigrants to settle, and to do this the land had to be surveyed. Charles Archambault was employed to conduct the new survey. He began on the Chateaugay, running anew the old lines and changed the numbers of the lots. Although deeds were refused, immigrants were readily granted permission to take up lots, a privilege of which a number freely availed themselves. Despairing of getting the tenure changed, Mr Ellice, in 1826, ordered Brown to grant deeds of concession, and by the end of 1827 20,000 acres had been conceded to 228 different persons. The terms differed slightly from those of the former deeds (page 36) in that there was no sliding-scale as to rent during the first years. The settler paid $10 for a location-ticket, sat rent free for three years, and after that paid $10 a year rent. The inability of Mr Ellice to sell the land was against its being taken up, for the immigrants had been mainly induced to cross the ocean in the hope of becoming owners of places of their own, and recoiled from the proposal to become

* It is probable that Mr Ellice made the transfer in person. He visited the province twice before his well-known visit in 1832.

† Brown had need of a secretary, for he wrote so vile a hand that he could not read his own manuscript when he forgot its subject.

tenants even on easy terms and with security of tenure. If the immigrants were shy about becoming censitaires, the habitants had no hesitation, and after some experience Brown preferred to deal with them, and he filled whole concessions with French which Ellice desired should be peopled with his own countrymen, for he looked forward to the time when one of his sons should go and live upon the seigniory.

The new policy, combined with the equally important innovation of steam navigation, caused Beauharnois to grow into a village. The first steamboat was the Perseverance, which plied between Lachine and Cascades, calling at Beauharnois or any other way-port when required. When she started I have been unable to ascertain, but she was certainly on the route in 1820, her chief business the conveyance of military stores for the fort at the Coteau and the passenger traffic with Ontario. With the exception of the road to Ste Martine and another that had been cut out from the Basin to St Timothy, there were no roads. In 1825 there were not over a score of houses, to which there were large additions made in that year. John Ross and William Becket came from Montreal and began business, and for the next score of years the only store worth speaking of was Ross's. A commodious manor-house was built on the east bank of the St Louis where it enters the lake, and an office alongside of it. The lot attached was reserved and in 1827 was used as a model-farm. Brown represented that the habitants succeeded poorly because of their ignorance of farming and contended that all they needed was to be shown how to do better. Operations were began on an extravagant scale and conducted in a still more wasteful manner, so that during the 14 years it was maintained it cost the seignior over $20,000. That it did some good is unquestionable, for there was a yearly distribution of young stock and seed-grain among the farmers. When Edward Ellice, the younger, visited Beauharnois in 1838 he pointed out that the farm could be of no advantage to the habitants; that the example it set was one to be shunned rather than imitated. In February, 1828, an agricultural society was organized, the inducement being a government grant of $200. Brown was appointed president, but the moving-spirit was the secretary, Mr Norval, who was an enthusiast in agricultural improvements, and who really carried on the work of the society for the next 20 years. Two shows were held, the first at Huntingdon, where $72 in prizes were awarded, and the second at the stone-tavern, Ste Martine, with $123 in prizes. On 12th October, 1829, a plowing-match took place on the farm of Jacques Forand, west of Ste Martine, when 7 Old Countrymen and 5 French Canadians entered. As the country became more thickly settled and the funds increased, the number of places where the shows were held were added to. About 1829 a weekly mail was secured, coming from Montreal by way of the Basin. Henry Bogue was postmaster. In that year St Clement ceased to be a mission and became a parish.

So slowly did the village grow, that, in 1832, it had only 300 inhabitants That summer was made memorable by the manner in which the cholera scourged it A steamer'touched at the wharf on its way to the Cascades, laden with immigrants, several of whom came ashore to buy milk. When she left, it became generally known there were cases of cholera on board. Next day the disease proclaimed itself, and for the ensuing fortnight its ravages were appalling. In one household, six took breakfast in apparent good health; before 8 in the evening, four were dead. Whole families perished, and the fatality was hardly less terrible than its suddenness. A lady noted a neighbor pass by to his own house, and a few hours afterwards saw a coffin carried to its door. She asked who it was for. It was for the neighbor she saw so short a time before. The dead were buried as they died, being put into rude coffins without preparation, and committed to the grave within a couple of hours of drawing their last breath. Amid the horrors of that awful fortnight, four men did honor to human nature. John Bryson, servant to Brown, and his coachman, Robert Finnie, (father of Dr Finnie of Montreal) with two Canadians* volun-

---

* I have been unable to recover their names.

tarily devoted themselves to attending the sick and burying
the dead, and were unwearied in their labors. Remarkable
to state, all four escaped the contagion. On the twelfth day
the mortality abated, and in a few days more the disease disappeared, after carrying to the grave 73, or one-fourth of the
total population—an unprecedented mortality. Afterwards,
to the mode of treatment adopted was ascribed much of the
excessive death-rate, the physician, Dr Fleming, insisting that
no liquids should be allowed. One patient, given up as lost,
in her intense thirst rose, in the absence of her attendants,
and finding in the kitchen a pan of water in which the dishes
had been washed, drank the greasy water as the most grateful draught she ever tasted, returned to bed and—recovered.
Dr Fleming, a young man who had arrived from Glasgow
a year or two before, was smitten by the contagion as it was
abating, and died. His body was prepared for the grave by
the two devoted men already named.

The year after this visitation a minister came, the Rev
Walter Roach. He was the son of an Edinburgh bookbinder,
was born in 1806, and after assisting his father in his trade,
was educated by him, at a great sacrifice, for the ministry.
He was licensed in 1832 and, there being no opening for him
in Scotland, early in the summer of 1833 landed in Canada.
The residents of the village having been long eager for a
minister, he visited Beauharnois and preached during July
and August, the seigniory-agent using his influence to form
a congregation and induce him to stay. Mr Roach was a
man of fine presence and agreeable in manners, but of ordinary ability; in the pulpit, loud and self-complacent. The
efforts put forth were successful, and, on the 1st December,
he was inducted as minister of Beauharnois, with a congregation composed of 14 heads of families, 36 adults and 39
children under 12. The following spring, work was begun
on a church, the corner-stone of which was laid by Brown on
the 23rd June, 1834. It was opened on the 15th March, 1835,
and was the finest Protestant church in the province outside
of Montreal. The entire cost was borne by Mr Ellice, who
retained the title of it until he disposed of the seigniory,

when he transferred it to the Presbyterian church of Canada. In those days, the English-speaking element predominated in influence if not in numbers in Beauharnois, and up to about 1850 it was essentially a Scotch village. The congregation grew until its attendance averaged 70, and it had a prosperous Sunday-school, which was started in 1835. The first collision with the incoming tide of French Canadians was in 1843, when the priest forbade the use of the Bible in the school. The Catholic ratepayers being in the majority, the Protestants had no redress, and withdrew. A site was given free and subscriptions were collected, of which $200 came from Montreal, to erect a school, which was opened and the education imparted within its walls was so superior to that of the older school, that a few Catholics dared the frown of their clergyman and sent their children to it. While Beauharnois had a common-school, it had several excellent teachers, among them being James Richardson, who subsequently distinguished himself on the geological survey.

The disruption proved a serious blow to the Beauharnois congregation, owing to so many of the families at Chateaugay Basin throwing in their lot with the Free Church, and Mr Roach found it useless to continue to hold service there, which he had done, on alternate Sundays, for 8 years. Thereafter he confined himself to Beauharnois and a charge he had established at St Louis de Gonzague. In 1849 his career abruptly closed. In the summer of that year cholera visited Canada for the third time and again scourged Beauharnois. Mr Roach was devoted in attending upon the sick. On the forenoon of the 27th August he entered the pulpit apparently in his usual health, and proceeded with the service in his customary manner. While in the midst of his sermon, his face suddenly grew ashy pale, and his voice faltered. Abruptly halting, he uttered the words, "We add no more," and repeating the Lord's prayer dismissed the congregation. After a brief rest in the vestry-room, he recovered so far as to be able to walk to his house, leaning upon a friend's arm. He had no pain and as he rallied from his fit of weakness, it was thought there was no danger. In the evening, however, he became worse, the dread disease developed itself in malignant form, and in a few hours the first duly inducted minister of the district had gone to his rest.

Beauharnois grew slowly, having no industry or traffic to attract population, and being simply the outlet for the surrounding country and a convenient place of supply. In 1848 it contained only 150 houses and 750 inhabitants. About that time grain-buying began, and under its stimulus Beauharnois knew its palmiest days. In 1826 Brown was appointed a commissioner for the trial of small causes, and held frequent courts until the office was abolished. The first judge to hold a court was McCord, who was appointed for this and the Missisquoi district in 1842.

In the chapter on Franklin further details will be given regarding the agents of the seigniory and their management.

CHAPTER XII.

CHATEAUGAY.

At the time when, in other parts of the district, the sound
of the settler's axe was only beginning to awake the
echoes, the seigniory of Chateaugay was showing signs of
decay. Every lot in it had been conceded by 1801, and along
the river there were in 1820 fields that had yielded 50 consecutive crops of wheat, and were lapsing into barrenness.
The outlet for the greater part of the lumber made in the
district, the place where the cribs were built into rafts, and
which took on their crews to run the Lachine rapids and to
make the voyage to Quebec, the Basin was a bustling place,
where much money was spent, where lumbermen were
always to be found in greater or less number—a place with
great stores of pork and biscuit and all manner of lumbermen's supplies. To regulate the trade, the legislature passed
an act in 1817, requiring all rafts coming down the St Lawrence to halt at the mouth of the Chateaugay, to be measured
and inspected, in order to see that their draft and strength
were sufficient to meet the strain of the Lachine rapids and
that they had a competent pilot and adequate crew. A small
fee was to be paid for each raft, the surplus, after defraying
the salary of the inspector, to go towards improving the
channel of the rapids, which was not done. The first inspector was James Milne, and who remained in office 5 years
His report for the first 3 years was—

	Rafts of Cordwood.	Fees 25c each.	Cribs of Lumber.	Fees 50c each.
1818	624	$156	910	$455
1819	480	120	1017	508
1820	468	117	613	306

All this, of course, did not come down the Chateaugay, but a
fair proportion did. Milne was also collector of customs, for

American goods and produce seem to have passed to Montreal during sleighing in considerable quantities; mostly
cattle, in all probability. In 1820 Milne reported that he
had collected duties on entries to the value of $60,000. In
1823 the office was abolished, the new collector at Coteau,
James Simpson, changing the system. William Dalton, an
Irishman, who had married a Canadian and opened a tavern
on the north side of the river, opposite the present steamboat
landing, succeeded Milne. In 1826 Arthur McDonald was
made inspector, the duties of which he delegated to Moses
Dalton. The rafts frequently formed a field in front of
Dalton's, with, perhaps, 200 lumbermen lounging about drinking. Fault was generally found by Dalton with the equipment, and as he kept oars and poles for sale, he made
something beyond his fee of $2. He took the draft of the rafts
and directed which channel was to be followed, none over a
certain draft being permitted to take the southern channel.
Extra hands and a pilot were hired; the latter was frequently
an Indian. It was rarely that a raft was wrecked in the
rapids, but injuries to the raftsmen were common. The chief
danger was to their feet, from the logs opening and closing
with the force of the waves. During the short period in the
spring when rafts could pass down the Chateaugay and its
tributaries, the Basin presented a busy scene. No sooner had
the ice moved, than the rafts appeared, and for a period that
varied from a week to a month, according as the weather
affected the height of the water, they continued to arrive.
As many as 500 raftsmen would be gathered at the Basin at
one time, and, being mainly young men, they celebrated the
close of their winter's work in modes that were not profitable
to themselves. When the last raft had left, the Basin relapsed
into its former dullness. Lumbering reached its height in
1825, after which it began to decline.

In 1823 two brothers, James and John Macdonald, sons of
the barrackmaster at Laprairie, opened a store and ashery on
the east bank, 5 miles from the Basin; and built up a business that brought in a fortune to John, who became its sole
owner. He was intelligent and well-educated, with polished

manners, and plausible of speech, and would have represented
the county in parliament had it not been for his unpopularity
arising from his grasping disposition.

Of the many hundreds of immigrants passing up the river
each season, none at first showed any disposition to settle at
the Basin, although there were plenty of habitants anxious to
sell, for the fate common fifty years ago to all old French
parishes had overtaken Chateaugay. Years of wretched
abuse of the soil had exhausted it, and its owners were
unable to wring from it even a bare subsistence. How
destructive of the fertility of the soil were the practices of
the habitants, until they learned better from the example of
the Old Countrymen, will hardly be now credited. The lots
in the seigniory of Chateaugay had been laid out 3 arpents
wide by 25 deep. The owner of a lot ran a rail-fence up the
centre, dividing it so far as his clearance extended. One-half
he cropped for two years, then he left it and cropped the
other-half for the same period. On the half that was not
plowed, he pastured his cattle, but as he did not seed it, grass
and clover seed being utterly unknown to him, the unfortunate animals got a sorry bite the first year, and needed all
the range of half the clearance to maintain life, upon which
the weeds were encouraged to grow to supplement the thin
fringe of grass. The cultivation of the portion cropped was
execrable. The plow was of the model their fathers had
brought from Normandy; a clumsy wooden implement that
hung between a pair of high wheels, which was drawn
generally by two yoke of oxen led by a pair of ponies. So
late as 1836 this style of plow was to be seen at work, with
a man guiding and another driving. The report of the Beauharnois agricultural society for 1829 notes with satisfaction
that the habitants were adopting the plow introduced by the
Scotch. The land was skimmed by the rude plow described,
which broke the upper-crust of it without rule or method.
No manure was used. An important bit of work for those
habitants whose dunghills had grown inconveniently large
during the winter, was to haul them on to the Chateaugay,
before the ice got weak, and let them float to the St Law-

rence. Pickles of different kinds of grain were sown alongside of each other, so that in the fall, when they were
ripening, the aspect was that of brilliant patchwork. The
chief grain sown was wheat. When the soil had grown so
exhausted that it was certain weeds would be more plentiful
than grain, wheat continued to be sown, for the habitant held
that it would be mistrusting Providence to sow anything else.
Wheat was the only kind of produce he had to sell. His
forefathers, when Louis was king, had exported wheat to
France, and he knew if he could get a bag or two to Montreal,
he would be paid its price in Mexican dollars to load the
brigs that sailed to the Clyde. Wheat always brought a
good price; rarely going below $1.20 the minot, and, as it did
in 1828 and 1836, rising as high as $2. To farm without
making wheat the leading crop was incomprehensible to the
habitant of that time, and he regarded the fields of potatoes
and turnips, of hay and oats, of the Scotch stranger with
amused wonderment. Livestock he had none to sell. He
had a hog or two for his own family-use, which he killed
after St Michael's day. To supply the wants of the town-
population and of the lumbermen pork was imported not
only from the United States and Ontario but from Great
Britain, and Irish pork topped the market. The report of
the Montreal agricultural society for 1821 declared it was a
shame that the city should be dependent for its supply of
beef on the United States: that not over one out of the 20
beasts slaughtered by its butchers came from the rich farm-
ing-country in sight of Mount Royal. They urged reform,
spoke of rotation of crops, of meadows and turnip-sowing; of
improved breeds of cattle and fattening on corn; of the
money the habitants were losing. They spoke to the wind:
Jean Baptiste went on attempting to raise wheat, until, in
1827, mildew appeared, and the crop thenceforth became so
subject, on old lands, to scourges of one kind or another, that
he was forced to change his course and copy a leaf from his
English neighbor. Raising few or no potatoes, and beef and
mutton equally rare, the diet of the habitants consisted of
bread (in summer-time more or less sour from leaven being

used instead of yeast and black and bitter from the presence of the moose-pea) and pork, boiled in making pea-soup. The soup was invariably good, the housewives having retained the custom of their ancestors in keeping the pot of stock always on the simmer. This diet, of bread, soup and pork, simple and strong, was also healthful, as was proved by the absence of disease and the longevity of the habitants. On fast-days, when pork was forbidden, they had boiled kidney-beans and fried flour-pancakes, and a favorite dessert was sour, thick milk (called in Scotland "lappered") beaten up with an equal quantity of fresh milk and a small amount of maple sugar. Of tea they had no knowledge, and the only article of groceries they bought was molasses, of which, after the opening of the trade with the West Indies subsequent to the Conquest, they came to know. Potatoes they regarded a luxury. If a bit of land was left after sowing what wheat they had, the strip was finished with a few potatoes, which were roasted in the oven, when they baked bread, and eaten with butter as a treat. The everyday clothing was all home-made, but from the opening of stores, with the advent of the British, the latent taste for finery began to be developed, and the wasteful expenditure in personal and domestic habits came to be a frequent topic of the curé's discourses.

Famine overtook the habitant, as can be seen by the numerous pitiful reports made by parish-priests and others between 1828 and 1840, but three circumstances prevented its becoming acute, as in Ireland, and tending to his extinction: 1st his wants being so simple, it was long before the soil failed to supply them; 2nd, the boundless extent of virgin land that surrounded him, and to which he moved when driven by necessity; 3rd, the advent of the Old Countrymen. Altho regarded with such jealousy, his presence resented as an intrusion, the advent of the British farmer was an unmixed blessing to the habitant. He introduced new methods of culture, broke the conservatism of ages, and practically demonstrated how the exhausted lands of the province could be restored to fertility. Whoever doubts this, may compare the state of agriculture in counties like Beauharnois, where there has been an admixture of the English element, with those counties on the lower St Lawrence where those who do not speak French may be counted on the fingers. But even in these counties the force of British example has been of saving efficacy. The implements they used have disappeared and better methods have been adopted. Counties in which, so late as 1845, the habitants were reported to be on the verge of want, are now thriving, and there is a slow but steady improvement and a gradual accumulation of wealth. The preservation of the habitant is due to the stranger he is too often taught, as the first article of his patriotism, to distrust and dislike.

The unfortunate condition of the habitant, at the period of which I treat, had been aggravated by storekeepers and moneylenders. The rapacity of these men cannot be exaggerated. The want of forethought, which enables the habitant to be happy by his not clouding the present with care for the future, rendered him an easy prey to the extortioner. When pinched for food, he would, for example, sell his oxen to the storekeeper, and then pay him rent for their use, or borrow a few dollars on his bon, at what seemed to be a trifle, for a month, not perceiving that he would be unable to pay then, and that the yearly interest ranged from 50 to 100 per cent. In every parish there were a few men grown rich by such methods, and who held the habitants by the score at their mercy. When the inevitable came, when the habitant could no longer get credit, his farm passed into the hands of the usurer and its occupant drifted to the city or into a new settlement.

It was at the juncture when the Basin was thus being abandoned, that the English appeared. In the deserted farms, in the fields overgrown by weeds and brush, the Scotch immigrants perceived the possibility of making comfortable homes with less labor than by going into the bush. The lots were offered cheap, and before many years there were a number in their hands, and being transformed by ditching, fencing, proper cultivation, and rotation of crops into a state of productiveness. The habitant watched them with astonishment, and it came to be a proverb with them, that an Anglais would get rich on a farm where a French-Canadian would starve.* The Scotch farmers were as so many unpaid instructors in their midst, and although they were slow to abandon the methods of their fathers and prejudiced against adopting innovations, example had its effect in the course of years; the old implements disappeared, better buildings were erected, grass-seed, beans and barley were introduced, potatoes grown as a regular crop, and stock fairly cared for, with the result of changing the condition of the habitants of the Basin from one of hopeless poverty to comparative comfort and independence. Among the first to come in were Robert Finlay, John Dale, George Burrell, who opened a tavern, and Charles Dewitt, who were quickly followed by James Holmes, Daniel Craig, Robert Elliot, James Clark, Joshua Walton, George McFadden, John Aitken, George Niven, William Watt, Robert Lang, Thomas Taylor, Thomas Duncan, John Cooper, Matt. McLean, and many others. The movement began about 1827, and continued until 1840, when, notwithstanding a number had left, there were over a score of families established along the banks of the Chateaugay for 5 miles above its mouth.

The year in which the Scotch farmers began to settle, 1827, was known among the habitants as "the Indian corn year." Wheat being a total failure, starvation stared them in the face, and to get food they loaded their traineaux with cordwood, and drew it on the ice to Montreal. As they could only take a third of a cord on their one-horse rigs, they rarely got over a dollar a load, which bought 3 bushels of salt. Returning home, and completing a journey of 30 miles,

*Patrick Shirreff, the famous East Lothian farmer, who visited the parishes along the south side of the St Lawrence in 1833, in his book of travels, remarks: "In many instances, soil of the best quality did not yield more than two seeds of wheat, while the crops were intermingled with truly luxuriant indigenous tares, thistles, and sweet-clover. I had often heard of the French Canadians clinging to their farms until starved from them—that is, until the soil did not yield them food to subsist on, and I had here evidence of the process and result of such an agricultural system."

they next morning started up the Chateaugay for the lines, where they traded the salt for corn, at the rate of 2 bushels for one of salt. On getting back to the Basin, they got the corn ground and managed to bake bread by sifting the meal and mixing the finer with the coarser after boiling it. Salt was then in great demand in Franklin county, for, from its isolated situation as regards New York, it was scarce and dear. Until the railway was built, it paid well to haul salt to Malone and adjacent villages, and Macdonald made much of his money by sending there trains of teams in winter with salt, and smuggling back tea, whisky, and tobacco.

The Basin in those days was a place of considerable traffic, for until the Beauharnois canal was opened, the Chateaugay was the main outlet of the district; the highway, both summer and winter, for immigrants and their supplies and the export of potash and lumber. When the stream of immigration fairly set in, a regular ferry between Lachine and the Basin became a crying necessity. The steamer that plied to the Cascades would occasionally, when a large load offered, as a favor take the channel inside Nuns' island, but she was no more to be relied upon than getting a bateau to hire when wanted. The loss and inconvenience immigrants sustained in getting across the river was very great. Gregory Dunning, an American who lived at the Basin, was the first to supply the want, and he endeavored, so far as wind and waves would permit, to make a trip each day, and in this he was aided by the Cascades steamer, which would give him a tow up the lake, casting his boat loose opposite the island. This was a great convenience, and he ferried over many hundreds of immigrants every summer, and, on the return trips, transported much potash. A sailboat, however, soon ceased to meet the requirements of the public, and on a boat propelled by horses proving a failure on the La Tortue ferry, from insufficiency of custom, it was proposed to her owners to move her up to the Lachine and Basin route, and, as an inducement, a number of the storekeepers along the Chateaugay took shares, which were placed at $20 each. The boat was placed on the route about 1828, and her captain and chief owner was Silas Dickenson, an American. She was propelled by 6 horses, which transmitted the power by their feet, they thrusting the treads on which they stood away from them. Peter Sinclair (afterwards a settler on the Ormstown concession) stood in the centre with a whip and kept them going, earning the whimsical title of "engineer of the horse-boat." It was found that the route was too long for the same team to come and go, so it was arranged that the landing-place should be $1\frac{1}{2}$ miles above Lachine. She could take a large load, the habitants driving on to her with their carts, and paying 50 cents. The charge for passengers was 20c, and for them the accommodation was not good. A railing protected passersby from the horses, but one afternoon a pensioner, returning from Montreal, where he had been drawing his allowance, fell upon the moving track and was trampled to death. Both he and his companion were drunk. She was of great convenience and made the Basin the outlet for a large extent of country. Her wharf was close to the present steamboat-landing, and was built by a Canadian, Pierre Reid, the horses being stabled at Dalton's. On John Smith's, an American and relative of Gregory Dunning's, beside whom he lived, building a wharf opposite his tavern, the boat ran up to it, which was about a mile farther, and he stabled the horses. This annoyed the residents near the old landing, who did not like the boat's passing them, and 6 of them clubbed together to purchase a rival in the shape of a steamboat. When steamboats were first introduced on the St Lawrence, it was the popular belief that one, sufficiently powerful, could not be built to stem the current above Montreal, and when an enterprising American was building one as a ferry to Laprairie his project was laughed at. One summer day in 1819 he demonstrated, in the presence of a great assemblage, that it could be done. His vessel, the Montreal, was small, and had a high-pressure engine, so weak that it took her from 2 to 3 hours to make her up-trip. This boat, superseded by a larger and much more powerful vessel, was for sale, and the malcontents got her for $1500. She proved a failure. Unless under full way, she was hard to steer, and her boiler being weak she lacked in power, and was constantly running aground. This gave her a bad name, while, at the same time, the horse-boat service was improved. By doubling the number of horses, and having a fresh team for each trip, she was able to run to Lachine and to pay less regard to the wind when it blew fresh. Both, however, were running without profit, and Dickenson offered to either buy or sell, when the Montreal fell to him. While she ran, she used a wharf erected by Michael Connolly alongside of Reid's, and who had left his farm in Ormstown to begin tavern-keeping at the Basin, and did not succeed. His property, after passing through several hands, was bought by John Jack, a Greenock blacksmith, and a man of genuine worth. The house he kept in connection with his smithy, was a true place of rest for the weary traveller, and was in such high repute, that many made it a point, even at a sacrifice, to push on and spend the night there. Perceiving that the horse-boat could not cope with steam and renewed competition being threatened, Dickenson was anxious to change, and on his relative, Horace Dickenson, of the Transportation company, replacing his boat on lake St Francis by a larger, he bought the discarded boat, named the St Francis. All went well for a time until Dickenson's death, when the company was dissolved and the steamer was bought by Jacob Dewitt, when competition was renewed. Passengers were carried at nominal prices and one boat endeavored to attract patrons by engaging a piper. The Dewitts prevailed eventually, after losses for which the subsequent profits did not recoup them, and they ran the Chateaugay, with John McEachern as captain, for a long period, extending their operations by placing the Fashion, an elegant vessel, on the route to Beauharnois. The traffic had grown to such an extent, that, up to the opening of the Beauharnois canal, the Chateaugay made two trips a day to Lachine, and generally with a barge lashed on either side of her.

The fate of Dundee and Laguerre eventually overtook the trade of the Basin, which left it for new channels. When the district began to be settled, Laprairie was its outport, and thither, through the woods from the southwards or along the river-road that passed by Caughnawaga, wended strings of carts and traineaux according to the season. Laprairie was deserted for Chateaugay, which, in turn, was left for Caughnawaga and Beauharnois, until the time came when the St Lawrence route was superseded by the railway. While it was the highway to Montreal, tavern-keeping flourished at the Basin, and no fewer than 16 came into existence. Of their owners, the statement that can be made of all those in other parts of the district stands true, the money they got by liquor-selling did no good to them or to their families.

When a bridge was placed across the Chateaugay I have been unable to fix definitely, but it is doubtful if there was anything better than a temporary one before 1830. The ice in 1843 carried it away, when the government gave a grant to replace it by a more substantial structure. The old gristmill (page 7) was now obsolete, with its two run of stones, and its bolts upstairs, to which the habitant had to carry them, and pay a penny (2c) a bag for the privilege of passing his grist through them. It was rebuilt about 1833, and the dam was raised. From the heightening of this dam, dates the ceasing of the Chateaugay as a fishing-stream. It was too high to jump for the multitudes of fish which had theretofore resorted to the upper waters to spawn. The nuns at the same time built a sawmill. The existing gristmill was built in 1856. The old mill was used for some time as an axe-factory and is now a ruin.

The spiritual needs of the settlement attracted attention, and in 1831 one of several catechists and lay-readers, Charles Forest, sent out by a Church of England missionary association, took up his abode at the Basin. He taught school, but his field otherwise was limited, the families, with a few exceptions, being Presbyterians. He visited the country farther up the river, and was gratified to find a number of families belonging to the denomination in whose interests he had come, and arranged for a fortnightly service in Ormstown. Archdeacon (afterwards Bishop) Mountain visited him in February, 1832, and was told by Mr Forest there were 45 unbaptised children in Ormstown. The Archdeacon could not go there, so, after baptizing 3 children, he left, arranging with Dr Bethune, in passing Montreal, that he should pay Ormstown a pastoral visit. In that year the Rev Alex. Gale, Presbyterian minister at Lachine, began to visit the settlement. Services were conducted in the house of James Lang, a man of sterling character and of singleness of purpose, who came from Scotland in 1831. In the summer of the following year the Rev Walter Roach (see page 216) visited the settlement with a view to a call. A congregation was formed, and he was inducted in Mr Lang's house on the 1st December, 1833, when 14 heads of families gave in their names, representing 36 adults and 39 children. Mr Lang and his father, who was living with him, had been elders of the West Kirk of their native place, Greenock, and they were chosen for the same office in the newly-organized congregation, and to the duties of elder the son added those of precentor, and until he reached his three-score and ten led the psalmody of the little body of worshippers. Mr Roach worked assiduously to establish the congregation with which he had been entrusted. There being pressing need for a place of meeting and a graveyard, in February, 1836, a lot was bought above the bridge. Mrs Jack's mother died while the transaction was pending, and her body was kept 10 days until the deed was passed, when the first grave was opened to receive it. Before that the Protestants had buried on the Dewitt farm. Preparations for building were begun that summer, but the work went on slowly from want of means. Besides the work they did, the people contributed $600, and Mr Roach collected a like sum by visiting Quebec and Montreal, and a brick church, 40 × 36 feet, was raised and opened for use in 1840. Means were lacking to seat the church, and benches were formed with boxes and planks, which sometimes gave way. Whether to lessen the chances of such catastrophes, or from the volunteers sitting together, the custom sprang up of the women occupying one side and the men the other, which survived until its demolition in 1881. Eventually Mrs Macdonald and Mrs Caldwell were instrumental in getting seats, which, rude as they were, added to the comfort of the people.

The settlement at the Basin differed from all the others in the district, in that the English-speaking farmers who joined it bought their lots ready for the plow, so that they experienced none of the privations or vicissitudes attendant on redeeming land from the bush, and of which it is the purpose of these pages to preserve some record. In course of time the disadvantages of being planted in the midst of a population who had little in common with them became manifest, and it began to dwindle, when the French reassumed the lots they had sold, and the English population came to be represented by a few families clustered between the bridge and the mouth of the river. Before leaving this settlement, a painful incident in its history has to be noted. The minister of the Congregational church established at Russeltown Flats, anxious to extend his connection, in 1840 established a preaching-station at English river, and gradually working down, as he became acquainted, held occasional services at the Basin. The connection thus formed seemed to be so encouraging, that it was severed from the Flats congregation, and in 1843 Chateaugay Basin and English river were constituted into a separate charge, with the Rev J. Bowles as minister. One Sunday evening in January, 1848, while driving home after preaching, he came down upon the ice. When near the bridge, the horse broke through, and dragged the cutter with its occupants, Mr Bowles and a lady, into the water. He was swept under the ice and lost. Buoyed up by her clothing, the lady was drifted by the current against firm ice, and, shouting for help, was rescued.

CHAPTER XIII.

Passing up the Chateaugay, habitants clustered as thickly on its banks, as far as the junction with the English river, in 1820 as they do to-day. The road on the west bank was the one used for reaching the upper settlements, owing to its having fewer hills and from the absence of bridges. Ste Martine from its situation, at the end of the Beauce road and a convenient stage-length from the Basin, naturally became a village. At first, it looked as if the village would be on the west bank, that it would spring up around the stone-tavern, but the erecting of the church and mill on the opposite side caused a change. The first house in the upper-village, and which stood not far from Bean-river, was that of Frs. Vallé, who built it before 1812. In 1820 the bishop divided the seigniory into two missions, the portion north of the Chateaugay constituting one, and that south of it the other. The first he named St Clement, the other Ste Martine. The names were chosen arbitrarily, and had no local significance, as some pretend. In 1823 a small chapel was built, the site of which was next to the existing edifice. The same year the seignior built a grist-mill, the work being entrusted to Peter and Daniel Macarthur. No dam was needed, a log being bolted to the rock to direct the water to the wheel, which was very high, some 16 feet, and narrow, on the undershot principle. Macarthur continued to build all his wheels thus until he saw the American plan of making them low and broad enough to take in the whole current of a narrow stream. The building still exists and is utilized as a carding-mill. The stones, two in number, were brought out from Scotland, and there were no bolts, the farmers getting back the stuff entire. It did an immense business for its capacity and paid the seignior its cost several times over. The first miller was Granbois.

The village received a great impetus from the exertions of a man remarkable in his sphere, Marc Antony Primeau, who opened a store, started an ashery, and carried on lumbering on a great scale. Centring his operations in the lower village, which he called Primeauville, he successively built a sawmill, tannery, carding-mill, and a brewery and distillery, which were managed by a Scotchman of the name of David Michie. The whiskey made was colored to resemble brandy, which greatly assisted its sale. When at the height of his prosperity, plank-roads had a great reputation, there being a craze about them which it is hard now to understand. Mr Primeau conceived the possibility of lifting Ste Martine out of the mud by the building of such a road. His first proposition was to plank the road to Beauharnois, which failed from the people of that town refusing to help. He thereupon resolved upon striking across the country, and opening a road to Ste Philomene, and thence to reach Caughnawaga, which had assumed importance from the proposal to build a railroad from there to the States. Primeau carried out his project, and the road was opened for traffic about 1849. It was of immense benefit to the district, by opening a more direct route to Montreal than that by Chateaugay Basin, which it entirely superseded, but was a dead loss to all who put money into it, the habitants using a hundred subterfuges to escape paying toll, while the perishable nature of the plank soon made it no better than a clay road. An able and successful business man, Primeau was unscrupulous and harsh towards those who fell under his power. The business he built up disappeared at his death, and the name Primeauville was forgotten, and the place came to be known as the lower village. Besides Primeau, Trottier has to be mentioned as a prominent storekeeper, and Dominick McGowan, an Irishman, who established himself in the upper village in 1833. The old name of the rapids at Ste Martine—rapides pêche aux saumons—indicates how plentiful the king of fishes once was in a river where he has been unknown for sixty years. On the rapids above, known by the English as Reed's or Campbell's and by the French as "Par-rouge," an American, James Perry, had a small saw-mill previous to 1820.

Of the priests who ministered in the parish, the name of Father Power deserves to be preserved. He succeeded Father Chartier, who went to the Grande Brulé and bore a prominent part in leading the rebels in 1837. Father Power was of Irish descent and had been educated by Father Macdonell of Glengarry and first Bishop of Kingston. He spoke French fluently, but was always glad to fall in with those who spoke English, and cultivated the acquaintance of the Scotch settlers on the Bean river and elsewhere in his neighborhood, impressing all as a man who sought to do what was right, and considerate, in speech and act, of those who differed from him in creed. One instance will suffice to illustrate the upright character of this noble Irishman. In the spring of 1835 wheat was scarce. Two Americans, calculating upon a rise in price, waited upon Father Power and offered him $2 a bushel for the tithe-wheat he had on hand, which was above the current price. He refused, and kept it to sell to the habitants on reasonable terms for seed. He came about 1833 and left at the close of the rebellion for Ontario, where he rose to be bishop of Toronto, and died through his devotion to his people during the visitation of cholera in 1849.

West of Ste Martine the habitants gradually extended, and began to creep up the Bean-river, where they were followed by the Scotch. Archibald Cameron, now of Tullochgorum, says:

My father (Donald) was a native of Strontian, Argyleshire, and a blacksmith by trade. We sailed for Canada in 1832, but arrived in Montreal too late in the season to permit of our going to the part of the upper Ottawa we had in view. While waiting in the spring for the opening of navigation, my father paid a visit to the Rev Mr Colquhoun at Georgetown, and who had come out in the same ship with us. He was urged to settle in Chateaugay, and, after examining the country, he bought lot 14, east concession of Bean river, which was held by a Canadian, who had a clearance of several acres on the river-bank. There were about 20 French families on the river, none of whom had been settled over 12 years. There were two English-speaking families, Hugh Henderson, a shoemaker, on lot 13, and Robert Pringle on lot 21, on the south-west concession. They had come the year before. The road from the Chateaugay had been opened on our side of the Bean river as far as lot 26, and on the other side from lot 3 to lot 22. Both roads were passable for carts. There was a bush-track to the Norton Creek, another on lot 21 leading to the Williamstown concessions, and a like track on lot 26. The country to the east of us was covered by bush without a break. The settlement grew rapidly during the 3 years after we arrived, and of the families that came the following remained : that of John Lowry lot 3, north-east concession; David Brown lot 15, John McLennan 41, and John McRae 44. On the south-east side of the river, James Ritchie lot 3, who made beer on a small scale up to the year of the rebellion ; James Cameron lot 2, Peter Henderson 9, and John Taylor and Edward Harsted on 22. My father set up a forge and got all the work he could do, while the other settlers did fairly well. A great quantity of potash was made, and neighboring settlers sold their ashes to those who dwelt on the Bean river, from their facilities for leaching. The river was not the shallow, stagnant creek it now is, but had water enough to float large timber down, and I remember one white pine log that was 4 feet across at the butt. A good deal of charcoal was made, and drawn to Montreal. The school we went to was that on the Irish concession, whose settlers were honorably distinguished by maintaining a good one from their first coming, and which we reached by a path through the woods. The prospect for several years was that the Bean river would be an Old Country settlement. After the rebellion, however, the French came crowding in from St Isidore, Laprairie, and Longueuil, until they occupied all the vacant lots. After that the Scotch began to sell out, so that now (1886) only two families remain. The St Urbain concession was an unbroken bush when we came, but in 1835 there were two houses, which stood where the church now is, and beyond them there was not another for a mile and a half. So wide a belt of bush separated us from the Scotch settlement (page 49) that there was no intercourse, but my father was told of it, and that they had Gaelic service on Sabbath, and he made up his mind he would try and reach them. So one fine Sabbath in June he followed the track that led southwards and, in due time, got through the bush and struck what is now known as the St Urbain road. After he had gone along it for about 2 miles, he began to see groups of people, in twos and threes, ahead of him, and all going the same way. He followed slowly until the schoolhouse was reached, and into which the people passed. When my father entered the services had begun, and he was much struck by the appearance of Norman McLeod (page 50) who conducted them. He was short in stature, and thin, with dark piercing eyes, and long flowing grey hair. His text was I. Kings xix: 5 and 6, and my father considered it as good a sermon as he ever heard. When the benediction was pronounced, an old man stepped up to him and taking him by the hand asked in Gaelic, "You are a stranger here?" and my father answered that he was, in the same language. The old man, on finding my father was a Highlander, took him by the arm and introduced him to the preacher and all the people, and insisted on his going home with him for dinner. The friendship begun that day between Finlay McCuaig and us was of long continuance. In the spring of 1835 I was sent to stay with him and attend Mr McLeod's school, for he still taught, though over 80 years of age. I liked him well. He was very kind to the scholars if good and just as severe with them if they did not do what was right. If ever there were two good men, it was he and Finlay McCuaig. McLeod was a relative of Dr McLeod of the Barony, Glasgow, and was an excellent English as well as Gaelic scholar and, when it became necessary, preached in both languages. He died, I think, the following spring. The schoolhouse was on lot 27, a mile east of Blackburn's corners, which were so called from the name of the man who kept tavern there. The 1st, 2nd, and 3rd concessions were fairly settled, and the people were comfortable and contented. The 4th and 5th were surveyed by Livingstone and thrown open for settlement in 1830 and rapidly taken up, and, unlike the Scotch settlement, the population was varied. The land looked well, being covered by a fine growth of hardwood, the name Beechridge being given to it from the number of large beech trees, and the newcomers did well by making potash and drawing cordwood to the city, but after the ridges were cleared there was little inducement to remain and farm the stony land.

On the death of McLeod the people sought a successor and the Rev Thomas McPherson, who had lately arrived from Scotland and was a brother-in-law of Dr Muir, was called and inducted in Dec., 1836, when a church was built on a site given by Pearson Nichols on lot 17, the contract being taken by one Robertson, an Englishman. Afterwards, on proving to be too small, 15 feet were added to it. Mr McPherson, after remaining 6 years, moved to Lancaster.

Of great benefit to the settlers throughout Williamstown was the opening of a store and ashery at Norton Creek by Nichols & Cantwell, about the year 1826. They were both Americans by birth, though Thomas Cantwell was almost an Old Countryman, his parents having been Irish Protestants. While a clerk with Jacob Dewitt of Montreal he became intimate with Pearson Nichols, who was a remarkably shrewd, active man, and who had become acquainted with the district of Beauharnois from his operations in smuggling goods from the States into Montreal. Their first store was a log building which stood near the mill, and here they sold an immense quantity of goods to the settlers, taking payment in ashes. So profitable did their business prove, that branch stores were opened at the Flats, Franklin, and Hinchinbrook. Nichols continued his smuggling to the last, his death in 1834 being caused by the exposure it entailed. Mr Cantwell carried on the business until 1863, when he retired with no inconsiderable fortune. The gristmill was built by the seignior in 1829 and was occupied by Robert Wheatly, an Englishman, who did not succeed very well owing to there being little grain to grind. When the mill was built the country was so near its primeval condition that the Macarthurs, on leaving their work on Saturday afternoon to spend Sunday with their families, lost their way in making for the Chateaugay, and another time were in danger from wolves. From its situation, the seigniory-agent thought a village would spring up around the mill, and named the place Brownville, after himself. The expectation was not realized. Along the creek there was some land fit for cultivation, but most of it was wet and to the southwards stretched great swamps, so that the attraction to settle was slight. When the lots began to be taken up, it was found necessary to pull down the milldams in order to drain them, so that the prospects of the village (now called Norton Creek) growing were blasted. Thos. Gebbie opened the first store at McGill's corners, and on his leaving for Howick, was succeeded by James Walker, who

sold to John McGill, and who did a large business. With his
brother Hugh he did much in clearing the land. John had
for neighbor a half-pay officer, Peter Meagher, an Irish
Catholic and the only justice of the peace for a long while.
His nearest neighbor was William Blair, who was a mile
below him, and beyond his place Nichols had a sawmill.
William Wiley and John Moore were first on the north
Norton Creek concession; the south concession was taken up,
almost exclusively, by Irish Catholics, none of whom came
early. Where the concessions ended on the creek were three
brothers, John, Martin, and Owen Dunn, remarkable for size
and strength. Stacy was blacksmith at McGill's, and beside
him was Newlove, a gunsmith. At Hope's corners, named
after George Hope, now known as Holton, a school was
opened about 1830, and in it one of the first Sunday-schools
in the district was held.

After 1840 the French began to move into the unoccupied
lands of Williamstown, and before other ten years the people
of the Beechridge and Scotch settlement saw themselves completely surrounded by them, and placed at the disadvantage
of being cut off from their fellow-countrymen in Russeltown
and on the English river. One after another left for Ontario
or the English-speaking settlements in St Malachie. About
1850 there was a large movement to the London district in
Ontario. The fewer they became, the greater the motive for
leaving, for apart from the want of suitable society, they
found it difficult to keep up school or church. In the Scotch
settlement, of which every lot was at one time occupied by
Old Country families, only six are now so held, and thus
the oldest settlement in Chateaugay founded by immigrants
from Britain, and for 30 years the most promising, may be
said to have become extinct. The church that was once
crowded to the door is now attended by a handful.

CHAPTER XIV.

THE first indications of the stream of immigrants that was about to set in, and which was to result in redeeming the upper Chateaugay from the wilderness, were to be observed in 1820, when several arrived, among them being William Carruthers, a Glasgow blacksmith, who set up his forge beside Reeves's house, William Donaldson, Peter Macarthur and his brothers, who obtained lots by purchasing the betterments of American squatters. Peter Macarthur paid $1200 for his 100 acres, which was considered an excessive price, despite the extensive improvements that had been made. In 1821 Alexander Graham, afterwards known as Squire Graham, got lot 30. He was from Cantyre, Scotland, and possessing some education and being of a peace-loving disposition, he made a very good magistrate. His common course on a case coming before him, was to speak privately to the parties and advise them to settle, adding significantly, "If you don't, it will be the worse for you." About the same time William Gardner, who came from Glasgow, secured lot 14. With 1821 ended the dormancy of the settlement, which, with the additions noted, had barely maintained its population and was dragging out an isolated and obscure existence; the few dwellers clustered, with one or two exceptions, on the north bank, living as one family and with no ambition beyond providing for their daily wants. Mr Ellice had resolved to fill up the seigniory, and ordered the making of surveys, the building of mills, and the advertising of its advantages for settlers. The stream of immigrants which his agents succeeded in directing up the Chateaugay set in strongly and aroused the section into new life and activity. The narrative of one of those who came in that year will present a correct representation of the Chateaugay settlement when he joined it, and of the drawbacks the newcomers had to overcome. Said William Grant:

I thought of going, on my arrival from Scotland at Montreal, to Perth, Ont., but my uncle, who had come out before me and was living in the city, said, "No; they are opening up the seigniory of Beauharnois for settlement and that is nearer Montreal." He went up with me, in June, 1821, to Beauharnois to see the agent, Brown, and we took passage from Lachine on the Perseverance, a small steamer that had begun to ply between that place and the Cascades. Brown informed us what surveys were in progress and where the lots were that we could get and the terms. Hiring a cart we drove to the Basin, and stayed at Dalton's overnight. At breakfast I remember there was a young Scotchman, newly out, who remarked that this "maun be an awfu country, for the beasts the fouk kept were maist bulls, and had kept rowtin a' nicht." Dalton laughed heartily at the mistake, which was not so inexcusable for the bullfrogs filled the country then by millions. The settlers on the Chateaugay said the frogs repeated the rhyme:

> William Ogilvie! William Ogilvie!
> Ralston! Ralston!
> Williamson! Williamson!
> Wright! Wright!*

We had pigeons, cooked in a variety of ways, at each meal, for the country was black with them. We walked from Dalton's up the north bank of the Chateaugay, along which ran a tolerable road as far as Alex. Reeves', (lot 26, North Georgetown). I chose lot 32, on account of the rapid, for I had been used to the sound of running water in Scotland. I then returned to Montreal and came back the following year with the necessary stores for settling. With the help of my neighbors I put up a log house, 20 × 18 feet, and I walked up to John Todd's, Dewittville, which was the nearest sawmill. I found him living in a small house with little comfort, but doing a good business. In the one room of his shanty, 18 of us slept that night. I bought what boards I wanted, for which I paid $8 the hundred pieces, equal to about 1000 feet. Owing to so many settlers coming in, he had put up

---

* The names of early settlers, already referred to. In different places, fancy interprets varied sentences in the croaking of the bullfrogs. In Ontario the words "More rum; more rum!" are generally attributed to these water-drinkers.

the price, which afterwards fell to $6. I made my purchase into 2 squares to raft down the river, and in prying one over the shallows on McNown's rapids, I slipped and fell, when the other square moved over me, so that I could not rise. After a while I got an arm out and reached my pole, when I pried up the lumber and crawled out. There was nobody with me nor near at hand, so that, had I not succeeded, I would have perished there. In running along through the long grass at Rapid Croche (just behind where Prejent's hotel now stands) a black snake sprang up and, in a twinkling, wound itself round one of my naked legs. In the impulse of the moment, I seized the reptile's head and jerked it away. All the way up to where Ormstown now stands, there were bits of cleared land here and there—the Meadows—the hay on which the settlers were allowed to cut by giving half to the seignior, for whom the Brysons acted and kept his stock. David Bryson was living in the old blockhouse at Allan's corners that had been put up in 1813, and above him lived William Bryson. Alex. McIntosh had come out that spring and was on lot 43. They were the only families between me and Ormstown, where old Jones lived. After a stretch of solid bush, small deserted clearings began again, which had been made by the Americans before the war. That same fall, Paddy O'Mullin, John Buckley, and Robert Leishman came out. The two first-named were Irish Catholics. O'Mullin was a blacksmith, and as the only one for many miles did well, and had soon a larger stock than any other settler. He lived on No 1, Ormstown, and Buckley on No 2, who only stayed a year. I went up with him, John McConachie (who had taken up lot 34 after I came) and Squire Graham, to help Leishman to put up a shanty on his lot, No 25, Ormstown. In returning after our day's work, in the dusk of the evening, the canoe bumped against a stone in Rapid Croche, and we were all thrown out except Buckley, who was steering. We managed to scramble back into the canoe, which, from having been split by the collision, soon sunk, and we were left floundering in the water. We could touch bottom, and got safely ashore. There being no house near, we walked to a barn on No 16, used for keeping hay cut on the meadows by William Bryson, and got in among it. I took off my boots, and next morning they would not go on, so I had to walk barefoot over the ground white with frost to John Williamson's, where we got break-fast. That winter I spent in clearing the land, cutting the trees into cordwood, which I piled on to a raft I formed of cedar. We had a cold winter with a great deal of snow, and

17

the break-up did not take place until April, which came in very warm with rain. The result was a great and sudden freshet, and my raft was swept away by the ice and lost. It was a great blow to me. There were about 3000 cords of wood lost in like manner on the Chateaugay that spring. We made a good deal of money that way. On reaching the Basin with our rafts, we took on 9 Indians, 4 with oars on either side, who got a dollar apiece, and a pilot, who charged $2. The channel of the Lachine rapids we ran is the same as that now used by the steamboats, and there was no danger except at the foot, where the big waves washed over the raft. We had splendid crops for many years, and could hardly sow too little seed. A peck of wheat or a bushel of oats to the acre was enough, and finer grain could not be wished for. The first grain I sowed was oats. They were put in on the 26th June, but the fall being late they ripened, and I had a splendid crop. Being a new crop on the river, the other settlers took them and gave me wheat in exchange, 1 bushel for 2 of oats, so I had enough for bread, and never wanted. The potatoes were equally good in yield and quality, and we fed so many to the pigs that the big pot was seldom off the fire. Pork sold cheap, $3 to $3.50 a hundredweight, but we had lots of it to sell. We made little potash, the timber not being very suitable, and paying us much better to sell as cordwood. Our chief need for money was to buy clothing, which was dear in those days, and many went to work a while in the quarries at Caughnawaga, where they were getting out stone to build the first Lachine canal. The year I settled the road was passable for carts as far as Morrison's; from there up the bridges were down and many obstructions, in the shape of trees felled so as to block the roads, done partly, I understood, during the war, and made worse by Milne to keep the Americans from returning to their lots. I helped to take away many of the logs. I cannot give the year, but it was soon after I settled, that Brown and the Grand Voyer came along. Brown asked me why I did not make the road across my lot. I answered I did not know where the line was left for one, for I had been told the present road was in the wrong place. "That is a mistake," replied the Grand Voyer, "the road is on the true line and is proces-verbaled." After that the settlers worked away to make the road more passable, but it was not until about 1829 that good bridges were built by the seignior, aided by a grant from government.

The same year that Grant settled on the Chateaugay, also

came what proved to be its leading spirit, Robert Brodie. He had visited Canada in 1815 and worked a while on the farm of Sheriff Boston, returning to Scotland. His old home in Ayrshire did not content him, and in the spring of 1822 he sailed from the Clyde on the True Briton, which chanced to have among her passengers those who were destined to be first settlers on the English river. Brodie's intention was to have gone to Ontario, but a visit to the Chateaugay prepossessed him in its favor and he bought from the American who held lot 20, North Georgetown. A man of means and capacity, and who was soon comfortably established, few immigrants passed his door without receiving help and disinterested advice. On the state of the settlement when he came, after 20 years' desultory labor, the following incident throws light. The lot to the west of him, Ralston's, had still a strip of bush running to the river. In crossing this one day, Sandy Campbell saw two cubs on a tree. He climbed up to it to catch them, when the bear appeared and began scrambling after him to protect her young. Swinging outwards, Campbell dropped to the ground, and ran for Brodie's. The animal, too content to rejoin her cubs, did not pursue him. A settlement where bears made their dens could not be far advanced. Primitive as it was, it now received its first minister. To Hugh Brodie of Petite Cote there came late in the fall of 1822 a minister newly arrived from Scotland, the Rev Alex. McWattie. Unable to do anything for him in Montreal owing to his want of credentials, he sent him to his brother-in-law, Robert Brodie, bearing a letter of introduction, in which he stated that it would be easier to corn than water him, which implied the sad cause of McWattie's coming to Canada. Of his antecedents little can be said, for, naturally, he was reticent as to his past life. It is supposed he was a native of Fifeshire, and he studied at Glasgow university, probably closing his collegiate career in 1805. Of what church he became a licentiate is uncertain—probably Burgher or Relief, and he received a charge in Dumbartonshire. Whatever the denomination, it had to suspend him for his intemperate habits, and he had to seek a home abroad. He was accompanied by his wife, a lady-like person who had evidently seen better days, and who wore a heartbroken expression. She was a native of Newcastle. The settlers were too well satisfied to get a minister to enquire into his antecedents, and Peter Macarthur gave an old shanty for a home and the neighbors stocked it with provisions. At the beginning of 1823 McWattie and his wife (they had no family) with all their effects, were driven on the ice from Montreal, and took up their abode in the humble hut prepared for them. On the 26th January, 1823, he signalized his entry into his ministerial duties by baptizing seven children. For a long while afterward, he was in frequent request for the same duty, for there were families with men and women grown who had not observed the first gospel ordinance. He was a good preacher and so many attended to hear him, that it became necessary to have a larger place of assembly than the settlers' houses, and the proposal of building a church was at once entertained. It was agreed to put up a church at Howick and another at Allan's corners, when the seignior stepped in, and offered lot 15, South Georgetown, as a glebe, the choice of that lot being made because of the burying-place that had been established upon its river-front. The brothers, Henry and James Wright, framed the building, which was about 40 × 60, and designed to answer both as church and manse, a partition dividing it in the centre. The settlers assisted heartily by bees, and the church was speedily completed. He, however, did not confine himself to it, but preached on the English river and at Rutherford's, near Ormstown. A life of usefulness was now open to McWattie, but in vain; his old habit of self-indulgence overcame him, and his dissipation became odious in a community by no means squeamish about drinking. An intelligent and agreeable companion while sober, he was a fool when drunk, and he drank to such excess that he became helpless. In his cups he abused his patient wife, for whose sake he was tolerated. So great was his craving for drink, that on visiting a neighbor who was laid up by a sore leg, on seeing him apply aqua fortis to it, he insisted on getting a drink, and took it diluted with water, without apparent harm. For him to pass from the pulpit to the nearest tavern was nothing unusual, though he had this characteristic, that he would not perform any ministerial duty while affected by drink. On one occasion, when sent for to baptize a distant family, he arrived under the influence of liquor and insisted on being allowed to sleep off its effects before proceeding. As the exhortations of such a man commanded no respect, those who attended his services did so from a sense of duty, but the number dwindled, until, near his end, he would preach to half a dozen. Of the contributions of the settlers he was soon independent, for he took up lot 11, South Georgetown, and proved to be a good worker. In 1829 he sold that lot and devoted his attention to clearing and cultivating the glebe. When he came he appointed elders and dispensed the communion, but that observance he speedily dropped. He preached with considerable force and the manuscript of several of his sermons which have been preserved, shows fair literary ability. He commented on the chapters he selected, and on reading that passage in Second Corinthians, where Paul narrates the trials he had undergone, he quaintly remarked, "Ay, ay, my brethren, doubtless Paul's sufferings were great, but he was never in so cold a place as Canada, nor had he to chop down trees." The poor man spoke from personal experience, for his existence depended upon his labors as a bush-farmer, and, as the church-end of his house ceased to be used for its proper purpose, its floor was utilized for threshing upon. In the spring of 1830 death relieved Mrs McWattie of her sufferings; he continued to live alone, his neighbor, Mrs Elliot, doing what she could for his comfort. He was often absent, and when he said he was going to Duncan's mill, it was known that he was bent on a booze with some boon companions in a neighboring drinking-place. His end was horrible. As 1831 was drawing to a close, he went one night to bed. There was no one in the house, and when the first neighbor visited it next day, he found him writhing in agony, from extensive burns about the head and breast. He lingered two days and died unable to give a coherent account of the accident that had befallen him. It was supposed he had gone to bed after drinking heavily, and awakening during the night rose to light his pipe, for he was a heavy smoker; that in gathering a coal at the open fire-place to put in his pipe, he had fallen on the burning logs and received the fatal injuries. A day or so after the New-Year he was buried beside his wife in Georgetown church-yard, where, though often proposed, no headstone marks the last resting-place of the first Protestant minister of the district. His register of births and marriages (he kept none of deaths) was irregularly filled, and on his death disappeared. As only marriages by ministers of the Episcopal church, Kirk of Scotland, or church of Rome were then legal, many whom McWattie married settled all doubts by being remarried. On the legitimacy of an heir to a farm on English river being called in question, the missing register was hunted up, copied by Robert Robertson, the schoolmaster, and a bill passed by the Quebec legislature making authentic all its entries. In personal appearance, McWattie was, as the people expressed it, a decent-like man, of a fresh complexion, and with a good voice and manner. He would be about 50 years of age at the time of his death.

The first year or two of his stay by the Chateaugay, McWattie eked out a living by keeping school in a shanty at the end of Brodie's house, and until a more capable schoolmaster came, who arrived in the person of a young man named Robert Robertson. He had been a fellow-passenger with Brodie on the True Briton and subsequently marrying a young woman whom he met on board, was content to assume the school McWattie was mismanaging. He was an excellent scholar and had been tutor in a gentleman's family in Scotland. Although he had no experience in managing a school, he speedily established a reputation that was wide extended and attracted a large attendance. On the government making the offer of $40 to any school that might be built, the settlers agreed to erect one on Peter Macarthur's farm. Before it was raised, a quarrel arose as to the location, which ended in the dividing of the lumber and the building of two schoolhouses, one on lot 14 and the other on lot 32.

Robertson selected the former, and as he grew older his habits and disposition changed, and he left behind him, on his death in 1855, the memory of a useful and pious man. The other school, Grant's, had Adam Patton for teacher, who took up a lot in South Georgetown. The first teacher the settlers west of Allan's Corners had was Alex. Shepherd (or Stewart), who was supposed to have left Scotland for his extreme Radicalism, and who taught in Robert Lindsay's shanty. Then came David Lind, well-educated but addicted to drink, for whom George Rutherford fitted up an old log-house on lot 17 as a temporary school. Preparations were made in the winter of 1826 for building a school for him, but before it was finished he died. The school, that of Stoney creek, was meant to be a warm building and had two layers of slabs for the ceiling with turf on top, and, after all, the first teacher, Adam Patton, complained of his heels being frozen. He was succeeded by (Squire) Harrison, who taught a few weeks, and by James Shields, a young Irishman of talent, who subsequently entered the U.S. army, served with distinction in the Mexican and civil wars, and was retired with the rank of general. After him came James Darby, a one-armed Englishman, a good teacher but unmerciful in his punishments.

As immigrants pressed in, the need of providing means for conveying them into the interior of the country became urgent, and Reeves gradually made their transportation a business. Immigrants found no difficulty in hiring carters to convey them from the Basin to his house, but farther they did not care to go, often could not go, for the road was not passable for over 5 miles beyond his house. Reeves supplied canoes, which went as far as Huntingdon. These canoes, like all the others used on the Chateaugay in those times, were of the pattern of Robinson Crusoe's. The largest available pine-tree was sought out, felled, and had the top cut off, when the trunk was shaped and hollowed. The canoes averaged 3 feet wide by 30 long, and were generally managed by 3 men, two to row and one to hold the steering-paddle. When rapids were reached, the men jumped into the water, and thrusting a stick through holes at bow and stern, worked the canoe up,

half-lifting, half-pushing it zig-zag among the boulders where
the water was deepest. The work was severe and slavish and
told on the strongest constitution. Each rapid had its name.
Thus the rapid at Ormstown was rapide croche, the one above
it, blotted out by the dam, rapide coteau, and the next, a mile
farther on, rapide savage. That at Dewittville was emphatically named the portage, for it was too shallow and rapid for
the canoes to be pushed, and they and their loading had to be
carried, the help of a yoke of oxen being called in. The
rapids at Huntingdon were too long to be passed (they were
named the long rapids) and the canoes ended their journey at
their foot. From Reeves' to Huntingdon, nearly 30 miles following the windings of the river, was a long day's journey
and, strange to say, the up-trip did not take much longer
than the down-trip, the current making little difference in
summer-time, when the water was low, and the men preferred low-water, as then the danger of striking boulders
and upsetting was less. The loading in ascending was immigrants and their baggage and provisions, and in descending
potash. The load was 2 barrels (950℔.) but there were
canoes large enough to take 3. The charge for conveying a
barrel from Huntingdon to Reeves's was a dollar, and thence
to the Basin was as much more for cartage. So large was
the trade, that Reeves started 3 or 4 canoes daily and the
entire upper country depended upon them for maintaining
communication with the outer world. When a settler wanted
anything, he hailed one of Reeves's canoes as it was passing
and gave his message, and was sure to receive, on its return,
what he ordered, for both Mr and Mrs Reeves were punctual
and honest. Dumochel, envying the profit of the trade,
started a line of canoes from his tavern above Ste Martine,
but did not succeed. As travel increased, Reeves enlarged
his house, until it consisted of three lengths of logs, when he
built a large stone-house, which stands now, changed in
use, a monument of early times on the Chateaugay. Its
walls were raised by John Metcalf of English river, in the
summer of 1834. He left his work on Saturday in apparent
good health and did not return, dying of cholera.

Connected with canoeing on the river, a sad accident occurred in 1825. It was the spring time, just at the break-up
when a canoe, having in it Willard, an American hunter, and
two squaws with a papoose, came down and touched the
bank at Sandy Williamson's, where Willard was advised to
stay all night. He answered, "No; I have a shilling burning
a hole in my pocket, and will go on to Reeves's tavern."
He was a hard drinker. Resuming their voyage, the canoe
got safely to Wright's when it was nipped between two cakes
of ice and sank. The papoose floated ashore and crowed when
brought into Wright's house, and the squaws were rescued
with some difficulty, but Willard never rose, and had probably
been stunned by a blow from the ice. Frost setting in afterwards, Williamson on going carefully over the ice saw the
gleam of the drowned man's powder-horn at the bottom of
the river, and so got the body, for which his poor wife, who
had come up from the Basin, where was their home, was in
waiting. A few years before that a French-Canadian known
as Mackinaw, perished by the river. He was sent by Reeves
with another Canadian in a canoe to Dewittville. They had
a bottle with them, and overcome by drink Mackinaw insisted
on lying down to sleep at Milloy's rapids. The night was
cold, and on his companion returning for him next morning,
he found the body frozen.

East of Reeves, William Greig, a Scotch blacksmith, bought
91 and 92, Annstown, and his farm became the place for
drilling the militia companies. On the opposite side of the
river from Reeves, came to live, some time before 1830, a
young man fresh from college and some service as a sea-
surgeon. Dr Syme was a native of Fifeshire and, despite
his falling into the social habits then prevalent, obtained a
high reputation, in this not belying the size of his head,
which was remarkable. An advice he gave a friend would
put an end to the use of patent-medicines and much self-
prescribing, "Be quite sure you are sick before you take
medicine." He met a premature death in 1851 by falling
from the bridge which connected Reeves' tavern with the
opposite bank. He was followed by Dr Harkness, also a

graduate of a Scotch college, who settled on lot 18, Ormstown, afterwards moving to Godmanchester.

Until the settlers cleared land sufficient to supply their wants, they depended upon provisions brought from Montreal, and to supply them a number of stores came into existence along the river. The first was that of Alexr. Rutherford, whose father, George, went to live on lot 16, Ormstown, in 1823. The means of communication with Montreal were so imperfect that both Reeves and Rutherford were often out of the commonest necessaries, and a settler would often make a long journey to them and be unable to get a pound of either meal or flour, and he deemed himself fortunate if he could borrow a loaf from the good-wife. Rutherford was an honest, considerate man, and, in a scarce time, when he got a quintal of oatmeal, would divide it among his customers according to the number of their families, giving this one two quarts and another 4 or 6. After him Crowley kept his store, with a good assortment of goods. Douglas & Wilkinson began business on lot 25, N. G., and did a thriving trade, adding an ashery, a blacksmith shop, and a tannery, the last beside the creek. In 1830, Robert Sutherland gave them competition on lot 27. An old account gives an idea of the prices then current. A scythe cost $1.10 and a handle for it 50c. Calico was 20c a yard, sugar 10c a pound, and shingle-nails 8c a pound. In 1827 Widow Cross, with a numerous family, and accompanied by her brothers, the Selkirks, bought lot 2, Ormstown, from O'Mullin, and kept a small store, which grew into a profitable business under her sons John and Robert, who added an ashery about 1833, and who gave in exchange for ashes, then worth 10c a bushel, peas and pork. The number of stores along the river bore no comparison with the drinking-places that sprang up, for taverns the majority of them could not be called, having no accommodation for travellers. They were an unmitigated curse to the settlers, and the cause of untold misery. At first the general drink was rum, sold at 60 to 75c a gallon, but soon superseded by Yankee whisky. On the opening of a passable cart-road to the lines in 1830, pedlers passed down from the States, calling at every house, selling tea at 25c which previously cost 75c, tobacco at 10c, and whisky at 25 to 40c a gallon. When from bad roads or weather they failed to appear in time to refill the jars, the grumbling was general. This abundant supply of a cheap spirit proved the ruin of hundreds of industrious men, and of those days most painful tales could be told of the results of its consumption—of sudden deaths, accidents, fights, and even homicides. One night three men left a drinking-place on the river, where they had been quarrelling. One failed to reach his home. A fortnight afterwards his body was found in the Chateaugay, bearing plain marks that he had been killed. His two companions were arrested, taken to Montreal, and tried, but were acquitted from want of proof. Long afterwards, on his deathbed a farmer told how, kept awake by the quarrelling of the three men, he watched them, in the clear moonlight, pass down to the water's edge and saw only two go over. On stealing down to see what had become of the third, he found the body, stark and stiff, hid in the wheat that grew luxuriantly. Next night he watched, saw one of the men return, lift the body, and throw it into the river. Fear of incurring the vengeance of relatives, caused him to hold his peace. The instigator of the crime, for his companion was overawed by him, died miserably some years afterwards. The drinking-habit led to many misunderstandings aggravated by Old Country antipathies, for, in those days, the feud of Highlander and Lowlander was revived on the Chateaugay, and neighbors quarrelled when the sense was obscured by drink, giving rise to numerous petty lawsuits, which were tried by Squires Graham and Brodie, who held their courts at Douglas & Wilkinson's, Sutherland's, or David Bryson's taverns, or the schoolhouse. Their clerk was the schoolmaster, Robert Robertson.

Of the state of the country when the immigrants began to crowd in, Mrs William Cunningham gives a good idea:

My father, William Cairns, belonged to county Derry, and we sailed for Canada in 1823. On landing at Montreal my father fell in with an Englishman who had a small contract on the Lachine canal, and who said he had bought a lot on the Chateaugay the summer before, and offered it for £50. My father bought it, and we drove to Lachine on our way to take possession. The captain of the steamer agreed to leave us at the Basin, but on the way something went wrong with the engine and she returned to Lachine. The freight-house was full of rough men, so we camped on the wharf, and had to stay there two days before the steamer was repaired. On reaching the Basin, Gregory Dunning agreed to cart our baggage, and we started after it on foot, grandmother, nigh a hundred years old, on top of the load, for she had insisted on accompanying father. When we got to Reeves's, we found the road to be unfit for wheels, and so stayed there all night and left next morning in two canoes, which landed us on our lot, on which was a small meadow, made by the Americans, and on the river-bank was a shanty the Englishman had started to build and which was ready for the roof. He had sown that spring some peas and turnips. We got the shanty finished and as we had brought a cow with us from Montreal and a good stock of provisions, we were not poorly off. Grandmother died 3 weeks after our arrival. David Bryson was our nearest neighbor. Robert Williams came the following year, and settlers came crowding in after that. The year of the Miramichi fire, it was so dark that we had candles burning, and even the pigs were like to die from the smoke. One woman came to our house in terror of being burned, and said she would "dook in the river gin the fire came up."

Several who went on to lots had to abandon them, from being too wet or from want of means, the absence of timber suitable for making ashes being a great lack in tiding over the interval until the clearing yielded enough to maintain the settler's family. This was partially supplied by rafting cordwood to Montreal, where it brought $2 to $2.50 a cord. While a number of the immigrants had some means, there were many who had nothing beyond an axe. On the best lots on the north bank being occupied, the immigrants quickly took up those on the south side. Probably the first to do so was Alex. Steel, a carpenter, from Forfarshire, who went on, in 1820, to the lot that had been abandoned by Logan (page 44) many years before. Above him, about a year later, an Aberdonian, Peter Reid, selected 20 of Jamestown, being induced to do so by its having 2 acres of an old American clearance.

The shanty he raised was considered a large one, yet in threshing grain in the loft, as he had to do until he got a barn, he had to half-kneel to find room for the sweep of his flail. On the extreme east, William Miller, from near Glasgow, took up lot 3, S. G., and a number of years afterwards his son James opened a tavern below Reeves's, which was a well-known halting-place for the stage. The seignior required the settlers to make the road across their lots, and, about 1827, employed Thomas Barlow to construct the necessary bridges. One settler, Michael Connolly, suffered by the straightening of the road. He had erected a large building on 5, Ormstown, designed for a tavern, when the alteration of the road left it in the middle of a field. He went away and on the lot coming to be sold by the sheriff in 1830, an old soldier, Sergeant Younie, bought it and became one of the best-known settlers on the river.

With very few exceptions, the settlers from Reeves's to Ormstown were Scotch, and they missed nothing more in their new homes than oatmeal. To mush and jonny-cake they did not take kindly, and wearied for the substantial parritch and toothsome oatcake of their native-land. Oats they raised, but there were no means of converting them into meal, and what oatmeal was to be had was brought from Montreal, and was consequently difficult to get and very dear. On one of his visits to Montreal Peter Macarthur saw a farmer, named Evans, erecting near Lachine a small mill to make oatmeal, placing it at the end of his barn and to be driven by horses. It struck Macarthur he could make one too. Hearing of a pair of stones being for sale at St Johns, he went for them with his cart, and then proceeded to make the gearing. The mill was started in 1828 and was hailed with satisfaction, there being instances of old men tramping 30 miles with a bag of oats to get the long-wished-for meal. The mill required 6 horses to drive it, though 4 sufficiently heavy to do so were eventually secured. It ground from 75 to 85 bushels a day, and was kept busy, save a short time in summer. The charge was 10 cents a bushel or the fifth quintal of meal, and the offal, and the seeds kept the horses fat. On hearing of what Macarthur was doing, Brown warned him that he was infringing upon the seignior's rights and would be prosecuted. Macarthur defied him to stop his mill, pointing out that it was not driven by steam, water, or wind as specified in the deed, but by horses, which was not prohibited; further that it was no injury to the seignior as it did not grind wheat, and none of the seigniorial-mills made oatmeal. To this Brown replied that the law gave the seignior the exclusive right of grinding grain, irrespective of how it was done, and that if Macarthur had no oatmeal mill, the farmers would grow more wheat. That the law was not clear on the point, as indeed it could not be, for oatmeal was unknown to the framers of the ordinances that regulated the seigniories, was shown by Brown's not taking legal proceedings to stop the mill, but he had Macarthur otherwise in his power. For work done by him in building the Norton-creek and other gristmills, the seigniory was due Macarthur a balance of $3000, and from this Brown deducted $100 a year as the value of the mouture, and, altogether, kept him out of $800 that was justly due him by Ellice. In building the Howick gristmill an oatmeal mill was added, and in time all the seigniorial mills were so fitted, when the horse-mill became obsolete, but in its day it did good work, and was the means of forcing the seignior to provide for the manufacture of oatmeal as well as flour. Before he broke with the seigniory, Macarthur built, at Norval's request, a threshing-mill for the model-farm. Its principle was that of beating the straw and then shaking it, and was driven by a sweep attached to a crown wheel. With two horses it would thresh as much as any modern mill, but it did not clean the grain. William Donaldson, on a neighboring farm, thought if Macarthur could grind with horses, he might saw with them, and put up a sawmill to be so operated, which did not pay.

The difficulty and danger found in crossing the river to go to church, suggested the erection of one on the north bank, which was set about in 1837, and by the fall of the following year a neat building was completed on lot 25, N. Geo. It was not long used until necessity for it was done away by the people turning out in bees and erecting a trestle-bridge, which they handed over to Turcot on condition that he should allow those going to church pass toll-free. The new church found use after the disruption, when Mr Fettes organized a highly respectable congregation within its walls. Henry Wright, on whose place it was built, was a stirring man, who engaged in many different occupations before the close of a long life. Before he left farming, he competed one fall, at the show held at Reeves's, with potatoes, which had a paper attached declaring the arpent of which they were part had yielded 410 bushels, 1 peck, and 7 ℔.

NORTH GEORGETOWN
RIVER FRONT.

1 François Vallé
2 Louis Leclere
3 Jules Daudien
4 John Simpson
6 Alex. Reeves
10 Nahum Baxter
14 William Gardner
15 James Wright
16 William Donaldson
17 Alex. Williamson
18 Vachon & Lachapelle
19 Peter Macarthur
20 Robert Brodie
21 John Ralston
22 John Harvey
23 Archd. Campbell
24 Zebulon Baxter
25 Henry Wright
   Douglas & Wilkinson's store
   Denio's tannery
   Dan. Kinghorn's black-
     smith-shop
   Presbyterian church
26 Capt. Morrison
   Robert Sutherland
27 Peter McKellar
28 John Simpson
   J. Reid
29 Robert Morrison
30 Alex. Graham

31 Daniel Morrison
   James Ogilvie
32 William Grant
33 Alex. McIntosh
   James Cowan
34 John McConachie
35 —— Blyth
36 James Bryson
37 Alex. Bryson
38 John Bryson
39, 40, and 41 David Bryson
42 Neil Campbell
43 Alex. McIntosh
   W. McWhinnie

FIRST CON. OF ORMSTOWN.

1 Patrick O'Mullin
2 John Buckley
   Widow Cross
3 William Cairns
4 John Carlyle
5 Michael Connolly
   Alex. Younie
6 Robert Williams
7 John Cunningham
8 John Williamson
9 Robert Lindsay
10 Samuel Cottingham
11 Robert Allan
12 William Bryson
13 Alex. Mills
14 Thomas Marratt
15 John Sangster

16 David Rutherford
17 Alex. Rutherford
18 Dr Harkness
19 Robert Nichol
20 John Carmichael
21 Thomas Sadler
22 Edward Jones
SOUTH GEORGETOWN,
    RIVER FRONT.
1 Alex. Logan
2 James Logan
3 William Miller
  Robert Robertson
4 William Carruthers
8 Robert Henderson
9 Dr Syme
10 Robert Henderson
11 Rev A. McWattie
12 Andrew Brown
13 William Reeves
14 Capt. Ogilvie
15 Glebe
16 Archd. Ogilvie
17 John Muir
18 John Boyd
19 William Anderson
20 James Williamson
   Craig Brown
21 John Cunningham
22 Daniel McArthur
23 —— Thomson, followed by
   David Baxter
24 Robert Robertson
25 John Taylor
26 William Greig
27 William Hamilton
28 Andrew Glen
29 Archd. Campbell
30 Duncan McCormick
31 Duncan Campbell
32 John Graham
33 John Morrison

34 Alex. Steel
35 Thomas Steel
36 Alex. Finlayson
37 Duncan McCallum
   William Gilchrist
38 Hugh Morrison
39 and 40 Hendry Craig
41 John Wilson
   Adam Paxton
42 James Cullen
43 Henry Craig
   Robert Greig
44 James Gilbert
45 Adam Patton
46 Rose Lily
   Archd. McCormick
47 David Bryson
JAMESTOWN—RIVER FRONT.
1 Michael Connolly
2 John Harvey
3 Wm. and Andrew Porter
4 John Scully
5 Robert Cairns
6 James Cairns
7 Donald McCormick
8 William McEwen
9 John Munro
10 William Bryson
11 William Smellie
12 Matt. & Patk. Kavanagh
13 Robert Allan
14 Samuel Baird
15 James McKegan
16 Robert Johnston
   James Mills
17 Thomas Thomson
18 Samuel Crutchfield
19 David Bryson
20 Peter Reid
21 John Sadler
22 —— Nolan
23 Reserve.

CHAPTER XV.

THE same year (1821) that the settlement on the Chateau-gay received so great an impetus from the setting in of the tide of immigrants, a beginning was made on the English river. From its mouth to Duncan's at St Chrysostom it remained in a state of nature. Reeves had bought Somerville's lot at Howick, but no person lived on it, and he sent men each summer to cut the hay that covered the clearing. On coming, one bright summer day, to begin this task, they found a brood of snakes sunning themselves on the roof of the log-barn that stood on the lot, and, attacking them, succeeded in killing 18, not one of which was less than 2 feet and a number nearly 3 feet long. Of the coming of the first settlers into this desolation, where so shy a reptile as the snake of this province flourished unmolested, William McKell tells the story thus:

My father (Matthew) was a shepherd, and we belonged to Lochwinnoch, Renfrewshire. We sailed from Scotland in the spring of 1821 and stayed about Montreal during the summer. It would be in September that my father, accompanied by David Wilson and Arthur Ritchie, hearing there was land to be had on the Chateaugay, started on foot to see it. They stayed overnight at Reeves', where Milne happened to be, and he told them the seignior would assign no lots that year, but next spring would open a large stretch of territory for settlement, and urged them to wait. On my father asking what he would do with his family until then, Milne offered the use of the blockhouse. Being told there was good land on the English river and anxious to get homes at once, my father and his companions accepted the offer of Brown of the Grand Marais to pilot them through the woods, and, joined on the way by Captain Ogilvie, they walked over next day and examined the land along the east bank, where they picked out lots. A fine flat on the river edge, a natural meadow, decided Wilson in his choice; the other two selected lots on which there was a good deal of oak. The prevailing timber was black hemlock, and the oak was considered, apart from its own value, to indicate better soil. They set to work at once, Captain Ogilvie trying to establish the bounds of the lots by measuring, for the survey was not completed. They knew nothing about chopping, and in felling the hemlock trees they lodged. On Mrs Wm. Ogilvie's walking over to see the new settlers, she took up an axe and showed them how to do. Poor bits of shanties were raised, the boards for the ceilings being supplied by Baxter, and brought round in a borrowed canoe by Logan's point. In October the families came from Montreal to take possession. Poor as were their habitations they proved warm, being embedded in the bush. That winter William Gardner and Stephen Patterson came in and joined us. There was not a track of a road to be seen. It was said there had been a bush-road that led to the States, but that, during the war, the British authorities had ordered to be closed by felling trees across it. There was a fair track half way across from where Howick now stands to the Chateau-gay. At the mouth of Norton creek there was a small clear-ance with traces of a house and a few apple-trees, but no other sign of anybody having been before us until you reached Duncan's at St Chrysostom. The winter was spent in chopping and the spring came in favorably, so that the first potatoes we planted were ready for use in six weeks. The other crops did well. Our nearest mill was at Beauhar-nois, but as it could not be depended upon, we went to the La Tortue mill, near Caughnawaga, which took 3 days, the journey being made in a canoe. Soon after we came, how-ever, the Ste Martine mill was built. The bush being almost entirely hemlock, there was no chance for making ashes, which was a great drawback, and the settlers for the first years depended on going to the States or lumbering nearer home to earn enough to pay the seigniorial rent, which, small as it may seem, was a great burden to people who had noth-ing for many years to sell. It was a common saying, that the settler who got in arrears for 3 years' rent ($30) might as well leave. Many went to work on the Lachine canal to earn a little. During the summer of 1822 the lots were laid off by Livingstone, and the seigniory fined us $20 each for having taken possession without leave. The survey showed that my father and Ritchie were on the same lot, when we moved to lot 97. That season settlers came in thick, and before very long every lot was taken up. Alex. McArthur and Alex. Taylor squatted on the west bank, which had not been sur-

veyed, but they were compelled to leave by the seigniory-
agent, and got lots on the other side. Until the dam was
built the Norton creek was as large as the English river.
There were no trout or salmon in the last-named, but it
abounded when we came with large pike. Both bears and
wolves were numerous, having their dens in the swamps and
ridges on both sides of the river. My father had 3 sheep
killed by bears, and a dead horse we left out was picked
clean to the bones by wolves.

This reference by Mr McKell to wild beasts, recalls a striking incident. While the Ste Martine mill was building,
David Wilson and his son were employed in blasting out the
tail-race. One Saturday afternoon a younger son, Robert,
left in a canoe to bring them home for the Sunday. On the
return journey, they got out at the rapids opposite where
Howick now stands to carry the canoe to the head of them.
It was a beautiful moonlight night, and while doing so,
sounds were heard from the top of the bank where Mr
Gebbie's house was long afterwards erected. The sounds
were so varied and human, that the boy took them for those
of men calling them to come up the bank to them, and was
about to do so, when his father told him it was a pack of
wolves.

The settlers were, with a few exceptions, Lowland Scotch,
in politics liberals to the verge of radicalism and, in religion,
largely dissenters. They were an intelligent and industrious
class of men, and comparatively few had been farmers, being
shepherds or tradesmen. Among the exceptions was Dennis
McNulty, an Irish Catholic, who came in among the first.
They were long in getting into stock from the difficulty in
providing feed. Trees grew to the water's edge, so that there
were no natural meadows along the English river, and those
who got a cow or a yoke of oxen had, until they cleared
enough to seed down, to draw hay from a great expanse of
wild meadow on lots 14, 15, and 16 on the Australia concession. One year, after the settlers had cut what they
needed, by the carelessness of some smokers who visited the
meadow in the fall, it took fire, and the stacks were consumed, causing much hardship that winter. In choosing

their lots on the river, these early-comers were guided solely by their comparative dryness, selecting those that had a high site for their shanty and first clearance. In this way, the most stony and undesirable lots were first occupied, but for many years their owners did best, as the ridgy land was brought under crop, while those who had low-lying lots had to work out half the time to earn money to buy provisions. For a long time lumbering gave employment during the winter, and great quantities of oak and pine were taken out. Of the size of the pine that grew, a canoe made by the Indians, 4 feet wide by nearly 60 long, is proof. Daniel Craig in 1823 tried to erect a sawmill at Aubrey. Knowing from the case of Duncan at St Chrysostom, that if he got the mill running he could defy the seignior, he endeavored to raise the building rapidly, cutting the tops off the trees on the site he selected high enough up to make the posts. Before he got the machinery in place, word was conveyed to Beauharnois of what he was doing, and a stop put to his proceedings. Craig, an ingenious man, ended his days at the Basin.

Back from the river, on the east side, the bush improved, hemlock being replaced by a splendid growth of elm, black ash, and hardwood. This attracted several and in 1822 James Davies and John Neal ventured into the first concession, which ultimately came to be known as Craig's, or the Scotch concession. They intended to live together and built a shanty on Davies's lot. When it was ready, all the expedients they tried to light a fire failed, and they started for the nearest shanty, that of Henry Bennie and Wm. Smyth, two young Scotchmen who had just settled on 92 and 93, and carried back a small pot filled with embers, a distance of 2 miles. The bush was remarkably thick and they did not dare to go far without blazing the trees. Their household goods and provisions they had to carry on their backs from the river. They were joined by Robert Hunter, John Craig, and John Metcalfe, and the first birth on the concession was that of a son to the first-named. William Miller says:

Hearing of the new lands that had been opened, I visited

with my father the district in the summer of 1823. As we
passed Ste Martine we saw the men at work on the first
gristmill and the first church. There was no road on the
English river, simply a foot-path on the east bank. The
west bank had not even a track and was unsurveyed. There
were very few settlers, and they were poor, having just come
in. I did not fancy the river lots, and chose the one I did
on the Scotch concession on account of the fine bush upon it,
hickory being especially plentiful. We returned home by
Beauharnois in order to see the agent. We asked first for lots
on the Grande Marais, which Brown refused, saying that he
meant to keep that concession for the French. We went to
take possession in the fall, going in a canoe to Capt. Ogilvie's,
whence we carried our goods on a handbarrow through the
bush to the English river, where we placed them in another
canoe that we borrowed. We got along smoothly until we
reached Goundry's rapids, when the canoe stuck fast in the
rocks. It was now late in the day with appearance of rain.
I said I would go and look for help and started up the river
bank, until I came to Allan Caldwell's (lot 96), where I met
a number of men returning from a bee. I told our situation
when one said, looking at the gathering darkness and the
rain that had begun, that he "wadna gae down the creek for
a dollar." I made my way back with difficulty, running into
the logs that strewed the banks, and found my father preparing to pass the night in the canoe. I said it would not do
for us to stay there on such a night, and just then I saw a
light at a distance, and we started for it. Although it did
not seem to be far off, I thought we would never get to it, for
they had been knocking down trees and it was hard to get
through them. The shanty was that of Charles McNulty,
who made us welcome, and we found —— Dickson there like
ourselves, finding temporary shelter. In the morning, they
would not let us leave until we had breakfast, when we took
another canoe to the head of the rapids and carried to it the
loading of the other, when we sailed up to Houston's (94)
where was the footpad that led into the Scotch concession.
The trees stood very thick and the only guide was the blaze.
We stayed with a neighbor until we got a shanty of our own
and that fall brushed on our lot. The winter was a very
snowy one, and on going back for the remainder of our effects
and a cow, we had to leave the latter with Robert Brodie.
We worked hard all winter and made quite a clearance across
the ridge. We had a good burn, and planted it in the
spring. The yield was wonderful, for we dug 200 bushels of

potatoes, besides the corn we cut. We never had any scarcity.
Settlers came in so slowly that it was often difficult to get
hands enough to raise a shanty. The first road we cut out
was along the base-line, which was done in 1825. That was
the year of the Miramichi fire. The country was full of
stifling smoke, which caused a feeling of sickness, and it was
so dark that we had to stay indoors. There was fire here
and there around, which, besides destroying much timber,
burned holes in the soil and obstructed passage in the bush
by toppling over large trees. My father was both a weaver
and a shoemaker, and we came from Kilmarnock. There
were only three shanties in the concession when we went in
—Robert Hunter, a carpenter, and afterwards engineer on the
boats to the Basin, who came from Lochwinnoch, James Davies,
from Kilbirnie and John Neal from Kilbarchan, who lived together, and John Metcalfe, a mason, from the north of England.
For many years we were troubled with wild beasts and at
night in winter, in going from shanty to shanty, women would
carry a fiery stick to scare the wolves. One night, when her
husband was away at work, Mrs Metcalfe was aroused by a
pack around her shanty, and looking out of its sole window,
a square of four panes, she counted 12. The wooden-latch on
the door was all that stood between her and them. One of
the settlers, William Linus, went out hunting, lost his way,
and when found his feet were frozen, which caused his death.
For a long time, and until the roads got anyway good, we
went to mill in a canoe or carried the grist.

The concession in front of the Scotch, that of the Norton
creek, although thrown open at the same time, was filled very
slowly. At the mouth of the creek was John Lang, from
Beith, who settled in 1822 and to the east of him was James
Wylie. The first to move into the concession were William
Airston, Alex. Currie, and Owen and Martin Dunn. At the
same time the third, or Irish, concession was settled, and of
it I cannot do better than give what was told me by the
last survivor of its first-settlers, Mrs David McClenaghan:

We belonged to county Derry and sailed from Lough Foyle
in the Harrison, which had 300 passengers, in May, 1824.
We had a calm passage of 6 weeks. My husband, who was a
gardener, got work about Montreal, where I remained until
July, 1826. Before that he had been up the Chateaugay
with his brother George and taken up lots on this concession,
built a shanty and made a clearance. There were several

before them. The first to move in was Samuel McKillin and his son David, three brothers, William, John, and Charles Abbott, and Nathanael Lannan, and, I think, an American, George Beach. The Abbotts and Lannan were related, and came from county Cork, and, like some of the others who took up land, had worked in making the Lachine canal. All the first settlers, except Beach and William Thompson, who was English, were Irish Protestants, which gave the concession its name. When I came, the sight was disheartening; the bush was mostly tamarac and the land was swimming in water. When you left the knolls you had to step from log to log. A good deal of the land had been burned over, and some of it was covered with bushes, which we called alderland, and a good part with brulé grass, which we cut in September and made into hay. There being no timber fit for making potash, the settlers had a hard time of it until discharges were made to drain the land, and enable them to grow grain. It was 5 years before we were able to raise wheat, but before that we had splendid crops of potatoes and corn. Most of the settlers worked out when they had a chance. My husband acted as gardener to Colonel Brown at Beauharnois for 11 summers, getting a dollar a day, and but for that we could not have lived until the land was brought in. There was no road when I came, and the outlet was across lots to the Bean river and so on to Ste Martine. The settlers were cheerful and hopeful and helped one another in a way people don't do now-a-days. We were long in getting a school, and the one first built was on the same place as the present, only on the opposite side of the road. I think it was in 1834 it was opened and the first master was Sutherland, who only stayed 4 months, when we got an excellent teacher from the city, named Lowry. Ministers came occasionally to preach in it, especially the two Laws, Isaac and James, who were Covenanters. About 1850 the old settlers began to sell out, several to the French, in order to go west, and have not left a soul to represent them. The lower side of the concession was so wet that none cared to go on what afterwards turned out to be the best lots, and the French got them.

William, a son of John Abbott, distinguished himself in the United States, and the graduate of the humble log schoolhouse of the Irish concession rose to be a member of the Senate. Quitting the Irish concession we find ourselves again on the English river opposite the site of Howick, and

Andrew, a son of its first settler, John Stewart, will tell how it came into existence :

My father was a native of Methven, Perthshire, but lived in Edinburgh, where he was doing a good business as a bookseller and bookbinder. Having several sons, a visitor from America advised him to emigrate for their sakes, and we sailed from Glasgow on the 3rd April, 1822, in the brig Jean of Irvine, which was the first ship owned by Alex. Allan and of which James Allan was cabin-boy. There were only 22 passengers and we were landed in the mud at Montreal, for there was no wharf, after a voyage of 7 weeks and 1 day. My father's intention was to go to Ohio, but he was advised to keep near Montreal, where there was a ready market at high prices, and he went up the Chateaugay. My father fancied 76, on account of the rapid, and applied to Brown for it, who said that the surveyor, Livingstone, had not sent in his report, but he would give a permit for the lot, and so my father, although there were others a year before him, was the first to get a deed for land on the English river. We came to our new home by way of Caughnawaga, and the carts took us to Rousseau's at the mouth of the English river, and where the road ended. We went up the Chateaugay to Captain Ogilvie's, and thence had everything to carry. The mill-road, which had been cut out in 1804, had grown up again, and the chief sign that it had been was a rotten bridge across the creek. We arrived here on the 1st of June. My father having some money set a number of men to work in clearing the land, and built a good-sized house, the lumber for which we got at Todd's mill, Dewittville, and brought it down the Chateaugay and up the English river on rafts. It stood where the road is now, a few yards from the bridge, and it came to be the best known tavern (named the Caledonia) on the English river. Until it was ready we lived with Andrew Glen. My father set up two kettles by the side of the river, where a large amount of potash was made, renting them to neighbors when not used by himself. Above us we had a number of neighbors, but were some time before we had any east of us, and not until James Holmes took up the lot on which was the old clearance (made by Somerville, see page 40), and from which we had got hay for our cows. Some years afterwards the grand voyer came, accompanied by Brown, and held a meeting in our house, when he made a proces-verbal for a road from the mouth of the river upwards on the baseline. This eventually caused much trouble, for when the French settled below us, they would make the road on the river-bank, which brought it out quite a distance from the road above. No 3 was then held by Gougeau, who did all he could to prevent them crossing his land to get to the road, and there was no end of trouble, which was finally ended on Brown's driving up the river and coming to a halt at the turn, owing to a deep ditch Gougeau had dug. He induced Gougeau to give a right-of-way to join the two roads for $50, and that accounts for the jog you find between 72 and 73. I cannot give the year, but it was some time about 1826 that the seignior engaged the Macarthurs to build a sawmill. The dam was erected by Henry Wright and was carried away, like a number of others, by the ice. Before it was thrown across the river, the settlers ran the rapids, which, except when the water was very high, was not dangerous to do. One day —— Dickson came along accompanied by his son. My mother advised him to leave the boy, when the father said there was nothing to fear. Near the foot of the rapids the canoe upset and the boy was drowned. The father took the body and buried it on his farm, where there are 3 graves. The sawmill was rather a primitive affair with a high and narrow wheel, not suited to streams that dwindle in volume during the summer. The power was so weak that David Wilson, reputed the strongest man in the district, undertook to hold it, and actually did so. His father managed the mill. The erection of the dam, necessarily high to suit the wheel, raised the level of the river, flooding the low lands for quite a distance above. Wilson's own flat was drowned, and for his damage and those of others the seignior refused indemnity. The mill ran until July, 1830, when it was accidentally burned. The seignior let to two Americans, Raymond and Lyman, the building of a sawmill and gristmill, which was to include a run of stones for oatmeal. They made a splendid job, and completed what was then the best mill in the province. They introduced the broad wheel of small diameter, by which all the water is made use of. They had trouble in procuring a settlement with Brown, and kept possession for several months after their completion, during which time they operated the mills. In the summer of 1832 they handed them over, when Robert King was installed as miller, and the verdict of the settlers was, that if ever there was an honest and just man it was him. Two Americans, Sears and Thomson, rented the sawmill. The building of a gristmill assured the future of the place as a village, and Arthur Ritchie, who had been selling grog in his shanty, determined to cross, and built, in 1833, a tavern on the north-west corner of the road where it crosses mill-street. He did not live long to occupy it. He was a weaver by trade, very intelligent, and much given to theological discussions, his views tending towards those of free-thinking, and he occasionally lectured or preached to the settlers. He had gone to church on the first Sunday of 1834 and while walking home with 2 friends, and criticizing what Colquhoun had said, he dropped dead. That year John Wilson, whose father had come from Scotland in 1816 and been very successful at Buckingham on the Ottawa, opened a store and tavern on the opposite corner (the east) to Ritchie's, and still (1887) lives there. John Gordon, a shoemaker, who had left East Lothian two years before, lived in Ritchie's house until it was bought by Peter Coutts in 1836, who kept store for 45 years, and was highly esteemed. Mr Gebbie, several years afterwards, bought a lot adjoining from Mr Gordon and put up a long, low building into which he moved and succeeded well. Before this, however, a bridge was built. The customers of the gristmill mostly lived on the east bank, and had to carry their grists across by walking the boom, which all could not do, so a bridge was a necessity. The seignior engaged Sears & Thomson to build one, the settlers on the east side of the river assisting; my father gave $25. A substantial bridge was raised. Like Raymond, they had trouble with Brown in obtaining what was due them, but they brought him to time, for on his driving the governor, Lord Gosford, while on a visit to him, up to Fort Covington, to see that place, they had Brown arrested, and would not release him until he gave security to cover their claim. Brown was extremely mortified at the indignity, and shunned the States thereafter. In the fall of 1848, on the ice on the river taking, 3 Canadians started to cross from Lavade's to David Wilson's and were drowned.

When Mr Gebbie took up his abode in Howick, about 1840, there were only three houses, apart from the mills. Mr Gebbie, who had been a grocer in Galston, emigrated in 1833, and came directly to Williamstown, from his obliging disposition and uprightness of character obtained the confidence of the people and became the leading man of business and largest property-holder in Howick, as the village was named after Lord Howick, at that time a member of the cabinet. In July, 1833, the seignior ceded in trust to John Stewart, David Wilson, and Charles Stewart a lot for a schoolhouse, which was built and John Clark placed in charge.

The west bank of the English river remained unsettled long after every lot on the opposite side was occupied. In 1827 Manuel was employed to make a survey of it, and that fall two brothers named Carson drew lots. One of them, Robert, said:

' We landed in Montreal from Belfast in the summer of 1827. We belonged to county Armagh. A friend told us about the lots to be given out on the English river and we drew 17 and 18, both being covered with the finest timber. My brother, who had a family, had to go at once to have a home for them, but I waited in Montreal to earn a little money, and followed him in 1830. The road had then been cut out as far as Norton creek but was very bad and not fit for wheels except in a very dry time. At Elliot's (lot 74) the cart we had hired stuck, and we had to borrow a yoke of oxen to pull it out of the hole. There were only two horses on the river when I came, and there was no road past the creek for several years afterwards, for it was I who took the job from the seignior to open the road upwards across the unconceded lots. When George Atkinson, an Irish Catholic, and who settled the same year as my brother, died, there was no road to take the body from his lot, and it was put in a canoe and conveyed to Ste Martine. That would be about 1835. We had a hard time until we could raise enough to keep us. We had food enough, but the money for boots and clothes was hard to come by. I have shouldered a bushel and a half of wheat to Ste Martine mill. My brother started a small ashery and he allowed others to use the kettles on paying $2.50 per barrel of potash. We brought a cow but there was no pasture nearer than a meadow a mile above us, and my wife, with the baby, paddled up morning and night to milk her. We cut fodder for winter on the beaver meadows west of us. The Indians then came in great numbers to pick berries on the rock, and they drew up their canoes on my lot. The water from the unconceded lands troubled all the settlers along our side of the river, coming pouring down on us and drowning the crops. It was not until a dozen years after I came, that the seignior agreed to dig a discharge, which gave us relief.

The early days of the English-river settlements were uneventful, yet there are a few occurrences which are worthy of preservation. Noted for the enthusiasm of its farmers in curling, it is interesting to know that this dates from the time of shanties with roofs of basswood scoops. In the winter of 1825 the ice was in such prime order that James Davies, a keen curler in Scotland, thought it a pity it should be allowed to pass unused and proposed to William Miller that they should have a game. They made blocks of wood, and going on to the creek had the first "gemm" played in the district, and of which Miller was the winner. The happy thought of substituting wood for stone removed the obstacle to the roaring game, and thenceforth curling was the recreation of the English river district. About two years after the introduction of curling, the first plowing-match was held. At one of the change-houses that had sprung up, William Airston and David Wilson, senr., got bantering as to which was the better plowman, and decided to have a trial. There being no land sufficiently cleared on the English-river or the creek, they had to go over to the Chateaugay, when the match took place on Captain Ogilvie's farm. A great crowd gathered to witness the match, of which Airston was declared to be the winner.*

Allusion has been made to the drinking-places which existed, and which were not peculiar to the English-river. The cheapness of whisky and the non-enforcement of the license law caused them to multiply, and they sprang up all over the district and in most unlikely places between 1825 and 1845, and were the cause of untold misery. Wherever an immigrant who had been a smuggler in the Old Country found a home, he erected a still, and of such persons the English-river had several. The most famous of its small stills was that of Daniel Gruer, who had learned the art of usquebagh-making in his native hills. His product obtained so wide a reputation that he could not supply the demand, though he charged more than double, 75 to 80 cents per

---

* The English river plowing association is the oldest in the district and one of the oldest in the province. It was organized in 1851, in the fall of which year it held a match on the farm of Moses Douglas, when the highest prize was $2.50 and the lowest 50c. William Woods was chairman of the association and Alex. Ross secretary.

gallon, what ordinary whisky could then be got for. His spirits he distilled from barley malt. "To switch the bowies" (to prevent the fermentation running over the tubs by beating it) was the occupation of the neighboring boys. Despite the excise laws, Gruer continued to make more or less until his death.

To change to matters more worthy of record, the settlers on the English river exerted themselves soon after they had established themselves to secure the means of education. William McGregor, a son of John McGregor, lot 14, S.G., and often called Doctor McGregor, from his affecting knowledge of medicine, opened the first school in a log-barn belonging to Henry Bennie. Previous to that, whatever education any of the children on the river received was by going over to the school kept by McWattie, which necessitated their living with friends on the Chateaugay, so that few were sent. On the 28th January, 1828, a meeting was held in the house of Stephen Patterson, when it was agreed they should erect a school to qualify the children of the settlement "to be useful either in church or state," that "no particular religious creed be taught the children" with their tasks, but "that a Sabbath-school may be opened" and the schoolhouse be open as a place of meeting for any religious denomination. It was agreed to buy from John Wilson 2 acres of the front of 91, and a committee was appointed, with Neill Primrose as chairman and James Craig as secretary, to carry the proposals into execution. Those present subscribed 1s 6d apiece (30 cents) to pay for the land. The work was vigorously commenced, bees being held to clear the site and roll the logs into the river, and on the 9th December the walls were raised. At the close of that day's work, a meeting was held, when the settlers organized themselves into a scholastic association and chose Henry Bennie, John Metcalfe and Barney Duigan as trustees, with Robert Hunter as chairman and Arthur Ritchie secretary. On learning the legislature had passed an act offering to pay one-half of the cost of schoolhouses that complied with certain requirements, it was resolved to put up a larger and better building, which would also accommodate the teacher and his family.　In the fall of 1829 the settlers again held bees but the project dragged for want of means, so that in June, 1830, the committee bound themselves personally for a loan of £10 ($40) at 6 per cent. from Lewis Lamont to finish the building, and it was completed that fall and William McGregor installed as teacher.　The building was an excellent one, a frame, clapboarded, and the people of the English-river section were proud of it.　Its total cost was $300.　A strange incident attending its opening, was the refusal of its use to McWattie to preach in, and a decision that it be only open to those "licensed by government to perform all the functions of a regular clergyman."　With the first Sunday of 1831 a S. S. was opened by Mr McGregor "for the purpose of instilling a principle of morality in the young and and rising generation in this settlement," nothing in the proceedings, however, was to be tolerated of a nature "to cause divisions amongst the people, on account of the many different principles of religion held by the community."　The collections at the meetings on Sunday it was resolved should be applied to buying a school library, but they were so trifling, seldom going over 20c, that this had to be dropped.　Great difficulty was found in maintaining the school, from the inability of parents to pay the fees, 20 cents a month, and the managers having no power to levy a general tax.　In October, 1831, it was agreed that those who were not members of the association in building the school should not be allowed to send their children to it unless they paid $1 entry.　A government grant, averaging $40 a year, greatly assisted, but the school, which was attended by from 40 to 60, was maintained at no small sacrifice on the part of those upon whom the burden fell.　McGregor continued to teach until the end of 1832, when James Easton succeeded him and was followed in 1835 by Wm. Smyth, an excellent teacher.　Adjoining the schoolhouse there came to live, about 1830, an old pensioner, Sergeant James Ferguson, who added to his income by working at his trade, that of a shoemaker.　There were a number of old soldiers among the first settlers.　On the west bank three lived, side-by-side, Murray, Johnson, and

Primrose, all sergeants who had seen service under Wellington. Mrs Murray had followed the regiment for 30 years, and had been previously married to a sergeant who was killed in action. On giving up school, McGregor, in company with Lewis Lamont, opened a store at the same place, now known as Riverfield, and occupied by Robert McLeod.

In securing so large a lot for the schoolhouse, the settlers had in view the using of part for a burying-ground, for which the need was felt, the custom being to convey in canoes the dead round Logan's point to the Georgetown churchyard or carry them across from Howick. The portion cleared in the winter of 1828 was apportioned in lots to the 36 subscribers to the purchase of the land, and when a second bee was held in 1830 to clear more of the lot, there was a grave, a death having happened in the Scotch concession. In the spring of 1831 a good fence was erected. It was well a place of burial had been provided, for there was soon sad need of it. In the beginning of August, 1832, a Canadian died in the sawmill after a brief illness. Nobody knew what ailed him, but before the week was out word came from Montreal of cholera, with a description of its symptoms, which were those of the poor man. The Canadians around Ste Martine were decimated, 40 dying within a mile of Reeves's. In the village, every member of one family perished, when the house was burned as the easiest mode of disinfection. Among the Old Countrymen there were only sporadic cases. The wife of Matthew McKell milked the cows in the morning, was dead before night, and buried with her daughter next day. McKell himself died while rallying from an attack. The wife of tailor Coutts died unattended and was coffined in a rude box as she died. The Scotch concession lost two of its pioneers, John Metcalfe and John Neal. The saddest incident of all was on the Chateaugay in the family of Duncan McCoig, newly landed from Scotland. In the morning the sons rudely coffined the remains of their father and took them in a canoe to the Georgetown graveyard. On returning from their sad errand, they found their mother had died, and had to repeat the same melancholy duty, for no neighbor would come near the house. The prevailing belief that to give a drink was to ensure death caused much suffering among the sick and, doubtless, several deaths. To the entreaties of one poor woman her daughter yielded, seeing that hope was past, and brought her a cupful of spring-water. It revived her, she got more, and recovered.

The first religious services held on English river were those by McWattie in John Lang's house. The providing of a schoolhouse did away with the necessity of going to private houses, and any preacher who came along held service in it. Colquhoun and Muir both regarded the English-river as a regular station. The majority of the settlers had been seceders in Scotland and their relations with them were not harmonious, so that they encouraged the visits of ministers of other denominations, at one time having services conducted by a Methodist. About 1840 the minister of the Congregational church at Russeltown was induced to hold a fortnightly service at the schoolhouse, and the attendance was deemed sufficient to justify raising a church, and a small building was erected by the roadside, near Wylie's creek, and was fairly attended. After the drowning of Mr Bowles (page 231) no successor was available, and the congregation united with the Free church. In 1838 a number of settlers offered sufficient inducement to the Associate Presbyterian Synod of the U. S., commonly known as the Covenanters, to secure regular visits from a minister, and in 1843 were formally organized, electing elders and constituting a kirk-session. A frame church was constructed on Houston's, lot 94, and a call extended to James Law, which he declined. Work on the church stopped for want of funds, and it remained in an unfinished state (available for use during summer alone) until the Rev James Fettes arrived in November, 1846, as a delegate from Scotland in the interests of the Free church. He passed the winter among them, and aroused intense sympathy for his denomination, so that the requisite funds were subscribed, the church was moved down to beside the burying-ground at Riverfield, and completed, and a strong and earnest congregation formed.

The lots between Howick and the mouth of the English river were secured by the French, who were so slow in taking possession that James Brown, who went on to lot 58 in 1832, found there was not a house between his and Caldwell's. The land between the English river lots and those on the Chateaugay remained in a state of nature until about 1850. For this there were several reasons, the frequent changes in the ownership of the seigniory, the desire to convert the land into free and common soccage tenure, and the expense of opening discharges to make the flats habitable. When it was decided to throw open the land contained in the peninsula formed by the two rivers for settlement, the work went on quickly. The surveys were made by William Barrett, assisted by William Edwards, between 1845 and 1848, and as soon as they filed their plans, the lots were taken up, largely by the sons of neighboring farmers. They were double ranges and were better known by the names given to them than by their numbers—Tullochgorum, Fertile Creek, Australia, California, Milwaukee, and Chicago. The first name was derived from an incident in its settlement. In 1848 Neil McEwan bought 38 and celebrated the completion of his house with a jollification, during which the giving of a name to the new settlement came up, when McEwan, who was in a convivial mood, suggested Tullochgorum, and Tullochgorum it was, and the party danced, as only Highlanders can, the reel of that name. Nobody suspected the extraordinary fertility of the land on this concession. Some time before 1830 a party of farmers from the Chateaugay had occasion to journey across it, which they did by jumping from logs and tree-roots, and while resting on a dead tree on No 1, S. Geo., and viewing the water that lay around, one of them exclaimed, "This will never be land," in which the others agreed. In those days it was flooded by the water from the Flat Rock and converted into a shallow lake, covered with cattails and scrub poplar. Its wetness saved its fertility, for the fires that periodically swept among the trees left the soil untouched. The lower end of the concession was settled in 1851, when the road was extended from Howick, and the year following Thomas

Chisholm made his way to the upper end, hauling in the lumber for a house by a bypath that ran along the ridges. With the opening of discharges, the land was brought in without difficulty. Fertile Creek concession was opened simultaneously, and was of the same character. The other concessions were different, being largely high and stony, and covered with good bush. An old Highlander, abandoning his farm in Williamstown, was asked where he was going. "To California," he answered, to which country there was then a rush. His reply gave name to the concession on which he was making his new home, and it naturally followed that the adjoining one should be Australia. After the first burn, the land on these ridges gave a great crop of fine wheat, which suggested Milwaukee, the A1 wheat of the market in those days, and Chicago. The seigniory did well by the sale of the lots on those concessions, charging from $4 to $6 an acre, according to the quality of the soil.

WILLIAMSTOWN—ENGLISH
RIVER CONCESSION.

58 James Brown
67 (?) James Wright
72 —— Andrews
—— Laviolette
73 —— Gougeau
John Elliot
74 & 75 —— Somerville
· Alex. Reeves
74 —— Bisson
J. Elliot
75 James Holmes
76 John Stewart
77 John Sawyer
78 Arthur Ritchie
79 Matthew McKell
James Knox
80 David Wilson
81 Daniel McArthur
82 Alex. McArthur
83 James Wilson
84 James Blair
85 John Currie
86 —— Hamilton
87 Charles McNulty
88 Dennis McNulty
89 —— Dickson
90 Robert Robertson
91 John Wilson
92 Henry Bennie
93 William Smith
94 James Houston
95 William Kerr
96 Daniel Craig
Allan Caldwell
97 James Wylie

FIRST DOUBLE OR SCOTCH
CONCESSION.

112 John Doherty
113 Robert Craig
David Fife
114 John Cousins
116 Allan Caldwell
117 James Davies
118 John Neal
119 Robert Hunter
120 William Miller
121 Thomas Maloney
122 James Donald

123 John Craig
124 George Thomson
125 Patrick Handlin
126 John Metcalfe
127 Daniel Owen
128 Alex. Maxwell
120 William Hazlie
    Arthur Hazlie
130 William Stewart
131 William Linus

SECOND DOUBLE OR IRISH
    CONCESSION.

132 Robert McClenaghan
133 David McClenaghan
134 George McClenaghan
135 Robert Adams
136 Francis Brennan
137 Samuel Egleston
138 Nathanael Lannan
139 Charles Abbott
140 John Abbott
    William Abbott
141 Samuel McKillin
146 John Roy
147 James Gordon
152 George Beach
153 Andrew McCracken
154 William Scott
    James McCracken
    —— Thomson

GEORGETOWN CONCESSION OF
    RIVER LOTS.

1 Howick village
2 John Stewart
3 William Gardner
4 —— Gagnier
5 Samuel McClymont
6 —— Malette
7 Hugh Henderson
8 William Currie
9 John Devine
10 John Lett
11 Michael Gaynor
12 Donald Gruer
    Daniel and Robert Gruer
13 James Murray
14 —— Johnson
15 Neill Primrose
16 William McKell
17 William Carson
18 Robert Carson
19 and 20 Alex. Logan
21 —— Reardon
22 William Currie
23 John McKell
24 Malcolm McFarlane
25 William Lang
26 George Atkinson
27 Nathanael Lynch

CHAPTER XVI.

WHEN the lots along the English river and the Chateaugay were occupied, it became necessary to open up more of the seigniory for the immigrants who continued to come, and it was decided to survey the land contained between the Chateaugay and the St Louis. Of the settling of that portion of it comprised in North Georgetown and Helenstown a better idea can be given by adhering to the narrative of the first to commit himself to its inhospitable wilds, than by separate descriptions of each concession. After perusing his simple tale of hardships endured and of indomitable perseverance under conditions the most discouraging, the reader will agree that the name of John Symons is to be honored for the intrinsic qualities of the man apart from the accidental circumstance of his being the pioneer of the wide expanse bounded by the two rivers named. In numerous conversations, the writer learned the following details :

I was born in Paisley in 1803, and was brought up to be a silk-weaver. Hearing that a beginning was about to be made in my department of that trade in Lowell, Mass., I resolved to emigrate, and sailed for Quebec in the fall of 1827. On landing in Canada I found I had made a great mistake in endeavoring to reach Lowell by the St Lawrence route, and that a long and expensive journey was before me. I fell in with the husband of an old neighbor, Robert Boyd, and he insisted I should go and see his wife, especially as he lived near Laprairie, which I would have to pass through on my way to the States, for there was then no outlet to New England by Quebec. He had a farm near Dunn's mills, about 5 miles west of Laprairie. I was kindly received, and was induced to forego my intention of pushing on to Lowell until the spring; the more easily because the weather had turned cold. I put my hand to whatever work there was doing. Boyd had an ashery, collecting the ashes from Caughnawaga and neighborhood, which was visited once a week. I learned the whole art of potash-making that winter, and it was lucky

for me that I did. Boyd had bought a farm on the Chateaú-
gay the year before and prepared to move on to it before the
sleighing left, and I assisted, which was the cause of introducing me to that section. I got acquainted with the settlers,
Sandy Williamson and Robert Brodie especially; I liked them
and they liked me, and they were very urgent I should give
up the notion of seeking work at my trade and take up land,
they promising to assist me. There was a vacant farm at
that time on the river, but it was beyond my means, and I
told them that I would have to start at the beginning and
clear a farm for myself. Williamson, who was a great hunter,
knew every inch of the country, and he advised me to take
up a certain lot on the fourth concession, which was then
being surveyed. I worked all that season among the settlers
on the river, learning a great deal, for I knew nothing whatever about farming. One day in the fall Robert Brodie
started with me to find the lot recommended by Williamson.
There was a lumber-road, formed by Macaulay's men, that
winded out and in across the country to the St Louis, and as
the season was dry we had no great difficulty in going over
it. When we reached the St Louis we found the surveyor's
pickets of the lines, but the lots had not yet been bounded.
Williamson told me to take the third lot, and Brodie, starting
at the river, stepped the 10 acres which should have brought
us to it, but did not, for we knew nothing about the gore-lot
being so wide, so were 4 acres astray. Well, Brodie picked
out a knoll as a site for my shanty, and after looking at the
timber, we returned home, and I went to Beauharnois and
took out my location-ticket, paying $10 for it, and agreeing
to pay 10 cents rent per acre a-year. After the New Year
some time, my friends made a bee and drove out to my lot.
Driving their horses and oxen round and round they tramped
a place in the snow where it was intended to build, and going
to work, the trees were soon falling, being shaped into logs,
and placed one upon another, so that before it got dark my
shanty was complete. No sawed lumber was used, the floor
and roof being split basswood logs. They left me in possession of it, and I was emphatically alone, for there was not
a living soul nearer me than 5 miles. At that time there
was not a clearing west of the corner of the Baker concession
on the St Louis road; in fact, the land had not been surveyed.
It was solid woods or swamp in every direction. Where St
Louis village now is, there was a hunter's cabane, a little east
of the site of the Catholic church, where a son of Bourbonneau,
a tavern-keeper in Beauharnois, lived when he was out on the

chase, and not another sign of life. I wrote to my wife to
join me, and went to work, chopping day after day, alone, in
order to have a decent home ready for her and the children,
never resting until Saturday afternoon, when I dropped work
and went to Brodie's, to stay until Monday, when I took
back with me provisions for another week. One day my axe
glanced, and cut my right foot. I bound up the wound as
well as I could and lay in my shanty unable to move and
suffering intensely. Saturday and Sunday passed and I
knew Brodie's folks would be getting anxious. I made shift
to crawl, rather than walk, over to their place, and found
that they were about to start for my shanty, fearing that
something had befallen me. The wound soon healed, though
it still affects my walking, and I was once more at work.
When the snow melted, I found the knoll on which my
shanty stood was an island, and that my lot was knee-deep
in water. I had not foreseen that it was so wet a lot, and
soon became convinced I could do nothing with it, for there
was no outlet and the water would have to lie until dried
by the July sun. I hurried to Beauharnois, and asked Brown
to change the lot. He said he did not expect me to live on
land that was under water, and gave me a ticket for lot 33,
which was the one I asked for, because it had a ridge on it.
I set to work on it with a will to make up for lost time.
Having no help, I could not log, so I just brushed the trees as
I felled them, and, dibbling round the fallen trunks, planted
potatoes and some corn. The track to the river being very
bad at that time, I did not go to Brodie's for Sunday, so that
for 11 days I did not see a human being. One windy day I
was chopping a large rock-elm, and from the wind blowing
on the top was uncertain which way it would fall. I was
watching it intently, ready to move out of the way when it
would begin to topple over, when a voice behind me said in
French, "It is not going." I jumped in astonishment, and
saw a French Canadian. For years after, when he would
meet me, he would laugh as he recollected my surprise. The
constant clutching of the axe affected the sinews of my hands,
which were unused to such a strain, and the fingers remained
bent for the rest of my life. Of the desolation of the country
south of me I had soon experience. I thought it would be a
great advantage to have a direct road to the Chateaugay
from my lot, and I determined to see if I could not get one.
I started one warm afternoon, scrambling over logs and sometimes going on my knees under them, and every now and
then climbing up a trunk to find out where I was going. I

always found I was surrounded by the trunks of blackened trees, and the ground covered by fallen ones, water, and cat-tails. So desolate was the scene and hopeless-looking the prospect of finding a way out, that the very dowg that was with me sat down at the foot of a tree and yowled. Night came on as I got a sight of a clump of green spruces, which stood where the Ormstown concession now is, and as I pressed on towards them it grew quite dark. I came to a creek, and to find the direction of its current, put my hand in its water. Just when I felt that I could struggle no longer, and might as well prepare to pass the night where I was, I heard a noise. My first thought was—a bear. I shouted, and, to my astonish-ment, got an answer. It was people on their way to their homes in the Ormstown concession, and I speedily joined them, and found the way to the Chateaugay. There were wild beasts in the forest, but they never gave me any annoy-ance. I only met a bear once. I was on my way to Brodie's one Sunday morning, when I suddenly heard the trampling of feet on the dry litter, and shortly saw two bears approach-ing me. The advice Sandy Williamson gave me for such a contingency, flashed upon me, and I bent my head until I could look between my legs and began dancing and capering. The brutes looked at me for a moment or two, and then, affrighted by the strange spectacle, turned and fled. Another time, John McConachie was helping me to chop, and on his having to go over a pile of logs, stepped up them, and was astounded, on raising his head over the top log, to find him-self looking in the face of a bear, which was scrambling up the other side. With a yell, he jumped down, and came running to me, but the bear did not follow. I got up a shanty on my lot, but before I had it ready, my mistress and the family arrived, and they had to stay in the old one for a while. I got two neighbors about the same time, William Patton, who had been a farmer in Scotland, and James Stewart; they sat down on either side of me. I had been saving my ashes all along, keeping them covered with elm-bark, and was most anxious to get a kettle and begin making potash. I had not a dollar and my neighbors were little better off. Stewart had enough to pay a French Canadian for sawing trees and making leaches and that was all, so I went to see if I could not get a kettle on credit. On entering Douglas & Wilkinson's store, I found Sandy Graham and Mr Brodie sitting there, and they burst out laughing at me, for I had no boots on and my trousers were rolled up above my knees, for I had to wade a great part of the way, and was dirty, ragged, and wet I told Douglas my errand and said, as an old clerk of Richardson, Forsythe & Co.'s I thought he might be able to oblige me. Brodie cried out he would be my surety for the payment, and Douglas agreed to get me a Three Rivers' kettle, which were the best, for they are thickest at the bottom. It arrived the week after, when I bargained with McConachie, who had a yoke of small oxen, to drag it into my lot for $4. He started in the morning and it was growing dark when the oxen stuck within sight of my lot, being fairly beat Next morning they were tackled to it afresh, and the kettle was placed on the line between Stewart and myself, for we were partners. That kettle was the saving of the fourth concession, for it brought to us the only money we could get for several years wherewith to buy provisions and pay our rent. Each settler could make two barrels, sometimes three, in a year, and as it was worth from $30 to $40 a barrel, the amount was of great consequence. We let neighbors have the use of the kettle and other apparatus for $2 a barrel, and, at least, 120 barrels were made in it. My potatoes turned out a remarkable crop, but the corn, from being planted late, did not ripen. Before winter set in, there were several lots taken up, and we could now have bees to log. The wetness of the land was the great drawback. James Dryden and James Hunter placed their shanties back on the bank of the creek to have a dry place, and a sort of a road began to be formed along it out to the St Louis. James Benning, an excellent farmer, who took my old lot, had to make a sort of a raft to get at his work in the spring. Several came and, after a short trial, left. There was Herring, a first-rate farmer, who was fairly starved out. He went and took up land near Ottawa, and became prosperous. George Steel boarded with me while trying to clear the lot he had taken up. One hot day, he came in from where he had been brushing, up to the ankles in water and with the mosquitoes very bad, and, putting on his coat, said he would not take it off again. He left all and, after several changes in life, died a wealthy banker in Chicago. The land was fairly drowned and we kept dinging at Brown to open discharges. He resisted, thinking he could force us into doing the work alone, but we set the right way about it, and the seignior was compelled to assist in making sufficient discharges. It would be the second fall, I think, when I sowed my first wheat. I went across the brulé to the Ormstown concession, and bought from Hood half a bushel of fall wheat, which I carried home on my back. I was afraid it would be too late for sowing if I waited until my potatoes (which were in hills) were ready to dig, so I pulled up the shaws and raked the ground, sowing my wheat. When I dug the potatoes, I hoed back the soil with the seed wheat in it, as well as I could, and the next season I had a wonderful crop. I was a poor thresher, having had no experience, yet I had 16 bushels to take to Beauharnois mill, and had the straw been right threshed would have had 20. That was the first wheat grown on the fourth concession, and all my neighbors had to get a pickle of the flour. Some of us had got cows and sheep, but none were able to buy a yoke of oxen, and for want of them we suffered much. The French Canadian carters charged us $1.50 a barrel to haul our potash from where Bougie is, about a mile east of the church, to Beauharnois, and a dollar more if they came up to the kettle for it, and often could not get them even at these prices. On an occasion when there were 13 barrels ready, I determined we should haul it ourselves. None of the others being willing to run the risk of going in debt for a yoke, I started out to the river, calling first on Williamson, who had no money on hand. I walked to Captain Ogilvie's, where I got the loan, and bought the oxen. They did all the hauling, I charging half a dollar to take a barrel to the mouth of the creek, or a day's work, which was generally given in preference. It would be about that time we got our first teacher, an elderly man who had been in a good way in Scotland, named Graves. I gave a spare building for a schoolhouse, and as there were only nine scholars to go to it, the fees had to be high, and were fixed at 4s 6d (90 cents) a month. It was well spent money, though hard for us to get, for he brought on the children wonderfully. He was an odd man, and would often, instead of rising in the morning, have the children stand round his bed, while he would hear them with his head on the pillow, and on fine days would leave the schoolhouse and take them out for a walk and teach them as they went along. Our food was coarse, chiefly potatoes, and often difficult to get, but there never was anything like want. We shared with one another, and if a family ran short, they borrowed until they got a fresh supply. Everything had to be carried on the back from Beauharnois or the Chateaugay. One neighbor, who was going to have a bee, started to get a supply. The day was very hot and he trudged along wearily with his bag on his shoulder. On reaching home, he told his wife what he had been able to get, a quantity of peas and 2 pounds of butter. She opened the bag, but there was no butter, simply a greasy paper. We had great joking as we supped the peas, that the butter was in them though we could not see it, for it had soaked into them.

The settling of the 3rd concession followed on that of the 4th, Robert Sinton and Archibald McEwen going into it in 1830, when lots were first given out, and James Howden finding a home on the 2nd the same year. In 1831 David Tait, an intelligent and worthy man, who lived to the patriarchal age of 90, arrived from his native parish of Cockpen, and joined them. Like the 4th concession, the 3rd was a mere frog-pond during the early part of the season and to find dry spots for their shanties the settlers had to go to the rear of their lots, which brought them close to the 2nd. The saving feature in the land was the splendid bush that covered it, more especially on the 2nd concession, and which, turned into potash, maintained the settlers until discharges were opened and crops could be raised. How thick the bush was, melancholy proof was supplied by a painful incident. Two daughters of Neil Conley, both girls in years, went out to gather sap, for it was sugar-time. They could not find their way back to their father's shanty. In their wanderings they separated. The youngest was discovered by the searching parties that were speedily at work, but of the older not a trace could be found. There were all manner of surmises to account for her disappearance; the most favored, that she had been kidnapped by Indians. Years rolled by, the land became cleared, and on 23, 2nd con., the fragile skeleton of the little maid was found. So dense was the forest, that the searchers had failed to see her, although within hail, almost, of the home she sought in vain to find. I could fill a page or two with the experiences of the settlers on these concessions, but they would be but a repetition of those given in Mr Symons' narrative. They, in time, reaped a rich reward, for the soil was of the best. In 1837 the settlers of the two concessions joined in raising a school, of which the first master was Thomas Cross. The lots on the 1st concession were passed by the Old Countrymen, who judged, from the timber on them, that the soil was light. In this they were mistaken, for the hemlock that abounded on this concession was second-growth, and the land equal to any in the district. The few Scotch families now on it, went in after 1840.

The "New Lands," as the concessions in the neighborhood of the St Louis were called, came to have a great name among those seeking homes, and were taken up as quickly as surveyed. At the lower end of the 5th range Ormstown, about 1835, a settlement of Old Countrymen was formed, including four brothers of the name of Selkirk and Charles Robertson. Some years afterwards they were joined by a few others. They had much difficulty in sending their potash to market, having to float the barrels down a great discharge that had been dug out to Bryson's creek, and thence to the Chateaugay, until the 4th concession road was opened, which was not for many years, for a great swamp stretched between lots 4 and 10, dividing the concession and rendering communication between the two ends, except on foot, impracticable. When it became probable the tenure would be changed, the seignior stopped conceding lots, which checked the settling of the New Lands for several years. When deeds of free and common soccage could be given, the concessions were speedily filled ; the 5th range mainly by habitants from Ste Martine and the Basin, who paid $4 an acre.

Along the St Louis the French Canadians kept creeping upwards from Beauharnois, but it was not until about 1834 that the first house was built on the site of the present village of St Louis de Gonzague. It was a small store, and stood on the southwest corner of the 4th concession road, owned by Charles Larocque, in many regards one of the most remarkable men the province has produced. His mother was a Highland woman, and he combined the best qualities of both races. After spending a number of years in the North-west, he returned to his native province and entered business, opening stores at different points and carrying on a large trade in lumbering and contracting. Wholly uneducated, he had to rely on his prodigious memory for records of his transactions, and it rarely failed him even in trifling details. His store at St Louis he placed in charge of his nephew

Isidore Larocque, afterwards the keeper of the first tavern in
Valleyfield. When, in 1835, Gilbert Cook and his brothers,
natives of Cantyre, took up lots, Larocque's was the only
house in St Louis. Many Scotchmen followed the example
of the Cooks, until they formed quite a settlement along the
road that divides the 6th and 7th ranges, and, slowly and
with many hardships, redeemed a section of country now
almost exclusively held by French Canadians. Below St
Louis village, few Scotch settled along the river, due in part
to Brown's being desirous to give the lots to the French and
to his demanding $15 for the survey, instead of $10. Habitants on the St Lawrence front drew them, and occasionally
worked at making clearances for several years before sending
their sons to occupy them. The bringing into close contact
of the two races in the St Louis district, had a peculiar result.
Watching the Old Country farmers, the habitants began to
imitate them, by raising coarse grains and roots, by going in
more for live-stock, and even seeding down an occasional
field. The priests were alarmed for the effect upon their
tithes, and exhorted their hearers to shun the innovations of
the Anglais and to do as their fathers had done, continue to
raise wheat. When Father Saya came he took a disinterested
view of the matter, and told his flock they would benefit
themselves by copying the farming of the Scotch. A decision
of the courts, which finally established that pease is grain
and therefore liable to tithe, removed in great part this
singular objection of the priesthood to a change in culture.
So few roots did they raise, that hardly a habitant had more
potatoes than would last over New Year, and the Scotch
settlers added largely to their incomes by selling to them in
the spring.

Mr Symons, finding in his neighbor at the corners, Charles
Larocque, a congenial spirit, became intimate with him, and
on his proposing he should join him as partner, he left his
farm and took up his abode in St Louis about 1841, which,
even then, was only a place of two or three houses. Mr
Symons entered into his new sphere of life with the same
ardor as he had shown in subduing the wilderness and was,

before long, engrossed in many projects. After Wakefield's election he was at dinner with that gentleman, along with Daly, known as "the everlasting secretary," and Derbishire, the Queen's printer. In the course of conversation, the subject of seigniorial-tenure came up, and Daly abruptly asked Symons what he had against the rule of the seigniors that he wished it ended. "Where I find most fault is," answered Symons, "that the seigniors are like the dog in the manger: what they will not use themselves, they will not let others get." He went on to explain that the settlement in which he lived suffered much from want of a sawmill, yet the seignior would neither build one on the rapids at St Louis nor allow anybody else to do so. Wakefield, on hearing this, said he was not aware that such was the case, and he would see to it that whatever powers were not wanted by the seignior would be sold to private persons. He was as good as his word, and singular to say, on the night following the day on which intimation was given to Mr Symons that he could have the power, Colborne's sawmill, built a few years before farther down the river, was burned by two habitants who alleged that its dam was drowning their land. Setting to work Mr Symons built a mill at the foot of the rapid, not being allowed to run a dam near the head of it, on account of the land that would thereby be drowned. The country above was still in a state of nature, and only two proprietors had to be settled with, one being Coté, who owned the present show-ground. The mill did famously until July, when the water failed, with a great stock of logs uncut. In casting about for a remedy, the report that lingered among old settlers, that a cut had been made from the St Lawrence as a feeder early in the century, came to Mr Symons's mind and he applied to Mr Norval for information. He knew nothing of the circumstance and disbelieved in it, and, when asked to do so, searched in vain among the seigniory records for any reference to it. Shortly afterwards he accidentally stumbled upon a small parcel of papers, which related to the feeder in question, consisting mainly of correspondence between Mr Richardson, the then seigniory agent, and Mr Winter, the local

agent and surveyor, and Thomas Fingland, who had undertaken the work. The locality of the canal and its dimensions
were described. Armed with these documents, Mr Symons
set out, accompanied by a French employé, to search for the
long-lost canal. Said Mr Symons :

Surveyors had run a line for a projected road from the
head of the Beauharnois canal, then being built, to Huntingdon, and I knew it must cross the feeder. We found the line,
and carefully followed it through the bush, walking so far
that I was afraid we had missed it, when my feet suddenly
gave way and I found I was in a ditch of mud and slush that
reached my waist. I called out to the man, that I had found
what we were looking for. We were so thirsty that, before
exploring it, we made our way to the lake, a mile distant, for
a drink. The feeder was pretty clear but stagnant, which I
found was due to the cut across the ridge to the north of the
St Louis not being deep enough, over which the water was
trickling. The feeder had been dug 3½ feet deep, and I saw
that all that was needed was to lower the cut across the ridge,
and there would be abundance of water in the St Louis at
the driest season. Satisfied that the project was entirely
feasible, I sent an application to the company that then
owned the seigniory to join me in doing the necessary work.

When Mr Symons' letter was laid before the directors, one
of them asked what sort of a man this was who proposed to
take water from the St Lawrence and give it back to it again,
when he was answered that he was not a rich man, but one
who never failed in anything he undertook. Authority was
given, and having the seigniory's assistance Mr Symons
cleared the feeder, and so widened and deepened it that,
thenceforth, there was sufficient water for his mill and the
seigniory's at Beauharnois. The cost was $4000, of which the
seigniory was to pay half. By this time the company that
held it was in difficulties, and, unable to pay cash, proposed
that Symons and his partner Larocque should take the 1400
acres of unconceded land that lay alongside their property at
$4 an acre, and the $2000 go in part payment, which they
had to do, but lost by the transaction, for much of the land
was marshy, and there was no road between St Louis and
St Timothy until Mr Symons undertook to make one, which
he did by laying the swampy portions with mill-slabs and

covering them with the soil dug from the ditches. The opening of the sawmill, with the consequent stimulus it gave to lumbering, brought in a number of French Canadian laborers and tradesmen, who put up shanties around it and the place began to wear the appearance of a village, to which the name of Rocqueville was given. On acquiring the 1400 acres, quarter acre lots were sold along the river for $30 a-piece, and the village, a long, straggling one, grew apace. About 1846 Mr Symons (with the consent of the seigniory agent) added to his sawmill a gristmill, which was copied from the Athelstan mill, and its construction still further added to the business of the growing village. To help it on, Larocque offered the glass, nails, and shingles for a church, and, about 1846, a wooden building was raised, and a priest of many virtues, Father Saya, was the first to hold a regular charge. He was a strong temperance man and used his influence repeatedly to defeat all attempts at opening a tavern. As the place grew the inconvenience of having no place of entertainment for visitors was felt, particularly by Mr Symons, whose house was almost a place of public resort. Representing this to the priest, an understanding was come to, that there should be a tavern and one only, and this compact has become traditional, for though St Louis is ten times larger now than it was then it has still only the one house of accommodation.

As to church matters among the Protestants, they, from their communication being better with Beauharnois than with South Georgetown and Ormstown, attended service there, and the Rev Mr Roach visited them regularly, and preached once a month in their houses. In 1842 the seigniory made present of 50 acres for a glebe, and on it a temporary building was raised as a place of meeting, and a congregation of nearly 50 families organized, to whom Mr Roach preached every third Sunday. The disruption broke up the little assembly, fully half following the Rev Mr Fettes, and building a good church at the eastern end of the village.

NORTH GEORGETOWN.

1ST CONCESSION.

1 Francis Turner, came in
.1842
3 John Galbraith, 1846
14 Wm Douglas, 1844
15 James Carruthers
16 John Carruthers
18 Rev Dr Muir
19 Alex Galbraith, 1854
20 Thomas Watson, 1848
21 George Penny, 1842
22 Philyre Martin, 1844
23 Michael Martin, 1844
25 Walter Patton, 1844

2ND CONCESSION.

2 John Howden
3 James Watt
4 Andrew Hunter
5 Robert Brown and Alex.
Craik
6 William Bursell and Jas.
Martin
7 Thos. Bursell and James
Brady
9 —— McNab
11 Lawrence Quig and
Anthony Rigg
12 George Downs
13 Jean Perrot and Joseph
de Grosseliers
14 Joseph Perrot
16 James Brodie
16 and 17 Peter McArthur
18 Alex. McArthur
19 Daniel McArthur
20 Robert Brodie, jr.
21 Robert Brodie, senr.
22 Duncan McCormick
23 James Hall, sold to Wm.
Hamilton
24 Andrew Elliot
25 James Dryden and Wm.
Cochrane, who sold to
James Tassie

26 James Howden
28 William Kilgour

3RD CONCESSION

1 and 2 John Alexander and
Robert Alexander
3 John Somerville and
James Alexander
4 William Donaldson, first;
Samuel Bursell, son-in-
law, 2nd
5 Robert Sinton
6 David Tait
7 Lewis Younie
8 Hugh Cowan, 1st; Adam
Paxton, 2nd; William &
Thos. Thompson, 3rd
9 Duncan Campbell
10 Archd. McEwen
11 John McCormick
12 A. McEwen, jr., & Andrew
Bennet
13 John Thompson, 1st; Robt.
Brodie, 2nd; A. McDougall,
3rd; Wm. Anderson, 4th,
and John Mair 5th
14 Robert Wilson, 1st, and
Wm. Black 2nd
15 James Hunter, 1st; Hugh
Cowan, 2nd; Robert King,
3rd
16 John Lockerby
17 Neil Conley
18 T. & J. Pullen, 1st; Hugh
McEwen, 2nd
19 Wm. Wilson & John Watt
20 Henry McKendrick and
Wm. Leith
22 Donald McCoig
22 Andrew Bennet and Neil
McNaughton
23 John Cheyne
24 Andrew McFarlane and
Wm. Maxwell
25 John Elliot, 1st; Wm. Hall
and Jas. Alexander 2nd

26 William Morrison
27 —— Roy

4TH CONCESSION.

1 Anthony Rigg
2 James Dryden
3 James Hunter
4 John Symons and James Benning
5 Hugh Symons and John Richardson
10 Michael Lynch
12 John Sawyer
13 Charles Cumming
14 Duncan Cumming
15 William Hall, junr.
16 John Hastie and Angus Menzies
17 John McCoig
18 John McNeil
19 Edward Thompson
20 Alex. Cumming
21 John Cumming and Patrick O'Mullin

22 Cornelius McKeegan and James Cowley
23 Robert Beatty
24 Captain Cook
25 Archd. McKellar
28 Duncan McMillan
29 William Wright
30 John Heron
31 Adam Tennant and John Somerville
32 Ralph Young and James Stewart
33 John Symons
34 William Patton
35 William Hall, senr.
36 William Kemp and John Hope

BEAUHARNOIS ROAD.

7 John Anderson, 1844
8 George Mitchell, 1841
9 Robert Sutherland, 1846
Robert Dunn's mill, built 1869

HELENSTOWN, SIXTH RANGE
Cadastral
No.107 St. L. James Anderson
105 William Baird
93 James Tait

No. 87 St L. John Gardner
69 David Brown
68 George Swanston
67 William Hunter
30 St Et. Robert Dunn

Occupants of lots in Ormstown will be found at end of next chapter.

CHAPTER XVII

THE sett'ement of the end of the 4th concession next the Chateaugay followed on that of the upper end. In appearance it was not inviting. The great fire of 1825 had swept over the section, leaving a wide track of blasted forest, the great pines standing, white and naked, like a forest of masts as far as the eye could reach, while, where the land was wet, the fallen trunks were matted by a thick growth of alder-bushes. The first to move in were John McNeil and Edward Thomson, who took up lots in 1829. The sons of the latter built a small sawmill on the creek which ran through his lot, called Evident, about 1840, which ran for several years. As the outlet of the lands west of it, which were all swampy at that time, it was a considerable stream, and kept the mill going until well on in summer. Duncan Cumming, son of John, says :

We came to the concession in 1831, when the only settlers before us at the south end of it were Thomson and McNeil. There was no road, and we had to carry what we brought in loads on our backs through the bush and brulé. Owing to so many immigrants having come in that season, provisions were scarce, and oatmeal and flour were the same price that winter, $5 the quintal (112 ℔). In the spring we ran out of food entirely, when, hearing John Harvey had peas, mother and I walked to his place, got a bushel for a dollar, and carried home the bag on our backs, by turns. The land was so very wet that many, in despair of making anything out of it, left. Oh, it was nasty, working in water nearly up to your knees. So little of the land was fit for raising grain, that for a long while we lived by potash-making, and the first year we made 9 barrels, for which we got $5 a 100 ℔. It was a number of years after we came before a road was cut out to the Chateaugay, and horses were only used in sleighing-time. At the north end of the concession the road was opened as far as John Richardson's, who was a tailor, but the swamp that intervened between his lot and McNeil's, was not spanned until 1841, when it was taken up by French Canadians, and is now a fine flat of fertile land. Alexander Cumming started a small still, which had the repute of making the best Scotch whisky in the district.

In his narrative of exploring the country between his new home and the Chateaugay, John Symons expresses his astonishment at encountering people who had settled on the Ormstown concession. That concession was surveyed by Manuel in 1826 and 1827, and before he was done settlers began to move in, and who were mainly young, unmarried men, few of whom knew anything about farming, being weavers, shoemakers, coal-miners, and the like. The first settler on the lower, or eastern end, was Alexander Fisher, a young man from Longue Pointe, whose people had sent him into the bush to be out of the way of evil companions. Mrs Robt. Barr thus tells the story of the coming of her people:

We belonged to Houston, Renfrewshire, and left in June, 1827. I had four children and my husband's parents, and my brother, Peter Lindsay, accompanied us. We had been advised to go to Sandy Shaw's when we reached Montreal, and telling him we wanted an empty house to stay in until we got land, he soon quartered us. My husband went to Mr Brodie of Petite Côté to make enquiry about a relative for whom he had a letter, when Brodie advised him to go to the Chateaugay. The men started off to hunt land, and went up as far as Trout river. The lower Ormstown concession had just been thrown open and everybody advised them to go in there, that the land was so good it would prove the garden of the district. They examined it and went to Beauharnois to draw lots 5 and 6 on the second concession, but they met at the seigniory-office William Rice coming out at the door after securing them and No. 7. My husband and Lindsay then took 5 and 6 on the 3rd range, and coming back to the city, we started together for our new home. At Lachine we went on board Gregory Dunning's bateau, and it took all day to get to the Basin. Next day carts brought us up to David Bryson's. The roads were muddy and I thought Canada a very dirty sort of country. The Brysons were very kind and offered us houseroom until a shanty was built, but we would not hear of that, there being so many of us, and asked for the use of their cow-stable, which we cleaned out and put up beds in. Building a shanty proved a long job, for my husband was a carpenter and he wanted to put up a good one. He squared the logs and forming a sawpit, they turned out boards with two frame-saws he brought with him and boarded the floor, ceiling, and roof. It was a good house. While they worked, I cooked and took out their provisions to them. There was no road and the land was so cut up with swamps that there was no travel through the bush, and the only way to get out or in was to follow the creek that comes out below Allan's Corners. As soon as we got settled down, I left to pay a visit to Hugh Barr and his wife on Trout river, who had been old neighbors in Scotland. Tying my shoes and stockings in my handkerchief and pinning up my skirts, I started, carrying my babe on my haunch. It proved to be a fearfully warm day, and I suffered much from thirst, for I could not bear the Chateaugay water, from its being soft. There was just one house at Ormstown, that of old Jones. A Frenchman passed on horseback and made signs he would carry the child, but I wadna trust him. Being new to the country and afraid of the bush, I asked if I would have to pass through any on my way, and was told no, but after I passed Dewittville there was nothing but woods until I reached Huntingdon, where there were only a few houses. I asked at one my road, and the woman said that Mrs Barr had just left, that she had had a quilting-bee (I never let on that I did not know what that was), and she pointed her out with others ahead of me. I started off, but did not overtake them. When I came in sight of Mr Barr's shanty, they recognized me and came running out, and he got well-water, and mixed homemade vinegar and maple-sugar with it, and bade me sip it. They were real glad to see me and so was I to meet them. When the house was ready, it was impossible to draw our luggage out to it, and it was a month before the New Year when there was frost and snow enough to allow of an ox-team going in with a load. There were other settlers who went in at the same time as we did. There were Robt. Beatty, an old soldier, who had a pension, who went on to lot 2, 2nd concession, and with him James Brown, who had drawn No. 1, stayed until his family arrived from Glasgow. He was a jokey, clever man, and a Deist. He came to a miserable end. Widow Hood, who came from Alloa, and had several grown-up sons, went on to lot 1, 2d con., and being strong in help (two of her sons were ship-builders), had a house finished before any of us. Rice was an Englishman and an old soldier, lacking a thumb that was shot off, and had been in the country some time, living at St Laurent; he did not move on to his lots, but sent up a man to chop and make ready. We spent the winter in enlarging our clearance and were eager about it. At the sound of every tree that fell, we would give a youp, and I would start it, so glad was I that a bit more opening in the woods was made. I went out and helped, brushing the tops of the trees, so that the men would have room to work. It was very lonesome and so difficult to get provisions in, having to walk sometimes through two feet of snow on the river to Reeves's to buy what we wanted. I have often walked there myself. Rice had sent a cow to his man, and on it proving farrow, he wanted to sell it, and we bought it, and a grand milker she afterwards proved to be. We got some hay from David Bryson that kept her living until the spring, and then I went over to the ridge and cut the yellow flowers (mayflowers) and brought them over to her by the basketful, for we had her tethered to a stump, being afraid we would lose her in the bush. We had a good bit of clearance ready when seed-time came, and I helped to log it. The potatoes we got to plant, we had to carry in from the river. Besides the potatoes, we planted some corn, and both did extraordinarily well. When the potatoes were dug, we hoed in some fall-wheat, which yielded abundantly. To carry it to the barn, my husband made a barrow of light cedars, and a heavy lift it was. We made no potash for several years, being unable to buy a kettle and coolers, so we saved our ashes, storing them under cover and digging a hole in the centre to put in the new hot ashes, so that they kept well, and at the first snow sleighs came in, from as far as Boyd's at Dunn's mill, and bought them, the price running from 14 to 20 cents the bushel. Our mill was at Huntingdon, and we carried out and in the bags to some house on the front, the bags going by Reeves' canoes. The wetness of the land was our great vexation. The water came down upon us from the lands of the 4th and 5th concessions in streams, and in summer lay about us in green pools. It was a wonder there was no fever and ague, but there was not. There being no proces-verbals in those days, it seemed impossible to get discharges opened. For two years running our crops of grain were drowned out, and we had to buy wheat to pay the seignior. The settlers were poor enough, but never wanted for food, there being aye enough of potatoes and jonny-cake, and we were as hearty and contented a lot of people as you would want to know. We missed oatmeal more than anything, the old folks especially, but after a while we always managed to buy enough for them. My husband was often for giving up and going to a city, but I urged him to hold on, telling him his pay as a carpenter would not keep us all, and that the land was our own and would be a home so long as we needed one. We never got oxen. Several years after we came we bought a mare from James Sadler. Once discharges were cut and the land dried, the settlement got on fast. I cannot tell the year the road was cut out to Paddy Mullin's; it was a good while after we came. It was not of much use, from the water running into it.

The road mentioned by Mrs Barr came out a little below Point Round and was the only outlet in that direction for a number of years, and until the concession-line was continued out to the 4th concession, which was effected with difficulty. Farther west, there was a path that followed the creek that empties below Ormstown. The side-line to that village was not suitable for travel until about 1840. The bulk of the settlers came in 1830, when John Cook, the Tates, William Elliot, Leitch, Ovans and others came in. The Tates were brothers and highly respectable Englishmen. Thomas opened a store on 12, the first on the concession, subsequently moving to the corners, when the road was opened to the village. That road ought to have been on the allowance left for it 4 acres farther east, but was placed where it is to suit the grist-mill, then planned. The worst lot on the concession was 15, which James Sangster describes as having been covered with hemlock and having no hardwood, and so wet that nothing would grow until it was ditched, and to do that they had to wait for the tree roots to rot. Until then the family lived by the father's labors, who was a shoemaker, and the young men made potash elsewhere. On the opposite side of the road were the McGerrigles and Robert McClenaghan, Protestants from the North of Ireland, and John Campbell, who came in 1827. Waddell, a brewer by trade, started a small brewery behind his shanty, which was the ruin of not a few. On the lots secured by Rice, was a ridge covered with a fine maple bush, to which, up to a late date, the Indians came every spring to make sugar. In 1832 a schoolhouse was raised on the corner of 13, of which Logan was appointed

teacher. He took up a lot, but was a poor hand at clearing.
It was said of him, that, to avoid the fatigue of working in
the sun, he would go to felling trees in the summer-nights by
the light of the moon, and in his nightshirt! Once the settlers
got a start, the concession advanced rapidly, and there are
now no finer farms in the province.

There were not the same drawbacks to contend with in the
upper end of the concession as in the lower, for the land west
of the side-line road was more easily drained and more
generally covered by hardwood bush. The first to take up
lots were William Graham, David Drummond, John Russell,
Jas. Leggatt, Archd. McDougall, and Jas. Kennedy, who moved
on lots towards the close of the season of 1827 or in the year
following. These families were all from Scotland, and were
followed by a fresh accession from the same country, John
McDougall, Robt. Wetherston, and James Cavers. The road
by which they got in was the path made by the American
squatters (page 51) before the war, along the east bank of
McClintock's (then called Smith's) creek, and the bridges they
had made across the smaller streams that flowed into it were
still standing. The first-comers, of course, selected the lots
with these old clearances, which gave them quite a start, for
they got some crop in at once, and they fared much better
than their neighbors. All the settlers were poor, Russell
being the only one that had brought money with him, and
the first few years was a struggle for existence, the land
being so wet that no seed could be put in until June. Had
it not been for potash, they could not have stayed. As it
was, it was potatoes three times a day with the most of them.
Russell, a worthy man, opened a store on his lot, and did a
fair business for a number of years. James Whithall, an
Englishman, who came out in 1832, gives this account of the
state of the settlement :

I landed at Montreal on the 22nd May and left at once to
see my brother, William. I crossed from the Chateaugay
road at Cain's, and came out on the Ormstown road-line at
William Watson's. The land was simmering in water and I
had to walk mostly on 'ogs. In crossing a creek, a rotten

piece of wood gave way, and up I was to my middle. I asked if there was no better road, and said if there was not, it was the last time I would travel it. When my brother's lot was reached, we found he was not at home, having gone to put up another house on a more favorable spot. Burton, who was with me, had been along with my brother as a coal-hawker in London, and as we got on top of a hill and my brother's new house came in sight, with himself on top shing-ling, Burton put his hands to his mouth and gave the coal-hawker's cry, when my brother sprang up and cried, "That is Burton." He was overjoyed to see us. Sammy Carruthers was helping my brother to finish his house and proposed I should buy his lot, No. 45. I wanted to go to Upper Canada, but finally was persuaded to buy. It cost me $100, and for 5 or 6 years I could not raise enough off it to keep my family. My brother was poorly off and glad to get the small legacy I brought him. The timber had been plundered off my lot, and the hemlocks would not make ashes. I burned a heap once, and after I had done so, a lad told me it was no use to leach such ashes, which sickened me with potash-making, and I turned to clear my land. To get my grain ground, I had often to put a bag on my head, arranged something like a night-cap, and walk along the logs that crossed the swampy bits to Dewittville.

The year before James Whithall came in, the concession-road had been chopped its entire length, but was not made passable for vehicles. A better road to the river than the trail along the creek being a necessity, the chopping out of the side-line road to Ormstown was begun in 1831, and was finished the following year, though it was not until the grist-mill was opened at Ormstown that it was stumped and made fairly passable. The jog of 4 acres between the upper and lower ends of the concession was done by the surveyor, in order to accommodate the line to the bend of the river, so that the lots might average 100 arpents each. Amid all their struggles, the settlers of the upper end of the concession were not unmindful of the need of education for their children, and in 1830 they put up a schoolhouse on the site of the present, hiring one Hall, who taught for a year, and was succeeded by the Rev James Miller, who during his stay of less than a year preached alternate Sundays at Ormstown and Huntingdon. He was succeeded by John Donaldson, who became closely identified with the concession. On leaving, Mr Miller taught a while in a new schoolhouse on Moore's lot. The Moores were Irish Protestants, and industrious and substantial.

From the upper Ormstown concession to the St Lawrence there were no settlements, the country being a tamarac swale, with clumps of pine on the ridges. The 4th and 5th ranges were surveyed by Livingstone in 1836 and 1837, and Edward Sproul was the first to move into the upper end of it, which he did in April, 1838. He was an Irish Protestant and had been for several years a resident of Hemmingford. He made a straight track through the bush on lot 38, 3rd con., to his lot, 37, and which was the outlet until the road was made by the yellow house 10 years later. Archibald, a son of Hugh McKellar's, followed, and took up 38. Others pressed in, and the few desirable lots were secured. They were sold in free and common soccage. The black flats had no attraction for English-speaking farmers, and were overspread by Canadians. Much of the tamerac, before the lots were sold, was cut into railway-ties and sent to England.

On the north bank of the Chateaugay, between Ormstown and Dewittville, the lots were slow in being cleared. James Sadler, who went on to lot 45 so late as 1835, says: "When I moved on the lot was early in the spring and I put up a log shanty with a sheet for the door, and managed to chop enough to get in a lock of wheat, oats, corn, and potatoes, and after that we had enough to eat. The stony ridges were best then. There was quite an old clearing on Furlong's point, and a small one in front of No. 44, both said to have been made by the Americans before the war, but the only opening on my lot was on the creek, where the deer had made a lick in coming to drink. The country back of my lot was full of deer and wolves." McEwen and Pace were among the first on the river and were followed by Michael Furlong, who came in 1824 and was joined the year after by James Finn, who, like him, came from Wexford, and whose presence led to the forming of a considerable Irish Catholic settlement.

40 & 41, bought by the Finns, had been taken up by 2 brothers, Scotchmen of the name of Anderson, who after doing some work, gave up the idea of being farmers and went to Montreal. Before them, however, had been Americans, for there were small clearances and a well upon them. That fall or in the following summer, they were joined by Patrick Mullin, John Murphy, John Scully, Patrick and Mathew Kavanagh, William Milloy, and Frank Hughes, who all settled within a communicable distance of one another. They were drawn together accidentally, for none had been neighbors in Ireland. Their struggles for the first five years were painful, owing to there being no timber on their lots fit for making potash. There were occasions when, for three months at a time, they had no bread, and lived mainly on potatoes. Poor as they were, they manifested a laudable anxiety to have a place of worship, and in 1827 they took the first step by fencing in a graveyard on lot 40, given by James Finn, the first to be buried being a child of James Keegan's. In the following year the contract was given to the brothers Wright to frame and put up a church, which was finished so far as to permit of being occupied for occasional service. The ten families who had erected the church were not content. They must have a resident priest, and they put up a log house to the south of the church and on the river bank. The first priest left under a cloud, and was succeeded in 1832 by Father Moore, a South of Ireland man, who remained many years and commanded the respect of the Protestants by his moderation and his efforts to promote the best interests of his people. He was a well-read man and delighted in gardening and other pursuits which were novel in the backwoods. In front of his house his name bloomed during the summer in flowers. In 1832 a belfry was added to the church, and at the raising of the bell Father Moore indulged in a practical joke. All the male portion of the congregation gathered to hoist the bell, which, with their imperfect appliances, had to be done by main strength. When about 5 feet clear of the ground, the priest, who was standing behind the group, took out of his pocket a sun-glass and concentrated with it the

sun's rays on a piece of punk upon the rim of the bell, when it burst into flame. One of the men conceived it to be a miracle, and exclaiming "Glory be to God!" sank upon his knees. His example was infectious, and the good father had difficulty in controlling his features. In 1835 the church was plastered and finished, and for a long series of years it was the only place of worship west of Ste Martine, and was attended by the settlers of Huntingdon as well as those of Chateaugay. It continued in use until 1861, when, on the 13th of October, the new church was opened at Ormstown. The old one was then levelled and the only indication of its site, are the tombstones in the disused graveyard.

The settlement of the concessions on the Jamestown side of the Chateaugay, above Ormstown, began in 1825, when a number of immigrants, mainly North of Ireland men, took up lots and placed their families upon them while they worked on the Lachine canal. Of these Francis Smith, a Tyrone Catholic, was the first to make much of a clearance, having several sons. He was led to select the lot he secured from a fine intervale of 10 acres, which is now a stony field. James Ross, who had chosen number 3, but did not intend to live upon it until the Lachine canal was finished, allowed Smith the use of it and he raised his shanty on the bank at the mouth of the Outarde. The rapids being too deep to ford, he built a scow. The difficulty of communication with the north side of the river was a great drawback to. Smith and his brother settlers, for there was no bridge at Ormstown until 1842. The Outarde flowed through solid woods, untenanted save by wild beasts, and wolves were so plentiful and bold that they came at night to Smith's door to snatch up the scraps that might be strewn around it. Matthew W. Harrison, a schoolmaster from near Dublin, took up two lots the same year as Smith, and when the population increased sufficiently opened school in his shanty, where he taught with success. He was "a character"—that is, his individuality was strongly marked. Among his peculiar habits was drawing in his firewood in the shape of a log long enough to afford him a seat at one end while the blaze of the other warmed

him. His substitute for a table was still more ingenious.
Spreading the food on the floor of the shanty beside the
trap-door to the cellar, he sat down, and enjoyed his meal
as heartily as if his legs had been beneath a mahogany table
instead of dangling' in the cellar. He kept no cart or other
vehicle, and gathered his hay and grain by dragging them
with a horse into a stack in the centre of the field. After his
marriage late in life, he built a good house and bought fine
furniture, of which he took slight comfort, for visitors found
a mahogany table upset across the door of the parlor, and
the room thereby fitted to hold grain. He was early appointed a magistrate, and in that capacity gave peculiar
decisions, the most singular being one where a man, who had
long been at enmity with his neighbor, brought him up on
some trumpery allegation. The Squire ruled that the court
adjourn to allow of the two men being shut up in a barn
alone to fight it out. This was done, and the quarrelsome pair
settled their differences for the time being by giving each
other a hearty pounding. In sitting on a case at Dewittville,
the trousers of his worship were so dilapidated that one of
his knees was exposed, but he maintained the dignity of the
bench by carefully covering it with the lapel of his coat.
With all his oddities and miserliness, the Squire was a good
teacher and neighbor, and a useful man in his generation.
His severity with his scholars was lightened by the humor
and drollery of his native country. Thus, on the occasion
of a quarrel among the boys, which had involved a number
in something approaching a riot, he held an enquiry which
made clear to him who were the ringleaders. Addressing
the school with due gravity, he said the custom was, in the
Old Country, to have such disputes settled by a boxing-match
between the leaders, and if both sides would agree to such an
arbitration, he would superintend the fight and see that it
was fairly conducted. The boys eagerly agreed, when he
ordered the two leaders to strip to their trousers. Picking
the two next most culpable in the row as seconds he directed
them to strip also, assuring them that was the correct style.
When the boys faced one another on the schoolroom floor,

waiting for the word to begin, the teacher suddenly drew out his tawse and laying it on the four pairs of bare shoulders, leathered the lads round and round the room, amid the shouts and laughter of the onlookers, and even of one of the sufferers who was more tickled by the teacher's witty craft than stung by his lash.

On the river front was Terence Smith, who, in 1831, set up a still and made poteen, to the injury of himself and his neighbors. On Jamestown island, James McCartney, an Irish Protestant, built a shanty on lot 7 in 1829 and was its first settler. He was followed by William Brown and Thomas Taylor, who was a superior man in many respects. He was a native of East Calder, Scotland, and had been educated for the Baptist ministry, but, unable to get a charge, became a schoolmaster, in which capacity he acted both in his native country and in England. In 1826 he, emigrated, and, having a family, was advised by Mr Snowdon and Mr Brodie of Petite Côté to take up land on the Chateaugay. In putting up his shanty, he asked the neighbors to make it long enough so that one end might do for a school-room, which was done, and there he taught the children of the settlers, who could give him little compensation, for 5 or 6 years. On the Sundays he held divine service in the little school-room. Like too many of the teachers of his day, he was very severe. Among the first settlers on the Outarde was Richd. Hamilton, who lost a son in 1830, while planting potatoes, by a tree being blown down upon him, an event that made a deep impression upon the settlement, and which the father, commonly known as the Duke of Hamilton, did not long survive. The first settler on the Outarde, lot 44, was an Irish Catholic, Francis Hughes, who came in 1827. Of the days of the first settlers on the Outarde the following narrative by John, son of Robert Woodrow, gives a graphic sketch:

We came from county Down and landed at Quebec on the 10th June, 1830. Several other ships with emigrants came in at the same time as ours, so that the steamer for Montreal was overcrowded; had 1100 on board. We were so close packed we could not lie down. In lake St Peter the steamer, the Richelieu, ran aground and we lay there half a day. By the time we landed at Montreal six or seven children were smothered. Complaint was lodged with the mayor, and I understood afterwards that the captain was punished by the suspending of his license. Our destination was the Gore, where we knew the Hendersons and Wilson, and we started for there. At the Portage (Dewittville) we stayed overnight with Todd, who was a kind man to the emigrants. He told my father that the Gore was a poor stony place and that he should, instead of going there, take up clay land. There was a carpenter, George Stewart, working at Todd's at the time, and he said he had 3 lots on the Outarde, with 20 acres cut and burned, and he would give us one, with the use of part of the clearance, and assist in putting up a shanty, if we would pay him in work. Father accepted the offer, and we moved on to the lot, on which a stick had not been cut, living in a tent of hemlock boughs until we could get a shanty raised. On the burned clearance we logged a piece and planted 12 or 14 bushels of potatoes, which we bought from Sangster, below Ormstown, and I carried them on my back, 1½ bushels at a time. In the fall we dug 340 bushels of the finest potatoes I ever saw. We have no such crops now. One year we had oats as high as Billy Finn, and he was the tallest man in the settlement, 6 feet 3 inches, and that, too, on land you would now declare the plow never passed over, for it is a stony ridge to-day, though then you would only see a stone peeping out here and there. I have sown oats as late as the 5th July, and reaped a bountiful crop, without a speck of rust, and planted potatoes on the 11th July, which grew full size, but were soft and we fed them to the cattle. The country was heavily timbered, particularly south of us, where there was great black ash and elm. I remember once of my father standing in the middle of our lot and asking me, "Will we ever get cleared this far back?" To-day there is not even firewood on that very lot. There was no road when we came or for 10 years after; we had no use for one, having neither horses nor waggons. We had to tramp along a blazed track that followed the Outarde to the rapids, where we crossed the Chateaugay in a canoe, and many a time I had to return home on finding the canoe on the other side. If we had ashes or produce to market, we had to carry or drag the load as we best could, and hire a horse and cart on crossing the Chateaugay. By and by we joined in building a flat boat, big enough to carry a horse and cart, and it was tied up at Hamilton's, with a good landing on either bank. The second year of our settlement I carried a bag holding 1½ bushels of rye to Henderson's mill (over 13 miles) Trout river. It was easier carrying it back, for they took big toll in those days. I had to go there, for the mill at Huntingdon had been stopped from injuries received during the freshet—the great July freshet of 1831—which filled the river with lumber and many farmers fished out good lots of 3-inch pine plank. Macarthur had started his oatmeal mill and we went to it by canoe, carrying the bags round the three rapids to make sure they would not be wet. When the bridge was built at Ormstown we cut out the road, but it was long before it was of much use, it was so full of holes. My father hearing the neighbors talk of the Land O'Cakes, thought it must be a good settlement to have such a name, so that the year after we came he sent me to visit it. The only way into it was a shanty-road cut out by Colborne, the lumberman, and it started from opposite Marratt's (lot 14, Ormstown). I followed it and came out at where the Fitzgerald brothers lived, and who had settled there the same year as we did. They were anxious I should get my father to move, but I saw that the land was poor, with a few good intervales. John Helm of Elgin, Alexander, and some more afterwards joined them. They had a hard time for want of an outlet, their only road being the ridge that runs out to the Chateaugay 3 lots below Ormstown, along which they dragged their barrels of potash and then put them on a canoe of Peter Reid's, and took them to Cross, or whoever was buying. In returning home I thought I would save part of the way by taking a short cut across the bush and lost myself. As there were wolves, I climbed a tree and did not close an eye all night. At sunrise I took my bearings as well as I could and struck, after a while, a lumber-road, which I thought was the one I had left. It was not, and I came out at the Blockhouse. I remember well old Mr Craige exclaiming, on seeing me, "Where hae ye cam frae?" On telling him, and adding that I was very hungry, his remark was, "My puir laddie, come awa in." I made a hearty breakfast of porridge, bread and milk. The great drawback of the settlement, the want of a proper outlet, was overcome about 1840, when the seignior built a bridge across the Chateaugay. After that, rapid progress was made on our side. When we came the Yankee war-road (the path cut out by Gen. Izard, see page 92) was quite plain. It ran the length of our lot and crossed the Outarde by what we called "the Yankee rapids" and then ran down the island to Terry's.

That there would some day be a village on lot 23 of Ormstown was apparent, from the fine water-power that ran in
front of it, but it was slow in coming into being. In 1823
Thomas Sadler, a county Cavan Protestant, went on to 21,
attracted by the American clearance on the point, and set
up his forge, for he was a blacksmith. About the same time
Edward Jones acquired 22. He was also a North of Ireland
man, had served in the army, and enjoyed a sergeant's pension. Although a tall, strongly-built man he did not care
about work and led a lazy, drunken life, varied by bickerings
with his wife, in a squalid and exceedingly dirty shanty which
stood on what is now village lot 283. In 1834 he sold to a
Montreal bailiff, Robert Lovell, who chanced that way on a
legal errand, and left a lot he had done almost nothing to
improve. Lot 23 the seignior would not sell, reserving it as
a mill-site and for the prospective village. The clearance on
its front, made by the American squatters, was in charge of
David Bryson, who raised an occasional crop of oats off it.
A level bit, west of the side-line road, was used for many
years as the place of assembly for the militia, when the
farmers turned out on the King's birthday, answered the
roll-call, and were treated by their captains. In the old
burial-place of the Americans a grave was opened early in
the winter of 1829 to receive the body of Andrew Foster,
who was killed by a tree falling upon him while working
on his lot, 34, 1st con. Ormstown. Word was sent to a son
of the lumberman Moreau, who was studying medicine and
anxious to get subjects. Accompanied by his brother, who
was studying law, they drove up from Montreal, resurrected
the body with difficulty, from the ground being frozen, and
started for their father's camp, near Dewittville, on their way
to the city. They had been observed at their unhallowed
deed, and the alarm being given, their traineau was pursued.
Being hard pressed, they flung the body over Finn's bridge.
Their pursuers passed it unobserved, and kept right on.
Near Dewittville they missed their prey, but after a while
got again on the scent, and, on arriving at Moreau's camp,
found the two youths innocently engaged in cooking a late

supper. They denied all knowledge of the deed, until, on searching the stable, their horse was seen to be covered with foam. Forcing the youths to go back with them, the sturdy backwoodsmen compelled them to carry to the sleigh the body from where they had flung it, to recoffin and bury it. On the west side of 23 lived the brothers McNeil and Leishman, who came in 1822. The first movement towards creating a village on 23 was an effort, in 1829, to build a church, a log-building, 20 × 26, that stood at the north-west end of the present church. The intention of the farmers was that McWattie should use it instead of going to Rutherford's, but he became so discredited that it was left unfinished, and in the summer of 1831 the Ormstown settlers joined with those of Georgetown in endeavoring to secure the services of a reputable clergyman and one whose official acts would be legal. In August, 1831, a memorial was signed by the settlers of the English river and the Chateaugay, praying the Glasgow Colonial society to send them a minister. They stated that "in the various settlements the lands are mostly occupied by Presbyterians, and a very great majority are by birth, principle and education, attached to the doctrine and discipline of the Church of Scotland." In furthering this memorial Dr Mathieson was the sole agent, and during the summer before McWattie's death he frequently visited the Chateaugay, preaching, baptizing, and even re-marrying several couples who had grown dubious as to the legality of the knot McWattie had tied. The Glasgow society favorably considered the request, and induced the Rev Archd. Colquhoun, a young man newly married, to accept the charge, they guaranteeing him $500 a-year for a limited period and assisting him in paying the expense of going to Canada. A short time after his ordination by the presbytery of Lochcarron, July 14, he sailed for Quebec, where he landed in October He was favorably received by the people of his new charge, into which he was formally inducted on the 14th November, and took possession of a small house that had been provided until a manse could be built. In anticipation of his coming, the Ormstown and Jamestown people united in providing a better

church than the log-building, which ultimately fell to William
Cross, who used it as a shoe-shop. The body of a good-sized
frame-building was raised beside the site of the present, and
after it had been partially boarded work was suspended from
want of means. When Mr Colquhoun arrived it was rendered
fit for occasional use, but it was not floored until 1835. Until
then, the sleepers in front were covered with loose boards.
In rear the people sat upon them, with their feet on the
ground. Of an ardent temperament, and finding the state of
society and his surroundings otherwise very different from
what he had anticipated, Mr Colquhoun applied himself to
work a change by pulpit denunciations, and before many
months he had come to look upon the leading members of the
Georgetown congregation as his enemies and the enemies of
the Gospel, and described their conduct and the consequences
it would entail with such force and plainness that they nick-
named him "Brimstone Colquhoun" and favored the proposal
to give a call to another minister who would preach in the
new church that was begun on lot 25, North Georgetown, but,
owing to subsequent events, was not completed until a number of years afterwards. Mr Colquhoun's position in Georgetown grew so unpleasant that he decided on leaving it and
on going to Ormstown, which was now formed into a separate
charge. Misunderstandings, chiefly financial, arose in time
between him and the Ormstown people, followed by painful
recriminations, which were ended, just before an examination
by the presbytery was about to be made, by his accepting a
call in Ontario. He left Ormstown in the spring of 1835.
From the time he withdrew, the adherents of the Georgetown
congregation were without religious ministrations other than
those supplied by the Montreal ministers and Mr Roach; Dr
Mathieson, especially, continuing to take a deep interest in
them, and again he was the means of getting them a minister.
In the beginning of April, 1836, he welcomed on his arrival
in Montreal James Creighton Muir, who had been sent to
Canada by the Glasgow Colonial Missionary society. Mr
Muir was born in Dumfries, in 1799, was educated at Edinburgh, and was licensed as a minister of the Kirk of Scotland

in 1832. After acting as tutor for a short time in the family of Justin McCarthy (father of the historian) he obtained employment in his proper calling as city missionary at Port Glasgow, which he followed for two years, when he decided on going to Canada, for which he sailed, by way of New York, in February, 1836. Dr Mathieson advised him to choose either Georgetown or Beechridge, both of which were anxiously waiting for ministers. As the sleighing was about done, no time was to be lost if he desired to recross the St Lawrence, and on the first Monday in April he started for Beauharnois. Dr Muir noted how cautiously the driver led his horse on the ice at Point Claire, and the rapidity with which he crossed. Leaving him at the house of the Rev Walter Roach, whom he found, with his then Old Country notions, engaged in a rather unministerial task, namely, taking away the banking of his house, the driver turned his cariole at once, and dashed for the crossing over the lake. The necessity for his haste he found out was the dangerous state of the ice, an awful instance of which had been given the preceding week, when a newly married couple, in returning from their wedding jaunt to Montreal, had broken through and disappeared, horse and all, in the twinkling of an eye. Mr Roach gave him a most hospitable reception, and drove him that week to Georgetown, the first house he stayed at being that of Robert Brodie, who was an elder of the church. Mr Roach then took him to Huntingdon, in order to introduce him to the Rev Mr Walker. To reach the house of the latter (now occupied by Dr Cameron, No. 190) they had to pick their way among stumps, while back of it was the virgin forest. As one of the sights of the place, Mr Walker took his guest to the bank of the river, where, in a clump of trees stood the wigwam of one of those Indians who made a practice of coming to the upper waters of the Chateaugay to camp during the winter, returning to Caughnawaga, when the ice broke up, with a canoe-load of furs and skins. The Indian they found engaged in skinning a muskrat for dinner. Having preached several times in the Georgetown church and in the English-river schoolhouse, a call was presented to him in the end of June, but from the presbytery in those days meeting seldom he was not ordained and inducted until the 29th September into a charge which he retained until death released him 45 years afterwards—a continuous pastorate without precedent in Quebec, and all the more remarkable that, from his fragile appearance, his people anticipated he would die young. His first duty was to visit and prepare a list of his congregation, when he found he had 110 families under his care, of whom only 10 had children over 14 years of age, showing that the overwhelming majority were young couples, recently come out, who had only infant families. Of the 110 families, 65 lived on the English-river. To meet the wants of the rising generation, he organized four Sunday-schools in different parts of his charge, which were attended by above a hundred children, and formed a congregational library. He preached regularly at South Georgetown, in the English-river schoolhouse, and in the church at Brodie's. In July, 1838, a session was formed and the sacrament was dispensed for the first time on the 5th August, when there were 180 communicants. The call presented to him was accompanied by a guarantee that he would receive a yearly salary of £90 ($360) payable in advance. Col. Brown, the seigniory agent, had subscribed £10 of the amount, and that was the first money he got. Of the total stipend promised he, for a long term of years, never got over £50, and he used to say that had it not been for the £10 from the seigniory (afterwards increased to £20) and the £30 he got from the clergy reserves, he could not have lived. The Sunday-school organized was not the first on the Chateaugay, for John Harvey (page 45) who was a conscientious man, had been in the habit of gathering the children of his neighbors in his house and hearing them read the Scriptures, which he explained.

Resuming the narrative of church affairs at Ormstown, peace was restored to the infant congregation by the induction, on the 14th July, 1835, of the Rev James Anderson, who was born at Cromarty in 1797, and was sent to Canada by the Glasgow Colonial Missionary society. After reserving a sufficient portion in front for the expected village, the seignior divided the rear of lot 23 between the Presbyterian and Episcopalian congregations, the latter receiving the eastern half. The congregation, not being able to build a manse, Mr Anderson bought a village lot and built, in 1838, a house at his own expense. He was a good man and an excellent preacher and served his people disinterestedly, for up to his death, in 1861, he received little from them. For a long time the annual subscription was $2, and the few who gave $4 were considered liberal. From his flock he never got more than $200 in any one year, and could not have lived had he not received an equal amount from the clergy reserves and the seignior. On his being settled over them, the congregation were desirous of completing the church, but it was 1839 before it was lathed, plastered, and otherwise finished, and until then there were no proper seats, except those a few of the farmers had made for themselves. When John Donaldson, the schoolmaster of the upper Ormstown concession, got married in 1838, a friend told him, as a favor, to take the bride to his seat, which had a back! Most of the work on the church was done by the farmers holding bees; the finishing was paid by a subscription, largely paid in wheat. Long before that time, however, the Episcopalians had a church. The missionary, Charles Forest, urged the adherents of the church he so zealously served to secure a place of worship and obtained some outside aid towards its cost. In 1831 the corner-stone of the foundation of a small church was laid by a son of Colonel Brown's, and on it was raised a good frame building, with a gallery at one end. It was built by Hugh McKinnon, a Highlandman, who also did the carpenter work of the Presbyterian church and of the one at Brodie's. Want of means delayed its completion, and it was not until early in 1834 that it was formally opened by Archdeacon Mountain. It stood at the west corner of the side-line road, and in its rear was a burying-ground, in which Robert Williams was the first to be laid. In 1836 the Society for the Propagation of the Gospel gave a grant of $2500 a year for providing missionaries in Lower Canada, when the Rev. William Brethour, an Irishman, and who had been laboring for some time in Leeds, was sent, and when in March, 1837, Dr Mountain, now bishop, visited the congregation, over 70 were presented to him for the rite of confirmation, at which he expressed great surprise. The concessions back from the river had a large proportion of Irish Protestants, mainly Episcopalians, and of Englishmen, so that the new church started with equally good prospects as the Presbyterian. When the old church had to be replaced, the new one was erected on the high ground north of the creek, and the site of the old church and graveyard is now covered with the houses of the village.

There were now two churches in the place and nothing more, until, in 1837, the seignior finally decided to erect a grist-mill, for which there had been long a crying-need. On this becoming known, a tavern was opened by Robt. Beatty in a log-house that had been erected by Lovell. David Rutherford in 1834 built what was at the time and for years afterwards the largest tavern in the district. He was told by his neighbors that he was making a mistake by building it on his own farm, for there would be a village yet on 23. He scouted the idea of trade ever passing his door, and the new tavern, named the "yellow house" from the color it was painted, did a large business. In 1835 he rented the place to John McEachern, but when the building of the mill was determined on, he gave up his lease and rented from Lovell Jones's old log-house until he could get a tavern of his own built, which was to be of brick. A substantial two story house was raised, which is still used as an hotel. The brick were made near to it, at the side of the creek. McEachern boarded the men who built the mill and for the next 40 years no house was better known than McEachern's, it being the usual place for all district meetings. The building of the mill was marked by the exercise of one of the extraordinary privileges vested in the seignior. Alexander Mills, a carpenter by trade, carefully preserved the pine and oak on his lot for future use. Brown ordered the contractor to go to his lot and take what he saw fit, which he did, and Mills had no power to prevent him. The com-

pletion of the mill was delayed by the rebellion and was not
ready to do work until the crop of 1839 was harvested, when
one McDonald was miller for a short time, followed by
Needler, an Englishman, who became popular and made
money. With the building of the mill, Wm. and Robt. Cross
opened a store and did a large trade. On the registrar of
Huntingdon, D. K. Lighthall, being notified to remove to
Ormstown, or rather Durham, as the infant village was then
named after Lord Durham, a warm friend of the Ellices,
he secured the room above Mr Cross's store as an office,
and opened his books there on the first of January, 1842.
An innocent pun amused the neighborhood. Sergeant Younie
called to see the new premises, and glancing round the room
the old soldier exclaimed, " This is a light-hall." William
McNaughton, a carpenter, who had been in the district since
1831, decided on taking up house in the new village, and on
its completion it was the fourth. A blacksmith came in,
Thomas Porter, who set up his shop in 1841. By this time
roads were being opened out to the back concessions and in
1842 a fine bridge was built, giving the people of Jamestown
ready access, and leading to the building, in the year following, of a sawmill at the south end of the dam by Enos Mills,
the American who had built the bridge, and William Cross,
with whom the seignior made the same arrangement as with
the Thomsons on Evident creek, granting a lease for 7 years,
at the end of which period he had the privilege of taking
possession at a fixed valuation. In 1844 John Gibson arrived
and erected a tannery, which was greatly needed and did
well. David Rutherford, finding that business passed his
door to the new village, moved into it himself, building a
large frame tavern, which hastened his financial ruin. The
yellow-house was rented by the government as a court-house,
and there Judge Guay held one or two terms until Justice
McCord was appointed for the district, and it was used on
several occasions as the polling-place for the county. Convinced by his own experience and what he saw around him
of the sin of using intoxicating liquors, Wm. McNaughton, in
conjunction with Jas. Lockerby, Edward Sadler, J. W. Bryson,

William Lindsay, and many others, organized a temperance-society, and some time afterwards built a place for its meetings, at his own expense, which were encouraging in their nature, and led to similar societies being organized in the surrounding country. The hall was used by the Methodists, who began to hold meetings about 1844; the first preachers were Charles Gage and John Lowrey. When a congregation was organized Ormstown was included in the Huntingdon circuit and served by its ministers until 1855, when it got a clergyman of its own. The church was built the year before.

JAMESTOWN,
OUTARDE CONCESSION.
23 John O'Mara
24 Finlay McMartin
25 Richard Hamilton
   George Sparling
26 William Patterson
27 Edward Murphy
28 Patrick Murphy
30 Robert N. Walsh
31 George Wilkinson
32 S.Wilkinson 2 John Skillen
33 Patrick Smith
34 Francis Smith
35 Nich. Smith 2 Hugh Smith
36 & 37 Matt.W.Harrison
38 Andrew Stewart
39 Thomas Stewart
40 Robert Woodrow
41 John McCaffery
42 Hugh Boyle 2 Jno. Gorman
43 John Hamilton
44 Francis Hughes
45 James McKee
46 James Carley
47 Andrew Cowan
48 Wm. Hamilton 2 J.Hughes
   Robt. Sadler
49 Jno.&Ab. Sadler T. Murphy
THE ISLAND
1 Donald Abercrombie
2 Terry Smith
3 James Ross

4 Andrew Strachan
5 Alexander Strachan
6 John Stewart
7 John Rodgers
8 Wm.Brown 2 OwenCollum
9 James McCartney
10 Thos.Taylor 2 John Tassie
11 Peter Robidoux
12 Wm.Finn 2 Ptk.McMahon
13 James & George Murphy
14 Jacob Monique
   Henry Whitaker
15 Louis Monique
16 Joseph Lapointe
ORMSTOWN.
1ST CONCESSION.
23 Village of Ormstown
24 Archd. and James McNeil
25 A. Leishman 2 A.Dickman
26 A.Struthers 2 Jas.Crothers
27 Daniel McNeil
28 John McClintock
29 William Smith
30 William Tremblay
   John Smellie
31 Matthew Furlong
32 Maurice & John Murphy
33 Peter McEwen
34 Hugh Morgan
35 Andrew Foster
36 James McNown
   Hugh McNown
37 Donald McEwen

38 John Pace
39 John Todd
40 James Finn
41 John Finn
42 William Milloy
43 Patrick Finn
44 Matt. W. Harrison
45 William Nolan
   Thomas Sadler
   James Sadler
46 Alex. Stevenson
47 John McDougall
48 Paul Monique
49 William Nolan
   2ND CONCESSION.
1 James Brown
2 Robert Beatty
3 Rose Lily
   James Harvey
4 David Sinclair
5, 6 & 7 William Rice
8 Thomas Barrington
9 Robert Lindsay
10 Thomas Barrington
11 William Smellie
   Thomas Hood
12 Thomas Tate
13 John Tate
14 Henry Tate
15 James and Geo. Sangster
16 Charles Robertson
17 George Elliot
18 Edward Sadler
19 Thos. and David Broderick
20 William Leach
21 John Campbell
22 John Clark
23 Robert Rember, senr.
24 Robert Rember, junr.
25 Richard Crothers
26 John McDougall,
27 John McDougall
28 Robert Wetherstone
29 George Douglas
30 James Cavers

31 William Cavers
32 John Young
33 Samuel Greer
34 William Dodds
35 Arthur Moore
36 John Russell
37 John McGregor
38 John Panton
39 Thomas Chambers
40 George Turner
41 Patrick Richard
42 James Liggett
43 David Corkindale
44 Hugh McConville
45 Mathew and Wm. Young
46 John McKee
47 Archd. McDougall
48 James Kennedy
   3RD CONCESSION.
1 William Hood
2 Francis Hood
3 John Wylie
4 David Ovans
5 Peter Lindsay
6 Robert Barr
7 John Lockerby
8 Adam Lynch
9 Alex. Waddell
10 William Knox
11 James Bothwell
12 James Grant
   John and Francis Cain
13 John Rollo
14 Thomas Harley
15 & 16 John Miller
   John & James McGerrigle
17 & 18 Alex. Fisher
17 John Cook
19 & 20 Robt. McClenaghan
21 William Sproull
22 Peter McEwan
23 John Brown
24 William Patterson
25 John Haig
26 George Brock

27 Andrew Brock
28 Joseph Hodgin
29 John Sinton
30 Michael Turnbull
31 John Bryden
32 David Drummond
33 Thomas Beattie
34 William Graham
35 James Hall
36 Archd. Muir
37 Isaac Philipson
38 John Fletcher
39 William Hodgin
40 John Liggett
41 Neil McLachlan
42 Hugh McKellar
43 Joseph and John Delorme
44 John Whittal
45 Samuel Crothers
46 Benjamin Burton
47 Irwin Armstrong
48 David McGill
4TH CONCESSION.
1 Robert Selkirk
2 James Brady
3 John Simpson
10 George Ainslie
14 James Bacom
Walter Bryden
William Cavers
William Traverse
John Beattie
Francis Beattie
38 Edward Sproull
39 Archd. McKellar
Martin Caveny
5TH CONCESSION.
1 & 2 Wm., John, and James
Selkirk & Wm. Bothwell
3 Charles Robertson
4 James Ainslie
5 John Lang
7 Dougald McNeil
8 John Carruthers

9 George Ainslie
10 & 11 George Brock
13 & 14 Robt. McMillan
John Rankin, senr.
Patrick Kelly
Charles Kelly
John Campbell
Dennis Campbell
James Whittal
6TH CONCESSION.
1 Archd. McGill
2 Neil Cook
3 Gilbert Cook
4 Donald Cook
5 & 6 Neil McIntosh
11 Robt. Rodger
12 John Cowan
13 & 14 Wm. Haire
15 Mrs Cowan
16 Robt. Murray
17 Anthony Wood
18 Wm. Johnston
19 William Thomson
7TH CONCESSION.
5 Archd. McCormick
6 Duncan McCoig
7 Alexander McCoig
8 Edward Thomson
9 David McCoig
11 & 12 Chas. Archambault
13 James Sangster
14 Nicol Porteous
15 John McKay
17 William Grieve
19 & 20 Robt. Rodger
—— Lumsden
8TH CONCESSION.
1 John McEwen
2 John McCracken
14 Daniel Murray
15 John Russell
16 John Sawyer
17 John Sawyer, jr.
—— Taylor

CHAPTER XVIII.

HUNTINGDON

In 1820 the sole indications of life on the site of the future village, were the sawmill of the Percy brothers at the upper bridge and the house of Palmer at the head of the rapids (page 139). These were the only openings in the forest, and beneath its shade the Chateaugay flowed in silence, unfretted save, at long intervals, by the ripple of the canoe of some lonely dweller on its banks as he journeyed to visit a neighbor equally isolated, or broken by a raft that glided, ghostlike, with its current to the St Lawrence. The end of the days of desolation were at hand; the dark curtain of the woods was to be rolled aside and life and activity break the silence and stagnation of ages. The Chateaugay, where it sparkled over limestone-ledges for nearly a half-mile, marked out the site of a village as a distributing-centre for the settlements that immigration now assured would spring into being, and it so happened that it preceded them. Huntingdon was an outgrowth from Dalhousie settlement, one of its visitors, John Hunter, becoming its founder. His eldest son, John, told me thus how it came to pass:

In January, 1821, I accompanied my father from Montreal to Dalhousie settlement, the purpose of our journey being to select a lot. We put up at David Brown's house, where I stayed, my father and James Brown, who professed to act for the government, going across the country to the Chateaugay to see the land there, and where he selected lot 17 (Major Whyte's), and returned to the city. I stayed with the Browns until March, when my father came back with two train loads, comprising the outfit and provisions needed for settlement. Along with him, was a French Canadian, Joe, whom he had hired to help in clearing the land. Starting through the bush, we reached the Chateaugay, and the 5 of us, (for the teamsters helped, and we all had axes) set to work at once in felling trees. It was near 3 o'clock in the afternoon when

we began, and soon after dark we had the frame of a shanty
up, 12 × 14 feet, and piling into it hemlock boughs for beds,
slept sound all night, warmed by a fire, which had a big backlog to prevent its setting fire to the wall. Next morning my
father went up to the sawmill owned by the Percy brothers
(James, Robert, and David) and bought a load of boards, so
that when we completed the walls of the shanty, we closed it
in and made it comfortable. The following day, father left
with the two traineaux for Montreal, and Joe and I had to
shift for ourselves. Our only neighbors, beside the Percys,
were Palmer and Pollica. Three weeks after, William Allan
came up from Montreal, by way of Dalhousie settlement, and
finding his way out to us by the Teafield, he stayed all that
summer. He was a hearty man and a good singer of Scotch
songs, and we enjoyed ourselves very much, the novelty of
our situation not having worn away. Mrs Pollica baked our
bread, and we managed the rest of the cooking. Louis Pollica
came the same spring as we did, and with an old man, Du-
mourier, lived in a shanty beside the mouth of Cowan creek.
They were poor and lived by day's work. After a while,
when immigrants came thick, Pollica kept a sort of a tavern,
though whisky was all he could give them. Late in April
father paid us a visit, walking along the Chateaugay from
the Basin, and by which time Joe and I had a piece chopped.
Father was a great walker, and thought nothing of going to
the city in a day, his only rest that while crossing the St
Lawrence. After remaining a week, he went back to Montreal, taking Joe with him, who was to return, but he did
not, so Mr Allan and I passed the summer alone. We missed
Joe, who was a good fellow and spoke fair English. While
high water lasted, the river was full of rafts, and during that
time we had no lack of company. In May father started
from Montreal to Lachine with 20 bushels of potatoes and 2
of wheat, which he placed on a bateau for Laguerre, where
he hired an old Yankee, Hosea Shaw, to draw them to our
shanty, which he did on a sled, dragged, over mere tracks that
wound through the forest, by a yoke of oxen. The potatoes
and wheat we put in the ground we had cleared. Father had
brought with him the plan of a house, and from looking at it
had no idea of what it would be, or he never would have
used it. He gave out the job to Bob Barter, and saw his
mistake when the frame was ready to be raised. There not
being men enough at hand to raise it, a messenger was sent
up Trout river, and two or three came from even across the
Lines. When the frame was up, the men all got dead drunk.

The house was 30 × 40 feet, and two and a half stories high.
My father called it "Hunter's Folly," and the name stuck to
it. To complete it, lime had to be burned and a kiln of bricks
for the chimneys. Its cost was not the worst part, for it
proved to be so cold that it was uninhabitable, and we had
to partition off a part for living in during the winter. When
we came, there was no house between Dewittville and Huntingdon, except the shanty of a German, Jacob Suttle, on the
point of lot 10. He was seldom at home, however, for he and
his son Henry were generally in the woods, either hunting or
making potash. At Dewittville John Todd had a sawmill,
and when the emigrants began to come in thick kept a house
of entertainment, such as it was. Macaulay of Glengarry
was lumbering on a large scale, getting most of his pine on
Trout river from Ford's rapids to Barlow's. Much was also
taken from the ridge that extends from Biggar's to New
Ireland. Oak was getting scarce, and what there was, was
manufactured into staves for the West Indian market, and
were worth from $36 to $40 a thousand. Much white ash
was split for ship's oars. There were a number besides Macaulay, who lumbered, of whom two, Thomas Fingland and
Kent Wright, had good large shanties. Judge Brown, an
American, contracted with the British government to get out
masts, and I have seen them taken out 90 feet long. Opposite
Dr Shirriff's place, where the bank is cut down, (cadastral
No. 235) there was a small clearance made by lumbermen to
form their rafts. It was hard work, for the men had often
to work up to the waist in icecold water, but they liked it,
on account of the excitement and high wages. The custom
was to have a bucket of whisky, on the bank, to which a
raftsman, when inclined, would go, dip up a tinful, and return
to his work.

Of the removal to Huntingdon a daughter of Hunter's (Mrs
McNee) relates—

My father having wound up his business in Montreal, the
family moved up in October, when the big house was habitable though not finished, for carpenters worked inside all
winter. The family drove out to Lachine. There was no
ferry at that time to the Basin, so father arranged with the
captain of the steamer that went to the Cascades to touch at
a wharf there was about 3 miles west of the Chateaugay. It'
was raining heavily when we went ashore, and there was no
house near. Father walked to the Basin to get carts, while
mother and the children huddled under the solitary umbrella,

getting wet to the skin. The carts came at last, and we and our luggage conveyed to John Smith's, who kept tavern, and with whom Gregory Dunning, his brother-in-law stayed. Next morning we got as far as Turcot's, where we stayed overnight, embarking next morning in canoes. A cow having been brought, father had to walk on the sort of track there was on the river-bank, driving her. In the afternoon the big barn erected by the seignior for storing the hay cut on the Meadows, and above Allan's Corners, was reached, when the Canadians who worked the canoes said this was the last place within reach where they could get shelter for the night. The Brysons were digging potatoes at the time and let us have all we needed. A fire was lit on the river-bank and they were cooked, my mother adding some boiled ham she had brought to the supper, which we all enjoyed. We all slept in the hay in the big barn. Next morning we took again to the canoes, except my mother, who did not like them, and preferred walking with my father. We had not great trouble until Dewittville was reached, when we had all to get out of the boats and land everything. A yoke of oxen was brought down from Todd's and dragged the canoes and the baggage over the portage to the head of the rapids. As it was getting late, it was proposed we should walk the remainder of the journey, which would be quicker than to go by the canoes, so we started. As there were no bridges across the creeks, when we came to one, father waded through, carrying us over, one by one, on his shoulders. It was dark when we reached our home in the bush, and we were glad of a rest, for it had taken us 4 days to make the journey—having left Montreal on Monday morning and getting to Huntingdon on Thursday evening.

The big house proved often small enough for its guests. Being on the corner of the road to the lake, and the first house on the road from Montreal, immigrants naturally sought rest and shelter beneath its roof, and none were turned away, for both Mr and Mrs Hunter were most hospitable. They were not destined to occupy it long, for they were soon notified that Stanley Bagg, a wealthy merchant of Montreal, held the patent for the lot they occupied, whereupon Mr Hunter built a block-shanty a little west, on the adjoining lot, on the S. E. corner of Cemetery and Wellington streets, but only to learn, before it was finished, that he was again unwittingly a trespasser, for one day a French Canadian,

Ducharme, dressed in an old red coat, showed it had been granted to him for services in the war of 1812. But I am anticipating.

During the fall, while Hunter was busy with his big house, there came tramping along an old salt, who gave his name as Bill Goudge, and who, as was afterwards ascertained, was a deserter from the Newcastle, the frigate which brought Lord Dalhousie, and on board which he had rated as carpenter's mate. Professing to be competent to teach, a shanty, or out-house, 12 feet long, which stood near where the mouth of the canal now is, was converted into a schoolroom, and 10 scholars gathered—4 Percys, 3 Palmers, and 3 Hunters—who however, learned little, for Bill was unable to teach them much. His want of learning he made up by the severity of his discipline, and the scholars retaliated by playing truant, and, when they could with safety, mocking his appearance, which was some-what singular, from his having lost an eye by a drop of hot pitch while repairing a ship. Often Bill was on hand in the morning, and not a single boy would appear. He remained 10 months, when he made for Quebec, and went to sea again. A few weeks after Bill Goudge's unexpected appearance, a physician paid the infant settlement a visit. Dr Fortune, a Glasgow licentiate, had come out in 1820, and was staying with old Mr Torrance of Montreal, for they had been school-mates. One winter's day, a fellow-passenger, Jas. Tannahill, called on him, told him of Dalhousie settlement, and the pros-pect of the country's fast filling up, and asked him to go and see them. Having little to do and no encumbrance what-ever, the doctor accepted the invitation, and started off with Tannahill in his traineau. The settlers pressed upon him to stay, which he did, for their habits suited him. He passed from house to house, living with each a while. Naturally he visited Huntingdon, and found the few settlers there as congenial, and lived among them, lounging a good deal in McFarlane's store when it came to be built. In the way of practice he got little to do, for the settlers were mainly people in the prime of life and enjoyed rugged health, and his resources in the way of medicine were limited enough, as may be judged by this incident. Hugh Cameron (probably in the summer of 1823) was taken seriously ill with dysentery, when Dr Fortune, having no medicine, prescribed brandy with eggs beaten in it. Neither were to be had nearer than Fort Covington, and thither Cameron sent one of his men with a $10 bill, the smallest he had. Not returning, Cameron was in imminent danger, when Palmer visited him, and told him to fill a bag with flour and boil it until he came back, which he did not until evening, when he brought a jug of new milk, which he mixed with the boiled flour, and made Cameron eat as much as he could, at the same time washing his body with vinegar. The treatment was successful, and was probably prescribed by Mrs Palmer, who had a wide reputation for skill in curing. The erring messenger returned in a week, without a cent, having spent the $10 in carousing with a party of Highlanders from Glengarry he had met at Dundee Lines. After staying some time in Huntingdon and vicinity, Dr Fortune went to Glengarry for a few years, eventually marrying and settling down at St Anicet village, where he acquired a large practice and a high reputation.

In the summer of the year (1822) succeeding that Hunter settled, there came walking from Lacolle, by way of Russeltown, a stout man past middle life. It was evening when he reached the river at the head of the rapids, and hailing the Palmers, a canoe went over and took him across, and he made his supper of corn boiled in milk. This was William Bowron, who had been promised the appointment of crown lands agent. He was a native of Crotherston, Yorkshire, England, where he was born in 1782. The family emigrated to America and took up their abode at Champlain, N.Y. On war being declared, Bowron moved across into Canada and lived in Montreal and Caldwell's Manor. During the war he, in company with Robert Hoyle, a fellow-Yorkshire man, secured the contract for supplying the British troops at Ile aux Noix with beef, and made a fortune out of it, buying the cattle from the American farmers along the line at a tithe for what their contract allowed and smuggling them across. Going into business in Montreal as a clothier he lost all, and left for Peru, N.Y., eventually drifting to Lacolle, where the Hoyles had settled. This was not his first visit to the site of Huntingdon, nor to the county. He had traversed its frontier during the war and had visited Elgin and Huntingdon the previous summer. Of that visit George Sayer gives this account :

In 1821 I was in Lacolle and found our old friend, for we came from the same place in Yorkshire, Mr Bowron, there. He told me he had the offer for an old song of 400 acres in Elgin from a Mr Whatman, and he meant to go and see what it was like, for Lord Dalhousie had issued a proclamation declaring the county of Huntingdon open for settlers, and warning all who held grants to make the requisite settlement duties within six months or their lands would be forfeited. In August we left Lacolle in a buggy, going south to Champlain, then west to Mooers-town, and crossed back into Canada somewhere near Sweet's, but darkness overtook us, and we slept in a log-house on the American side. Next day we called, in passing, at Sweet's, Stafford's, and Widow Gilfillan's. On bending down Covey Hill, there was a place where we came over the rocks like a wall. The entire road was overshadowed by second-growth. Halting at Gentle's, where we got a drink of sugar and vinegar mixed with water, we learned he had gone for the cows, and overtook him on the road. He was a rough, active, determined-looking man, and carried a long stick. On Mr Bowron telling him of the government's change of policy, in no longer trying to keep the frontier in bush, Mr Gentle struck his stick on the ground and exclaimed he was "Glad to hear it, for what better defence can there be than a loyal farmer with a gun in his hand!" We drove on to Squire Manning's, where we put up for the night, and he agreed to go with us. As the road would not farther allow of wheels, we started next morning on horseback. The first house we came to was Frosty Campbell's, so called from his white hair, and to distinguish him from Uncle Campbell. Here we had dinner. Squire Manning had put a big hunk of salt pork in one end of his saddle-bag and a loaf of bread in the other; Campbell supplied good hot tea. Bowron could not go the raw pork, but I did. We crossed Hampton's road, (the track cut by Izard, page 92) which was not much changed. We called at one or two houses on the 1st concession of Hinchinbrook, among them that of Granny Reed's, but she was not at home. At Powerscourt there was a new log-house up to the square. On riding down the river-bank, I noticed docks and nettles where Sandilands now lives and said it was the first good land I had seen since leaving Lacolle. There was a bridge across the Hinchinbrook and the frame of the old sawmill was standing; it was near the site of the present gristmill. We rode on to Jack Elliot's, who lived on Peter Munro's place (lot 28, 5th con.) and stayed all night. Elliot said he was unable to guide us to the lots we had come to see, and went for Zeb. Baxter, who lived farther down the river (lot 25), who being a hunter and familiar with the whole country, would likely be able to serve us. On Baxter's coming, he readily agreed to guide us. We started early in the morning, and followed Oak creek, which we crossed by my felling a tree. After passing a good deal of wet land, we reached the 400 acres, the posts of which Baxter readily discovered. We saw it was splendid land, and Bowron determined to close the bargain for it. Returning to Elliot's, we stayed with him a second night, and before starting for home, rode down to see Percy's sawmill, where Huntingdon now is. James lived where Boyd does, and his brother Robert's house stood where the road now runs. We went back to Lacolle the way we came.

I quote this narrative not merely to show how Bowron came to be connected with the county, but its state—that of a wilderness with a few Americans, or descendants of Americans, scattered along its frontier. On his acquiring the 400 acres from Whatman, Bowron applied for the appointment of crown lands' agent, and in that capacity came, as stated, in the summer of 1822. He boarded with James Hamilton and at the Hunter's, bringing some pork as his contribution to the larder, until he got a shanty up on the river-bank on the Hinchinbrook side, lot 16 (John Ewart's) having bought the block of land from Hamilton's line up to the present sideroad, 7 three-acre lots, from Scheffalitzky, a Pole, seignior of Chambly, for 75 cents an acre, and the 2 lots west of it from a Mr Gray of Montreal at $2 an acre, and the third at 75c. These people sold believing the land to be comparatively worthless, and because they did not wish to do the settlement duties. Bowron saw that the rapids naturally marked the site for a village, and resolved to have it laid out as one. Soon after he came, a surveyor arrived, authorized by the government to remark the concessions of Hinchinbrook and lay out the lots. This was Thomas Carlisle, who had for an assistant, Duncan McCallum, who afterwards studied medicine, and became eminent as a physician in Montreal. He was then newly out from Scotland. Carlisle made a survey of concessions 4, 5, 6, 7, and 8 of Hinchinbrook between the 26th of August and the 12th of October, when he had to desist. William Lalanne was entrusted the following year with the laying out of Godmanchester.

There were several other arrivals during the summer of 1823. Charles McHardy and his wife came and he worked for some time at his trade, that of blacksmith, before moving on to a farm in Hinchinbrook. Then there was Peter McFarlane, a blacksmith by trade, and who had been in business in Glasgow for many years. He had come over in the Rebecca on her spring trip, and on going to see his brother in Glengarry was strongly recommended to cross the St Lawrence and join the new settlement at Huntingdon. Mr Bowron by this time had taken up his residence in James Percy's old house, having bought it and the sawmill, Percy moving into a house he had built that summer on the riverbank (No. 306) and which he had made large enough for a tavern. That winter he went heavily into lumbering in partnership with Bowron, and came out a beggared man. Bowron received McFarlane cordially and rented to him a room of his dwelling-house for the purpose of opening a store. That winter McFarlane got a shanty raised on Chateaugay street, a short distance east of Lake street, whither he moved his stock of goods, which was very small though their prices were not. His stock was so limited that he was often out of the commonest necessaries, though rarely out of whisky, of which he sold enormous quantities. He was a good man for the settlers, being ready to trade with them, taking potash and their services in assisting him to lumber, in payment of goods. In the following summer a former apprentice of McFarlane's in Glasgow, Duncan McNee, arrived and he placed him in charge of the store, devoting the most of his own time to lumbering.

When McFarlane built his own store, he raised on the opposite side of the street a shanty for a Scotchman, Jock Best, who was a blacksmith. He was a man of great strength, reputed to have a solid sheet of bone instead of ribs, so that he suffered lightly in his numerous fights, for he was sadly addicted to drink, and ready for a scrimmage in his cups. One anecdote has been preserved illustrative of his strength. When Cameron wished to finish his mill, Bowron, who sought to prevent him, came with several of the men from his mill to throw down what had been done. They had pulled off one large timber, when Jock interfered, drove them back, and seizing the displaced log hoisted it to its place. Farther down the road, opposite the upper bridge, was a hut or wigwam of poles and bark, where camped the Hugh Cameron already referred to, a native of Perthshire, who had left Scotland in 1815. While working at his trade of millwright in Glengarry, he heard of the new settlement, and was told that there was an opening for a mill and a splendid privilege. He crossed to Dalhousie settlement and saw Brown. He found the site of the village brulé, covered with scrub timber, cedars, and raspberry bushes, and very wet. On the high ground around where the Academy now is, the original bush still stood and was so dense that in following the drumming of a partridge he wished to shoot, he lost himself in it, and only recovered his bearings on hearing a rooster at Percy's crow. He considered there was a fair opening for a mill, and arranged with the Percys to get water from their dam, he purposing to build on 258, (opposite the Methodist church). One day while at dinner, he was surprised by Mr Bowron, whom he had known in Montreal, dropping in, and telling him he had at last received his formal appointment as land agent. He said he would confirm Brown's grant of a millsite to him, and was glad indeed a man of means (Cameron had $4000) had come to supply what the country needed so badly—a gristmill. Before the winter set in, Cameron had a warm house up for himself and the frame of the mill completed, with much of the machinery. He did almost all the work himself, what few castings he used being brought up by canoe from Montreal. The millstones were cut out, by plug and feather, from boulders lying in what is now St Andrew's graveyard, by Robert Barrie and John Brown, of Elgin. The mill was not destined to be completed, however. Bowron coveted the property of the Percys, and as they were only squatters, succeeded, after their losses in lumbering, in getting them to convey to him their betterments, and accepting in payment two lots on the road to Athelstan, where James lost his life by falling down the cellar hatchway. No sooner had he effected the exchange, than he notified Cameron that he would not be allowed to draw water from the dam, and litigation ensued. That summer (1823) Joseph Bouchette, surveyor-gen'l, visited Huntingdon,* when he advised Cameron to drop the action, and if he would, he would get him a grant of 300 acres at Dewittville, where there was an equally good opening for a mill. Cameron accepted the advice, and conveying the machinery down the river by canoes and rafts, opened a mill that fall. It was a primitive affair, having one run of stones, driven by a large undershot wheel, and could grind 12 bushels an hour. He received little custom for there were only a few farmers between the mill and Allan's Corners, but that winter he brushed out a track to Hungry bay, when, during sleighing, habitants came from both sides of the St Lawrence, and even from as far as Ile Perrot, often 20 or 30 arriving in a day. The frame of the mill at Huntingdon, Cameron sold to McFarlane for a store, but he delayed moving it, until, one spring, the ice carried away the foundation, and a raft striking the frame, the timbers tumbled on to it and were borne to the foot of the rapids. The 3 raftsmen (James McDonald was one) were unhurt.

On acquiring the Percy property, Bowron began at once to prepare to raise a gristmill, which he placed where Boyd & Co.'s old machine-shop stands. It was, of course, a rude affair, containing 2 run of stones, hewn out of boulders taken from

---

* Mr Bouchette, on the visit alluded to, called all the settlers to meet him at Mr Bowron's and took down the number of acres they had under crop, number of live-stock, etc.

the site of the old Methodist church, and dressed by an American named Tripp, who was the first miller. The bolt was upstairs, had 2 boxes and was turned by hand, so that when the farmer got his bag full of flour, he carried it upstairs, and bolted it himself. The machinery was driven by an undershot wheel. The mill was not put in operation until 1824, and, primitive as it was, was a great boon to the settlers, who had, up to this, to go to the mill at Brighton Hollow, at Constable, or the red mill at Fort Covington, all across the border. The only way of taking the grain at first was by carrying it on the shoulders, but soon the track was so cleared to Trout River Lines that an ox or a horse could pass, when with 1½ or 2 bushels of wheat, divided between two bags, slung across their backs, the settler trudged by their side through mud and water, endeavoring to keep the bags from slipping off. Among the most useful of these 4-footed carriers, was Bob Barter's bull, which was often hired, and could carry 2 bags as well as any horse. Hunter was the first to get oxen, Bright and Daisy, followed by a horse, whose main duty was to go to mill at Fort Covington, taking two days to the journey. Mr Hunter often came back with his grist late at night, and wet to the middle, guided through the darkness by holding on to the horse's tail. The difficulty in getting to mill was so great that the settlers were frequently without bread, and sometimes tried to make a substitute by shaving ears of corn with a jack-plane. At one time, owing to the impossibility of reaching mill, the Hunter family were without bread for 6 weeks. Their main diet was potatoes and venison, with occasionally pork, which they got from Dalhousie Settlement. The mill-toll was one-tenth, but the bran was not sifted, and that the settler had to do himself by hand-sieves. When Bowron acquired the Percy property, he, as already noted, left his shanty on lot 16 and moved into James Percy's house, which he improved. The house he raised for the miller, which stood between the mill and the road, was the scene of the first fire. Smoke was issuing in volumes from its roof, when one of the Percys ascended with an axe and cutting into the blazing portion extinguished it. Taylor had built an oven in the basement and baked bread for sale, for he was a baker as well as a miller.

I must go back, however. For quite a while after Goudge left, there was no school, when Mr Bowron went to Montreal and brought up Geo. Davies, a Highlander from Invernessshire, who had a taste for drawing and engineering, and was well-educated, but with no particular talent for teaching. The settlers united to put up a schoolhouse, a small frame building, a short distance above the foundry and close to where the canal is. This was in the fall of 1825. The society for the advancement of learning gave a grant of $72 towards his salary. Davies was respected, and all the more so from the sympathy felt on account of his domestic unhappiness, for, soon after coming, he lost his wife, when he married a daughter of Widow Suttle's, who made his life miserable. Unable to live by teaching, he engaged as clerk with Lewis & Ames. After him there was a succession of teachers, and the saying was that Huntingdon could not give a living to one.

In 1824 Halcomb & Latham opened store a little south of the new schoolhouse, and, expecting to do a large business, put up an ambitious building, with an unusual allowance of windows, but did not succeed, and turned their attention more to lumbering, having built a sawmill at Powerscourt. On leaving, their store became pretty much common property, having a succession of tenants and made use of by many immigrants as a temporary shelter. From the successive patchings and the abundance of broken glass, it came to have the name of Castle Clouts. A more important event for the settlers than the new store, was the building of an ashery to the west of the upper bridge by Peter McFarlane. Here ashes were pearled for the first time in the winter of 1823. In September of that year there was a flood in the river, which was followed by an influx of salmon, when Palmer, Bowron, and Percy speared a large number and barrelled them. Young John Hunter tried his hand with an extempore jack and succeeded in killing 3, though from his inex-

perience the fire was quenched by the canoe's dipping at
every lounge he made. Standing by the north end of the
dam he and Hugh Cameron counted 93 large salmon jump
it. A few days afterwards, they went down again.

On the 4th October, 1824, the grand voyer, L. R. C. de Lery,
came to see about making roads. The grand-voyer in those
days was regarded as a man of wonderful authority, being
vested with supreme jurisdiction in laying out roads and
ordering how they should be paid for. He came, accompanied by Col. Brown of Beauharnois, and lodged at Bowron's,
where the settlers gathered to meet him in the afternoon in
such numbers that they adjourned to McFarlane's store. The
result of his visit was his preparing a proces-verbal, ordering
a bridge to be built across the river below the mill, to be supported by 6 trestles made of logs a foot square, bearing 5
sleepers 12 inches square and 40 feet long, and a flooring of
squared logs 6 inches thick, edged with a 3-foot railing. The
total length of the bridge was 240 ft. The road was ordered
to be made from the bridge to the lines at Burke, with a
branch connecting Russeltown. The bridge across the Hinchinbrook was to be 60 feet long, supported by 4 trestles.
De Lery left for Hemingford, and nothing proves better
the rugged state of the country at that time, than that he
departed for Manning's in an oxsled. It was probably about
this time, that a party of settlers met in McFarlane's to agree
on a name for the village. Some one in joke proposed Best-
town, after the blacksmith, but Bowron village was agreed
upon, and prosperity to the new village drank, and the
locality henceforth ceased to be known as Long Rapids.

The need for the bridge was great, for as settlers increased
the necessity of crossing the river became of almost hourly
occurrence. Passengers got over in canoes, or, when the boom
was up, if they were steady-headed, they walked over on it,
or when the water was very low, a temporary bridge was
made by placing planks from boulder to boulder, but for
freight it was different, and settlers coming in from the east
or anxious to cross to Hinchinbrook from Godmanchester,
met with serious difficulty if the water was deep at the ford,

which was situated at the head of the rapids and over the flat rock there. It was expected that the grand-voyer would have ordered the bridge to have been built there, where it would have cost less, been safe from ice, and been on the direct road from the lines which had existed for over 20 years. His changing the route was done at the instance of Bowron, who desired the bridge to be convenient for his mills. The contract for building the bridge was let to 2 Americans from Burke, Nimes and Grissel, for $1000. The amount was to be raised by a tax of 50 cents on the lots designated by the grand-voyer in Hinchinbrook and Godmanchester. Much difficulty was experienced in collecting the money, partly owing to the poverty of the settlers and partly to their refusing to pay owing to the bridge not having been built at the head instead of the centre of the rapids. They argued that as Bowron had got the bridge placed to suit him, and given out the contract without authority, he should pay for it, and, eventually, he had to pay more than his share, for he had become responsible to the contractors when they undertook the work.

The year following the visit of the grand-voyer, Lord Dalhousie issued an order-in-council to lay out the village, which was done by William Lalanne, and his plan was entitled the village of Huntingdon. His laying the streets out parallel with the township lines, instead of taking the river as the base, led to those angles and gores which have proved such a nuisance. The river-banks were left in common, not so much with a view to the healthfulness or beauty of the future village, as from Bowron's desire to retain the water-power in his own hands and prevent claims for water damages. That year (1825) was remarkable for its bush-fires. The summer was hot and dry, but it was not until the leaves began to fall that the full danger from fire was realized, for, when a spark fell, the fire ran along the ground, and wrapped the trees in flames. For some time before there was any fire in the neighborhood of Huntingdon, the country was covered by a dense pall of smoke, afterwards believed to have come from New Brunswick, where, especially along the Miramichi, the fire caused appalling loss of life and property. There had come to the village that summer, from Hemingford, two young men, Archibald Henderson and Andrew Anderson, who had undertaken to build a frame-barn on 302, and which is now converted into a double tenement. It was ready for raising, and a number of settlers had come to the bee, when the alarm spread that the bush was on fire all around, and that the big house, Hunter's Folly, was in danger, when they ran to save it. No sooner was danger averted in that quarter, than there was a second report that Mr Hunter's barn on his lot, No. 24, was on fire, which proved true, and it was consumed with all its contents. Soon after Palmer's cattle broke the fence and ate his potatoes. These losses, joined to his successive disappointments in taking up land, so discouraged Mr Hunter that he resolved to go back to Scotland, and actually did sell part of his effects, when an obstacle arose, in the difficulty of finding a cash buyer for his farm, when he took up his abode in Huntingdon, opening there a small store, and lived for 40 years in the village he saw grow up in the bush, he dying in 1862. Back of the village the fire did much damage, and where the park lots now are was brulé ever after. Until between 1840 and 1850 these lots were mostly untaken, and formed a common, from which the villagers hauled many a load of cordwood and pastured their cows

That winter (1825-6) a young man, Fisher Ames, came driving up the ice on the Chateaugay, and announced his intention of opening store. He had served in John Hoyle's store at Lacolle, and hearing much from him of the new settlement at Huntingdon, had agreed with his fellow apprentice, Benjamin Lewis, that they would start in business there. Acquainted with Bowron, and recommended to him by his relative, Hoyle, he rented a small building from him opposite the mill,* and opened out; Lewis, whose apprenticeship did not expire until then, joining him in June. They subsequently moved to a larger house on the opposite side of

*The building is incorporated in that of C. S. Burrows' bakery.

the river, and finally, on Lewis's acquiring Lalanne's lot at the north-west end of the village, built a large store. Benj. Lewis was regarded as the cleverest man in the settlement, and with his partner Ames, and his brother Joshua, who came in 1827, did the largest business for a number of years. Except what little money the new-comers brought, there was none in circulation, so having to give long credits and making many bad debts, they took heavy profits on what they sold. For the first 6 or 8 years the entire settlement depended more or less for its supply of food upon Montreal, it being long before even pork enough could be raised. By the line of canoes started by Reeves, which ran first to Dewittville and eventually to Huntingdon, the settlers not only sent their potash but received flour and pork as well as groceries. One time the canoe failed to come, and day after day passed without her anxiously looked for appearance, and scarcity, if not starvation, threatened the settlers. Neighbor shared with neighbor, and it may be guessed how low the stock had come, when it is stated that Mr Bowron's family lived for 3 days on milk and vegetables. McFarlane, at last, went down the river to find out what had happened, and learned that the ferry-boat from Lachine to the Basin had been wrecked.

To illustrate the scarcity of money and show how Lewis came into possession of the lot (W ½ of 20) on which he built his store as stated, this story was told by John Hunter:

William Lalanne, the surveyor, bought lot 20, paying $4 an acre, and erected a house and large shed, which subsequently came to be Thomson's tavern. He and Benjamin Lewis went to Montreal, part of their business being to buy cooking-stoves. They got them at $5 apiece, Lalanne giving his note, which Lewis endorsed. When the note came due, Lalanne gave a bond promising to pay Lewis on a certain day or, in default, give him up his farm. The bond was deposited with my father. When the day came, Lalanne found he was unable to raise the money, and Lewis called on my father at 10 o'clock in the forenoon and demanded possession of the bond. Father declined, and said he ought to wait until the day was near its close. He returned in the afternoon with a witness, and renewed his demand in so imperative a manner, that my father got angry, and told him the day was not done until midnight. Sure enough, after 12 struck, Lewis came to our door, made my father get out of bed and give him the paper, and so the farm went for a cook-stove. This would be in 1828.

To change from temporal to spiritual, it is well here to note the first occasion on which religious services were held. In the winter of 1822-3 Peter Horn, then newly settled on the 1st concession of Elgin, had got the consent of Janet McFarlane to be his wife, and the Rev Mr McWattie was sent for to tie the knot. On his way, he was detained at Huntingdon by a heavy fall of snow, and arranged that on his return he would preach, so word was forwarded to the most remote settlements. The place appointed was James Percy's bar-room, it being the largest room in the village, and it was crowded. McWattie was long in coming, and when he did appear it was plain he was only getting over the previous night's excess, and trembled so much that he frightened his little congregation by letting his Bible fall. He got through the service creditably, however, preaching from John 5:40, and baptized several children. No sooner had he pronounced the benediction, than he asked for a glass of rum and water. Of a very different type was the service held by Bishop Stewart.*

*He was a younger son of the Earl of Galloway and from his devout temperament was led to study for the ministry. Offering his services to the S. P. C. K., he was sent to this province early in the century and appointed missionary at Frelighsburg, then called Slabtown, and whose inhabitants were so coarse and irreligious that they resented his settling among them, and he could not find a boarding-place. He found shelter with a widow a few miles distant, overcame the prejudices of the people, and built 2 churches. Though rich he spent nothing on himself, and lived in so plain a manner that when more than two called upon him, he had to draw the box which held his books from under his bed for a seat. In presence he was very plain, having protruding front teeth. His remarkable success was due to his earnestness and deep spirituality. He traversed the Eastern Townships regularly, but does not appear to have again visited Huntingdon. He died in 1837. He never married.

In the course of one of those tours which he took every winter
to the new settlements, he came to Huntingdon, and stayed
with Mr Bowron,* when word was sent round that he would
preach. Percy's bar-room was again crowded by the settlers,
who listened with reverence to the prayers and sermon uttered
by this pure-hearted servant of God. After his visit, Doctor
Townsend of St Johns came occasionally, generally during
sleighing. On one occasion, after baptizing 8, a mother came
in with her infant, when he declined to repeat the ceremony,
with the remark that she ought to have been in time. While
the village rarely saw a clergyman of any denomination, it
was now and then visited by wandering lay-preachers from
the American side, who, on their arrival, sent round word
that they would preach in the schoolhouse on such a day
and hour, when everybody would go, more from the event
being a break in the daily monotony than any other reason.
One American notified the villagers personally, and after
making his announcement in a shoemaker's shop was asked
who was to preach, when he oracularly replied "Come and
see." There were only two residents who attempted preaching: Whadby, whose attempts were marred by his practice,
for he was not a sober man, and James Gordon, who had a
farm on the ridge and kept, on 215, a cooper's shop where
Dalgliesh's store stands. He was well-meaning but ignorant,
being unable even to read, and his sermons were tedious
and incoherent.

In 1827 the village took a decided start. In March of that
year David Fitch entered with his worldly effects on several
sleighs and accompanied by 4 cows and 40 head of sheep.
He was a tanner and shoemaker from Mooers, N.Y., and a
man of some means. The appearance of the village on his
arrival he thus described. Entering it by the Athelstan-road
the first shanty was a little west of the mouth of the canal,

---

* Mr Bowron, when he came, was not a church-member.
His parents and connections were Quakers, and while being
visited by the latter they held two or three meetings in the
schoolroom. On the Episcopal church being built, he attended it.

and occupied by Richard Rice, an Irish Catholic, then working as a laborer, but who afterwards got a lot on Victoria
settlement. The next house was Claud Burrows, a shoemaker,
and in Castle Clouts was another shoemaker, an American
named Nutting. Near to it, was the schoolhouse and then
came Bowron's house, a long wooden edifice, with the saw
and grist mills; between the latter and the road stood the
miller's house, where Robert Taylor was installed. On the
opposite side of the road was the tavern, kept by James
Percy, and north of it Lewis & Ames' store. Crossing the
river, and beginning at the extreme western limit, stood
Palmer's shanty, then, after a long interval, a house and
shed put up by William Lalanne, but not occupied. Next
came McFarlane's store, near the eastern corner of Lake-st.,
left in the charge of McNee and Cairns, and his house to the
east of it. His store was the better-stocked of the two, and
the profits charged may be judged from the fact that for
white and blue calico 50 cents a yard was the price. On the
river-side, in front of McFarlane's, stood Best's blacksmith
shop, and an ashery, and on the east side of the road, leading
to the bridge, the shanty where Stinson, the saw-miller, lived.
Old Mr Hunter built his house nearly opposite where St
Andrew's now is, and then there was no shanty until 219
was reached, where Burnside dwelt. Farther east, on 183,
was the dwelling of Davies the teacher, and then solid bush
until the extreme east limit of the village, where, on 287,
dwelt Suttle. At the river-bank, opposite the end of the
island, the canoes landed their cargoes, for, until the lower
dam was built, the current was too strong for them to ascend
farther.

Fitch had not come with the intention of remaining per-
manently, as he had Upper Canada in view as his destination,
and meant to rent a house and work up the leather he had
brought with him. No suitable place was to be had, and he
bought from Burnside the frame of a building, large for those
days, which he meant to erect on the field west of the old
Methodist church. On the snow going away, he saw the field
was low and wet, and determined not to build there. He-

bought lot 181 and hauling the timbers to it, proceeded to build. To do so, he had first to chop down the trees on the site. He started a shoe-shop at once, and also took steps to open a tannery, employing some half-dozen men altogether, and giving quite an impetus to the village. His best customers for many years were the farmers on the Meadows, who drove or walked up to deal with him. From them he got hay for his cattle, which they hauled up on the ice. His sheep he had to let out to James Gordon, then living on the Ridge That same summer, David Hall, a waggon-maker, and Sweeny, a tailor, both Irish Catholics, arrived, and built at the lower end of the village, and David Hunter put up a house at the corner of Chateaugay and Bouchette streets. Hall had acquired from his brother, a Dublin doctor, whom he had assisted in hospital, some knowledge of physic, and as the settlers had a profound belief in the benefits of being bled regularly every spring and fall, he was always ready to oblige them in opening a vein, and also prescribed, the medicine having to be procured from Fort Covington or Malone. He also pulled teeth and attended any call for his skill. He made no charge, and his patients, if they chose, could leave at his door a bushel of wheat or peas. He was a decent, liberal-minded man, and was much respected.

The growth of the village was sustained the following year by the advent of several new settlers, chief of whom was Dr Bell, a Scotchman. He had travelled much, been in both Indies and visited the chief cities of the United States, and came to Huntingdon a stranger, expecting to find an opening in it from its being a new settlement. He boarded at first with Fitch, and it was 3 months before he developed the reason of why a man of his talent should have sought the backwoods. He was subject to periodical sprees, drinking so long as he could have liquor brought to him, for he would not go for it or drink outside his own room. While under the influence of drink he invariably refused to exercise his skill, and the answer of his housekeeper (he was unmarried) to callers was, "that he was not at home."

The removal of the store of Lewis & Ames to the north-west

corner of the village led to the establishing of an American
colony around them, of whom the chief and best was Orson
French, a shoemaker, who added a tannery to his business,
placing it on the river-bank of 325. Besides him, there were
some half a dozen others, constituting an anti-British element,
and dividing the village into two factions, the head of the
other being, for a time, Bowron. The jealousy grew with
the years. A rival school was built on 251 (Oney's); indeed,
the rivalry extended through every relation, even to religion,
for the Americans favored Universalism. A curious mode of
giving it expression was by writing insulting or satirical
communications, and fastening them to the front fence or
slipping below the door under cover of night. Ames was
the leading spirit in this mode of expressing the feelings of
the American party and defending their reputation, and to
Dr Bell the other side entrusted their replies. The missives
of both were coarse and grossly personal.

Tea and tobacco were the chief commodities on which the
Canadian government raised revenue, and as they were cheap
in the United States and dear in Canada, there was a great
deal of smuggling, men making it a regular business to supply
from the Champlain district the retailers of Montreal. Owing
to the wretched roads of Huntingdon, little was done in this
irregular trade, save in winter, previous to 1830. In 1825 Capt
March, the customs officer at Lacolle, was instructed to extend
his supervision over Huntingdon, and paid two or three visits
yearly thereafter. On hearing of his approach the storekeeper would hide whatever tea or tobacco he had, and on
the captain's entering would cordially greet him, and, producing the bottle, engage him in a chat. Rising to go, he
would ask if there were any dutiable goods on the premises,
and being invited to look for himself, would remount his
horse and leave. Remonstrated with on one occasion for his
easy mode of dealing with the storekeepers, he said his instructions were to keep in check the wholesale trade of supplying the city and not to interfere with small storekeepers
who smuggled in a petty way. Several times he chased
smugglers whom he found on the road with loads for the

Basin, but without success. A noted smuggler, Gill Dickie, thus detected, he pursued down the Trout river road. On reaching the door of Thomson's tavern, Gill shouted for the best horse in the stable to change for his own blown beast, and dashed off as the officer came in sight, and was closely pursued to Dewittville where he wheeled into a byroad that led to the back settlements, and over which March was afraid to follow. The few who followed this desperate trade always drove poor horses, so that, if caught, their loss would be slight. The inducements to smuggle were great. Tea that could be bought across the lines for 25c cost $1 if brought from Montreal, and there was a considerable, though less disproportion, in the prices of dry goods. Parishville whisky could be had at 20 to 25 cents a gallon, while in Montreal rum was 50 to 60 cents. Men made a business of peddling American whisky and tea and waited at every settler's door without concealment, and, without, in a single instance, being molested by the Crown. Major Hingston was appointed a sort of deputy to March, but did not care to exercise his powers.

In the spring of 1829 an accident happened which caused a deep sensation and proved a sad blow to the infant settlement. McFarlane, the storekeeper, had engaged during the winter in lumbering to a greater extent than ever before, having about 40 men employed. When the ice moved, he started his rafts, and followed them to Dewittville, being most anxious to get them to market. He stayed during the night with Hugh Cameron, and, early in the morning, crossed the mill-pond between the two dams to see his men and give them their dram. He got into a canoe to return for breakfast, having along with him a negro, Charley Freeman, and a tailor who had recently come out from Scotland, McCallum by name. The negro alone understood the management of a canoe, and owing to the carelessness of one of the others, it upset above the pitch of the lower dam. The negro and McCallum swam back to the north bank, but McFarlane was swept over the dam, in sight of over a hundred raftsmen, who were powerless to save him. His body was not recovered for some 6 weeks, and was found 1½ miles below where he was drowned. It was buried beside his house, near the sidewalk on 243, chains being placed round the coffin, with the intention of lifting it to send it to Glengarry, but his relatives took no interest in the matter, and there his dust still lies under one of Huntingdon's stores. He left no will, and his clerk, Duncan McNee, was engaged by the creditors to collect the assets, and ultimately they made over the business to him.

The monotony of life in a hamlet buried deep in the woods was broken in the fall of 1828 by the arrival of Col. Brown and Mr Norval, who had come to hold an agricultural show. It was held on "the green," the open space between Bowron's house and the canal and mill—a place where children played and on summer evenings housewives gathered for social gossip. It was a meagre affair, of course, a few horses and more oxen; a group of cows and an odd sheep or two. $72 was paid out by Mr Norval in prizes and then the day was celebrated by a carouse. With the exception of 1830, when the funds would not permit, shows were held yearly thereafter, generally during the last week in September, and were of increasing interest. Of the one in 1832, the report states that the turn-out "manifested the great improvement going forward in a country that ten years ago was little less than an impenetrable bush." The attendance grew more quickly than the exhibits, show-day coming to be regarded as the harvest holiday, and, noting this, one report declares that the shows "promote cordiality and good-will, amalgamate persons of different races, and spread information." The "relaxation and festivity" that characterised thus early one of Huntingdon's peculiar institutions has increased with time and lost its grosser features. As funds grew more plentiful, competition in crops was added, which were judged in the field; in the case of roots, a square patch was measured off and dug in the presence of the judges, the yield being weighed. The prizes were good, $6, $5, and $4 for horses, and $4, $3, and $2 for cows. After a while, the shows were held on Prince Arthur square, and began to partake of the nature of fairs, the settlers coming in to buy and sell. Of buyers from a distance, two McShanes (father and cousin of

James McShane, M.P.P. for Montreal West) were prominent, and came up with rolls of bills in the pockets of their long coats and leather breeches. The evening was given up to drinking, and the taverns and stores were scenes of disorder. When James Percy left the village there was pressing need for a house of entertainment. On acquiring Lalanne's lot, Lewis converted the stable into a good-sized tavern, joining Lalanne's log-house to one end of it for a bar-room, and it was the first house where decent accommodation could be had. It was kept successively by Benj. Lewis, James Love, Charles Hibbard, Orson French, —— King, Thos. Crawford, and John and Harrison Thomson—all Americans or of American descent—none of whom, except the Thomsons, kept it long. Mr Fitch adapted his dwelling-house for a hotel on his raising another, and rented it to John Thomson in 1832, who did not keep it long, moving up to opposite the bridge, and finally renting Lewis's hotel. In 1835 Mr Fitch moved in and kept hotel himself, and continued to do so until he handed over the business to his son-in-law, William Barrett. David Milne, who had a farm on Trout river, sold it to Robt. Murray, and opened a tavern which stood east of the Methodist church, on 245. The securing of a tavern had become a necessity to Lewis from his having taken the contract to carry the mail. Up to 1829 there was no postoffice in the district, and settlers depended upon Montreal or the U.S. offices for their mail-matter, and losing one or two days to send a letter or find if there was one for them. When a settler visited Montreal, he would ask at the postoffice for letters for all his neighbors. A letter to Great Britain cost $1, and seldom took less than 6 weeks to go. On the 6th April, 1829, a mail-route was established, having Laprairie, Chateaugay and Beauharnois as offices. On the 6th July, 1830, François Maurice Lepallieur of Chateaugay started in fulfilment of a contract he had entered into to convey the mail to Dundee, with liberty to cross to Fort Covington. He made one trip a week, performing the journey on the back of a sorrel pony when the roads were bad and in a French cart when they permitted; the only offices on the route,

Reeves' and Huntingdon; and his remuneration $240 a-year.
The rate of postage was 18 cents a letter for any distance
not greater than Quebec. There were not half a dozen
newspapers in the bag. They were dear, the annual subscription being $4, and, in addition, there was 80 cents
postage. The postmaster at Huntingdon was Dowie Kettle
Lighthall, who came through the Hoyles. His habit, when
he had sorted the mail, was to read out aloud to the crowd
that never failed to assemble when Lepallieur hove in sight,
the address of each letter. The plan had the advantage, if
the person was not present, of some neighbor who was,
telling him. When St Andrew's opened, he put the package
of undelivered letters in his pocket and after service handed them to their owners. Lepallieur had been making his
rounds a considerable while, when there came to Huntingdon
an American named Campbell, who had fled from his creditors. Among other property he brought with him were a
number of horses and a stage-waggon. A long-mooted project had been the establishing of a stage between Ogdensburg
and Montreal, and Campbell undertook to perform the duty
on the Canadian side. The experiment proved that it could
be made a success in competent hands, and a company composed of Lewis, Schuyler, Ames, and Love bought him out.
Sending to Albany for two of the best stage-coaches then
made, they opened in the summer of 1832, making two trips
a week, and when Lepallieur transferred to them his contract
of carrying the mail. The route was well-patronized by Americans and was a popular means of communication between
Northern New York and Montreal until the canals were
opened. Leaving Ogdensburg in the morning, Fort Covington was reached in the evening, when a few hours of rest
were allowed. At 2 in the morning the horn was sounded
and the journey was renewed in the Canadian stage, which,
drawn by 4 horses, drove down Briggs street to the lines
and then reached Huntingdon by the Ridge-road in time
for an early breakfast. The horses were pulled up alongside the ferry-boat at the Basin in the afternoon, and on the
boat's nearing Lachine another stage was seen to be in wait-

ing, which landed the passengers by nightfall at the door of the Ottawa hotel, then kept by Hall on St James street. The fare from Fort Covington to Montreal was $3.50, and from Huntingdon $2.50, with half a dollar additional in winter, when the stage drove straight across the ice to the city. The management of the line was bad and the company became insolvent, when Joshua Lewis got sole control. Falling under suspicion of being in sympathy with the rebels, the postoffice department, then managed by the Imperial authorities, withdrew the contract ($1000 a-year) of carrying the mail from him, and gave it to George Pringle in 1839, who took the stage from Lewis and ran it tri-weekly for 14 years, using 3 horses instead of 4. In 1842 the steamer agreed to take the stage on board, which saved the transfer of baggage. The establishing of the stage led to additional postoffices being opened, and bags were made up for Ste Martine, where Primeau was postmaster; for Widow Cross's at Point Round; for Durham (Ormstown) Wm. Cross postmaster; and Dewittville, James Davidson. The starting of the stage-line, as important an event in those times as the opening of a railway in ours, ended the prosperous days of the canoes, which, thereafter, were resorted to only for conveying heavy goods. Reeves deplored this, for he had brought his canoe-line into fine working order. "Before the stage began," he said, "people looking for land had to stay overnight and the same going back, but now they go right on and all they leave is three coppers for a dram."

The starting of the stage-line was rendered possible by the improvement of the roads by grants from government. After years of persistent refusal to aid in improving the communications of the country, it dawned suddenly upon French members that if they gave $5 to open up roads in the townships they could take $20 to improve those in the parishes. The revenue, then raised by custom-duties levied at Quebec and Montreal, was advancing by leaps, owing to the rapid influx of immigrants into the Townships and Upper Canada, so that there was no lack of money. In 1829 the first grants were made, and for the next four sessions the chief business of members was the promotion of petitions for grants to make roads and bridges in their counties, and grants were made by the hundred, and the expenditure of most was attended by bare-faced misappropriation. In this distribution of public funds, a part fell to the district of Beauharnois. $4000 was given to improve the road from Caughnawaga to Beauharnois, half of which was spent in building a bridge at the Basin. A like sum was given to cut out a road from St Timothy to St Regis. Col. Davidson was given a part to build the Dundee end, and during 1830 cut a track 6½ miles long through the woods and corduroyed 560 rods between Salmon river and Laguerre. Dr McGibbon and Mr Bowron were entrusted with $2000 to make a road from Laguerre to Huntingdon, and thence to Dewittville. The work was finished in 1832. The contract for the bit of road from Huntingdon to Dewittville was taken by Thos. Barlow and Peter Outterson in 1831, when it was straightened somewhat. The roads, where they passed through the woods, were cut 36 ft. wide and measured 20 ft. between the ditches. Subsequently, on the grant for the road from St Timothy proving insufficient, $4800 more was granted, when the existing road along the lakeshore of Ste Barbe and St Anicet was made. Grants were also secured for roads and bridges in the seigniory, the chief one being a road from Beauharnois up the St Louis, high trestle bridges spanning the creeks, and to the road from St Remi to Huntingdon. While it was an inestimable boon to the settlers to have roads where there were none before, they were execrably made, and in spring and fall were impassable for wheels. During the first 10 years of its existence the stage had more than once to be suspended, and the mail-bag forwarded on horseback. During such a time, the carrier was found dead in a ditch near Helena, from his horse having stumbled in the dark. The opening of waggon-roads to the frontier revolutionized the trade of the district, which, instead of depending upon Montreal, now drew its supply of store-goods from the United States and continued to do so with impunity until the union of the provinces, when the fiscal laws were more strictly enforced.

Indeed, no attempt was made to uphold any of the laws in the early days of the village. In 1826 Mr Bowron was made a commissioner for the trial of small causes but seldom exercised his powers from having no means of carrying them into effect. The inhabitants included a good many roughs, one of whom, an Irishman named William McCoy, kept the place in terror when drunk. He lived by fishing and hunting, and habitually carried a double-barrelled rifle. One day he quarrelled with another notorious fighter, a Welshman named Davis, who threw him, and would have kicked him to death but for the interference of bystanders. Both afterwards went West, and Davis was hung in Ohio for murder, confessing before he was executed that he had killed 2 men previously while drunk. When sober he was civil and active, and was well educated. Drink, indeed, was the curse of the young village. On Saturday men came straggling into the village, spent the day in idling and drinking, and by nightfall were drunk and quarrelsome. It was a common occurrence to see 30 or 40 men in front of McNee's struggling and fighting a la Donnybrook fair, from no other cause than that the whisky they had drank had removed all restraint from their strong, passionate natures. The consumption of liquor was enormous, and to meet the demand Mr Bowron raised a building on the south-side of the river, opposite 267, for a distillery, but abandoned his project before the machinery was required. The want of courts to settle disputes and enforce the collection of claims was much felt, and an act having been passed to reconstitute the magistracy in 1832, a petition was got up, and carried round by John Gilmore asking that Huntingdon be included, when William Lamb and Charles Dewitt were appointed. They held a monthly court, at which not only offenders were tried, but proces-verbaux were homologated and much of the work that now falls to municipal councils was done by them. They held their first court in French's house; Orson French being clerk. Shortly after a commissioners' court was organized, which had sufficient business to require a monthly session, the court sitting in a log-house at the upper end of the village. These courts developed two pettifoggers, Sam Pelton and Tom Barlow, who made a double profit, for they also acted as bailiffs, and served their own papers, which they carried in the crown of their tall hats. The mode of dealing in those days was conducive to the disputes that lead to the law-courts. There being hardly any money in circulation, business was done by trading, and the dickers or turnings-in led to misunderstandings which necessitated suing. Of more benefit than the courts, was the establishing of a registrar's office in 1830, John Munro being the first registrar, and who, from an accident in childhood, was dwarfish and deformed. He kept his office in the store of Lighthall, who was appointed his successor, on his death, and in 1841 was ordered to move the office to Ormstown, where it remained 13 years.

Primitive and difficult of access as it was, Huntingdon received visits from two governor-generals. In 1829 Sir James Kempt, desirous of seeing the settlement, drove up in company with Colonel Brown. While visiting Lewis's store, half-a-dozen petitions were handed to him by settlers who had grievances regarding their lands, when he testily exclaimed, "Damn it; do you think I have come here to hold a court of justice?" and pitched them aside. They were taken in charge by an attendant, however, and justice was subsequently done to all by the department. Dissatisfaction with the management of the local-agent was of long standing, for as early as the fall of 1823 a petition was sent to the governor by the settlers asking that he be relieved. The second governor who came was Lord Gosford in 1836. The village had sufficiently progressed to justify its entertaining him to a dinner, for which a shed was erected in front of Milne's hotel, whence it was supplied, the dishes being handed out at the window. The governor, who lodged with Mr Lighthall, stayed overnight. While crossing the upper bridge he recognized Henry Turner, who had been brought up on his father's estate, and cordially shook hands with him. For the rest of his life Turner was known as Lord Gosford. The vice-regal party, which included Sir George Simpson, visited Fort Covington and there Brown was arrested (page 266).

The population of the village up to 1830 was exceedingly fluctuating, partly owing to lumbering being its main dependence and partly to many coming who left disappointed in their expectations of the place. In 1829 Bouchette found its population to be only 125, which was less than it had been, owing to the depression in lumbering. A striking proof of the paramount importance of the lumbering industry in those days and how everything else was made to defer to it was shown in an agitation that stirred the village for several years. The placing of the bridge by Mr Bowron where they suited his mills, led eventually to their removal. Raftsmen complained that it was so close to the dam, that it was difficult, after shooting it, to steer between the piers of the bridge. Point was given to these complaints by the drowning of one man, William Wilson of the Gore, and the numerous narrow escapes the bridge had from being wrecked. A raft of boards caught on a pier and hung there all summer. Masts were constantly being caught. Hugh Cameron, not forgetful of his wrongs, urged the lumbermen to compel the removal of the dam, which was 5 feet high, as an obstruction, and the farmers above the rapids joined, they declaring the backwater flooded their land. To avoid a legal decision, Bowron lowered his dam and engaged Barlow to dig a canal from the head of the rapids, thereby hoping to secure all the power he required. In this he was disappointed for in summer there was not head enough and in winter the canal choked with anchor-ice. To remedy the one he first tried bolting a boom to the flat rock and then endeavored to meet the other by deepening and widening the mouth of the canal. The stone that was blasted in the operation, which was prosecuted in 1831, was sold at 12½ cents a load to McNee, who used them in building a store and dwelling-house in front of the lot on which now stands the Methodist church. It was the first stone building in the village, which up to then was composed of mean-looking frame and log-houses. The improvement in the canal had little effect on the anchor-ice, and Mr Bowron decided to get out of the difficulty by rebuilding his mills on another site, and was the more inclined to do so

from the fact that, by this time, both his mills were nearly
worn out—the sawmill no longer cutting evenly and the
gristmill liable to get out of order and making such poor
flour that the settlers often preferred to go to Fort Covington or to the Trout river mill. To satisfy both raftsmen
and farmers, and secure ample head, Bowron chose a site for
the new dam near the foot of the rapids, and preparations
for building a mill were begun in 1831. The summer of
that year was long remembered for its July freshet. It
rained for six days with little cessation, filling the swamps
and swelling every stream. In the spring the water had
been so low that many rafts had been unable to reach the
St Lawrence, and they lay stranded along Trout and Chateaugay rivers. With their withes warped and shrivelled
by long exposure the flood easily tore them from their
fastenings, and swept them along, unmanned and unguided,
until broken up, covering the swollen waters with boards and
logs. The flood was at its height on Sunday, and, there happening to be service that day, the villagers had just left the
schoolhouse, when the bridge yielded to the pressure and
went with a crash. A man had barely stepped off it when
it began to move. It was replaced by another trestle bridge,
the piers of the present one not being built until 1843. The
backwater stopped the gristmills all over the district, so that
many families were without bread for a fortnight. All the
low lands were flooded, ruining both the hay, which it filled
with sand, and the grain growing upon them, but for the poor
settlers worse was to come. When the clouds passed, the fierce
heat of the July sun evoked malaria from the soaked soil,
and, for the first time, fever and ague visited the settlement.
Many, when struck down, knew not what ailed them, so
unknown was the disease. Dr Bell was kept busy, and, to
add to the distress, he had little of either quinine or the
bark. The winter proved one of scarcity, and had it not
been for the village storekeepers giving credit, many settlers
would have suffered from hunger. The succeeding summer
brought no improvement, for cholera broke out at Quebec
in the first week of June, and spread at once to Montreal,

causing a complete stagnation of business. For a long time it seemed as though Huntingdon was to escape altogether, so much so that when Benjamin Lewis was starting with the stage one morning, he was asked where he was going, he replied that he was proceeding to Montreal to bring back the cholera to kill off some of the poor people about Huntingdon. He did his business in Montreal and started for home apparently well. At Miller's tavern the stage halted for dinner, of which he partook, but afterwards became suddenly ill, determined to go no farther, and died that night. He was buried in Georgetown graveyard. After that there were scattered cases along the river, but the disease never became epidemic. It was worse at Dewittville than anywhere else, a number of French Canadians dying and several Indians, who happened to be encamped there. One afternoon the stage dropped a passenger at Dewittville who had taken ill, and drove rapidly to Huntingdon to send back Dr Bell, who succeeded in curing the patient. While in the East Indies Dr Bell had seen the disease, and affirmed if sent for in time he could cure it, but was not disposed to undertake any case that had advanced beyond the first stage. To James Davidson, son of Colonel John Davidson of Dundee, who had by this time established himself at Dewittville, in charge of a sawmill, the Doctor entrusted a quantity of medicine to be administered on the first appearance of illness, and after that there were no deaths. In Boyd Settlement, John Telford died of the disease and in Huntingdon there was another victim, Wallis Green's daughter. Benjamin Lalanne, who was subject to epileptic fits and was greatly disfigured in the face by having fallen into the fire while attacked by one, was taken ill at Athelstan, and died at Munro's. At the time of his death, he was preparing to build a store on 148, of which the foundation is still to be seen. His brother the surveyor had left by this time, and died, about 1850, in Hemingford. They were natives of the Eastern Townships; English by their mother's side, and Protestants. The summer following the visitation of cholera, two young men alighted from the stage one evening, who became prominent among the villagers. One was Francis W. Shirriff, who had graduated a few months before as a physician at Edinburgh. Dr Bell sent for him, and said he had learned he had decided on remaining and as there was not practice for two, if Dr Shirriff would give him $100 he would leave. The money was paid, and Dr Bell left for near Allan's corners, where he died soon after from an overdose of morphine. Dr Shirriff, notwithstanding, did have opposition. The American party induced a Dr Misisoom to come, who endeavored to eke out a living by keeping a small drug-store. The people, who could not catch his name, called him Dr Methusalah, and by that appellation he was best known. The young man who accompanied Dr Shirriff and who came from the same part of Haddingtonshire, was John Somerville, who alternated between farming and business. His brother, Robert B., arrived the same year and became the leading public man of the village and ultimately of the county.

The new gristmill was opened in the fall of 1832 and the frame of a sawmill erected a few rods above it. The new mill had 5 run of stones, driven by turbine wheels, and cost $6000, one-half of which was advanced by Archd. Henderson, who now became a partner with Bowron in his milling business. Walker Needler, who had been for some time in the old mill, was placed in charge of the new one. After the New Year, there was a great thaw, when the ice broke and left the river, carrying the frame of the new sawmill down the stream several hundred feet and breaking a corner of the gristmill. The village wags one night took down the sign of a storekeeper and nailed it to the mill, informing passers-by they could get groceries and dry goods on the ice. The sawmill was afterwards drawn back to its place by a sweep, and bolted down.

The old gristmill was not long without a tenant. In 1832 one Daniel Gorton of Malone rented it to make paper, supposing that from rags being cheap and nearness to Montreal he would do well. These were the days before machinery had come into general use for paper-making, and Gorton fol-

lowed the old method, dipping the pulp up by hand. He was
a decent man and persevered for some time, making printing-
paper only, which he sent to Montreal by means of a canoe
of his own that plied to the Basin. The difficulties of transportation, especially in winter, caused him to abandon the
enterprise, and the next tenant was another American,
Stevens, when the old mill was fitted up for carding and
fulling cloth, something which had long been wanted, and
which enabled farmers to turn their wool into cloth. The
old mill met its fate in the Fall of 1836 and was the cause of
the death of four of its occupants. One day Stevens left to
visit Fort Covington. The weather was cold, and to prevent
the oil from congealing about the machinery during the
night, a pan of hot ashes was placed under the carding-mill.
When all were asleep, it was conjectured the dripping oil
caught fire from the ashes, and the whole building was almost instantly wrapped in flames. The occupants slept in
the second story, and as the boards curled off from the heat,
they were seen lying in their beds, apparently having been
smothered to death long before the flames reached them.
The victims were, Mrs Stevens and her child, and the two
mill-girls, Emmons and Stone. Stevens firmly believed the
building had been set on fire by thieves, who had stolen webs,
measuring about 1000 yards, which were in readiness to be
taken to Fort Covington to be dressed and finished, he not
having the machinery for doing so. The only circumstance
that supported his supposition was the absence of any
charred remains of the cloth where it was piled. As may
be imagined, this tragedy caused a deep sensation, and, like
the drowning of McFarlane, formed a waymark in the history of the village. The mill was rebuilt by Hoyle, who
had owned the property for some time, and in 1839 was
rented to Briggs, an American, who made very good cloth.
Almost as unlooked for an industry as paper-making, was
tried to be established in the village and about the same
time. An American, Shirley Norton, got a building convenient to the new sawmill, which he fitted up as a foundry,
his fan being driven by the sawmill wheel, and the blast

conveyed across the mill-yard by a leather hose. He made such small castings as the settlers then needed, especially moulds for baking johnny cakes, but attempted nothing large. The cartage of the raw material was so expensive that he had to desist, and the building was applied to other use. Mr Bowron, in building his new mills where he did, had in view the moving of the village over to the east bank, which he had a surveyor lay out in streets and lots, but, from some cause, abandoned his intention. On completing the mills, he built a two-story residence for himself, the second stone-building in the village, now the property of the Hendersons (296). At the same time Andrew Smith, a saddler, engaged his brother-in-law, Killaly, to build a stone-house for him on 265. R. B. Somerville, who owned the property on the opposite side of the road, did all he could to prevent it but to no purpose. The house was built and an example set of infringing upon the common, which was readily imitated by others, to the destruction of the beauty of the village, for had the front street been built only on one side as designed it would have been as spacious as picturesque. The refusal of its squatters to do road-labor or pay assessments, led to application to the government to survey the common and make it part of the village proper.

In his "Tour Through North America" Patrick Shirreff tells how he drove up the Chateaugay to see his friends at Huntingdon, and says of it: "The village of Huntingdon consists of 30 or 40 wooden houses, with grist and saw mills; paper and hat factory and a postoffice. There is a school, and a church is soon to be erected." The school alluded to was that near the canal; there was, however, another. The leading villagers, strange to say, were strongly imbued with the notion that boys and girls ought to be taught separately, and as early as 1829 opened a girls' school, which Miss Badgely of Fort Covington kept in Percy's old tavern. She was succeeded by Miss Dowd of Ile aux Mott, and the school was maintained, with occasional intervals when a teacher could not be got, for over 25 years, when the people became reconciled to mixed schools. When the government began

making grants to assist in building schoolhouses, the leading
men of the village united in an attempt to erect an academy,
and petitioned, in 1834, the legislature for a grant of $1000,
which was not given. The church alluded to by Mr Shirreff
as being in prospect was St Andrew's, and to trace how it
came to be built needs a slight retrospect. Huntingdon was
unfortunate in not having among its founders any who
exerted an active influence for good, they being careless and
worldly. For the first ten years there was no religious life
to speak of ; no organized effort in spiritual things. Sunday
was spent in idleness, in visiting and gossip, the day passing
heavily; the more youthful went fishing or hunting, or, if the
weather did not permit, played cards. As already stated,
religious services were rare and irregular, and conducted by
persons who commanded no respect. McWattie paid a few
visits, but only came when sent for to perform some ministerial duty. A few staunch Presbyterians walked to Ormstown on the days he preached there, and until disgusted by
his habits. The first Presbyterian minister from Montreal
to visit Huntingdon was Dr Mathieson, who, in 1828, came
to see Peter Horn of Elgin, who had been an old schoolmate.
He rested at Huntingdon, staying with Hunter, who insisted
on sending round word that he would conduct a service.
"Being a paper-reader, (the Doctor tells this himself) I had
to erect a pulpit by the fireside, which was easily extemporized by 2 chairs, back to back, and a four-legged stool laid
across and covered over by a piece of carpet." He repeatedly
visited the settlement after that and so did Dr Black. None
of the Montreal ministers attempted to establish a congregation, and their visits were regarded chiefly as being useful in
furnishing an opportunity for baptisms and marriages. The
first resident minister, was an Englishman, Rev Mr Kingsford, a Baptist, who came to Canada in 1831, with a letter of
introduction to Col. Davidson, who referred him to Bowron.
Renting his old house, for he had gone to live near his
new mills, Mr Kingsford and his wife remained for over a
year, he preaching in the schoolhouse and baptizing in the
mill-pond three converts. Mrs Kingsford, a most estimable

lady, assisted by engaging as mistress of the day-school for girls, and on Sundays had a Bible class in her house, which was largely attended. The field not being encouraging, this worthy couple, who had no family, left, and eventually settled in Pennsylvania. Apparently a year or so before the Kingsfords came, a Sunday-school was opened by Joshua Lewis in the schoolhouse, assisted by his future wife, Eliza Ames. It was attended by the young people for miles around, many of them barefoot. Learning that the Methodist Episcopal conference was to meet at Fort Covington in 1827, Wm. Dalgliesh, a Scotchman, who had then a farm on Trout river, and John Ingles, an American squatter on the Ridge, walked all the way to attend it, represented the spiritual destitution of Huntingdon, and urged that it be taken under its care. The utmost the conference's resources permitted, was to order that the minister of Fort Covington should include Huntingdon in his circuit, and make appointments so far as compatible with his duties on the American side. This meant very little, for the Fort Covington minister had little time to spare after attending to his own people, and the bush-tracks into Canada were bad beyond belief. The best he could do was to include the schoolhouse at Kensington in his preaching-stations, several years elapsing before regular appointments were made for Huntingdon. Before that, the arrival of the Rev James Miller (page 296) led to the organization of a Presbyterian congregation. He was born at Polmont, Stirlingshire, in 1791 and received his elementary education at the parish school and at that of Falkirk. He entered Glasgow college, in 1810, and read theology under Doctor Lawson of Selkirk. On completing his studies, he united with the Congregational church at Falkirk, and by it was licensed to preach. Unable to find a charge, he became a schoolmaster and followed that honorable occupation for 16 years, preaching as occasion offered. In 1828 he joined the U. P. Presbytery of Falkirk and Stirling, when he was appointed a city missionary in Tradeston, Glasgow, and labored for 2 years, when, at the instance of Dr Wardlaw, he consented to go to Canada under the auspices of the Glasgow Mis-

sionary Society. He arrived, by way of New York, in
Montreal in December 1830, when, by the direction of a friend,
he went west by Dundee, driving up the Chateaugay to Huntingdon, and proceeded as far as Brockville. Finding no better
opening, he returned to Ormstown, and engaged as teacher
until there was a vacancy for him as a settled minister.
With that in view, he seized an early opportunity to revisit
Huntingdon, when he stayed with Hunter, who, on learning
that he was a minister, made him promise to come back on
Sunday and preach. Word being circulated, he had a large
congregation in the schoolhouse, and so well pleased were his
hearers that they asked him to come and be their minister,
promising to build a house for him, which was raised on 232
by bees in the spring of 1832, and was the first house on
Hunter-street. He was installed in the schoolhouse, teaching
in it during the week and preaching on Sunday. He discharged both duties excellently, the school being crowded to
excess and his congregations large and interested. In the
winter he had no less than 120 scholars on the roll, many
of them men-grown. The American school (page 336) was
then at its best and no good feeling existed between the
scholars, there being skirmishes on the ice during recess,
ending usually in the Yankee boys being chased to their
own door. A man of decided views and with the courage of
his convictions, Mr Miller set his face against the drinking-
customs that prevailed, and organized a temperance society
in the spring of 1832. The pledge was merely against distilled liquors, but it did much good, by preparing the way for
a more sweeping covenant and by directing people's minds
towards considering the sin of using intoxicating liquors.
The time was favorable, for many farmers had become uneasy in conscience regarding the drinking at bees, yet none
had the courage to set the example of banishing the keg.
The temperance reform supplied the required countenance
and motive for their new departure, and thereafter many
farmers had no drink at their bees. On the evening of the
4th May, at one of the meetings in the schoolhouse, Thomas
Danskin delivered a lecture so excellent that it was printed

after his death. Very soon Mr Miller's hearers began to think of building a church, and as to the site there was no difference of opinion. The point below the bridge had been covered by a grove of giant oaks and pines, which had been among the first to fall before the lumberman's axe, and forming a clearance when all around was bush. When the village came into existence this clearance was used as a washing-green, and there, for many years, the goodwives slung kettles, washed their linen with water taken from the river, and spread them on the grass and the stumps that abounded. At the corner next the bridge, lot 260, Bowron put up a shanty for his sawyer, an American, named Schofield, who planted potatoes in the clearance. In the summer of 1832 a child of Bryant's (a blacksmith), died, and he asked Schofield's permission to bury it by the riverside. Armstrong conducted the religious service, and the body was committed to the ground, the first of many destined to follow. The second to be buried was Andrew Cowan, drowned from off a raft at Dewittville, who was buried where the postoffice block stands, and dressed as he was recovered from the river, boots and all. After this, as if by common consent, the strip of land became the burial-place of the neighborhood and the corner of Percy's old cornfield (a few yards east of the old Methodist church), where one or more of that family had been buried previous to 1825, and used subsequently on several occasions by the settlers, was no longer resorted to. The Old Country idea, that the church should be with the graveyard, decided the members of Mr Miller's congregation on where they should build. In the Fall of 1833 they had bees to take out the timbers, which were framed by Elijah Matthews, an Englishman, who came from Odelltown, and had been in Huntingdon several years. His wife was Irish, and though they had no family, were kept poor, it was currently believed, by their enormous appetites! The frame was raised and, to use the phrase of those days, it "stood in sticks" for a year, for the people were unable to finish it. In 1834 they managed to enclose it, the contribution of many farmers being packs of shingles they had shaved themselves. The following year it was clapboarded and finished, but not seated. Singular to relate, the cause of all this activity in church matters, never preached in the new edifice. The Presbytery of Montreal refused to recognize him, owing to the insufficiency of his credentials, and, despairing of his induction as minister of Huntingdon, in 1835 he accepted a call from Chateaugay, N.Y., and died there, after a prolonged and useful incumbency.

During the first year of Mr Miller's stay in Huntingdon, the religious differences between the American and Old Country inhabitants of the village came to a climax. The former had brought the Universalist minister at Malone, Rev Mr Bellew, to preach several times. Mr Miller replied to him, and a controversy ensued, which aroused such deep interest that people came from as far as Georgetown to hear the disputants. Mr Miller, at first, took the same text as his opponent, preaching on it the following Sunday, but, finally, came to close quarters, and replied on the spot. In this he had a great advantage, as Bellew got on ill without a manuscript, and was further at a loss from being only superficially acquainted with the Greek Testament. On one Sunday, he was so decisively refuted, that he never returned, and Universalism, which, for a while, looked as if it would gain a footing in Huntingdon, became unknown.

In the fall of 1834, the Rev William Montgomery Walker, a native of Ayrshire, arrived in Montreal, having been sent out by the Glasgow Colonial Missionary Society. He was ordained by the Presbytery of Montreal, and in November proceeded to Huntingdon accompanied by Dr Black. The church not being ready, he was inducted in the old sawmill, and afterwards preached in the schoolhouse. Of his first sermon, the odd comment of Dr Bell has been preserved. While a knot of the people were discussing the new minister, the Doctor was asked his opinion of the sermon, when he replied that he thought the preacher had been too hard on the devil! The force of expression thus indicated was characteristic of Mr Walker, who placed undue emphasis on whatever idea possessed his thoughts for the time being and, consequently, was vehement in his language. Though very unequal, he was acknowledged to be a great preacher by his flock, whose tastes he suited. He read his first sermon, but on learning that the people disliked the paper, he said it was all one to him, he could do without it, and never after used manuscript. At the congregational meeting Dr Black used all his persuasive powers to induce the people to subscribe more liberally to the support of the new minister than they were inclined, when Robert Taylor, the miller, exclaimed, "It's a' very weel, but you never minded us till noo; you let us a' go to hell thegither until there was word o' this money comin' frae the clergy land." The money spoken of was that of the clergy-reserves, which formed the backbone of the minister's salary. Mr Walker organized a kirk-session; George Danskin, Hugh Barr, and James Tully being elders. Mr Barr was precentor. The first couple he married was Alex. Anderson (the laird) and Elizabeth Tully, whom he cried in the Scotch fashion. Being the first church, the settlers, irrespective of denomination, took seats in it, and during Mr Walker's incumbency it was always crowded. His energy was not bounded by Huntingdon, however, for he established preaching-stations all around the village, and after the service in the church, taking a piece of bread and cheese in his hand, he started off at once on foot to his second appointment, preaching on alternate Sundays at Marshall's and Elgin schoolhouses, with occasional services in those at Munro's (near Athelstan) and Dewittville.

On the completion of the church, a move was made to fence the graveyard, for, in muddy weather, it was used as a short cut to the bridge, and cattle browsed unmolested amid the graves. A rumor, that a pig had uprooted and devoured a child, stimulated the movement, and in 1836 a tolerable fence was erected. The highest subscription was $1.50, and only $11 in cash was collected. The people were unequal to the building of such a manse as Mr Walker wanted, so he bought a lot on the north-east corner of Prince and Bouchette streets and raised, what was considered in those days, a very fine house at his own expense.

For quite a while after the church was opened, the only

vehicles known were ox-sleds during winter and ox-carts in summer, their occupants squatting on pease-straw. For many years Mrs Rose and Mrs Reid, who led society, attended not only church but made their visits in a Scotch cart. The condition of the roads rendered the use of lighter vehicles impossible. Even in the village the mud was terrible, women, if they wanted to go out, having to don long-boots. In returning from the lower end of the village one evening, R. P. Somerville had one of his boots drawn off by the tenacious clay. Dr Shirriff was the first to get a two-wheeled spring cart.

The congregation of St Andrew's had barely got their church completed, when a split took place among them. Joseph Johnston of Laprairie had become interested in Huntingdon from having bought an insolvent estate, in charge of which he placed James Adam. Noting the inability of the settlers to do more than earn a living, he represented their case to the Montreal branch of the American Home Missionary society, and they sent Miss Pearson and Miss Gordon to teach and do what evangelistic work they could. Miss Gordon took charge of the girls' school in the village and Miss Pearson of the school on the Ridge. They were both Americans and of exemplary life. In the winter of 1836 Mr Johnston succeeded in getting a promise from the Rev W. F. Currie, one of the society's agents, that he would visit Huntingdon, and of the nature of the work he did I cannot give a better idea than transcribe the narrative of one who came under his influence, William Caldwell:

I was in the bush working, when somehow my mind got full of thoughts and I sat down on a log, when I heard the horn. It was too early for supper, so I supposed somebody wanted to see me, and taking up my axe went to my home, where I found supper on the table. My wife said that Miss Pearson and Miss Gordon had been in, and left word that there was to be a prayer-meeting at the school (then on McNair's hill) for a revival of religion. The expression was new to us all, but I felt as if something was coming, as if it were a cry "Awake, thou sleeper." I went to the meeting, which was attended by two from Huntingdon—Adam and Johnston of Laprairie. They made the announcement, that

Currie, a revivalist, was coming. Fears were entertained that Mr Walker would not give him the church to preach in on Sunday, but he did, and during the following week meetings were held every night in the sort of court-house where Oney now is (lot 251) but the church was refused the second Sunday. This bore on my mind, and, after a struggle, I felt it my duty to go and see Mr Walker about it. He received me kindly, said he perceived there was a great change in me, asked me the names of the converts, so that they might be watched for 10 years, to see if their change was genuine, and offered to lend me any books from his library. He would give me no satisfaction about allowing Currie the use of the church, but promised to attend one of his meetings. I asked him to let us unite in prayer. He shook like a leaf, though he consented, and I, who could not have prayed a few days before, had full utterance. Mr Walker attended as promised, and was as Saul amongst us, for he was very tall, interested in the service and joined heartily in the hymns. He, however, turned against the movement more and more as time went on, and some 32 of his people withdrew and formed a congregation.

Mr Currie, as may be supposed from this narrative, was a man of force and eloquence. He only remained 3 weeks and never revisited Huntingdon, yet during that short time he set in motion the most remarkable revival of vital Christianity the place has known, for when he left hundreds were under deep convictions to whom religious feeling was unknown when he came. Mr Walker was disposed to countenance the movement, and his subsequent opposition was attributed to the influence of the leading members of his congregation, prominent among whom was Major Gardner, who ridiculed the revival in dogerel as wretched as the sentiment. The older people regarded the doctrine of instant conversion with doubt, and unhesitatingly condemned prayer-meetings and hymns as innovations without warrant, but the cause of antipathy among the majority was Currie's uncompromising denunciation of the use of strong drink. He uttered no uncertain sound; the sin of the drinking practices, then universal, he laid bare. That people to whom whisky was more familiar than tea, and who had been brought up to regard it as a necessary of life, should resent the views laid down, was natural, and the feeling among the majority of the attendants of St Andrew's was that those who believed what Currie taught should not be allowed to remain among them. The result was that a secession of the best people took place, including such men as the Caldwells, the Clydes, the Biggars, Dunsmores, Cunninghams, Cowans, Lairds, and the Whites. The prospect was that those who left would, before long, be the stronger, body, for in two years they counted 200 members. They organized as a congregation of the American Presbyterian church, and received as their first minister a Mr Wells, an excellent preacher. Like all Americans, he was suspected during the insurrection of sympathizing with the rebels ; in his case unjustly. In the winter of 1838 he had occasion to visit Fort Covington and it being late when he returned he stayed overnight at James Clyde's. One of the mounted patrol, who disliked the new movement, saw him enter and perceived a chance of annoying its leader. He rode to Huntingdon and reported to Colonel Campbell that a suspicious-looking stranger from the States had put up at Clyde's. He denied that he knew him, and expressed his belief that the stranger was a spy. Three troopers were detailed to go and arrest him. Mr Wells was taken from his bed, in spite of his protestations and those of his host, and hurried to the village, where, of course, he was immediately released with voluble apologies. The insult affected Mr Wells so deeply that he left, and the Rev Mr Dobie came as his successor. He was zealous and sincere but most indiscreet, struck off from the roll as members many excellent persons whom he adjudged unsound in the faith, so that the congregation declined. It worshipped in a log-house, that stood on lot 233 until 1842, when a good frame church was raised on the opposite side of the street, lot 323.

The completion of the Presbyterian church was followed by the organizing of an Episcopal congregation. In the fall of 1834 Archdeacon Mountain, (afterwards Bishop) came to Huntingdon by way of Ormstown, and· on Sunday held service in the barn of Catten, lot 27, on the Chateaugay, which was so filled that many had to stand around the open door.

He administered the holy communion on the occasion. In the afternoon he preached in the schoolhouse at the village, "where (he says) the people were jammed together in an oppressive degree, and there were also auditors on the outside of the windows." This visit had a stimulating effect upon the Episcopalians, of whom there were a great many, chiefly North of Ireland people. In 1835 a catechist, a Mr Harvey from Kingston, arrived, and took up house, for he had a family. He preached in the schoolhouse and also at the Gore, where he resided when he left, which was in about 18 months. He was a decent, conscientious man. It was his custom, before passing the threshold of any of his people, to invoke a blessing upon the house. On Sunday he read the service and a sermon out of a book. At the beginning of 1837 the bishop returned, and gives us this pretty picture as an incident in his journey : "In emerging from a wood, on the road to Huntingdon, into a clearing full of stumps, we were at a loss to pursue the right track, and drove up to a log-hut, where, by a light, I saw a mother reading the Bible to her children closing round her knees. She was rejoiced to see me, and, bringing out a lantern, walked in front of us for some distance through the snow, and set us in our right course." Who this good mother was I have been unable to ascertain. The bishop goes on to say : "I preached at Huntingdon, in a small edifice of squared logs, contrived a double debt to pay, being constructed for holding the sessions of the magistrates and adapted also for use as a schoolroom. I had 39 communicants, baptized 11 children and churched the mothers." Before he left he succeeded in starting a movement to build a church, Bowron and Lewis taking part in it. The contract was given to William and David Lamb, who were paid mainly by a grant from the Society for the Propagation of Christian Knowledge. It was completed in 1839, when the Rev William Brethour, missionary at Ormstown, arranged to have stated services in it. That year the first meeting of the Bible Society was held in it, at which Colonel Campbell presided, and named a committee of two from the Episcopal, Methodist, and Presbyterian congregations. The church was on the site of the present one ; the lot was given free by the government. At that time the Episcopal church had more adherents than either of its sister denominations, and the prospect was that it would prove the strongest of the three. Before many years, the larger portion of its members had joined the Methodists. The Rev D. B. Panther was the first resident minister.

Although last to have a church and the organization it signifies, the Methodists had been an active element from 1830. At first, the only Methodists were a few of the American squatters, and their example did not recommend the body they professed to belong to. Mr Dalgliesh, already alluded to, was the first Old Countryman to join them, and in 1830 there came an awakening that thenceforth gave the Methodist body a standing in the community. It arose in this way. Henry Denio, a blacksmith of the town of Fort Covington, had got into debt, and as money was more plentiful on this side at that time, came to the Ridge, and arranged with a man named Dank, near Clyde's corners, to work for him on condition that he be permitted to make ashes in his bush. In 6 months he had managed to send to Montreal 3 barrels, with the price of which he returned to the States and paid his creditors and never returned. During his brief stay he was active in more than making potash. He was an ordained local preacher of the M. E. church, and in the evenings and on Sundays was persevering in his efforts to arouse those with whom he came in contact. He preached in Ingles' house, in Page's on Trout river, and in another near the Pine Plains, and in all three formed class-meetings, which proved most effective in drawing outsiders and grounding them in the faith. The work he began was taken up by another layman, David Armstrong. He was a native of Tyrone, Ireland, and was of a good family, whom he offended by marrying below his station, which led to his enlisting as an artillery-man. Being made deaf by the sudden explosion of a gun, he was discharged with a pension of 12 cents a-day, and sent to Canada, where he was placed in charge of the ordnance at Chambly. With a view to providing a home for his wife and family, and a place to which he could retire when relieved of duty, he came up to Huntingdon in search of land in 1828, and chose 27, 4th range of Godmanchester. He made frequent visits to his family and during them promoted the work Denio had started, for he, also, was a Methodist and a local preacher. In 1832, on Chambly being abandoned as a military post, he was transferred to Ile aux Noix, which he did not like, and he retired and joined his family. Not needing to work, his sons managing the farm, he devoted his declining years to labors which might shame many a member of the regular ministry. He made periodic tours throughout the western portion of the district, visiting the settlers in their homes, advising and praying with them, and preaching as he had opportunity. His sermons were poor enough, and largely repetitions, but they were plain statements of the Gospel by a man whose daily walk showed he believed in what he taught. The class-meetings Denio organized he maintained, assisted by John Lowrey, the son of a Hinchinbrook farmer and the ablest local preacher the district has produced, and by Mr Dalgliesh, who was of kindred spirit, and made a local preacher in 1832. Indeed, the saying ran in a community that looked with no favor on Methodists, that there were, at least, two good men among them, old Mr Dalgliesh and old Mr Armstrong. In 1837, while attending the conference at Fort Covington, they were ordained as ministers by Bishop Hedding. Mr Dalgliesh did not use the authority given to him, but Mr Armstrong thenceforth married occasional couples and baptized many. He continued to travel within a circuit of a dozen miles of his home until near to his death, and in many settlements his were the only services they knew. Wesley, son of Benjamin Palmer, assisted in those days when the work fell mainly to laymen. He, as well as Lowrey, afterwards entered the ministry.

The ministers of the Fort Covington circuit improved the ground broken by Denia, and endeavored to visit Huntingdon once a month. Their appointments extended with their labors, and included New Ireland. The earliest to visit Canada were Loviss, Redington, Johnson, and Barney. The minister of Chateaugay in 1833, Emms, paid a stirring visit to Huntingdon. The quarterly meetings they held in the Ridge schoolhouse. They came on horseback save when there was sleighing, and one of them was so poor that at such seasons he kept his appointments by driving in an extempore sled made of a crockery crate set on runners. To get to New Ireland, they went on foot from Dewittville. Their labor was one of love, for the contributions from the Canadian stations were trifling. These American ministers were good preachers and excellent organizers. They continued to come until the outbreak of the Rebellion, when, in 1838, the Canadian Conference caused the Russeltown circuit to include Huntingdon; Barnabas Hitchcock being the first minister. During the time of the American ministers, there were too few Methodists to form a congregation in Huntingdon, and the nearest approach, was the organizing of a prayer-meeting, which was kept up from 1830, and held on Sunday evenings alternately in the houses of Palmer and Fitch. In 1839 the building of a church was begun at the head of Lorne-street and completed the following year with great sacrifice and exertion on the part of the members, who were few and had little to spare; Mr Dalgliesh was chapel-steward at the time.

CHAPTER XIX.

GODMANCHESTER.

OF Todd and Cameron establishing themselves at Dewittville mention has already been made. The presence of their two mills ensured the springing up of a village, and more people flocked into the neighborhood then than now. Up to 1845 it was the centre of the lumber-trade on the Chateaugay, and immense quantities were handled long after rafting had ceased at other points. Todd, who had borrowed money from Jacob Dewitt at high interest, got into difficulties and his property passed into Dewitt's hands, who thereby got a standing in the county which he turned to account by becoming its representative. Before leaving Dewittville for the farm he had secured below it, Todd accommodated the travelling-public in his house. He was a bluff, free-hearted man and no immigrant passed his door hungry, whether with or without money. Besides Todd's sawmill, an American, Wright, put up another which Samuel C. Wead of Westville, N.Y., rented in 1826 and did a large business, under the style Meigs & Wead. It, with the gristmill were burned in September, 1828. The fire was the work of an incendiary, for he was seen in the moonlight running from the mill by a woman, an immigrant, who was passing the night on top of a cart-load of luggage. Cameron was insured and began at once to prepare to rebuild, but the company contested his claim, and although he proved it, the costs of litigation ate up the award and, finding himself unable to replace the mill, settled down to farm on the west bank. When the property was sold by the sheriff, James Davidson bought it and built a sawmill and store, and for the next 30 years was the leading man of the place. The want of a gristmill now became pressing, for the lots along the river were taken up and every settler had a few bushels of wheat to grind, which he had to

take either to Ste Martine or Huntingdon. Peter McArthur
(page 253) wished to lease the power at Ormstown, but the
agent of the seignior refused, being willing neither to build
nor let others do so. He thereupon travelled up the river to
Dewittville, when he saw that by throwing a dam across to
the island at the head of the rapids he could have a fall of 4
feet without injuring the power of the sawmills, which were
below. In 1830 he bought the lot from Dr Munro of Montreal for $400, and set to work to clear an acre, for it was
under dense bush. In 1832 the mill opened, having a run
for wheat and another for oatmeal, the power being supplied
by an undershot wheel, 14 by 16 feet. The mill did a good
business until the Ormstown one was opened, which was not
for 7 years afterwards.

The lots between Dewittville and Huntingdon were slow in
being settled, which was mainly owing to their having been
granted to non-residents, though their wetness made them
undesirable. Of the low esteem in which these lands were
held this anecdote will illustrate. Charles McNarland was
at Blakely's tavern (a notorious place at Dewittville, in the
lumbering days, for drinking and rowdyism), when an old
pensioner stepped in. He had come up from Montreal to see
the lot he had drawn, and finding it wet and covered by thick
underbrush, was disgusted, and offered to give a deed of it
for a pint of whisky. McNarland, who had enough to do
with what land he had, declined, and afterwards learned that
Blakely had got the ticket from the man for his night's
lodging and breakfast. The lot was No. 8. On the point of
No. 10 lived a Dutchman, Benjamin Suttle, or Sawtell, who
sold his betterments in 1822 and moved back to New Ireland.
The purchaser was Robert Lowrey, a baker, from the North
of Ireland, and who had been some time a resident of the
States. At the mouth of the Hall creek was the hut of a
negro, Black Jim, whose wife was white. While the front
was left almost in a state of nature, the back lots were taken
up and the settlement of New Ireland begun. In 1822 the
Charles McNarland, mentioned above, left county Derry and
hired a year with John Simpson, collector of customs a the

Coteau, when he heard of the land being open for settlement in Huntingdon. He crossed to Dalhousie settlement to find out, and travelled by a lumber road from Thomas Brown's until it came out on the beaver meadow at lot 9. He examined the land and finding that a fellow-countryman, William Cox, who was living on the Chateaugay, owned lot 7, on which he had made a small clearance, he bought it. There was no house on the lot. He went back to Coteau and moved over that winter. His only neighbors were Suttle, who had moved from the river because game was more plentiful and ashes easier made, and an Irish Catholic, John .Caughlan. The following year two of his acquaintances in Derry, John Douglass and Jonathan Sparrow, joined him. They had been employed in building a house for Roebuck, near Coteau, when they heard of what McNarland had done, and took up lots beside him. They moved over in the fall of 1824, and so far removed were they from help, that they had to raise their shanties on Sunday, in order to get the assistance of Bagg & Waite's men, who were lumbering near by. Where they settled the land was good and dry, but on every side they were surrounded by marsh and soon found the mistake they had made in choosing so inaccessible a spot. The bush was favorable for potash-making, and they were not careful in discriminating where they felled their plan heaps, for, as McNarland remarked, "It was all God's land," and there was no cne to dispute them. A track was made to the Chateaugay by the Hall creek, which, however, could only be used in winter or very dry seasons. A better outlet was gained by following the ridges towards the seigniory-line, connecting them by rollways, and ending on Wm. Milloy's, 42, 1st range of Ormstown. The barrels of potash were dragged in jumpers over the more solid parts of the road by oxen, then rolled on the rollways by hand until Milloy's was reached, where a long dray-cart, bought by Charles Mc-Narland, was kept. On it the barrels were loaded, the oxen yoked to the pole, and the journey made to the Basin. Mc-Narland made no charge for the use of the cart, his only condition being that it was to be safely returned to Milloy's.

In the fall of 1825 the smoke was so dense that Douglass lost his way, and wandered 3 days in the bush, suffering much, yet all the while close to his home. An equally dangerous adventure was that of Sparrow, who one evening came upon a pack of wolves, climbed a tree and remained there until daylight caused his besiegers to seek their 'dens. The swamps were the refuge of the wild beast, and a score of years after wolves and bears were unheard of in the other settlements, they troubled New Ireland, as this one ultimately came to be called, though it was known for over a score of years by no other name than the Sparrow settlement. Following Douglass and Sparrow, two Irish Catholics came, Daniel O'Donohue and John Waters, a blacksmith, who set up his forge, and proved a most useful addition. The settlement quickly filled up, and was divided between Protestant and Catholic Irish, the latter the less numerous, who lived in great harmony. Their great want was an outlet to Huntingdon and 20 years after the first lot was taken up, they had no road fit for a wagon, and depended upon ox-sleds when the swamps were dry, and when wet had to carry whatever they wanted on their heads over logs laid lengthwise. McNarland one day slipped from the log with his bag of wheat, and for many a ' year the place was known as Charley's Hole. It was a common sight for the villagers to see a string of New Ireland men file across Prince Arthur square, each bearing on his head a bag of wheat to be ground at the mill. The common load was $1\frac{1}{2}$ bushels, though a few had strong enough necks to carry two. There being no bridge for quite a while at the new mill, they crossed on the boom. Their isolated situation so intensified the hardships natural to all new settlers, that only the unwillingness to change with some, and inability with others, constrained them to remain, and eventually the close dependence which that situation entailed, evoked a spirit of clanishness which made New Ireland the brightest spot in the world to them. It was a day long to be remembered when the first plow was brought in. Robert Douglass had got a field sufficiently clear of stumps to render the use of a plow possible, and he got the blacksmith to make one of the bull pattern. The whole settlement gathered to see it start and a good crop of oats rewarded the venture. The introduction of the plow, caused horses to be used, and they gradually superseded oxen. For many winters, habitants from the lower parishes would come in traineaux leading a string of 4 or 5 ponies, which they dickered with the settlers. The first religious service was held by John Lowrey, who, one Sunday evening, preached in Jonathan Sparrow's shanty, having the settlement as his audience. After him, the Methodists held meetings at regular though wide apart intervals. When Mr Harvey came to the village, he held regular service every second Sunday evening, walking both ways, and often coming in with his boots full of water. In case of danger from bears, the settlers gave him an escort back across the swamp. By this time, a schoolhouse had been built on No 5, where he held his meetings. The first teacher was named Leitch, passionate and harsh and fond of drink. On the death of his wife, Jonathan Sparrow set apart a plot in front of his farm as a burying-ground, and it was used generally for a long series of years, owing to the difficulty of access to the village. Mrs Lattimore was the second to be placed to rest in it.

First to settle on the land between New Ireland and the river was Owen Heffernan on lot 13. One who was a hunter in those days, relates his entering Owen's house, tired and hungry, and finding the wife getting supper ready. The table was a log of split basswood, and on it Mrs Heffernan emptied a pot of potatoes, which they ate with no other relish than some salt. The same difficulties had to be contended with as in New Ireland, the land being wet, but there was, of course, not the same trouble in getting to the village. For a long while the settlement was known as Connaught; 25 years ago it was given the more appropriate name of Victoria settlement. The first to settle west of it was Robert Cowan, who came from county Derry in 1831, and who said:

When I came on to this lot, 15, there was not a tree cut, and they stood so close to the shanty that my wife came out when one was about to fall. I put the shanty on a ridge and

my wife helped me to roll the logs down it to form heaps.
All the road to Pollica's in the village was a swamp, and
we had to walk on logs. I was brought up a weaver, and an
old neighbor, Edward Dawson, coming to stay while sick, I
got him to make a loom, which he did, picking up in the
woods dry poles for lumber. After that, I did not work
much out of doors.

On the stretch of country between Cowan's and Clyde's
corners the first settler was James Biggar, who came from
the Borders, and arrived in Canada in 1819. After trying
Dundas county, he resolved on taking up land in Huntingdon
and visiting it acquired 25, and moved his family over the
last of sleighing in 1823. There was no road of any kind,
but one of the American squatters to the west of him, Force,
undertook to draw his stuff from Laguerre in an oxsled,
which he managed to do. • Those Americans had come in
from Trout river, the attraction being the splendid growth
of timber for ashes. They shifted along the Ridge, staying
in no place long, making potash and working for the lumberers. The first Old Country neighbors Biggar had were
three brothers, John, Robert, and James Dunsmore, from
county Derry, who left Ireland with the intention of settling
near Fort Covington, but moved from there to lots 21 and 22
on the 5th range of Godmanchester. They were joined by
their cousin, William Cunningham, in 1825, whose narrative
is as follows:

I sailed from Londonderry on the 5th May, 1825, on the
Harrison, an old man-of-war, a fast sailer but crazy from age.
Owing to rough weather and head winds, it was 6 weeks
before we reached Quebec. There were 750 passengers, all
Catholics except a score or so. They domineered over the
Protestants, refusing us our fair share of water and keeping
us from the caboose, until we joined and asserted our rights
by force. I came up to Montreal in the Lady Sherbrooke,
and went to Lachine in a French cart, where I got on to a
Durham boat, bound for Coteau. Being afraid of my chest
being stolen, I lay on top of it and tried to sleep, but could
not, for the jabbering of the Indians and Frenchmen over my
head. I wanted to go to Fort Covington, where I understood
my cousins the Dunsmores were, but when we reached Coteau
I met a young North of Ireland woman at Simpson's, who

25

told me they had moved to Huntingdon, and that my best way to reach them was to go to David Brown's, near Port Lewis, and walk from there. She hired a man to row me to Brown's, and I started, there being another passenger, a woman. When half way across, a squall burst on us, when the boatman wanted to throw my chest overboard to lighten the canoe, but I would not let him, and giving the paddle to the woman, I took one of the oars, and, for I was used to boating in Ireland, kept the canoe's head right, and let her drift to an island, near the north shore, the only inhabitants of which were some fishermen, who had a sort of summer-shanty. They gave us some eels, which we roasted, and ate with some bread I had in my chest. Next morning, the lake was very rough, too high for the boat to venture out, and on learning by signs that the water between the island and the shore was not deep, which I could see from its being studded with rushes, I got a rope and slinging my chest on my back, waded the distance. I hired a cart to take me back to Coteau, where I found the Durham boats still lying, having been unable to sail from the storm. Being told one was bound for Fort Covington, I went on board, and Capt. Lucas agreed to give me passage, and his wife made me breakfast. I reached the Fort without more trouble, and there learned that the Dunsmores had all gone to Canada, being unable to get land of their own any nearer. Being directed which road to follow, I started on foot. The road was good until I got to Trout River Lines, where I rested at John O'Reilly's. My feet were sore by this time, and O'Reilly told me to pull my boots off, and bringing a tumbler of spirits, with part he rubbed my feet, and made me drink the rest. It was the Fourth of July, and the Americans were celebrating it. The road along Trout river was very bad, fit only for oxen, and I met two of the Elder boys working on it. There were quite a number of small clearances. Towards evening I reached John Wallis's, where I went in to rest and ask my way. There I found James Biggar, who told me he was a neighbor to my cousins, and I went with him. The road from Wallis's to the Ridge was merely a blazed track. I stayed all night at Biggar's, and started next morning for my cousins. I soon came on their clearing, and there I found the 3 brothers at work in their shirts only, for the day was oppressively hot, logging. John was the first to recognize me, and rushing towards me, he flung his arms around my neck, knocking me down, and rolling over me in ecstasy of joy. I agreed to work with them, and stayed altogether 6 months. They were living on lot 21, in a shanty 10 × 14, and as they had only been there since the spring had little done. I wrote my father, telling him of what the country was like, and leaving him to decide whether he and the family should follow me. To post the letter, I had to walk to Fort Covington, 22 miles, that being the nearest office. That fall an answer came, that they would join me in the spring. I thereupon squatted on lots 18 and 19, put up a shanty and made a small clearance. Afterwards I had to pay the seigniory, which claimed these lots, $2.50 an acre for them. Father and the rest of them came next summer, and there being 4 brothers of us, we were strong in help, and went at the work with a will, chopping all day, and logging in the long evenings, often working late into the night. Once my sisters came back to see what had happened, for it was 1 o'clock in the morning. We had been busy, and never thought of the time. The timber was heavy, and the ashes we drew down to the creek, near Cemetery-street, where father leached them and made salts, which we sold first at Fort Covington but afterwards drew to the village and paid Reeves $2 a barrel for conveying by canoe and cart to the Basin. We got as high as $35 a barrel. My father having some money, was able to get oxen and cows, with pigs and sheep. In 1827 we sowed 10 acres of fall wheat, which yielded 20 bushels to the acre, and, being early, was free from rust, which ruined the crop that year. At the bee we had for reaping it, I met my future wife, and in going to Montreal that winter to sell a load of it, I stayed at her father's (William Cairns, Ormstown,) and completed the engagement. I sold the wheat for 75 cents. We were married in March, 1829, when I bought lot 20   The timber was very heavy. One elm near the house was 7 feet across, and took nigh an acre of timber to burn it. We worked very hard to make a home, and were the more eager from having bad luck, our first cow dying, and our second being drowned in the spring in a hole made by a fallen tree. After underbrushing, I determined to clear an acre each week, got up before daylight, did my chores, and was out with my axe by sunrise. My wife helped me at everything, and placing our first baby in a sap-trough beside us, would lend a hand. There was a great swale between us and Huntingdon, which was hard to pass in the spring. I have often carried two bushels on my back to mill, when oxen would sink. The Biggar creek in those days was quite a stream, and when high you could not wade it. I don't think there has been any change in the

·climate, only the land is now drained. In 1827 we had a great snow fall on New Year's night, so that the stumps were covered, and when we felled a tree it disappeared, and oxen could only haul small loads.

The first to settle west of Biggar was William Caldwell, who, on finding that the lot he had taken near the lake was claimed under a former grant, moved in 1824 to the Ridge, and, with his sons, acquired most of the land to within sight of Clyde's corners, so named after William Clyde, who settled there in 1826, and who possessed qualities that made him respected by all. From the number of American squatters, the locality was named the Yankee ridge. On 38, 5th range, was a tall, lame man named Force, who provided a number of leaches, supplied directly from the spring which forms the remarkable creek that flows through the lot, and which then abounded with trout. To these leaches his countrymen brought their ashes. The extent of the destruction wrought on the bush by these trespassers, was indicated by the heap of leached ashes they left behind them, for on Patton's securing the lot, he found they covered nearly quarter an acre and deep enough for him to dig a cellar for storing his potatoes. Their outlet was an ox-track that angled across from McNair's hill and came out on Trout river on 41, called the Shaw road, from his brushing it.

The road to Huntingdon was a track that followed the ridge and came out near Cemetery-street. The first school was on 19. When the government gave a grant for a road from Huntingdon to Dundee, Bowron, in 1829, engaged Col. Pettis, an American who lumbered a good deal and who lived on 37, to lay out and clear one, which he did by beginning at the village a few rods west of Thomson's tavern, and following the ridge as far as it extended, and so secured a dry and direct road, although it cut up the lots badly. The present road substantially follows the line he brushed. The contract for making the Huntingdon end was given to Barlow, who completed it in 1832. The Dundee end was finished 3 years later. On the range behind the Cunninghams, Dunsmores, Biggars, and Caldwells a settlement sprang up which came to be known as the Laird settlement. Alexander Lunan says :

We came from Dundee, Scotland, in 1819, and were led to take up land at Lapigeonniere through a relative who lived there, and where my father bought 500 acres. We did not like the place, and, hearing of the new settlements in Huntingdon county, my brother George visited them, and drew the east half of 26 on the 4th concession. There was no settler then upon it, and the two acres he chopped was the first that was cleared. After making the clearance he left with the intention of returning. In 1826 James Laird moved on to 24, leaving the river because he could not have lots beside his own for his sons. In 1824 my father visited Huntingdon, and bought 25 from Ellice for $3 an acre. He thought the land good, for the stones did not show, being covered with the forest litter, and was nice and dry. We moved in April, 1825, I driving an ox-cart, which contained among its contents a potash-kettle. On reaching Dewittville, I was told I would have to leave my cart and put my effects on a canoe. The spring was a dry one, and I determined to push on, and succeeded with some difficulty, and found that my cart was the first to reach Huntingdon, only ox-sleds having been able to struggle over the track, along which the roots had been notched to allow of the runners of the sleds slipping over them. Past Huntingdon the cart could not go, for there was only a blazed track back to the Ridge. Our land was covered by a splendid bush, with no underbrush, so that you could drive between the trees. We set to work, and by the end of June had a barrel of potash ready. How to get it to Huntingdon was our next difficulty, and we succeeded by laying long poles across Biggar's swamp, along which we rolled it, and then I dragged it on a sled through the woods to Peter McFarlane's. The day was very hot and on reaching his store-door, one of the oxen fell down dead, melted by the heat. I daresay I looked very rueful, for McFarlane took pity on me, and told me he would get me another yoke, for which I could pay at my convenience. A settler was rich who had a yoke of oxen and a potash-kettle, and I paid McFarlane in timber the following winter. The 2 acres chopped by my brother in 1823 we logged and put in wheat and potatoes, and had a great crop. When they could not raise a spear of grain on the river-front for wet, we were having splendid crops. In 1836 I had 300 bushels of fall wheat, and took down part to Montreal, where I got 6s. and 4d. for it, though 5s. was the usual price. I remember my father rubbing out some heads of our first crop, and looking at it, exclaim "It's as guid as ever grew on the carse o' Gowrie." Bowron's mill was going when we came, but the stuff it ground was awful. There would not be over 30 to 35 pounds of flour to the bushel of it. The fall we came was that of the Miramichi fires. The largest was behind the village and along the creek from lot 17, making a great slash. A year or two afterwards the fire again ran, and burned the fallen timber and the black muck down to the clay. It did not come our way. From the knowledge I acquired of the woods, when Mr Armstrong came on his regular visits, every three months, while still living at Chambly, I was sent to lead his French pony, which was laden with provisions and necessaries for his family. One very dark night I made my way home by taking off my boots, for I knew when I got off the track by feeling the leaves, which had fallen. Wolves and bears were plenty. In one fall I had 13 fine fat sheep killed by the wolves. When the Laguerre road was made, we cut a track to it along the ridges, and did our trading at Laguerre, or Godmanchester village as it was then called.

Where this track came out on the Laguerre road is an eminence, called from the first owner of the lot, McNair's hill. James McNair, a native of Inveraray, was among the number at Dalhousie settlement, and had to leave from his land being claimed. After living near the lake for 4 years, he moved to 33, 4th range, in 1826. He is to be remembered not only from having left behind numerous descendants who are worthy members of society, but for his extraordinary age, 108. His widow, born 1782, is still living, in the enjoyment of her faculties, and a pattern of a tidy Highland-woman. About 1832 a schoolhouse was built on the hill, so as to suit both the Ridge and the Laird settlement, and a belfry was added, it being designed to be used on Sundays for worship, and there Mr Armstrong conducted it for many years. None of the descendants of the first families are now to be found in Laird settlement. It is different on the Ridge, and there the children and grand-children of those who redeemed it from the bush, many among them men of sterling character, still possess it, and have too firm a hold to be easily shaken.

Returning to the river-front, I would tell somewhat of the settlers from the village to the frontier. From their accessibility, the river lots were taken up first, though the choice was often rued, for the land was so flat and so drowned by the water that drained from the ridges behind, that it was impossible to grow crops to any advantage until it was ditched as well as cleared of bush. James McDonald related his experience thus :

Our family belonged to Melrose, and we left Scotland in the spring of 1820. My father, Henry, who was a miller, got employment with Robert Buchanan at Fort Covington, and stayed there a year. Anxious to have a place of his own, on hearing of the newly-opened lands, my father and I proceeded to Port Lewis to see James Brown, who, we were told, was agent. He gave us all the information he could, and told us to pick out what lots we saw fit, and to notify him of our choice. We started by the newly-cut out road to Huntingdon, which was only a soft path or track, and rested a while at Hamilton's. On reaching the Chateaugay we found that the raising of Hunter's new house had been begun that day, and the men employed were lying drunk; a gable chained to a stump to prevent its falling. We slept with the Hunter boys in their shanty, and started next morning to examine the lots. We did not think much of the land from Huntingdon up to Murray bridge, it being covered largely by hemlocks. Above that point, the timber was large elms and black ash. The ridges were heavily timbered with maple. Everywhere we saw pine stumps, showing where the lumberman had been. Having chosen our lots, we returned to Port Lewis to see Brown, and went back to Fort Covington. Late in the fall we started for our new homes. This time we drove along the States' side until we reached Trout river lines, where we turned north, and found, following the river, a fair road to Morrison's (lot 41). From that downward there was only a track which could be used for vehicles in winter, so we had to borrow a canoe from Davis and sailed down to our lot. There were few residents along that part of the river, perhaps half a dozen, and all American squatters except an old soldier who lived on lot 30, maintained mainly by his pension. From our lot to the village there was nobody except an American, Benjamin Stebbins, son-in-law of Palmer, who had a bit of a clearance on the east half of 22. Cooper Anderson, after living a while in the village, built a shanty on 23. Deacon Allen came about the same time to 24. We were helped by our neighbors in raising a shanty, Palmer being the most serviceable, as he had a yoke of oxen, with which he hauled the logs. We had brought provisions with us and worked hard, late and early, even by moonlight, in chopping. In the spring, just before the snow went away, Hugh Barr arrived with his father-in-law, James Laird, in traineaux from Cornwall, by way of Laguerre, the first going on 26 and the latter on 25. They brought some stock with them, and a quantity of ready-baked bread and boiled pork. We planted among the logs potatoes and corn, which yielded tolerably. The following winter, my father had to carry a bushel of flour on his shoulder all the way from the Fort. The road along the river was made gradually and very slowly. In front of my own lot, near my house, it was so bad that I had to lengthen the chains for the oxen while drawing logs. We sent for a potash-kettle to Montreal, and it came up by a bateau to Laguerre. Though it weighed only 800℔. it took two yoke of oxen nearly two days to drag it home. We sold our ashes to McDonald at Dundee. Deer were very plentiful, which was well, for we were long before we could raise much. Though we lived on the river-bank, our clearances were on the ridge, for the flat land was so wet as to be useless. The year of the July freshet, I had fever and ague for a month. We got along by changing works with our neighbors; one having a yoke of oxen working for us a day in return for our logging for him, and so on. It was quite a while before we got a cow, which lived by browsing in the woods, chewing twigs nearly half an inch thick. The woods were full of wild leek, but we were glad of the milk, despite its flavor. There were no trout or salmon in Trout river when I came.

Hugh Barr, mentioned in this narrative, had come from near Paisley, Scotland, in 1819, and stayed in Glengarry until he moved to Huntingdon. He proved to be one of the leading men in the community, of staunch character and devout disposition. His father-in-law, James Laird, also a truly good man, left the river for the 4th concession, as has been already told, William Lamb, an Irish Protestant, taking his lot, and who lived to be one of the leading men of the township. Cooper Anderson brought a spinnet with him from Scotland, but his daughters found they had something else to do in Canada than play on it, and it stood in their shanty as an ornament and dresser by the fire-place. One spring, on a neighbor dropping in, he found that a lamb, which had been like to perish from cold, had been placed in the enclosure beneath its keyboard.

West of McDonald, the first settler to move in was John Wallis, who came from Roxham, and took up lot 30. On the point lived a pensioner, Duncan Cameron, and Macaulay, who had a road from it straight to the Ridge, made up his rafts there. Wallis was an Englishman and had been in Canada before the war. Although short of stature he possessed great strength, and could lift a barrel of potash, nearly 600℔., on to an ox-cart. Possessed of some means he built a stone house in 1825, bringing a mason, James Moore, from Hemingford, to whom he gave 100 acres in Roxham in payment, and John Perry of Covey Hill did the wood-work. It was an ambitious structure and stood until 1883, when, being too ruinous to live in, it was pulled down. It was the first stone-house west of Franklin, the second being a small one built by Jonathan Sparrow and John Douglass for Abraham Suttle in New Ireland. Macaulay's operations in lumbering were large, his limits extending from New Ireland to Lee's corners. Among those who lumbered on a smaller scale were Thomas Fingland, Kent, Wright, John Ingles, Campbell, —— Town, Isaac Davis, —— Adams, Samuel and David Page, Colonel Nimes, Judge Brown, Thomas Barlow, and many others. Barlow was a pushing American who could turn his hand to anything. He had come to live on Trout river previous to the war, and married a Frenchwoman. Like all others who risked their earnings in lumbering, he died comparatively poor. The plundering of the crown lands of their merchantable timber, was a corrupt piece of jobbery and a grievous injury to the settlers. Mrs Robert Ford, who settled with her husband on 28 in the fall of 1828, gives a graphic account of the state of the country at that time :

The banks both of the Chateaugay and of Trout river were different from what they are now, being green and grassy. Cutting down the trees removed the roots that preserved their shape, and the water washing away the loose earth, the banks gradually became as they are now, broken and unsightly. The roads were dreadful, being full of stumps and mudholes, and ran through the woods, we coming every now and then on a little opening in them, with a small shanty in the middle, and most of them having shanty-roofs. In passing McDonald's we saw him hauling in his grain on an ox-sled. When we came to our lot, which was all under bush except a bit by the river strewn with decaying pine-logs left by the lumbermen, oh, but we were disappointed; it was so different from the glowing descriptions of the bush we had believed while in Scotland. My father-in-law, an old man, was so stunned by the change, that he was never himself again. We had brought a cow from Montreal, and tying a bell round her neck let her roam in the woods for a living. A bag of oatmeal was among our stores, and being seldom seen, neighbors came and got a bowlful each. The mosquitoes were a great plague, and we could not sleep for them. We lived in a barn of McDonald's until a house was raised, and moved into it before quite finished, and had a dreadful winter of it. Every morning I had to thaw and dry the blankets where our breaths had struck them and could not touch a knife or fork until they were warmed. At that time Canadians drove up from the lower parishes to exchange wheat for corn, and we bought some; it made horrid flour, being full of wild-pea. Our neighbors had plenty of food of its kind—mostly potatoes and jonny-cake. The village-stores were miserable and dirty, smelling of rum and tobacco. What little they had to sell was very dear. People were thinly clad, for sheep were scarce, and they had no money to buy cloth. Young girls went round asking for spinning, and when Briggs started he would make a yard of cloth for 1¼℔ of wool. Everything was paid by trade or turning-in. I used to say I had no need of a pocket, for I never saw a sixpence. When spring came we planted pota-toes around the roots of the stumps in our bit clearing and I added some corn. The pigeons came and ate it. I planted a second time and sat on a big stone during the day until the corn was big enough. The potatoes yielded abundantly but the corn did not ripen. That spring Mr Wallis brought me a few apple-trees to set-out, for he had an orchard on his lot. My husband set his face against supplying drink at bees, and on having one the first summer, when the people came and heard there was to be no whisky, part of them were for leaving at once, but the others got them to stay and raise the building, which was a carpenter's shop. After that, a few farmers would have no drink at bees. We had our mis-fortunes, of course, but got over them. One fall we had a splendid field of wheat and after cutting it, the weather changed and became so wet that not a bushel was saved. That winter my husband drove to Beauharnois to buy wheat

and we had often to make pea-scones answer for bread. Some
time after we came, a relative, Learmont, was leaving and
my husband to oblige him bought his oxen, though he did
not really need them, giving his note in payment. The first
day he had them in the woods, where he was getting out
square timber, a pine he was felling proved rotten, and in
falling snapped in two, and one piece killed the oxen. Paying for them was a sore trial, as the only cash to be got was
for ashes, and for 3 cows we offered the holder of the note
he allowed only $30. My husband made an ox-cart, one of
the few on the river, and we drove in it to church, using bed-
blankets for buffalo-robes. We had such a smart-stepping
yoke, that they would trot half a mile on starting. The
winter-roads were good in those days. I heard Mr Barr say
he made it a point to have his firewood drawn by the first of
March, as the blows came after that date. It is different now,
when the roads sometimes drift full in December.

Between McDonald's and the mouth of Beaver creek, the
first Old Countryman to settle on the river was Thomas
Marshall, one of the members of the Dalhousie settlement
party (page 153) and obliged to leave his improvements.
His son James said:

We moved in the early spring of 1825, driving on the ice
to the Laguerre and up the river until we struck a track
that led into the Shaw road. There was quite a settlement
of American squatters along the river, who were making a
poor living by potash and lumbering. Most of them had
come in 1812 to avoid the draft. I heard one frankly say
he did not want to fight and had slipped across the lines into
the bush to have peace. The Davis's, who were on the lot
next to us (41) were decent people. Abram Davis, in company with another American, named Wright, had built a
sawmill several years before, close to where the bridge now
is, and the remains of the dam are still to be seen. The
summer before we came the machinery had been bought by
Barlow, and moved into the mill he had built on 44, which
was up but not covered in, waiting for boards to be cut by
its own saw. The first school was held in a house owned by
Davis in 1826, the teacher being an American, Mrs Brewster.
Afterwards, a house on Barlow's lot was made into a school,
and taught by a man named Shepherd, who was very severe.
The first preaching was by Bellew the Universalist, when on
his way to Huntingdon. He preached in the upper flat of
Barlow's house, which was 2-storied. Our crops for many

years were splendid. A stook, 12 sheaves, gave a bushel of wheat. Deer were plenty, and in the morning we often found them with the cattle. Our nearest mill was at Constable, No. 3, as the settlers called it, and we had to carry the bags on our back. The fire in 1825 did no damage, our woods being green, but the smoke was very thick. The first burying-place was on 39, which is now plowed up.

Of the state of this part of Trout river Mrs Merrill Cooper gives a lively description :

We belonged to Vermont, and land being dear there my husband went out prospecting and selected this lot, 10, 4th range, on the Elgin side of Trout river. We moved in 1830, having 2 waggon-loads of stuff. There was no bridge across Trout river, and the road from Constable down would do for oxen but not for horses, as we had to drive round the stumps. My husband being weakly, I had to help him to log up, and to put in the crop and take it off. I put my hand to everything, and was not ashamed of any work so long as it enabled us to earn an honest living. The Yankee squatters, who were our chief neighbors, were a lazy, shiftless set. We brought a year's provisions with us from Vermont, but one after another came borrowing, saying they had nothing in the house, until our store was exhausted in 4 months. There was a small clearing by the river, which had been made by a squatter named Dewey, and my husband enlarged it, we making potash of the logs. In the spring (1831) we sowed every bit of it with corn, which grew splendid, and we looked for a large crop. The season was very dry, so much so that you could step across the stones at the fords without wetting your feet. One afternoon in July it began to rain, and poured down so that next day the river was so high that cribs crossed over Johnston's point. Everything was swept away, and Barlow's dam with the rest. Our corn was ruined, and we did not have 13 bushels. There was great scarcity that winter and until the next harvest. Those who had money, went across the lines and bought beans. The wife of one of the Yankee squatters told me that during the following summer, and before the potatoes were fit to dig, they had been without solid food for 48 hours, and all they had was the milk of 2 cows. The pickle bran the hens laid in, she sifted, and made into a cake. Her boy, 12 years old, went out and ate blue clay, and was found by Dr Taylor, who gave him a large dose of salts. He got better. The family of another squatter lived on rice. The Yankees had begun to leave before we came, and soon were all gone, except 2 families. They had lived by plundering the woods for lumber and potash, and had to move as their lots were taken up by others, who gave them something for their betterments. My husband seldom went to Laguerre, preferring Fort Covington, as being a better road, though it took him 3 days with an ox-team. We always traded our potash for provisions, but the regular thing with most settlers was tea, tobacco, and the re-filling of the 10-gallon keg. For a long while the settlers lived very poorly on potatoes, rye, and corn. The Dr Taylor I spoke of lived above Helena, and came from Milton, Vt. He had no horse and visited his patients on foot. He was frequently out of medicine, and had to supply their place with the herbs he collected. He was very skillful, and never lost a patient by measles, scarlet-fever, or the like. He remained until he became frail, when he went back to his native place, and died at a great age.

From Marshall's to the Lines may be described as the centre of the Trout river settlement, for within these 6 miles the Americans most abounded and the first Old Country-men took up land. As stated on page 140, Elder and Terry were the forerunners of the immigrants, and were followed by John White, from Kelso, Scotland, in 1820, he settling on 51. One day, while working in the bush, his shanty took fire, and he lost everything, whereupon he crossed to the Elgin side, and took 1, 2nd concession, which was higher and therefore drier, and where he made much potash. Massam (page 140) followed, and William Nesbit, a Scotch blacksmith, in the spring of 1822, losing his tools by the ice breaking on the Laguerre, and taking up 49. The same year there came the Buckhams and Tullys, both of whom had emigrated from the Scottish borders in 1814. Tully was placed by Lord Dalhousie in charge of his farm on the St Foye road, and who, on Huntingdon being opened, gave him an order for 400 acres in Elgin, but he only got 200. Sending a man in the fall of 1821 to put up a house and make a clearance, the family moved the following May, going from Lachine to the mouth of the Laguerre in a Durham boat, and to Ogilvie's in canoes. The Shaw road was so bad, that the horse they had brought was useless to draw, and was led in by the son, while

Ogilvie sent 2 single ox-sleds to drag what they most needed, the family, which included several young girls, walking. On coming to opposite their lot, they crossed by canoe, soon followed by a raft of cedar logs, which Tully got made by an old French Canadian soldier, Bombardier, who lived with his wife and a negro on 46 ; the raft was so made that it could be drawn back and forth with ropes, and large enough to bear a horse. The infant settlement got on very poorly, having many difficulties to contend with, the chief being the wetness of the land and their want of an outlet. Barlow's dam had flooded much of the low land, which was wet enough before. Their only road, the Shaw, was a succession of mud-holes until the ridge was gained, and to encourage his oxen to dive into them with the sled bearing the barrel of potash, Mr White would take a few ears of corn out of the bag he had provided, and place them a few yards ahead. Had it not been for the potash, the settlers could not have remained. The land was so difficult to clear and became fit for the plow so slowly, that they would have starved, but for the potash which they exchanged for food and clothing, and, happily, at that time there was a good demand for it and prices ranged high. The only settlers whose land was all low, having no ridge whatever, was Nesbit and McBeth, and they had a hard time of it. Even in potash-making, the ridges were superior to the river-flats, for their maple was almost equal to the elm of the swales. The privations of those years, the want of everything save the bare necessaries of life, in no way broke the spirit of the immigrants, for those who survived to reap the fruit of their exertions, declared they were happier when they shared their loaf with their neighbor than when their granary was filled with wheat. Their main article of diet was jonny-cake, made with cold water, and potatoes. Wheat grew well among the stumps, but the diffi-culty was to get it ground. The nighest mill was that at Constable, which involved a tiresome journey through the woods, and which was often at a stand-still from want of water. Barlow got a small contract on the first Lachine canal and returned in the winter (probably that of 1821)

with 3 old horses and as many tom...eau. These were the
first and only horses from the Lines to the Meadows, and he
hired them out, with a boy, at $2 a day to take grist to mill.
A long bag was chosen, in which a bushel of corn or wheat
was put in each end, and then, tied in the centre, was slung
across the horse, the boy riding. $2 was a big sum to the
settlers, but they could not better themselves, for carrying a
bag on their shoulders or taking a canoe to go down to Huntingdon was exhausting and involved much loss of time. By-
and-by the road got better cut out, and in winter ox-teams
got along with ease, but it was not until near 1830 that there
was a decent road for wheeled vehicles to the Fort.

.The first school was opened in a shanty by the riverside at
Kensington by Mrs Hezekiah Barter, an American, and the
second was taught by Daniel Sutton, who was lame, and
member of a numerous family who were American squatters.
He taught in a shanty on the river-bank near Tully's bridge.
He was a fair scholar and something of an artist, for at the
examinations he held, his prizes were colored drawings from
his own pencil, and which were greatly prized by his scholars.
He boarded with his brother Abram, on 49, and on which another brother, Hiram, had a small tannery. They all left for
Ohio, John White buying their betterments.

Lumbering was actively pushed along the river, and all
the pine, and most of the oak had gone before the Old Countrymen came in. Shaw took out most on the north bank
and Barlow on the south. The first sawmill after Davis's
was one built by an American, Colonel Allen, on lot 54,
nearly behind where the custom-house now is, and engaged
David Smith, who long after lived on the road to New
Ireland, to run it. He sold out to Col. Pettis. The great
want of the settlement was a gristmill, and it was not until
1829 it was supplied. In the preceding year Andw. Anderson,
who was acquainted with mill-work, and Archd. Henderson
bought the privilege at Kensington, and built a small mill
on the Elgin 'side, with 3 run of stones, operated by a large
board wheel,' so high that the machinery had to be on the
second story. The first miller was a Canadian, who spoke

Engl'sh fluently, Julien, followed by Peter Taylor, and in 1836 by Robert Clark, who gave the mill a wide reputation. During the July freshet of 1831, part of the dam was swept away, and, in rebuilding the opportunity was taken to erect a sawmill on the Godmanchester bank. It is unnecessary to say that this mill was a great boon to the settlement, though the Scotch deplored its inability, for many years, to make oatmeal, and when McArthur started his horse-mill, not a few travelled down to it for a bagful. The first store at Trout River lines was opened by an American, James V. Dickie, about 1823, and soon after Squire Stearns, also an American, opened one at Helena, and subsequently added an ashery and pearling-oven, but did not succeed, owing to his habits. About 1820, Dr Taylor, spoken of in Mrs Cooper's narrative, came and began to practice. He was an uneducated man, with a taste for medicine, who had received some training under a physician. His success as an accoucheur aided him, but after all he made a poor living, and was wont to go on his visits on foot, carrying in a pair of saddlebags slung over his arm his medicines and instruments.

That section of Godmanchester called the Beaver was late in being brought under cultivation owing to its wetness. The first to venture in that direction was Thomas March, and the circumstances attending his settlement are thus related by his son John :

We belonged to county Fermanagh, Ireland, and sailed in the summer of 1823 from Sligo, taking 7 weeks and 3 days to reach Quebec. We proceeded by way of Laprairie to Lacolle, where my uncle, Charles, was comfortably established, having a pension for service in the army and being customs-officer. He recommended my father to go to Huntingdon, where the land was to be got free, and we made our way to it by Odelltown and along the American side to Trout river, when we lodged with Brewster until our house was ready. Father knew nothing about the fitness of land for settlement, and like all new-comers thought it a great thing to be owner of a farm of any kind. He had gone back of the settlement on Trout river and seeing a nice hill on lot 57 of the 5th range at once concluded it was desirable, and drew it. The shanty was not quite finished when we moved in, and to reach it we had to walk through the woods. The roof was so open that daylight came through, and looking up the Dutch chimney we could see the trees waving overhead. It was December when we moved in and it was very cold. Father was strong and hardworking and to earn a little money, which was seldom seen in those days, went to Briggs street (which is on the American side) and worked for the farmers, who were better off, and earned enough to get a cow in the spring. When his job was thrashing, he could earn his bushel of wheat a day, which meant thrashing 10. Wheat was good in those days and 12 sheaves gave a bushel. He made salts, which he had to drag to Fort Covington, where it brought $3 the cwt., and it was a good burning that yielded $10. Our crops were good, but we soon found that it was impossible to clear much of our lot, which was mostly under water. The north half we could not do anything with. There was no other settler on the range besides ourselves. To the east of us on 54 was a Canadian, Gagnon, who lived poorly by making baskets, brooms, and maple sugar and working odd times for the farmers, but he had only a small clearance and did not increase it. Our first neighbor was a friend of our own in Fermanagh, Thomas Wilson, who took up 56, and who left long ago. The next was William O'Rielly, who came in 1824. The flats along the creek were covered with a splendid cut of bush, as you may suppose, when one pine made 6 logs of 12 feet. Lumbering was being actively carried on and an immense quantity of masts, square timber, and sawn lumber was rafted to Montreal and Quebec. The Hall limits included the best of the pine. A great many Highlanders were engaged in the woods and among them was Archie Mc-Master, whose people lived in what we called the Scotch settlement, in Dundee. He married and settled down on 61. I remember the wedding-feast as if it were yesterday. A sort of covering was made with boards and bushes between the house and the barn, and there the dancing and feasting was kept up for 3 days. Besides a fiddler they had a piper, liquor was served round like water, and the people came from far and near. It would be about 1829, if not earlier, that a schoolhouse was built next to McMaster's, and I think Jamieson was the first teacher. A grant was received from government. The road in those days was a track that led out to Helena, fit only for ox-sleds. Except in 1837 there was no scarcity. In that summer flour was not to be got, and for several weeks our only bread was made of barley. My mother often walked to Fort Covington to trade the butter she made.

CHAPTER XX.

ELGIN.

THE dispersion of the settlers at the lakeshore led to the settlement of Elgin. Owing to part of the township having been set aside as crown and school reserves and a portion ceded to non-residents, the lots available for the settlers were few, and mostly situated on the 2nd concession. They were distributed, so far as they would go, among the hapless inhabitants of Dalhousie settlement, and in the fall of 1822 they set forth to visit their future abode. Following the road, or rather foottrack, they had opened to the Chateaugay, they found a path little better which led from Hunter's house upwards along its bank until it met Trout river, along which, as already stated, the shanties of a few settlers were thinly scattered. Opposite the residence of Jonas Spencer, they crossed the river by a ford, which until bridges were built, was to be their main means of communication with the outer world. Spencer was one of the Americans who had squatted on Trout river, and was an industrious and active man, whose recreation was hunting. Familiar with the woods, he undertook to point out their lots, a duty which a negro, Black William, did to others of the party. With the exception of a small clearance made by a farmer, named Palmer, where the church at Kelso now stands, these pioneers found the township in a state of nature, the only evidence that man had ever traversed the woods they struggled through being the discovery, at long intervals, of the posts with which the surveyors had marked out the boundaries. Palmer lived on Briggs-street, directly across the lines, and had been in the habit of making a yearly incursion into Elgin to make ashes, and in the clearance he had thus made had sown some wheat. The lot on which this clearance was, fell to John Gillies, and he had need of it, for, as he was wont to tell, all he brought

with him to Elgin was a York shilling (an English sixpenny
bit) and an axe. He lent the shilling and lost it. Behind the
axe were a pair of strong arms and a cheerful spirit, and he
carved out in time from the wilderness one of the best farms
in the county and a modest competence. Having ascertained
their lots, the pioneers cleared small patches and put up
shanties; then they returned to the lakeshore to prepare for
moving so soon as the approaching winter would give them
a road by its ice and snow.

The winter of 1822-3 was a busy one with them, and witnessed the transfer from their homes on the lake, which they
left with some anguish of spirit, relieved by the hope that in
Elgin they would have better land and more of it. By New
Year the smoke was curling into the frosty air from a row of
shanties hid among the woods on the 2nd concession, and the
reclamation of the wilderness had begun. Had it not been
for their mutual helpfulness, their living together as one big
family, they could not have succeeded, so poorly provided
were they for the task to which they had set themselves.
But where each one would divide the last handful of meal
with his neighbor and was ever ready to lend a willing arm
to log or do other heavy work, the impossible became possible.
In the community of hardship and suffering at the lakeshore
and during the first years of their second settlement, is to be
traced the origin of that unity which is, even in the third
generation, so striking a feature in the character of the people
of Elgin. A visitor to their poor shanties a year after they
came, said bread was rare, and the staple food cornmeal porridge, and broth, made as nearly after the Scotch recipe as
possible where butcher-meat was seldom seen and few vegetables obtainable. In the magnificent growth of elm and
hard maple that abounded along Oak creek they had for
years an unfailing treasury, and, by painful labor, the trees
were transmuted into potash with which both food and
clothing were bought. Those whose lots had little ridge
were worst off, for where a good piece of high land could be
brought in, abundant crops were invariable. David Anderson,
whose lot was mainly gravelly, made money by selling wheat

when others could not raise enough to suffice themselves.
The marshy land along the banks of the creek gave much
labor to reclaim, and for years the settlers worked in the
wet, finding difficulty to get the trees burned, and cutting ·
ditches with incredible labor. Although named Oak creek,
the oak had disappeared before they came, having been plundered many years before. The Indians, who, long after the
settlement, frequently raised their wigwams on its banks
during the winter, called it Otter creek, from the abundance,
at one time, of that animal. The matter-of-fact settlers, viewing its sluggish stream and slimy bed, gave it a third name
—Mud Creek. On its banks Peter and Parlan McFarlane
started an ashery, employing Black William for the leaches.
This was a great convenience to the settlement. The starting
of the ashery involved the buying of an ox-cart, which was
lent at a shilling a day, when a settler found his ox-sled un-
suitable. The potash was mainly drawn to the Laguerre.
The marriage of a sister of the McFarlanes was the first in
Elgin. The 20th Dec., 1823, was set for the ceremony, and
bride and bridegroom, with the whole settlement, awaited the
minister, McWattie. The hours slipped by without his appearance, and finally the company determined they should
not be cheated out of their merry-making, and all night the
woods rang with the jollity of the company in the little
shanty. In the forenoon the minister appeared, and at once
proceeded to tie the knot. Standing bareheaded out-of-doors
he twice informed the snow-laden trees that there was a
purpose of marriage between Peter Horn and Janet Mc-
Farlane, and the trees making no objection he went on with
the service. Crossing to the Ridge he, the same week, united
James Paul and Ann Caldwell, whose hopes had been deferred
a year by his building his shanty through mistake outside
his own line and on the lot which Barnabas Lanktree, an
Irish Protestant, a native of Cork, bought, and moved on to
New Year's day, 1823. His brother Thomas came beside
him and they, with the Sayer family (page 321) were the
exception, all the others being Scotch. The first concession
remained longest in a state of nature, owing to a great part

having been granted to non-residents, who asked higher prices than immigrants could give. Elias Wallis said :

I came in June, 1824, with my uncle William to see the lots we had bought. We rode on horseback, following a trail from the Chateaugay. We found Gilbert McBeth the only settler near our lots, and he was living, with his wife and 2 children, in a lumber-shanty, which he had found standing when he came. It was most uncomfortable. At one end a flooring of slabs was laid, on which stood the bed ; the rest of the shanty was bare ground ; with the fire on a pile of stones. We had to sleep on the floor, and our horses, for which we could get no hay after leaving Franklin, we tethered at the edge of the clearance to browse on the trees. The clearance was small, and the blackened stumps stood up in it 10 feet high, for the depth of snow during the winter had prevented cutting low down. McBeth was engaged planting corn among them when we arrived. The road not being cut out and the surveyor's posts rotted, we were unable to find our lots, and had to get Black William, who lived where Donnelly does now, to point them out, and in 2 days I had marked out my limits and cut my half of the road, when I returned home, and did not return to settle for another year. Black William was quite a gardener and in the fall went round the settlement to sell water-melons. I brought a horse and 2 cows. The cows were of little benefit, as we had to turn them into the bush to pick up a living, would often be absent 4 days, and soon ran dry. The horse was of no use, and I exchanged it with James Dickie, who had opened store at the lines, for provisions. My first wheat failed from mildew, and my second crop was spoiled by chess. I traded 40 bushels of it for an old cook-stove, which was the first in the settlement. My first success was 4 years after coming, when I hauled a load of pine boards to Champlain, N.Y. I only took clear stuff, and, when the sleighing was good, could go in 2 days and come back in one. It was sawn in a mill started by my neighbors Scriver and Hamilton, from whom I bought 50 M. At that time clear pine was worth $60 in New York city, so that I did well. But for the trade I thus opened, with my old neighbors in the east, I would have starved, for my land was low and wet, and it was long before I could get it sufficiently drained to make crops certain. The first I would know of a new neighbor would be hearing a voice or the falling of a tree.

The Scriver here spoken of was Joseph Scriver, who also

came from Roxham, and lived to be the first mayor of Elgin. He was a blacksmith by trade and worked 2 years at Helena, beside the store that had been opened by Stearns. James Donnelly with his 7 sons settled west of Wallis, and for many years were the only Catholics in Elgin. Moving down Trout river, the settlers on the Elgin bank were seen to be progressing fast, despite the difficulty of fording and the flats being cedar-swamps. The July freshet of 1831 was a sore blow to them, but a worse calamity was the frosts of 1836, which were more severe along the river than anywhere else. On the night of the 18th August it froze hard, as it did also on the two following nights. All the grain that was not ripe, was ruined, and the potatoes were touched. In the midst of their consternation at this staggering blow to their prospects, the hearts of the settlers were touched by the calamity that overtook a neighboring family. Benjamin Burnside was an American, who had been led to settle in Canada from having accompanied Wilkinson in his hapless expedition. He worked for Barlow in his saw-mill, and did not return home on the evening of the 21st August. After an anxious night, his wife walked to the mill at the first streak of day, to make enquiry. Again there had been frost, and the ice on the puddles in the road crackled beneath her feet. All was silence in the mill. First she saw his cap, and looking up beheld her husband hanging in the machinery. In adjusting the saw, which had got loose at the head, the frame had moved, and he had been caught, and there being no one to release him, had died. The widow lost not heart, for, with thrift and energy, she managed the farm and brought up reputably her young family. The season continued cold and in digging potatoes the soil came up in lumps, out of which they were knocked with an axe. Had it not been that the gristmills brought in wheat from the Basin, where fall-plowing had enabled early sowing, and Montreal, there would have been no bread, and before the winter was over wheat was selling at $2.50 a bushel, and oats at 80 cents. The settlers were badly off, and ground barley and peas together as a substitute for flour, which was better than the

Indian meal sold by an American storekeeper across the lines, which, from having been mixed with sawdust, caused serious illness. The season of 1837 was favorable, but until the crop was reaped the privation deepened, and Robert Clark, the miller at Kensington, told of one settler who, seeing some bran and shorts below the bolt, begged for it and (as he told long afterwards) mixed with the berries on which he and his family lived for 3 weeks. The dinner which many of the children took with them to school that summer consisted of boiled half-ripe ears of corn and nothing else.

Owing to its wetness, the northern end of Elgin settled slowly. The first one to break ground was George Sayer, a Yorkshireman, who, with his two sons, Matthew and George, drew the first location-ticket Bowron issued in the fall of 1822. The land being wet, they made their living by potash, which they found to be hard work in summer. One spring they had pork and nothing else. The potatoes saved for seed were picked over for a mess, but the neighborhood was scoured in vain for a pickle of flour or meal, until Hingston's was visited. Major Hingston, so styled from his command in the militia, was an Irish Protestant, and had risen from the ranks to be adjutant in the 100th regt., which served in Ontario during the war of 1812. Hingston was in all the fighting on the Niagara peninsula. At Lundy's lane he was struck by a spent bullet on the forehead and at other engagements had received injuries, he counting 7 wounds. He had twice married Catholics. After his second marriage he sought to leave Montreal for the country, and visited Huntingdon, with which he had some acquaintance from having hunted through it, to select a lot. He decided on 30 and 31, 5th range, and moved in 1824. He lived an easy if rude life, spending most of his time hunting and fishing, and adapting himself to backwoods' habits. Two years after coming, he lost a son under circumstances that shocked the community. On the bank of Oak creek the potash-kettle had been placed, and the young man was left with it all night to keep up the fire to boil down the lye. He fell asleep on the slope above, and awaking suddenly, turned, and thrust his legs into the hot lye. He died the following day. On the reorganization of the militia in 1827 Hingston was appointed major of the 4th battalion, the duties of which were nominal, for all the men were required to do was to muster on the King's birthday, answer to their names, and be treated at the expense of their captains. His militia rank conferred many of the powers of a magistrate. On his death in 1832 he was buried on his lot with military honors, Captain Hudson collecting a firing-party. No stone marks the resting-place of the veteran. To the west of Hingston, settled Capt. Charles, who had been an ensign in the 32nd regt., and John Ruston, who preached occasionally, he having been a Methodist local preacher in England. Both families came in 1824. The crown reserve long lay in a state of nature, an American squatter, Page, living on the river point of 5, and in an adjoining pine-grove the first camp-meeting took place. The reserve eventually, at a comparatively recent date, was surveyed and sold.

The want of religious ordinances caused Thomas Marshall, John Caldwell, William Clyde and a few others to organize a Sunday-school, held in Peter McFarlane's shanty, where the children repeated verses and questions from the shorter catechism. By-and-by the older people got into the way of holding a prayer, or fellowship, meeting at its close, and these gatherings were kept up until Danskin came. Thos. Danskin was the son of an intelligent and pious man, a Cumbernauld weaver, and one of eleven brothers, of more than ordinary ability. Born in 1802 and brought up to a life of toil, he aspired to "wag his heid in a poopit" and attended Glasgow college for two terms. To economise, he took both the arts and divinity courses together and yet devoted his evenings to teaching in a night-school. Privation and overwork broke him down and he was advised to seek change of life and climate. He sailed in 1827 for Canada, having in view an old acquaintance of his family, David Anderson of Elgin, who heartily welcomed him and his coming was looked upon as opportune, for the settlement had been long in want of a schoolmaster. He entered upon his duties at once, and until a schoolhouse could be built, he moved from one neighbor to another, beginning at Helena and ending at Charles's, teaching a week in each shanty, the scholars following him. He had completed four rounds before the school was ready for occupation, which was in the summer of 1828, and henceforth, until, long afterwards, the stone-church was built at Kelso, the humble log-house answered for a place of worship, and behind it a burying-place was formed, the first body interred being that of Archd. Fleming. Attending the fellowship meeting, the schoolmaster expounded with so much acceptance, that he was asked to preach, and for two years held regular service on Sundays. Although a Presbyterian, his belonging to the United Secession body caused Dr Mathieson and Dr Black to look askance at him, and there was no prospect of his being ordained. On his marriage in the fall of 1830, he took up a farm, which he had to relinquish, being unequal to the hard labor, and accepted the Huntingdon school. His health continued to decline, and he died in 1832. His grave, that of the poor scholar, is among the unmarked and unknown behind St Andrew's. There was other evidence in Elgin of intellectual life beside the organizing for worship and education. In the winter of 1832 a number of the settlers formed themselves into a debating-club, for which John Danskin drew up the constitution and by-laws. The meetings were held weekly in the schoolhouse. The rules required that the two leaders should open the debate with written essays, and the leaders were generally the teacher and Robert Barrie. What the latter lacked in scholastic gifts he made up for by a ready humor that set the audience (the room would be crowded) in a roar, his store of stories, and an insensibility to defeat. These meetings not only gave much innocent pleasure but stimulated thought and gave the members of the club the habit of expressing themselves in public.

The material progress of Elgin was unaided by government grants. What the people accomplished in the way of building bridges and roads they did themselves. For a period that goes beyond the limit of this narrative, that curious ridge that spans the township, and named the hogsback, was the chief outlet from the 1st and 2nd concessions to Athelstan, a cart-track following its windings.

Instead of giving the narratives of individual settlers in Elgin as I have done of those of other localities, I thought it well to combine into one what several told me and present a connected picture of a settler's life, which will make plain to readers unfamiliar with the bush, much that has been alluded to. In the townships all unconceded land was given free to actual settlers. For instance, on an immigrant arriving in Huntingdon, he would call on the crown-agent, Bowron, and ascertain what lots were still ungranted, visit them and choose one. For that lot, containing 100 acres, the agent would give him a location-ticket on his paying $12. The conditions of the ticket were, that he should erect a house, live continuously on it, and make a certain amount of clearance within 3 years. If he did not, the lot reverted to the crown; if he did, he could apply for a patent, or deed, from the government giving him absolute possession. In Huntingdon, as has been seen, much of the land had been conceded to non-residents, and many of the difficulties in settling it arose from that circumstance, for these absentees not only held their land at exorbitant prices, but refused to make roads or ditches through them, increasing the hardships of those in their vicinity and keeping the country back. Had the crown issued the lands of Huntingdon solely to the men who stood ready to go and live upon them, it would have been settled in a much shorter time and made much faster progress than it did. Having secured a lot, the next step of the settler was to erect a house upon it, which was a simple matter. In choosing a site for it, there was slight scope. Covered by a dense forest, he could not well tell where there was eminence or hollow and the best he could do was to pick out the driest spot he could find near to where the future road would be made. Then he turned to cut logs for the walls, choosing, if he could, those trees that were of medium-size and lightest grain, for heavy logs were difficult to handle where help was scarce. When sufficient were cut, the raising took place, and as many men as possible were got together. The logs, notched at the ends, were laid, one by one. The first few were easily got into place, but as the wall rose, the lifting of green logs by main strength into their place strained the muscles. On the ease with which the shanty rose and its comeliness, all depended upon whether there was an experienced ax-man to take the lead. If there was, a square and shapely hut was the result, if not, there was an unsightly and rude abode. The size varied with the necessities and means of the settler; the common sizes were 12 feet square and 12 × 18. In front was the door, purposely made large to allow of big back-logs being hauled in. At one end was the fire-place; at the other the solitary window. When the walls were up, the rear one would be higher than the front, to allow of a slant for the roof, which was made either of basswood or elm bark, or, what was better, basswood troughs, that is the rounded slabs split from basswood logs, which are curved, and when placed overlapping, the convex edges resting in the concave centre of the one next it, shed the water perfectly so long as they remained sound. The openings between the logs and roof were packed with moss, as were also the interstices between the logs of the walls, which were afterwards plastered with mud. If the floor was dry and hard, it was left as it was; if not, planks split from straight-grained basswood logs were laid down and hewed as smooth as practicable. In many shanties, the only sawn boards used were those that formed the door and framed the window. One end of the shanty was devoted to the fire-place. For this flat stones were gathered and, if it could be got far or near, enough of lime to make some plaster, with which a wall, called a Dutch back, was built against the logs, ending in a frame of sticks, generally cedar poles, which formed the chimney, and which, when plastered inside and out, became perfectly fire-proof. Lime in Elgin was never scarce, for an abundance of flat lime stones, called shell-lime, could be picked up on every lot, and were easily burned by being put into a log-heap. The chimney finished, the shanty was ready for occupation, and in its construction not 3 pounds of nails had been used.

Coming from across the seas and separated from town and city by almost impenetrable woods, the settler, even if he had the money, could not get furniture. In a few rare cases, a mahogany "kist of drawers" had been painfully brought from Scotland, and, more often, that outward sign of respectability in old times, an eight-day clock; as a rule, the settler had nothing at first but the trunk and boxes which had contained his clothes and goods, and they answered for seats and table. Bedsteads were generally made by the settler himself out of poles picked up near his shanty, shaped with help of ax, adze and auger, bottomed with elm bark and placed end to end at one side of the shanty. The fire being on the floor was difficult to keep in if the wood was green (which it generally was, for years elapsed before settlers adopted the plan of having a year's supply ahead) and gave no end of trouble to the housewife, whose cheeks were either scorched by its flames or her eyes smarting from smoke. The bigger and drier the back log the steadier the fire, and settlers who had the luck to have a horse often trotted the animal into the house hauling one they could not have handled. Few shanties had andirons, their place being supplied by two flat stones, and on these smaller sticks were piled, resting against the backlog. Matches being unknown, when the fire did go out, a trip had to be made to the nearest neighbor and a smouldering punk, carefully covered from the wind, brought back. The cooking utensils comprised a frying-pan, "the big pot," and the chaudron, or Dutch oven, a flat pan that answered as an oven, sometimes of tin, more often of iron, but always with a tight lid. When the dough was ready, it was put in the chaudron, which was placed upon a heap of hot coals carefully raked from among the blazing logs, and heaped around its sides. In its bed of glowing ashes, the bread cooked quickly, and its progress was judged by occasionally lifting the lid and thrusting a knife into the doughy mass, the wetness or dryness of the knife showing how the heat was affecting it. Where the housewife was skillful as sweet and wholesome bread was the result as ever came out of the finest oven, but, alas, for the first settlers whose wives had never seen household bread baked in the Old Country, the loaves produced were commonly sour and heavy. Their difficulty was in the raising of the dough, generally effected by leaven left over from the last baking, and sour as vinegar. There was little variety in food. For many years deer were plentiful, but few settlers cared about hunting, so that venison was not common, and soon tired of. The deer fat was preserved and made into candles. Bear meat, named bush pork, was much more palatable than venison, but many a settler never tasted it. From the first, as to-day, pork was the staple animal food, for after the first crop of potatoes a pig was easily kept. The main article of diet, however, was cornmeal, in the form of jonny-cake or porridge. In Elgin the saying went, that their bill of fare, three times a day, was "parritch and a spune." The impossibility of getting oatmeal, was a sore cause of complaint among the Scotch, with whom potatoes made up poorly for "the halesome parritch" and jonny cake for the farls of their youth. Milk was far from plentiful. Having no pasture, the cows wandered through the woods, returning with half-filled bags and the milk so often tainted from wild garlic or other herbs they had eaten as to be unpalatable. The wisdom of these cows in finding their way in the woods was remarkable. To enable their being found, a bell was hung round their necks Tea was an unattainable luxury to the majority, and its place was supplied by roasted corn or a toasted piece of bread soaked in hot water. Few of the Old Countrymen cared about the herbs which the American squatters used, though those who acquired a taste for sage or hemlock tea found it not ungrateful.

The dress of the settler was a serious matter, for in those days, when the steam-loom was unknown, cloth was very dear, and the daily attire of himself and family, after the stock brought from the Old Country was exhausted, was a thing of shreds and patches. From no one cause, did more suffering arise than from the cold in winter owing to the lack of clothing, men facing it in cotton shirts and the women in print dresses. As soon as able, the settler bought two or

three sheep, and their wool the wife or daughters spun and
dyed, when the yarn was taken to some settler (and there
was no scarcity of such) to weave. Where a mill was not
near, the fulling was done by hand, but in no case, for many
years, was dressing of the cloth permitted—the thicker and
heavier the cloth the better. A pair of pants of such fabric
and a flannel shirt was the daily wear of the men, and many
had none else for Sunday. The women wore calico dresses
in summer and flannel in winter. The Scotch settlers brought
with them "their Sabbath claes," but found such scant occasion for wearing them in the backwoods that they decayed
more from time than use, seldom being taken out of the kist
except for a funeral or a preaching—the former, in a country
made up of young and healthy people, an event so rare that
settlers for a radius of a dozen miles would flock to one, the
latter unknown in one Sunday out of a dozen. The first
sheep were almost exclusively Cheviots, and their supplant-
ing by Leicesters was a doubtful improvement.

So much for the indoor life of the settler. His first task,
after getting his shanty in habitable shape, was to make
warfare on the trees. There, on every hand, they stood,
walling him in, even shutting him out from sight of sun
and star, of all sizes and kinds. Here was a monarch who
reared his head far above his fellows and whose trunk a
giant could not, with outstretched arms, span; there the
sapling that a child could snap. Littered on the ground
were the remains of old trees in every stage of decay, from
the veteran overthrown by the last gale, carrying in its fall
a score of its neighbors, to the trunk half resolved into the
soil that had for ages fed it. Where the land was low,—
swales was the local term—the trees formed thickets that
were impassable, and in the swamps cedars shut out the
day. Unlike the forests that covered the greater portion
of Ontario, the bush of this district had a thick under-
growth, which made the clearing of it more laborious. All
the trees of value for export—the oak, pine, and white ash
—had been taken away before the settlers came, so that
those left were available only for potash, and had it not

been so much of the timber was fit for making that alkali their hardships would have been intensified. The transferring of the trees into potash was laborious. Our settler, having no oxen, would begin work by forming a plan-heap. His object being to make a clearance round his shanty, he would select two of the largest elm or ash trees that grew close together, and endeavor to fell them so that they would lie side by side. Deciding on his trees, the swinging axe would gash their sides, and if an expert hand, he could so cut them as to secure their falling in the direction he desired. The axes used were, in those days, mainly made by the local blacksmiths, and weighed not less than 5 ℔s. The settler bought them as they came from the anvil, with an edge about an eighth of an inch thick, paying $2 for one, and afterwards slowly ground it himself on a grindstone, every shanty having one at its door. The helve, or handle, he shaped out of the hickory trees in his bush. When he had felled the two large trees that were to form the foundation of his plan-heap, he cut off their branches, and then turned to the smaller trees that stood near, felling them so as to be conveniently rolled by the handspike on to the pile. When the heap became as large as he had strength to make it, fire was applied. Even in dry weather the heap would burn slowly, and necessitate constant watching, so as to keep the glowing logs close enough together to make them blaze. When all was burned save, probably, some black remnants of the thickest trunks, the ashes were raked into a pile and covered by sheets of elm bark in case of rain. By neglecting this precaution many a settler saw the results of a week's toil lost by a thunder-shower washing the strength out of the ashes. As near to water as possible the leaches were made, formed of battened boards or elm bark peeled in long slices. In these troughs the ashes were packed and water poured upon them, which, soaking slowly through, escaped from a hole at the lower end in lye. As the buckets filled with lye, they were carried to the potash-kettle and emptied into it. The kettle was a large circular pot, that held 20 pailfuls. It was slung over a hot fire, which kept the lye boiling violently, and as it boiled away more was added, until the mass became so thick that it would not boil, when it was stirred into a molten mass and ladled into a barrel, as black salts, worth generally $6 the 112℔. The labor involved may be guessed from the fact that it took 15 bushels of ashes to make that quantity. When an ashery was convenient, the ashes were sold as taken from the plan-heap at 12½ cents the bushel, which saved the leaching and boiling, which could be done more cheaply and quickly in the asheries, which were specially fitted up for their work, and the majority of which had also ovens, for converting the potash into pearl-ash. The narratives of settlers given, have shown the great importance to them of the money potash brought, and it was exceedingly fortunate that the district had sufficiently advanced in husbandry before it was discovered by Leblanc that potash could be made much more cheaply from salt than wood-ashes. Had potash then been worth no more than it is to-day, large sections of this district must have remained unsettled.

When a settler had a yoke of oxen, or could "change works" for one, he would go on felling the trees on an acre or so without regarding how they lay, and then, choosing a dry time, burn the brush and smaller limbs. The field would then be a blackened fallow, covered with the charred trunks of the fallen trees. A bee would be called and these would be hauled by oxen and rolled into heaps, to be burned into ashes. Any way it could be taken, the work was dirty and exhausting, especially in hot weather, when the settlers, black as negroes, toiled in piling the logs together to burn them.

In the land, thus cleared, potatoes or corn was planted with the hoe, and perhaps a handful or two of wheat dragged in with a bush. The virgin soil never failed to respond with a generous yield, and the best crops ever known were procured by this rude cultivation. Insects or blight of any kind was unknown, and the only enemies were the wild beasts of the woods, which at night would help themselves

to a late supper off the settler's clearing. The farming of
the backwoods was unique. When the first crop of potatoes
was taken up, fall wheat, either red or white chaff, was
sown, and for many years never failed. The clearings, imbedded in the woods, were sheltered from the blasts of
winter, and the snow lay deep and even until April, so that
winter-killing was impossible. From the same cause, the
soil was kept moist in summer, and the sunlight warmed it
without producing drouth. The humidity of the atmosphere,
caused by the ever-present bush, was the best possible for
plant-life. Then the virgin soil was not only rich in vege-
table food but free from those weeds that are now the
farmer's plague. After hilling the potatoes, the settler had
no need to hoe them. Harvest was thus described by an
Irish settler of Godmanchester: "Whate as high as your
head, and when you scraped away the dirt where you
planted potatoes, you found them like a hen's nest." Plentiful as the yield was, when the clearings were small potatoes
had to be carefully hoarded, and with the setting-in of cold
weather the seed-end was carefully cut off each mess as
selected for food, and laid away for spring, thus saving the
cutting of whole potatoes for planting. When the land came
to be passably clear between the stumps, timothy was sown,
and it grew wonderfully, the crop being often so abundant
that it had to be spread on the stump-tops to cure. Clover
was then almost unknown. Haying was most laborious,
from the unevenness of the land and the number of stumps,
and, owing to the greater moisture of those days, was later,
sometimes extending into Sept'r. Toiling under an August
sun, the mower would halt to take off his shirt and wring
it, dripping with perspiration. One more nice in his ways,
took a spare shirt with him, so that one was always drying.
Of the feats in mowing in those days, big stories have come
down, but that men have cut 3 acres in a day for a wager
is undoubted. The grain was reaped with the sickle and
stooked, Old Country fashion. About 1835, John Gilmore
and David Cairns, left Huntingdon on a visit to relations
in Ohio, where they saw, for the first time, a cradle. Cairns

was so delighted with it, that he brought one back, which
led to their adoption, and the disuse of the toothed hook.
The first blight to visit the wheat was smut, which was a
dreadful catastrophe, as the mills then had no means of
cleaning it, and the bread was as black as if the flour had
been mixed with soot. Following the smut, came rust, and
to it (though I am now beyond the days of first-settlement)
succeeded the fly, which rendered the growing of fall wheat
impossible, and led to the adoption of Black Sea wheat. It
was so difficult to thresh, that something more powerful than
the flail was needed, and it was found in the niggerhead—a
heavy log about 10 feet long, studded with oak pins. The
wheat was strewn on the barn-floor, or a clean bit of ground,
and a horse dragged the niggerhead over it. The first thresh-
ing-mill was brought to Trout river by David Elder.

A very interesting subject is opened up on coming to speak
of fruit-trees. The first apple-trees were brought from Caldwell's Manor and vicinity, and so early as 1812 there were
trees in bearing in Hemingford and Franklin, and ten years
afterwards they were being exchanged for grain with the
new settlers. In 1828 there settled on the river below Huntingdon John Cassidy, who was a gardener by trade, and he
started a nursery. Unquestionably, however, almost all the
trees came from the American side of the line, and consisted
of natural fruit. Owing to the difficulty in fencing, orchards
were not a success with the early settlers, and, on the clay,
apples were not plentiful until of late years.

The live-stock was drawn mainly from the French parishes,
and therefore Canadian horses and Canadian cows were predominant, and for their size there is nothing better in the
world. The lumbermen were of some service in introducing
heavy teams and imported many large yokes of oxen from
the States. The first impetus to the improvement of cattle
was the obtaining of bulls from Henry Hoyle of Lacolle,
who was a noted breeder in those early times. The sheep
were generally good, being off imported stock obtained from
the Scotch farmers on the island of Montreal. As the settlers
became able to pay for service, a number of horses, more or

less thoroughbred, came from the United States. As early as 1835 the father of the Somerville brothers sent them as a present a Clydesdale stallion and several Leicester sheep. The horse was badly bruised in the voyage and had to be left at Lachine to recuperate. He was of grey color and a good specimen of his breed. The settlers were unable to patronize him and after holding him for a season or so, John Somerville sold him to a resident of Ottawa for $200, who resold him for a good figure, and he died from bursting a bloodvessel while going west. In 1845 John Somerville brought out another Clydesdale, a black, named "Clyde," which left numerous progeny. He was sold subsequently to Robert Graham of Hinchinbrook. Another horse brought out with him was secured by Mr Dods of the Island of Montreal, he tossing with Mr Somerville for the choice. The one he selected was the handsomer of the two but proved to be inferior as a stock-horse.

I have got beyond the date of which I was treating, however, and will return to the settler during his first years in the backwoods. Every fall and spring he would turn to the stumps, endeavoring to reduce them in size by burning, and tearing up their roots, but years would pass before their hold on the soil loosened sufficiently to be pulled out by a yoke of oxen and hauled into piles to be burned or to form a fence round the rude fields. The toil was unceasing and exhausting. Not only had the clearing to be labored, but it had to be enlarged, and every yard gained on the bush told on the constitution of the settler, a majority of whom became broken-down and aged before their time. But the life had its compensations. There was the sense of satisfaction, inexpressibly sweet to men who had been laborers or tenants in the Old World, that they were land-owners and that they were working for themselves—that, for the first time in their lives, they were lords of a portion of God's footstool and their own masters. This feeling of independence was strengthened by their being free from all the restraints of organized society and almost totally exempt from taxation. All the paraphernalia of law was unknown in the backwoods and the only taxes they paid they did not feel, being the custom duties, then only 10 per cent., on whatever little imported goods they bought. To people who had been ground down by taxation, to whom the rate-collector, the sheriff's officer, the poor-house master, the factor, the magistrate, the county gentry, had been objects of terror, the relief in being placed where no one domineered over them and no one exacted a portion of their earnings, was a solace for the pinching cold, the coarse food, the exhausting toil of the Canadian bush. Such an Arcadian state of matters could not last long, yet in Huntingdon it continued until 1845, when the adoption of a municipal system involved taxes, and the increase of wealth necessitated the establishment of a simple system of administering justice. The burdens were nominal, however, for another quarter of a century, and it was not until Confederation was adopted that the Canadian farmer felt that a portion of his earnings were going to pay taxes. Again, there was the gratification that came to the settlers from a sense of continued progress; every week saw some improvement effected or the bush rolled farther away. The sunlight no longer struggled through interlacing branches, but fell in one golden volume upon the clearing hollowed out of the woods. The prospect widened. The day came when the leafy curtain was so far lifted, that the inmates of one shanty could see their neighbor's, and in time the hills to the southward stood revealed, and the sense of loneliness that had so long oppressed the family passed away. By this time the settler felt he could afford a better house, and a block-house—one of logs hewn flat on their face—would rise, with pitched roof and an attic-room, and when the family entered it they thought it a palace, while the shanty was used as a pighouse or stable. With improved circumstances, however, there came no increase of happiness—rather the reverse—for as hope merged into its realization it was found that the joy of expectation was greater than that of possession. A community of settlers struggling in making their first clearances were bound together by the strongest ties of mutual helplessness, and the knowledge that they could not

exist without the aid of their neighbors, broke down all feeling of exclusiveness, and their hearts warmed to one another
just as their hands were extended to help one another. No
democracy is so perfect as that of the backwoods; no scheme
of socialism can ever approach it. If a settler was in want,
he had but to ask if his neighbor had to give him; if one
was sick, his crops would be put in or reaped as the case
might be. If there was a widow, there would be bees to
help her; if orphans they would be adopted. Of the hundreds with whom the writer conversed in preparing this
book, all save one, a woman, admitted, that, despite its
privations and excessive toil, the happiest period of their
lives was when they were struggling for existence in the
bush, and many spoke with bitterness of the exclusiveness,
the ostentation, and other forms of selfishness which came
with increasing wealth.

Living as one family, the settlers of a concession shared
the advantages of any superior capacity they individually
possessed. One would have an aptitude for making ox-sleds
and the like, another for framing buildings, a third skill in
treating sick animals, and in every settlement was one man
the tacitly recognized leader and spokesman. Thrown upon
their own resources, almost as much as if wrecked on a
desert island, the settlers developed in themselves unsus-
pected capabilities. Extraordinary expertness with the ax
came from daily use, but necessity forced them to be carpenters and waggon-makers, shoemakers and harnessmakers,
and even to try tinkering and blacksmithing. From the
small tanneries that sprang up all over the district, where
they sold their hides, they took in exchange sides of leather,
which were made into boots by shoemakers who passed
from house to house, and the boots so made the settlers
made a shift to patch themselves. Clothing was commonly
made by the women, except the coats, which were cut if not
also sown by itinerant tailors. Until their clearings were
large enough to raise sufficient food, their struggle for existence was a hard one, all the potash they could make going
in exchange for provisions. There was no other mode of

earning money. Labor was cheap yet it was rare to find a settler able to pay for it. An able-bodied man counted himself fortunate to get $7 to $8 a month and board, and in harvest the highest that was paid was 50 cents in cash or a bushel of wheat for a day's work that lasted from sunrise to sunset. A tradesman, a carpenter for instance, would be paid 75 cents a day, and in no case more than a dollar. During the winter, expert axmen got $15 a month in the lumbering-shanties and in the spring $1 a day was offered to men for running rafts and the pilot got no more than $1.25. Modes, therefore, of the settlers earning money apart from making potash, could hardly be said to exist, and pinching economy was requisite. It was not strange that, under such circumstances, they came to place an undue value upon money, and that, when better days came, and the necessity to save and deny no longer existed, there was a tightening rather than a loosening in the hold upon the world's substance, and that the old age of too many was made odious by a miserly and covetous disposition, which gave tone to these of their descendants.

The constant struggle for existence diverted their minds from other concerns, and it cannot be said truthfully of any of the settlements in the district that they had, at first, a religious tone. The seemly habits of the Old Land were suspended, if not lost, in the backwoods, and the Sunday was devoted to visiting, to idling, and, among the youngsters, to fishing and hunting. In no case, however, was work done upon it, and if it had not to them a spiritual value it was, at least, a day of rest. There were no clergymen and the lay preachers, whether itinerant or local, commanded slight respect. When the effort was made, as years passed, to establish churches, the training of the settlers stood in the way. The Scotch, mainly members of the Kirk of Scotland, had never been called upon to contribute to the support of their minister, and their dropping a copper coin into the collection-box had represented all they gave. It was the same with the North of Ireland settlers who were Episcopalians and to a degree also with those who were Presbyterians. Being called upon to support their minister came strange to men who had never been accustomed to give for such a purpose, and as a consequence, even for their limited means, their contributions were scandalously small and given reluctantly. While it will not do to ignore their more energetic methods, undoubtedly the more vigorous growth of the Methodist and secession Presbyterian churches is to be accounted for largely by their members having been trained in their native land to the habit of giving. But though these infant settlements were not religious in the sense of observances, they were in morals. The poverty and crowding together in small shanties had no deteriorating effect on their self-respect and they were truly a well-living people. When the day's work was over, and the family gathered around the blazing logs, with perhaps a neighbor or two dropped in to see them, there was plenty of fun, but it was innocent. The father talked with his wife as she sat at her wheel of his work and the simple "news" of the settlement, the daughters, engaged in carding wool or some other task, joked with the neighbor lads, while their brothers were doing the same with the girls of some adjoining shanty. There were husking bees and quilting bees and other less regular gatherings, and each family made it a point to have two parties in the year, at which the guests were welcomed with a heartiness unknown in more refined days and the amusements, singing and dancing, engaged in with a gusto that told of pure hearts and simple tastes. In Elgin the singing in concert of Scotch songs by Thos. Brown and William Morison was famed far and near and Robert Stewart played the fiddle to the dancers. New Year's week was a period of festivity, while Christmas was passed unnoticed.

The shadow to the picture was the prevalent drinking customs. The cheapness of whisky removed the chief check on its use, and for what a bottle cost in Scotland or Ireland, the settler here could buy a couple of gallons. It was used habitually and its use gave rise to nearly all the calamities that befell the settlements. Were it not that it would pain their descendants, a harrowing catalogue could be given of those who met their death from accidents while drunk, while it was the ruling cause of failure to families in the battle of life. That the liquor used did not affect these hardy first settlers more, was owing to its weakness and their active habits in the open air. A stronger spirit came into use in course of time. In Elgin William Wattie, in Godmanchester, Donald McIntosh, and others on the Ridge, built stills in which they made whisky from barley after the Old Country method, and it was followed by the more potent spirit of highwines that Molson began to make in Montreal. Considering the universality of the drinking-custom among the early settlers, it is most remarkable that its hold should be so slight among their descendants. Then not a house was to be found without its jar; now it is the exception to find a house with one. Then no bee or social gathering could take place without the circling bottle; now, it would be an insult to offer it.

The schools of these early days were uniformly bad. When a man was too lazy or too weak to wield an axe, he took to teaching without the slightest regard to his qualifications for the position. Men who could not read words of many syllables and whose writing was atrocious, were installed as masters of schools. Worse than their ignorance was the bad habits that characterized the majority, for drunkenness was common, and a teacher seen without a quid of tobacco in his mouth or smoking while setting a copy or puzzling over a sum was exceptional. Discipline was deemed by these usurpers of the teacher's office as the great qualification, and their cruelty was past belief. The petty tyrants vented their irritation after a debauch, or when out of tobacco, upon their helpless scholars, girls as well as boys, with a severity that was revolting, and for which there was no compensation in what they taught. The main study was the catechism. With the impartiality of indifference, the teacher heard each scholar recite from the catechism of the church to which he belonged, the strap descending when a word was missed. There was great lack of schoolbooks, and the family was counted well-off that had a couple of readers for the children.

Many of the scholars having no book, the reader was passed along the line. Copies were universally made out of fools-cap, the master "setting" it with a heading. No other pens than quills, plucked from geese or other fowls, were known. Ink was scarce, and often supplied by boiling the bark of the soft maple. In many schools, there was not an arithmetic, the master giving out sums which the scholars copied on their slates. Male teachers were universal, and it took over 25 years to convince parents that women could manage boys, and that a good female teacher was very much better than an indifferent male teacher.

The schoolhouses were in keeping with their masters, sometimes unfloored, and if floored it was with loose boards. The benches and desks were of a rude description. They were always log buildings, and in one school a couple of short pieces were worked loose by the boys, making, in warm weather, a convenient exit. The roofs were covered as often with slabs or boards, eked out with turf, as shingles. What the scholars suffered from cold is not to be described. The modern woodpile was then unknown. The fuel was drawn in log lengths, and the first boy in the morning had to apply himself to chop off enough to start the fire, and as it needed replenishing, the master detailed one or two boys to renew the task. Each family supplied half a cord for every scholar sent under a certain number. Walking several miles through the snow, insufficiently clad, and having only for dinner "the piece" they carried, such pursuit of knowledge could only have been possible to the hardy children of a hardy race. Occasionally the schoolmaster occupied one end of the schoolhouse as a dwelling, so that the scholars were tickled by hearing what passed on the other side of the board partition and by the oft appearance of the wife to consult her husband. One master utilized the loft above as a winter roost for his hens, and, when they scraped, a shower of dust descended on the heads of the scholars below, who would be excited by suppressed merriment when, on a biddie's clucking, they overheard the remark of the house-wife, "Eh, but the gudeman will hae an egg the morn."

Up to 1829 the only government aid towards education was extended through the royal institution, which was badly managed by an irresponsible body of placemen. The Williamstown school was the only one in this district that derived a yearly grant from it, and Norman McLeod received $120 from 1825 until his death. An occasional grant was made to the Huntingdon school. In 1829 a law came into force by which a small allowance was allotted each school, ranging from $10 to $80, the average being $40. This act was followed by another, making grants towards the building of schoolhouses of from $40 to $100 each in proportion to their cost, and under this stimulus nearly every settlement erected one. By subsequent acts, small subsidies were given to keep up the schools, but they were paltry and irregularly paid. In 1833 it was enacted that $16 additional be paid English schools that taught French, and vice versa. It is superfluous to state, that every English school was returned as teaching French and every French school as teaching English, so that the act was annulled. The grants were distributed by county visitors, who were supposed to examine them once a year. Charles Archambault, one of its representatives, was visitor for this district, and discharged his duties in an easy manner. He would listen to a scholar read a few sentences and, with the words, "Good scholar; good scholar," pass on to the next. The $1.80 allotted as prizes for each school he seldom had, and excusing himself by saying he would pay the best scholars 4d apiece at his next visit, passed on to the next school. Like many others in similar positions, he embezzled the school grants. Having no power to levy a rate to sustain them, the maintenance of the schools depended on the few zealous settlers who took the lead in their management and on the small fees paid by the scholars. The salary of the master never exceeded $200 and often fell under one hundred. Up to 1828 there were only 6 schools in the present district; in 1829 there were 13, with 650 scholars, all English. In 1831 the number rose to 41, with 1300 in attendance, of whom about one-fourth were unable to pay fees. Bouchette, writing of his visit to the district in 1828, states that the French had no public schools. "Among the few French Canadians," he says, "who have any wish to give education to their children, the practice prevails of taking a teacher into the house of one individual and collecting there the children of as many parents as are desirous of this benefit, each paying his quota of the expense. Of these private schools there are not more than 4 or 5. Their benefit is very limited, and little else than the catechism is taught." The first French schools were two opened in the seigniory of Chateaugay in 1830, followed by one in St Clement, and, in 1831, by one each in St Timothy and Ste Martine.

1ST CONCESSION.

Village lots, John Donnelly, sr.
William H. Caldwell
Henry Wilson
——— Beattie
3 & 4 Edward Donnelly
5 Captain William Wallis
6 Thomas Wilsie
  Elias Wallis
7 Joseph Scriver
8 David Russell
  James Forbes
9 William Moore
  Peter Horn
10 Jno. Potty; 2 Jas. Crawford
11 William Glennie
12 John Cunningham
13 John Ronald
14 Charles Crawford, senr.
14 Wm. Marshall; 2 John McBean
15 John Wattie
   Alex. Thomson
16 Duncan Stewart
   John Graham
17 William King, junr.
   Thomas King
18 William Johnston
   John Patterson
19 Charles McFaul
   Patrick McFaul

John Fee
20 Michael Fee
20 Joseph Scriver
21 Holcomb & Latham

2ND CONCESSION.

1 Anderson & Henderson
2 William Dickson
  James Spencer
3 James Gavin
4 Andrew Buckham
3 & 4 James Donnelly
5 Alex. Shaw
  Gilbert McBeth
6 Andrew & William Morison
7 Parlan McFarlane
  David Brown
8 Peter McFarlane
  David Anderson
9 William McIntyre
10 James Johnston
   William Wattie
11 James Glennie, senr.
12 John Wagstaff
   Barnabas Lanktree
13 Alex. Shearer
14 Thomas Way
   James Wilson
15 William Watson
15 William Hay
16 William King, senr.
17 John Richardson

George McDonald
17 & 18 Stephen McCrae
19 Neil Mathieson
20 Samuel McCane
    James Ewing

3RD CONCESSION.

1 George Elder, senr.
    Gabriel Buckham
    James Tully
2 George Ewart
    John Elder
3 Alex. Smaill
    Robert Smaill
4 James Tannahill
    John Gillies
5 Thomas Brown
    William Smaill
    —— Rorison
6 James Paul
    Robert Barrie
7 Thomas Lanktree, senr.
8 William Wattie
    John Caldwell
9 William Ruston
    Nicholas Ruston
10 John Ruston
10 & 11 Edward Charles
    Major Hingston
12 Thomas Stott
    John Seely
13 Hiram Seely
    William Stewart
13 & 14 John Anderson
14 Hugh King
15 & 16 Donald McIntosh
    William McIntosh
    Alex. McIntosh

4TH CONCESSION.

1 Cl. R. James Bowles, 1838
2 John Caldwell, 1833
3 William Morison, 1833
4 & 5 Ephraim Pelton, 1836
6 Robert Nelson, 1838
7 Thomas Lanktree, 1844
8 William Stark, 1837
9 Mrs Thorn, 1833
10 Merrill Cooper, 1830
11 Barnabas Lanktree, 1833
12 Robert Henry, 1833
13 William Carr, 1841
9 Cr. R. Wm. Minor; 2 Joseph
    Carr
9 James Learmont
7 Joseph Corpron
    Robert Moore
2-6 Page Brothers
2-6 John Brown
32 Page ; 2 Thomas Cairns
31 Andrew Gilmore
30-1 —— Gargett
29-31 George Sayer, senr.
28 Samuel Lamb
    Thomas Cairns
27 Robert Raven
    William Rose
25 & 26 Robert Murray
24 William Lamb
23 Z. Baxter

5TH CONCESSION.

27 Hazelton Moore
28 J. Elliot; 2 John Seely, sr.
29 & 30 Major Hingston
31 Thomas Hingston

CHAPTER XXI.

HINCHINBROOK.

WHEN the tide of immigration set in, the first to penetrate into Hinchinbrook was James Hamilton, whose narrative I give entire:

I am a native of Motherwell, Scotland, and left the day after my marriage for Canada, being accompanied by my brother William. We took passage from Greenock on the Alexander. On getting to Montreal, we helped a while in the search for land made by our fellow-passengers, but left on a visit to our uncle in Vermont before a decision was come to. We thought very little of Vermont, and when we heard where our old friends went, we determined to join them, and set out for Dalhousie settlement in March, 1821, and cast in our lot with theirs. The land had been all taken up facing the lake, so we had to move back, and the first solid land ungranted was south of Teafield. James Brown, who assumed to have authority, gave my brother lot 20 on the 4th range, and to me lot 17. We made some sugar at Wylie's, with whom we stayed, and then we moved to our lots, agreeing to make the first clearance on mine, for my brother was not married. My wife, of course, had to walk, and she was the first woman to cross from the lake to the Chateaugay. We raised a shanty, and fitted the ground for a crop by hewing down the trees, lopping off the branches, and planting potatoes and corn between the logs. We had bought potatoes in Glengarry and corn in Fort Covington. As we had to carry everything on our backs, neither horse nor ox being able to pass Teafield, we cut the potatoes into seed, to make the burden less. As it was, we sank to our knees in water in places. My brother carried a grindstone on one of our trips, the heaviest load ever so brought. The season was favorable and we had a large crop, but were troubled by the deer digging up the potatoes with their hoofs and eating them. In October, after husking the corn and storing it away, the three of us, my wife, brother and myself, started to see if we could not get a more cheerful location by the river's bank, for we were just buried in the woods and saw

nothing, and decided on moving to a ridge, where the river
takes a fine sweep, on lot 15. Satisfied with our choice and
talking cheerfully of our arrangements for moving, we walked
through the bush to the site of our shanty, when, on arriving
at it, we were astounded to find the house in ashes—a spark
from the open fireplace, we conjectured, had fallen among the
corn husks that strewed the floor and set the shanty ablaze.
Everything was consumed, even to my wife's rings, and we
were left homeless and destitute. We had just daylight
enough to return to the river, and found shelter for the night
in a corner of the house that Hunter was building. On viewing the devastation the fire had wrought, I exclaimed that I
did not care if my axe was spared, but it too had been in the
flames. I took the head to Dalhousie settlement, where there
was now a blacksmith, an Englishman of the name of Hatton,
who had extemporized a forge on a large tree stump and he
retempered it so hard that it flew into pieces on my putting
it to use. We tried to overcome our misfortune and set to
work, and, unaided, put up a shanty of round logs on our new
location, being the first house on the Hinchinbrook side of
the river, below the village. Fortunately we had some money
and our big chests had been left in Montreal, and for these,
after a winter spent in chopping 5 acres, I went early in the
spring. They were brought up in a traineau to river Beaudet,
and from there up the Laguerre and out by a lumber-road to
Marshall's, and then down Trout river. That season (1822)
we had a good crop of wheat, corn, and potatoes, but were
sadly troubled by the favor the squirrels showed for the corn.
There was no settler on the Hinchinbrook side of the river
besides ourselves until the summer of 1822, when James Armstrong and James Gardner arrived. Of the desolation of the
country I cannot give you an idea. One afternoon Mr Bowron
and myself walked back from my clearance to the Outarde,
to see what the country there was like, when it came on dark,
and we could not find our way back and had to camp until
daylight. The potash-kettle we bought in Montreal, was
brought up by canoe from the Basin. In November I went
to Pointe Claire for a cow, which a relation of my wife's,
Robert Benning, had secured for me, and this I led by a rope
of withes, carrying a load of 16lb. on my back, and driving a
ewe lamb. Such was the state of the road, or rather track,
that it was after dark when I reached Dewittville, where, on
learning my wife had been confined, I left my charge and
started for home. The night was so dark that I could only
tell where I was by throwing chips into the river and being

guided by the sound of their plashes. On getting opposite the point on lot 14, I called out to Armstrong, who crossing with his canoe, took me over to the south bank. On reaching home I found my wife well, but the child (our first-born) dead. Singular to relate, in the wilderness this country was then she had had medical attendance, for Dr Fortune had been staying with us. In bringing home my 4-footed companions next day, I feared the lamb would not take the water, but on seeing crummie, to which she was much attached, plunge in, she followed. After that my brother and I bought each a 2-year old steer, and that was our first yoke of oxen. To feed our livestock during the winter, we had cut a stack of beaver hay at the lake, and this we drew in on narrow sleds, each attached to an ox, during sleighing, leaving most of the load sticking to the branches along the narrow road. Our neighbor Hunter brought from Montreal the first horse, and this we borrowed to take our wheat to Percy's mill at Brighton Hollow, a bag being slung at either side. The road was wretched, and to make a passage over a mudhole near Athelstan a long slab was placed, which the horse walked, the only one I ever knew to do the like. The land we settled on Ellice claimed, and we ultimately had to pay $360 for it. The year of the Miramichi fire I lost a heifer from being smothered by the smoke. The flames came very near the shanty, but I lost nothing else. Up to that time there was no slash or brule in the woods. While the fire was burning, 3 young bears crossed my clearance, the only time I ever saw that animal. I lost 2 or 3 sheep, and blamed the wolves, whose cries we heard almost every night. For many years after I came, the Indians visited us every winter, making wigwams of poles covered with birch bark, the smoke coming out at the top of the poles. They slept with their feet to the fire and their heads to the poles. The point opposite my house was a favorite camping-spot, and when the river came to be well settled, they moved to the Outarde, and their last camp was at the mouth of the Hall creek. The men hunted, and the women sought for dry logs among the snow for firewood, did the cooking, and made baskets. They were harmless neighbors, but if they got drink were furious, and then the women would fly to the woods pursued by the men yelling and flourishing their tomahawks. In the spring they made sugar and as soon as the river opened left in their canoes for Caughnawaga.

Owing to most of the land from Hamilton's down to the seigniory-line being claimed by Ellice, its settlement was much hindered, although Brown encouraged applicants to go upon it and make clearances, telling them that though the seigniory-office was not prepared just then to give them titles, bargains would, in a short time, be made with them for the purchase of the lots. Not a few of the lots were occupied under these representations, and there came to be a row of shanties from Dewittville to Huntingdon. There being much fine elm, they cut it down and made potash, by which they lived, for the land was wet, save the strips they cleared on the river-bank. Their uncertain tenure of the land troubled them much, and when a message came from Beauharnois for the heads of the families to attend there on a certain day, they thought their suspense was to be ended. On arriving they were separately admitted into the office where Colonel Brown sat, with his clerk and two strangers. They were questioned as to how long they had been on their lots, their number, what the land was like, and particularly what buildings they had raised and how many acres they had cleared. After all had been examined, the settlers were told by Col. Brown that he was not yet prepared to give deeds, but when he was they should have the first offer. They withdrew satisfied, but a month or so afterwards they learned that they had been the victims of a dishonorable scheme. Ellice held these lands as he held those of Dalhousie settlement, merely by the purchase of the location-tickets of those to whom they had been granted. He had no patent, and could get none until proof was furnished that the settlement-duties had been performed. The object of sending for and examining the settlers was solely to ascertain how much land they had cleared and what improvements otherwise they had made. When they were gone, the 2 strangers who had sat listening to them and who had noted their answers, made affidavit that the settlement-duties had been performed, whereupon the government issued a patent to Ellice for the lots, when a demand was sent to the settlers to either pay $4 an acre or leave. With an exception or two, the defrauded and broken-hearted men had to choose the latter alternative, and it was fortunate for them that at that juncture the lots on the Gore concession were being given out, and to it they moved. The first settler on the 7th con., or the Gore as it came to be known by, was Samuel Foster, a Connaught Protestant, who had come to Canada in 1819 and lived in Montreal until the fall of 1823, when he moved on to lot 10, several young men accompanying him from the river settlement to put up his shanty. Before the snow left next spring, Haws and Peak followed from the river, and, though they had pick and choice, made what proved to be poor selections of lots. Mrs Peak said : '

My husband was an artilleryman, sent out from England at the close of the war, and discharged at Prescott, where I was married to him when a girl of 15. On hearing of land being given out free in Huntingdon, we came over in 1822, and squatted on lot 12, on the river. Unable to pay what Ellice asked for it, we moved with Haws to the Gore. Haws was a U. E. loyalist; his father had to leave a 200-acre farm in Maryland and fly to Canada. They stayed first at Quebec and then moved to Sorel, where Jasper enlisted in the service of the Northwest company, and spent a good part of his life under them. We had two cows when we moved to the Gore, and cut beaver hay to feed them. Such as it was, we never wanted for food. Nightly we heard the screaming of the wolves, and once my husband, while driving home at night, was followed by a pack, which did not come near him however.

In the spring of 1825 the Johnstons, Peterkin, and Armstrong followed the example of Peak and Haws and a survivor, Alexander Johnston, supplied this narrative :

We belonged to county Tyrone, and sailed from Belfast in the spring of 1823. Our design was to go to Ontario, but on landing at Montreal my father (John Johnston) met Todd of Dewittville, whom he had known in Ireland and who induced him to come to Huntingdon county. We took up lot 11, on the river, and had to leave it owing to the trouble with Ellice. All we got from Lowrey, who bought it from Ellice, for our 2 years' improvements was $35. We moved in the fall of 1825, 3 weeks before the great fire broke out, and put up our shanty on 11. The land was all in splendid maple, which was easy to burn, and the stones, being covered with leaves and forest litter, we did not see. When the smoke and fog of the fire came we were in great distress; surrounded by the bush on every side and unable to see a rod ahead. Foster on coming

to visit us, had to feel along the fence we had put up to reach
our house. The tongues of the cattle hung out a foot, and
they would not eat grass or hay, so we sliced potatoes for
them and gave them what slop we could to keep them alive.
When the smoke lifted, we saw fire all around us, and my
brother and I had not our clothes off for 11 days, fighting it,
to save our property. The leaves had fallen, and the flames
ran in every direction. On the Outarde the fire raged fiercely,
and felled so many trees that we were unable to reopen our
outlet to the river until the winter was well on. That winter
there was barely enough snow to put out the fires. Our road
was just a blazed track, coming out on 10, and we either
dragged our loads on ox-sleds or carried them. At the river,
we crossed in a canoe to the track on the other bank which
ran from Dewittville to Huntingdon. Our mainhold at first
was potash-making, and dragging the barrels across the creeks
was awful work. If the water was too high for the sleds to
go through, we would fell a hemlock and roll the barrel across
upon it, reloading on the other side. Oxen were so slow that
when we could carry the load, we did so, and a number of us
would start for Huntingdon in the morning, each with his
bag of grist on his shoulder, and return before dark. One
settler, Murray, an Irish Catholic despite his name, who was
a very powerful man, could carry 2 bushels. Foster, in 1827,
was the first to get a horse, but had no harness for it, and
many a bag it bore on its back to and from mill. Haws
after that got an old black horse. We never had any actual
scarcity, though our food was coarse, chiefly potatoes. The
year of the frost (1836) the tops were killed, so that they did
not ripen properly, and were not good eating. So soon as the
land was fit for it, we had had splendid crops of both fall and
spring wheat. I remember of our getting 4 bushels of red
chaff wheat from Upper Canada, and reaping 96. We had
plenty of hay from the first, there being beaver-meadows here
and there, especially one great meadow on Foster's. There
was no pine on the Gore to speak of, but on the Outarde
there was a fine cut both of it and oak. Settlers came in
thick and before 6 years every lot was taken up. They were
all Irish, and mainly Protestants. One settler, Lavery, was
a main instrument in inducing many to come, for he wrote
glowing accounts of the settlement to his old neighbors' in
county Down. The Coulters are descended from James who
came in 1828 and Henry who came in 1831, the year when
William Anderson and Law arrived. The Hendersons and
Wilsons came in 1829. We kept up the celebration of the

Twelfth of July from the first year we came, always having some kind of social gathering. We escaped both visits of the cholera. In the fall of 1831 there was fever and ague in every other house, and it continued a year or two after. We were divided about the cause. Some ascribed it to the vapor from the rotting stumps, and the water we used, for there were few wells sunk, and surface-water was all we had, but as the disease was almost all among men who had hired out to help farmers on the river during haying, we thought they had got the infection there. Ship-fever was brought by immigrants, but did not spread to the settlers. Our first religious services were conducted by the Rev Mr Merlin, who came to us so soon as he heard of the new settlement. After preaching at Black's, he walked over through the woods, and preached in one or other of our houses in the evening. He made all his journeys on foot, and would come when asked for a wedding. After that, Wesley Palmer and John Lowrey, the two Methodist local preachers, came occasionally. The catechist, Mr Hervey, was the first Episcopalian. Our great drawback was an outlet, the reserves for sideline roads being in sections so wet that we could not make them. After a great deal of opposition we got the road opened to Dewittville, and later on the one to Huntingdon.

These recollections may be supplemented by those of Archd. Adams, a nephew of the Armstrongs, and who joined them in 1825 :

The settlers had a good many drawbacks and had a sore struggle for years. The potash was often hauled out to the Hinchinbrook, the track that way being drier than out by Muir's. It was consigned at first to Reeves, who told the settlers he would sell for them in Montreal at the highest price and charge nothing if they would take the price out in trade. He made money both ways, however, declaring the ashes had graded low and charging high prices for his goods, 25 cents a yard for calico and $1 a pound for tea. Afterwards they sold in Huntingdon to McNee, who took delivery at Athelstan. While everything was so dear, all the lumberers paid for men was $6 to $7 a month. After clearing a bit of land, we put in corn and potatoes, and, in the fall, wheat, which, on being reaped, gave place to rye, which I have seen on what is now the poorest land on the Gore 6 feet high. The rye was used mainly for bread. The living was plentiful but poor. The mills having no machinery for cleaning the grain, the bread was often black, from smut or weeds. At a bee, the food was bread and hot water colored by having had a piece of toasted bread boiled in it, and without sugar. In Elgin I have heard at bees the variety was potatoes in their jackets and champit. The only year of real scarcity was 1837, caused by the frosts in August of the year before. The potatoes having been first frosted and then winded became bitter, which caused many to vomit them. That year flour was $5 a quintal, and oatmeal $5.50. I brought two or three loads of meal from Montreal that summer, and to one man, who had no money, I gave half a hundred on credit. That fall, when he had a glass, he told me he would never forget me, for when I had let him have the meal he and his family had been without food for three days except the milk of their solitary cow. There was often scarcity between the last of the old crop and the new one, but neighbor shared with neighbor. The Rev Mr Merlin visited the settlement from the first, coming once a month or once in three, according to the state of the roads.

To these two narratives, little can be added of the history of the settlement of the Gore. In May, 1828, an immigrant named McKinney died of ship-fever—the first death in the settlement. He was buried in a corner of Haws's lot. A year after another immigrant, a woman, died, and was also buried there, whereupon Haws gave an acre to be set aside as a graveyard. In 1829, when a schoolhouse was mooted, it was placed on this reserve, and a brother of Dr Harkness engaged as teacher. This schoolhouse was used for religious services. In the early winter of 1837 Bishop Mountain found his way to it and in his diary he says: "In a schoolhouse of squared logs I preached, administered the Lord's supper to 32 communicants, baptized 11 children, and churched the mothers." The settlement was equally divided between the two denominations, Episcopalian and Presbyterian, and this delayed their uniting to put up a church, and caused some feeling. On the old school being burned, in 1838, from a coal dropping between the flooring, it was not rebuilt, but one placed on Foster's lot and another on Johnston's. The refusal of the former on one occasion to the Presbyterians, when the Rev Mr Austin came to hold service, led to their building a church. A misunderstanding prevented the Episcopal church being placed on the Gore, and it was built at Herdman's corners.

Returning to the lots on the river left by the founders of the Gore, I would note what became of them. Col. Brown winked at a succession of squatters who occupied them, for they were enlarging the clearances and making them more valuable for the purchasers he awaited. In the summer of 1827 Archd. Muir walked along the river in search of land, and was attracted by a clearance on the long bend in front of 10, the crop on which indicated, to his experienced eye, superior soil. He set off for Beauharnois and bought the lot for $300 and gave the squatter upon it, Masson, $100 for his improvements. A skilled farmer of the Lanarkshire school, Muir set to work with his two sons to reclaim the land, and long before his neighbors had a large portion under crop. The year after William Cowan settled west of him and in 1831 John Donnelly, who had a large family of sons. That year three of the McNaughtons came, drawn to this section from their relationship to the Muirs, and in 1832 the father with the remainder of the family arrived. It is related of the old man that the relative who accompanied him to find a lot, exclaimed to a son, after several days' search, "That father o' yours is bound to settle in a swamp." Like the Muirs the McNaughtons were good farmers, and knew the soil that would prove best, and cared nothing about lumbering or potash-making. Taking up lots on both sides of the river, for there were several sons, the section came to be known as the Muir and McNaughton settlement, and their modes of working land and managing stock had its effect in raising the standard of farming. There stood on Muir's lot an old shanty, put up by lumbermen, and this in 1830 was fitted up as a school and a half-cracked being, named Dalzell, engaged as teacher. It was not until 1834 that the road was opened fit for vehicles to Huntingdon, and until then the traffic was by canoe or the road on the Godmanchester side. On the beautiful reach of the river opposite 9, a sad fatality took place. Two girls were rocking themselves in a canoe when it upset. A French Canadian, Louis Giroux, was passing at the time on horseback, and gallantly plunged in to their rescue. Sad to relate all were drowned, the horse included.

The concession lying between the river and the Gore, now called Boyd settlement, was begun in 1823. In the fall of that year John Grant settled on 10, which he had drawn as a free grant. He was from county Wicklow, Ireland. A fortnight after John Telford moved in. His daughter, Mrs Robson, gave these particulars of his coming :

My father was a Cumberland farmer, and we left England in 1818. After visiting Upper Canada my father returned east, convinced that he could do better near Montreal, owing to prices being so low in Ontario, wheat selling there at 50c a bushel in trade. In the fall of 1823 he came to Huntingdon and secured this lot, cleared a bit and put up a shanty, also cutting a stack of wild hay, which was plentiful along the Outarde. We were then living at Moulinette and in Feb'y, 1824, left for our new home. We drove up the Laguerre, crossed by the Shaw road to Trout river, and then down. We brought 6 cows, 2 young beasts, a yoke of oxen, and 8 sheep. Up through Muir's lot there was a rude lumber-road which ran back to Foster's on the Gore, and this took us to our new shanty. Except Grant, we had no neighbor east or west of us. The woods stood thick around us, although they had been plundered of the best pine and oak. During 1824 Wm. Irwin settled east of us and James Logan in 1826 a good bit to the west. The year of the Miramichi fire we had a dreadful time of it. It was so dark we often could not see 3 feet away. Our chief care was to save the stacks of wild hay cut for the winter-feed of our live-stock, and we were kept busy sweeping away the leaves (and they were unusually plentiful that fall) from the ridge on which they stood. We succeeded and lost none of our animals, which my father as-cribed to putting some salt in the water he gave them. The fire left the bush on the ridges, but made an awful slash on the low grounds. When we came the Outarde was a fine clear stream, but so many trees fell into it and across it during the fire that it got choked and after that the swales never dried, and we had fires every other year, making matters worse, but, after all, they helped to clear the land. Wolves were not plentiful when we came, but increased afterwards. One fall, when there was a little snow on the ground pre-venting the sheep from running well, the wolves killed 12 out of 14 ; 8 were found dead on the spot, and 1 within 20 feet of where the schoolhouse now is. Deer were very plentiful. In 1826, when the snow was deep with a crust, my brother with a dog ran down 6 in one day and 6 the next. On going on the 3rd day to haul them home, 5 more were killed. The Americans came and killed a great many for the sake merely of their hams and their hides. In 1832 my father, while haying on a lot he had bought on the river, ate some green peas, which were at the time in the pod. Old Mr Muir brought him home ill with cholera. Dr Bell was called in and his treatment included the withholding of all liquids. My father died in an agony of thirst, calling for water. Muir took the disease but recovered. There were no other cases.

The filling up of the concession went on slowly, owing to the land being held by Ellice and other non-residents and the immigrants were either unable to give the prices asked or would not pay for land until the free grants were exhausted. The want of a road to it and the long stretch of swamp between it and the village also retarded its progress. In 1831 John Boyd went on lot 15, being the first to go so far west. As he had a large family and was joined by his brother William, their work began to tell and as others went in beside them the name Boyd settlement came into use. For many years the only mode of access was a track that followed the ridges through to the swamp, which was crossed by stepping from log to log. Up Boyd's lot there was a track to the Gore. Another road to the new settlement passed up 12. Except in a very dry time, even an ox-sled could with difficulty reach the settlement, and when the swamps were full everything had to be carried on the shoulder. Until the land was ditched, potash-making was the main reliance of the settlers, who, with a few exceptions, were from the North of Ireland. James Flynn, who arrived in 1832, was the first Catholic. The Kellys, who came so late as 1837, found the settlement still in a backward state. Robert Kelly said :

I bought my lot (12) from Ellice, for $4 an acre. It was all bush, and the flat south of the Outarde was a dreadful swamp, often preventing passage to the Gore. The only way to get a little cash was to make black salts, which were placed

in a trough hewn from a basswood log and dragged by oxen
to Huntingdon. Everything was very cheap, a cow with calf
would fetch $8 to $10, and I have sold butter for 8c. The
first wheat I got was a bushel given me by Wilson on the
Gore for helping him to thresh. I carried it on my shoulder
home, often like to drop it, for the water was high, and then
to mill, and it was the first flour we had. My wife, of course,
knew nothing about baking but having heard hops were
necessary, got some and mixed them with the dough, and our
first loaf came from the chandron as hard as flint and bitter
as gall. When she learned the right way, none could beat
her for good bread. In the spring of 1838 I got a cow, and
cleared up enough of broulé land to sow 2 bushels of wheat,
and from that time never wanted bread. I have had oats
eaten by bears in the back fields. Our great trouble was
want of roads. The settlers on front opposed our opening a
concession-line, as they would have to help to make it, and
wanted us to be content with opening a side-line through 12
to the road they had made on the river. We stood out for a
regular front road and ultimately got it, though it was years
after before the side-line road was opened to Huntingdon,
compelling us to trespass on our neighbors to get out. On a
move being made to join the school at Muir's, at Watt's hill,
and our own into one, the present stone schoolhouse was
built, and it served as church and a place for public meetings.

The lower end of the concession, that east of Robson, was
somewhat longer in being opened up, owing to the want of
a road to Dewittville and the difficulty of clearing the land,
the flats having been repeatedly burned over and the fallen
logs intermixed with scrubby second-growth, but by 1834
all the lots were bought and a thrifty settlement was in
progress.

Owing to their nearness to the village, it would be supposed that the lots between Huntingdon and Athelstan would
have been quickly taken up, but such was not the case, and
there was a large settlement on the 3rd range when the land
between it and the Chateaugay was untouched. This was
partly due to its being owned by non-residents and partly to
the belief that the land was poor, from its being covered
with soft wood, mostly second-growth poplar and hemlock,
with some pine. Except in summer, it was a marsh, and
during that season, on Sunday afternoons the lads and lasses

of Huntingdon roamed the expanse, known as Canova's swamp, as far as 26, picking blueberries, and between Nelson Vosburgh's clearance on its river-point and Baxter's on 24 there was no house, as there was none from Baxter's to that of Claud Burrows in front of 21, where the village began. From being held by non-residents, no labor was put on the road, which became notoriously bad at a time when all roads were execrable. For hauling it was useless, so that the journey to Athelstan was made by canoe as far as Munro's hill, and when the water was too low for loaded canoes to go up the shallows, the freight was landed at "the oaks," as the burial-place by the road-side on 28 was named, and where several of the American squatters and a few Old Country people rest. The current belief, that a number of Hampton's men were buried in it during the retreat, has no foundation. A little farther up, a bridge was thrown across the river to give an outlet to the settlers on the Elgin side, and named Seely's bridge, from his living at the west end of it. At the other end of it, about 1827, a store and ashery was started by an Englishman, Wilson, who was succeeded by Joshua Lewis, and who, on removing to Huntingdon, sold to M. G. Teel, an Italian, who disappeared soon after. On the grant of $1200 being given to make the road from Franklin to Huntingdon, a considerable portion was absorbed by the section, namely from 22 to 26, on the river, held by non-residents, who had thus their property improved at the public expense and that of the actual settlers. In 1834 William Rose, a farmer from Aberdeen, and a neighbor, James Reid, who had been, for a short time, an ensign in the 78th, came in search of land, and the former bought out Vosburgh and the latter Richard Catton, who had a clearance on 27. George Blaik settled beside Mr Rose, and gradually the lots to the village came to be taken up, although as late as 1840 the greater part were unimproved. Once the land was cleared and ditched, it was seen there was no more fertile flat in the district.

. The first Old Countryman to settle near Athelstan was James McBeth, who left Dalhousie settlement in 1822 and took up 18, range 3. Two years afterwards, Allan Munro came from Ontario, to see about 1700 acres in Hinchinbrook that his mother had inherited from her brother, a Scotch officer, Deneen, who had served in the war of 1812. Munro selected as his abode that portion of his land (lot 28, range 5) on which John Elliot was squatted, who moved to 20 on the 3rd and built his shanty by the brook, and where he had several other Americans for neighbors. To convert the timber on his land into lumber, Munro set about building a sawmill on the rapids of the Hinchinbrook, but was unable to complete it, when he sold to McNee, the Huntingdon storekeeper, who ran it for 2 years, when he found a purchaser in a prominent newcomer, Thomas McLeay Gardner, who had been unsuccessful as a farmer in the Lothians, and emigrated from Scotland in 1827. Accompanied by two neighbors, George and David Pringle, and by David Sandilands, a Fifeshire farmer, he came to Huntingdon in search of land, when Bowron told them all the crown lots had been granted and they would need to buy, recommending them where to go. Hiring a canoe, they paddled up to the junction of the Hinchinbrook with the Chateaugay, where lived one Kater, who readily sold to Gardner, who subsequently bought the adjoining lot from Judge Gales, making 400 acres. He built his house near the mouth of the present feeder. Sandilands bought the adjoining property and built beside him. On the river, a short distance above him, a Dutch American, Hogle, had a sawmill. The road to Powerscourt was a wretched one, being the old track cut out by Hampton, which bent east at Sandilands' house and followed the ridge. Work on the new road, by the river-bank, proces-verballed by the grand voyer two years before, was begun that August. Mr Sandilands had three sons, one of whom, George, was a superior man, and made his influence felt for good, taking a part in all public matters. He was an ardent Liberal in politics, as, indeed, were all the immigrants of that time, save the few who had a little money and affected to be superior to the common herd. William Gardner took part of 18 and opened a store and pearling-work, and assumed charge of the sawmill. Going back to Scotland for his family, Gardner gave such glowing descriptions of the locality in which he had settled, that he created quite a stir in the East Lothians, and a number of his neighbors decided on emigrating. On the ship in which he sailed in 1828 were John Pringle, Alex. Lumsden, and James Johnston, and a number followed. On arriving, Lumsden raised a shanty on the east side of the road near the present bridge as a home and on the other side of the road a shop, for he was a blacksmith. These were the first houses in Athelstan. Going largely into lumbering and the sawmill being kept busy, people were attracted to the place, and it soon became large enough to get a name and was known as St Michaels, until, 30 years afterwards, it was called Athelstan. In 1832 the growing population was provided with a school, placed some distance north of it, to suit the settlers on the Elgin side. It was a low pavilion-roofed log building, placed by the road-side on 28. Thos. Taylor (p. 301) taught the first year and held service on Sunday. Sir John Rose attended this school as a pupil and subsequently taught it for a term. In 1834 William Kerr, who had been a calico-printer in Glasgow, and had given up business from losses by endorsing, came and Gardner proposed to him to join in raising a gristmill, and he agreed, supplying the funds. The mill (now used as the oatmeal mill) was built by Waldie, a mason, and was fitted up in a very cheap manner, the spindle of the wheel resting on a hemlock knot. It had 2 run of stones, one for flour and one for Indian meal. Following this, Kerr was induced to make advances towards building a distillery, which, however, never began operations, the poor gentleman having lost his all. Soon after the sawmill had been opened, Patrick Grady started a tavern at the corners east of it, and was induced by Gardner to move into the infant village, and in 1838, beside the gristmill, a house was raised which became known far and wide. To show that whisky-selling was even more profitable in those days than now, it may be stated that a 40-gallon barrel, for which Grady would pay Mitchell, the storekeeper on the Lines, $10, he took in $60, besides what the family used or gave in treats. In addition to Kerr and Gardner, Rose and Reid, several others came who brought some money with them. There was Patrick Walker on the 1st concession, Alexander Copland, an Aberdeen advocate, John and R. B. Somerville, Dr Shirriff and Dr Whyte. The last-named, who came in 1836 from Elgin, was a physician of reputation, who did not practise, and a very intelligent gentleman. Drawn from a class different from their neighbors, and not having to plod daily to earn their bread, they formed a small circle of their own, and exchanged frequent visits. They endeavored, so far as the changed surroundings would permit, to keep up the customs and style of the Old Land, but the imitation was rather pitiful. During the winter each in turn gave a dinner, which was attended with much formality. On the ladies withdrawing, the toddy was brought in, and there were few of the company who left the table without disposing of 5 tumblers. When, in consequence of the rebellion, Huntingdon became a military station for a few years, and the society of officers was added to the select circle, the dissipation and whist-playing increased, with other extravagances added, as horse-racing. On the whole, the existence of a sort of gentry during the early period of Huntingdon's history, was not of any benefit, and it is very remarkable that all who brought money with them from Scotland lost it.

Behind Athelstan, on the 6th concession, a prosperous settlement sprang up, the first to go in being John Pringle. His son James gave the following account of his early days in the bush :

In 1827 my brother John went to Canada and the family followed in 1828. We took 10 weeks to reach Quebec from Leith, and it was a two days' journey from Lachine to Dewittville. On arriving at Huntingdon we found carts could not go farther, the road was so bad, and we embarked in canoes at the head of Palmer's rapids which landed us at Allan Munro's. From Allan we bought part of 25, 6th concession, at $1.25 per acre and half of 22 from an American named Phillips, who left for the States. How long he had been on his lot I cannot say, but he had a clearance of only about 6 acres. The only other settler on the concession was Samuel

Hudson, who lived on the other half of 25, and left in 1835, when he sold to Dr Gibson. We moved into Phillips' house. There was no road, just a track over which oxen could drag a sled. The land was so very wet that my father bought 15 acres of ridge on 24 until his own land was fit to cultivate. There was a splendid bush and we made a great deal of potash. Fire had never touched the woods and did not until 1840, when a great one raged along the Outarde. The winter after we came was fine and what we got in during the spring yielded well. For several years our only crops were corn and potatoes. That summer, 1829, Malcolm Munro came in, and took up 300 acres at the upper end of the concession. He was a Highlander and had a large family. James Waldie, John McWilliam, and Wm. Anderson came in 1836. Owing to the land being so wet where the allowance for the concession road lay, we could not open it where it ought to have been, and laid it out so as to keep the high ground. It was several years after we came that the road was cut out, when each settler did his own portion. My eldest brother, John, died of the cholera in 1832. He was in no way exposed, but, from the first report of its having reached Montreal, was in mortal dread of the disease. He never left home, yet took ill and died in 4 days. Dr Bell, who attended him, said it was Asiatic cholera. One of my sisters caught the infection but recovered.

The lots to the rear of those on the ridge road, and on the 5th range, remained in a state of nature to a much later date, from their being held by non-residents who asked high prices for them, and one, Nye, would not sell at all. The flat west of the Outarde bridge had been terribly swept by fire during 1825, and the outlets so choked by fallen trees that it was converted into a deep swamp. When it did come to be reclaimed, the roots of great cedars were found under the second-growth timber that covered it. When a settlement came to be made in this dreary expanse, which was towards 1850, it was named "the lost nation," and the title has remained, although it long since lost its appropriateness, the section being a fine and accessible one.

The Samuel Hudson mentioned by Pringle as living at the corner of the brook road, had, with his brother Robert, moved from Eaton, in the Eastern Townships, to Fisher-street, Hemingford, at the close of the war. Robert had served with

gallantry at Lacolle mills, and was with the army at Plattsburgh. On seeing how the men were being swept from the
stringers of the bridge as they endeavored to cross the Sar-
anac, he took it upon him to countermand the thoughtless
order that was sending brave men uselessly to death, and
expected to be punished therefor. Instead of that, he was
promoted to be lieutenant. In 1823 he moved into Hinchinbrook, taking up 25, range 6, and his brother followed in the
spring of 1825. Two nights were spent on the road. The
second was in the house of John King, who had come in
1823. He was a Scotchman and a bachelor, in which state
he continued until his death. He was very kind to the new-
comers, producing table-linen and silver, relics of his family
in Scotland, and which contrasted queerly with the rudeness
of his small shanty. Years afterwards, he lost all by the
burning of his house while absent. He was a carpenter by
trade and had come with Robert Higgins and Archibald
Fleming, a mason. These were the only neighbors the Hud-
sons had, save Baxter, already referred to, and Wells, also an
American, who lived opposite to him on the south side of the
road. Robt. Hudson, anxious for the education of his family,
induced a sister-in-law, Miss Cross, to open school in his house,
and she taught in 1825, followed by his sister, Mrs Leggatt.
After that Major Gardner had a governess, no public school
being opened until the one already referred to, near Athelstan.

The settlement along the road between Athelstan and Herdman proceeded very slowly, there being no settler beyond
King until 1825, when James Terry left Elgin and took lot
26, and, east of him settled John Kennedy, John Trainer,
Robert Johnston, John Kelly, and Stephen McCrea. These
were all from the North of Ireland, and, except one, Protestants. Their countrymen on the Gore turned out to put
up shanties for them, and it was long remembered that in
going to raise that of McCrea they could hardly find their
way, owing to the darkness of the smoke of the Miramichi
fire. The start the settlement thus obtained it kept, and immigrants came thickly until every lot was occupied. The road
so late as 1829 was a mere track along the bank of the Hin-

chinbrook. In that year something was done to straighten it and chop it out, but it was not until 1832 that, with the aid of a small government grant, a rude bush road was formed.

The origin of the hamlet at Herdman's corners does not date far back. In 1826 an American, Henry Sweet, from Champlain, bought 29, and sold a couple of acres to Duncan Campbell, who opened a store and pearling-work on the east-side of the road. He continued to carry on business until 1838, when, disgusted by the collapse of the rebellion, with which he sympathized, he went back to the States. Of the coming of the family who gave their name to the corners, Arthur Herdman said :

Our family sailed from Belfast in 1830, and we left Montreal for Huntingdon by way of Laprairie and Russeltown, reaching the house of William Gibson (whose wife was my sister) after a two days' journey. My father, Henry, bought 30, and my brothers chopped out a clearing and put up a log-house, into which we moved that fall. Sweet and McCrea were our neighbors, and had only small clearings. We had a yoke of oxen, and made much potash. It was terrible work dragging out a barrel in a sled over the dry logs to where a cart could be used. The settlers were poor but hopeful, and the household was thought well-off that had a loaf baked in the chaudron on Saturday for Sunday. In 1832 Perkins Nichols and Duncan Campbell opened store on the south-east side of the corners, and in 1836 my brother Paul started tavern opposite them on the north side of the road.

The taking up of lots proceeded more actively east of Herdman than west of it. Nearness to Franklin induced settlers to move in and John Black, Joseph Arthur, Archd. Mather, William Gibson, and James Downs came in 1820, and formed a small neighborhood. Being entirely ignorant of bush-life they had a hard time of it at first, and but for mutually assisting each other could not have held their ground. In 1822 Hy. Rennie and Robt. Gibson came, the first securing 35 in a singular way. The lot was vacant and the first who took possession would secure the patent. One of the Duffins fancied the lot and hearing of Rennie's intention to settle on it, determined to forestall him. Getting word of

this on a Sunday, Rennie set himself to defeat him. As he
could not legally take possession on Sunday, he was constrained to wait at Arthur's until another day begun. There
was no clock in the settlement, so he and Arthur sat up until
the cock crew, when, knowing it would be about 1 o'clock
Monday morning, they sallied forth, reached the lot, and
swung their axes with such good effect that by daylight there
could be no question as to who was in possession. His shanty
was erected on the little hill east of the graveyard. From
his lot being midway between Rockburn and Herdman the
school came to be placed upon it, the first teacher being
Christy Campbell. In 1829, by a great effort, a small church
was built, which stood in the present graveyard. It was a
frame building, with balloon-roof, 24 feet square, built by
Brewster and McHardy, and subsequently 6 feet was added
to it for a belfry. In 1831 Mr Rennie lost an infant son,
who was buried beside the church, which began the use of
the plot as a graveyard, he giving a deed for an acre and
keeping a burial register, which his nephew (James Rennie)
has continued. The Rev Mr Merlin preached as his other
appointments permitted. When asked as to his next visit,
he would reply, "I will come sometime." He was not punctual and the congregation were always kept waiting. Wm.
Taylor of the 1st concession precented. No contribution was
made towards Mr Merlin's salary. The situation of the
church was convenient to the residents on the 1st concession
for the only road east of the Powerscourt side-line to the 3rd
concession was the military road cut out by the Americans
during the war. It followed the line between 34 and 35
until the swamp was reached, when it bent east and came
out opposite to the present church. Lewis McKay, who
visited Huntingdon for the first time in the fall of 1822, and
drew lot 35, range 3, said "the Blacks were engaged reaping
their first crop, and, though the season was dry, the only
way I could get to Athelstan was by passing np the war-
road to the 1st concession, and along it to Powerscourt,
where I took the Chateaugay road. The country was very
wild at that time and I often trapped beavers to the north

of my farm. Venison was the only meat we had, and I shot
deer from my own door. Bears gave us a good deal of
trouble, for they came from the swamps to the north in
search of food."

The first settler at Rockburn was Matthew Shearer, who
took up 44 in 1821. Selling to Robert Rennie he moved to
Russeltown, and his name became associated with a story of
a pedlar alleged to have been murdered at the Flats in the
fall of 1826. Shearer, from being involved in the radical
riots, fled from Scotland in the fall of 1819 and eventually
drifted to Hinchinbrook, where Robert Gibson became his
neighbor, and with whom he lived. On transferring his lot
to Rennie, he worked with several farmers in Franklin,
finally marrying and settling down at the Flats, where he
had a small house next to John Forbes. One day, in September, 1826, there came along a French Canadian pedlar,
with a great pack of goods, and was readily given permission
to stay overnight. His goods were much too fine and costly
for the settlers, and finding, after a considerable stay, that
he could not sell them, he resolved to cross into the United
States, and succeeded in getting a man to convey his goods
thither. For their kindness in entertaining him, the pedlar
presented Mrs Shearer (a daughter of William Brisbin) with
silk enough to make a dress and left behind a box and other
valueless articles, until his return. As he never came back,
the story got abroad that he had been murdered, and it was
generally believed. It was entirely unfounded, for the cause
of the pedlar's non-return was, that on the road to Plattsburgh he met an American, A. Rand, who purchased his stock
of goods in bulk, when, having no need to go back to the
Flats, he struck out for fresh pastures. Shearer moved to
the Bay of Quinte, where he throve, and probably remained
unconscious of the unjust suspicions he left behind him.

The fine water-power of the Mitchelbrook at Rockburn
was turned to account in 1829. James Allen, unable to restore his mill at the Flats, for the seigniory-office was now
zealous in upholding its privileges, resolved on building a
gristmill in Hinchinbrook, and there was a great bee to

raise the frame that fall. He operated it successfully until he left the country, when Robt. Needler bought his property and supplemented the water-power by a steam-engine. Following the erection of the grist-mill, William Dunlop, some distance farther down the stream, placed a sawmill. On the upper Mitchelbrook Thomas Blair, about the same time, built a sawmill, and in 1836 the Craiks engaged Nelson Proper to erect one on their lot. At a much later date, David Craik, a born-mechanic, bought a part of Blair's lot and proceeded to build a small gristmill. Near to these mills on the 1st concession, a Scotchman, George Blain, opened a tavern. The stream that thus supplied power to so many mills in the short space of 2 miles, dwindled as the country got cleared to such an extent that all have been abandoned except the one originally erected by Allen and now owned by John Stewart. There was no store at Rockburn until 1862, when one was opened by Andrew Oliver, and the place assumed the character of a village.

The forest east of Rockburn was first broken by a party of Scotch, who landed in Montreal late in the summer of 1820 and worked at quarrying stones and at the laying down of water-mains until the following spring, when they drew lots in the eastern extremity of Hinchinbrook and moved, by way of St Remi, to occupy them. Leaving the women and children with the settlers on the Beechridge and Franklin, the men pushed forward to erect shanties. The families were those of William, Andrew and James Lauder, William Easton, Henry Wilson, David Lecky, and William Craik. None of them knew anything about bush life, and Craik, in attempting to fell his first tree, began by nicking it all round, when Gentle, who came over to see him, arrived opportunely to direct him. All remained and succeeded in making homes for themselves, except Lecky, who left. Craik was a man of education and some means, and about 1830 opened a store and pearl-ashery on his lot, by the side of the road, near where the spring is, and did tolerably well. In accord with the natural law of settlements, the nationality of the first-comers determined its future. Other Scotch families moved in and up to a comparatively recent period Rockburn and neighborhood was mainly Scotch and Presbyterian. East of Craik was John Manning (page 20), who had left Hemingford owing to losses entailed by misplaced trust, and who had bought 44 from a squatter, Asa Smith, who claimed to have come in from the States in 1792. Mr Manning took possession in 1820, enlarged Smith's clearance and erected suitable buildings. In the early spring of 1822 he moved his family, severing his connection with Hemingford, which the people of that township regretted, as he had been their chief man of business and their only justice of the peace It is proof of how much public sentiment has advanced with regard to the liquor-traffic, that this worthy man had not a doubt as to the legitimacy of manufacturing and selling whisky, and the first summer completed a building fitted up for distilling potato-whisky, to supply the material for which he planted 10 acres, and that fall, no excise laws then hindering, the manufacturing was begun. The spirit was sold at 25 cents a gallon. The squire lived to regret having ever had anything to do with the liquor-traffic, and gave his influence to the side of temperance. As a magistrate his services were sought in other than his judicial capacity, and, in disregard of the statutes, he performed the marriage ceremony. He died in 1854, attaining the patriarchal age of 89, and was buried on his farm.

The 8th concession was not taken possession of until subsequent to 1830. Three brothers, Matthew, Hugh and James Simpson, Hugh Calhoun, William Small and William Lindsay (the two latter Scotch, the others Irish Protestants) were the first to go in and had many difficulties to contend with, the chief being the want of an outlet, their only road being a track through the bush to Rockburn. A fine cut of black ash and elm was their support for many years, they turning it into potash.

The settlement of the first concession began with the century (page 54) and, at the time immigration set in, was fairly occupied. Of the condition of the concession and its progress I can give no better account than that told by Wm. Taylor:

My father was a weaver in Paisley: a man of natural ability and deep piety, who preached on Sundays to a small knot of Baptists, who, in those days, represented that denomination in the small Scottish town. Among his hearers were Matthew Tannahill, brother of the poet, and David Coats, who afterwards became the great thread-manufacturer. I was born in 1801 and when I became old enough learned my father's trade. In 1820, the radical year, trade was very dull, so that I could not find work, and my thoughts were directed to emigrating. The government was offering unusual inducements to go to Canada,—100 acres in county Lanark, an axe, nails, glass, etc., and $10 in money—and I joined the first party of 300, which sailed in the Buckinghamshire from Greenock on the 19th April, 1821. From Lachine, the passage was made in 30 Durham boats, the emigrants helping to tow them up the rapids, a Canadian heading the tow-rope and we falling in behind him. We were carted back to our lots in the bush. The land was stony and the poor people had a hard time of it, though those who persevered eventually made comfortable homes for themselves. Towards spring the settlement was visited by Jacob Hart, who had been educated by the Rev Dr Ewing, Independent minister of Glasgow, as a missionary, and who came to Lanark to see the Huttons, with whom I lived, a family with which he was connected by marriage. He told me that he was living in the county of Huntingdon, (p. 155) where the land was much better. In April, 1822, I determined to go and see for myself, and footed it the entire distance, being ferried across at St Regis, and coming down on the American side to Chateaugay, from whence there was a rude road to the 1st con. of Hinchinbrook, not straight, but angling across the lots until it got to the centre of them, when it ran east. The first settler's house after crossing the boundary-line was that of Joe Silver, a Canadian, who had just sold to Adam Patterson but had not left. Then came 5 Americans, who afterwards sold out to Old Countrymen and left, and after them a Dutchman, Kidner, on 27, who sold to Wallace, which brought me to McLatchie, who held then 600 acres and was very comfortable; still farther east were Peter McGregor and his father-in-law, Captain Barron, and John Campbell. I was so pleased with the land that I determined at once to remain, and walking to Huntingdon I found Mr Bowron and took out my location-ticket for part of 30. Pittenwright, an Aberdonian, took up the lot opposite me, which he sold afterwards to Donald Fisher. George Gillis drew part of 31 and as he was, like myself, a single man, we worked together, making potash. Our living was potatoes and salt and salt and potatoes. Gillis sold in 1824 to William Burns. To make a little money I hired out the fall I came, at $6 a month, to Peter Campbell, and remained with him 15 months. Being ignorant of farming this was an advantage to me, for Campbell had to teach me even to mow. In 1824 an Irish Catholic, Charles Mooney, arrived and built a sawmill on the east side of the Hinchinbrook, and afterwards, in 1828, a gristmill on the west bank. The latter was operated by a breastwheel 30 feet high and the machinery was very simple, mostly of wood, Sandy Lumsden making what ironwork there was. The stones were hewn out of boulders in the adjoining field. They moved slowly and turned out poor flour, but for all that, the mill was a great convenience. His coming induced a number of his countrymen to follow, and every Irish Catholic immigrant met on the road would ask the way to Mooney's. At the east end of the concession there settled the McMullins, Felix McCormick, James Condron, the Duffins, (Henry lived on the site of the Catholic church) and the McDonaghs. The Learys came later on. A few years after he built the mills, Mooney sold the property to one Murray, who died market-clerk of Montreal. The same year that the sawmill was built, John Mitchel, a Dutch Yankee, built a store at the lines, on the road to Chateaugay, where all our trading had heretofore been done. The new store was very convenient and Mitchel was liberal, giving credit to the new settlers, who had often to get trust for their first axe. They paid in potash, which Mitchel hauled to Athelstan and sent to Huntingdon by canoe, having a large one for that purpose, which held 3 barrels. From Huntingdon to the Basin Reeves took them in his canoes, and often conveyed for Mitchel as many as a hundred in a season. An American from Plattsburgh, Standish, established an ashery and store in the fall of 1825 at the lines, but shortly after sold out to his clerk, George McCoy, and the place is still known as McCoy's lines. He shipped in a season as many as 120 barrels of pearl-ash. Near by, Judge Smith had a store, and sold a great quantity of whisky. Our first school was opened on 34 in 1827 and was taught by Miss Hudson. She and subsequent teachers boarded round, one week for each scholar, and the subscriptions to the salary were paid in grain and orders on the storekeepers, with very little money. My wife taught in 1828 and 1829, and on our marriage, I settled down in earnest to improve my land. The Rev Mr Merlin was our first minister, though Adam Patterson and a few neighbors engaged for a short time a

Baptist, Elder Smith. We had occasional visits from Methodists, but the first Canadian one was Father Hotchkiss, who
began to visit us in 1838. He belonged to Missisquoi bay
and had been a blacksmith. He was just suited to the backwoods, and could talk about and give advice on building,
cattle, farming, and so on, so that even the Catholics were
eager to see him and get his opinion. He was a loud, strong
preacher, but had so limited a stock of sermons that he gave
us one on Noah three times. He preached in the schoolhouse.
On Mr Merlin ceasing to be able to keep up his visits, the
Black church was unused. One winter night John McIntosh
was driving when he passed a standing sleigh. Thinking
something was wrong he halted and turned back, when he
found it was a neighbor and his wife, who had lost a mitt,
for which they were searching. They were going to a prayer-
meeting at James Gamble's house, and asked McIntosh to go
with them, which he did. He attended one or two afterwards, when Mrs Black said she had the key of the church,
and as it was not used, they might meet there. They did so,
and that led to the Franklin minister including the Black
church in his appointments. There was not a wheeled vehicle
used on the 1st concession when I came or for years after; it
was all ox-sleds. Clearing an acre of land was counted in
those early days worth $10. The school at Powerscourt was
opened in the winter of 1833. The Johnston burying-place
at Powerscourt is not a very old one. It contains a good
many Irish Catholics, whom, for some cause or another, the
priest would not bury in consecrated ground.

This narrative is sufficiently full regarding the 1st concession. A little south of Powerscourt, Holcomb & Latham,
while they kept store at Huntingdon, built a small sawmill,
which, on their failure, they transferred to a creditor, a Montreal merchant named Buck, by birth an American, in payment
of their debt. In 1827 Buck built a gristmill on the Elgin
side, in which he gave some interest to Holcomb, whom he
engaged as manager. The mill was of the greatest service to
the settlers, who came to it from great distances. In 1833
Fisher Ames was engaged as manager, when the mills were
refitted and a run of stones put in to shell oats. The small
sawmills on the Chateaugay and its tributaries from 1830 to
1850 did a large business in sawing pine lumber, which was
sent to Quebec. In the winter of 1833 Major Gardner made

a great effort to have a large output, the sawmill being kept going night and day. The spring of 1834 came early, and the rafts he had ready started and went down easily until the Blockhouse was reached, when it was found the ice below was firm. After waiting a good while, it moved, when the rafts followed, but the water fell rapidly, and there was not sufficient to float them over the rapids at Ste Martine. The cost of teaming the lumber to the Basin swallowed the profits, and the season was long remembered by lumbermen as a disastrous one. In those days farmers never paid for sawing, giving half the lumber as toll. Hemlock was rarely drawn, millers having a prejudice against sawing it, especially in winter, from its flinty nature being hard on their saws. The western end of the 1st concession road was long in being chopped out, the settlers using the track made by the old American squatters that circled round to Mitchel's. About 1835 the road was cut out on the proper line, and the cedar-swamp that lay west of Burnbrae was cross-wayed, and many years elapsed before it was covered with soil and converted into a solid roadbed. Speaking of Burnbrae, the only death from cholera on the concession occurred there. Mr and Mrs Walker had visited the city, and he returned ill with the disease. Dr Shirriff was sent for, succeeded in overcoming the attack, and went to bed, congratulating himself on the recovery of his patient, but did not sleep long until he was awakened by Mrs Walker, who cried that she was very ill. The doctor rose and entered her room, when he found her in a state of collapse, and she died in the morning.

NOTE. At the close of this chapter, I would direct attention to the neglected condition of the graves and burial-grounds of the first settlers. No effort has been made to preserve them, and, in a few cases, the plow passes over the bones of those who led the way into the wilderness. Surely something might be done to ensure respect for the few square feet of land they now claim. In Hinchinbrook the grave of Capt. Barron (p. 56) will soon be lost sight of; and it is the same with others. The interesting burying-place on the Chateaugay, named in the foregoing chapter "the oaks," is in danger of falling a prey to the plow.

CHAPTER XXII.

THE era of immigration affected Franklin less than any other part of the district. The northern section had, as already described, been taken up by Americans; the southern was held by non-residents; the crown had no lots to grant. Compared with the western part of the county, it was an old settlement, and, therefore, does not present the same material for narration. In 1826 Amos J. Fassett, an American, opened store on the upper road, on the gore lot, and did business for about 6 years. He was backed by Keyes & Hotchkiss, for whom he bought ashes. At Stacy's corners, in 1830, George Smith, who had moved from the Hill, began a blacksmith shop. It may be here remarked, that stores and taverns were more numerous along the frontier in those early days than they are now. At one time or another every cross-road has had its store or tavern, and much business was done at corners which are now deserted. The decline of the drinking-habit reduced the number of taverns, and as roads were opened and improved, business centred more in the villages. On the Moe place (lot 4, 9th range) stood the first school, built probably about 1822, which had a succession of teachers, mostly from the States and none of them competent, until a son of Wm. Easton took charge. This old schoolhouse remained in use until the stone-schoolhouse, long the place for council and public meetings, was erected at Stacy's corners, or Manningville as it was then called. That name passed with the post-office to the hamlet at the point where the road crosses the Outarde, which, 40 years ago, was a busy place, sawmills being built on either side of the bridge, and eventually a tannery was opened and a store by Ames & Fargo. About 1830 Cantwell & Nichols opened a branch store at Franklin Centre which did a large business. While on his deathbed in 1834 Nichols bequeathed half an acre of his farm, 13, as a graveyard, and he was the first to be buried in it. William Cantwell said: "I came from Troy, N. Y., in 1835, when I bought the Franklin store from my brother. This section, even then, was pretty much under bush, and there was not a French Canadian at St Antoine, on the Black river, or in St Jean Chrysostome. It was not until 1840 that the French began to move into the Black river country. Potash was the great commodity, and I have sent away 85 barrels at once. They were sent on sleds, dragged by two yoke of oxen, to St Remi, and sometimes they took 2 barrels when the road was good, but generally one was a load. There was not a buggy then in the county." The opening of a store at the corners added to its importance. Job Douell, an American, opened tavern, and after keeping it some time sold to a brother countryman, Abram Samson, who was succeeded in 1837 by an Irish Protestant, Thomas Wilson. Willis Pelton, before that, opened a whisky-shop, a class of places numerous all over the country. After 1835 the whisky was nearly all smuggled. It could be had at Malone for 20 cents the gallon, was worth 80 cents at Franklin, and $1 at St Remi. The business of smuggling was followed systematically and immense quantities of liquor brought in. About 1830 a schoolhouse was built on the site of the existing one, large enough for meetings on week days and Sundays, and within its walls, eventually destroyed by fire, the Rev Mr Townsend and others held service. Some time after the war an American physician, Dr Walbridge, took up his abode on lot 18, 2nd range. He was found dead in his bush, having been killed while dragging a tree home for firewood. He was succeeded by Dr Austin, who lived near or on 16. Walbridge's lot was bought by Robert Dunn in 1821, and who became a prominent settler. On 14 was Jacob Abbott, a native of Maine, who kept travellers from an early date. He was the first to introduce a wheeled vehicle, getting an ox-cart made in Montreal, which he used in going round to collect ashes, for he had an ashery. In 1825 he sold to Frederick Border, an Irish Protestant, who, until his death at an advanced age, occupied a prominent position in the township. He was the cause of others of his countrymen coming to Franklin, among them being Jas. Tate on 13, range 3, and his brother William. The growth of that section of country which forms a gore between the old Hemingford and Hinchinbrook lines, extending from the Flats to near Rockburn, was blighted for 25 years by an attempt to prove that it was part of the seigniory of Beauharnois. From the beginning, there had been a doubt as to how far the seigniory extended southwards. Anxious to have the country settled, the first seigniory-agent, Winter, told those who were purposing to take up land in what is now Franklin, that he would make them safe by giving them permits, which few accepted, the majority regarding that an unnecessary precaution, being persuaded that not only Russeltown and Edwardstown, but a strip of Williamstown were outside the bounds of the seigniory, and therefore belonged to the crown. Milne was so dubious about the seigniory owning these lands that, in a case where he wished to favor a family, he would not give a deed. When Brown came all doubt as to the designs of the seignior were ended. The Hon. John Richardson and he resolved to begin with the Williamstown settlers. The Highlanders were summoned to attend at Beauharnois one day in October, 1821. Asked what they had to say for themselves, they told how they had sought homes nine years before in the forest, (p. 48) and how, when informed that the owner of the seigniory claimed the land they had selected, two of their number had gone to visit Milne and wanted to arrange with him, for they wished to act honestly, and he refused to deal with them in any way and, thereupon, they had taken possession. Richardson perceived the simple character of the men and he proceeded to bully them. Affecting to be in a rage, he denounced them as trespassers and land-robbers, whom he would cause to be punished with the full rigor of the law— he would take their lands from them and imprison them until they paid what they were due. The unsophisticated children of hill and glen, without a friend, unable to communicate with those around them, for they spoke Gaelic alone, were struck dumb, and when, as a great favor, they were told they would be allowed to compromise by paying lump sums in proportion to the length of time they had held possession and by agreeing to become censitaires, they complied, and signed an obligation to that effect, the amounts ranging from $25 to $200, and which they had much difficulty in paying. The next move was made upon the Russeltown settlers. Manuel was sent to make a survey. The settlers would not let him; told him their lands belonged to the king, and that Ellice could not treat them as he had done their Highland neighbors. Manuel returned to Beauharnois and reported that many of the settlers had been in undisturbed possession for nigh 20 years, that they had clearances of 30 arpents and over, with fine orchards, and were not the stamp of men to be imposed upon. There the matter rested, and as year followed year without further molestation, the settlers concluded Ellice had abandoned his claim and gave no more thought to the matter. It was in the spring of 1828, while they were plodding along at their weary work of subduing the wilderness, that they were astounded by the announcement that Mr Ellice had taken steps to make good his claim to their farms. They had never doubted that the land they held belonged to the crown, and it was in that belief they had gone on improving it; indeed, many had paid for it under that supposition, for not a few lots had changed hands several times, and always at an advance in price in proportion to the increased improvements. No settler had troubled himself about applying for a patent, for so long as the government did not disturb them, they were not anxious to settle with it. The demand of Mr Ellice, that they recognize him as their seignior and pay rent, shattered their dream of fancied security in their possessions and set them enquiring into the foundation of his claim. The question was a rather involved one, and turned upon the correctness of the surveys of the boundary-lines between the seigniory of Beauharnois and the Huntingdon townships. In 1787 W. Chewett was ordered to survey the township of Godmanchester, which then included St Anicet. It was of course essential for him to

establish the western boundary of the seigniory, and the
proper way to have done so was to begin at the boundary
(which had been then legally established) between the seigniory of Chateaugay and that of Beauharnois, and from that
point measure 6 French leagues, which would have brought
him to the western limit of the seigniory of Beauharnois
and the starting-point for the new township he was to survey. Instead of that, he started at St Regis, and measuring
eastward struck the river Chateaugay which he followed
until he either arbitrarily fixed the western boundary of the
seigniory or, what is probable, accepted some old post that a
previous surveyor had planted. Having settled in his own
way the seigniory's landmark on the river-bank, he ran his
line north-west to the St Lawrence. The following year
Henry Holland was sent to survey Hinchinbrook. Without
examination, he accepted Chewett's line as correct, and continued it south-east until it struck the province-line in the
centre of 51. In 1791 Joseph Kilburn was engaged to survey Hemingford, and just as Chewett and Holland had
established the western boundary of the seigniory, it fell to
him to ascertain its southern boundary. This he did by
starting from the south-east landmark of the seigniory,
which had been established, and ran a line south-west until
it intersected that run by Holland. This he struck half a
mile north of the United States, when he concluded that the
western line of the seigniory was to that extent short of
the six leagues. Alexander Ellice, who was then seignior,
demanded compensation for this deficiency, and, in 1801,
the government, without enquiring into the merits of the
case, ceded to him 6600 acres in the township of Clifton,
Sherbrooke county. Thus the matter rested for over a
quarter of a century, during which the settlers were painfully and slowly subduing the forest and changing an unproductive wilderness into a fertile country. The agents of
the seigniory, the Hon. Mr. Richardson and Colonel Brown,
perceived this. They envied the prosperous settlements
which fringed the southern border of the seigniory and
resolved to appropriate them under the pretence that they

fell within its limits by virtue of the old and forgotten
surveys above described. If these surveys were correct, the
claim of Mr Ellice's agents was indisputable, and the whole
question therefore turned upon their accuracy.

Nothing could be plainer than the limits defined in the
original deed by the French king. The Marquis of Beauharnois was to have a square of land 6 leagues long facing
the St Lawrence, and 6 leagues deep, the side-lines to run
south-west. A square of this size would contain 254,036
arpents. The questions to decide Mr Ellice's pretensions
were : Did his seigniory have a front on the St Lawrence
of 6 leagues; did his side-lines measure 6 leagues in depth;
did they run truly parallel ? Thus tested, it was ascertained,
1st, that instead of a river front of 18 miles, he had one of
18½, Chewett having made a mistake in allowing half a mile
more to the seigniory than it was entitled. 2nd, that the
west side-line was unduly prolonged by Holland, and, instead
of being short, as judged by Kilburn, was the reverse. 3rd,
that Chewett had run his line on the wrong angle, and by
going too far west, had given the seigniory a breadth in
rear of 19 miles instead of 18. In addition to all this, the
three surveyors had overlooked the circumstance that the
St Lawrence took a bend from the dividing-line between
the seigniories of Chateaugay and Beauharnois, and that
the great projection of land northward, including Grande
Isle, should have been taken into account, and the southern
boundary been made to conform to it, by slanting it northward from the end of the eastern-line. The result of all
these errors was, that if the boundaries of Godmanchester
and the other townships were to be accepted as the boundaries of the seigniory, then it contained 32,000 arpents
more than the deed of the French king authorized, and
the farms of Manning, Gentle, and the 150 others east of
them were part of the surplus.

To these representations, Ellice's agents had but one answer, that the surveys placed their lands within the limits
of the seigniory, and the settlers pleaded in vain that Ellice
could claim no more land than his deed gave him, namely,

a square of 18 miles, and the gores between· the township lines and the true limits of the seigniory were simply unconceded crown lands. No error of a surveyor could increase the bounds of the seignior beyond what he had legal title to. It was in vain. The agents of the seigniory saw the catch the error in the surveys afforded, and laid claim to all the land east and north of the boundary-lines of the townships as drawn by Chewett, Holland, and Kilburn. Knowing what was brewing for them, the settlers appointed a committee to wait on Felton, the agent for the crown lands, who lived at Sherbrooke, and negotiate for the issue of patents for their lots. Mr Felton declined, saying he had no authority to interfere with lands about which there was any dispute. Hearing of the effort to obtain titles from the crown, Brown decided to proceed to extremities with the settlers, and, as a necessary preliminary to instituting actions against them, had to offer them deeds of concession. In the summer of 1828 he notified them he would visit Russeltown and to meet him and show their titles to holding the land they occupied. There was a large gathering, for over 150 families were affected. None had any deeds to show beyond the conveyances of those they had bought from, but a few had permits from Francis Winter, as agent of the seignior, authorizing them to take possession of the lands they were upon. These Brown scoffed at, and demanded that all should take deeds of concession from him. They refused, contending that their lands were outside the seigniory. He threatened them, when one of the settlers stood forward and said they wanted no law and, as a compromise, if he would accept of a copper and a quart of wheat as rent per acre, instead of the 12 coppers per acre he demanded, they would take deeds of concession. He laughed at the man and left the meeting with the assurance that the next visit they would have would be from the bailiff. Without any delay, writs were served on 13 of the settlers most prominent in resisting the seignior's claims, among them being such old residents as Andrew Gentle, Aram Moe, William Adams, and Ichabod Allen. The demand made upon them was, that they take deeds of concession from the seignior at $10 yearly rent per 100 arpents, pay up all arrears of rent, including lods et ventes, where there had been transfers, or settle for the past by paying the lump sum of $800. Unable to bear the costs of so many suits, the settlers, at a meeting held in the school-house at Moe's, agreed to abide by the decision of any one, and John Manning's was agreed upon. Money to defend the test-suit was hard to get, and in the hope of swelling their own poor contributions, an address, dated 12th January, 1829, was issued to the censitaires of the neighboring seigniories stating that the time had "arrived when the great question is to be tried, whether the seigniors are to extort what quantum of rent they please, or whether the tenant has a remedy in law to reduce and establish the amount," and asking aid for the defendants in the cases then before the court of King's bench, Montreal, which disputed the amount of seigniorial rent as well as the liability to pay it, as they were "mostly of that class whose misfortune in life it is to be poor and unable to support the defence." The response to this appeal was discouraging. On the 27th April, 1830, 11 settlers* met at the house of John Forbes and drew up a plan of levying a subscription of $8 per lot, payable in instalments, which was generally fallen in with. In the hope that the government might be induced to intervene in their favor, Manning went to Quebec, and laid the matter before the governor, Sir James Kempt, who expressed himself as averse to interfering, as being little acquainted with the affairs of the country, in which he had arrived a short time before, and this he proved by asking such a foolish question as if the settlers would not be as well to have their lands under the seignior as the crown, followed by his statement that he "understood it was a common thing for seigniors to claim beyond their limits in Canada." He closed by telling Manning that he would leave the matter to the courts, adding

* The 11 were John Manning, Aram Moe, Abraham Sampson, James Duncan, David Gordon, Daniel Parham, Nathan Pettis, Abraham Welch, Perkin Nichols, Robert Dunn and Jacob J. Manning.

that he "thought you Americans are a little troublesome"—
a gratuitous insult to a U. E. loyalist like Manning. The
case proceeded slowly, and when it came up for argument,
Duval, who appeared for the defence, simply pleaded that the
lot occupied by Manning was ungranted land and therefore
belonged to the crown. This threw the onus of proof upon
Ellice, and as his counsel could not show that he had a
title to the lot, the court in February, 1831, dismissed the
action, with costs against him. The settlers were jubilant;
if the government would not help them, they would fight
the wealthy seignior alone, and henceforth they maintained
a defensive union, each settler to pay in proportion to the
land he occupied, and Squire Manning being chosen their
agent. Fortified by this decision of the court, he again visited
Quebec, and asked the governor to grant the settlers crown
patents for their lands. No promise was given, and he had
to leave the papers for "future consideration." Subsequent
events proved that the governor was being influenced against
the settlers, for the interests of Ellice were those of several
of the most prominent citizens of Montreal, men like Peter
McGill and John Richardson, and more than one of whom
had a seat in the council. To keep up appearances in a
case where the right of the crown to 32,000 acres was at
stake, something had to be done, and the something resolved upon by the council was designed not to protect the
interests of the government but to strengthen the claim of
Mr Ellice. They ordered that Kilburn's line be retraced,
naming on the part of the crown Alexander Stevenson and
the seigniory choosing Olivier Arcand. The instructions
given by the government to the two surveyors revealed the
true intent. They were not, as the settlers supposed, when
they rejoiced on hearing of the order for the survey, instructions to examine whether Kilburn had laid down his
line in the right place, but whether the line was properly
drawn, and to replace his wooden posts with stone ones.
Nobody disputed the straightness of Kilburn's line; the contention was that, while it might be the best line ever drawn
by surveyor, it was in the wrong place; that it was laid

down over a mile south of where it ought to be, and that the correctness of his starting-point and not the straightness of his line was what ought to be looked into. Stevenson and Arcand came on in 1830, discovered the old post at the north-east corner of the seigniory, followed up Kilburn's line to the Outarde, set stone-posts at intervals, and reported that they had found Kilburn's line a straight one and had re-established it. Their proces-verbal was accepted and thus the government, in a sense, committed itself to acknowledging Kilburn's line the true boundary of the seigniory. All this was unknown to the settlers, who waited impatiently for the answer of the governor to Manning's request to grant them patents. In December they were thunderstruck to read the legal notices that Ellice was about to apply to have the unconceded lands of his seigniory converted from seigniorial tenure into free and common soccage. They saw at once that the scheme had, for one of its objects, the investing him with a title to the lands they held, which he would obtain by the regrant from the crown, taking the line of Kilburn as the southern boundary of the seigniory. Manning called a meeting of them to decide on what should be done, and was the more keenly instigated in doing so by the defection of Abraham Welch, who criticised the steps he had taken and insinuated that the funds contributed by the settlers had not been properly applied. The meeting took place in the Flats schoolhouse (Kirkfield, it was then termed) on the 1st February, 1832, which was packed to the door. The squire read a long address, in which he elaborately and ponderously described Welch as the personification among them of the spirit of evil, and himself as the pilot who had steered the ship so far successfully and was willing to again brave the storms that lay between them and the haven of rest. The meeting sustained the squire in all he had done, re-appointed him as their agent, pledged themselves to sustain him, and characterized Welch's conduct as "spiteful, malicious and persecuting." The meeting thus resulted in reconstituting the association for the renewal of the contest with the seignior. Their first act was to send a memorial to Quebec, praying to be declared possessors of the lots held by them, their second a protest against the regrant of the seigniory, as prayed for by Ellice, and asking, if their prayer were not granted, that, in any back claims he might make, he be limited to the rents authorized by the old French law, namely 2 coppers, or 1 copper and a quart of wheat, yearly, for each arpent. The government handed the documents to Ellice's agents for reply, and a controversy ensued in which the legal acumen was on one side and right and equity on the other. The case for the settlers was wordily and blunderingly presented by Manning and Jacob Dewitt, then one of the members for the county; the strongest points they made being that the decision of the court in dismissing Ellice's action against the 13 showed he had no legal title to the lands in dispute, while, it was asked, "What better title can that man have who has cleared and cultivated the land, who, with the very sweat of his brow, has fertilized and rendered it productive? It is true the settlers took possession of their lands, but they did so when they were wild and uncultivated, and it is only now, when their labors have rendered these lands valuable, that the seignior makes an attempt to wrest them away, or, at least, to impose heavy and burdensome conditions upon the retention of them." The papers were referred to a special committee of the executive council, who made their report in December 1832, which, though long, may be summed up in few words. The question was, where lay the boundary-line between the lands of the crown and those of Ellice? In the opinion of the committee, it was the line run by Kilburn, and re-established by Stevenson and Arcand, therefore as the crown cannot set up a claim to the strip of 32,000 acres in dispute, John Manning and the other settlers were still less competent. This decision was a severe blow to the settlers, but in no way shook their resolve to fight for their rights to the bitter end. All opposition being quashed, the proceedings to extinguish the feudal tenure of the seigniory were hurried. John Davidson of Dundee was named by the crown to value with the Hon. Mr Bell the unconceded lands, and, in doing so, they deducted as valueless 8000 acres of Teafield, 10,000 acres of Blueberry rock, and 5000 acres devastated by the fire in 1825, and which afterwards (Tullochgorum was comprised in the section) proved to be the best land in the seigniory and sold by it for a high price. The remaining 95,000 acres of unconceded land they estimated at 60 cents an acre, and the fine of 3 cents, being one-twentieth, was tendered and accepted by the government, which, in May, 1833, issued a proclamation declaring the unconceded lands of the seigniory to be held by Ellice in free and common soccage. And thus, for the sum of $2765, Mr Ellice became absolute owner of over one-hundred-thousand acres of land. The prospect now was black indeed for the settlers; the government had not only refused to come to their assistance, but had cut away their main defence; their opponent was one of the wealthiest and most influential merchants of his day. For 20 years and over they had labored to make homes for themselves, and now, apparently, their properties were to be at the disposal of a seignior, and they were to be treated as trespassers on the lands they had redeemed from the forest. All the spirit of independence and sense of right which characterizes backwoodsmen revolted at the thought, and they resolved to lose all rather than be defrauded. Their resentment was not so much towards Ellice, whom they believed to know nothing of the merits of the case, as against his agents, more particularly Brown, whose rapacity and duplicity had long made his name a byword in the district, while his lewdness disgusted decent people. His taking advantage of Kilburn's error in running the Russeltown boundary was regarded by the settlers solely as a scheme to obtain money to maintain him in the extravagant and shameless mode of life he maintained at Beauharnois.

The year the tenure of the seigniory was changed, Mr Ellice visited Canada. The first Sunday after his arrival at Beauharnois he went to the door of the Catholic church, and, with Peter McGill standing by his side, announced, as the congregation came out, that he would be at Reeves's tavern on a certain day to hear any complaints his censitaires might have. There was a large gathering, and he was overwhelmed

with astonishment at the number and variety of the grievances
of the people, and finally grew irritated and angry. Brown
kept many back from speaking by fair promises, but enough
came out to show Ellice how the people had been wronged.
When old Mr Elliot of English river stated the grievance of
the settlers with regard to the mouture, the answer, that he
had not received a penny from the revenues of the seigniory,
that he had been even drawn upon for $2000 to pay for the
Norton creek mill, silenced his astonished hearers, for it is
hard to complain to a landlord whose property is a source
of loss to him. They knew that, between lumber and rents,
a large sum was paid yearly at Beauharnois, and their indignation was subdued with pity for the London magnate who
was being bled by his servants. Mr Ellice impressed the
settlers as anxious to do what was just and he made many
promises, which, as he left Brown to perform them, were
not fulfilled. Touching the question of the Russeltown lands,
he declined to interfere, letting it remain with his lawyers.
After a brief stay, he departed, leaving behind him an agent,
named Bull, professedly to assist in the seigniory office, but
in reality as a check on Brown.

Negotiations were re-opened with the settlers, and in July,
1836, the seignior made a written offer to give clear deeds for
$4 per acre for lots marked by their surveyor "superior," $3 for
lots marked "middling," and $2 for "inferior," one-fifth of the
price down and the remainder as agreed upon, with interest.
The offer was to remain open until the end of the year, and
all who did not accept were to be prosecuted for unlawful
possession. None accepted the proferred terms, and in 1837
fresh actions were taken out against a number. By consent,
those against Squire Manning and Jeremiah Dunn were
selected as test-suits. Before they were called in court, a
change took place which caused indefinite delay. The summer of 1838 young Ellice arrived in Canada and happening
to be at Beauharnois on the outbreak of the rebellion, was
so disgusted by his arrest and treatment while a prisoner,
that he returned to England determined to get quit of the
seigniory, and the following year he succeeded in inducing

Mr Scott, a London banker, to purchase it, and who appointed Lewis Lyman of Montreal his agent. Owing to severe losses in his business, Mr Scott was unable to retain the seigniory, whereupon he organized a company, the London Land company, to take it over for $750,000, of which $150,000 was paid to Ellice, who was elected a director. Edward Colville, of a noble Scotch house, a lad of 23 and fresh from college, was sent out to manage for the company. Brown, who had been retained by Ellice to look after his interests until the whole of the purchase-money was paid, soon threw his wiles around the lad and led him into excesses which destroyed his usefulness. This was his associate's object, for, above all things, he desired to see the former régime restored with himself in his old position. The change of proprietorship caused a stay in the proceedings until 1844, when they were resumed in a desultory manner, which was particularly harassing to the farmers, who ardently desired the question settled, and well they might, for so long as their right to their lots was disputed they did not care about improving them, and shuffled along, from year to year, as they best could. The settlement was almost at a standstill, and the young people, who, under other circumstances, would have spread over the adjacent country and formed strong English-settlements in Edwardstown and along the Black river (now occupied by the French), left for Ontario and the United States. About 1835 a craze prevailed regarding the Bay of Quinte, and there was a large emigration to that fine district. Roads and water-discharges were neglected, and whenever any improvement was mooted the cry was, What use to work for the benefit of the seignior? As they would get no compensation for their betterments, should the cases go against them, the old log-shanties and the meagre clearings were enough for them to lose. The uncertainty as to title affected their credit. Storekeepers did not like to trust them too far, and as they could not give mortgages, they were at the mercy of the money-lenders. To their honor be it said, the settlers took no advantage of their situation, and all obligations on their

lands were paid. The stagnant appearance of the settlement was no reflex of the minds of its inhabitants, which
were kept awake by never-ceasing anxiety. Hopes of an
early decision of their suits were born to be blasted, and
rumors excited them but to die away and be succeeded by
others as unsubstantial. There were spies in their midst
and wires were pulled to cause divisions and bickerings
among them, but these maneuvers of Brown were futile,
beyond exasperating public feeling. The Land Association,
as they called their union, stood intact, and when Fisher
Ames moved into Franklin it gained an unwearied and
fertile-minded secretary. The weak point in the case of the
seignior, that he could not prove his right to more than the
254,016 arpents granted by the French king, was perceived
by Ames, and he perseveringly pressed the government to
order a survey of it, and here it is to be noted that, after
the union, the government ceased to be the obliging friend
of Ellice and refused all assistance to defeat the farmers.
The persistent efforts of the settlers to obtain a decision on
their cases were baffled by the lawyers for the seigniory,
who entered demurrers and made motions with no other
end than to weary the defendants and impoverish them by
the costs, for which frequent assessments had to be imposed.
New actions were constantly being taken out, with no other
view, of course, than to frighten the weak into yielding and
to annoy resolute opponents, for one case would settle the
merits at stake as well as fifty. The settlers retorted by
taking steps to dispute the title of the seignior to much of
the land that had been heretofore considered as his beyond
dispute. William Barrett and William Lalanne were employed to make a survey of the seigniory. The work was
one of danger and difficulty. Mr Nicolson of the seigniory-
office was deputed to prevent the survey being made, and,
sustained by a strong posse, he vigorously hunted the two
engineers. Ordered by the seigniory-office, the habitants
along the river forbade them to put a foot on their farms.
Foreseeing this trouble, the winter had been chosen to do
the work, and the surveyors scanned the shore from the

ice. Where the current was rapid this was dangerous, and, on one occasion, the spot where they had levelled their instruments was open water next day. The chief difficulty was providing shelter for the party at night, and this was undertaken by Joseph Towns and William Wilson, who succeeded in securing board and lodging. Creeping along the ice that edged the bank, even where the rapids foamed and roared, the surveyors fulfilled their task, and when January, 1847, closed, they had obtained a correct outline of the river-front of the seigniory. The running of the sidelines was easy, and when they completed their calculations, they demonstrated with mathematical precision that the seigniory contained 32,503 arpents over the 254,016 secured by the French king's deed. They petitioned the government to order a new survey of the seigniory and to reinvest in the crown whatever surplusage of land might be found. The lawyers of the seignior pleaded French law and custom as to defining boundaries, and insisted that Kilburn's line, re-established by Stevenson and Arcand, was final as to the southern limit of the seigniory and that the letters-patent issued in reconveying the seigniory in free and common soccage confirmed the title to all other lands in dispute. This latter contention would have been unanswerable had the letters-patent described the extent and limits of the seigniory, which it did not, merely naming its divisions, as Jamestown, Russeltown, and Edwardstown, without defining their boundaries.

The year 1851 had not passed many days when Colonel Brown suddenly died, and thus an obstacle to a settlement of the wearisome dispute was removed. There were other circumstances favorable to such a result. The company which bought the seigniory had been obliged to relinquish it, for owing to Colville's mismanagement the receipts had barely sufficed for the expenditure, and they arranged with Ellice to take the property off their hands, he to retain the payment of $150,000. James Keith was appointed successor to Brown and he applied himself to bringing the dispute with the settlers to a bearing. John Rose, now Sir John

Rose of London, then an advocate in Montreal, was entrusted with the case, and as the government of the day was amenable to the influence he could bring to bear, an advantage was gained upon the settlers they had long dreaded. What successive governments had refused, namely, to give the use of the name of the crown in the actions carried on against them, the Morin administration agreed to, and Mr Rose was informed that all pleadings against the settlers could be made in the name of her majesty, provided a bond was furnished to save the crown from costs. Actions were taken out against 17 settlers and the request to select one of them as a test-case was peremptorily refused. The settlers saw the ground of their defence thus cut away, for it would be preposterous to contend that the crown owned their farms when the crown prosecuted them to surrender them to Edward Ellice. There is no more shameful instance in Canadian history of the government lending its powers to a private individual to further his selfish ends. It was in the hope that, some day, the government would vindicate their cause, that the backwoodsmen, who had spent their lives in giving value to the property sought to be wrested from them, had cheered themselves through the long struggle, and now, instead of that, the government had sided with their enemy. Nelson Manning, who had taken his uncle's place on his becoming incapacitated by age, went to Montreal to consult with Mr Cherrier, then at the head of the bar. He advised a settlement on the basis of what they would have to pay the crown for the land if they won the suit. On the lawyer for the association, Andrew Robertson, stating he coincided with the advice, a compromise with the seignior began to be entertained, and negotiations were instituted. They dragged over a year, and until 1853, when a personal conference was arranged to take place between the committee of the settlers and Mr Keith at Mrs Young's hotel, Franklin Centre, on the understanding that if no agreement was reached, what was said on either side should not be used as evidence in court. On the meeting taking place, Frederick Broder began by asking Mr Keith if it was like a gentleman to be disturbing loyal men in their holdings. Keith rose to leave the room, saying if such talk was to be tolerated the meeting could have no good result. He was persuaded to remain and the business for which they met taken up. The committee frankly stated that if they won the suits, and their farms declared to be crown lands, they would have to pay the government 75 cents per acre. If the seignior would agree to take that and give them a clear acquittance, they were ready to pay him. Mr Keith demurred. That the seignior would win the cases, he declared himself satisfied, and the settlers would have to pay the $6 per acre he was selling other wild lands at, with damages in addition, but he was willing to take much less to amicably settle a dispute that had now lasted over 25 years. Finally it was arranged to pay a dollar per acre. To come to an understanding about who should pay the law costs of the seignior was more difficult, for Keith insisted that the settlers should pay them all. When asked what they amounted to, he could not tell, but roughly estimated them at $2000. Finally, he said he would agree to the seignior paying $200 of the amount, whatever it might be. The conference was suspended to allow of the committee consulting with the farmers in attendance outside. Nelson Manning pointed out that if the bill of costs was left to the lawyers, there was no telling how large a sum they would have to pay. He suggested that they offer a lump sum and then they would know where they were. To Mr Keith he pointed out, that whereas $1000 was a small sum to Mr Ellice it was a serious one to the farmers, and that as they were yielding so much in acknowledging his title to their lands, he might make a financial concession. His words had their weight with both sides, and on the committee tendering $800, Mr Keith accepted, and the conference ended. It was subsequently ascertained that the seignior's taxed costs were $3000 and the association's $1600. In apportioning how the dollar per acre should be raised, the settlers agreed that all who had held lots over 30 years should pay 60 cents per acre, those who had held lots for a less period 80 cents per acre if on the high land and $1.40 on the flats, making the average of one dollar an acre all over. The costs, including the $800 to be paid to the seignior, amounted to $2,400, and they were assessed on each lot. A few of the members of the association dishonorably refused to pay their share of the costs, which had to be made up by the others.

And thus ended the most famous lawsuit the province has known; famous on account of the parties to it, a body of poor backwoodsmen against a wealthy London merchant and prominent English politician, and famous from the stake at issue—the homes of 200 families and the right of ownership to 32,500 acres. Neither side could claim victory. Ellice got a portion of the money he sought; the backwoodsmen vindicated their claim that their land was not seigniorial, which the government soon after acknowledged by including the larger portion of it into the reconstituted county of Huntingdon and still later into the township of Franklin. The removal of the incubus of the lawsuit wrought a wonderful change. Once more assured that the lands they cultivated were their own, the farmers set about improving them with spirit. The neglected aspect of the country disappeared and in 5 years more progress was made than in the 26 during which the renowned contest had lasted. One settler, James Lamb, a Scotchman, alone refused to enter into the agreement, and retained Andrew Robertson to defend him. The case was carried to England. He won, but he lost his farm, which went to pay his costs.

CHAPTER XXIII.

Of the country that spreads in wide extended flats at the foot of Covey hill, I will endeavor to give a consecutive history from its first settlement. The stony ridges and gravelly slopes, which form the base of Covey hill, spring abruptly from a plain of fertile soil, watered by the Black and English rivers, Norton creek and several brooks. When the first-comers gazed down on this plain, they named it "the flats," and that title has adhered to the north-western portion of it. When the great inland-sea, that stretched from the Adirondacks to the Laurentians, receded, and when Covey hill reared its head as an island in its icy waters, it left a thick deposit of alluvial soil around its base, with a number of small streams trickling through it. On these flats sprung up a heavy growth of black-ash and elm, which the New Englanders, forced to leave their own sterile valleys in search of new homes, were not long in discovering. When the first of these pioneers set up his shanty on the banks of Allen brook or of the English river is not known, but it is doubtful if it was before the beginning of the century. The only authentic record of these first-comers is contained in the narrative of the son of one of them, Willis C. Roberts:

My father, Benjamin, was of English descent, and lived at Deerfield, N.H. He sided with Britain in the revolutionary war, and, so soon after the peace as he could do so, he moved into Canada, and took up land in Stanstead. What caused him to leave there I do not know, but in 1811 he moved westward and squatted on lot 16, 5th range. There were other settlers before him, very few, however, and I cannot give all their names. Humphrey Brayton was among them, and his shanty was on 205. My father did not like his location, for, owing to the brook being filled with driftwood, it was liable to sudden floods, and one spring his shanty was surrounded with water for quite a while. I was born in Sept. 1813, and my mother being very ill a neighbor walked to Laprairie, which was the place where the nearest doctor lived. On the following New Year's day my parents were invited to a merry-making at Sweet's (p. 22). My mother, of course, took me, but left my two little sisters behind, getting a son of Brayton's to remain in charge. About midnight the lad was awakened by a crackling sound, and saw the rafters overhead on fire. Snatching up the youngest child he rushed out, and driving the pigs from their pen, laid her in their nest, and returning brought out the other girl, being burned by a falling coal in doing so. Neither of my sisters was clad and the brave boy was barefoot. Everything was consumed. We spent the winter in Sweet's house, and in the spring my father rented David Stockwell's farm, lot 9, 4th range, and he prepared a new place for himself beside it. Stockwell was a blacksmith, and for many years the only one in this section. My father was the first to take up land between him and the flats, but he soon had neighbors, for Robert Hunkins squatted on 173 and Daniel Gordon on the opposite side of the road in 1818. In that year the settlers along the track, for it was not a road, that led to Franklin, were as follows: East of St Remi, the settlers were French; where the village is now, lived Dewey, Struthers and Robt. Dunn, and west of them the woods were unbroken until Beechridge was reached, where a Dutch American, Hope, had built his shanty. The settlers on the flats in passing homewards, picked up the shell limestone that abounded on his lot, and burned them in their log-heaps to secure the lime necessary for the lye-leaches. Why the Beechridge got its name is hard to say, as spruce was the predominant tree. Leaving Hope's clearance, the woods closed in again and continued until the Norton creek appeared, and on its banks were several houses. First were two of the Nortons, and James Brock, whose shanty stood where Thomas Cantwell afterwards built. On the west side, where the gristmill stands, was a Dutchman, Burgot, who afterwards put up a large blockhouse and lived a long while. In the fall of 1813 two sons of his were working in the bush when they heard the roll of musketry to the north of them, and realized that an engagement was going on, for they had not heard that Hampton had crossed. Hurrying to the house, they snatched up their rifles and pushed across the country to the Chateaugay, reporting themselves at the British headquarters before sunset, when the officer, glancing at the stalwart frames of the loyal backwoodsmen said: "I am glad to see you, but the job is done,"—the Americans having fallen back. The next houses to that of Burgot were those of Proper and Mosher, the latter an American deserter, Walker, and another of the Nortons. Now came an unbroken stretch of forest, 3 miles long, for, until 1820, there was not a clearance in or near the site of the village of Chrysostom. As the track turned southwards to the flats, three Canadian families were met, Sylvia, who came in 1815, Richard, and Percheron. On the north side of the English river were Levi Grimshaw, who came, accompanied by Petty, from New England in 1812. Petty on 205, and Goodwin on 16. Brace was on 15, and raised a large frame building still standing (1887) and which he sold to Samuel Brisbin, when he moved down from the hill. The next shanty was that of an Old Countryman, John Wilson, an Irish Protestant, who came in 1818. He put it up on a spot that faces the existing church door, but failing to get water, built another on the west side of the road. His neighbor to the west of him was James Allen, who, probably as early as 1815, erected a small gristmill, with a single run of stones, on the brook which bears his name. Next to him was Wm. Campbell, a Scotch shoemaker, who came in 1818 with his brother Hugh, and who had beside them, on lot 206, a singular character, Zebulon Huntington, a shaking Quaker, who had been a farmer of some consequence in Vermont. On leaving he invested the proceeds of his real estate in livestock and drove them before him into the Canadian wilderness. He cut some hay for them on the beaver-meadows along the brook, but seldom fed it, preferring to winter his beasts on browse. Each morning in winter he started out with his axe over his shoulder, followed by his drove of cattle, and felled trees for them. Sometimes he killed one, by a tree accidentally falling as they pressed around him. You may think it poor feed, but the truth is, the tips of the maple and basswood are very nourishing and so well relished that cows will leave hay for browse. I have known the wives of settlers go to a tree when felled and break off the branch points, which crack off easily in frosty weather, to feed their cows. In course of time Huntington cleared, to secure browse, the side of the hill on lots 128 and 9. He had also a large flock of sheep, and at times was troubled by wolves. When he suspected a pack of them being near, he sounded a conch-shell he had, and we would hear it sound until after midnight. Huntington was useful as a source of supplying the settlement with oxen and cows. He was of a peculiar nature, seldom speaking, and passing neighbors without notice, and was currently believed by them to dance naked round the trees, "whipping the devil round a stump." He had a fine family of daughters; his only son was killed by a cyclone in the West. One day he brought home a few yards of calico which his wife had asked him to get, and, on coming in from the stable, and finding her tearing it into strips, he got into a rage at what he considered her wanton destructiveness of property, and never after spoke to her. She was shredding the calico to make a quilt. He had a most wonderful memory, and could repeat what he read or heard without mistake. He moved to Ohio, where he died. West of the lot of this strange man, whose name is perpetuated in that of the brook that waters the western end of the flats, lived John, Charles, and Alanson Allen. With the few exceptions named, all the settlers were Americans, and a light-hearted, improvident class of New Englanders they were. The outbreak of war caused, in the majority of them, no apprehension sufficient to drive them away, and the few who did leave, returned, though none entered the British service save my oldest brother, who enlisted in the Invincibles, and fell at Chrystler's farm. Either not hearing or unheeding the bugle when it sounded to retire, he remained and fell pierced with many bullets. The slash of timber made east of Chrysostom (page 63) named the American blockade, gave the settlers no small trouble, as they were refused passage with their teams, and would have been shut out from their only market but for Abram Welch, who had got authority to pass the lines. Welch was a singular being, well-educated and of great natural ability, but a notorious swearer, and so wild in manners that children were terrified of him. He came from the state of Maine and had imbibed in his youth free-thinking notions and confused the simple-minded by arguments from Paine, delighting to shock the religious. One Sunday, while the Methodists were flocking past his house to a quarterly meeting, he hammered with all his energy on the roof of a new building he was erecting. His speech was the worst of him, however, for he was honest and abstemious, and freely lent his aid in surveying land, at which he was surprisingly accurate, and in building. He settled first on 14 and 15 and then moved west to 136. During the war he acted as a secret agent for the government, for though an American he was loyal to Britain, and rendered valuable service to the settlers in taking loads of potash to Laprairie and returning with much-needed provisions, for the clearances then made were insufficient to sustain them.

The magnificent cut of timber that surrounded their shanties appeared to those American squatters to be a source of inexhaustible wealth, and potash-making was their constant avocation. Bees were of almost daily occurrence, for as soon as one had a sufficient quantity of timber chopped, he called in his neighbors to log and burn, when there was a jollification, but nothing to that when the barrel was filled, hauled to Laprairie, and the proceeds brought back in the form of provisions and a replenished keg. It was working in the woods by day, and fiddling and dancing at night. Had they gone soberly to work, and cleared the land for cultivation, they would have become comfortable, instead of leading a careless life with only the potash-kettle between them and starvation. Patches of corn, wheat, and potatoes were raised on the knolls, but what they grew was insufficient, and the bulk of the provisions was brought from Montreal. Of the difficulties of the journey thither it is impossible to now form any conception. There were no bridges save a floating one across the La Tortue, and long stretches of swampy land had to be traversed. With an auger and axe to replace the runners as they wore out, the settler started with his barrel for Laprairie and often a week passed before his return. A fair day's journey for a yoke of oxen was 16 miles, and 20 was counted good. Horses were useless, for, owing to their stepping quickly, they smashed sled or cart against the succession of obstructions. If the ground was dry, causing the sled to rub hard, and he did not intend to bring a return load, the barrel was laid on a sort of cradle, cut from a large log, which was left behind at Laprairie, and the oxen returned light. The bush in those days differed from the present, in being so free of underbrush that in an hour's travel the axe would not have to be used once. Winding out and in between the forest monarchs, the settlers drove their ox-sleds in every direction, as fearless of losing themselves as the Arab in his native deserts.

The first impulse to the prosperity of the settlement came in 1820, when an American, James Duncan, quietly threw a dam across the English river at St Chrysostom, and raised the frame of a sawmill. He knew he was breaking the law, that it was illegal to build a mill in the seigniories without the consent of the seignior, but he relied on a decision lately given, that where a seignior neglected to build a mill where required, or when a mill was in running-order when he became cognizant of it, he could not compel the owner to remove it. Duncan acted in concert with James Allen, and as soon as the frame of the building was ready, Allen floated down upon a raft the machinery of a small sawmill he had failed to work from want of water. Long before word reached Beauharnois, the mill was going and had cut boards to enclose itself. The agent, Richardson, was furious and threatened all manner of penalties, but Duncan defied him. According to law Duncan could not renew or rebuild the mill after notification by the seignior, but this difficulty he got over by quietly replacing each .timber as it showed signs of decay, which he did without difficulty, being an excellent mechanic. For over a quarter of a century the mill was a thorn in the side of the seigniory people, not only because it absorbed profits they elsewhere monopolised but because it sawed the timber which the settlers plundered off the ungranted lots. Up to this time the settlers had roofed their shanties with elm bark and floored them with split basswood, but now they got boards, and entered into the profitable business of rafting sawed lumber to Montreal. For a long while Duncan was the only resident of Chrysostom, and did a large business. He did not confine himself to the lumber-trade, for he erected an ashery and built a canoe large enough to carry down to Reeves's 7 barrels at a time. The existing gristmill is on his mill-site and Mr Boyd's residence stands where his shanty did. About 1828, an American shoemaker, Ichabod Munsill, set up beside Duncan, and on the south side of the road, where Robert Stewart now is, an Englishman, John Parnby, opened a blacksmith shop. There was no appearance, however, of a village until after 1840. On the double concession the first Old Countryman to take up land was John Severs, who had been a butcher in Hull, England, and lived, on coming to Canada, for some time at La Tortue before moving to Edwardstown, which he did about 1820, opening a tavern and store as the needs of the country required them and being the means of bringing many immigrants in, until the lots between the English river and Norton creek were, with few exceptions, occupied by English and Irish families. Among the first of the latter, was that of Andrew Currie and of the former Geo. Toynton, whose grave is near the Episcopal church. William Creasor, with his sons Philip, William, and John, all stout Yorkshiremen, were prominent settlers. In 1828 the population was sufficiently large to justify the erecting of a school, when Capt. Severs gave the land for it, specifying in the deed that part was to be used as a burying-place and that the schoolhouse was to be open for the preaching of the gospel by any Protestant minister. Robert Hope was teacher and had 36 scholars during 1829. A large and prosperous school was maintained during the week, with service on Sundays, conducted by Methodist, Presbyterian, and Episcopalian clergymen for over a score of years, when, owing to the English-speaking ratepayers having become outnumbered by the incoming French, the school was appropriated by the Catholic commissioners, who, despite the stipulation of the granter of the land, refused the use of it for worship, and now (1887) are taking steps to compel the Protestants to pay their rates towards its support, although, from the sectarian character of the tuition imparted, they cannot send their children to it.

The stream of immigrants, once directed into Edwardstown, naturally spread wherever there were vacant lands open for settlement, and thus all the concessions north of that I have been describing were filled. The first to seek a home on the English river, south of the Norton creek, was Malcolm Ross, from Lochalsh, Invernessshire, who raised his shanty on the river-bank on lot 8, in the fall of 1821, and one of whose sons is now a great railway contractor. The following year, James Hamilton, who had kept a grocer's shop in Glasgow, took up 10, 11, and 12, intending the two extra lots as farms for his boys, John and James. He placed his shanty by the river, but was so troubled by freshets that he removed to the ridge that skirts the stream some distance back. The presence of Ross induced several Highlanders to come beside him, among whom was James McDonald, who could not stand the hardships of the bush, and being consumptive sickened and died under his roof. The young mountaineer was buried on the clearance and a railing set around his grave. The present owners (Morris brothers) have plowed over it. On 3 was Sandy Taylor, who found help to make a living by fishing out oak from the river, for in those days its bed was strewn with the wreck of rafts. The flats along the upper waters of the English river were dotted with giant oaks, fellows that yielded logs 3 feet square, and from 30 to 40 long, which took 3 yoke of oxen to drag, and so heavy that rafts of cedar often failed to float them out of shallow water. On 9 was Colin McCrae and Daniel McIntosh held 18. Josiah Black says :-

My father owned a printfield at Partick and we sailed from the Clyde in 1827. In Montreal my father fell in with a shoemaker, Gardner, who had a lot for sale on the English river, one of those that had belonged to Hamilton, and which they had found necessary to sell. We went to Lachine in a boat towed by horses, and a bateau was hired to take us to the Basin, where we were landed at Smith's tavern. Carters were hired to take our baggage and my father and the rest of the family went with them, while we boys set off in carts up the Chateaugay with a friend, White, a sea captain. We landed at Bryson's, Allan's corners, and stayed overnight. Having got directions how to go, we walked down the river and crossed at Ogilvie's, and found a fair track to the English river, which we crossed on a dam at Howick, which had just been finished. We followed a footpad along the river, and the captain halted at every house to ask for bread and milk for us boys, for we had become ravenous, but not one could spare a morsel. It was what the settlers called "the hungry month" (August) and they had not enough for themselves. The captain, who got an occasional glass of grog at the shanties, cheered us with the assurance we would get plenty when we reached Hamilton's, but when we did, we found they were like the rest, and were out of bread. Father with the supplies had not arrived, and the captain took Hamilton's advice, although it was now evening, to strike across to Severs's, which we reached at dark, and the bread and milk Mrs Severs

THE NORTON CREEK CONCESSIONS.

hurriedly got us, was the sweetest meal I ever sat down to. The carts had great difficulty in getting along, part coming by the Beechridge, but finally reached Duncan's. They had begun to cut a road from his mill down along the river, but it was barely passable. Duncan yoked his oxen to a sled, and the men taking axes to chop out any obstructions, they got our effects to the shanty Gardner told us was on the lot. We found it had been used for leaching ashes, and was in a great mess. Sunday as it was, we had to set to work, and got it cleaned out, made fit to live in, and slept there that night. Lumbering and potash were the mainhold of the settlers until the land was cleared.

It was somewhat remarkable, that the people south of Norton creek had little intercourse with those north of it, which was due to that stream being, so to speak, the watershed of two distinct modes of communication with Montreal. Those north of the creek found an outlet by Beauharnois and the Basin; those south of it, by St Remi and Laprairie, and their material interests therefore lay in with the settlements on the flats, Covey hill and Hemingford. How little communication there was between the lower and the upper settlements on the English river is shown by the fact that the road from Howick to St Chrysostom was not continuous until 1832, when the seignior gave James Houston the contract for cutting out the portions that were untouched. The two concessions divided by Norton creek were settled between 1826 and 1830. The timber that covered them was mixed with a number of pine-roots left by the lumbermen, of whom McGillis was chief, and which gave the settlers much trouble to get rid of. There being so little bush fit for making potash, the settlers worked out a great deal, going to Montreal and wherever public works were in progress to earn a little until they had clearances large enough to support them. The south concession was largely occupied by Irish Catholics, and their presence was the cause of inducing others to come in and take up the land to the south and east. Archd. Craig, who bought 96, north concession, from Allan Caldwell in 1826, was a Paisley silk-weaver, but, despite his calling, proved to be a successful settler, being the first to get a yoke of oxen. He set up a loom and, with Samuel

McClymont, did the work of the neighborhood. On 119 William Gray opened a tannery in 1843, which did a fair business. Aubrey had no existence until a late date, the point on which it is now built remaining covered with trees. In 1852 Andrew Orr bought 500 acres from the seignior on the west side of the English river with the water-privilege and built a sawmill that fall. The work it gave attracted French Canadians and a small village sprang into existence. In 1849 the seignior offered for sale the lands on the west side of the English river, south of Aubrey, and the lots were chiefly bought by French Canadians at $6 an acre.

Returning to the Russeltown flats settlement a few points in its progress may be noted. At the close of the war James Allen placed a gristmill of primitive construction on the brook which bears his name. The gearing being all of wood it soon wore out, when he brought, in 1820, from Napierville John Parnby (p. 464) to renew it in a more substantial manner. When seigniorial rights were more sharply enforced, Allen, after persistent threats of lawsuits, moved the machinery to Rockburn in 1829, as has been narrated, the more moved to do so, as, from the Allen brook beginning to fail, the mill was frequently stopped during summer. In 1822 a great boon was bestowed on the settlement by an enterprising American firm, Keyes & Hotchkiss, who hired John Wilson to clear for them half an acre on lot 205, and proceeded to build a store thereon. They dealt largely in potash and lumbered heavily, giving much work and facilitating the supply of groceries and provisions. The ashes they shipped to Laprairie in rude carts drawn by 2 or 3 yoke of oxen, according to the state of the roads. The development of the lumber-trade gave a much-needed stimulus, securing employment to the settlers during the dull season of the year and circulating money that would never have come otherwise. Keyes & Hotchkiss soon had a competitor in another American, John Forbes, who built a store near where the Presbyterian church stands. Each spring he sent down the English river an immense number of logs, but made little by it. In the fall of 1831 he sold out to two brothers, James and

Wm. Cochrane, who had newly arrived from Lanark, Scotland. They had considerable money but little knowledge of business, especially of business in a new country. They were made the dupes of all the rogues in the vicinity, gave credit to men who never intended to pay, bought what they had no need for, and kept a large staff of idle men. They opened a branch-store in castle clouts, Huntingdon, which received no more attention than their business at Russeltown. The crash came in the spring of 1833, when the Montreal creditors took possession of the assets. The young men sailed for Scotland, which they never reached, the ship being wrecked on the way.

Of far greater benefit to the settlement than the coming in of business men and the development of the lumber-trade, was the construction of a leading-road. Up to 1832 the road from St Remi to Stacy's corners was simply the track beaten out by ox-sleds. In 1831 the legislature granted $2400 to turnpike it, and Squire Manning, Robert Dunn, and John Forbes were named commissioners to expend the amount. The first difficulty to be met was the line to be followed. Grand-voyer de Lery visited the county and held a meeting in Craik's store of those interested. It was represented that although the road, in great part, angled across the lots, yet it kept the best ground for a dry, hard road, and to remove it would cause inconvenience to those who had built along the track. The grand-voyer agreed and prepared a proces-verbal, directing that the new road should follow the existing track, his deputies to straighten any crooks where advisable. As to the short bit of road from Stacy's corners to the lines there was more trouble. The people wanted it to go between lots 48 and 49 ; the owner of the land, Aaron Priest, demanded that it follow the township-line. The grand-voyer acceded to the request of the people and Priest appealed against his proces-verbal. Meanwhile the work on the main-road was begun. The deputies who staked it out straightened the crooks by taking sights from one prominent shanty to another, which accounts for the road from Stacy's to Stockwell being a succession of angles. From there to the flats, the cld track was abandoned, and the road placed on the dividing-line between Russeltown and Huntingdon. The work on the flats was heavy, logs having to be hauled to cross-way the swampy portions, which were numerous. Under the sweeping provisions of the proces-verbal, the owners of lots at a distance on either side were brought in, and the road-officers used their powers in an arbitrary manner. One of them, Lewis Norton, so exasperated the settlers, that they rode him on a rail. So much of the money went in paying officials and buying tools, so heavy and clumsy as to be of slight use, that little was left to pay the farmers, who received only $2.50 per lot. It shows the cheapness of labor in those days, that David Manning took a contract of 110 rods of new road for $1.45 per rod. On Priest losing his appeal, the road was completed, and in 1835 the commissioners reported that it was open from the province-line to St Remi. This was not all, however. A grant of $1200 had been given to form a road from Stacy's corners to Huntingdon, of which Squire Manning was named superintendent. The same course was adopted as with the other road, the existing track being adopted, which caused it to angle across the lots from Black's church to near Athelstan. It was completed in the fall of 1832, the average sum paid each farmer for making the road across his lot being 25 cents a rod. In his report, the squire states that, when he began, the road was impassable for a loaded waggon from Huntingdon to Rockburn; when he finished, one could drive the whole way. If such was the case, it did not last long, for during the next ten years it was not uncommon for waggons to be so firmly imbedded in the mud-holes by the Chateaugay, that the horses had to be unhitched and leave them for the time being.

The year that a grant was made to open the road, a mail was established, leaving Montreal weekly for Squire Manning's house, by way of Laprairie and St Remi. The first carrier, Harty, died, and on the failure of the storekeeper, Fassett, who had taken over the contract, it was given to Hiram Gentle, at $160 a year, who held it until 1837. He left Manning's in the morning, and called at the several

offices on the route—John Forbes on the flats; Thomas Cantwell, Norton creek; and St Remi—reaching Laprairie in the
evening. The following morning, he started homewards.
The journey was made at first on horseback, but on the
completion of the new road Mr Gentle used a wagon, and
carried passengers, the fare to Laprairie being $1. The bag
was a light one, and contained only three newspapers—the
Vindicator for Reid at Norton creek, and the Herald for,
Jacob and Squire Manning.

The saying about New Englanders, that the church and
the school appeared without delay on the hill-top of every
valley they entered, is not substantiated by their record in
this district, for in all their settlements they were careless
alike about religion and education. The Russeltown colony
was no exception; so heedless, indeed, about Sunday that
they often lost count of the days of the week, and, in making
engagements, spoke of "the day after to-morrow" and the
like. Brayton was a close communion Baptist, professed
to be a religious man, and, occasionally, held services. He
was of a singularly lymphatic temperament, so much so that
in praying he sometimes dropped asleep, and during his prosy
exhortations shared the slumbers of his hearers. A Baptist
minister, Elder Smith, straggled into the settlement from the
States and stayed about a year. He was so given to drink,
that he often preached with a handkerchief bound round his
forehead to ease the headache of a late debauch. The first
graveyard was formed opposite where the Presbyterian manse
now is, and there the settlers buried until about 1820, when
they abandoned it, owing to graves being so hard to dig, for
a new spot on 205, where the soil is sandy. The first to be
buried there was Fanny, a daughter of James Allen, and this
spot was used until the church was built. Both these old
graveyards are now plowed-land, and the sole trace they will
furnish in future years will be the upturning of bones. The
first school was opened in a disused shanty on the Stafford
place in the winter of 1819, and had for teacher Aikins, an
American, of worthless character. An effort was made to
secure a permanent school, and one was built on the north

side of the road on lot 11, 5th range, the spot still being
marked by two apple-trees, and to which the children went
for miles around. The master, Alexander, was a deserter
from the U. S. army, and an excellent teacher. On Goodwin
settling on 169, about 1830, a schoolhouse was built on the
west side of his lot, and used by Methodists and Episcopalians
for service on Sundays, and it became the custom to bury in
rear of it. All trace of this burial-place, which lies near the
western fence of the enclosure of the show-ground, is ob-
literated. The use of schoolhouses for worship was now to
be superseded through the efforts of a woman. The wife
of John Forbes was full of energy and fertile in resources.
Soon after coming to the flats she began to agitate the building of a church, and the work was undertaken. She begged
for it on both sides of the lines. Money there was none, so
she took the subscriptions in cheese, grain, lumber, and the
like. She also purchased cloth and set the girls to making it
into articles of wear, which she sold, and collars and breast-
fronts (then called dickeys) became common. Providing a
framer, the settlers turned out and raised the building, all
the outside work of which was done by bees. The building
was raised in 1826 but not finished for some years afterwards.
It was to be used by the Methodists and Congregationalists,
and a minister of the latter denomination, an Englishman, the
Rev James Noll, was secured about 1830, part of his salary
being paid by the Canada Education and Home Missionary
Society. He remained until 1836. During the incumbency
of the Rev J. Bowles a deed was secured for the property,
and he was entrusted with its registration. On his death
by drowning (page 231) all trace of the document was lost,
and the church remained vested in Mrs Forbes, who in 1853
transferred her rights to the Church of Scotland in Canada
on condition that they added a steeple to the building and
paid her $100 which she claimed was due her.

Before the settlement had a clergyman it had a well-
qualified physician in Dr Austin, who came from the States
in 1824, and took up his abode on lot 6, 5th range, subsequently moving into Franklin. He was handsome in person

and agreeable in manner and became popular. The habits of
those around him had their influence, and from a temperate
man he became a drunkard. He often foretold that he would
be found dead on the road, and, sure enough, he was discovered one cold night insensible on the highway with a jug
of whisky. He was carried to a house and placed before the
fire, but all efforts to restore him were in vain, dying in the
morning.

On the Black river and west of it a few American families
continued to live, among whom were Alard, Pettis, Samuel
Brisben and Gould, a Methodist local preacher. Pettis was a
good mechanic, and, for Brayton on 169, put up the first
frame barn. In 1829 an Englishman, John Parnby, bought
out one of them, Seaman Brown, who occupied the lot upon
which St Antoine Abbé village is now built, paying $30 for
the betterments. Another Englishman, James Parmalee, came
beside him and set up a blacksmith shop. James Cassidy, an
Irish Catholic, bought out Joseph Allen and was followed
by P. Brady in 1835 and other of his countrymen until they
formed a little colony. .

Between the flats and Covey hill wound, for a few miles
east of Stockwell, a track which the new road replaced in
course of time. On it a few American families lived, but,
generally speaking, the clearing of the country south of the
flats was the work of Old Countrymen, chiefly Irish Protestants. The first was Joseph Allan, a member of a good
English family, who ran away from school, and went on
board a ship for America. The vessel was wrecked on a
desert island off Newfoundland, which he, with only sixteen
others, reached, and lived there 6 weeks before rescued by
a vessel bound for Quebec. He drifted into Huntingdon
and secured the east-half of 134 about the year 1820. He
had west of him the family of James Gilfillan (p. 24) who
moved to 135 on being forced to leave Woolrich's land, and
beside him came to live Jos. Larabee and Chas. Colston, related
by marriage. The old man died in 1818 and several years
later his widow sold the lot to two Englishmen, Jeremiah
Dunn and William Wright, distinguished for strength. Going

to Champlain for provisions, Wright bought a barrel of pork, which he emptied into a sack and carried home—a burden of 200℔. To the north of them was a Scotch blacksmith, James Douglas. Despite these and a few others, the new road settlement was essentially a North of Ireland one, its founder Daniel Mannagh, who went on to 128 about 1823. He was from Monaghan and on the trouble arising in Sherrington with regard to the tenure of the land, a number of his brother countrymen, who had found where he was, moved beside him. Among those who did so between 1826 and 1830 were James and Robert Dundas, John˙ and George Fiddes, Wm. Saunders, Thomas and James McCort, Christopher Irwin, Joseph Ball, Joseph McKee, James and Andw. Keese, and Miller. To the east of them were Thomas Doris Palmer, known as Peem, and Joseph Stafford, who was on 126. What is true of the Ulstermen on the new road, is true of the Irish Protestants as a whole who came into the eastern end of the county,—they were a hard-working, thrifty, self-denying and persevering people. Land which the Americans thought could never be reclaimed, they transformed into good farms, and in a few years wrought a marvellous change in the aspect of the country. As they took up their lots, they cut their share of the concession-road that crossed them. Receiving no government help, it was long before it was complete, and it was not until 1839 that it was possible to pass over it from Stockwell to Hemingford. The road from the flats to the top of Covey hill was more actively pushed, and was fit to use by 1837, when the old road that started from 33 and came out at Stockwell fell into disuse and ultimately closed. The experience of W. C. Roberts upon it during the fall of Miramichi fires is worth preserving: "I was (he said) coming down Covey hill with a load of corn, when I saw the fire darting from the west. Unhitching the oxen, I ran with them and just got across in time. Although there was little wind, the fire passed like lightning over the ground, the extreme dryness of the soil from great drouth and the thick covering of fallen leaves being favorable. You may suppose how quick the fire ran, from hens dropping dead into it from their roosts on fences and trees. Where the sled was left happened to be a hollow, and being moist around it, the fire did not touch it or the corn. Many settlers had outbuildings burned and the smoke from the mucky land to the north was so pungent that we were like to be suffocated. The low ground was badly burned, and long tracks of blackened trees channelled the forest."

From the point in the east, where the land begins to rise, to the Hinchinbrook line, a length of a dozen miles, came to be known as "the hill." From the account given in chapter III. it has been seen that the eastern face of the hill had settlers from an early date, but the western remained in a state of nature until long after the northern ranges of Franklin and Havelock were thickly occupied. This was owing to the drawbacks attending living on steep slopes and to the land being held by grantees, who demanded a high price. To what has been related of the old O'Neill settlement, there is little to add. As the immigrants came seeking for land, the Americans sold out to them at reasonable prices, many crossing into Clinton county and others going to Ohio. Among the first to buy were Geo. Marshall and John Gray. Once the movement began, it proceeded smartly, and what was once an American settlement became British in its tone and customs. Two of the more prominent settlers were John Edwards, who had been in business in Dundee, Scotland, and who bought part of 81 in 1834, and, 2 years later, William Barrett, an Englishman, and a surveyor by profession, bought the east half of 81, and during a long life pursued his calling, getting much to do from the seignior. On lot 30, an American, Aikins; who sometimes preached, built a small sawmill on the Allen brook about 1832, and Capt. Edwards raised another, which proved to be of great benefit to himself and to the neighborhood. The McDiarmids first lived at the foot of the hill, subsequently buying Covey's old lot, 33, on to which they moved, and were among the best known residents. A block log schoolhouse, built by William Brisben about 1825; and which stood opposite where the Union church now is, was the only place for meetings up to a late date. West of the settlement, on the summit of the hill, lived William Danford, who made a living by hunting.

Mrs Mountain of Cornwall held 2400 acres on the second range, a grant to her father, Major Scott, for losses during the American revolution. Abram Welch was her agent, and the price was $3 and $2 an acre, according to quality, in instalments. Her dealings with immigrants formed a striking contrast to those of Ellice and Woolrich, being considerate and honorable. In 1823, an Englishman, John B. Oldham, bought from her 89 and the following year an American, Humphrey Tolman, settled beside him on 90. In 1826 came the Stevensons, the advance of the class who were to possess the western portion of the hill. Robert Stevenson said :

We belonged to county Armagh where my father was in comfortable circumstances. Receiving urgent letters from a brother in Ohio he decided to join him, impelled thereto by the consideration that he could establish his numerous family in a way of doing for themselves more easily than in Ireland. He sold out and we sailed from Newry in May, 1824, and had a splendid passage, dropping anchor at Quebec on the 28th day from weighing it at Newry. A steamer came alongside, and we stepped on board of it in good health and spirits. On arriving at Montreal father complained of feeling poorly, and it soon became clear he was ill of the ship-fever. One after another took it, until the whole family, ten in number, were down with it, save myself, who was the oldest. Not one could help the other even to pass a cup of water, and I had to attend them. I can give you no idea of the misery of that time. The doctors came twice a day, and it was half-a-guinea each time, and there were, of course, other expenses. All got better in time except my mother, who was the last to become sick and the trouble kept to her longest. One of the doctors, Dr Stevenson, took a more than common interest in us, perhaps from our name, and he advised father to move out of the city, for he said the family would not gain strength by remaining in our lodgings, and he would get mother admitted to hospital. By this time father had found out what a mistake he had made in sailing to Quebec instead of New York in order to reach Ohio, and giving up the idea of going there he went out to Sherrington, where he heard land was for sale, and bought a lot with a clearance and a shanty on it. We

went and took possession, and all got well as the doctor said
we would. Poor mother, lying in the hospital, was worried
in her mind about us and was eager to get away. Dr Stevenson warned her that if she left she would be liable to a relapse,
but she insisted on leaving, and father got a covered waggon
and brought her to Sherrington. He had hired a woman in
Montreal to keep house for us until she recovered. Well, she
took the fever, and, in her delirium, was outrageous. On the
fifth day after leaving the hospital, mother had a relapse. On
the eighth I went to the French settlement and bought some
chickens, one of which I took and made soup with. I made
it as nice as I could, and when it was ready I raised my
mother's head and held a spoonful to her lips. She swallowed
it, and I asked her if it was good. She answered "yes," the
last word she spoke, for on giving her another spoonful she
choked and I felt her stretching out her body and stiffening
in my clasp. I knew she was dying, but said nothing to the
children, who were playing in the room beside us, for they
were too young to know what death was, and father was out
at the time.——After that, we had no more trouble from
sickness, and we got on fairly well, the land giving us plenty
of food. I hired out with Joseph Scriver and in the fall of
1825 went with him to Elgin, to see the lot he had bought
there. Some snow had fallen and we found it disagreeable
crossing the creeks, which we had to wade. We went to
Athelstan along a sort of lumber-road and then up to Powerscourt, and along the first concession, the only shanties on
which I recollect were those of Horn and Brown. We built
a shanty and made a little clearance. I felled the first tree,
a small maple. Having thus prepared for his moving in next
spring, we returned home. My brother Thomas and myself,
wanting to have places of our own, resolved to move into
Huntingdon, and selected lot 91 on Covey hill. We started
from home in December, 1826, to take possession, and came
by way of Clelland's corners. The settlers after leaving there
were, Goodsill, Sweet, Robson, Spearman, Brisben, George
Marshall, William O'Neill, Keenan, who lived on a lot owned
by Shedden, the mill-owner at Mooer's, N.Y., David Musgrove,
Oldham and Tolman. These were the only settlers between
Clelland's corners and our lot. That year James Hall came
and took up the west half of 90 and Hugh Carson went to
live on 93. William Haire and Francis Anthony came that
winter and were followed by William Brooks, the Brown
brothers, and William Hamilton. In fact, the settlers came
so quickly, that in a few years every lot fit for cultivation

on the hill was bought. All were North of Ireland Protestants and nearly all had, like ourselves, been a while in Sherrington. The country was in a state of nature, and we barricaded our doors at night, for the cries of the wolves and panthers were awful. At the south end of my brother's lot Colston had a bear-trap, using corn as bait, in which he caught several. We were all poor and depended on potash for the means of procuring food. The hill was covered with beautiful timber, mostly maple, with some birch, there being very little black ash or elm. The first year my brother and I made 4 barrels, which we drew by way of the flats and St Remi to Montreal. It took generally five days to go, and one to come back. The money we applied to meeting the instalments on our land. One of my sisters came to keep house for us and father carried to us at intervals provisions. We often ran short, for neighbors from Sherrington in search of land would stay in our shanty, and the supply would give out sooner than father calculated upon. Forbes had opened a store on the flats, but it was more of a groggery than anything else, and he had seldom provisions to sell. Our neighbors were often pinched themselves, so that if you were starving they could not give you a bowl of flour or meal. The first fall we got out of provisions altogether, and for two days had nothing more than the milk of our only cow among the three of us. We were mowing at the time and kept on working, hoping every minute to see father come in sight. On the second day my brother gave out from weakness and had to go and lie down, but I kept on, and that evening father came. The land yielded good crops of potatoes, corn, rye, and wheat, and when a settler got clearance enough there was no more lack of food. On finishing a barrel of potash, we turned to and cleared the land fit for cropping. The want of a mill near us was a great drawback. We had to shoulder our grists to Shedden's mill, at Mooers, N.Y., and it took a day to go and another to come back. The first year we had to roll our logs by hand, but the second we had a yoke of oxen, and horses began to be got, but were used mostly in taking grists to mill, two bags being tied by their mouths and slung over the beast's back. There being so much heavy work to do, bees were common and at every one there was whisky, which was so plenty from its cheapness that on going into a house they would sooner offer you a tinful of it than of water. Several of my neighbors besides myself did not like the drinking and quarrelling that resulted, and although there was no talk then of teetotal societies, 5 of us agreed in 1827 to

abstain for one year. We all kept our pledge and finding the
benefit of it continued to abstain, and, for myself, I did not
taste liquor for 5 years. Our example at bees, in refusing to
taste, had its effect upon others, and many followed our example. On the authority of the grand-voyer, I suppose, David
Manning had cut a road between the 1st and 2nd ranges, 18
feet wide, but it was grown up with saplings when we came,
and each of us had to cut out the road in front of our lots.
Mrs Mountain was good in allowing us credit for work done
in cutting the road across vacant lots. It was a long while
before it was fit for wheels. It was 1839 before the byroad
was made. In 1829 father joined us and in 1831 the neighbors united in building a school on our lot. It was well-
finished and comfortable. Miss Parham (afterwards Mrs N.
Manning), was the first teacher and she was a good one. The
Rev Mr Dawes and the Rev Mr Bond (afterwards Bishop)
preached in it when they visited our settlement and, after a
while, it was made a station by the Methodists of the Hemingford circuit. The Rev Mr Merlin did not visit us. One night,
after it had stood about 5 years, the schoolhouse was set fire
to and destroyed with all the schoolbooks and Bibles left in
it. It was burned from hard-feeling that had arisen regarding its location and the payment of the salary of the teacher
then engaged, an excellent one, Mr Bird, to whom more had
been promised than some were willing to pay. Although ours
was a Protestant Irish settlement, we had no set observance
of the twelfth of July, beyond not working and spending the
day in visiting, until lodge 41 was organized by Samuel Orr,
who was the heart and soul of it, and was chosen the first
master.

When the Irish Protestants had overspread the eastern half
of Covey Hill they pushed westward until all the vacant lots
were occupied. Benjamin, (son of Edward) Johnston thus
told of the experiences of those who took up land at the
Franklin end :

We belonged to county Cavan, and my father's case illustrates much of the cause of Ireland's troubles. He married
young and when he had only a holding of 3 acres. He soon
found that what had been enough for one would not do for
two, and on the birth of his first child, he asked and obtained
a reduction of rent. After he had two children he found
himself worse off than before, and asked another reduction in
rent. The landlord refused, telling him it would be no kindness, that to comply would be only to encourage him to remain

and raise a family of beggars and that he had better emigrate. He took the advice and we sailed to Canada, and father occupied a lot in Sherrington. He believed the land to belong to the crown and helped to dispute the claim to make it seigniorial. When the case went against the settlers, he would not stay and pay rent, and followed those who had left for Covey Hill, which was in March, 1831. I recollect our halting at Stevenson's to rest ourselves, and that the roof of their shanty was made of basswood scoops. Our lot was 46 and we brought with us a horse and 3 cows, which we would have been better without, for, the first winter, hay to feed them cost a dollar the hundredweight. The land was covered with as handsome a bush as could be imagined, the trees being large and set so wide apart that you could drive a yoke of oxen, there being no underbrush and few fallen logs. There were many butternuts, some of them 3 feet across and giving 3 logs without a branch; they were of no value then, and had to be burned, giving us much trouble, for it is wood difficult to burn either green or dry. On the 2nd range there was a good deal of hemlock, which caused it to be shunned, for the settlers thought the land was poor where it grew. It was a mistake in this case, for the 2nd range is better than the 1st. There was no sign of the land being stony, and it was not until cleared and it came to be cultivated that we found out how plentiful they were. There was no road, and we went whichever way we liked through the bush, carrying our loads on the shoulder. I recollect of Marshall Hall going all the way to the Flats to buy a bushel of rye, backing it home, and then carrying it to the mill at Rockburn to be ground, and home again, all in one day. Not a few backed meal or flour all the way from Champlain, for at times it was not to be had any nearer. None of us cared about cornmeal or rye bread, and it was a while before we had wheat. Both it and the rye were very subject to smut, causing the bread to be bitter. The settlers for the first few years, and until their clearances yielded them enough to live upon, depended on potash-making. They were all Irish Protestants, excepting Hugh McGarr, a Catholic, on 23, who did not stay, selling out to Wm. Brooks. Those who wanted stock and could not buy, sometimes went to Robert Dunn of St Remi, who would rent a cow for three years on condition that she be then returned along with her first calf. The steers he thus obtained he made oxen of, and leased out at $12 a-year. When he died, he owned a great number of cattle all over the country. When land was seeded down, we had immense crops of hay, two ton and more to the acre, so that feed became very plentiful and not only were the log barns filled, but you saw stacks all over the country. All the lots were quickly taken up, except 49, which Vanvliet, the owner, did not sell until about 1850, and 48, owned also by an outsider, McCallum, who had Frederick Broder living on it in charge when we came. The 3rd concession, except the lower end, where Jeremiah Dunn and Archd. Muir lived, was also late in being occupied. I cut out the road myself upon it towards 1850. The settlement on the 1st and 2nd ranges was delayed in getting a school owing to disputes between the east and west ends of it as to the location. Finally it was decided to have two; one was built at Stevenson's and the other on Hall's lot, 45, about 1836.

The northern portion of Franklin was late in being opened up, owing to its being inaccessible and to the dispute with the seignior. Those who went in, squatted, Welch marking the boundaries of the lots for them. When the seignior sent surveyors, the settlers pulled up their stakes. Between the 7th and 8th ranges there was a prosperous little settlement formed between 1830 and 1833. On lot 11 Charles Meehan had a small sawmill.

THE NORTON CREEK
CONCESSIONS.
Williamstown Side.

96 James Hay; 2 Allan Caldwell; 3 Archd. Craig
97 Thos. Gould; 2 D. Stewart; 3 Ralph Murdoch
98 James Knox; 2 Jas. Wiley
99 Alex. Currie
100 David Smith
101 James Henretty
102 William Wiley
103 William Allan
104 John Campbell
105 James Easton
106 Neil McNulty
107 Charles McNulty
108 John Moore
109 Archd. McDonald
110 James Black
111 Robert Carr
112 John Kelly
113 James Bulger
114 Thomas Bulger
115 Andrew Walsh
116 James McDonald
117 Bernard Harkin
118 John Dunn
119 William Gray
120 James Rossiter
121 Philip McIntyre

Edwardstown Side.

1 Barnabas Diggins
2 Martin Dunn
3 Owen Dunn
4 John Fitzwilliams
5 William Airston
6 Robert Pullar
7 Thomas Fitzsimmons
8 Patrick Fitzsimmons
9 Robert Jamieson
10 Joseph Chatel
11 Pierre Mabe
12 James Blackburn

13 William Blair
14 Peter Rooney
15 Daniel Cross
16 Luke Bulger
17 Michael Maher
ENGLISH RIVER CONCESSION.
1 John Lang, 1829
2 Alex. McRae
3 Alex. Taylor
4 John Angel; 2 Daniel Mc-
  Intosh; 3 Thos. Bruce
5 ——McKay; 2 John Robb
  1829
6 Duncan McRae, 1826
7 John Mitchell
8 Malcolm Ross

9 Colin McRae, 1826; James
  Craig, 1841
10 Hugh Carr; 2 Josiah Black
11 James Hamilton
12 Alex. Black
13 David Davies; 2 James
  Middlemiss, 1829
14 John Toolan; 2 Moses
  Douglass
15 Frs. Robidoux
16 John Charters, senr.
17 John Charters, junr.
18 Daniel McIntosh
19 Ichabod Munsill
20 John Wilson
21 James Duncan

DOUBLE CONCESSION.

I failed to get numbers of lots, but the following list of names, furnished by Mr William Creasor, gives the order of the settlers :

North.	Norton Creek.	South.
Andrew Dewly		George Wheatleay (given
—— Davis		erroneously on p. 237)
Walter Claflin		Philip Burhart (Burgot)
William Gleason, ½ lot		William Ryan
—— Santoire "		Michael Dcolan
Pierre Arbor "		George Hart
Timothy Gorman "		Timothy Gorman
James Walker		Daniel Mosher
Patrick Gregory		Philip Hart
John Severs, 2 lots		William Barron
Philip Hart		Hugh Levy
William Creasor ·		William Creasor
James Swords		—— Duston, ½ lot
Andrew Currie		John Becket "
Thomas McComb		John Briggs
George Toynton		Robert Grasby
James Tassie		—— Carr
St Chrysostom village		John Gregory, ½ lot
		John Sylvia "
		Francis McComb, ½ lot
		William Briggs "
		D. Proper
		John Charters

CHAPTER XXIV.

THE movement of Old Countrymen into Hemingford began soon after the war, when a few took up lots, but they did not remain. The first to stay was William Robson, a Northumberland shepherd, who came to Montreal in 1816, near which he rented a farm. In 1818 he bought 70 on the 1st concession of Hemingford from an Irishman, Dady, for $800, and added to his purchase until* he had a block of 600 acres, for he desired to give his 7 sons a farm a-piece. All strong-bodied, industrious men they speedily effected a great change in their lots and made a great deal of money by potash. East of them on the same road, and two years after their coming, Thomas Clelland, a native of the upper ward of Lanarkshire, bought 13, and began to work at his trade, that of a blacksmith. On the 26th April, 1822, he went to a bee at the corners, now known by his family name, to raise a barn for Daniel Scriver, when he was killed by the falling of a bent. He was buried in an acre of land given by Colonel Scriver, and was the first of the great number since interred in what is now the general burial-place for the Protestant population of Hemingford. On the road between the 3rd and 4th concessions James Brownlee was the first of the immigrants to take up land. He said:

I came from near Carluke, Lanarkshire, and was brought up to be a carpenter. Trade being bad, in 1819 I took passage for myself and wife on the Rebecca for Montreal, paying 8 guineas each. We had a good voyage, and on reaching Montreal, I found work at my trade. The following year there was great dullness in business and I resolved to try farming, and bought 142 from a man I happened to meet at St Johns. In November we started to take possession, and

---

* His tombstone says 1823—an error to be accounted for by its erection long after his death.

had great difficulty in reaching Scriver's corners, owing to a heavy snowstorm that came on. The schoolhouse that stood where the store of Scriver brothers now is, had just been finished (p. 145), and we found shelter in it, and the day following got to my lot, on which was a shanty and a small clearance. The snow all melted and the frost came out of the ground, so that my brother and myself were able to delve a good bit of the clearance. The frost did not set in until after the New Year. On the ridge in rear and front of my house, was a string of clearances made by American settlers, which they had abandoned when the war broke out. These clearances were called "the commons," and farmers in Sherrington sent their cattle to graze upon them. In 1822 my brother-in-law, Archibald Stewart, came from Scotland, when I sold him my lot and took up 179, on which I opened a store soon after, and did a good business. Thomas Stewart took up 97 about 1824. In 1832 I went to town to buy goods, and the two days I was there proved to be the worst days of the cholera, which was then raging. If I buy goods (I said to myself) they may be the means of introducing the infection into Hemingford, and so I returned without making any purchases. I wound up the store and devoted myself to farming. There was no pride in those days. When there was preaching in the old school, Mrs John Scriver came dressed in a flannel gown of her own spinning, and a square of the same cloth drawn over her head for a bonnet.

The year following that on which Brownlee settled, 1821, arrived Andrew Spence, an Edinburgh printer, who bought 107 and lived and died on it, and two families which have left their mark in the township. John McFee of Russeltown said :

My father and Finlay McNaughton, of Glenelg, Inverness-shire, were brothers-in-law. They embarked at Tobermory on the Glen Tanner of Aberdeen, which had a numerous body of emigrants, many of whom became settlers on the Beech ridge and adjoining concessions. We landed at Quebec after a voyage of 7 weeks and 3 days. Our intention was to go to Ontario, but at Montreal we met a namesake, a surveyor, who was going to see some land in Hemingford that had been granted to a gentleman in Glengarry. My father and uncle went with him to see the country, with the result of both buying there. My father bought 99, on which young Starnes was living, and he moved out to make room for us. McNaughton bought 108, a bush-lot, from Judge Sowles of Alburgh, Vt.

Had they known enough, they could have gone into the crown reserves and taken up land for nothing. There was a small clearance on our lot but none on McNaughton's, and to provide shelter he bought 50 acres adjoining his lot on 108 with a shanty from Comfort Brayton. We arrived in Hemingford on the 11th September. We had neighbors and a passable road but McNaughton had neither, the path to his shanty being a track that followed the ridge, in order to avoid the swamp. Our dependence was on potash, and if settlers had not timber on their lots suitable for making it, they just went into the reserves.

In 1822 Andw. Starnes, a merchant who had 1000 acres in the vicinity, built a sawmill on the Little Montreal river, a short distance north of Cleveland's. At this mill was the landing for canoes, for, when there was plenty of water, the settlers preferred floating down their potash as far as Napierville, and bringing back a return load by canoe, to the weary journey through bush all the way to Laprairie.

The first Old Countrymen to seek a home on the road that runs north from Hemingford village were Robert Moore, who squatted on No 5, Cr. R., and Graham, who took up a lot a little north of him. This would be in 1820 or 1821. Both were Irish Protestants and on Moore's visiting Montreal in the fall of 1822 he fell in with John Reay, who had been his neighbor in Carrickfergus, and who had just arrived from Ireland with his family. Moore advised him to try Hemingford, which he visited and bought No 1, 200 acres, from Joshua Odell, on which he raised a shanty. In the spring of 1823 he brought his family from the city, and they found the location a most lonely one, for there was not a house between them and what is now the village, and to the north of them, were only Odell and Moore and Graham, both of whom subsequently went west. Reay, who was a man of sterling qualities, set manfully to work, and, although a linen-weaver by trade, succeeded in creating a comfortable home in the bush. He toiled hard and endured many privations. Wild beasts abounded, and he lost calves more than once by prowling bears. As the country filled up, he resumed his old work as a weaver, only now it was woolen yarn instead of flaxen he handled. The first one to settle near him, was John Reid, and he, like the bulk of the immigrants for many years, was an Irish Protestant. There was a great influx of immigrants into Sherrington, and the overflow naturally passed into Hemingford.

The acquisition of the year 1823, however, was the Rev John Merlin. He was born in Maghera, county Derry, Ireland, in 1781, and, when old enough, was apprenticed to be a mason. Having aspirations beyond his trade, he sought to qualify himself for the ministry, and attended several sessions at Glasgow and Edinburgh. Unable to get a church after his ordination as a minister of the Irish Presbyterian church, he obtained a succession of situations as schoolmaster, and taught for some time in an academy in Dublin. Despairing of getting a charge, he resolved to emigrate, and sailed from Belfast in 1823, leaving his wife and 4 children with her people, who lived near that city, until he provided a home for them. On his arrival at Montreal, he called on the Rev Henry Esson, who advised him to go into the new settlements in the county of Huntingdon, towards which the current of immigrants was setting. He acted on the advice, and after examining the country and living in it some time finally selected 184 as his home, and the neighbors raised a shanty for him. In 1825 his wife and family joined him. The people were so very poor that they could pay him no salary, and all he received for many years was occasional presents from the better-off among them. To live, he had to cultivate the land and teach school, which he kept at first in his own house. He was engaged as master of the school at Scriver's corners, succeeding several Americans who had taught for brief periods, and in 1828 induced his neighbors to raise a school next his dwelling-house, which he kept open several months in the year. There was a great scarcity of text-books, the New Testament and Webster's speller being the only ones known for a long period. When a family moved in, whose parents desired their children to be taught geography, it was regarded as an astounding innovation, and, after that, if a scholar could get hold of any American school-

book he brought it. From the first month of his arrival he
began a system of itinerancy which he maintained until too
feeble to bear the fatigue. While absent on his western appointments, which occupied a fortnight of each month, his
wife endeavored to fill his place in the schoolroom. From the
Sherrington-line to the Gore of Hinchinbrook he had appointments, and maintained religious ordinances when, but
for him, there would have been none. His journeys were
made, as a rule, on foot, though latterly he used a horse. In
going to the Beech ridge, where he preached once a month,
he floated down Norton creek in a canoe when the water
permitted. He was far from punctual, and his expectant
congregation was frequently on the point of dispersing when
he appeared. In his labors he was perfectly disinterested,
asking for no recompense and being offered none until the
later years of his pastorate, when the circumstances of his
parishioners had improved. His fee for marrying was moderate—two dollars—which he rarely received. His lack of
punctuality caused some inconvenience at a good many wed-
dings. At one the hour came and went without tidings
of him, the fun and dancing were kept up until midnight
without his arrival, and finally the guests set out, by the
bright moonlight, down the road he would come to see what
hindered him, and met him leisurely returning from a visit
to a distant settlement. He performed the service and the
merry-making lasted until daylight. In marrying he insisted
on crying the banns. Some time after he came, finding there
was sufficient material, he organized a session, Alex. Walker,
a worthy Scot, John Reay, and the minister's brother, Joseph,
being the first elders, and held regular communion-seasons
in the old schoolhouse at the village which answered until
1842, when a stone-church was built. All the while he had
maintained his connection with the church in Ireland, which
did nothing for him. Yielding to the remonstrances of his
brethren, in 1841 he and his congregation united with the
Church of Scotland in Canada, when he became entitled to
a share of the revenues from the clergy reserves. On the
visit to Montreal when he received the first payment, he was

accompanied by Dr Black to the wharf from whence the Laprairie boat sailed. The day was gusty and the river had
an ugly look. Mr Merlin expressed some apprehension as
to the boat crossing in safety. "What!" exclaimed the Dr.,
"you are not afraid of losing your life?" "It's no that,"
answered Mr Merlin with unselfish simplicity, thinking of
those at home whom it would benefit, "it's the money in my
pouch"—some $60. In 1855 he resigned on a retiring allow-
ance from the clergy reserve fund, and 11 years afterwards
ended his long and useful life.

Before Mr Merlin came Hemingford was visited at rare
intervals by ministers from the States and Townships who
held services. Among these was the famous Bishop Hedding,
who preached at Scriver's corners. Mr Judd, an Englishman, who had lived in Roxham, and who was a Methodist
local preacher, made stated visits to the corners, and after
him Mr Kilburn, an American, who pursued his trade as
cooper on the outskirts of the village and did something in
medicine, held alternate services with Mr Merlin. He was
a Baptist and a consistent Christian. From the first Method-
ism had obtained a strong hold upon the settlers of American
descent, prominent among whom were the Scrivers and Odells,
and quite a number of the immigrants fell under their influence, for those were the days of protracted meetings, at
which personal influence was exerted in the most direct and
stirring form to awaken souls to a sense of their duty. In
1834 the Methodists set about raising a church, in which
they succeeded with much difficulty, the greater part of
the subscriptions being made in produce and labor. When
closed in, its use was tendered to the Presbyterians for,
to them, a somewhat singular use. The holding of revival
services had been adopted by the American Presbyterians
who were his neighbors, and Mr Merlin had resolved on following their example. He announced that "a four days'
service" would be held, in which he would be assisted by
the Rev Mr Foote of Champlain, N. Y. The announcement
aroused widespread interest and it became evident that the
schoolhouse would not hold all who intended coming, where-

upon the Methodists tendered the use of their church. The order of the services was to open with an enquiry meeting in the schoolhouse, which was held at about 10 o'clock, and from it those who attended walked to the Methodist church, at 11 o'clock, where an expectant congregation was found in waiting, and a service similar to that of Sunday, except that the prayers and sermon were of an awakening character, was held. Like meetings were held in the afternoon and evening. So deep an interest was awakened that the meetings were continued for a fortnight instead of four days, and a large number declared their resolve to turn to God. Of these the greater part became Methodists or fell away, for the regular ministrations of Mr Merlin were not calculated to draw and hold the young, being monotonous and prolonged, never lasting less than two hours. The second year after the Methodist church was built, 1836, Hemingford was included in the Odelltown circuit, and thereafter enjoyed stated services.

The Episcopalians, of whom there was a fair proportion among the North of Ireland immigrants, were late in organizing. In the fall of 1838 William Dawes was engaged by a society in Montreal as a travelling missionary among the settlements bordering on the Richelieu. He was an active and earnest worker and established stations in every settlement where there was sufficient encouragement, which he visited once a month. In January, 1840, Bishop Mountain visited Hemingford for the first time, confirmed 65, and stimulated the movement to build a church, and one was raised in 1845 in the north-eastern part of the township, known as the Starnes neighborhood. The Rev Mr Bond succeeded Mr Dawes, who was ordained and died the death of a martyr while attending immigrants stricken with ship-fever during the dreadful summer of 1847.

The Roman Catholics were not numerous in the township until after 1840, for there was no influx of them while the Ulstermen were pouring into it from Sherrington. There were, however, a few families, the first to come that of Daniel Heffernan and the second that of John Ryan, in 1828, who lived first on 145 and afterwards bought out the Nortons on

112. In 1843 they united to raise a church, forming a cemetery in rear. Previous to the building of the church, the Catholics buried in a small plot near Johnsons station, close to the railway-track.

The settlers of Hemingford were peculiar in that few of them came directly into it from Montreal. The majority lived one or more years in Sherrington, which they crowded into under the belief that it was ungranted crown land and left owing to a dispute similar in nature to that waged between the settlers of Russeltown and Ellice. Sherrington was debatable land, and on those who contended that it was granted land winning the day, the Old Countrymen left, being resolved that they would not pay rent. They were the more induced to do so from the land not being inviting, consisting in great part of stony ridges with marshy intervales and from the neighborhood being a rather turbulent one. For instance, in April, 1823, after a row of more than usual violence, part of Captain Wallis's company of militia was sent to arrest the ringleaders. Two of them, John and Michael Kenny, they found working in a fallow, when they ran to the house, and on the militiamen surrounding it, John thrust a gun through a chink of the door and threatened to shoot. Col. Scriver rushed forward and grasped the barrel, and in turning it upwards the fellow drew the trigger when the bullet lodged in the shoulder of Ben Spearman. The brothers were seized and sent to Montreal but were not punished. After repeated application, the legislature granted $300 indemnity to Spearman. In surveying Hemingford, a portion was, as already described, set apart for crown and clergy reserves, which, by mistake, was in excess of the one-seventh prescribed by law. The excess was designated blank lands, and were left unsurveyed. The reserves constituted the eastern and northern parts of the township, and into them the people from Sherrington passed, among the first being John Orr, a county Cavan man, Henry Figsby from Monaghan, and John Jackson, also from Ulster. They found on the crown reserves a number of French and American squatters, who had gone into the bush to make potash, with

no intention of remaining and who readily sold their betterments at from $50 to $100 and moved to another part of
the bush to repeat their speculation. If there was nobody
on the lot, and it suited the immigrant, he forthwith took
possession by raising a shanty. The government had made
no provision for selling the lots, and its agent who had
charge of them lived at Sherbrooke. In course of time he
(Mr Felton) visited the township and demanded high prices
for the lots under penalty of ejectment. Col. Scriver, when
matters were coming a crisis, went to Quebec to intercede for
the settlers. During the disastrous attack on Plattsburgh,
he had an opportunity of showing some kindness to the
captain of one of the regiments. That captain was now
governor-general, and Colonel Scriver sought and obtained
an interview with him. Sir James Kempt recognized in his
visitor the brave backwoodsman whom he had met on the
Richelieu and cordially acceded to his proposal, namely, that
the settlers should pay 50 cents an acre, for, being reserves
set apart for the benefit of certain funds, they could not be
given free. This favorable arrangement quieted the apprehensions of the settlers. Many years afterwards, on the
blank lands being surveyed, patents were issued to those in
possession on paying from 75c to $1.25 per acre according
to the quality of the land and situation. By this time Col.
Scriver was carrying on an extensive and profitable business
at the corners then known by his name and now designated
Hemingford village. The first store there was opened by
Bartlett Nye, in a 10-foot square shanty, which he abandoned
in a year or two, when Joseph Corbin and the colonel undertook the business, which Corbin left in 1826 to build, in
company with Finlay McNaughton, a sawmill on Norton
creek. Born with the trading-facylty and always ready for
a dicker, the business prospered in the colonel's hands, and
although the settlers had no money they never need leave
his store without what they wanted, for they could "turn
in" their lumber, their produce, or their labor in payment.
He was considerate in his dealings with the settlers, and to
his help in their struggles during the early days, many

owed their subsequent prosperity. At first he kept liquor and sold large quantities, but becoming convinced of the immoral character of the traffic, in 1831 he gave up keeping it and became a rigid total abstainer himself. Probably there was not, at that time, another country store in the province that did not sell intoxicating liquor, and in this, as in several other respects, Colonel Scriver was in advance of his age. His shrewdness, energy and executive ability would have made him a leader anywhere, but in Hemingford his preeminence was enhanced by his being then the only man possessed of resources that enabled him to assist others. He always kept a number of hired men and whether it was lumbering or potash-making or clearing up land did so on a scale that nobody else could emulate. To the improving of existing roads and the opening of new ones he labored strenuously. When the government grants to roads were being made, he was a persistent petitioner, but Hemingford got less than its just share. His request was that assistance be given to open the road between the 3rd and 4th ranges, to complete the road eastward, and to make good the road from the Napierville line to the province line. To the latter, in 1832, $800 was given, to make "the road from the province-line on No. 10 to the house of John McFall." In 1834 $600 was given to make passable the road from Stockwell to Vicars (then called Mannagh's corners), when communication was possible from Hemingford to Franklin, and the upper road was less used. The same year an additional grant of $600 was made to the road from Clelland's northwards. In October, 1831, a mail was granted from St Remi to Hemingford, Colonel Scriver being postmaster.

The trials and disadvantages of settlers in Hemingford were so similar to those already described of their neighbors in Havelock that one narrative will suffice, and I select that of William Barr:

We belonged to county Tyrone, and sailed from Belfast in the spring of 1830. My father and mother died soon after leaving port. I was led to this part of the country by a married sister, who had preceded me and lived in Sherrington. I bought for $400 lot 66 on the 2nd range. There was a shanty and a bit of clearance, made by a squatter. From Clelland's corners to Covey hill was solid bush, with the exception of the clearings of Clelland, the Robsons, Sweet, and the Spearmans, James and Simon, both blacksmiths, by trade and Irish by birth. The road had been straightened the year before, and the pieces across the swamps cross-wayed. Before that, the road had crooked southward to avoid the swamps. Francis and William Horn, two as decent Scotchmen as ever lived, and William Pullar came the same year as I did, and settled near me. My father, thinking it would be better to take linen than money, had packed up 500 yards with a quantity of thread. I found it hard to exchange. Colonel Scriver took part, and from him I bought a yoke of oxen. I had sufficient money to furnish my shanty save to buy a stove, and I went to William Horn to beg the loan of $20. Remarking that by lending a man generally lost both his money and his friend, he said he would trust me, and when, the following spring, I went to repay him he refused to accept of any interest, and on pressing him, he exclaimed, "Weel, weel; give me a day in hairst," and so I sheared a day for him that fall. I set at once to clear the land and make potash, which was then selling high, $25 to $30 per barrel, in order to pay for my lot. My lot was finely covered with maple and elm but it was fearful work chopping in summer —often had I to take a drink from the brook every few cuts. That winter I did a good deal at lumbering, and became very expert with oxen. In 1835 I joined with Hosmer Corbin, who belonged to Champlain, in building a small sawmill on the creek that runs through my lot and did very well, selling the lumber chiefly to Colonel Scriver. Corbin brought 50 pigs in the spring from Champlain and they were turned loose in the bush. In the fall they came out fat, fed mostly on beech-mast. In 1838 Corbin left me and built a mill for himself on the English river, on lot 117, and Colonel Scriver at the same time raised his tannery a short distance above it.

Several years before Corbin built his sawmill, an expensive gristmill, with oatmeal-mill attached, was erected on the same lot by Colonel Languedoc of St Edward, replacing the old Woolrich mill. He sold them to Humphries Nesbitt, and while in his hands the gristmill was burned. The sawmill and carding-mill he kept running for many years. In the eastern end of the township, in 1835, Andrew Starnes built a small gristmill on the Little Montreal, but that stream proved insufficient to keep it going during the summer, and, after a few years' trial, it was abandoned, and the farmers had again to rely on Judge Moore's mill at Champlain, or Shedden's at Mooers, both on the U. S. side.

Previous to 1829 there were only two schools in the township—one at Scriver's corners and the other in the Robson settlement, which was opened about 1827, and stood at the corner of the sideline. Shortly after the Robsons raised a block building near the site of the present one, which had Duncan Young as teacher. The building was occasionally used on Sundays by itinerant preachers, the more frequent being Methodists. On the Rev Isaac Law's visiting the English river, a congregation in connection with the U. S. Associate Presbyterian synod was organized. In speaking of the Robson neighborhood I would relate, in the words of Richard Sweet, an extraordinary event that happened in it :

In April, 1824, Mr Merlin was sleeping at the Robsons, when he heard a commotion among the live-stock. Waking the household, they went out, when they found a wolf chasing the cows and sheep round the yard, the brute barking and snarling. Rousing the adjoining family of Robsons (Walter's) and securing a lantern, they came to my father's, towards which the wolf had run. Hearing the noise, my father rose and went out. While they were telling him of the cause of their coming, the pigs were heard squealing in our pen, and presently the wolf jumped out, holding a pig by the ear. Roger Robson fired, but the gun did not go off. Bringing it to the light in the house, they found the cause to be that the flint had slipped. Replacing the flint, they issued forth, and the wolf being still in the yard, gnawing the pig, Robson fired and broke the brute's leg, when it went close to the barn. Father's gun was in the barn, and slipping in, he got it and going up to the wolf fired into its breast, killing it. The wolf acted most savagely, snapping continually. Bringing it into the kitchen to skin it before the fire, they found it to be of unusual size and with only 3 legs, one having been lost in a trap. While skinning, mother suggested that they ran some risk, for the brute might be mad, and, sure enough, her conjecture turned out to be true, for every animal, except the sheep, it had bit became mad. Some of the sheep died from

their injuries, but none went mad. We supposed it was because the wool had cleaned the teeth of the virus before
entering the flesh. Cows and pigs went mad one after another and had to be killed, and all the dogs. A bull of
Robson's, while mad, was a dreadful sight in his fury, which
was stopped by a shot. We had a cow that we thought had
escaped, but in August she too turned mad. We had used the
milk in the interval and without harm. The horses that
night were in a stable some distance apart and so escaped.
My father lost every horned critter he had, and the Robsons
7 or 8   The symptoms in dying began with paralysis of the
hindquarters. The pigs were full of droll antics when seized.
Wild beasts were very plentiful about that time, and deer
were seen in herds, often of half a dozen. One day when all
the men were away, a dog was seen to have a splendid deer
at bay close to the big stone by the road. The only man in
the house was a travelling tailor, Jim Segar, who got the gun
and went out, but the flint would not work. Mother ran
for a coal, which went out; she returned for a second, and
dropping it on the priming while the tailor pointed the gun,
the charge exploded, and the deer killed.

CHAPTER XXV.

WHEN, five days after Wolfe's victory, Quebec surrendered, the English found that the responsibility of providing for the government of the people they had overcome was thrust upon them. Gen. Murray, soldier-like, solved the difficulty by issuing a proclamation declaring French law abolished and English established, and naming certain of his officers to attend to its administration, a colonel being chief judge. For fifteen years that system prevailed, English civil and criminal law administered by military officers, and during those years French law was as dead in Canada as if it had never existed. The lawyer left the Custom of Paris on its shelf in his library, and, pleading before a gentleman who held a commission in a marching regiment from George III., quoted from the statutes of Great Britain, from Coke and Blackstone. The notary was in a perplexity; Pothier he laid aside and attempted conveyancing after the English style. No tithes were collected, no body of churchwardens levied tax to build or repair church or parsonage; whatever the habitant gave towards the support of religious ordinances he gave of his freewill. The military commandant was considerate and respectful towards the subjugated people, even going so far as to issue a general-order that officers and privates on meeting a religious procession should salute by touching their hats, but on the point that English law and English precedent should prevail he was inflexible. The habitants were satisfied. For the first time they knew a government that respected the rights of property. For generations the word government had represented to them officials who appropriated their grain and cattle for the king's service and impressed the young men into his regiments. From the despotism of rogues who robbed both them and the king and by their pilferings reduced the colony to a state of beggary, the habitants passed under the rule of soldiers who paid for every bullock and minot of grain and preserved them undisturbed in their holdings. The first murmurs of discontent came from, the priesthood. The conquest had reduced them from a paramount position over their flocks to one of obligation and they intrigued for the restoration of their former privileges, for they had discovered that, without the compulsion of the law, the habitant would pay neither tithe nor fabrique-tax. In an evil hour for posterity, the Imperial government decided not only to put an end to its military rule, but to divide Canada into two provinces. That Great Britain, in entering upon the seven years' war, acted wisely in concentrating her strength upon the overturning of French rule on the continent of America, cannot be asserted. Her success rendered possible the independence of the American colonies, which meanly took advantage of the enormous sacrifices she made to free them from the menaces of the French power, which had encircled them on the north and west and threatened their existence, while it threw upon the Imperial government the most perplexing problem a constitutional country can be called upon to deal with—the treatment of a conquered people. The success of British arms had cleared the Mississippi, the Alleghanies, the great lakes, the New England northern frontier, and the maritime provinces of the element that had so long imperilled the existence of the American colonies, which thus reaped all the benefit, while it left the management of Canada as a bad legacy to England. Three courses were open to her—to abandon Canada, which several military men advised, to hold it as a conquered country and govern it as she governed Bengal, or to introduce a large loyal element and give it self-government as a whole, in the expectation that the new element would control and in time assimilate the old. The Imperial cabinet rejected the first proposal and adopted a bungling compromise between the other two. Canada was divided into two provinces, thus ensuring the perpetuation of the national divisions it was not only the truest statesmanship but the truest kindness to the French to blot out. Had Canada been left a unit, the moulding of the two elements would have been effected by this time. It was divided, with the result that the stream of immigration which would naturally have overspread the waste lands behind the French parishes on the St Lawrence, swept past them, because few immigrants had a mind to make new homes in a province with a French legislature. In the 16 years after the province of Upper Canada was created, it added 80,000 English-speaking immigrants to its population; Lower Canada did not add 8,000. By this one error of dividing Canada in 1791, we have a divided Canada still.

The settlers of Upper Canada used the privilege of self-government entrusted to them to their great advantage; the French settlers of the lower province accepted the, to them, novel boon suspiciously, and used it gingerly at first, and then perverted it into an instrument to undo what Wolfe and Murray, Amherst and Haldimand had done. Before five years, the ministers in London realized their folly in localizing and giving to a recently subjugated people the power of self-government. Every mail brought them despatches from the governors telling of attempts to restore French rule, and before long there was established a chronic war between the legislature and the executive—the one struggling to re-establish French law and customs the other to maintain English law and institutions. The liberals of England heard of the struggle and misapprehended its nature, supposing it to be a struggle between people and prerogative instead of one where popular institutions were being used to destroy British connection. No governor more clearly realized the situation than Sir J. H. Craig, and he wrote bitterly to London of how, at every point, the legislature was endeavoring to restore the old régime so far as change of circumstances would permit, how all his efforts to promote the settlement of the townships were thwarted, and how he found the priests endeavoring to estrange the habitants more and more from the British government. The priests were not alone. The cities of Quebec and Montreal abounded in young men descendants of officials in the time of Vaudreuil and Bigot, who, despising trade, hungered for office. The endowing of Lower Canada with a legislature opened a career for them. They fanned into life among the habitants the worst prejudices to secure their election, and notaries and lawyers who took their religion from Voltaire and were lost in admiration of the American republic, appealed for votes on the score that they were true sons of the church and devoted to the French nationality. Craig complained that the house was largely made up of advocates and notaries, and that of the other members 2 signed by mark and 5 could scarcely scrawl their names. In this assemblage the two Papineaus gained the ascendency, and round the tavern stoves in the evening harangued the habitant members, who next day (evening sessions were unknown) voted as they had been instructed without debate. The aim of the leaders was the establishment of a French Canadian republic, and every move they made, no matter under what form, had that end in view. All that had been effected during the period of absolute rule, in the way of reconciling the habitants to the new order of things, was undone, and the conviction was implanted deep in their minds that the driving out of the English was possible, and a song was popular among them which had for its burden that Napoleon was the man who was going to help them to do it.

In no more mischievous form did these national aspirations show themselves than in the opposition to the settlement of the wild lands of the province by immigrants. Not only were grants refused to open them by roads, but votes to provide the new settlements with means for the administration of justice and registry offices were rejected. East of the Richelieu were populous settlements of intelligent and energetic men who were unrepresented in the house. In 1823 the council sent down a bill to give them 6 members. Papineau declared that the interests and feelings of the inhabitants of the townships did not correspond with those of the French Canadians, and therefore he would not consent to allow them a voice in the legislature. The bill was killed by an amendment that would have added 18 French Canadian members. A proposal to unite with Upper Canada was voted down on the ground that such union would endanger the peculiar laws and institutions of Lower Canada. So determined was the opposition to union with the upper province, that the money required to build a canal between lakes St Francis and St Louis was steadily refused. From the year 1807 it was the avowed purpose of the house of assembly to retain the province of Lower Canada as the exclusive inheritance of the French Canadians, and the demand was that seigniors who had vacant lands should be compelled to concede and the parish system be extended to the townships, so that the children of the habitants might find homes for themselves. This, in a hundred forms and under innumerable pretences, Neilson, Papineau, Viger, and Cuvillier endeavored to accomplish. To prevent the extension of the parish system to the townships, however, every governor was resolute, and in 1826 the matter was set at rest by the Canada tenure bill, passed by the Imperial government, which declared the tenure of all land outside the seigniories to be that of free and common soccage, and gave power to the owners of seigniories to convert the tenure of unconceded lands. This act, received with shouts of chagrin by the disaffected, really saved the townships, and their settlement proceeded apace. But if the King could give the people of the townships assurance that they should enjoy their properties under English law, he could not give them representation, and until 1830, while Papineau and his followers were declaiming against the tyranny of being taxed without representation and of the preciousness of self-government, the 80,000 English-speaking settlers between Salmon river and lake Memphremagog had no more to do with the making of the laws or the spending of the taxes they paid, than the trees they were industriously hewing down. The sentiment that denied the townships representation was at last the means of giving it to them to a partial extent. A scheme was prepared by the house for Frenchifying the province and in order to ensure its passage by the council, a few members were allotted the English settlements. Under this act, the old counties were swept away and new ones with French names substituted. Huntingdon was blotted out and Beauharnois, Laprairie, and L'Acadie took its place. It was the same everywhere. The old English names of the counties were superseded by French ones. So far as regarded the Old Countrymen of old Huntingdon, they found themselves electorally no better off under the new name than the old one, for the act provided for only one polling-place and it was located at the town of Beauharnois, from 30 to 50 miles distant from the bulk of them.

The new distribution of seats increased the French representation and emboldened its leaders, who now defied the executive and succeeded in bringing the business of the province to a standstill by refusing the supplies. For their conduct they could give many plausible reasons. Like all irresponsible bodies, the legislative-council had deteriorated, and charges of filling offices with incompetent relations, of passing bills favorable to private interests, and of conniving to conceal frauds upon the revenue, could be substantiated. With all its faults, however, this fact must be recognized, that but for the council the townships would not have been settled, and that the existence of an English-speaking element in Quebec is due to it. Under all the ostensible reasons given by the agitators, the councillors recognized that their true motive was the subversion of the crown, and to thwart them they lent their influence to the successive governors. Had the imperial government conceded the demand upon which the agitators finally concentrated their strength, that of an elective council, the English element would have been wiped out. To sticklers for constitutional rights, like Sir James Mackintosh, it seemed monstrous that the will of the majority in Lower Canada should not prevail, overlooking the fact that the majority were clamoring for the constitutional powers in question with the object of wrenching the province from England and of expelling the English people from within its bounds. Was the Imperial parliament going to grant constitutional powers to the Lower Canada legislature which would enable it to undo on the floor of its house all that Wolfe had effected on the plains of Abraham? A majority of the members at Westminster saw this, and refused the demand; they were denounced as despotic by men, able and generous, who carried their theories of self-government to that extreme that, on the same principle, the victor in a fair fight would restore to the vanquished weapons to renew the battle.

There were a few among the English who, while acknowledging the service the councillors were doing the minority, could not let it condone their conduct otherwise, and who, therefore, to a certain extent supported Papineau in his demands by favoring the reform of the council. Then the American element in the townships, which at that time was large and influential, sided with him, in the belief that his success would lead to annexation. This blatant Yankee element in their midst, whose resolutions were quoted by the French agitators as representing the English sentiment, annoyed the Old Countrymen greatly, and they followed with meetings and resolutions declaring their determination to uphold British connection. Such a meeting took place at Huntingdon in 1833. It was announced to be held in the schoolhouse on the south side of the river, but so large was the attendance that it was made an out-door meeting. The speakers did not mince matters, and the sentiment of the brawny men who stood thickly around, clad as they had left their work in the bush, was shown by their shouts and exclamations to be that they would fight to the death in resistance to the threatened attempt to take the province from under British sway. The meeting, like all the others then held in the townships, refutes the popular notion that the causes of the rebellion in both provinces were identical. It is safe to say that had Lyon McKenzie been a resident of Montreal instead of Toronto, he would have shouldered a musket to put down rebellion instead of leading one. The class to which he belonged, the Scotch radical, was the predominant one on the banks of the English river, the Chateaugay, and Trout river, yet nowhere in the province

were more resolute opponents to Papineau, nor more eager
volunteers for the Queen's service. In Ontario, the rising
was measurably one in vindication of civil rights; in Quebec
the appeal to arms was to restore French domination. But
the Huntingdon meeting was more than an expression of
sentiment, for at it the important decision was come to,
that, despite their distance from the poll, they would nominate a candidate at the approaching election and endeavor
to break the custom of the county's sending supporters of
Papineau. A subsequent meeting was held at Brodie's, N.
Georgetown, to nominate a candidate, when Wm. Bowron
was decided upon, and an exciting canvas was begun, as
may be imagined when a staid man like the Rev Mr Merlin
was led, in the course of a sermon at Hemingford, to ex-
hort his hearers to support the crown by voting for Bowron
and Primeau. No sooner was the benediction pronounced,
than Colonel Scriver rose to protest against what had been
said, when he was anticipated by Joseph Merlin, who remonstrated with his brother for introducing the subject on
such an occasion. Refused the use of the schoolhouse, Wm.
Lalanne, John Hynes, David Heffernan, and David Manning
called a meeting in favor of Dewitt, which was held on a
pile of boards in the village. There were four candidates,
Primeau, an advocate, of the Cedars, who sided with the
British, Bowron, and the two retiring members, Jacob Dewitt,
a hardware merchant of Montreal, and the surveyor, Charles
Archambault, a man of no principle. Dewitt, an American,
acted with Papineau in the hope that his success would
bring annexation. Archambault, anxious for his return, approached Bowron's friends, and told them they were mistaken
in supposing he was in league with Dewitt, and that if they
would drop Primeau, who had no chance, and vote for him,
he would instruct his supporters to vote for Bowron. They
fell into the trap, and when the Old Countrymen went to
Beauharnois to vote for Bowron, they carried out loyally
the agreement with Archambault by voting for him also.
A large number of votes had been polled before it was found
that Archambault was playing false, and that his supporters

were voting not for Bowron but Dewitt.   The Old Countrymen were indignant, and refusing to vote any longer for
Archambault, they were hustled out of the polling-room by
the French, and no more were allowed to vote.   Being in a
hopeless minority, they could not assert their right by force.
A Montreal lawyer, Armour, who had come to represent
Bowron, appealed to the returning-officer, who told him to
quietly bring his friends to the back of the building, and
he would take their votes through an open window, which
was done.   It was soon plain to be seen that the contest
was hopeless, and Bowron withdrew his name.   The poll
ended by declaring Dewitt and Archambault elected.   Before
the next general election the law was changed, so that instead of one polling-place for the county, the returning-officer
moved from village to village, continuing in each a certain
number of days.   From that election dates the active interference of the Old Countrymen in public affairs, and the
quick succession of events intensified their interest.   When
the new house met the famous 92 resolutions were submitted, which embodied every imaginable grievance without
declaring the animus that dictated them—namely, the desire
to expel the English-speaking inhabitants of the province
and to convert it into a French republic.   That this could
be accomplished Papineau was assured, for he declared "not
only were republican institutions to prevail throughout the
whole of this continent, but America was destined, at some
future day, to give republics to Europe."   The American
·residents in Huntingdon village called a meeting to endorse
the 92 resolutions, which was held in the schoolroom where
Oney's house stands.   Joshua Lewis presided, Ames read the
92 resolutions, and a resident of Malone, Hutton, harangued
in their support.   Brown and Norval with others of a different way of thinking were present, and changed the complexion of the meeting.   When the house refused to vote the
supplies and brought about a deadlock, it became apparent
a collision was approaching which would decide whether the
province was to continue part of the British empire or be
changed into a French republic.   While Papineau was ad-

dressing immense gatherings in the parishes, the people of
the townships met to organize in self-defence. At the meeting in Hemingford, which filled the Methodist church, Col.
Scriver caused a sensation by rising and saying that he
knew he was suspected by a majority present because he
had supported Dewitt and because he believed many of the
reforms advocated by Papineau were necessary, and which
he wished to see effected in a constitutional manner, but
when the real issue came to be, as was now the case, whether
the province was to be French or British, his sword and
fortune were at the service of the crown. The old militia
companies were filled up and volunteer ones formed wherever
English was spoken, and the determination expressed that
they would show whether they were, as styled by the
church-door orators, intruders and trespassers in a colony
where the union jack floated.

As no overt act took place in the district of Beauharnois
during the first year of the rebellion, it would be beyond
the scope of this book to touch upon it, further than to
note its influence upon what followed in the succeeding
year. The rebellion of 1837 failed from three causes, 1st
the cowardice of the leaders, 2nd the failure of the aid
anticipated from the Americans, 3rd the decision at the last
moment of the hierarchy to discountenance the revolt. The
utmost clemency was shown to such of the leaders as were
caught, none being executed, and a number, like Cardinal
of Chateaugay, who was one of the members for Laprairie
(the seigniory of Chateaugay was then part of that county),
and Dr Perrigo, were left untouched. Mercy to the vanquished was not mercy to the province, for had a stern
example been made in 1837 there would have been no rising
in 1838. The leniency of the government was misconstrued
by the habitants into proof of its weakness, and the fellows
who were set at liberty swaggered about the parishes boasting that the bureaucrats did not dare to punish them. How
the ignorance of the habitants was imposed upon by the
demagogues who were leading them to ruin, it will suffice
to state that many were induced to take up arms under the

representation that the throne of William IV. having been filled by Victoria, they ran no risk in rising against a girl. The leaders were guilty of worse than misleading a credulous people; the accession of a new sovereign required the members of the house to be resworn. Four months after they had taken the oath of allegiance to Victoria, they were in arms to overthrow her authority in Canada. The outbreak stimulated the placing of the militia in an effective condition, and the forming of volunteer companies. Arms for the Beauharnois district were hurriedly sent to Caughnawaga, whence they were brought in carts, and from the 1st December the younger men were kept on guard, receiving 20 cents a day and rations. When spring approached, so convinced were the authorities that all danger had passed, that the companies were disbanded six weeks before the expiration of their term of enlistment.

On the surface, everything wore a most tranquil appearance; the agitation that had filled the province for a score of years with its clamor had ceased, and the habitants had resumed their ordinary occupations. Unhappily their submissive aspect was assumed to cover their purpose of making a second attempt to drive out the English. Their late failure had taught the leaders several lessons, by which, safely ensconced in the United States, they profited in devising a fresh conspiracy. Ascribing their want of success to the betrayal of their plans and the incompleteness of their organization, they devised a society elaborate in detail and secret in operation. It was called the Raquet or Chasseur society, with four degrees, and, after the manner of secret societies, its oath was administered impressively and under threats of vengeance if violated. The signs and passwords were simple yet effective. During the summer of 1838 emissaries traversed the province, initiating members and forming lodges, and carried on their propaganda so unobtrusively that the authorities had no suspicion of what was going on. In the counties of Beauharnois and Chateaugay the women were the most active in promoting the society, and by them the oath was frequently administered. So very quiet and

friendly were the Canadians, that the Old Country people
were completely thrown off their guard, and believed that,
in the catastrophe of the preceding fall, the insurrection-
ary idea had perished and that the French had become
reconciled to the existing state of affairs. The calm, however, was so profound that it caused suspicion among a few,
but none scouted the idea of a second rising being brewing
more emphatically than Colonel Brown and Mr Norval, and
no other two in the district had greater facilities of knowing
what was going on, or were more thoroughly acquainted
with the Canadian character. The degree of deception used
is indicated by men like them being so completely deceived.
The providing of arms and material was a more difficult
matter than the obtaining of recruits for the lodges, and for
the means to purchase them the leaders depended mainly
upon the Americans. All over the Northern States of the
Union large meetings were held, at which resolutions of
sympathy for the French Canadians "in their aspirations
for freedom from the British yoke" were enthusiastically
adopted, and, in defiance of their own neutrality law, subscriptions were opened to buy arms and ammunition to
make war against a nation with which the United States
was at peace. Along the northern frontier, many of those
American sympathizers formed themselves into secret societies, called Hunters' lodges, the object being to aid the
French Canadians in their effort to convert Canada into a
republic not only by collecting subscriptions in their respective neighborhoods but by organizing military companies,
to march to their support when the flag of insurrection was
raised. These Hunters' lodges were most numerous in Vermont and in St Lawrence county, N.Y. Despite the contributions of the Americans and the sacrifices made by a few
of the Canadian leaders, the Chasseurs were indifferently
provided with arms when the time of rising approached.
What muskets they had were mainly old flint-locks that
had been used in 1812, and these were eked out by daggers,
pikes, and pistols. The pikes were made clandestinely by
the parish blacksmiths. Stranger than even these rude

weapons, was the boring of logs to make wooden cannon. If arms were deficient, the leaders had, by means of the Chasseur or Raquet lodges, undoubtedly secured a fairly organized body of men, and were thus in a much better position than when they took the field the year before.

How the authorities obtained word of what was going on has not yet been fully revealed, but there is no question that the first definite information as to the extent of the danger was made known through the Catholic ecclesiastical authorities of Montreal. Apart from the consideration that they foresaw the second rising would be a second failure, and were anxious to prevent the impoverishment of their people, their act was one of self-interest. The rebel leaders by this time had imbibed American ideas of church and state, and had adopted as one of their measures of reform the abolition of tithes. Careful as the priesthood had ever been to identify themselves with the French Canadian nationality, sparing no effort to impress the habitants that their patriotic aspirations were indissolubly blended with the church of Rome, they had no intention that they should be realized if it cost them the power to tax and tithe. Better British rule with tithe, than French without. The information supplied to Sir John Colborne was so precise that he knew not only the plans of the conspirators but the extent of their resources. He was warned too late to be able to nip the plot in the bud or even to warn the militia officers in the districts affected, and all he could do was to organize to crush it before getting headway. The rebel plan, in brief, was that there should be a simultaneous rising in the corner of the province that lies west of the Richelieu, and that the American contingent was to join them by way of lake Champlain and by crossing the frontier of New York state. With the triangle of country in their possession they would have a base of operations against the rest of the province.

The night of the 3rd November was fixed for the rising and the chief blow was to be struck by the habitants of the county of Laprairie, which included the seigniory of Chateaugay. They were to attack and capture the barracks at the village of Laprairie. The chief agent was a habitant, one Desmarais, who had devoted his time to inducing his neighbors to join the movement, and it is proof of his energy, that no other section was so well-organized. He had been implicated in the rising of 1838 and there was abundant proof for his conviction, but the government, in its mistaken clemency, had set him at liberty. The seigniory of Chateaugay he entrusted to Cardinal, who was to make a night-march on Caughnawaga, surprise the Indians and seize the muskets and ammunition with which the government had supplied them the year before, and then proceed to assist in the attack on Laprairie barracks. . Cardinal was a slow and somewhat heavy man, regarded by many as soft and stupid and by a few as cunning and ambitious. He was certainly callous and ungrateful. The steamer from Lachine, the Chateaugay, was late that Saturday, and it was dark when she reached her wharf. She had a full load, and among her passengers were a number of Old Country farmers. The night was cold and wet and the roads bad, so that it was some time before they got under way. The first to get as far as the bridge was John Lewis Grant, a Lachine farmer, who was on his way to his brother-in-law, John McDonald, to warn him that the Canadians had marked him among those they had designated for assassination.* In front of Mrs Duquette's tavern he met a great crowd of Canadians, who seized hold of his horse's head, and dragging him from his gig, carried him, for he was half-drunk, into a room, where they searched him, thinking he was the bearer of despatches to his brother-in-law. There was no letter but they found a pair of pistols in his pocket, which Duquette

*There was a plot to kill McDonald. It had been arranged with a worthless fellow to do the deed for a sum of money, and was given a knife and pistol as instruments. The plan was that the assassin was to go with a neighbor to McDonald's store and ask him to examine a pile of the bons storekeepers then issued, and, while so engaged, either shoot or stab him. The neighbor refused with horror, and caused, too late, McDonald to be warned of his danger in the manner stated.

appropriated. Shortly afterwards, a string of other passengers came along, when they also were halted and made
prisoners. One of them, John Stewart of Howick, resisted,
when Duquette drew his sword and threatened to run it
through him, when his sons persuaded him to submit. The
crowd was constantly increasing and all were in great glee,
laughing and gesticulating. That the province would be
theirs within a couple of days they had not a shadow of
doubt. By-and-by Canadians appeared who had been sent
for, chasseurs and raquets who had repented at the twelfth
hour and been forced to turn out by patrols sent for them.
Meanwhile two detachments of considerable strength were
marching down the river, visiting the houses of all the Old
Countrymen. The first house they went to was that of
John McDonald, and surrounding it knocked loudly for admittance. McDonald, who was getting into bed, asked their
errand, when they shouted they were going to declare their
independence that night. Delaying to give them admittance,
threats of setting fire to the house were made. His servant
advised resistance, but McDonald said two could do nothing
against so many, and told him to go and hide and seize the
first opportunity to fly to Beauharnois and let Col. Brown
know that the Canadians were in arms. The servant having
hid under a bed, the door was opened, when the rebels crowded in. Their leader, Jean L. Thibert, a neighboring farmer,
ordered him to dress and go with them to his store, for Mc-
Donald was a merchant as well as a farmer. There they
seized some powder and shot, but touched nothing else. Returning to the house, they searched every nook of it for arms,
finding a gun. Reforming their ranks they began their march
to the bridge, taking McDonald with them as prisoner. At
the house of every Old Countryman they came to they halted
and rousing the inmates from their sleep demanded instant
entrance under fearful threats. Taken thus unaware, resistance was impossible, and amid the tears of wife and children,
the head of the house, and, if he had any, his grown-up
sons, were compelled to leave their beds, to huddle on their
clothes and be taken away as prisoners. The hardship was

the greater from the nature of the weather. A piercing blast was sweeping over the country and at intervals heavy showers fell, so that the prisoners, as they dragged their weary way through the mud, were chilled and drenched by wind and rain. At one house the goodwife appeared to answer the summons, and declared that her husband was from home. The Canadians knew better, and told her unless he appeared they would set fire to the barn. She pointed to the chimney, where he had taken refuge, whence he was dragged with laughter and his wife was compelled to supply a piece of rope to tie his arms behind his back, the man telling them he would live to see his captors yet hung with it. In the house of James Holmes, they found the Rev Mr Roach, who had come to hold service on the morrow, and marry a couple on Monday. He also was made prisoner, and there was neither service nor marriage.* At Dickson's house was Robert Findlay, who, on hearing the errand of those who were demanding admittance, jumped out of his bedroom window and made for Caughnawaga, told the Indians of the rising, got them to ferry him over to Lachine, whence he was driven to Montreal and was the first to give Colborne in-

---

* This house-to-house visitation did not pass off as harmlessly elsewhere. A few miles east of the Basin, at La Tortue, two sturdy Yorkshiremen, warned in time of the rebels' approach, stood at either side of the door, musket in hand. The Canadians fired a volley, when Aaron Walker fell back dead in his wife's arms. David Vitty, after discharging his gun, stood his ground, and shouted he would pierce with the bayonet the first Canadian who crossed his threshold. A second volley was fired, and he was wounded in four places. The rebels then rushed in, and found Mrs Walker, clasping a nine months' old infant, bending over her dead husband. Recognizing among them a neighbor, she said, "You have murdered a man who never injured you." "It is good for him and you too," he replied, as he roughly pushed her aside. Vitty, who was dabbled all over with blood from his wounds, asked for a drink, and as one of the household was raising it to his lips, a French Canadian dashed the cup to the ground. A troop of Hussars, from Laprairie barracks, warned by a messenger sent by Walker, were heard approaching, when the rebels fled.

formation that the outbreak had taken place. Every house was searched for arms, but beyond a few fowling-pieces none were found. When the party reached Duquette's they had 19 prisoners, who were led to Madame Boudria's office, where Cardinal had his office. He received his neighbors with complacency, the majority of whom, a few months before, had signed a petition to the government to condone his offence of sharing in the rising of 1837. The leaders consulted, when the farmers were released, excepting McDonald, an Irishman, McLean, who had acted as drill-sergeant to the militia the year before, and a young Aberdonian named Innis, who provoked the Canadians by telling them the Huntingdon men would soon be down to whip them. The release of the passengers by the steamer was refused. The party sent to visit the houses between the Basin and the bridge, took all the arms they could find but made no prisoners.

Having finished their task of making sure that the Old Countrymen had no arms, the order to fall in was given, when Desmarais picked out 150 as the corps to capture the arms at Caughnawaga, and, at the first streak of daylight, they started. About a third had muskets, the others pikes and staves. The road was a mud-track, but, where it would permit, a semblance of military order was maintained, the men marching in platoons. Generally they presented the appearance of a scattered crowd, making their way as they best could on either side of the road. Many by this time had come to think seriously of their situation and the enterprise upon which they were bound. Ignorant as, with the exception of the leaders, they all were, they knew that rebellion was punishable by the halter, and they felt that to disarm Indians in daylight would not be so easy as surprising Old Country farmers in their beds. Any attempt to fall behind was checked, however, by the threat that all who turned would have their brains blown out. Afterwards one of the rank and file related a conversation he had upon the road with Cardinal, which showed that getting the arms of the Indians was not all he aimed at. He told his follower that their American friends objected coming to their assist-

ance until they had achieved some success which would give
them the status of combatants. "If," argued Cardinal, "the
Americans come now and are captured, they will be hanged
as murderers; if they come after we have obtained the standing of belligerents and are captured, they will be treated as
prisoners-of-war," and so he saw in the disarming of the Indians and the capture of their village more than a merely
prudential step.

On reaching the vicinity of Caughnawaga, the Canadians
were ordered to halt and lie concealed in the woods, which
surround the place, while Cardinal and Duquette would go
to the village to reconnoitre. Quietly as they had advanced
and early as was the hour, they had been observed by a
squaw, who was looking for her cow, and she, young and
fleet of foot, fled with the intelligence that armed men were
lurking in the bush. A brave was sent out as a scout, and
he speedily returned, confirming the girl's statement. George
Delorimier, the head-chief, to whom he brought the word,
connecting the presence of the Canadians with the tidings
Findlay had brought during the night, concluded at once
that the rebels meant, improbable as it might seem, an attack
on Caughnawaga. The bell was ringing for first mass and
part of the congregation had assembled. Delorimier sent
the priest word, who stopped the service, while messengers
passed from cabin to cabin summoning the braves to assemble at the may-pole with their arms. All this was done
with the silence and secrecy which are characteristic of the
Red Man, so that when Cardinal and Duquette came walking
into the village unconcernedly, and as if paying a customary
visit, they could not tell by any sign that the Indians were
aware of the force they had within hail in the woods or that
they were ready to fight them. Cardinal went to the store
of Delorimier and sounded him as to the arms and ammunition the Indians had and where they were kept, said he
would like to see the chiefs and hinted he would pay a
good price for any guns they would sell him. In further
conversation with the chiefs, he told them the whole province
had risen in arms during the night and that they were sure

to make Lower Canada independent. If the chiefs would
join them, or even lend them their arms, they would not
only be well paid, but would be allowed to keep their seigniory under the new government. When asked what they
wanted the arms for, Cardinal said to go and aid in taking
Laprairie. He used no threats, did not tell them if they
did not give up their arms, he would take them by force; in
fact, thought he was going to succeed by diplomacy. When
word was brought that all was ready and that the braves
of the tribe had assembled at the flagpole prepared for fight,
the chiefs threw off all dissimulation and made their two
tempters prisoners. Wondering what detained Cardinal and
Duquette three others of the leaders came walking carelessly
and unarmed into the village to find out, when they likewise were detained. If they advanced into the woods, the
Indians knew that the Canadians, after firing a volley, which
might do them some injury, would scatter and fly, and so
escape them, which would not suit their designs. They resorted to a very simple stratagem to capture them. Picking
out a few of their number, they sent them into the woods
to endeavor to induce the Canadians to come into the village.
By this time the habitants had grown restive. Exhausted by
the excitement and exertions of the preceding night, cold
and hungry, they were in no mood to fight the Iroquois, so
that, while waiting in the bush, many took the opportunity
of stealing off to their homes. Lapailleur was now left the
sole leader, and, on seeing a few of the Indians approaching,
among them a chief, and apparently without arms (they had
their tomahawks and scalping-knives concealed under their
clothes) he concluded that a friendly arrangement had been
made by the leaders who had gone to the village and went
forward to meet them, accompanied by one of his men. After
the interchange of a few friendly words, one of the Indians
playfully snatched away his pistol, which was his sole weapon,
when his companion ran back to the Canadians and ordered
them to advance. Lepailleur forbade them to fire and said
they were going to settle matters with the Indians like
brothers, and the Indian messengers confirmed this by a

general shaking of hands. "Would they not come to the village?" The Canadians answered, "Perhaps if we go to the village you will make us prisoners." "Don't be frightened," retorted the chief, "I will take care of that." Thus assured they walked towards the village, and on coming in sight of it saw the Indians drawn up in line. With fatal indecision they did not fire, and in a few moments they were surrounded, the war-whoop sounded in their ears, their guns were wrested out of their hands, and they were made prisoners, the Indians thus capturing the band without striking a blow. Disarmed, the Canadians had to bear the jeers and laughter of their captors as they examined the mode in which many of them had loaded their guns. Getting their canoes ready, the Canadians were marched down to them, and, with only 2 or 3 Indians to each as a guard, were forced to take the paddles and row themselves over the St Lawrence to Lachine and captivity. On reaching the north bank, from the earliness of the hour and the day being Sunday, only a solitary trooper was to be seen. Here was a second opportunity to escape, yet no effort was made to break away, and they passed on to the prison, which two of them, Cardinal and Duquette, left for the scaffold, and 4 for the hold of a convict ship.* The sight of the captive rebels, as they were marched through the streets of Montreal, had a strong effect in deterring sympathizers from rising, and the effect was deepened when it became known that, on reaching the jail, the prisoners had been eager to save themselves by turning Queen's evidence, and that even Cardinal's brother-in-law had made a deposition criminating him. But the Indians were not done with the Chateaugay rebels. Finding out next day that they had established a guard-house at the

---

* Desmarais was not among the prisoners. When the Canadians were waiting in the bush, he suspected all was not going well, and, being on horseback, he rode to the outskirts of the wood, and on learning of the capture of the poor men he had helped to delude, returned to Chateaugay and subsequently escaped to the United States. Newcomb, a Canadian Yankee, also got away. The Indians took 75 prisoners.

Basin, they haunted it, and, during a heavy shower of snow, a band of them suddenly dashed into it, seized the muskets, and kicked the astonished guard out of doors before they knew what had happened. After that, a well-known Indian appeared one day on horseback at the headquarters at the bridge, with a message which he alleged came from the chiefs, to the effect that they wished to have friendship re-established with their French brothers, and if they would send some of the patriot chiefs they would talk over their differences and, perhaps, make an alliance with them. The rebels deliberated over the message, when it was decided to send the deputation asked for. They had just entered the Caughnawaga woods, when they were pounced upon and sent prisoners to Montreal. Among the captured was an American, a brother of Jacob Dewitt, and the Indians arguing that whatever belonged to the rebels was fair spoil, a party of them, bearing raft-oars, boarded the steamer Chateaugay and began rowing her to Caughnawaga. They were with difficulty induced to give up their prize on the representation that the vessel was needed for the Queen's service.

It will be recollected that when the Canadians surrounded the house of John McDonald, he told his servant to hide himself and to take the first opportunity of fleeing to Beauharnois to give the alarm to Colonel Brown. This the young man, Bean, did, for, so soon as the rebels had left, he slipped out to the stable, saddled a horse and struck out for Beauharnois. By riding hard, he entered that town by midnight, and drew rein at the door of John Ross, the leading store-keeper, to enquire where he would find Brown. He was told, and was turning his horse's head, when curiosity caused Mr Ross to ask the object of his errand at so late an hour, when he told him of the events at Chateaugay—of the Canadians having risen in arms and of McDonald's being taken prisoner, and then hastened on. Mr Ross, who was captain of the volunteer company, at once dressed and proceeded to warn his men to get under arms. On Bean's rousing Col. Brown, he received his story with incredulity, until, on cross-questioning, he found that it was too true, when he hastened to the mansion-house to warn Mr Ellice, and then went to Mr Ross's to get out the volunteers, and was gratified to find that already a dozen had assembled. The astonishment of the group in Ross's store is not to be described. Of all events, a second rebellion was the most unlooked for by them. Living in the heart of a French population they had not detected a sign of preparation, and even yet thought that Bean must have misapprehended what had passed at McDonald's house. Only one of them, John Bryson, had no doubts on the subject. He told how, that evening, he had gone to pay an account to a French Canadian, when a dispute arose, during which the man exclaimed to him, "In two or three hours see what will happen to you damned English." He did not understand then what he meant, but he did now. Others had remarked, that while the Canadians had gone early to bed and no lights were to be seen in their houses, they had noticed in passing men peering out at the windows, more particularly of Prevost's tavern. These men were watching for the arrival of the contingents from Ste Martine and St Timothy, which was to be the signal for them to come forth. From there being a volunteer company in the village, and the capture of the seigniory-house with its inmates being regarded as an undertaking of responsibility, the disaffected of Beauharnois did not consider themselves capable for the task alone and had stipulated for outside help. When Lord Durham came on his mission to Canada, Edward Ellice, eldest son of the seignior, accompanied him, and took up his residence at. Beauharnois, Brown moving out of the mansion-house for his accommodation. He had kept up great style, Lord Durham, among other notables, paying him a visit, and on the night of the rising had several guests. The design was to have surrounded the mansion-house so soon as the inmates had gone to bed and taken possession. Time passed and neither the St Timothy nor the Ste Martine contingents appeared. The watchers in Prevost's had noted the arrival of the horseman, his calling on Ross and Brown, and the assembling of the volunteers, and had sickening doubts that they had been betrayed. It was long after midnight when

Dumouchel rode up to Prevost's, with the word that the Ste
Martine men were collected behind the Catholic church, and
were waiting impatiently for the St Timothy force. It was
resolved to strike without waiting for them, so, while Col.
Brown was out on his errand to see about getting the volunteers under arms, the party at the tavern sallied forth and
divided, one portion going towards the house of Ross the
other to that of David Norman, a storekeeper, who was
quartermaster of the volunteer company and kept their
arms. Norman had been notified by Ross of the rising,
and as the rebels went along the street they met him while
hurrying from house to house rousing the members of the
company. He was seized and taken to his store and ordered
to open the door. He refused, and, despite threats of immediate death, persisted in refusing, whereupon the door
was burst in and the muskets together with a barrel of
powder taken possession of. The moment the men left Prevost's, the village suddenly burst into life. Every window
was lighted and men, women, and children filled the streets,
excitedly shouting and running hither and thither. The
houses of nearly all the English-speaking residents were
entered and the men made prisoners, among others those of
Duncan the baker and of Robert Wilson, carpenter. The
party detailed to go to Ross's store met on the way Robert
Finney, whom they took prisoner. They had scarcely done
so, when several volunteers appeared, whereon the rebels fled,
except one, who fell on his knees and begged for mercy. In
another part of the village, a volunteer, Robt. Johnson, stopped
a man on horseback, and made him prisoner. He proved to
be Louis Dumouchel, a tavern-keeper of Ste Martine. While
detaining him until assistance should come, Dumouchel took
advantage of his captor's attention being momentarily distracted, to put spurs to his horse and gallop yelling up the
hill, when he was answered by a chorus of shouts, which was
the first intimation the volunteers had of the force at the
Catholic church, and Brown and Ross at once decided that
it was necessary they should advance with the few men they
had and cover the entrance to the seigniory-house. This was

done, and the men formed in line at the gateway. Hardly
had they done so, when, through the darkness of that stormy
night, the Canadians, with a tremendous yell, came rushing
down the hill and across the open field at the foot of it, the
voice of their leader, Joseph Dumouchel, shouting "Ho, my
comrades : forward !" and firing their guns. Colonel Brown
was shot in the thumb, but no one else was hurt, the Canadians having aimed too high. Firing a few ineffective shots,
the volunteers ran into the house, where they found Mr Ellice
helping the ladies into the cellar. Colonel Brown told him
there was no use in resisting, and counselled surrendering on
the best terms they could. The cowardly advice was assented
to by Ellice, and the Canadians were admitted on promising
to respect the ladies. They rushed in, when the few volunteers, some 10 or 12, handed them their muskets. Brown
asked what they meant by such conduct, when he received
a hurricane of answers from the excited crowd who swarmed
everywhere. "We have suffered long enough," "the Canadians must have their rights," and "we want the country
for ourselves." The premises were searched, and 11 barrels
of cartridges and some dozen muskets were found, at which
the rebels were much disappointed, for they had believed,
from Colonel Brown's having been entrusted by the government with the distribution of arms for the district, that
several hundred muskets and three cannon were stored on
the premises. The Canadians were beside themselves with
joy over their success, and confidently expressed their belief
that the province was theirs. So well-informed a man as
Dr Brienne said 6000 Americans were to have crossed the
frontier that night, but his followers declared the number
was 30,000, and that they would have to pay no more
seigniory-rents and dues and no more tithes ; all their
American allies had asked was that they make way for
them and they would do the rest.

Mr Ellice was disgusted and cowed by what was going on
around him. He was a big, softish sort of man, without
much energy or presence of mind, and who, had he not been
wealthy, would never have been heard of. At that time

there was an infatuation as to the efficacy of constitutional government as a sovereign remedy for the ills of society. The creation of the American republic had started it, the French revolution had aided to develop it, and the prolonged agitation over the reform-bill had grafted it in men's minds that there was a magical efficacy in the government of the people by the people, and constitution-making was regarded as of the first importance. Mr Ellice was one of the circle of whose opinions the Edinburgh Review was the exponent, and he had rather pitied those who were opposed to granting the demands of Papineau. It was a great shame to deny the French Canadians a full measure of self-government, most illiberal to distrust how they would use it; remove all checks and throw the entire responsibility upon them of governing themselves, and you will see what wonders will be wrought. Such were the sentiments of this Englishman on the 3rd November, 1838; on the 4th November of the same year he had not a word to say in favor of the virtues of paper-constitutions or of his protegees. In one hour the French Canadians had turned a friend into an enemy, and a theoretical politician into a practical one, prepared to acknowledge that the Imperial authorities ought to be satisfied on two points before entrusting a dependency with self-government, 1st, that its people possess sufficient intelligence to use it; 2nd, that they are loyal to the head of the empire. When it was intimated to him, that he was to be taken a prisoner to Chateaugay Basin, he was overcome with fear that his life was in danger. Before daylight, he, along with Brown, Ross, Norman, Onslow, and Bryson were put in carts, and, guarded by some 40 men, started. On reaching Norval's house, which was outside the village, a halt was cried, and the rebels bursting in the door entered his bedroom. Altho' taken unawares, Mr Norval resisted, when he heard the voices of his friends outside shouting to him to submit. When he had dressed, he was hurried out, and, being placed in the caleche beside Brown, their wrists were tied together. All the other prisoners were similarly bound, except Mr Ellice, who had also a seat for himself, probably on account of his

being a very stout man. The procession then dragged its
way to Chateaugay, over roads deep in mud and under a
pouring rain. What galled Mr Norval and the others most
of all was that the Canadians who were treating them in
such a manner were their intimate neighbors, whom they
had helped in their necessities a hundred times, and who,
up to the last hour, had professed the greatest friendship.
When the cavalcade halted in front of Duquette's tavern at
Chateaugay bridge, the rebels came swarming around it in
scores, and were greatly elated on seeing Ellice and Brown
prisoners. On Mr Ellice's alighting, the coachman, Finney,
wheeled his horses to return to Beauharnois, when a rebel
raised his musket. A comrade beside him prevented his
drawing the trigger by seizing his arm, and shouting to
Finney to halt; he left his seat, which was taken by a Canadian who drove the team to Ste Martine, where the horses,
fine blacks, were used as mounts by the rebel leaders. At
10 o'clock the exultation of the party at Duquette's was
dashed by Edward Dalton, who came riding at post-haste
with the intelligence of the capture of Cardinal and his
party. It was now all the leaders could do to hold the habitants together, and even they felt that circumspection was
needed. The decision was come to, that the passengers by
the steamer be allowed to go on promising not to bear arms
and that the Beauharnois captives with McDonald be kept
in close confinement, as they might be of value yet in com-
pounding with the government for their own safety. In the
afternoon they were removed to Mallette's house, and confined in a large room; the shutters were closed, a guard
posted, and all communication with the outer world cut off,
even the wives of the prisoners being denied permission to
see them.

When the party at Beauharnois had disposed of Ellice and
the others by sending them to Chateaugay, they began preparations for their next enterprise, which was the capture of
the steamer Henry Brougham, which plied between Lachine
and the Cascades, forming a link in the communication with
Upper Canada. She was to leave the Cascades before day-

light, and would touch at Beauharnois on her way down about 5 o'clock. The plan proposed by Charles Rapin (then a bailiff and afterwards a well-known hotel-keeper) was that a few men should be on the wharf as usual to catch the lines, and that, when securely moored, a rush should be made by the party in concealment behind the buildings. Everything turned out as anticipated. The steamer came unsuspectingly up to the wharf, was moored, and captured in a twinkling by a number of Canadians rushing on board. One of their number, Rochon, a carriage-maker, unscrewed the starting-bar of the engine and took it away, so that the vessel could not possibly escape, but, to make doubly sure, a hole was bored in the hold and she was scuttled at the wharf. The passengers, 17 in number, and who were all from Upper Canada, were made prisoners, and taken up to Prevost's tavern. Ultimately they were removed to the Presbytery, where Mrs Ellice and the ladies who had accompanied her from England were also placed. Altogether there were some 40 prisoners in the house, and, except overcrowding, they had nothing to complain of, the priest, the Rev M. Quintal, being exceedingly kind. A strong guard was kept round the doors, and they were not allowed to go out. The other Old Country people, who were not confined here, were yet, in a measure, prisoners, as the sentries posted on the different roads would not let them pass. Very few remained to be thus treated, for, after the surrender of the mansion-house, the majority of those who apprehended molestation, took canoes before daylight and escaped to Lachine. The week that followed was an exciting one to the rebels who, to the number of about 500, held possession of the village. There was a succession of rumors causing marches and counter-marches to Chateaugay and Baker's. Among the leaders there was only one stranger, Chevalier Delorimier, a Montreal notary, who maintained a disguise by dressing in grey and wearing green goggles. On the forenoon of the 10th there was great excitement caused by a small steamer seen approaching from Lachine. It ran close in shore and then headed for the Cascades. It was laden with arms for the

Glengarry militia and its menacing Beauharnois was a piece
of bravado. The rebels felt that they were more likely to be
assailed from the land-side than from the lake, and in a field
westward of the village, above Buisson point, they converted
a stone-fence into a barricade and flanked it with wooden
cannon. This was the only direction in which defence was
needed, for to the south the village was covered by the camp
at Baker's and to the east by that at Chateaugay.

Sir John Colborne's plan was to assail the rebels both from
the east and the west. Colonel Carmichael was stationed at
Cornwall with a detachment of regulars and he was instructed
to organize a force to attack Beauharnois from above, while
Captain Campbell was ordered to cross with the Lachine
brigade to Caughnawaga, and with the Indians march on
Chateaugay and, breaking up the camp there, pass on to
Beauharnois. Campbell used the utmost secrecy in his movements, crossing the river after dark, and advancing swiftly
on Chateaugay, but it was to no purpose, for the rebel camp
had broken up that morning. After a week spent in drill,
the decision had been come to that they would unite with
the rebel army at Napierville, where they believed there was
a huge army, including a large number of Americans. On
the morning of the 10th they started, taking with them
Ellice and the other prisoners, 11 altogether, in carts, and
bound with ropes. The week spent by the prisoners had
been a miserable one. They had not lacked for food, the
priest and the nuns having daily sent them baskets, but close
confinement in a dark room had told upon them. When
Ellice one day opened a shutter, the guard levelled his
musket at him. After that, as a favor, candles were allowed
them. When the column reached Lapigeonniere the news
of the rout of the rebel army met them. The prisoners
were taken into a house and the leaders hastily consulted
what they should do. They agreed to make for the United
States. And what about the prisoners? One hinted at shooting them, when another remarked that they would be hunted
down and shot next. The prisoners were bundled into the
carts again and the journey resumed. They were greatly

alarmed and, when a halt was made in a lonely part of the road, and they overheard the words, "Won't this place do?" they looked blankly in each other's white faces, believing their last hour had come. At that moment the trampling of horses was heard, and a body of Hussars came in sight. Instantly the French vanished in the woods, where the cavalry could not follow. Overjoyed at their rescue, Brown took charge and succeeded in hiring conveyances to take them to Laprairie, and they reached Montreal in sore plight. Ellice was so thoroughly disgusted with Canada, that he started at once for New York and England, determined to induce his father to sell every acre he owned in the Province.

Colonel Carmichael had no trouble in getting all the men required for his expedition. On the report of the rebellion reaching Glengarry, the county rose en masse, the loyal Highlanders burning with but one desire, to get an opportunity to crush it. They came to his headquarters in hundreds, beseeching him to give them the privilege of striking a blow for their Queen and British connection. As fast as he got them enrolled and supplied with arms, he sent them by steamer to Coteau, where he meant to start from. By the 9th his arrangements were completed and at daylight next morning the Neptune with two barges in tow crossed with the first detachment. There was then no wharf on the Beauharnois side, and the wind was so high that great difficulty was experienced in landing the men at Knight's point, and still more in landing the horses. With all the expedition possible it was noon before the last of the force was brought over, and the march for Beauharnois begun. The frost had transformed the mud into stone, making walking unpleasant and cutting the boots of the men. The troopers went ahead reconnoitring and seizing carts and horses for the use of the army. At 6 o'clock they were within 2 miles of Beauharnois, when a halt for half an hour's much-needed refreshment was called. Ensign Cox, who, at great risk, had gone forward to note the enemy's position, returned with the report that neither the barricade nor the stone gristmill were occupied, as had been feared, but that the rebels were concentrated around the priest's house on the top of the hill and that the bridge was intact. Carmichael's plan was to cross the St Louis river and then let the cavalry ascend the hill to the east, deploy and surround the rebels on the south, while the infantry would assault them in front. Silently, in the dim moonlight, the force resumed their march, and crossed the St Louis bridge at 8 o'clock, wheeled, occupied the mill and other buildings, and were facing up the hill, when the whole plan miscarried through the ardency of a bugler, who, rejoiced at the capture of the dreaded stone gristmill, sounded a joyful call. The rebels, who had got word late in the day of the crossing of the expedition at Hungry bay, had not supposed it was so near, did not believe it would approach Beauharnois until daylight, now learned of its arrival by the untimely bugle-call. They quickly gathered at the head of the hill, and when, in a short time, they heard the tramp of the advancing column, fired a hurried volley and fled. By their scattering fire 3 of the loyalists were wounded; one of them, Private Turner of the 71st Highlanders, was shot through the head, and lay in an insensible state until morning, when he died. He was a Scotchman and well-liked by his comrades. The return fire did no execution. A scene of bustle and excitement followed. The prisoners in the priest's house, who had taken refuge in the cellar at the sound of the musketry, were rescued and French Canadians, suspected of being rebels, were arrested on every hand. Soon the village was lit by the glare of burning buildings. The loyal inhabitants, known to be indignant at the rebels getting off so easily the previous year, were accused of starting those fires, and if so, they punished themselves for their wantonness, for the fires spread, and much property belonging to loyal people was destroyed. Next morning 4 of the Lachine troop rode in with a message from Campbell telling of his unopposed occupation of Chateaugay. There, too, the torch wrought mischief, many houses and barns being destroyed and much property taken by the Indians. The Glengarry men had a special eye for the Canadian ponies, and Sir Francis Bond Head declared they went to Beauharnois infantry and left it cavalry. When the Lord Brougham was refitted, she started for Lachine with 82 prisoners, a rebel flag, and a wooden cannon, which· was about 5 feet long, made of layers of plank, bound together with numerous iron-hoops.

Comparatively few of the Beauharnois rebels were caught. The country being then nearly all bush, they had ample cover, and they fled towards the United States, especially to Fort Covington. The Old Countrymen of St Anicet had organized a guard to watch the Valleyfield road, and it was stationed at the end of the bridge that spans the small creek on lot 11. On the evening of the 11th, the three who were on duty saw, suddenly emerging from the wood, a band of 29 men, marching in military order, and all save two with muskets. They were a body of Beauharnois rebels making for the Fort. Despite their superiority in numbers, on seeing the 3 men on guard at the bridge, they broke rank and fled into the bush. As they were disappearing, the last man turned to take a look, when Barney McGuire fired and the bullet broke the bridge of the rebel's nose—Charles Rapin, who afterwards kept a tavern in Beauharnois and became crier of Her Majesty's court, of which another, concerned in the outbreak at Beauharnois, Louis Hainault, was made sheriff. The fleeing men were pursued by the settlers, who quickly turned out, but there was no tracking them in the marsh. It was afterwards learned part returned to their homes and part safely reached the Fort. The following day one of their number, Jacques Goyette, was found in the house of the fisherman Legare, which stood on the shore of Hungry bay. He had Norval's sword and having been a leader, was sentenced to transportation to Botany Bay.

Having traced the course of the rebellion along the St Lawrence, I would now narrate the events that happened in the Chateaugay valley during the week. The sun had not long set on Saturday, 3rd November, when the habitants, intent on rebellion, began to gather at Miller's tavern on the outskirts of Ste Martine and in that village. The village then, as now, was purely French Canadian, so that the only

Old Countrymen were the few who happened to be in its taverns on their way to or from Montreal. Among them was Archibald Henderson, the Huntingdon mill-owner, who, at the first alarm, went to the barn and hid among the hay. The rebels, after searching the house, came to the barn, exclaiming, "They must be hid here," and began to prod among the forage with their pikes, the point of one wounding Mr Henderson in the thigh and discovering him to his searchers, who, in an excited manner, dragged him to the tavern, when the wound was dressed by Dr Brienne. The other English-speaking guests taken prisoners were in no way molested beyond being deprived of their liberty. Having thus established their supremacy at Ste Martine a detachment was sent to the Bean river to assist in seizing the Old Countrymen of that section and another and much longer force, led by Dr Brienne, Louis Dumouchel, who kept a tavern at Ste Martine, his brother Joseph, and François X. Touchette, a blacksmith, started across the country for Beauharnois to help their brethren there, and which they did in the manner already narrated, returning to the Chateaugay next morning. The Bean river contingent was late in leaving and operations there were not begun until daylight. I leave David, son of Donald Cameron, (p 234) to tell what they did:

We had not the faintest suspicion that the French Canadians were contemplating a rising and neither had any of our neighbors. They worked for us and we went in and out among them as usual. We went to bed on the evening of Saturday, 3rd November, without dread and with a full feeling of security. In the morning we were awakened by the noise of a number of men rushing into our shanty. The door was only latched, and they came in without difficulty. We were all in bed. Day was just breaking, it being about a quarter past six, and a dull morning, rain falling in a Scotch mist. The intruders were all armed in one way or other. Some had fowling-pieces, others pitchforks, and a number reaping-hooks (sickles) set at the end of poles, in the way they were then used for cutting peas. I knew them all, for they were our neighbors. I comprehended at once their object, and realized they had risen in a second rebellion. I calculated in a flash how many I could handle, and thought I might dispose of five, and springing up I went at them.

One of them grasped me by my night-shirt and lifting me threw me out of the door, where I lay naked, the shirt having been torn. I now saw there were fully 60 men, and that it was folly to resist. I could see my father struggling with a number of them, pushing and wrestling, and shouted to him to desist, that the French were in force, and resistance was of no use. He kept up fighting them, however, until over-powered, when he was thrown out violently beside me. I told him it would be wise to submit, and finally he agreed to go with the rebels if they would give him his clothes. A rebel asked for them and while my mother was carrying them out, another (Chaloup) struck at her with his weapon, a sickle set on a pole, which missed her breast and cut a gash on her right arm, the mark of which she carried to her grave. The rebels were under command of Joseph Patenaude, a neighbor of ours. I asked those who were guarding me, what object they had in rising. "Oh," answered one of them, "we are going to get tithes and (seigniory) rent put away, which will be a good thing for you too." I then asked what they were going to do with us. "We are going to take you to Ste Mar-tine to see King Papineau." They seized the two muskets we had as volunteers, and the place where they were was pointed out by two Canadians who had been working for us the day before. Having hastily put on our clothes, we were hurried away. While crossing the gully near our house, my father made another attempt to wrench himself away from his guards, but was again overpowered and thrown down. A habitant, a neighbor, untied the sash from his waist and proceeded to bind my father's arms with it. While so doing, my father gave a backward kick that sent him sprawling. There was again a great outcry, and my father was roughly used. All being got in order again, we were forced forward, proceeding to Hugh Henderson's house, who was surprised in bed as we were, and he and two Irishmen from Norton Creek, who had been working for him and unable to go home the night before from its being so dark and the roads bad, were made prisoners. The houses of Peter Henderson, Jas. Ritchie, and John Lowrey were successively visited, and in all 10 prisoners were made. The house of James Thomson had been visited before ours, and he was in their hands when I went out. In fording the Bean river, Michel Patenaude, who had a great respect for my father, insisted on his getting upon his back, which he did and was carried over dry-shod. We had gone about 2 miles when my father, who felt at being taken into Ste Martine with bandaged arms, got them loosened on promising he would not try to escape. We were marched up to Joseph Demers' tavern and given some bread and cheese. The tavern stood opposite the church, and the priest, Father Power, was walking up and down in front of the presbytery. The two Irishmen from Norton creek, who were Catholics, wanted to go over to speak to him, but were refused. After waiting some time, word came that we were to be taken to Dumouchel's, and the party was got ready. Another prisoner had been added to our number, Dominick McGowan, the Ste Martine storekeeper. On coming opposite Dumouchel's, we were crossed in a scow. On entering his tavern, we found Joseph Dumouchel busy in serving out ammunition and weapons to the men who crowded the bar-room. My father at once complained to him of his treatment, when Dumouchel, who was a customer and a good acquaintance of father's, professed much regret that violence had been used. "Why," he said, "I took Brown and Ellice prisoners last night, and did not hurt a hair of their heads." On his saying he wondered neighbors like us should be against the French Canadians, my father replied that we were not against the French Canadians, but were resolved to maintain the Queen's authority and British connection, which, if they would only think it, was best for both them and us. Dumouchel said if we would take the oath of allegiance to King Papineau he would let us return to our homes, and produced a Bible, which I saw was an English one, and bore Perrigo's name. The two from Norton Creek and McGowan were disposed to comply, but none of the others would, my father telling Dumouchel he would take no pledge but perform his duty to his Queen so far as circumstances would permit him. After a good deal of talk, we were unconditionally released, were treated at the bar by Dumouchel, and got home in the middle of the afternoon, and much relieved those we left behind us were on seeing us come. While at Dumouchel's we saw the Canadians assembling at Baker's, and towards the camp there a constant stream was flocking.

It was part of the rebel plan to have treated the settlers on the English river and on the Chateaugay above Baker's in like manner to those of Bean river, but it was not carried out, probably because the risk of going into thickly populated settlements, where many were members of volunteer companies, was too great for the courage of those to whom the task had been allotted. On Sunday morning, the first sign to the Scotch farmers west of Baker's of the rising of the preceding night, was finding that their French Canadian servants had deserted and that not a man was to be seen in the houses of the habitants near them. It was speedily ascertained that a camp had been organized at Baker's and the French everywhere were in arms. The tidings flew westward like wildfire, and the expectation in every household was that the rebels would speedily appear. As to a common centre, the settlers crowded to Sandy Williamson's, to get the news and decide on what was to be done. The general opinion was in favor of each one going back to his own home and defending it to the last extremity. In the midst of their consultation the Rev Dr Muir arrived and perceiving the danger of such a course and that their only hope lay in united resistance, he pleaded earnestly with them to keep together and not to allow themselves to be captured in detail as they would did they adhere to their first determination. Of the soundness of the advice thus tendered they were ultimately persuaded, and it was resolved that each man should go home and get his gun and then assemble at the church at Brodie's, which had just been finished, all save the pulpit and seats. This was done and by noon there was a band of resolute men inside its walls, who would have disputed their advance had the Canadians left their camp, which they did not, being busily engaged in organizing the reinforcements that were hourly arriving.

Wherever the alarming intelligence reached an Old Countryman, he shouldered the musket he had received as a volunteer at the rebellion of the year before, resolved to die sooner than let Canada pass from British sway. The blockhouse was regarded as the place to make a stand by the men of Jamestown and Ormstown, and Captain John Tate had soon a large body of loyal men mustered within its walls. At Huntingdon the people were gathering for worship, and some had gone into St Andrew's to take their seats, when Archibald McEachern (afterwards Colonel McEachern, C.M.G.) galloped past, coated with mud, and went into Milne's tavern, where Colonel Campbell, who had charge of the volunteer service, happened to be staying, and told

him of what was happening at Baker's. The colonel at once
sent out messengers to warn the volunteers to assemble.
The congregation by this time had gathered in St Andrew's
and the Rev Mr Walker had begun the service, when Mc-
Eachern came in and walking up to the pulpit whispered to
the minister that the French had again risen in rebellion.
"Is that so?" queried he in astonishment. "Yes," answered
the messenger. Instantly Mr Walker slapped the open Bible
before him together, with the words, "Then it is time we
were away from here." Leaning over the pulpit he told his
astounded hearers that the French had risen in rebellion and
exhorted them to fly to arms, and march instantly to put
them down. The congregation crowded out and, before many
minutes, a number had their muskets, Mr Walker himself
being prominent, as he stalked back and forth, his tall form,
though bent, towering above the throng, with a gun over his
shoulder. All were not of his mind, however, and the maiden
sister of an industrious settler was heard exclaiming to him,
"Come awa hame, Jock; gin the minister wants to fecht let
him dae't himsel." The reception of the alarming news had
a different effect on another, though smaller congregation,
that had met that morning. The Rev. Ashbel Parmelee, the
Congregational minister of Malone, had come to conduct
service for those who had recently formed themselves into
a congregation in connection with the American Presbyterian
church. They had met in the schoolhouse at the northwest
end of the village, and were engaged in prayer, when one of
the Danskins came to the door, and shouted that the French
were on the way and would soon arrive to kill them all. Mr
Parmelee, with much dignity and composure, said quietly that
the men should leave to meet the enemy, but the women and
children remain, for, if death was coming, they could not meet
it better than while engaged in the worship of God. This
was done, those able to bear arms left, and to those who
remained, Mr Parmelee preached a striking sermon from that
passage of Ezekiel where, under the figure of a river, the
Deliverer from sin is revealed. Long before he was done,
Colonel Campbell, accompanied by his man-servant Mulhol-

land and McEachern, were on the way to the scene of alarm, and reached Bryson's in a few hours. What he there learned caused him to send back McEachern with a despatch to Col. Davidson, ordering him to march with his command at daylight to Reeves's.

The facts of the rising had, as usual in times of excitement, been grossly exaggerated. For instance, the report was spread far and wide that day, that the' Canadians were marching victoriously towards Huntingdon, burning everything before them, and had reached the Portage (Dewittville). The alarming news by no means disconcerted the Old Countrymen, who all day came flocking into the village to join the companies. The chief drawback was the want of arms, for there were not muskets enough, and many of them were in wretched condition. Sandy Lumsden, blacksmith, of Athelstan, was set to work in the church repairing them, and not a few were brought to him with the flints tied to the hammer, while Willie Stark was kept busy shoeing horses for scouts and messengers. Such a Sunday had never been known in Huntingdon, the street being crowded with an excited throng, and St Andrew's made the rendezvous of armed men. In the confusion a musket was discharged and the bullet went through the roof of the sacred edifice. At night its floor was covered by sleeping men. Early on Monday morning they fell into rank, when it was found there were 150 men sufficiently equipped to go forward, and they began their march; watched until out of sight by women with moistened eyes and sad misgivings as to what might happen them ere they returned. The present aspect of the country gives little idea of what it was on that eventful morning, for the road from Huntingdon to Dewittville passed through almost solid bush, the clearances being small and the houses log-shanties. From Dewittville onwards the clearances were larger, yet they were only notches in the forest, which extended without a break on the north. The road could hardly have been worse; so bad, indeed, that the men preferred the fields, along which they tramped, jumping ditches and fences. As each man had been ordered to take a day's food in his pocket, the

halt at the yellow house was brief, yet with all expedition
it was late in the afternoon when the blockhouse was reached, and to which they were ferried in a scow, and there the
wearied men found food and rest within its walls and those
of the neighboring shanties. To their eager enquiries, they
were told the French were encamped at Baker's, and their
numbers were grossly overestimated. Except along the St
Louis and the 4th concession they had not molested the Old
Countrymen. There a body of 200 had visited every house
and seized what arms they had. After a miserable night, for
the blockhouse was overcrowded and its atmosphere dense
with smoke, the chimneys being out of order, the men fell
in and renewed their march, Colonel Campbell leaving in
charge of the blockhouse the company of Captain John Tate,
raised mainly from the 2nd and 3rd concessions, with orders
not to leave it under any circumstances.* The force in a
couple of hours reached Reeves's tavern and found that there
was no change in the position of the rebels.

The ground they had selected possessed no military
strength. The country is a great flat plain, with the Chateaugay winding sluggishly through it. Along its banks
and for some distance back from them were cleared fields,
with a background of forest. The road from Huntingdon
to the Basin followed the river bank, and at Baker's, where
the rebels had formed their camp, a road that led to Beauharnois struck off. At the corners, formed by the joining
of the two roads, stood George Washington Baker's house,
a large 2-story wooden building, painted yellow. Baker was
of American descent (page 46) and strong for annexation,

*This order gave rise to a strange misunderstanding. Three
days afterwards a trooper appeared on the opposite bank and
shouted that Colonel Campbell ordered Capt. Tate to join him
with all his men save 10 who were to be left in charge of the
blockhouse. The captain was in a quandary, and asked Sergt.
Younie's advice, who, a shrewd old soldier, said the trooper
had no written despatch and an order by word of mouth
could not supersede the express one, personally given, not to
leave the blockhouse. This seemed so sagacious, that the
trooper's order was disregarded.

and in so far as the rebels were likely to bring that about he was favorable to them, but he was too astute a man to believe they could succeed. He told them only failure was in store for them, as they had neither plans, arms, nor a fit leader. In his brother-in-law, Dr Perrigo, (p. 137) who lived beside him, the rebels found more encouragement. In 1837 he was deep in the rebel secrets, and set down as a colonel in their army. The clemency of the government, in withholding from prosecuting him, had had no effect beyond making him believe its mercy arose from timidity, and he unhesitatingly threw in his lot a second time with the rebels. Baker's conviction that failure awaited them did not prevent his house being chosen as headquarters, and the rebels from Ste Martine and the adjoining parishes made for it, on the morning of the eventful Sunday. Being a wealthy farmer, they found abundance of provisions in his cellar and barn. Hoping to save something, Baker affected to go in with them, and sending away his family to a neighbor's for safety, remained. West of Baker's were three stone houses, where the Leclere brothers lived and beyond them was Reeves' tavern, but the habitants who swarmed around Baker's made no move to take possession of them. Their decision was to stay where they were, and await any attack that might come from Huntingdon. The timber of a stranded raft was hauled up the river-bank and with rails and slabs a barricade was made, some 4 feet high, crossing the road and extending about 150 feet into the neighboring field. On the road a wooden cannon, made of staves strongly hooped, was planted, to rake any approaching force. On Monday evening they threw out a picket-line, which had its headquarters in Jean Leclere's house. On Tuesday, on the Huntingdon column's arrival, Campbell ordered 8 of them to occupy it. Creeping up behind a barn, they fired into the window that faced it, and reloading ran for the house and entered it. The men had fled to the camp, leaving a number of women and children stricken with fear. None had been hurt by the bullets, which had lodged in a cupboard and smashed the crockery it contained. The inmates were

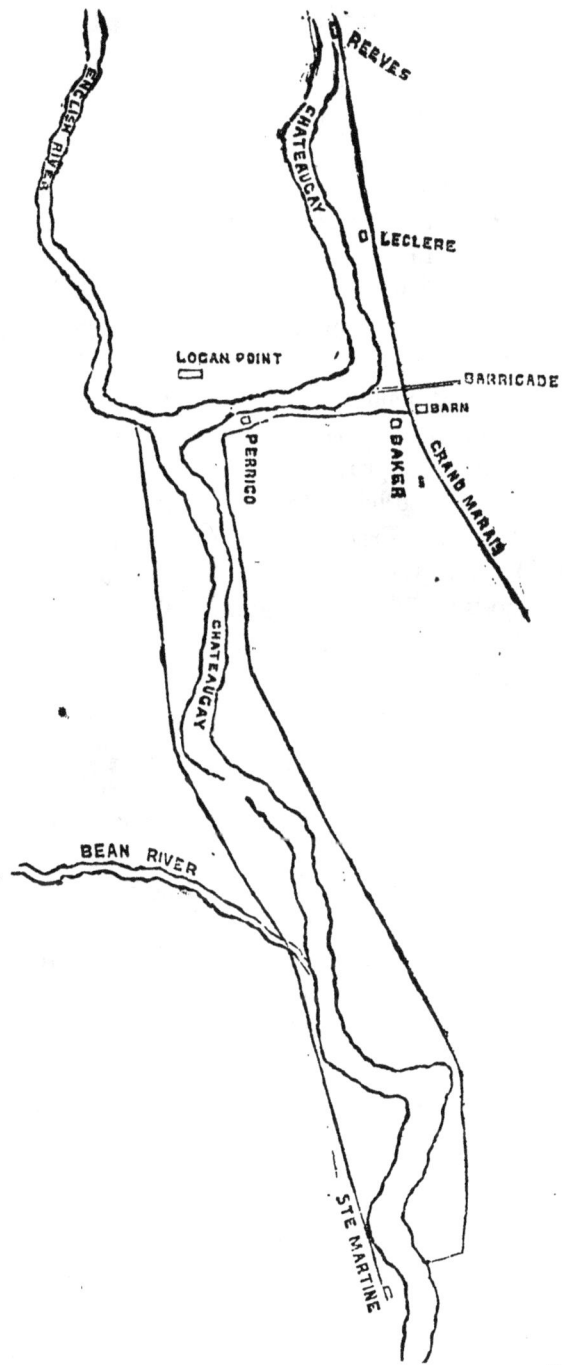

MAP OF THE SCENE OF OPERATIONS

conveyed to other shelter, when the windows were planked and loopholed, and a guard stationed in it, each man being assigned his post in case of attack. A straw-thatched barn, between the house and the rebel camp, which would give shelter to an attacking party, was set fire to after dark, and its burning spread consternation among the rebels, who were seen flying towards Ste Martine. On Tuesday and Wednesday morning further reinforcements were received from Huntingdon and more men came in from the English river and the neighboring country than there were arms for. Shelter was found for them in the houses around Reeves, and there was no scarcity of provisions. The settlers' wives, for miles up the river, baked bread to send to them, hogs were slaughtered, and old Mr Brodie brought them a number of cheese. The volunteers, however, did not trust their commissariat entirely to such friendly hands. They lived, to use the phrase of one of them, at heck and manger, rumaging the deserted houses and barns of the French. In one house only the women were found, but when the volunteers were helping themselves to potatoes in the cellar, Jean Baptiste was unearthed himself, and, once assured of his safety, proved to be a hearty good fellow and a kind host.

On Wednesday morning the men were eager in their desire to assault the rebel camp, the weakness of which was now apparent. Colonel Campbell refused, saying a majority of the volunteers were married men, and he would not be responsible for the butchery which might ensue. In this decision he was largely influenced by Dr Muir and several of his friends, who held that the prudent course was to await the reinforcements that were on the way from Glengarry before assuming the offensive. A strict disciplinarian, he issued orders to the captains to complete the organization of their companies and keep up constant drill. Baker, anxious to get out of his predicament, sent a message by George Cross, who had passed the lines unseen, asking Col. Campbell to give him a meeting. That evening, walking quietly down by the river's edge, he met Baker, and before coming up to him, called out, "That you, Baker, eh? you'll be hanged for a rebel !" The salutation so alarmed Baker, who suspected that he was going to be seized, that he turned and fled, and next morning threw in his lot with the rebels and shouldered a musket. His intention was to have acquainted Campbell of the true position of the rebels and showed him how he could have won a bloodless victory. Reinforcements kept arriving almost hourly at Reeves's, being farmers from the upper country, chiefly from Hinchinbrook and Godmanchester, very few being from the village, where the expectation was that American sympathizers would come down from Chateaugay, N.Y., and so they remained, under control of Major McGibbon, to defend their property from such a danger. The Jamestown company (Capt. Strachan's) was stationed at the gristmill at Ormstown, which had just been built and into which the machinery had not yet been put. The neighboring French Canadians were arrested as found and placed in its cellar, until it became full. Beyond being kept in custody until the danger was passed, they were not injured. The men of Williamstown and Edwardstown, forming 4 companies, were stationed in the Norton creek gristmill, as a check to any advance the rebels of St Remi might make. An incident of their occupation is worth recording. One day the volunteers on the upper-story detected a lurking figure in the neighboring bush, and guessing he was a spy, who was examining their position, stole quickly out and caught him before he knew he had been perceived. His name was Lafrance, and he had been sent from Napierville to reconnoitre. Without more ado, his hands were tied and his eyes bandaged, and the guns were pointed to shoot him, when Mrs John McLennan, who had accompanied her husband to the mill and acted as cook to Finlayson's company, rushed out, and at her intercession, he was let off. His narrow escape did not frighten him out of his treasonable courses, for he went back and took part in the fight at Odelltown church.

The settlers of English river formed a company under Captain James Craig. On hearing of the trouble on Sunday morning, they marched to the blockhouse, where they remained until ordered to reconnoitre St Louis, where it was reported the rebels were gathering. The men proceeded up the 3rd concession, meeting with no opposition, and after burning a house at the head of it, where they were told the rebels had lodged, came back, and slept in the church at Brodie's, leaving next morning for Reeves's.

The appearance of the Huntingdon volunteers greatly disconcerted the insurgents in Baker's camp, many of whom seeing that matters were going to prove more serious than anticipated, took every opportunity to desert. A messenger was sent in hot haste to Beauharnois for reinforcements and he found the rebels having an easy time of it, lounging about the taverns and the mansion-house, the cellar of which contained on ample supply of food and drink, and taking what else they wanted out of the store of Mr Ross, causing the clerk to keep an account, as they said all would be paid for when the French republic was established. The leaders consulted and agreed they could spare the help asked for. On Wednesday, after dinner, all who had guns were marshalled in front of Prevost's, and over a hundred volunteered to go. They were commanded by Prieur, a St Timothy storekeeper, and Delorimier, the Montreal notary, and their arrival did much to restore the confidence of those at Baker's.

The discontent in the loyal camp at their continued inaction was growing to the verge of mutiny, the men threatening they would make an assault without orders. There were urgent reasons for bringing matters to a crisis, for the suspense throughout the English settlements was painful, and the majority of the volunteers were so situated that they could not remain much longer from home. In many settlements there was not a man, all having gone to the front, and women not only tended the live-stock but hauled firewood and threshed. Colonel Campbell was not to be moved from his policy of remaining on the defensive. He had seen some service while a subaltern, and was wounded in the leg at Waterloo, but his experience had made him a martinet without giving him the dash and courage of the soldier. When his officers, as a few dared to do, remonstrated with him, he

represented the danger of assaulting the rebels with an un-
disciplined force, and implied his distrust in the men he commanded. He would make no move until the force he had
been advised of arrived from Glengarry. On Thursday a
collision was precipitated by accident. On the forenoon of
that day, Captain Somerville walked from Reeves' towards
the rebel camp, and seeing no signs of life about it approached very near. The log-house, in which the rebel
picket lodged, a few acres west of their camp, was apparently tenantless. Mr Somerville came to the conclusion that
the camp had been deserted during the night, and returning
to Reeves' reported what he had seen to Campbell, who decided he would make a reconnoissance. After dinner, Capt.
Reid's company was ordered out and, accompanied by a few
mounted scouts and several officers of other companies, he
proceeded to do so. The men, 25 in number, were arranged
in open order, 6 paces apart, and advanced steadily, throwing
down the fences as they went, which was a stupid act, as,
in case of opposition, it deprived them of all cover. No
enemy appeared until the small creek was neared, when,
suddenly, from Baker's house and barns the rebels came
streaming out like bees from a hive, and ranged themselves
along the road and behind the stockade, with Prieur, mounted
on one of the black team stolen from the seigniory stables,
endeavoring to get them in order. Those who had guns were
posted in front and those who had only pikes stood behind.
There were about 200, and all wore blue tuques. The advancing volunteers saw this, but Colonel Campbell, who had
halted in the centre of a field and was trying to fix a tele-
scope upon the rebel position, was unconscious of the danger.
The space narrowed until the volunteers were within 300
yards of the stockade, when the French fired a volley.
Startled by the sound, Campbell shouted to the volunteers
to halt, which they did, remarking they had come to reconnoitre and not to fight, when, on the rebels continuing to fire,
he gave the order to retreat, which the men heard with disgust, for they expected the next order to be to charge the
enemy's position. Their captain, James Reid, lost no time

in obeying the order to retire, and ran off, the new recruits of his company following his example. The body of the men fell back slowly and irregularly, for they had their overcoats on and all their equipment, and the field they had to traverse was a plowed one. Colonel Campbell commanded them not to return the rebel fire, which was superfluous, for few of the volunteers could have got their muskets to go off. Rain had begun to fall in big drops which dampened what priming had remained dry after scrambling over the fields and ditches. Some of the men, when they came to examine their muskets afterwards, actually poured the water out of the barrels. The French kept up a sputtering fire, so illdirected that it did no harm, and, despite the colonel's command, a few of the volunteers, especially those who had rifles, fired back, possibly 20 shots altogether. When nearly out of range, and approaching where a line fence had been pulled down, William King, of the 1st concession of Elgin, was hit. His exclamation "I'm shot!" startled those near him and his comrades hastened their pace. In the rush, the author of this shameful scene, Colonel Campbell, slipped and fell, and being slightly lame from his wound, was unable to rise. As the men hurried past him, he bawled out, "You rascals, are you going to leave your commander." Robert Morrison, who was mounted, tried to lift him on to his horse but could not, when James Coulter and Abram Foster of the Gore caught hold of him and assisted him off the field. Before leaving, he told Morrison to order the volunteers to keep the rebels in check, for they showed an inclination to move northwards to flank his force. A few shots caused them to again seek the shelter of the barricade. Poor King, though conscious of his wound, jumped a broad ditch and made for John Leclere's house, where John Anderson was waiting, and asked for a drink. Anderson went out and got a dipperful of water, when, as King raised it to his lips, he fell in a faint. While some of his comrades, who had now assembled, went for a horse to take him to Reeves', one of them, a powerful fellow, caught him up in his arms and carried him across the 3 lots. By this time all the rest of the force were under arms and hastening to the point of danger, the Rev Mr Walker at the head of Captain Somerville's company, waving a sergeant's sword and exclaiming that their captain might be killed but he would lead them. At sight of their comrades, Capt. Reid's men halted, and for a few seconds the general expectation was the order to advance and carry the French position. Colonel Campbell would not give it, however, and told the captains to march their companies back to their quarters. The mortification was great and the feeling was intensified by the order that came later to prepare to withstand an assault by barricading the windows of the houses occupied by the companies and it was remembered how reluctantly Sergeants Ford and Corbett nailed them up. Hogs were slaughtered, provisions laid in to stand a blockade, and, instead of outposts, that night two men stood guard at each window. Campbell's apprehensions of a night attack, which caused such orders, were entirely groundless, for the enemy had not the remotest intention of assuming the offensive; in fact were so sick of the whole affair that the majority were watching for a chance to desert and were only kept in camp by the threats of their leaders and the cajolements of Delorimier, who assured them that, although the Americans had not yet appeared, they were certain to come. Unconscious of the state of matters in the opposing camp, the volunteers spent an anxious and sleepless night, deepened by the weather, for it rained heavily, and by the knowledge that poor King was dying. He was carried to an upper room in Reeves's and attended by Dr Shirriff, who could do nothing for him, as the ball had passed from the back through the lungs and lodged in the breast. With the childishness of small souls placed in positions of authority, Campbell had all along exercised much mystery about paltry matters, and King's sickness was no exception. His condition was kept a secret and no information communicated to the men, and, when, after prolonged agony, he died, an hour before midnight, the body was taken to a room in the attic, put in a hastily-made coffin, lowered out of a window at daylight, and sent home. Such attempts at concealment only embittered the state of feeling among the rank-and-file. As the body was on its way to Elgin, those in charge of it met the Cornwall militia, and a band of 70 St Regis Indians hurrying to reinforce Colonel Campbell. The meeting took place east of Ormstown, and at sight of the coffin the Indians raised the war-whoop, which, echoing over the forest, was heard with dismay by families many miles off.

' How the Glengarries and their dusky allies had come to be there can be told in few words. Colonel Turner, who was in command at Cornwall, had received orders to send reinforcements to Colonel Campbell, and he detached from his command a battalion of the 1st Stormont regiment of militia, 250 men, under Colonel Æneas MacDonnell, and he also had a fighting chaplain, in the Rev John McKenzie. The force went on board the steamer Neptune at Cornwall, which landed them at Dundee, where they were met by the St Regis Indians under their agent, Captain Solomon Chesley. This was the forenoon of the 6th. They at once formed into line and took the road for Huntingdon, which they reached, after a fatiguing tramp, late that night, which was rainy. . They resumed their march the following day but owing to the awful state of the roads were overtaken by darkness when they reached Ormstown. They were heartily welcomed by McEachern, who did all he could for his brother Highlanders, the rank-and-file finding quarters in the church and barns, while the gristmill was given to the Indians, who managed to get some whisky and kept up a constant yelling. Early next morning they resumed their march, hastened by messages from Campbell, and met the coffin of King as narrated. When the sound of the bagpipes reached the camp, the volunteers were ordered to line the road to greet them. On the Highlanders came, great stalwart men, with swinging stride, and swept by, amid cheers, their pipers proudly playing "The Campbells are Coming," and never halted until they reached the front and established their headquarters at Leclere's. Shaking hands, Colonel Campbell asked when his men would be ready for the assault. "As soon as they get their over-coats off," replied the dauntless Macdonnell, but Campbell was not prepared to avail himself of such promptitude, wanted to wait until Col. Carmichael reported from Beauharnois, and the afternoon slipped by in like inaction to the three that preceded it. That day a messenger from Napierville arrived in the rebel camp, with a letter asking for reinforcements. This was so contrary to the expectation of the habitants, who had been buoyed up by promises that the great combined army of Americans and patriots at that place was coming to help them, that desertions increased, and the leaders, not caring to await the assault they knew was inevitable after the arrival of the Glengarry men, decided on abandoning the camp. Before daylight they began their retreat, were crossed at Ste Martine in two scows, and took the road for Napierville. Before they had gone far, news of the defeat at Odelltown church met them, and then it was every man for himself. Their abandonment of their camp was discovered early on Saturday by Peter Gibson who, rambling about in his simplicity, crossed the barricade and found nobody. After breakfast the advance began, the Indians and Glengarry men leading, who tossed the barricade aside and passed on to Ste Martine, wading the river. As the others followed, Baker's and Perrigo's houses were emptied of what provisions they contained and then fired. It was noted as proof of the quantity of hay and grain they contained, that fire smouldered in the ruins of Baker's barns for a fortnight. On every hand prisoners were made, the rebels submitting so meekly, that a trooper might be seen driving a score before him. Entering Ste Martine the Indians instantly overspread the place, and robbed every house they found tenantless. When Colonel Campbell entered the village he accepted Father Power's invitation to breakfast, who interceded on behalf of his neighbor, Joseph Brazeau, but the colonel was firm. Brazeau had been one of the leaders and they must be punished. As he left, the match was applied to Brazeau's store. The habitants, on giving up what arms they had, were dismissed to their homes. Taking the Bean river road, the column marched to St Remi and their march was a trail of spoliation. The Huntingdon men refrained but the Glengarries and the Indians showed not the slightest compunction in plundering the houses they passed, and when they left for home, there were few who had not a bundle of household effects tied to their shoulders or conveyed in a cart. One Indian was seen to coolly empty out the feathers from a mattress and take away the tick. The worst thieves of all, however, were unprincipled men who roamed in the rear of the troops and stole the horses of the habitants. Before the column came in sight of St Remi, word was received that the place was already in the hands of part of Colborne's army and their services were unneeded. The day they arrived a most painful incident took place. Thos. Gebbie, lieutenant in Finlayson's company, was ordered to go with a detachment and arrest certain rebels in St Remi. The duty, a most distressing one, for the majority were found in the midst of their families, he performed, leaving for Norton creek mill with 15. Among them was Grenier, a storekeeper, who had been a captain in the rebel ranks. Asking as a favor that he be permitted to ride, he took his horse. A few minutes after Lieutenant Gebbie had left, a troop of Hussars galloped into the village, and their sergeant waited on the priest to get information. The father, who spoke English imperfectly, said a body of rebels had just left, and pointed the direction they had gone. Taking it for granted he spoke of a body of fleeing rebels, the Hussars put spurs to their horses, and galloped after them. Coming in sight of a party of men, dressed like farmers, with muskets over their shoulders, plodding through the mud, the Hussars shouted to them to halt and in a moment were upon them, each one seizing a man. Mr Gebbie, who had a pistol levelled at him by one horseman and a sword held over his head by another, was about to explain they were laboring under a mistake, that they were not rebels but a party of loyal volunteers in charge of rebel prisoners, when Grenier, either frightened by what was going on or seeing a chance for escape, slipped off his horse and ran for the fence, in going over which a bullet, fired by a Hussar, struck him, and he died an hour afterwards.

The rebellion being over the volunteers were discharged,

and they returned homewards. Those from Huntingdon got
back after an absence of exactly ten days, during which time
few had their clothes off, had undergone much privation,
and borne most fatiguing marches over execrable roads in
the worst of weather. To the widow and infant son of King
they voted a day's pay, which, for a private, was 24 cents.
The government gave her no compensation.

I would now shift the scene to Hemingford and describe
what took place there. While Colonel Scriver was on his
way to Troy, he learned on the lake Champlain steamboat
sufficient to convince him that a second rising was imminent,
so, instead of prosecuting his visit, he returned home and
made preparations for getting the militia companies in readiness. On Sunday morning, 4th Nov., the intelligence was
brought of the French having risen in St Remi and the
parishes east of it, and throughout Hemingford there were
lively apprehensions of an invasion by them. There was
great spirit shown by the settlers, who not only turned out
themselves but brought their sons, if old enough to carry a
musket. The militia companies were soon filled, and volunteer companies then formed. Alex. McFee raised one in the
northern part of Havelock, John Edwards another on Covey
hill, and Thos. Woolrich a third on the 1st and 2nd ranges
of Hemingford. There were not arms for all, so they took
what they had, and the majority had only fowling-pieces.
Guards were posted at the Flats, Perry's corners, and other
roads leading from Chateaugay county and the States. The
French leaders had assiduously striven to coax the Irish Catholics to unite with them. Whatever dissatisfaction with the
British government lingered in the minds of the Irish Catholics who had become settlers, they were not going to be led
by it into cutting the ground from beneath their feet. They
took a commonsense view of the situation, perceived plainly
that the motive of the rebellion was one of race, and that if
they helped the rebels to drive the English-speaking Protestants out of the province, the turn of the English-speaking
Catholics would come next. They therefore rejected the ap-
36

proaches of the French, and joined their neighbors in the ranks. In Colonel Scriver's opinion no attack was to be apprehended from the French parishes; the source of danger was the United States, and the defeat of ,any body that might enter from there by way of Mooers or Rouse's Point was imperative. With this in view, he notified his captains to hold themselves in readiness to march. Captain McAllister with the Sherrington company arrived at Hemingford on Monday, 5th November, and were billeted there until the move was made. On the forenoon of the 6th, a message was received from Colonel Odell, stating that he had positive information that the rebels were gathering at Rouse's Point, and asking Colonel Scriver to be prepared to come with all the men he could muster. He made instant preparations to do so. The day had been damp and lowery, but towards evening the sky cleared and a sharp frost set in, which formed a crust on the mud. The little hamlet of Hemingford was in a state of excitement. Every house was overcrowded with men anxiously talking over the prospect, whose number was each minute increased by the arrival of others, who came prepared to march. There was no talk of flinching among those hardy backwoodsmen, the overwhelming majority of whom were from the North of Ireland. Their instructions had been to bring a day's provisions, pork and oatbread, and this with the muskets they shouldered constituted their equipment, for they had no uniform. In order that they might distinguish friend from foe in the dark, Col. Scriver had each man tie a strip of white cotton cloth round his arm. Midnight came and went and still the expected order to march was not given, Scriver being in doubt as to the point of attack. Captain Woolrich's company came in late from Clelland's corners, and cartridges were served out—20 round to each man, one cartridge having 5 buckshot besides the bullet. Two o'clock drew near, when a mounted messenger emerged from the darkness with a letter. It was from Odell, and stated that the rebels were crossing from Rouse's Point and, fearing they would overwhelm him, asked for immediate assistance. Colonel Scriver wrote a reply, that he would be

with him by 10 o'clock at the latest, and the messenger left,
while another was sent to Capt. Shields of Sherrington to
join with his company at Roxham corners. The order to fall
in was given, and in the starlight the companies mustered
quickly on the road. Woolrich's company was placed in
front, and following it were the companies of Donald McFee
and McAllister. Colonel Scriver, who alone was mounted,
briefly told the men they were going to Odelltown to meet
the rebels there. He knew that many among them had unjustly suspected him, but he would now show them what
sort of man he was. He exhorted them to act bravely, and
added, if any of them saw him act as did not become a man,
to shoot him. Up to the moment of this announcement, the
impression among the men was that they were to go to St
Edward's. The word to march was given and the wretched
journey began. The road, soaked by the recent rains, and
the mud cut up by the unusual travel of the past few
days, would have been almost impassable but for the frost,
which made firm footing where the puddles were not deep.
No wagons were taken, and each man stumbled forward in
the dark, weighted by his musket, the 20 rounds of ammunition, and his day's provisions. No apprehension being entertained of a surprise, the column, with no further precaution than having their guns loaded, pushed forward through
the swampy flats, covered by a dense growth of tamarack
and brush that marks the dividing-line between Hemingford
and Lacolle, the strains of the bagpipes, played by Dryden, a
Highlander, relieving the tedium. Soon the column emerged
on the cleared lands of the Roxham settlement. Four miles
and a half were traversed and the corners reached, when the
order sounded through the night air to halt. Capt. Shields
with his company had not come up, and the column would
have to wait their arrival, one of the 3 mounted despatchmen
in attendance being sent to hurry them up. While the men
waited they munched the crusts they had brought and the
neighboring farmer, Charles Stewart, brought out all the milk
he had. The eastern sky was whitening with the coming
day, when Shields' company came up, raising the little force

to a total of 220 men, and, falling in at once, the hurried
march was resumed. Leaving the rocks and knolls of Roxham, with its strips of forest, a fine open country was entered.
On reaching the turn that leads to Beaver meadow, the road
was left, and a short cut taken across the commons. Scriver,
who from the start, had never ceased to ride up and down
the column, encouraging the men, here remarked, "If the
rebels will give us a chance on a field like this, we will show
them what we can do." It was now broad day, and in front
spread the beautiful flats of Beaver meadow, which were then
in as high a state of cultivation as they are to-day. The turn
was taken to Harper's house, a roomy two-storied edifice, and
here a brief halt was made for breakfast. Men were detailed
to visit the nearer farm-houses to get what food they could
spare to eke out the provisions the men had in their pockets.
Here the 3 despatchmen left their horses and took their place
in the ranks. Scriver alone kept his mount, a powerful buff
colored horse, which he rode with grace. Eight miles had
now been got over, and the rising ground along which Odelltown-street runs was in sight. The men's spirits rose as the
hour of encounter approached, and the anxiety was great to
find where the enemy awaited them. It was 8 o'clock when
they fell in and as they took the turn up the slope to Eldredge's corners, which is marked by a lonely graveyard on
the north side, two men were seen waiting. One of them,
who wore a blue military cloak, advanced and taking it for
granted the approaching straggling column of men in the
ordinary attire of farmers was a portion of the rebel force
from Napierville or St Remi coming to unite with the expedition that had gathered near Rouse's Point, and which he,
with his companion, had been sent to meet, walked confidently up to the front ranks and addressed them as French
Canadians. He was quickly undeceived, for in a twinkling
both were made prisoners. Following this incident, the distant boom of cannon was heard in front. The pace was
quickened and the corner of the Odelltown road gained, when
one of the finest landscapes on the continent burst upon the
view of the wearied but excited men. The morning was a

[Map illustration with labels: RICHELIEU, LAKE CHAMPLAIN, REBELS, ROUSE'S POINT, ALACOLLE, BARNS, O CHAMPLAIN, HOUSE, CHURCH, ODELLTOWN, FLORBACKS CORNERS, BEAVER MEADOW, ROXHAM CORNERS, BOUNDARY LINE, HEMINGFORD]

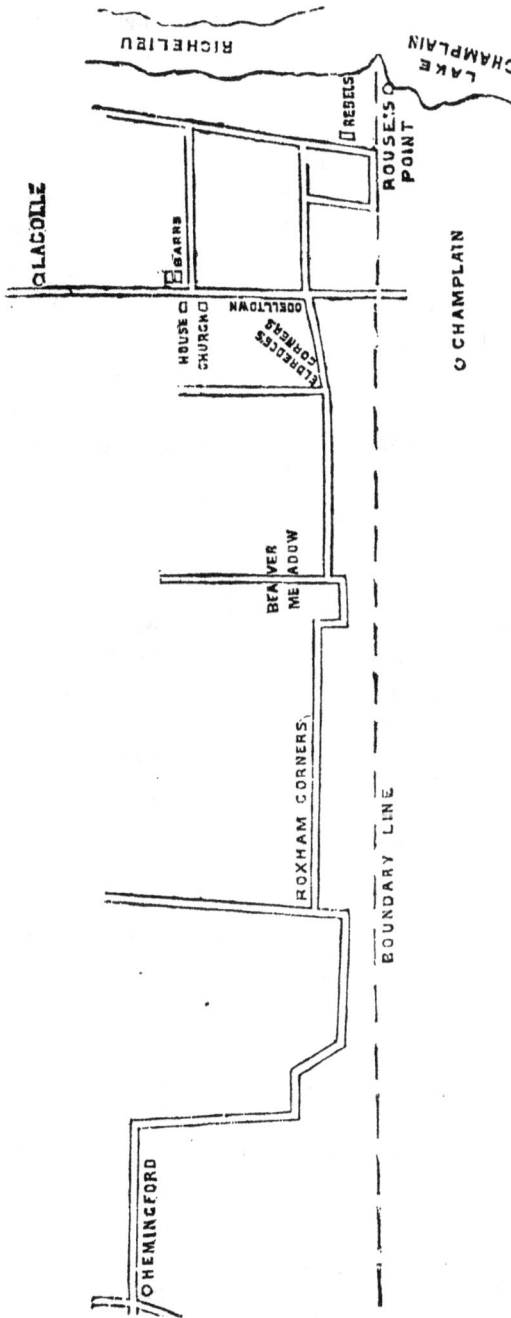

glorious one—bright sunlight permeating the frosty air. To the south-east were ranged, sharp and clear, the ranges of the Green Mountains; every outline of Mansfield and Camel's Hump traced against the cold sky. Midway in the great plain that stretched between them and the peaked heights of Vermont, the sunlight fell on the gray masonry of the bastions of Fort Montgomery, and between it and the clustering houses of Rouse's Point was seen the shimmer of lake Champlain. In front the level fields, outlined by their fences, of Odelltown and, beyond, of Caldwell's Manor, were depicted as on a map. The Hemingford men were looking on the cradle of their township, where its pioneers had been reared, and many of whose fathers had helped to clear this fertile plain. Not a few of them, reared in the bush, for the first time saw smooth fields, free from stumps and stones. Northward the great plain, lightened at uncertain intervals by the gleam of the waters of the Richelieu, stretched until lost to view. From the name Odelltown the reader is apt to be misled into supposing that it designates a village or town. Among the refugees from the tyranny of the victorious Republicans in the war of the American revolution was Joshua Odell, who took up land a short distance across the frontier from the town of Champlain, and on the direct road to Montreal. After the custom of the country his name was used to designate the settlement of which he was the first and leading member, and as his family was large and took up farms around him, the whole section, a strip of several miles, came to be known as Odelltown. But there was no village, not even a corner-hamlet, simply a fine concession of farmers' homesteads. In front of a stone-building, erected by Squire Odell for a store, was drawn up in line the Odelltown force, consisting of a battalion of hastily enrolled militia and March's company of Lacolle volunteers, who alone had uniforms, consisting of white blanket suits. Passing to the head of the line, the Hemingford men halted, and Scriver stepped into the house with Colonel Odell and his officers. While they were consulting, the rank-and-file had an opportunity of viewing the position of the enemy. Odelltown-street, as the road they stood on is named, follows the crest of the western side of the valley of the Richelieu. The height above the river is slight, but the slope downwards is so gentle, and the great plain it overlooks so perfectly flat, that every object for miles can be distinctly seen from it. To their right, and over a mile away as the crow would fly, at a point on the road parallel to them, where stood a log-house and barn, could be seen a black cluster of men, and from the glitter that momently flashed from it, it was apparent they were armed. More palpable proof was given by the cannon, which stood between the house and the barn, firing an occasional shot in pure bravado, for they were beyond its range. The rebel force was com-

posed of French Canadians who lived on the American side
of the frontier, and who, the evening before, had crossed from
Champlain and Rouse's Point to reinforce their brethren at
Napierville. Selecting the road that leads to Montreal from
Rouse's Point, they had crossed the line and taken up their
quarters at a farmhouse about 200 yards in Canada. Here
they awaited the arrival of the Americans who had promised
to join them from Vermont, and who came straggling in all
night, the most of them rowing up the river in boats. At
daylight a barge and a scow moved slowly up, and landed
some 40 American sympathizers, with several hundred stand
of arms, a large quantity of ammunition, and a 6-pounder
field gun. These were conveyed to the house. The total
force was nearly 400, commanded by a French officer, tall
and pock-marked, named Touvrey, assisted by Dr Côté, a
respectable physician of Napierville, who had been led into
the rebellion from entertaining republican views, and Gagnon,
a vulgar agitator. All three had left Napierville the previous
day to lead the movement. The contingent of Americans
called a farmer of Alburgh, Benjamin Mott, their captain.
Their information being that Colonel Odell, whose force they
could see distinctly on the Odelltown road and on which they
tried shots from their cannon, was afraid to assume the
offensive, they took matters coolly, believing that, before the
day was over, their force would be overpowering. Breakfast
was got ready in the house and the table had been filled and
refilled repeatedly, when a lad came galloping up the road on
a steaming horse, with a message from a friend in Champlain
to Dr Côté, that the enemy had received word of their movement and that Scriver had left Hemingford to fight him. Dr
Côté had hardly read the letter, when the Hemingford column
could be seen defiling down the slope from the Odelltown road.
The rebel officers acted with indecision. There was still time
to go back to the United States or to take up a defensive
position in the scrub of a small swamp that stood in rear of
the house. They did neither, but remained to receive the
onset where they were.

All this takes some time to record, but the consultation

between Scriver and Odell only lasted a minute or two. Odell said, though superior in rank he had not had Scriver's military experience, and his desire was that he should assume command, to which Scriver, a man of few words, consented, and leaving the room went out to where the men were resting on their arms. His plans were quickly made. Captain March was ordered to lead, and endeavor to get between the rebels and the frontier-line, a maneuver which the screen afforded by some bush and a deep ditch favored. Captain Weldon's company was told off to march east and, then striking south, prevent the enemy from retreating towards the Richelieu. Odell, with the remaining companies of his force, was to follow as a reserve, while he himself would attack the rebel position with his own battalion. The orders were given in quick succession, "Try if gun is loaded and primed," "Fix bayonets," "Shoulder arms," "Right wheel: march!" The men marched swiftly down the side-line road from Odelltown street, turned southward at where a stone-school stood, and were soon opposite the enemy, a broad field intervening. The word was given, the 4 companies wheeled, faced the fence, and jumped into the field. At this moment the rebels fired their cannon loaded with grape. The gun had been pointed too low, and the shot tore the earth up in front of the charging-line, though one bullet hit a rail and carried it with the volunteer who was crossing it some distance. The order to fire was given, and a fair volley was delivered at the rebels, who were kneeling behind the road-fence, and who returned the fire individually. The attacking party got excited, broke rank, and began running across the field, firing as they went. Again the cannon belched flame and smoke, and again harmlessly. In correcting the first mistake, it had been trained too high, and the shouting loyalists heard the grape shriek above their heads. Every eye was fixed upon Colonel Scriver, who rode fearlessly in front, waving his sword as he encouraged his men, and that he escaped with his life was solely due to the nervousness and inexperience as marksmen of the rebels. Half the field had been crossed, the cannon had sent another harmless volley of grape into the air, and the rebels were now fairly within the range of the old Brown Bess muskets of the volunteers, when Col. Scriver shouted: "Cease firing: charge!" Instantly a cheer burst from the loyal lads, who dashed forward at the French as they crouched behind the log fence, and, as instantaneously, the rebels jumped up and fled, running at the top of their speed in a slanting direction towards Rouse's Point and finding early cover in the scrub that then covered the plain. Dashing on to the road, the volunteers found the fence that a few moments before was alive with rebels deserted, and not one of them in sight. It was like a transformation scene on the stage. The cannon was there, half-loaded for another shot, behind the fence lay in order a number of pikes, ready to use as bayonets to resist a charge, and in the house blazed a huge fire in the open chimney, and on the table pans of potatoes and meat, as the rebels had left them while breakfasting. Ranged in the house was a great store of muskets, 500 in all, pistols, bowie-knives, and bayonets, brought in from the States to arm the habitants. In the barn were 30 horses, ready saddled, and in the stable-yard the corpses of two rebels lay stretched as they had fallen. Behind the house 6 more dead bodies were seen, and 3 were afterwards discovered. The wounded had crawled or been carried away. Only one prisoner was taken, Captain Mott, found hiding below the sill of the barn. Great was the indignation against Captain March and his blanket-men, for the Hemingford lads stoutly held that had they shown equal zeal to theirs, and been less heedful of the ditch, they could have cut off the rebels' retreat. While still excited by the encounter, Capt. Weldon's men appeared in the east, and narrowly escaped being fired upon, being mistaken for a fresh rebel force. As many of the arms in the house as could be carried were taken out and then the building set on fire, while ropes being attached to the cannon it was dragged in triumph by the volunteers to Odelltown-street. But, alas, they had burdens more sad. Two of the Hemingford men had fallen. William McIntyre, soon after crossing the fence, while halting for a moment beside a small oak tree to take aim, was hit in the groin.

He made no exclamation, but, turning ghastly pale, fell dead. His brother Robert, who was near him, said, "Oh, my brother is shot!" and running up to him found he was dead. He wasted no time in vain grief. The blood of an Irish loyalist coursed in his veins and he turned more eager than before to do his duty against the foe. He hurried forward, and while in the act of taking aim at a rebel behind the fence, was struck in two places, one bullet severing the femoral artery, and he sank to the ground with the words upon his lips, "I am a dead man." Twelve hours before, in leaving home he said to his young wife in parting, "I go to fight for my Bible and my country, and I hope I will do my duty." Their bodies were reverently placed on doors and passing muskets underneath their comrades bore them away with heavy hearts and buried them in their clothes in shallow graves until they could be removed to Hemingford. James Allen of Sherrington was carried in like manner. He was sorely wounded, and despite the medical skill of Dr Adams died that night. The other volunteers who were wounded recovered. The escape of the rebels with such light punishment was attributed more to the volunteers having fixed bayonets than the shelter they enjoyed behind the rail fence. The fixing of the bayonet on the old musket was clumsy, and made correct shooting difficult. It is also to be borne in mind, that few of the loyal forces were marksmen; indeed, many fired a musket that day for the first time.

The men straggled back to Odelltown-st. as they pleased, no effort being made to reform the companies on the field. The impression was, that the engagement had killed the rebel movement in that neighborhood and that there would be no further need of their services. Knowing how anxious their families would be and how much they were required at home, a number started at once for Hemingford. In the afternoon, Colonel Scriver, leaving 20 of Woolrich's company under Lieutenant Sims to reinforce Odell's command, ordered those who remained to fall in, and they followed, the object of the quick return being a dread that the rebels at Mooers would make a like move to that they had checked from

Champlain and Rouse's Point. On reaching Hemingford and learning all was quiet at Mooers, the men, wearied alike from exertion and want of sleep, were permitted to go to their homes, with a warning to assemble next day.

Apart from those under Sims, all the Hemingford men did not leave Odelltown. A number remained to haunt the scene of the late excitement in the expectation that it would soon be renewed. That the rebels who hid under the shelter of a pretendedly friendly power would make a second raid into Canada was not supposed; the seat of danger was to the northwest. On the afternoon of the previous Saturday, the 3rd November, under the direction of one Trepannier, the rebel element in Napierville suddenly asserted itself, by appearing in the streets in bands, armed in a rude fashion, who arrested the loyal inhabitants, some 50 in number, placing them in prison, and posting guards at all outlets so that no message could be sent to the authorities of what had happened. Soon after reinforcements came straggling in from the neighboring parishes, St Remi, St Valentine and Lapigeonierre, among others, furnishing contingents. At four o'clock Lucien Gagnon came marching in with a strong band of habitants and with Dr Côté assumed command. The rebels had it all their own way; the few loyalists were in custody, all the rest of the population were in sympathy, and the ease with which they had gained the upper hand created a feeling of unbounded confidence, which caused every man able to bear arms to crowd into the little town, so that when Sunday dawned there was the raw material of a little army. All was excitement in view of the expected arrival of Dr Robert Nelson* and the American contingent, and they went out to meet him. The previous evening he had embarked on a barge

---

* Dr Nelson was a native of Montreal, and was led to sympathize with the revolt against the crown from his being an ardent republican. He was arrested for complicity in the rebellion of 1837, was released on bail, and taken in charge by Jacob Dewitt, who sent him from Lachine to the Basin on his steamer, and he was driven from there to the lines by the mate of the vessel. When it was discovered, too late, that he

at St Albans, accompanied by two officers from France, Hindenlang and Touvrey, the boat having for cargo 250 muskets. Dropping down the river to lake Champlain, a course was taken for the Canadian shore and early in the morning she tied up to an obscure wharf near the mouth of the Richelieu. Nobody awaited the leader of the contemplated revolution, and the guide left to get aid. After waiting an anxious hour, he was seen returning with half a dozen habitants, whom he had roused out of their beds, and three horses. Getting into the saddle, Nelson and his two aids-de-camp rode to Napierville, the arms and ammunition following in 4 French carts. The road was so bad, that it was drawing towards noon when the little cavalcade was met by the delegation that had come out from Napierville to receive them. With shouting the procession entered the village, when the rebels formed a hollow square in the market-place and Dr Nelson was formally welcomed. In responding the doctor denounced Britain as a tyrannical nation, and declared that the hour had come when its power should be overthrown in Canada. Of the assistance coming from the United States, which he had left a few hours before, he gave a glowing account. Turning to the two gentlemen who were on horseback beside him, he introduced them as officers from old France, exiles on account of their republicanism, and who had come to assist in freeing Canada from the curse of monarchy. The habitants yelled with delight and believed the day of English rule was at an end. The waggons were unloaded and they exchanged their pikes and scythes for fine new American muskets. The French officers set to work to organize the habitants into companies and to teach them something of drill. The commissariat was simple, consisting of the confiscation of the property of the English-speaking residents. The goods in their stores were appropriated for the benefit of the new

had passed through Ormstown and Huntingdon, there was loud indignation against those who had sheltered him. Once safe in the United States he actively co-operated with the French Canadian refugees in organizing another rebellion.

army as were their cattle and grain. Before evening two
elaborate documents were promulgated. The first was an
imitation of the American declaration of independence, giving
reasons for throwing aside allegiance to the British government and for erecting a republic, followed by an enumeration
of the reforms that were to be made in "the State of Lower
Canada." The second was simply a declaration that they
had taken up arms and that they would not "lay those arms
down until we shall have secured to our country the blessings
of patriotic and sympathizing government." To those who
would assist the hand of fraternity and fellowship was extended; on those who opposed them they would "inflict the
retaliation which their own terrific example has set before
us." Dr Nelson signed these documents as "president" and
as "commander-in-chief of the patriot army." The troops
paraded with two small flags, blue with two white stars, and
a large white flag with two blue stars was hoisted on the
village flag-pole. It was the flag of the new republic. A
perfect furore possessed the habitants on hearing of these
doings at Napierville, and by Tuesday it was estimated that
there were 4000 of them who had come to support the rising.
There were more recruits than there were arms for, and the
arrival of fresh supplies from the United States was anxiously waited for. On Tuesday morning Gagnon, Côté, and
Touvrey left for Rouse's Point to hasten the reinforcements
of men and supplies, and next morning were routed by Col.
Scriver as already described. The tidings of this defeat fell
like a thunderbolt on Napierville, and the habitants, true to
their volatile nature, dropped from exultant confidence to
blank despair. That night a large number deserted and returned to their homes, and their place was by no means
supplied by the few who came in that day and next from
Chateaugay and Beauharnois. Dr Nelson saw that if he was
to effect anything at all, he must strike at once. The intention had been to advance on St Johns, and had that town
been captured it would have afforded a base for operations
and a convenient rendezvous for the parishes that lined the
St Lawrence. Instead of striking a bold blow for the cap-

ture of St Johns—the only place of the slightest strategetical value within his reach—he weakly determined upon falling on Odelltown and restoring his communication with the United States. Hindenlang had, with miserable success, striven during the past 5 days to lick the crude material, of which there was such abundance, into something like an army, but it was still little better than an armed mob. All Thursday, it rained, preventing any movement, but on the morning of Friday, the 9th, the order to march was issued and the rebels, to the number of 1200, took the road that led to Odelltown. They moved in companies, the officers being on horseback, and were fairly well-armed, 800 having muskets, the others pikes. Opportunity favored them, for the loyalists had not expected such a movement, and were taken unprepared. An easy-going man and satisfied that the rebels would not assume the offensive, Colonel Odell had the day before, which was very rainy, freely allowed such of his men as wished to visit their families, with orders to muster after dinner on Friday, when Scriver with the Hemingford men were to return and an attack be made on Lacolle. The consequence was that he was left with few men beyond the Hemingford volunteers who had remained, and who were billeted at Fisher's tavern or the Methodist church, where Lieutenant Sims was posted. At 9 o'clock Colonel Taylor, of the regular service, who had been sent the previous winter to organize the militia on the frontier, arrived at Fisher's tavern from St Johns to take command of the designed attack on Lacolle, and for which he brought a quantity of ammunition. He found everything quiet and not a suspicion of danger being close at hand. While resting quietly a messenger came galloping up with a message from Capt. Weldon, who held the advanced post, about half a mile from Lacolle, that the rebels were advancing in great force, and that he was falling back before them. Surprised by the startling news, the colonel ordered out his horse, sprang into the saddle and galloped up the road. He had not gone far when he saw, in front of the Methodist church, a cluster of volunteers gazing earnestly northwards. Among them were

Captain Weldon and his men. They were watching the head
of the rebel column as it appeared above the rise in the road
a little to the north of them. All told there were not 200
men about the church, but Colonel Taylor had no intention
of retreating. The cannon that had been captured two days
before had been left in charge of Lieutenant Sims, and it was
wheeled to the middle of the road and pointed at the advancing column. It was handled by a member of Capt Edwards' company, Lieut. Curran, an old artilleryman, who had
become a Covey hill farmer, and Sergeant Beatty, of the
Royals, a regular, detached to act as adjutant in Woolrich's
company. When about to apply the match, Colonel Taylor,
who was watching the approaching rebel host with his spy-
glass, said, "Wait a minute; I will give the word." In a few
moments he cried, "Fire now!" The gun was badly directed,
and the shot riddled the adjoining fence. At the report, the
rebel column halted, and, dividing, one-half deployed on to
the fields to their right and the other to those on their left,
when they resumed their advance behind the shelter of the
trees and buildings that lined the road. The movement was
well-executed, and its object Colonel Taylor perceived. From
the church there ran backward an old fence with a deep
ditch which continued some 200 yards when it reached a
graveyard. This ditch and the graveyard were promptly
occupied by the loyalists, and the attempt to flank the
church checkmated. As the rebels drew near they set up a
dreadful yell, and opened fire. Up to this time the cannon
alone had been brought into requisition, and, though energeti-
cally served, did no damage to the enemy beyond making
them cautious in advancing. The conduct of the gunners was
admirable. Beatty stuck to his post until disabled by a shot
in the calf of the leg, and Curran had the powder-horn
carried away by a bullet while pouring in priming. When
he shouted that he had no wadding for another shot, a volunteer took off his coat and, tearing out the lining, handed
it to ram home the charge. The rebels after halting a while,
began to edge nearer the church from the northeast when
Colonel Taylor, fearing they designed to make a charge to

capture the field-piece, ordered it to be dragged into the
church. He received a coarse refusal. A minute afterward,
it became apparent it was impossible to stand by it, owing
to the stealthy approach of sharpshooters, and an effort was
made to run it from the road up the steps of the entrance
into the church, when it was found too heavy to handle, and
was left in the ditch. Captain McAllister, whose long white
locks and simple piety alike commanded respect, was standing at the church-door watching the movement. At the
engagement of Wednesday he bore himself bravely, and
when the day was won was overheard to exclaim, "Glory be
to God for this victory." Now he scanned the coming foe
with unblanched cheek, when a rifle bullet, fired by an unseen rebel, struck him on the breast, passing through his
body, grazing the right arm of a loyalist behind him, and
denting the door of the church. Without uttering a word,
the stout-hearted Ulsterman, for he was an Irish Protestant,
fell dead. Colonel Taylor's order, that all should go inside
the church, was unneeded, and the door was shut. It contained 60 men, of whom half were from Hemingford.

The scene of the engagement thus begun has changed but
little during the intervening 50 years. The church was a
plain stone-building, about 45 × 50 feet. In the gable, facing
the road, was the door, with a window on either side of it,
and above 3 small windows, which lighted the gallery. On
each side of the building were 3 windows, and in the rear 2
more. The door opened into a vestibule, ceiled by the gallery
above, and small doors led to the aisles. The pews were high
and square, yet the pulpit towered above them, and faced the
gallery that filled the opposite end. The windows were high
set, so that the bullets, which now began to come whizzing
through them, passed over the heads of those standing beneath.* When it became plain that they were in for a siege,
the courage of the men did not quail. They recognized their

---

* The church is different now, having been remodelled and
modernized, with long gothic windows and new pews and
pulpit. The windows that were behind the pulpit were built
up and the exterior of the walls plastered.

danger, and one sentiment animated them, that they would die at their posts rather than save their lives by surrendering. One drawback there was, they did not like their commander; had contracted a prejudice against him while organizing the companies. To such a feeling Colonel Taylor was indifferent, for his faculties were absorbed in devising means to defeat the rebels. Watching from a window he could see a mass of them moving along the fields to the east of the road with the intent of surrounding the church. It was a moment of supreme anxiety, relieved by seeing Colonel Odell marching up the road with some 140 men. Gallantly they came on until Colonel Odell discovered the overwhelming numbers of the enemy, when, abandoning the idea of attack, he formed a defensive line along the road from Fisher's tavern to near the church, which kept up so steady a fire that it checked the rebel advance. Thus balked on the eastern side of the road, the rebel commanders tried the western flank of the loyalist position, and assailed the grave-yard. From behind the tombstones and the bushes and apple trees between it and the church, came so well-directed a fire that the rebels would not face it. Captain March held the line from the church to the graveyard,* and held it firmly to the close. Finding a flank movement either east or west too difficult for them, the rebels concentrated their efforts upon the church, and their best shots crept forward, finding shelter in fence and tree, until a storm of bullets assailed it on every side except the southern. Their strongest position was the two log barns and the stone fence that surrounded the barn-yard to the north-east of the church, and which Col. Taylor had neglected to occupy.† When the contest outside had re-

* James Brownlee of Hemingford was among those in the graveyard. On asking him if he hit anybody, he answered, "I used to do some poaching in Scotland and I could shoot a bird on the wing or a dog running. That day I did my best."

†The map on page 549 indicates the situation of the church, house, and barns. The house was not occupied by the loyal-ists because it was a frame one, clapboarded, and therefore not bullet-proof.

solved into a duel at long range between combatants under
cover, those in the church felt that they were surrounded
by enemies, of whom a few were within 50 yards of them.
Cooped up in a small building, with musket-bullets pattering
against its walls and flying through its windows, all they
could do to prevent assault was to keep up a hot fire
upon their assailants. As each man loaded his musket, he
cautiously approached a window, took aim, and fired, instantly retiring to give another his place. The danger was
extreme. More than one was pierced while delivering his
fire, and hairbreadth escapes were of momentary occurrence.
Lieutenant Sims, a capital shot, stationed himself at one window, and fired as quick as 5 of his men could supply him
with loaded muskets. A private of the regulars, an Englishman named Negrass, one of the Royals, and adjutant to
Odell's battalion, took possession of the pulpit, and fired out
of the windows in the rear as fast as muskets were handed
up to him. The supply of ammunition being limited, Colonel
Taylor dreaded its giving out, and his voice was heard ever
and anon warning the men not to waste a shot. Father
Kooney, the minister of the circuit, who had been educated
for the priesthood and converted under the Methodists, a
truly sincere and zealous man, was among those shut up in
the church. Visiting the volunteers quartered in it that morning, the rebel advance had surprised him. When told the
enemy was coming he dropped on his knees in prayer, but
as soon as the fighting began and his services were needed,
he became assiduous in attending the wounded and in encouraging the men to contend for their queen and faith.
Small need was there for such exhortation. The stubborn
courage of the British race was roused, and the resolve was
to fight to the bitter end. The conduct of the enemy tended
to encourage them. They could see the rebel officers urging
their men to make a rush for the church, and the habitants
skulking away. Decoigne, dressed in the uniform of the
French army, flourishing his sword, rushed forward repeatedly, but not a man would follow him. Hindenlang's voice
they could hear shouting, "Forward, we are sure to win!"

but all in vain. To use Hindenlang's own words, "The greater part of the Canadians kept out of the range of shot, threw themselves on their knees, with their faces buried in the snow, praying to God, and remaining as motionless as if they were so many saints, hewn in stone." With such remarkable soldiers, the bravery of Hindenlang and Decoigne went for nothing. They had the loyalists at their mercy. A rush of a hundred yards over the open would have brought them to the walls of the church, when they would have been safe, for its windows were too high to allow of a raking fire. To burst in the door would have been the work of a moment, when, with their overwhelming numbers, the few loyalists would have been overpowered. The rush was not made, and the fight went on, 60 men holding at bay 1200. And now the danger foreseen if the fight should last long overtook the gallant band. Their ammunition was running short. A violent snow-squall had come up and the big soft flakes darkened the air. Col. Taylor saw his opportunity. Volunteers were called for to go for a fresh supply of flints and cartridges, and 4 answered. They had not far to go, for in Fisher's tavern, to the south of them, there was plenty stored, and the road was held by Colonel Odell and his men. They ran fast and returned safe with a full supply. When the snow flurry passed away, it was seen that many of the rebels had improved the opportunity to get closer to the church, and now from every tree and bush and fence, even to within 30 yards of it, came the flash of muskets. The storm, however, if it had given them a better position, had impaired their fire. The soft snow had wet many a flint and pan, and the priming failed to take fire. Still, the bullets came thick and fast, and mingled with the reports were shouts from the rebels to give up and they would receive quarter. They were answered with cries of derision and defiance. The little garrison was now desperate and acts of daring that verged on recklessness were enacted at every window. The scene was repulsive. In several pews lay stretched dead men, in others the wounded, writhing in agony, for whom nothing could be done, for there was not even water to give them. Every man was blackened with the smoke of gunpowder and many were smeared with blood. But there was not a whisper of surrender. Colonel Taylor retained perfect composure and coolly directed the men where to aim. The fire from the barn-yard being peculiarly galling, it was determined to put a match to the nearest barn, when James Rodgers and John Crystal, both Huntingdon men, volunteered to do the work. For a minute the fire from within the church was concentrated upon the barnyard, so that not a rebel dare lift his head above his cover. The result was, that when the door was opened, and Crystal and Rodgers sprang out, the one with a smoking portfire the other holding a brand snatched from the stove, they were not seen. A short rush across the road and they were in the nearest barn, the combustibles thrown among the straw in stall and mow, and then a dart back to the church, which was safely gained. A yell of exultation from its defenders at the completion of the gallant deed, and the column of smoke springing upwards, told the rebels what had been done. The adjoining barn caught, and the heat and smoke obliged the rebels to leave their shelter. And here a strange incident took place. Instead of following his companions, one of the rebels ran up to the church shouting "Me fight for the Queen!" A shot from within brought him down, but he managed to drag himself to the door and was admitted. After all was over, while walking across the church, he dropped dead.

But not alone in the church did the men of Odelltown and Huntingdon bear themselves bravely that day. On the line along the road, in the graveyard, and the cover that stretched between it and the church, were deeds of daring done, which explain how it came that the rebels, though four to one, were held at bay for over two hours. In the ditch next the church were some 16 men, mainly Huntingdon volunteers, and among them was Robert Rodgers.* The ditch made a

---

* Now Colonel Rodgers of Franklin Centre and of H. M. Customs, to whom I am indebted for not a few details embodied in this account of the fight. James was his brother.

fair trench, and loading within its shelter, they rose and.
fired, keeping their position throughout the engagement and
having only one wounded, William Moore of Covey Hill. A
bullet struck him on the forehead, when, failing to penetrate
the skull, it ran up between it and the scalp. After recovering from the momentary stun, he tied his handkerchief round.
his head to stop the bleeding, and went on loading and firing
as if nothing had happened.

The fight had now lasted over two hours and the rebels
were no nearer capturing the church than when they began.
Relief was nigh at hand. That morning Scriver had left.
Hemingford with his battalion to join in the expected attack
on Lacolle. On reaching Eldredge's corners, he cried a halt,
and the men rested on the knoll, where the graveyard is laid
out, and munched the food they had in their pockets. The
colonel went about the companies, encouraging them, and
urging the officers to set an example and keep up the spirits
of their men, for they would have a tussle with the rebels
before night. He was in no hurry. Two o'clock was the
hour when he was to join Odell, and it was now only noon;
he would give his men a good rest. Had he only known that
within a mile of him, a handful of loyalists were holding at
bay a horde of rebels, he would have rushed to their rescue,
but no messenger came with word of their peril, and, the
wind being west, no sound of the firing reached his ears.
Help arrived more swiftly from another quarter. Captain
Vaughan, with his company, the Clarenceville Rangers, had
started that morning from Caldwell's Manor to join Colonel
Odell's force, and were now seen coming up the side-line road
down which the church looks. They were a mere handful,
but the sight of them was enough to complete the discomfiture of the rebels, now heartily sick of fighting. Hindenlang
says, "Presently some 20 bureaucrats (loyalists) appearing
from a wood, struck such a terror into the Canadians, that
forthwith the little army was like a flock of sheep, flying as
fast as legs could carry them." The panic was as complete
as sudden. Dr Nelson who had posted himself to the west
of the church, shared in it, and galloped towards Napierville

at the head of his redoubtable army. Colonel Taylor,* on
seeing the movement, ordered out the men in the church to
pursue, which they did, but nothing short of cavalry could
have got wind of them. They disappeared in a minute,
leaving the fields strewed with muskets, pikes, and even
poles, with points hardened by fire, and not a few of their
dead and wounded. The rebels never halted in their flight,
and, sweeping past Lacolle, late in the afternoon straggled
into Napierville, covered with mud, exhausted, and starving.
The leaders saw that all their hopes were blasted and that
night they fled for the United States, and the patriot army
became a thing of the past. The dauntless defenders of the
little Methodist church had given the rebellion its deathblow.

Unconscious of the importance of their achievement, that
little band was intent solely on getting something to eat.
They had had no breakfast, and two hours and a half of
fighting had sharpened their appetites. Father Kooney had
got a great cooler filled with potatoes, whose boiling he looked
after, and the carcase of a sheep was set to roast. When
served, the heroes sat around the church with a rib in one
hand and a potato in the other. Ere their frugal meal was
ready Scriver arrived, and learned, to his vexation, what
service he could have rendered had he been earlier. "And
why didn't ye come sooner?" asked a Hemingford man of
his neighbor. With a glance of admiration at the powder-
blackened hero, whose achievement would have been lessened
by sharing with others, and another of caution at the dead
and the wounded, he answered with the exquisitely witty
equivocation, "An, troth, I think, we came soon enough." The
losses on neither side were heavy. The loyalists, though fighting under cover, had 5 killed and 10 seriously wounded out
of their small number. The rebels left 6 dead and 9 wounded
on the field. They had removed those who fell during the
early part of the engagement to Lacolle. Afterwards it was
ascertained that their total loss was about 50.

*On his return to England he was appointed to the com-
mand of the 29th regt., and fell in the Sikh war, being killed
while acting as brigadier at the battle of Aliwal.

*   *   *   *   *   *   *

The crushing of the rebellion was the work of the English-speaking minority. Of course, the army with which Colborne was slowly moving to the scene of danger, would have done what Scriver, Odell, and Taylor effected, but that does not change the fact, that it was the farmers of English speech who gave the blow that extinguished for a time the movement to convert Lower Canada into a French republic. Even had Colborne with his battalion of regulars delivered the finishing stroke, it would still have remained true that it was the dogged opposition of the English minority to the effort to snap the chain of British connection that defeated the agitation which Papineau represented. This great service has not been hitherto recognized, but to the existence of a handful of farmers born in the British isles, and scattered over the province, future historians will point is due the preserving of a united Canada. Had the rebellion succeeded, Lower Canada would have ceased to be British, and, as the gateway to the west, all the rest of Canada would have been driven into annexation. That we have a united Canada, destined to be the theater for the development of all that is good and great in British institutions, untrammelled by the hereditary hindrances that clog the footsteps of the motherland, is to be ascribed to those Irish, Scotch, and English backwoodsmen, who, no matter how small the community they formed, set their faces as flint against the aspirations of the majority among whom they dwelt. Can the Dominion at large afford to permit these communities to be wiped out? Have the fifty years which have elapsed wrought such a change that no menace to British institutions or the consolidation of Canada is any longer to be feared? Had circumstances permitted me to complete this work in the form designed, I would, by simply tracing out the chain of events, have answered those questions. As it is, the sense of duty to my country will not allow me to drop my pen without touching on points of vital bearing alike on the future of Canada and the well-being of the English-speaking minority, the history of no inconsiderable portion of whom, I trust, the reader has followed with some degree of interest. The narrative of this book leaves that minority, prosperous, aggressive and hopeful. To-day they show signs of decay, are lethargic and disheartened. Once they controlled seven counties. It is questionable if the next census will show them to be a majority in more than three. Whole settlements have disappeared in those fifty years and the strongest of those that survive no more than hold their own. The most sanguine person among them acknowledges that, at the existing rate of decrease, the extinguishment of the English-speaking farming communities is simply a question of time; and that, unless a speedy change in the laws is effected, that decrease will go on with accelerating rapidity.

In 1838 the English-speaking population of Quebec was full of vitality, expansive and self-assertive: in 1888 it is the reverse. What has caused the change? I submit, that it is to be found in the extension to the townships of French laws and customs. When, after the rebellion, the constitution of Canada was recast, the cause defeated in the field won victory after victory in the domain of politics. The bait of gaining the support of a solid phalanx was too much for the patriotism of the Ontario politicians and they bought coalitions with the French party with what they ought to have held inviolable. From 1841 to the present day the political history of Canada has been largely that of compacts with a party whose aim is to strip Quebec of its distinctive British features. For ten years after the union the supreme qualification to entitle an applicant to become a servant to the Queen was that he had borne arms against her, and the national aspirations that had caused so much trouble were revived and strengthened by the spectacle of seeing the public offices of Quebec placed in such hands. Every concession has increased those aspirations, so that while we find a Papineau declaring in 1837 he would be content with the abolition of the veto of the council, by making that body elective, we have now a Mercier who protests against the federal veto and demands for Quebec nothing short of complete autonomy. To the class-legislation which has been building up Quebec as a province peculiar among its sister provinces, and enjoying powers and privileges that pertain to none of them, is to be ascribed the decline of the English-speaking settlements. How this class-legislation affects them a single instance will illustrate. The first aggressive step was the act that extended the parish-system to the townships, whereby the priests resident in them enjoyed the same powers as those in the seigniories, and could, by force of law, collect tithes and taxes to build and maintain churches and presbyteries. Both taxes being collectable off real estate alone, a strong monetary motive was thus supplied by the legislature to the priesthood to get as many of the farms in the townships into the hands of Roman Catholics as possible. So long as a farm is owned by a non-Catholic, it is unproductive to the church; the moment it changes owners and passes into the hands of a Catholic, it yields a 26th part of its grain towards the priest's salary and whatever tax to build or repair church or house the churchwardens may levy. A systematic scheme was inaugurated and is carried on with growing vigor, to push out the English-speaking farmers and substitute habitants. Surely, of all the shortsighted and foolish acts passed by a popular legislature, that was the most superlatively imprudent which offered a premium to a wealthy, disciplined and ambitious organization to get rid of the Old Country farmers of Quebec. I believe the act to be more than unwise, that it is unconstitutional, and do so on these grounds. That after the conquest English law took the place of French law is undeniable, for there is the proclamation of the king to that effect. The point to be settled is, Was not that proclamation superseded by the act of 1774? The Hon. J. W. Horton, than whom there could be no more competent authority on the subject, was one of the witnesses examined before the parliamentary committee in London in 1828, and, in reply to a question, he declared that "so far as regards the townships that proclamation (of 1763) has never been repealed." Several French witnesses were examined, but none of them disputed that statement, and they could not, for the act of 1774 expressly states that the French law and custom is restored to the fief land alone. The distinction is plainly and broadly drawn between the seigniories and the townships; between fief and non-fief land. The people residing in the first were to enjoy again the civil law and customs that had prevailed in the days of Vaudreuil; outside the limits of the parishes and over all the rest of the province, English law was to continue and English law alone. For obvious reasons, French politicians always refer to the act of 1774 as one that covered the entire province, but, in truth, it applied only to a very small portion of it. French law and the power to tax and tithe was conferred not upon the province of Quebec, but the 82 parishes that then existed and them only. It was a limited concession, in no sense applied to the territory outside those 82 parishes. This was proved in Craig's time, when Bishop Plessis was not permitted even to annex new territory to existing parishes or to rearrange their limits. From the beginning, the intention of the Imperial government was that, while they might have to submit to French law and usage lingering for a time in the strip of settled land that fringed the St Lawrence, the province at large should be English to all intents and purposes. Whatever land was surveyed, was measured by acres and not by arpents, and the divisions were named townships and counties, and not parishes and seigniories. The Canada Tenure act, passed in 1826, declares "the law of England the rule by which real estate is to be regulated and administered in the townships," and the report of the select committee of the Imperial parliament in 1828 re-affirms this in these words: "The provision of the act of 1774, providing 'that in all matters of controversy relating to property and civil rights be determined agreeably to the laws and customs of Lower Canada,' there is a marked exception to this concession of French law, namely, 'that it should not apply to lands which had been or should be granted in free and common soccage.'" This condition of affairs continued without alteration until after the union. The two tenures and the two laws existed side by side. In the parishes, seigniorial tenure and French law; in the townships, free and common soccage and English law. From 1841 to the present day can be traced a succession of statutes assimilating the law in Quebec, not by adapting the French law to the English, but by superseding the English law with the French, ignoring the plain rights of the townships and producing the effect, already noted, of weakening the English-speaking population and driving it away.

The question naturally arises, seeing the Old Country settlers of the townships were induced to immigrate and take up their abode under the promise of King George's proclamation, that they were going to a colony where they would be under English law, a promise confirmed and ratified by subsequent legislation of the Imperial parliament, whether it was in the power of the legislature of Upper and Lower Canada, or is even in that of the present Dominion parliament, to violate those terms? The townships of Quebec were settled under certain conditions entered into by the king and his parliament. Can these be violated by subordinate legislatures? In other words, is not the legislation, since 1841, affecting the status of the townships of Quebec ultra vires? When the priest sues a townships farmer for tithes, when the churchwardens lay on his land a tax to build a church, when a bishop steps in and forms a parish with municipal powers* out of township land, are the statutes by whose authority

---

* While the book was in press, Judge Bélanger decided that Archbishop Fabre was within his prerogative in creating Ste Barbe. See page 164 for details.

they act, conformable with the compact under which the townships were settled? Nay, more than this, can land held under English tenure, be made liable to the servitudes imposed under the French law upon seigniorial land? When the crown issued its patents, vesting the settlers of the townships in their farms in free and common soccage, is it constitutional for the legislature afterwards to violate that concession, by giving the priesthood a vested right in those lands, a right which sleeps while it is held by a non-Catholic, but comes into force the moment he leaves? Surely it is contrary to common sense, that upon land conveyed to a settler by crown patent, the priesthood of Quebec should hold a conditional lien, and yet that is what the extension of the parish-system to the townships means.

The inhabitants of the townships are neither strangers nor intruders. They are the descendants of men who settled in them at the invitation of their sovereign, who had become possessed of the country by the most absolute of all titles, that of conquest ratified by the cession of the former owner. In settling in those townships they dispossessed nobody, they were in a state of nature, and by what labor they redeemed them the narratives in these pages bear testimony. Why should they be placed under disabilities that tend to dispossess them of these lands? Why, for nigh fifty years, should successive governments have legislated for Quebec on the assumption that it belongs to the French, and that their wishes and prejudices should be deferred to? The French Canadian has the same rights as every other subject of the British throne, and no more. He has no claim to exceptional legislation or to be treated otherwise than his fellow-subjects of English speech. Their orators talk of treaty-rights—talk unheard until the present generation— it is mere rhetorical flourish, for they can quote no article guaranteeing what they term their peculiar institutions. They are the majority, they have skilfully exchanged their votes for the assistance of Ontario politicians, and they have abused their power to trample upon the rights of the minority, to invade the townships with laws and customs from which they were to be preserved and entangled the English-speaking farmers in the net-work of a system which stifles enterprise, independence, and progress wherever it falls. The hope of the English minority lies in THE VINDICATION OF THE RIGHTS OF THE TOWNSHIPS: that there shall be restored to them that independence which was secured to them when they were founded. With that reform, the injury done in the past would not be repaired, it would not even save many English communities now grown so weak that they are unable to maintain school or church, but it would ensure the continuance of the great body and give a strong stimulus to their prosperity. And that minority, weakened as it has been, is still a considerable body. In the county of Huntingdon there are ten thousand of English speech, in Chateaugay four thousand, in the province at large there must be fully 150,000 who live on or by the land. Surely an intelligent and hard-working farming population of that number is worthy of preservation, and yet there is nothing more certain than that, unless existing laws are abolished and reforms instituted, it will become extinct, and that the sole representatives of the English-speaking minority will be found in the mercantile, manufacturing, and professional circles of the province.

But not on this ground, sufficient though it be, is the plea rested for the help that is called for. How can the Canadian, whose heart glows with love of his country, hope for its having a glorious future, while the Dominion is shackled and weighted with a province, which, at every step, claims peculiar and exceptional treatment and casts the shadow of medieval institutions over the entire Confederation? Can we have a pure and patriotic parliament while three score of its members have an interest in bartering their support with any faction that will, in return, agree to assist them in maintaining the union of church and state in Quebec? Is the public policy of our country to continue, as it has since 1841, to be one of constant compromise between the bounding aspirations of freedom and a clutching backward at feudalism; between a national spirit, broad and benign, and a greedy sectionalism, as narrow as it is intolerant? Freedom will take her flight from a land where one arm is bound and a nation is not to be built upon pillars of unequal height. When the Dominion shall realize her great destiny and show the world a community spanning the American continent, permeated with the spirit of liberty and loving, honoring, and, if need be, supporting the land from which it sprung; standing thus in vivid contrast with the people of that republic who smote the breasts that nursed them, and make an element of their patriotism the reviling of their own kindred; it shall be upon the basis of equal rights and equal laws; a policy that shall make no distinction between its subjects on the score of origin or religion, but shall have the one law and the one measure of administering it for every man whether he be French or English, Catholic or Protestant. That is what the finger of Patriotism points every true Canadian to work for; that is all the English-speaking farmers of Quebec ask of their brethren in the more favored provinces of the Dominion.

NOTE.—Only one treaty was made between France and Britain, so that, if such a thing as "treaty rights," touching the peculiar institutions of Quebec, exist, they must be contained in that document. The treaty, that of Paris, ratified 10th Feby. 1763, contains but one article, the 4th, which refers to the religious or social concerns of the inhabitants of Canada, and it reads as follows : "His Britannic Majesty, on his side, agrees to grant the liberty of the Catholic religion to the inhabitants of Canada; he will consequently give the most effectual orders, that his new Roman Catholic subjects may profess the worship of their religion according to the rites of the Roman Church, as far as the laws of Great Britain permit." When the Canada bill was contemplated, the government obtained the opinion of Wedderburn, afterwards Lord Chancellor, on the meaning of this article, which he gave in 1772 as follows: "The 4th article of the Treaty of Paris grants the liberty of the Catholic religion to the inhabitants of Canada, and provides that His Britannic Majesty should give orders that his Catholic subjects may profess the worship of their religion according to the rites of the Roman Church, as far as the laws of England will permit. This qualification renders the article of so little effect, from the severity with which (though seldom executed) the laws of England are armed against the exercise of the Roman Catholic religion, that the Canadian must depend more upon the benignity and the wisdom of Your Majesty's Government for the protection of his religious rights than upon the provisions of the treaty." There have also been deliverances by our own courts on the intent and scope of the article. On the petition to declare null the Charlevoix election on the ground of clerical influence, Judge Routhier rejected it for, among other reasons, "that the priests of the Church of Rome in Quebec enjoy exceptional privileges by virtue of certain treaties." The petitioner appealed to the supreme court, which rendered judgment in his favor on the 28th Feby. 1877, when Judge Taschereau stated that the article in the treaty "merely confers on the priests and Catholics generally the privileges allowed by British law in the toleration of their faith." Judge Ritchie was more minute and equally explicit on the point. If there is one thing more certain than another in our history, it is that the exceptional privileges which exist in Quebec, have no better authority than that of statutory law, and the greater part of it of recent date.

The proclamation of King George, referred to several times in the preceding chapter, was issued Oct. 7, 1763. The following extract is decisive as to English law being made the law of Quebec and all immigrants to it being guaranteed its continued enjoyment: "Whereas it will greatly contribute to the speedy settling of our new governments that our loving subjects should be informed of our paternal care for the security of the liberty and properties of those who are and shall become the inhabitants thereof, we have thought fit to publish and declare, by this our proclamation . . . . that all persons may confide in our royal protection for the enjoyment of the benefit of the laws of our realm of England."

FIRST SETTLERS OF GODMANCHESTER.

Settlers on Chateaugay and Trout river lots, ranges 5 and 6.

1 Jas. Millar   Jno. Monique
2 John Todd
3 Alex. Stewart   Wm. Hassan
4 John Purse, erected a carding mill and hat factory in 1834
5 Peter Kearney
6 Wm. Dickson   John Purse
7 John and Patrick McArdle   Louis Giroux
8 James Mitchell
9 Felix Hughes   T. Blakey
10 Peter McNaughton   Alex. McNaughton
11 Jas. Freeland   Jno. Davidson
12 John McLean
13 Ptk. Sherry   Jno. Humphrey
14 Jas. Brown   John Telford
15 Alex. Cowan   Jas. Hamilton
16-17 Butterfield   Dr. Whyte
20 Wm. Lallanne   Benj. Lewis
21 Benj. Palmer   2 D. McNee   James Adams
22 Benj. Stebbins   Geo. Hunter   John Hunter, jr.
23 Jas. Anderson   Thos. Smith
24 Jno. Hunter, sr.,   Jas. Robb   Jas. Laird   David Milne
25 David Milne   Wm. Lamb   Robt. Murray
26 Hugh Barr   Geo. Danskin   Henry McDonald
27 Jas. and Andrew McDonald   Benj. Lucas
28 Robert Ford
29 Robt. Nelson   Danl. Wallis
30 John Wallis
31 S. Richardson   Wm. Black   Matt. McCrae

32-3 Wm. Stark   John Smith
— Miner 2   Jas. Black
H. Logan   And. Grennan
34 Maj. Wright   Wm. Dalgliesh
John & James Creighton
35-6 Kelicate   McKittrick
Wm. Johnston
37 Green   Jas. Stephen
38 Jno. Reed O. Force R. Clark
39 Stone   John Tannahill
Peter Booth   Wm. Arthur
40 Saml. Pelton   Thos. Dryden
W. Lanktree   N. Waggoner
41 Hitchins Isaac and Orange
Davis 2   Wm. Morrison
42 Thos. Marshall
43 Rbt. Jamieson Jos. Vaughan
44 Thos. Barlow   Wm. Wattie
Longdale Bradbury
45-6 Thos. Barlow   Alex. and
Arthur Anderson
Bpte. Deschambault
47 Jos. Bombard B. Burnside
John Tannahill
48 Sutton brors.   John White
49 Wm. Nesbitt
50 Geo. Elder   John Massam
Dempsey Peter Donnelly
51 The Barters   John White
Archd. Henderson
52 Wm. Barter   Hartle
James Lunan
53 Jno. Wilson, Henry Starnes
storekeeper
54 Allan McGowan
55 Jas. Donnelly 56 Pk. Solan
57-8 Sylvester F. Healy
3RD RANGE, NEW IRELAND.
1 R. Ferguson   E. Dunsmore
David Kennedy
2 John Reid   Wm. McMullen
David Nicholson
3 John Dunsmore
4 Thos. Elliot John Douglass
5 David Reid Wm. & Geo. Bell

6 Jno. Coughlan, S. Dunsmore
7 R. Douglass   C. McNarland
8 Jonathan and Jas. Sparrow
9 James Sparrow
10 Wm. Feeny   Robt. Stewart
11 Cushing & Clawson
2 Alex. Young
12 Alexr. and William Sadler
4TH RANGE.
1 Martin and Patrick Caveny
2 Jno. Waters   Thos. Whealy
3 Richd. and Major Feeny
James Feeny   Wm. Wilders
4 John and Wm. Montieth
Peter Flynn
5 Ptk. Kiernan   2 C. McHugh
6 H. Suttle   2 Benj. Douglass
7 T. Donohoe   R. McNarland
8 Jas. Gardner   John Reid
9 Bar. Flynn   John Dowler
10 Jas. and Thos. McCartney
11 Jno. Barnes   Jno. Howlett
12 Richard and Joseph Rice
13 O. Heffernan   Jno Rooney
14 Ant. Murphy   Alex. Cowan
Charles Brown
15 Robt. Cowan   David Smith
16 John Gilmore   Daniel and
John Murphy
20 James McNab
22 Hugh Kinniburgh
23 Mrs Hingston
24 James Laird, senr.
Jas. Laird, jr.   Jos. Laird
25 Alex. and James Lunan
26 Geo. Lunan   2 W. Henderson
Patrick Reardon
27 David Armstrong
28 L. Charlebois   A. Duheme
29 Hugh Wiley   Jno. Tannahill
John Tannahill, jr.
30 Walter Barr   Wm. Danskin
31 Arch. Buckless   Jos. Lafleur
32 Geo. and Thos. Danskin
M. McVeay   W. Dalgliesh

33 James McNair
34 Ricord   Michael Murphy
    S. Ingles   James Smith
35 Dank   Michael Curran
    Dewey   Mrs Burnside
36 Wallis Green Jas. Stirling
    D. Nichols J. B. O'Connor
37 John Ingles James Coslow
38 Donald Stewart Campbell
    Robert Taylor
39 Thos. Murphy   ·Rielly
    Donald McIntosh
40 Jno. Hamilton   T. Murphy
41 Peter Phillip Geo. Stephen
    John Christie
42 Asa Campbell Jas. Warden
    Patrick Keogh
43 Miles O'Neil
44 Jas. Sweeny   Jas. Leahy
    M. Donovan   Jas. O'Neil
45 T. Tamerson Jno. McCarty
    J. Cunningham J. Leonard
46 John Bannon JosephVann
    John McGee
47 N. Campbell Thos. Walker
    Cor.Whealey James Smyth
48 Philips   James McManus
    James Lee
49 Peter Welch Richd. Welch
50 John Armstrong, jr.
    James Moore Ths. Murphy
51 Michael and Thos. Fallon
55 Nichols C. Waggoner
56 Charles March
57-8 Thomas McGarvey
59-61 Arth. Moore J. McCarthy
    Jas. Clark Wm. McDonald

5TH RANGE.

17 James Hamilton
18 Alex.and Jas.Cumningham
19 R.Cunningham G.Mentieth
20 Wm. Hamilton
    Wm. Cunningham
21 John Dunsmore
22 Robt. and Jas. Dunsmore

23 Jos. Hutton   Eb. Danskin
    Alex. McPhee Jno. Dunlop
    Archd. Elliot
24 D. McPhee Alex. Danskin
24-5 James and Wm. Biggar
26 Alex. Caldwell
27 Capt. James Gordon
    James and And. Caldwell
28 Jordon J. Laird R.Graham
29 Wm. and Peter Caldwell
30 Hugh Wiley   John and
    Brian McDonagh
31 Wm. Caldwell, jr.
32 Hugh Logan   Wm. Clyde
    Jno. Smellie Benj.Prevost
33 George Reid   John Mack
34 Peter Booth   Robt. Mack
    John Pettis   Jas. Smellie
35 Chas.Filow MauriceO'Neil
    Thos. Clyde
36 Wm.Smith   Hosea Shaw
    Peter Boban
37 John Wright   Patk. Burns
38 Wm. Wright   Jas. McNab
40 Thos. Dryden   Geo. Patton
    Oliver and Solomon Force
47 Archd. Henderson
48 W.Wilson 51 Ptk.McComb
52 W. Tannahill 54 Jas.Tallon
55 Matt.Connell   Patk. Tallon
    Peter Brady
56 Peter Grant   Peter Brady
    Wm. Brady
57 Thomas and Charles March
    John McArthur
    Mathew McRae
58 Rood   W. Kerr
    Charles O'Reilly
    Walter Sutherland
59 James Walker   B. O'Neil
60 Wm. O'Reilly   M. O'Neil
61 Owen and Patrick O'Reilly
    Alex. and John McMullen
    Dougald Cameron
    Charles Gray

1ST RANGE.
23 Jos. Silver 2 Ad. Patterson
26 Andrews Job Sylvester
   Gibson Ptk. Walker
27 Chas. McHardy Peter Hall
   Peter Comstock
28 James McClatchie
29 Rev. Jacob Hart
30 Wm. Taylor
31 Geo. Gillis 2 Wm. Burns
32 Chas. McCurry Creamer
33 Capt. Barron John Nichols
34 Peter McGregor
35 Peter and Danl. Campbell
36 Duncan Campbell
38 John Barron
38-39 Felix McCormick
   Wm. Shaw
39 James Duffin Daniel Leahy
   Thomas Rielly
40 Henry Mooney John Grace
41 Henry Lavery Martin Iby
42 Ptk. Kelly Robert Riley
43 Jno. Fitzcharles Danl. and
   Wm. Leary
45-46 And. Craik Thos. Blair
   2ND RANGE.
22 Robert Percy
23 T. Cockburn 24 — Smith
23 Henry Platt 24 Wm. Reid
   John Kidnell
26 Duncan McGregor
27 David Robertson
28 P. Middlemiss Jn. Brewster
29 Richd. Gillis — Pittenricht
   Dnld. Fisher G. McClatchie
30 David Barron — Murphy
31 M. Kehoe — Henderson
32 Patrick McElroy
34 Hugh Lavery James Miller
35 Capt. Wm. Steel
36 John & Archd. Mather
37 Alex. Rennie & Jas. Wilson
38 Jas. Condron & Edwd. Cody
39 Hy. Duffin & Robt. Gibson

40 P. Mooney & Jno. Mahoney
41 Daniel McMillan & Peter
   McDonaugh
42 Wm. McMillan & Daniel
   McMillan, sr.
43 Isaac Cain & Robt. Rennie
44 Felix McCormick & John
   C. Manning
45 Abraham Manning
46 Hy. Wilson & Wm. Craik, sr.
47 Julius Manning
   3RD RANGE.
17-18 Thos. McC. Gardner
18 William H. Pringle
19 George & David Sandilands
20 John Kelly & Patk. Grady
21 John Cook Robt. Higgins
22 John Outterson
22 John Patterson
22 John White 23 John King
23 Wm. Kerr & Jas. McBeth
24 Thomas Edgerton
25 Matthew McCrea
25 Wm. Johnston 26 Jas. Terry
26 John Kennedy
27 Robert Johnston
27 John Trainer
28 John Kelly S. McCrea
29 Danl. Sweet Jas. Allen
29 Patrick Keirney
30 Paul & Henry Herdman
31 Wm. Gamble 32 P. Brisben
33 Jas. Black 34 John Black
35 Hy. Rennie & Lewis McKay
36 Saml. & Thos. Gibson
37 Wm. Gibson & Ed. Downs
38 Jos. Arthur & Arch. Ramsay
39 William Arthur
40 S. Leckie & Jos. Arthur, sr.
41 John & James Eston and
   William Esdon
42 Jas. Logan & Jas. Leckie
43-44 Andrew, James, and
   Wiiliam Lauder
43 2 Dominick Solway

38

44 Ant. Sarsay & Jno. Manning
     8TH RANGE.
1-2 Alex. McIntosh & James
    Simpson
3 Hugh & Matthew Simpson
4 Jno. Murphy & Thos. Eaton
5 Hugh Calhoun, Wm. Small
   & James Stewart
6 Alex. McIntyre
8 Joseph Watson
9-11 Alex. & Chas. Broadfoot
     7TH RANGE.
3-4 James Anderson
6 Jas. Graham, Saml. Dalzell
   Peter Walsh
9 Hy. Mulholland & Ptk. Fury
10-11 John & David Johnston
12 Henry Henderson
13 Thomas Gibson & William
   Henderson, sr.
14 Robt. Todd & Jasper Haws
15 Wm. Peake 16 J. Armstrong
17 Martin Armstrong & Archd.
   Adams, sr.
     6TH RANGE.
1 Benj. Neely & Hy. Coulter, sr.
2 John Rutherford
3 John Neely and Jas. Coulter
4 T. Whiteside and Jos. Greer
5 Samuel and Wm. Henderson
6 Jas. Gallagher and Robt.
   Knowles
7 Sherick Crump and Daniel
   Gilmore
8 Patrick Walsh and John
   Campbell
9 Jno. Henderson and Henry
   Murray
10 Fred. Sheets and S. Foster
11 Jas. Foster and Ptk. Briniff
12 John Todd and Robt. Howe
13 Andrew Wilson
14 Thomas Docherty
15 John Johnston
16 Archd. Johnston

17 Wm. Irwin and M. Campbell
18 Wm. Johnston and Archd.
   Adams
19 Peter and Martin Munro
20 Wm. Anderson, Jno. Collince
   Alex. Pringle, Jn. Patterson
21 Jas. Waldie and Mal. Munro
22 John Harrigan, John Mc-
   Williams, James Baird,
   and John Pringle
23 James Johnston, Samuel
   and Robert Hudson
24 Edwd. Boyce 25 Pk. Grady
26 Alex. Lumsden
     5TH RANGE.
1 L. Monique and O. Eutaw
2 Archd. Cameron and Wm.
   Menzies
3 Donald and Duncan
   Robertson
4 Thomas Moore
5 T. Ouimet Archd. Cameron
6 Donald Downie
7 Pk. McCaffrey Wm. Irwin
8 Hugh McConville
9 John Telford   Jas. Kelly
10 John Grant   Wm. Robson
11 H. Telford   Wm. McClean
12 Robert Kelly
13 Jas. Davidson Jno. Barnes
14 Melvin Kelly   John Boyd
15 Wm. Boyd Sarah Douglas
16 Wm. Nicol 18 Peter Lukin
19 John Grant Jas. Hampson
20 William Hampson
22 Arth. McCarthy S. Brown
24 James Watt   Wm. Cairns
25 R. Pringle Alex. Lumsden
26 Alex. Anderson & Sons
   Thomas Way
27 James Reid
28 Allan Munro John Seely
29 John Wilson
     4TH RANGE.
1 Francis Lapointe

2	James and Alex. Davidson		Jas. Logan Robt. Kelly
	Hugh Cameron	15	James Edgar James Flynn
3	Peter McArthur		Wesley Cox
4	Alex. Reeves 5 Pierre Moss	16	Wm. Hamilton Jas. Ewart
6	James and Alex. Davidson	17	John Somerville
	Robert Gordon	19	S. H. Schuyler
7	Malcolm McNaughton	21	Claud Burrrows
8	Jas. Hall 9 Neil McCallum	21	James McCallum
9 & 10	Archd. Muir		Robert McCracken
11	Robert Lowrey	23	William and Samuel Fee
	Malcolm McNaughton		Thomas Burrows
12	Wm. Cowan Jno. Donnelly	24	Thomas Gage John Hyde
13	John Cassidy Jas. Gardner	26	George Blaik Wm. Rose
13	Jas. Gardner T. Dickinson		Thomas Cairns

GLEANER TALES.

JEANIE MORISON, A tale of Elgin.
AN INCIDENT OF HUNTINGDON FAIR.
LOST IN THE WOODS, a Hinchinbrook Incident.
THE SETTLER'S FIRST GRIST, a Story of Dundee.
THE DROVER'S WEIRD, a Scotch Story.
ABNER'S DEVICE, an incident of the War of 1812.
WHAT A FIRST SETTLER TOLD ME, a Picture of Old Times on
    the Chateaugay.

It is from such endeavors as that of Mr Sellar—endeavors
to depict what he has really seen—that we may expect to
obtain a Canadian literature hereafter.—Toronto Globe.

The stories are extremely well-told, and display quite a new
phase of Canadian pioneer life in an interesting and entertaining manner.—The Week.

Some of the tales bear the stamp of reality; they are all
racy of the soil.—Montreal Gazette.

All who are interested in preserving the records of the
heroism of the peasants and crofters who, in so many cases,
have been the pioneers of Canadian civilization, will enjoy
these simple tales of sacrifice and suffering, of toil and triumph.
—Toronto Mail.

Price 50 cents.   Sent free by mail on receipt of price.
Address :   THE GLEANER,
                    Huntingdon Q.

INDEX

www.ingramcontent.com/pod-product-compliance
Lightning Source LLC
Chambersburg PA
CBHW060545280326
41932CB00011B/1405